CIVIL WAR II

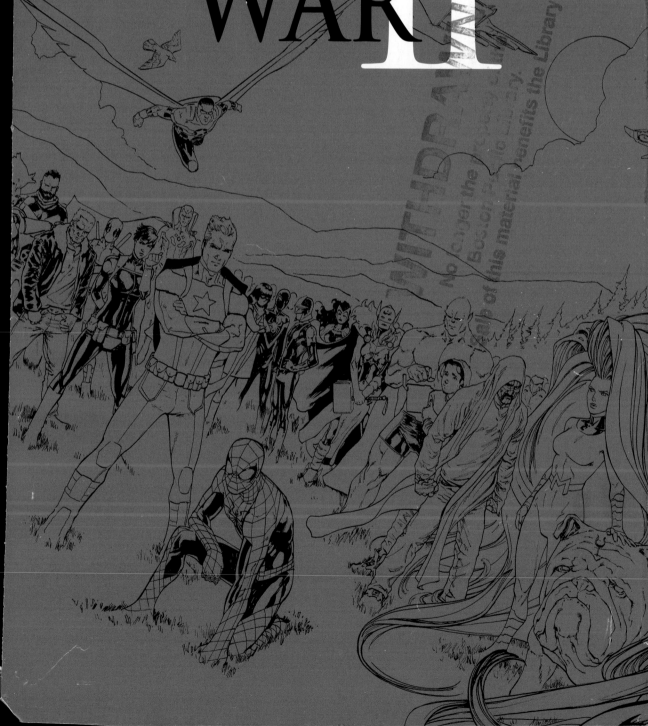

CIVIL WAR II

COLLECTION EDITOR: **JENNIFER GRÜNWALD**
ASSOCIATE MANAGING EDITOR: **KATERI WOODY**
ASSOCIATE EDITOR: **SARAH BRUNSTAD**
EDITOR, SPECIAL PROJECTS: **MARK D. BEAZLEY**
VP PRODUCTION & SPECIAL PROJECTS: **JEFF YOUNGQUIST**
SVP PRINT, SALES & MARKETING: **DAVID GABRIEL**
BOOK DESIGNER: **JAY BOWEN**

EDITOR IN CHIEF: **AXEL ALONSO**
CHIEF CREATIVE OFFICER: **JOE QUESADA**
PUBLISHER: **DAN BUCKLEY**
EXECUTIVE PRODUCER: **ALAN FINE**

CIVIL WAR II. Contains material originally published in magazine form as CIVIL WAR II #0-8 and FREE COMIC BOOK DAY 2016 (CIVIL WAR II) #1. First printing 2017. ISBN# 978-1-302-90156-1. Published by MARVEL WORLDWIDE, INC., a subsidiary of MARVEL ENTERTAINMENT, LLC. OFFICE OF PUBLICATION: 135 West 50th Street, New York, NY 10020. Copyright © 2017 MARVEL No similarity between any of the names, characters, persons, and/or institutions in this magazine with those of any living or dead person or institution is intended, and any such similarity which may exist is purely coincidental. **Printed in the U.S.A.** ALAN FINE, President, Marvel Entertainment; DAN BUCKLEY, President, TV, Publishing & Brand Management; JOE QUESADA, Chief Creative Officer; TOM BREVOORT, SVP of Publishing; DAVID BOGART, SVP of Business Affairs & Operations, Publishing & Partnership; C.B. CEBULSKI, VP of Brand Management & Development, Asia; DAVID GABRIEL, SVP of Sales & Marketing, Publishing; JEFF YOUNGQUIST, VP of Production & Special Projects; DAN CARR, Executive Director of Publishing Technology; ALEX MORALES, Director of Publishing Operations; SUSAN CRESPI, Production Manager; STAN LEE, Chairman Emeritus. For information regarding advertising in Marvel Comics or on Marvel.com, please contact Vit DeBellis, Integrated Sales Manager, at vdebellis@marvel.com. For Marvel subscription inquiries, please call 888-511-5480. **Manufactured between 12/9/2016 and 1/16/2017 by LSC COMMUNICATIONS INC., SALEM, VA, USA.**

10 9 8 7 6 5 4 3 2 1

I

WRITER
BRIAN MICHAEL BENDIS

CIVIL WAR II #0

ARTIST
OLIVIER COIPEL

COLOR ARTIST
JUSTIN PONSOR

COVER ART
OLIVIER COIPEL & JUSTIN PONSOR

FREE COMIC BOOK DAY 2016 (CIVIL WAR II)

PENCILER
JIM CHEUNG

INKER
JOHN DELL

COLOR ARTIST
JUSTIN PONSOR

CIVIL WAR II #1-8

ARTIST
DAVID MARQUEZ

COLOR ARTIST
JUSTIN PONSOR

BANNER CONVERSATION ARTIST
OLIVIER COIPEL

ART ASSIST, #5
SEAN IZAAKSE

OLD MAN LOGAN ARTISTS
ANDREA SORRENTINO & MARCELO MAIOLO

FUTURE ARTISTS
ADAM KUBERT, LEINIL FRANCIS YU, DANIEL ACUÑA,
ALAN DAVIS & MARK FARMER, MARCO RUDY,
MARK BAGLEY & JOHN DELL AND ESAD RIBIC

COVER ART
MARKO DJURDJEVIĆ

LETTERER
VC'S CLAYTON COWLES

ASSISTANT EDITOR
ALANNA SMITH

EDITORS
TOM BREVOORT WITH WIL MOSS

CIVIL WAR II #0

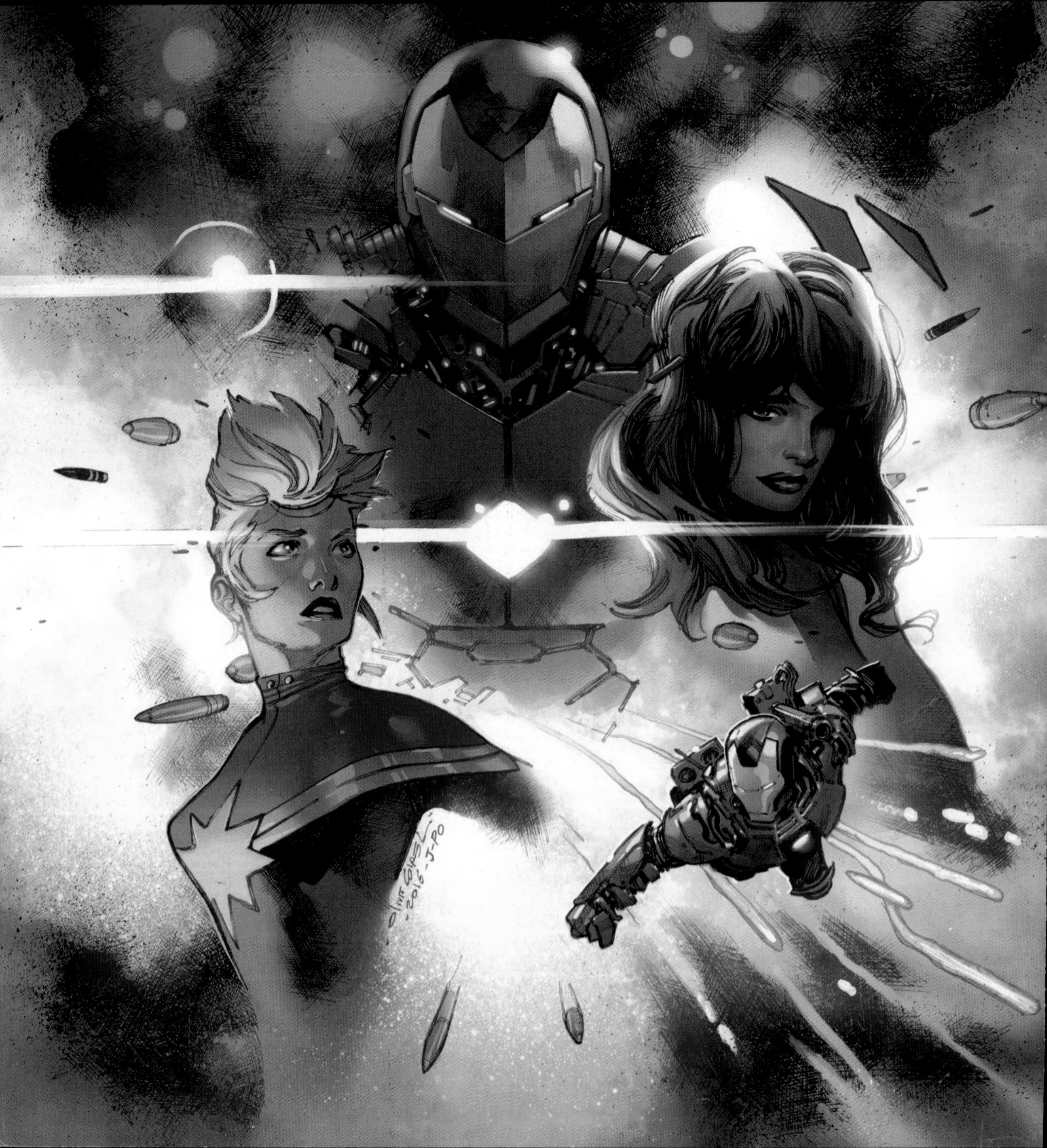

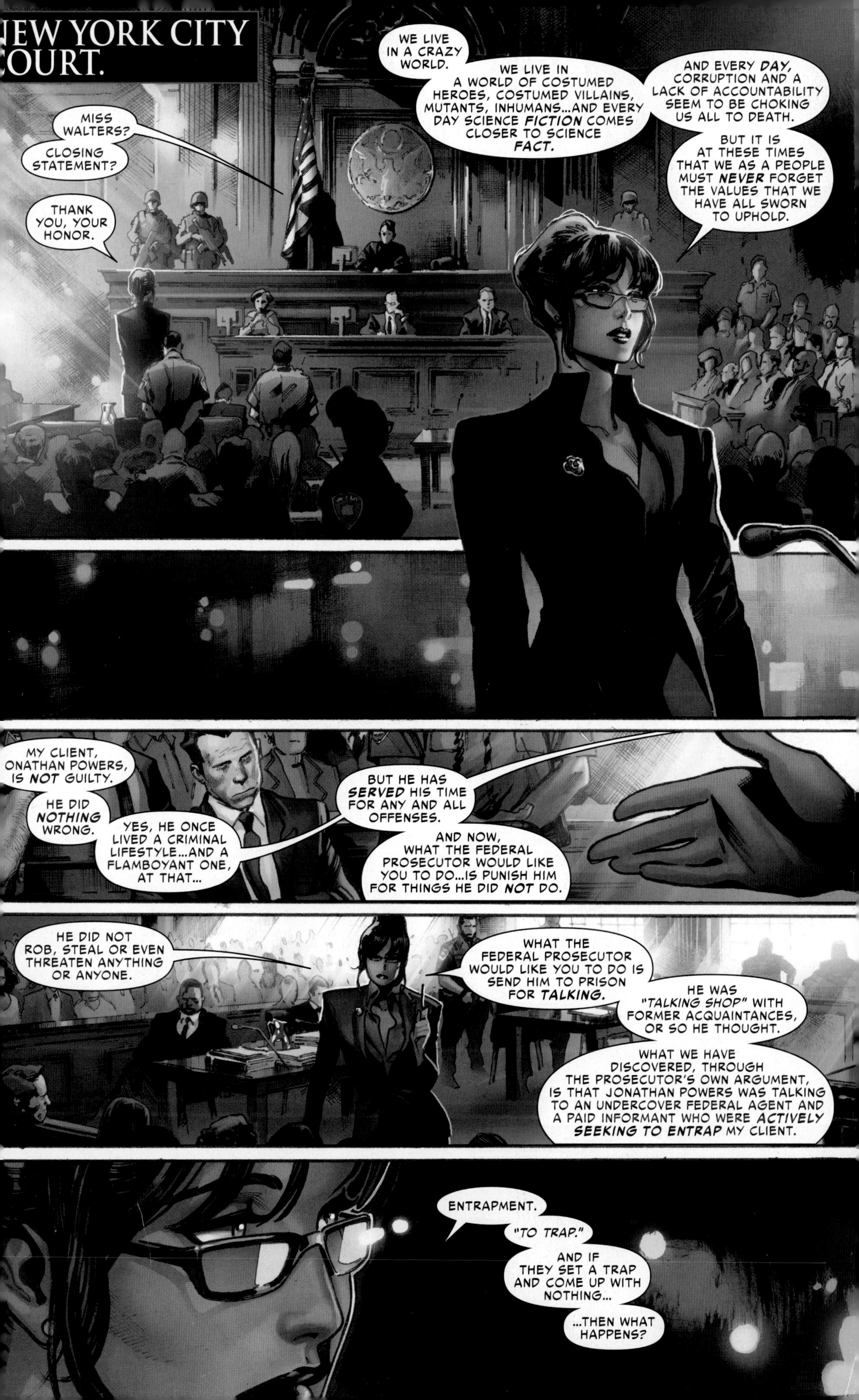

NEW YORK CITY COURT.
MISS WALTERS?
CLOSING STATEMENT?
THANK YOU, YOUR HONOR.
WE LIVE IN A CRAZY WORLD.
WE LIVE IN A WORLD OF COSTUMED HEROES, COSTUMED VILLAINS, MUTANTS, INHUMANS...AND EVERY DAY SCIENCE FICTION COMES CLOSER TO SCIENCE FACT.
AND EVERY DAY, CORRUPTION AND A LACK OF ACCOUNTABILITY SEEM TO BE CHOKING US ALL TO DEATH.
BUT IT IS AT THESE TIMES THAT WE AS A PEOPLE MUST NEVER FORGET THE VALUES THAT WE HAVE ALL SWORN TO UPHOLD.
MY CLIENT, ONATHAN POWERS, IS NOT GUILTY.
HE DID NOTHING WRONG.
YES, HE ONCE LIVED A CRIMINAL LIFESTYLE...AND A FLAMBOYANT ONE, AT THAT...
BUT HE HAS SERVED HIS TIME FOR ANY AND ALL OFFENSES.
AND NOW, WHAT THE FEDERAL PROSECUTOR WOULD LIKE YOU TO DO...IS PUNISH HIM FOR THINGS HE DID NOT DO.
HE DID NOT ROB, STEAL OR EVEN THREATEN ANYTHING OR ANYONE.
WHAT THE FEDERAL PROSECUTOR WOULD LIKE YOU TO DO IS SEND HIM TO PRISON FOR TALKING.
HE WAS "TALKING SHOP" WITH FORMER ACQUAINTANCES, OR SO HE THOUGHT.
WHAT WE HAVE DISCOVERED, THROUGH THE PROSECUTOR'S OWN ARGUMENT, IS THAT JONATHAN POWERS WAS TALKING TO AN UNDERCOVER FEDERAL AGENT AND A PAID INFORMANT WHO WERE ACTIVELY SEEKING TO ENTRAP MY CLIENT.
ENTRAPMENT.
"TO TRAP."
AND IF THEY SET A TRAP AND COME UP WITH NOTHING...
...THEN WHAT HAPPENS?

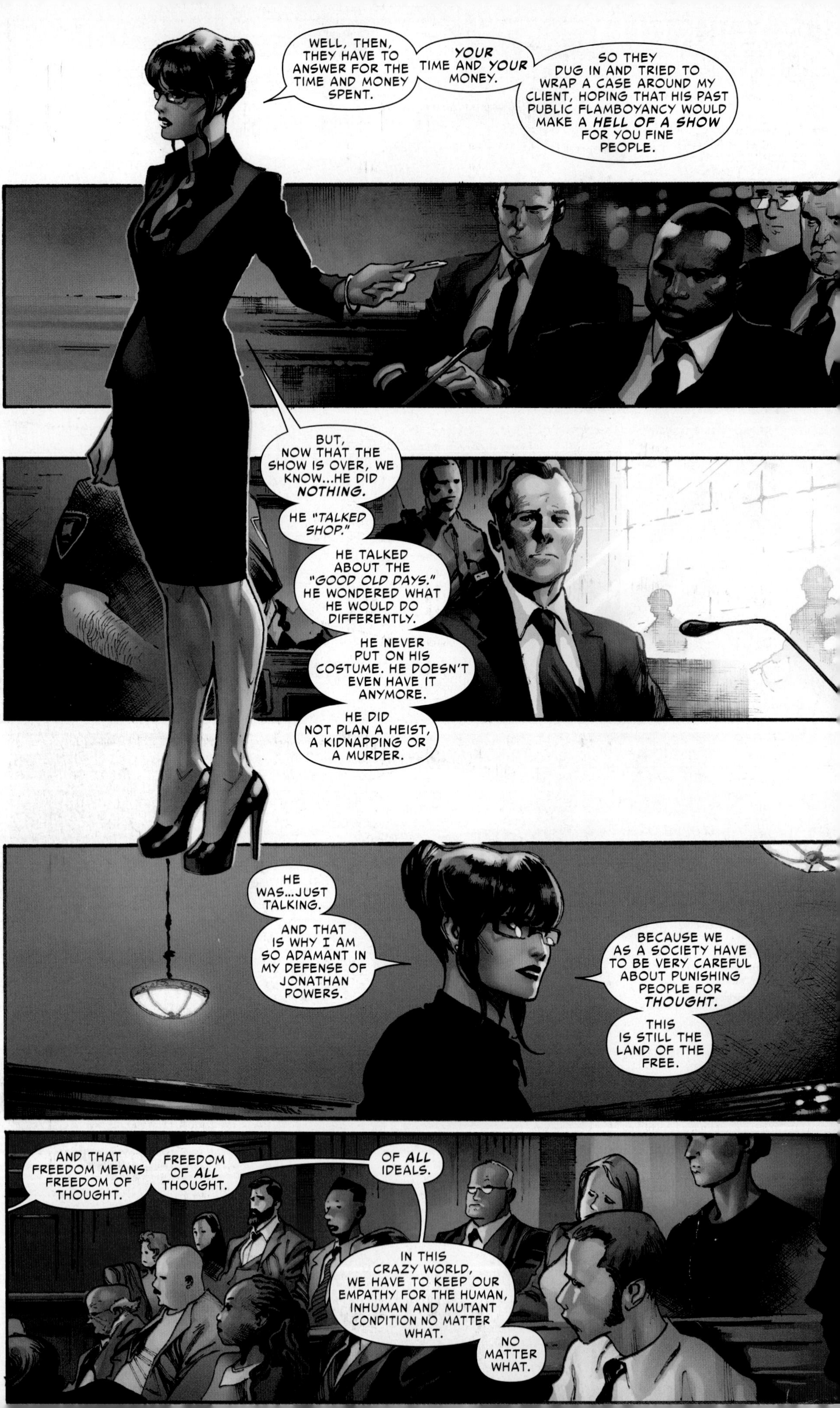
WELL, THEN, THEY HAVE TO ANSWER FOR THE TIME AND MONEY SPENT.
YOUR TIME AND YOUR MONEY.
SO THEY DUG IN AND TRIED TO WRAP A CASE AROUND MY CLIENT, HOPING THAT HIS PAST PUBLIC FLAMBOYANCY WOULD MAKE A HELL OF A SHOW FOR YOU FINE PEOPLE.
BUT, NOW THAT THE SHOW IS OVER, WE KNOW...HE DID NOTHING.
HE "TALKED SHOP."
HE TALKED ABOUT THE "GOOD OLD DAYS." HE WONDERED WHAT HE WOULD DO DIFFERENTLY.
HE NEVER PUT ON HIS COSTUME. HE DOESN'T EVEN HAVE IT ANYMORE.
HE DID NOT PLAN A HEIST, A KIDNAPPING OR A MURDER.
HE WAS...JUST TALKING.
AND THAT IS WHY I AM SO ADAMANT IN MY DEFENSE OF JONATHAN POWERS.
BECAUSE WE AS A SOCIETY HAVE TO BE VERY CAREFUL ABOUT PUNISHING PEOPLE FOR THOUGHT.
THIS IS STILL THE LAND OF THE FREE.
AND THAT FREEDOM MEANS FREEDOM OF THOUGHT.
FREEDOM OF ALL THOUGHT.
OF ALL IDEALS.
IN THIS CRAZY WORLD, WE HAVE TO KEEP OUR EMPATHY FOR THE HUMAN, INHUMAN AND MUTANT CONDITION NO MATTER WHAT.
NO MATTER WHAT.

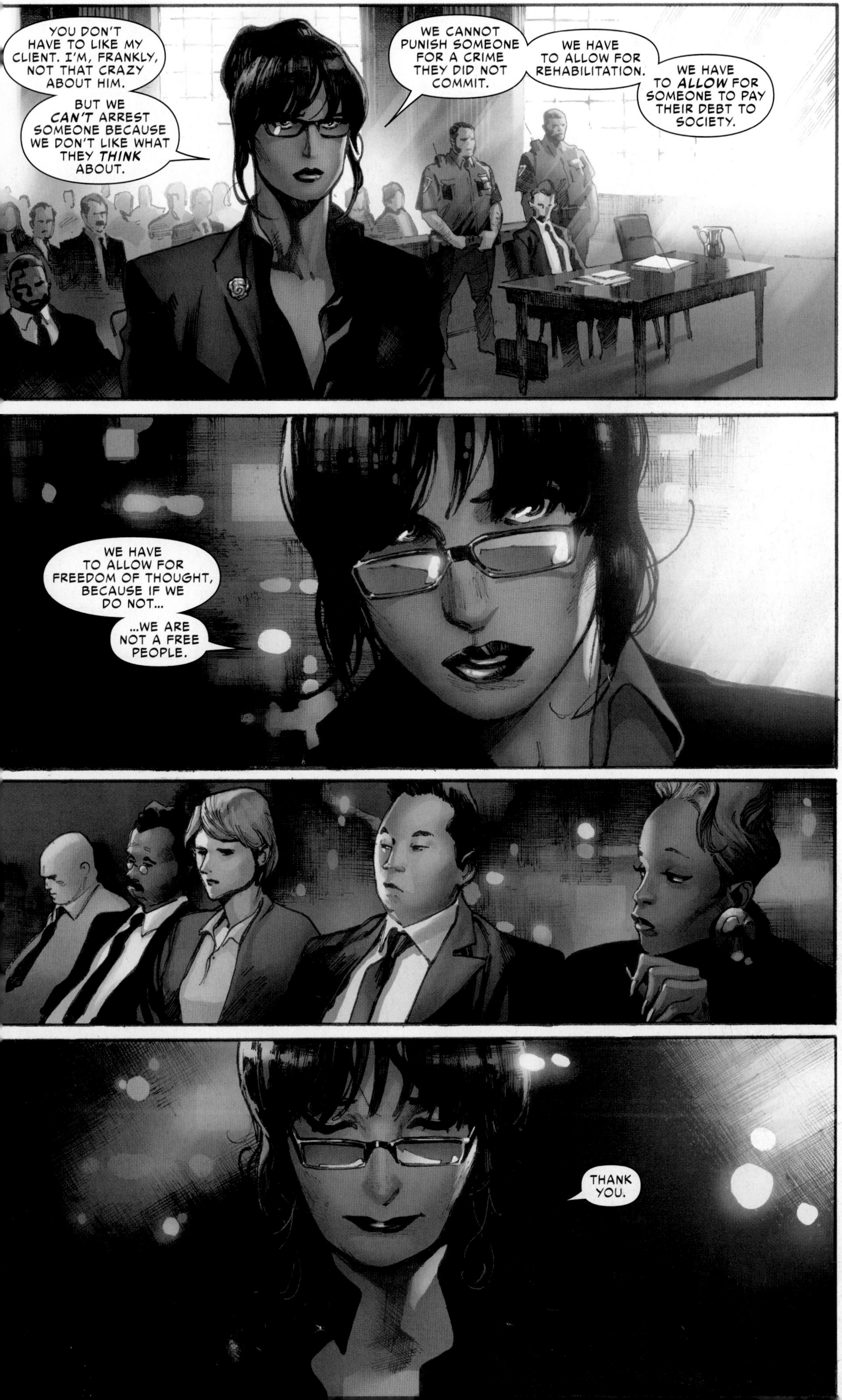
YOU DON'T HAVE TO LIKE MY CLIENT. I'M, FRANKLY, NOT THAT CRAZY ABOUT HIM.
BUT WE *CAN'T* ARREST SOMEONE BECAUSE WE DON'T LIKE WHAT THEY *THINK* ABOUT.
WE CANNOT PUNISH SOMEONE FOR A CRIME THEY DID NOT COMMIT.
WE HAVE TO ALLOW FOR REHABILITATION.
WE HAVE TO *ALLOW* FOR SOMEONE TO PAY THEIR DEBT TO SOCIETY.
WE HAVE TO ALLOW FOR FREEDOM OF THOUGHT, BECAUSE IF WE DO NOT...
...WE ARE NOT A FREE PEOPLE.
THANK YOU.

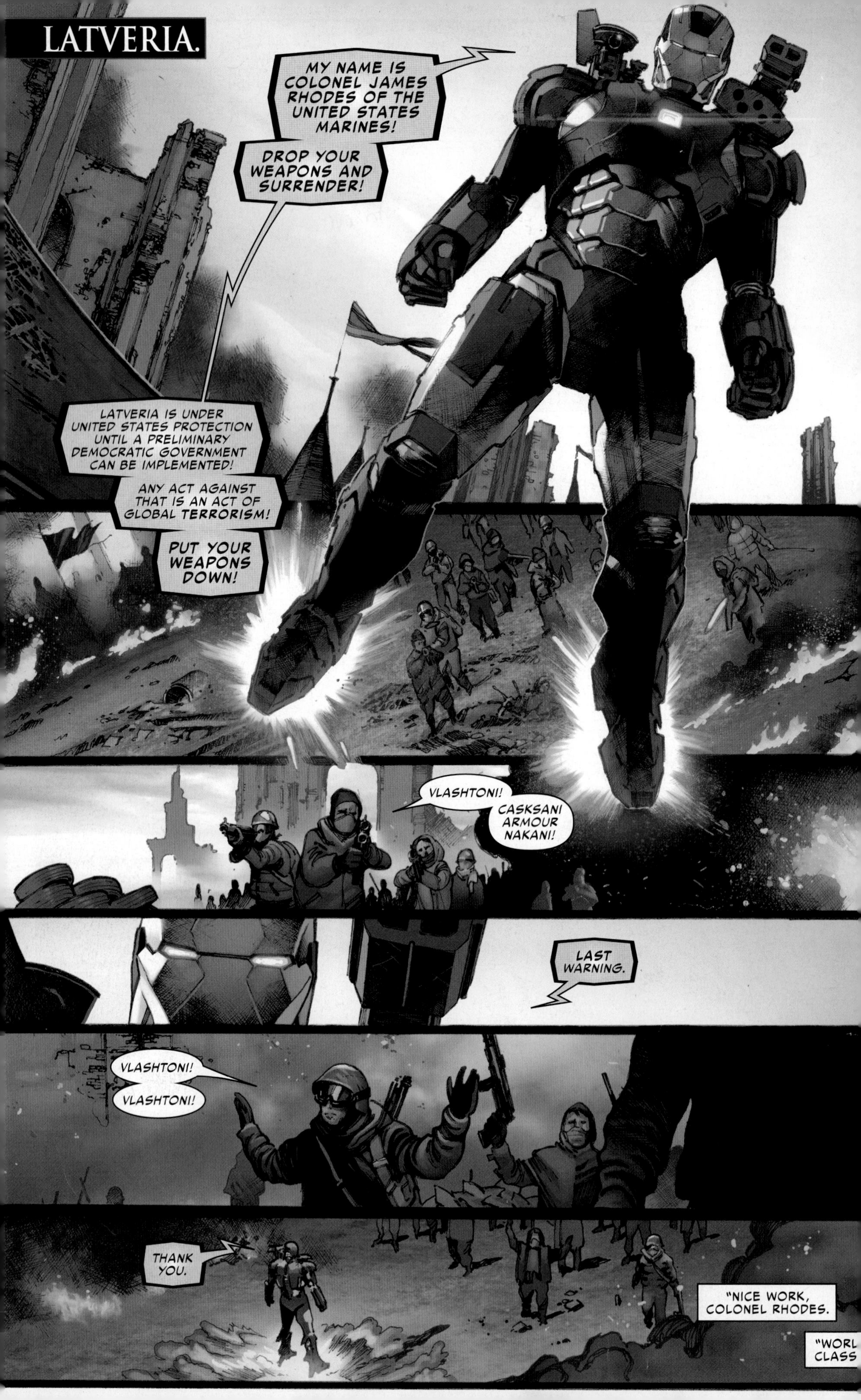
LATVERIA.
MY NAME IS COLONEL JAMES RHODES OF THE UNITED STATES MARINES!
DROP YOUR WEAPONS AND SURRENDER!
LATVERIA IS UNDER UNITED STATES PROTECTION UNTIL A PRELIMINARY DEMOCRATIC GOVERNMENT CAN BE IMPLEMENTED!
ANY ACT AGAINST THAT IS AN ACT OF GLOBAL TERRORISM!
PUT YOUR WEAPONS DOWN!
VLASHTONI!
CASKSANI ARMOUR NAKANI!
LAST WARNING.
VLASHTONI!
VLASHTONI!
THANK YOU.
"NICE WORK, COLONEL RHODES.
"WORL CLASS

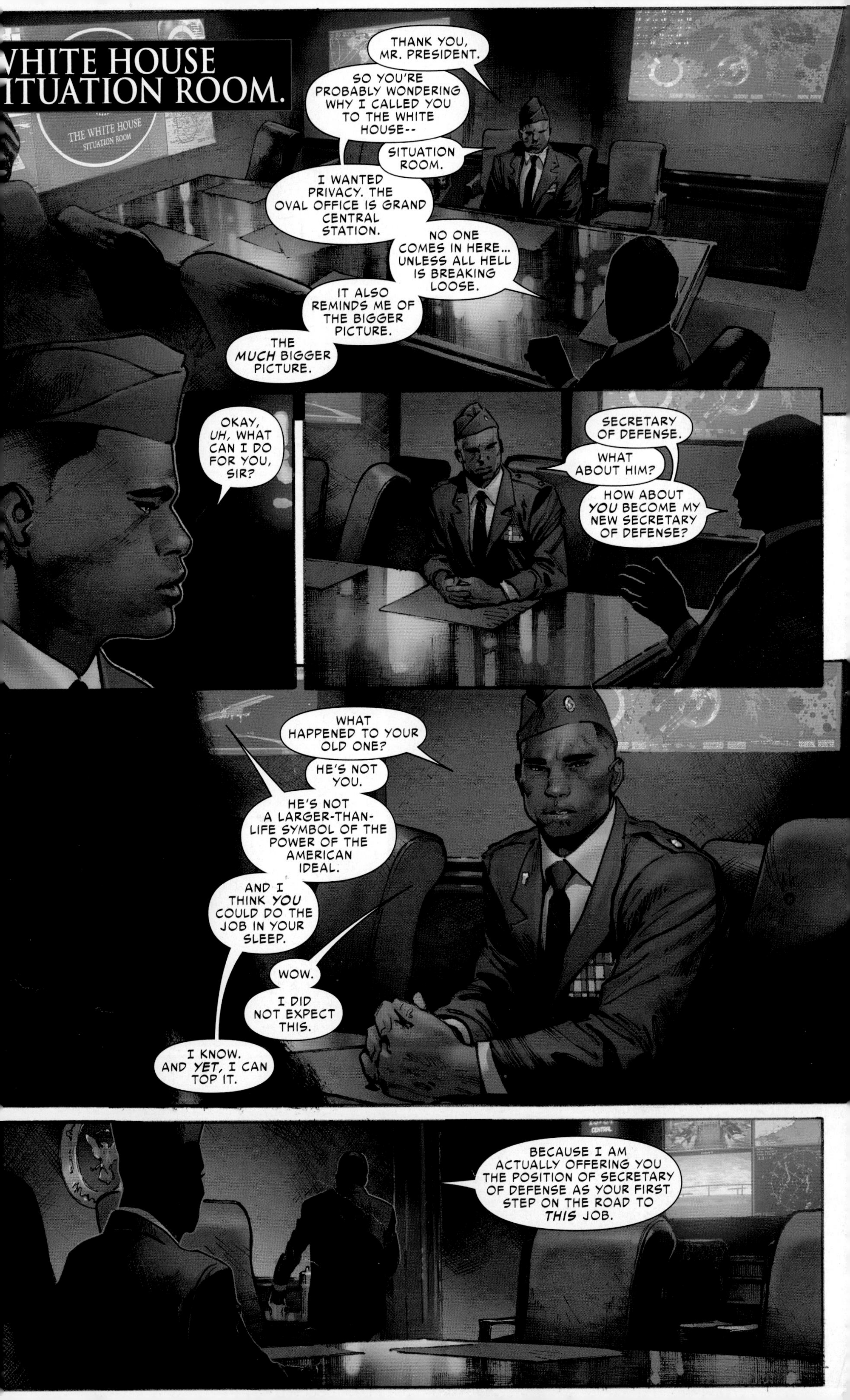
WHITE HOUSE SITUATION ROOM.
THE WHITE HOUSE SITUATION ROOM
THANK YOU, MR. PRESIDENT.
SO YOU'RE PROBABLY WONDERING WHY I CALLED YOU TO THE WHITE HOUSE--
SITUATION ROOM.
I WANTED PRIVACY. THE OVAL OFFICE IS GRAND CENTRAL STATION.
NO ONE COMES IN HERE... UNLESS ALL HELL IS BREAKING LOOSE.
IT ALSO REMINDS ME OF THE BIGGER PICTURE.
THE *MUCH* BIGGER PICTURE.
OKAY, *UH,* WHAT CAN I DO FOR YOU, SIR?
SECRETARY OF DEFENSE.
WHAT ABOUT HIM?
HOW ABOUT *YOU* BECOME MY NEW SECRETARY OF DEFENSE?
WHAT HAPPENED TO YOUR OLD ONE?
HE'S NOT YOU.
HE'S NOT A LARGER-THAN-LIFE SYMBOL OF THE POWER OF THE AMERICAN IDEAL.
AND I THINK *YOU* COULD DO THE JOB IN YOUR SLEEP.
WOW.
I DID NOT EXPECT THIS.
I KNOW. AND *YET,* I CAN TOP IT.
BECAUSE I AM ACTUALLY OFFERING YOU THE POSITION OF SECRETARY OF DEFENSE AS YOUR FIRST STEP ON THE ROAD TO *THIS* JOB.

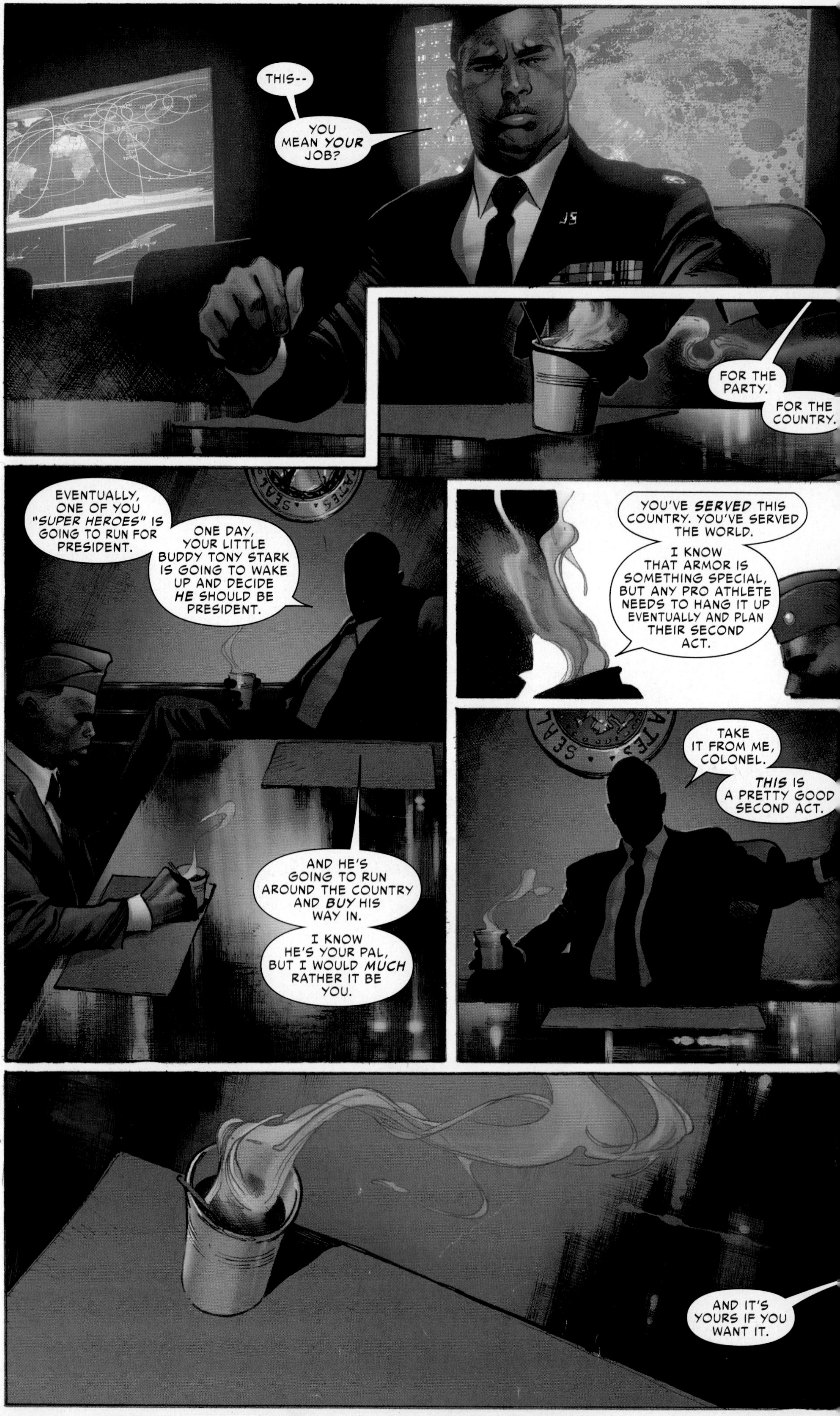
THIS--
YOU MEAN YOUR JOB?
FOR THE PARTY.
FOR THE COUNTRY.
EVENTUALLY, ONE OF YOU "SUPER HEROES" IS GOING TO RUN FOR PRESIDENT.
ONE DAY, YOUR LITTLE BUDDY TONY STARK IS GOING TO WAKE UP AND DECIDE HE SHOULD BE PRESIDENT.
AND HE'S GOING TO RUN AROUND THE COUNTRY AND BUY HIS WAY IN.
I KNOW HE'S YOUR PAL, BUT I WOULD MUCH RATHER IT BE YOU.
YOU'VE SERVED THIS COUNTRY. YOU'VE SERVED THE WORLD.
I KNOW THAT ARMOR IS SOMETHING SPECIAL, BUT ANY PRO ATHLETE NEEDS TO HANG IT UP EVENTUALLY AND PLAN THEIR SECOND ACT.
TAKE IT FROM ME, COLONEL.
THIS IS A PRETTY GOOD SECOND ACT.
AND IT'S YOURS IF YOU WANT IT.

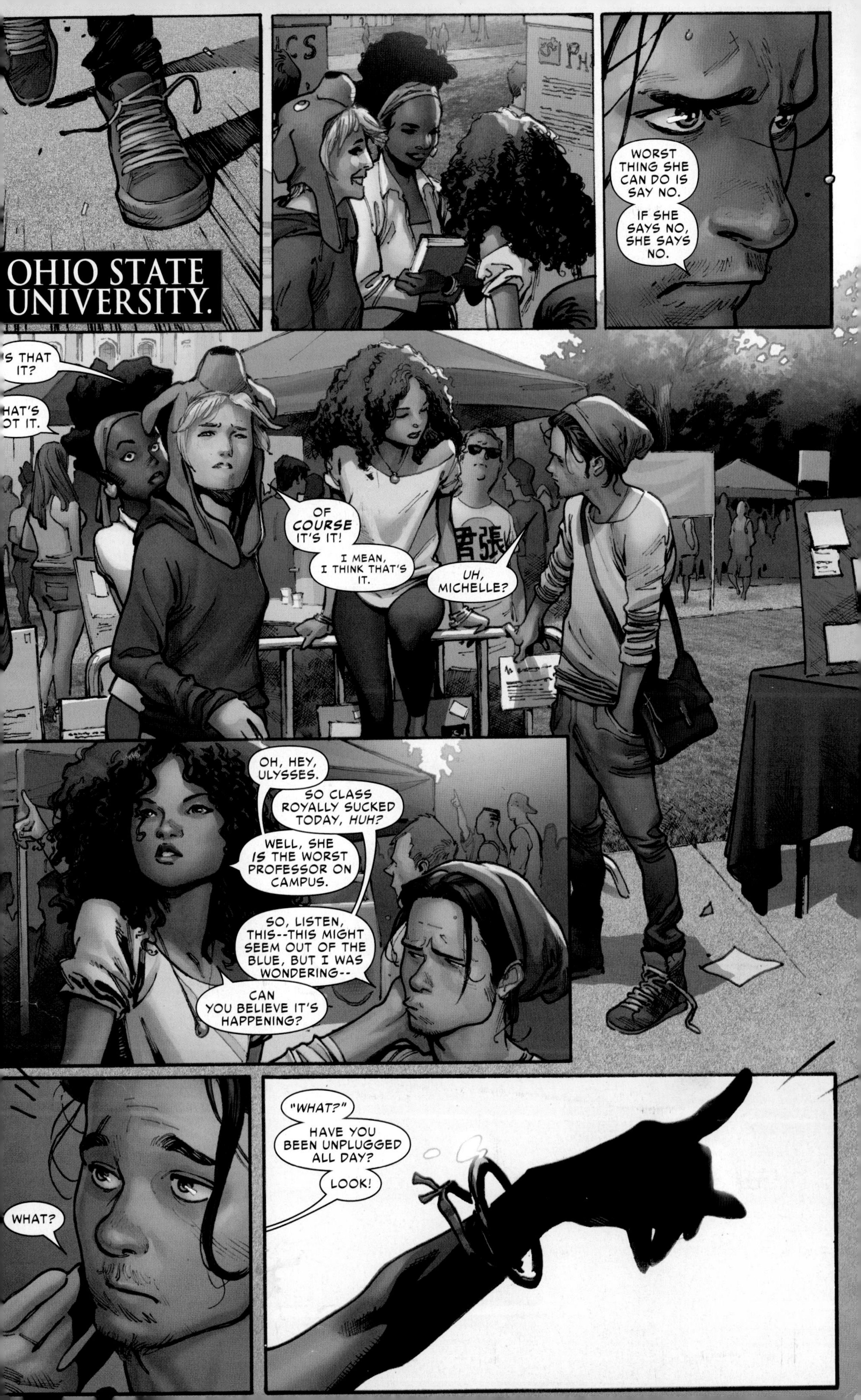
OHIO STATE UNIVERSITY.
WORST THING SHE CAN DO IS SAY NO.
IF SHE SAYS NO, SHE SAYS NO.
'S THAT IT?
HAT'S OT IT.
OF COURSE IT'S IT!
I MEAN, I THINK THAT'S IT.
UH, MICHELLE?
OH, HEY, ULYSSES.
SO CLASS ROYALLY SUCKED TODAY, HUH?
WELL, SHE IS THE WORST PROFESSOR ON CAMPUS.
SO, LISTEN, THIS--THIS MIGHT SEEM OUT OF THE BLUE, BUT I WAS WONDERING--
CAN YOU BELIEVE IT'S HAPPENING?
WHAT?
"WHAT?"
HAVE YOU BEEN UNPLUGGED ALL DAY?
LOOK!

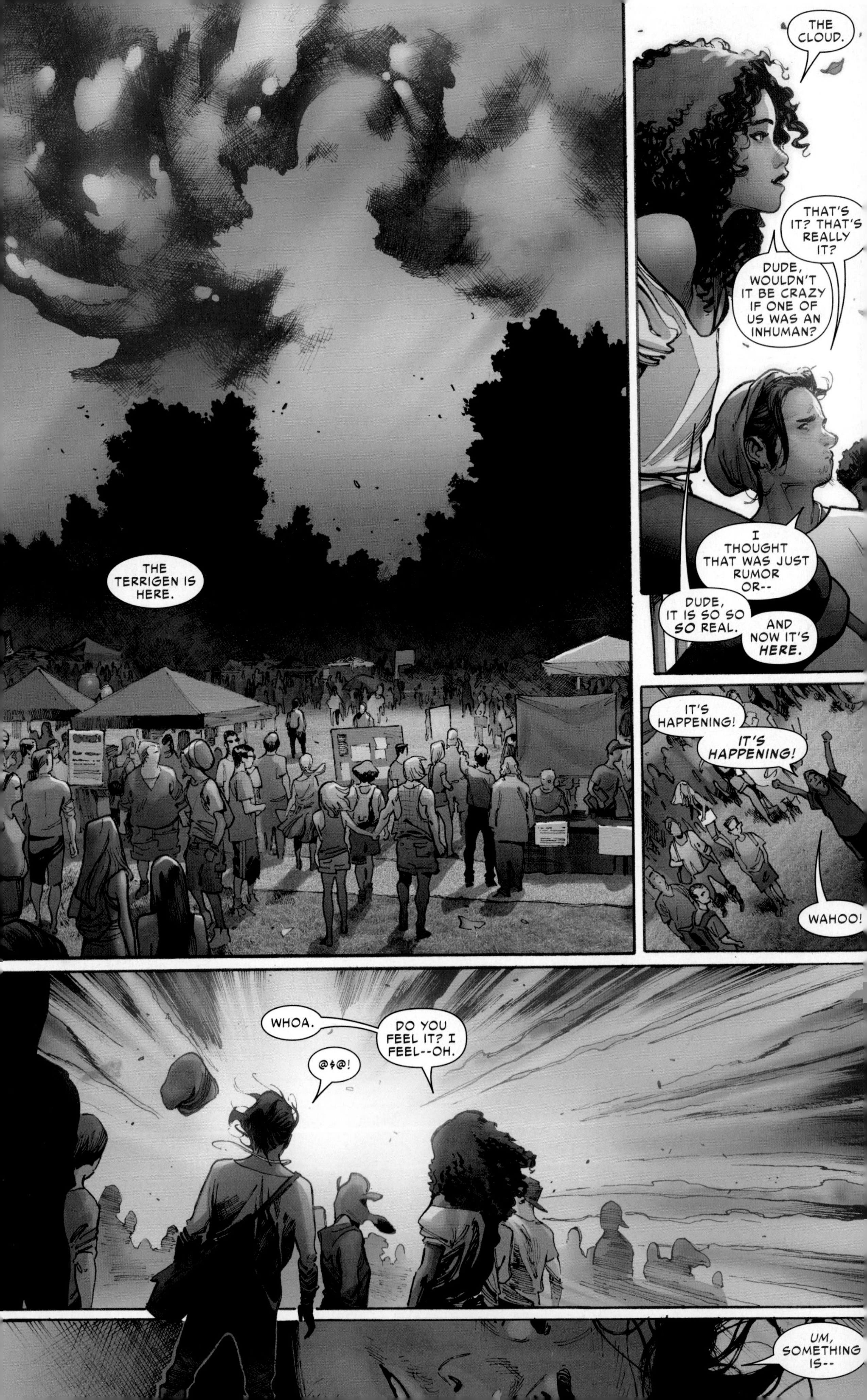
THE TERRIGEN IS HERE.
THE CLOUD.
THAT'S IT? THAT'S REALLY IT?
DUDE, WOULDN'T IT BE CRAZY IF ONE OF US WAS AN INHUMAN?
I THOUGHT THAT WAS JUST RUMOR OR--
DUDE, IT IS SO SO SO REAL.
AND NOW IT'S HERE.
IT'S HAPPENING!
IT'S HAPPENING!
WAHOO!
WHOA.
DO YOU FEEL IT? I FEEL--OH.
@$@!
UM, SOMETHING IS--

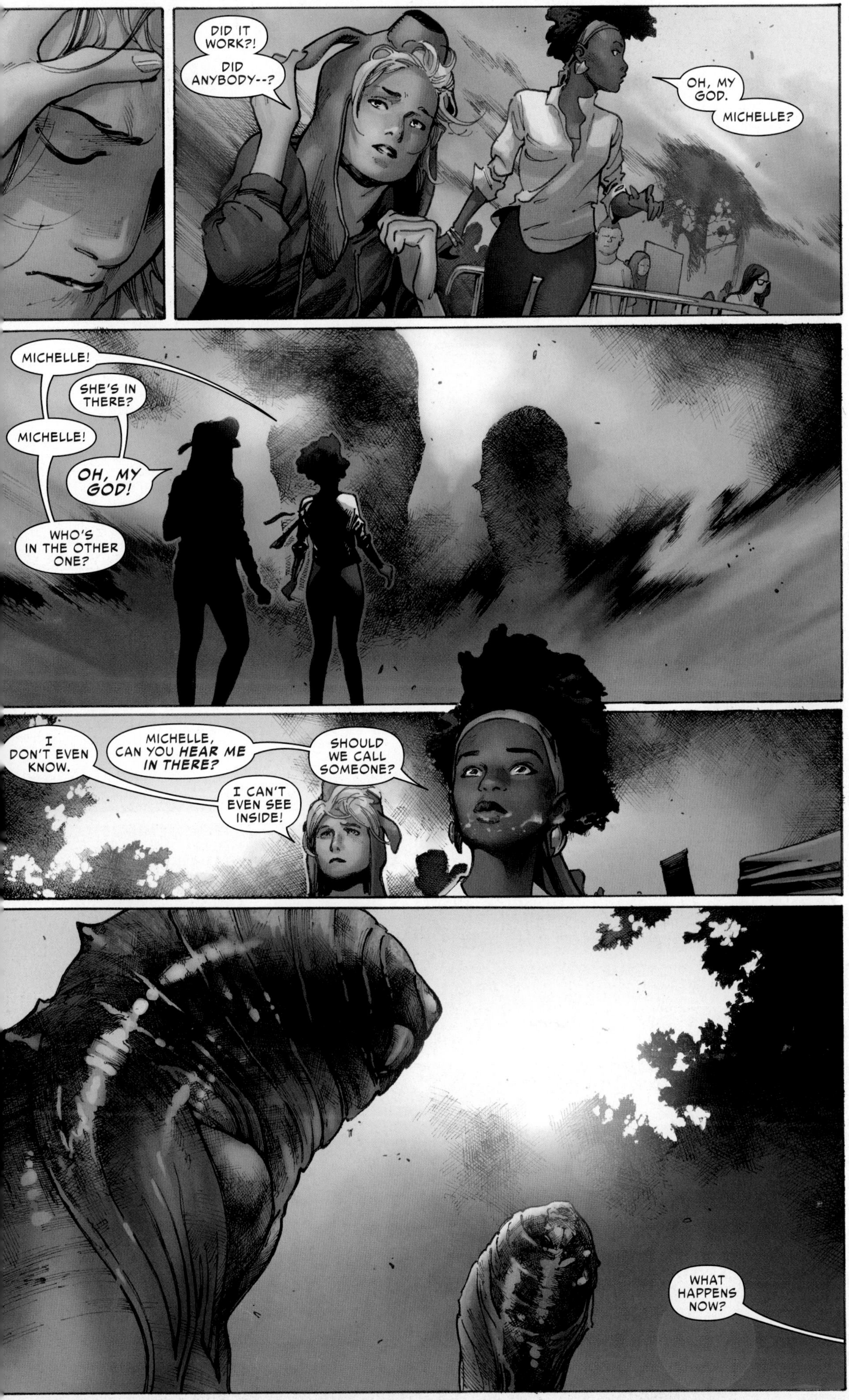
DID IT WORK?!
DID ANYBODY--?
OH, MY GOD.
MICHELLE?
MICHELLE!
SHE'S IN THERE?
MICHELLE!
OH, MY GOD!
WHO'S IN THE OTHER ONE?
I DON'T EVEN KNOW.
MICHELLE, CAN YOU HEAR ME IN THERE?
SHOULD WE CALL SOMEONE?
I CAN'T EVEN SEE INSIDE!
WHAT HAPPENS NOW?

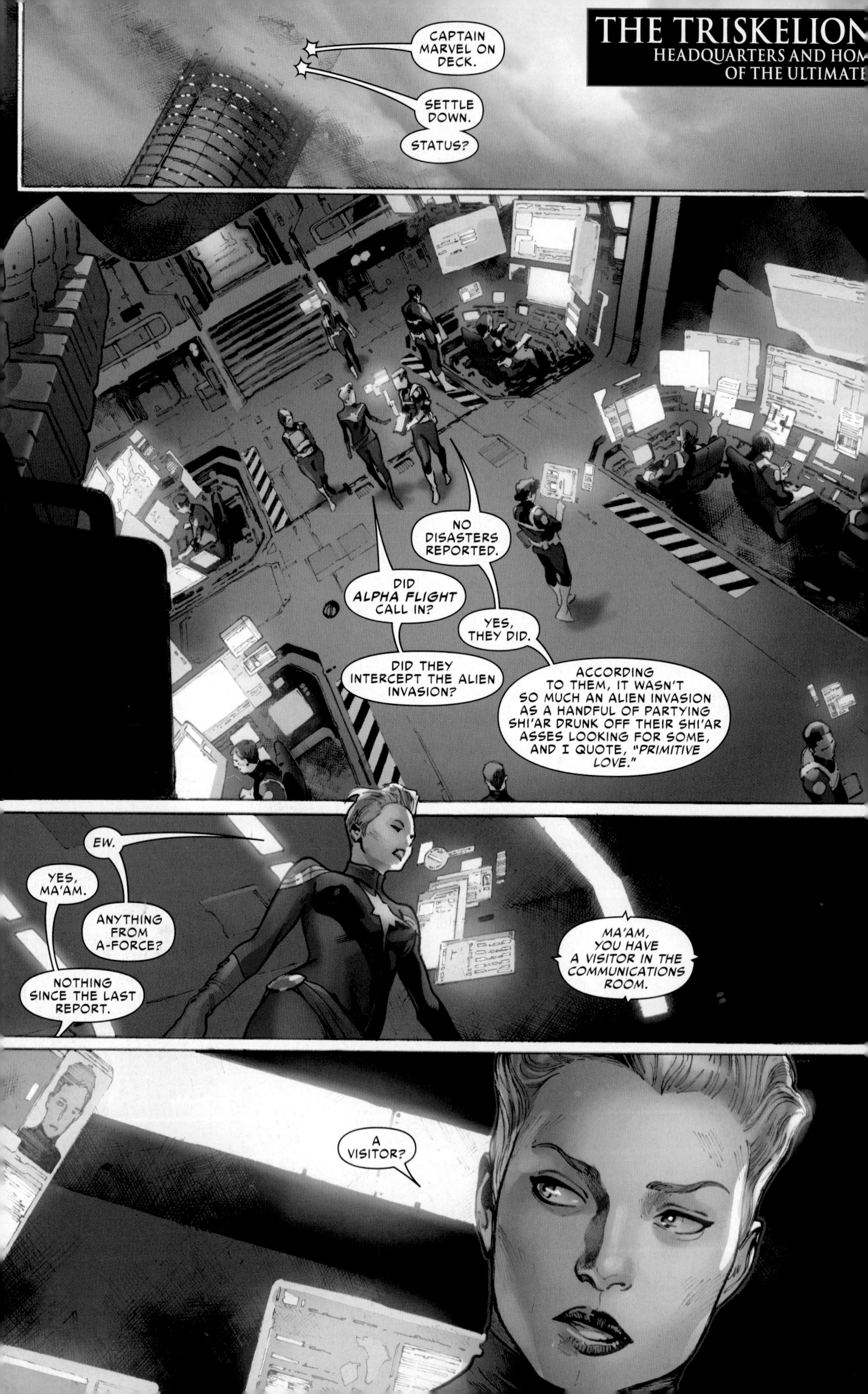
THE TRISKELION
HEADQUARTERS AND HOM
OF THE ULTIMATE
CAPTAIN MARVEL ON DECK.
SETTLE DOWN.
STATUS?
NO DISASTERS REPORTED.
DID ALPHA FLIGHT CALL IN?
YES, THEY DID.
DID THEY INTERCEPT THE ALIEN INVASION?
ACCORDING TO THEM, IT WASN'T SO MUCH AN ALIEN INVASION AS A HANDFUL OF PARTYING SHI'AR DRUNK OFF THEIR SHI'AR ASSES LOOKING FOR SOME, AND I QUOTE, "PRIMITIVE LOVE."
EW.
YES, MA'AM.
ANYTHING FROM A-FORCE?
NOTHING SINCE THE LAST REPORT.
MA'AM, YOU HAVE A VISITOR IN THE COMMUNICATIONS ROOM.
A VISITOR?

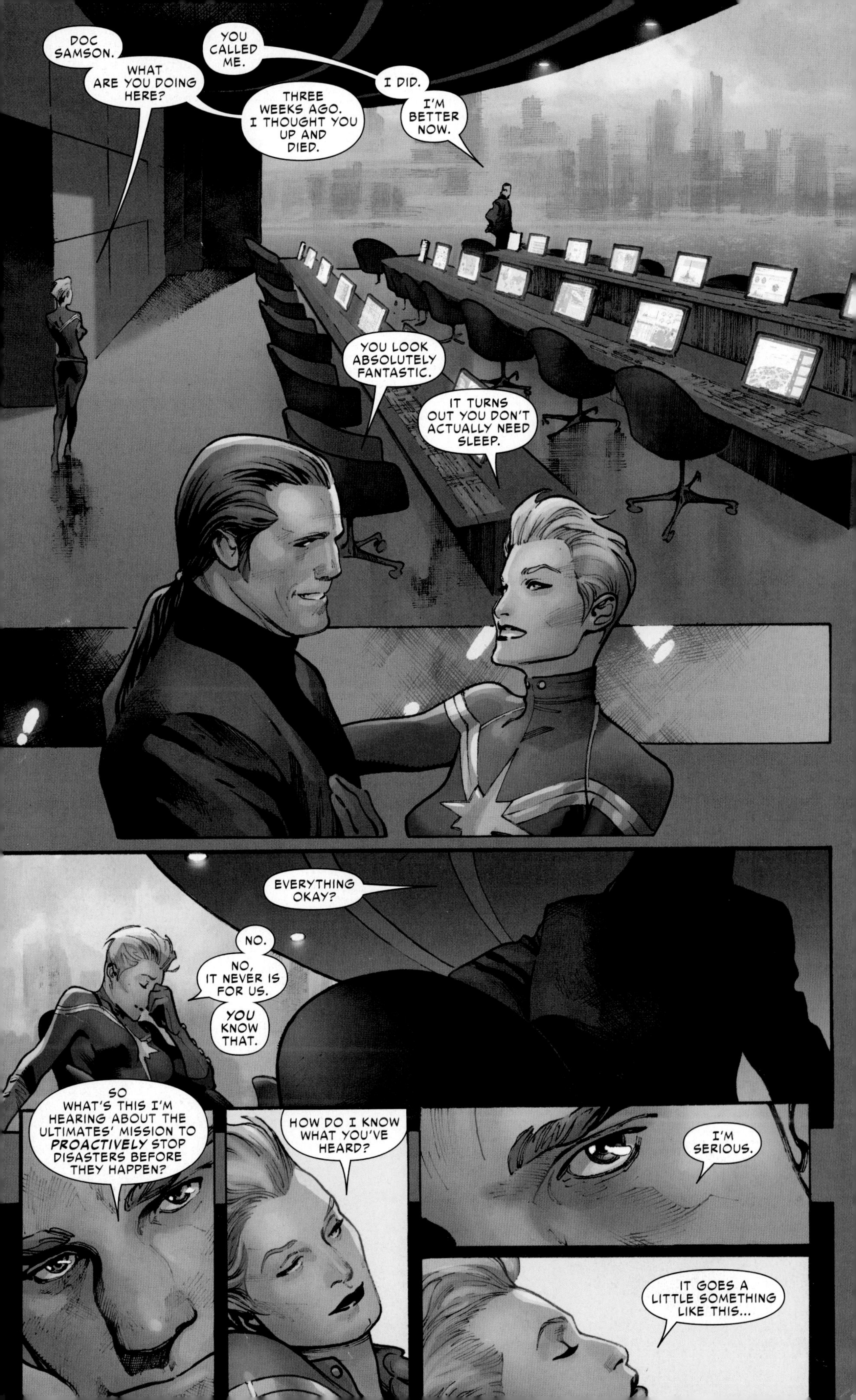
DOC SAMSON.
WHAT ARE YOU DOING HERE?
YOU CALLED ME.
I DID.
THREE WEEKS AGO. I THOUGHT YOU UP AND DIED.
I'M BETTER NOW.
YOU LOOK ABSOLUTELY FANTASTIC.
IT TURNS OUT YOU DON'T ACTUALLY NEED SLEEP.
EVERYTHING OKAY?
NO.
NO, IT NEVER IS FOR US.
YOU KNOW THAT.
SO WHAT'S THIS I'M HEARING ABOUT THE ULTIMATES' MISSION TO PROACTIVELY STOP DISASTERS BEFORE THEY HAPPEN?
HOW DO I KNOW WHAT YOU'VE HEARD?
I'M SERIOUS.
IT GOES A LITTLE SOMETHING LIKE THIS...

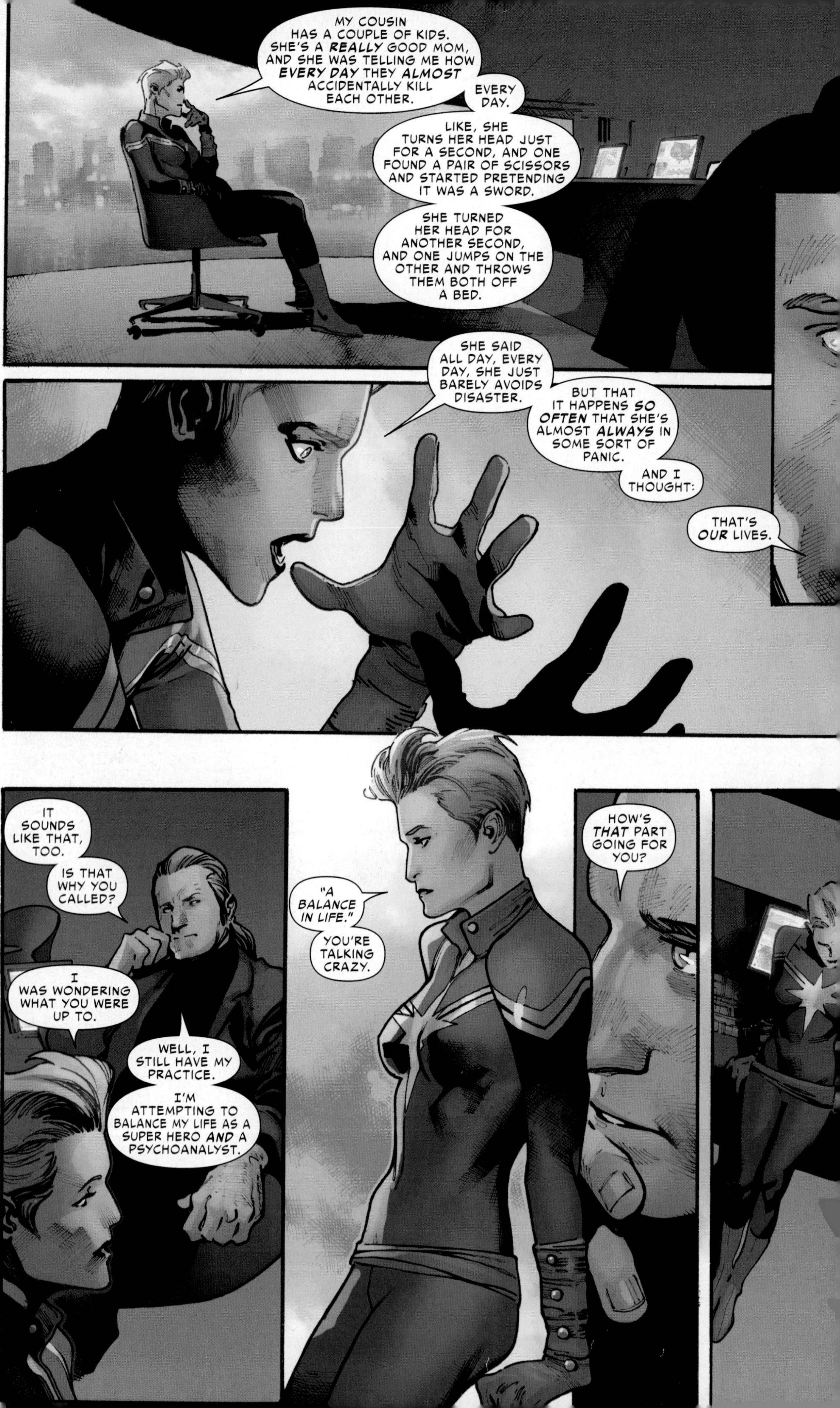
MY COUSIN HAS A COUPLE OF KIDS. SHE'S A REALLY GOOD MOM, AND SHE WAS TELLING ME HOW EVERY DAY THEY ALMOST ACCIDENTALLY KILL EACH OTHER.
EVERY DAY.
LIKE, SHE TURNS HER HEAD JUST FOR A SECOND, AND ONE FOUND A PAIR OF SCISSORS AND STARTED PRETENDING IT WAS A SWORD.
SHE TURNED HER HEAD FOR ANOTHER SECOND, AND ONE JUMPS ON THE OTHER AND THROWS THEM BOTH OFF A BED.
SHE SAID ALL DAY, EVERY DAY, SHE JUST BARELY AVOIDS DISASTER.
BUT THAT IT HAPPENS SO OFTEN THAT SHE'S ALMOST ALWAYS IN SOME SORT OF PANIC.
AND I THOUGHT:
THAT'S OUR LIVES.
IT SOUNDS LIKE THAT, TOO.
IS THAT WHY YOU CALLED?
I WAS WONDERING WHAT YOU WERE UP TO.
WELL, I STILL HAVE MY PRACTICE.
I'M ATTEMPTING TO BALANCE MY LIFE AS A SUPER HERO AND A PSYCHOANALYST.
"A BALANCE IN LIFE."
YOU'RE TALKING CRAZY.
HOW'S THAT PART GOING FOR YOU?

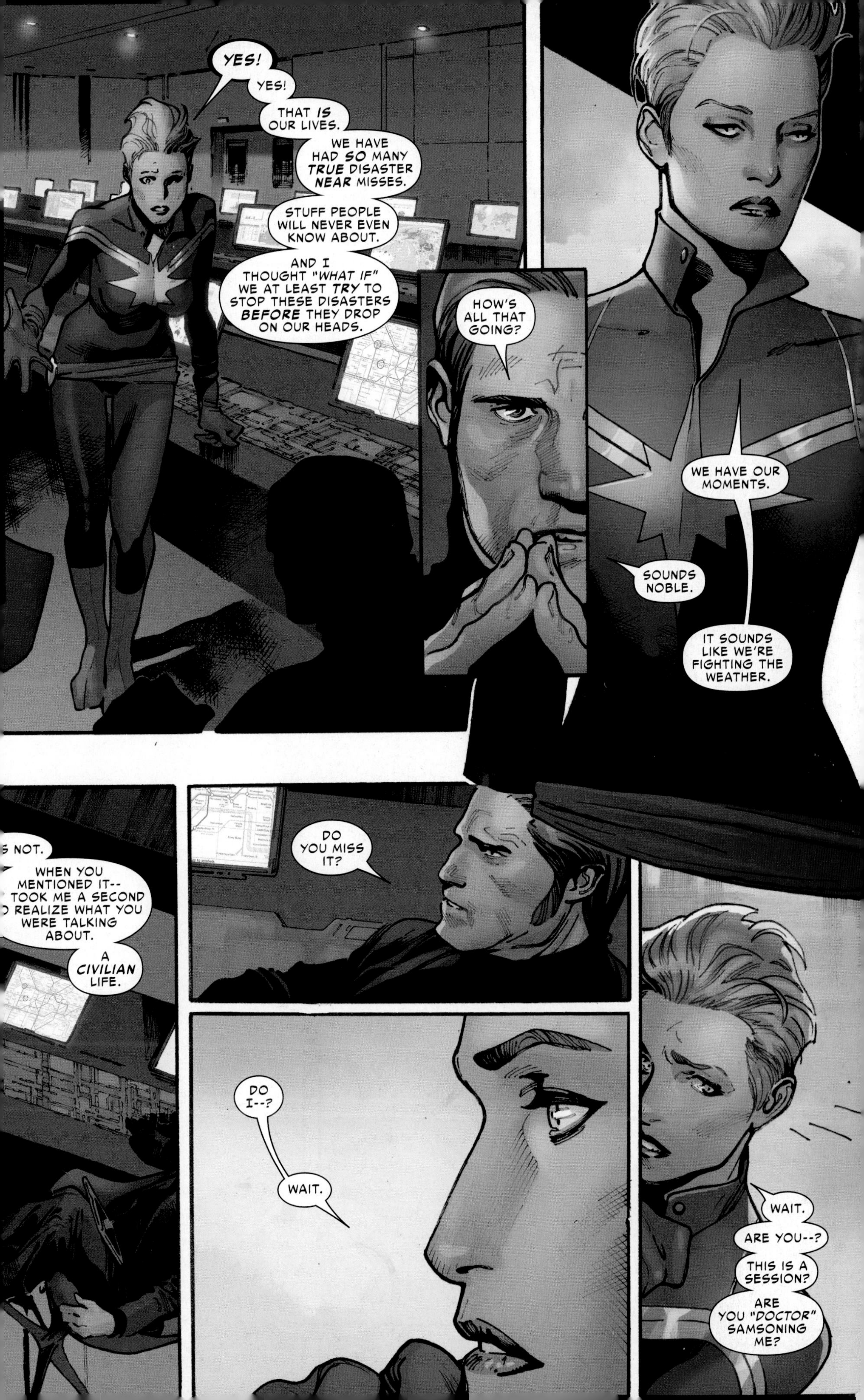
YES!
YES!
THAT IS OUR LIVES.
WE HAVE HAD SO MANY TRUE DISASTER NEAR MISSES.
STUFF PEOPLE WILL NEVER EVEN KNOW ABOUT.
AND I THOUGHT "WHAT IF" WE AT LEAST TRY TO STOP THESE DISASTERS BEFORE THEY DROP ON OUR HEADS.
HOW'S ALL THAT GOING?
WE HAVE OUR MOMENTS.
SOUNDS NOBLE.
IT SOUNDS LIKE WE'RE FIGHTING THE WEATHER.
S NOT.
WHEN YOU MENTIONED IT-- TOOK ME A SECOND REALIZE WHAT YOU WERE TALKING ABOUT.
A CIVILIAN LIFE.
DO YOU MISS IT?
DO I--?
WAIT.
WAIT.
ARE YOU--?
THIS IS A SESSION?
ARE YOU "DOCTOR" SAMSONING ME?

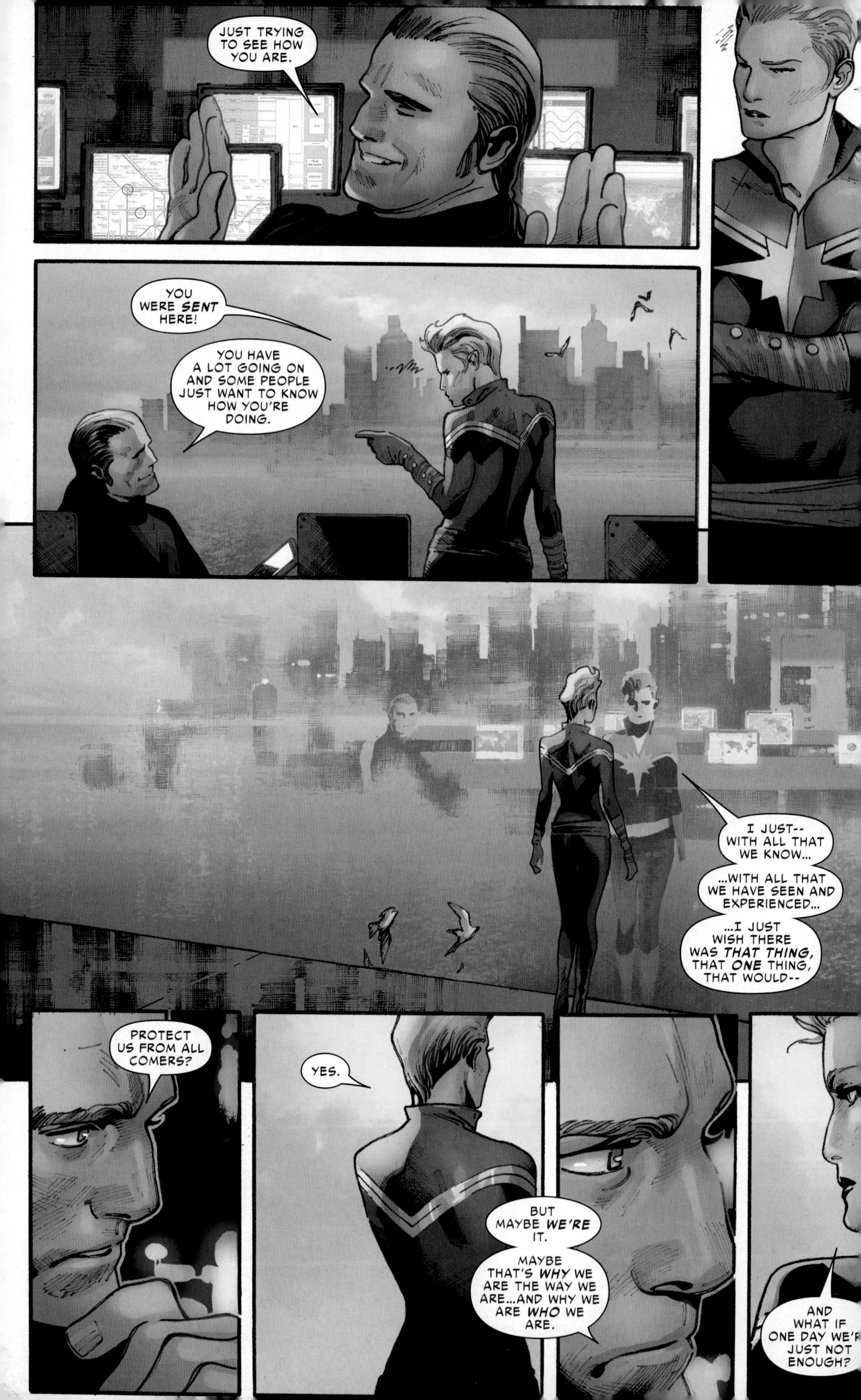
JUST TRYING TO SEE HOW YOU ARE.
YOU WERE SENT HERE!
YOU HAVE A LOT GOING ON AND SOME PEOPLE JUST WANT TO KNOW HOW YOU'RE DOING.
I JUST-- WITH ALL THAT WE KNOW...
...WITH ALL THAT WE HAVE SEEN AND EXPERIENCED...
...I JUST WISH THERE WAS THAT THING, THAT ONE THING, THAT WOULD--
PROTECT US FROM ALL COMERS?
YES.
BUT MAYBE WE'RE IT.
MAYBE THAT'S WHY WE ARE THE WAY WE ARE...AND WHY WE ARE WHO WE ARE.
AND WHAT IF ONE DAY WE'R JUST NOT ENOUGH?

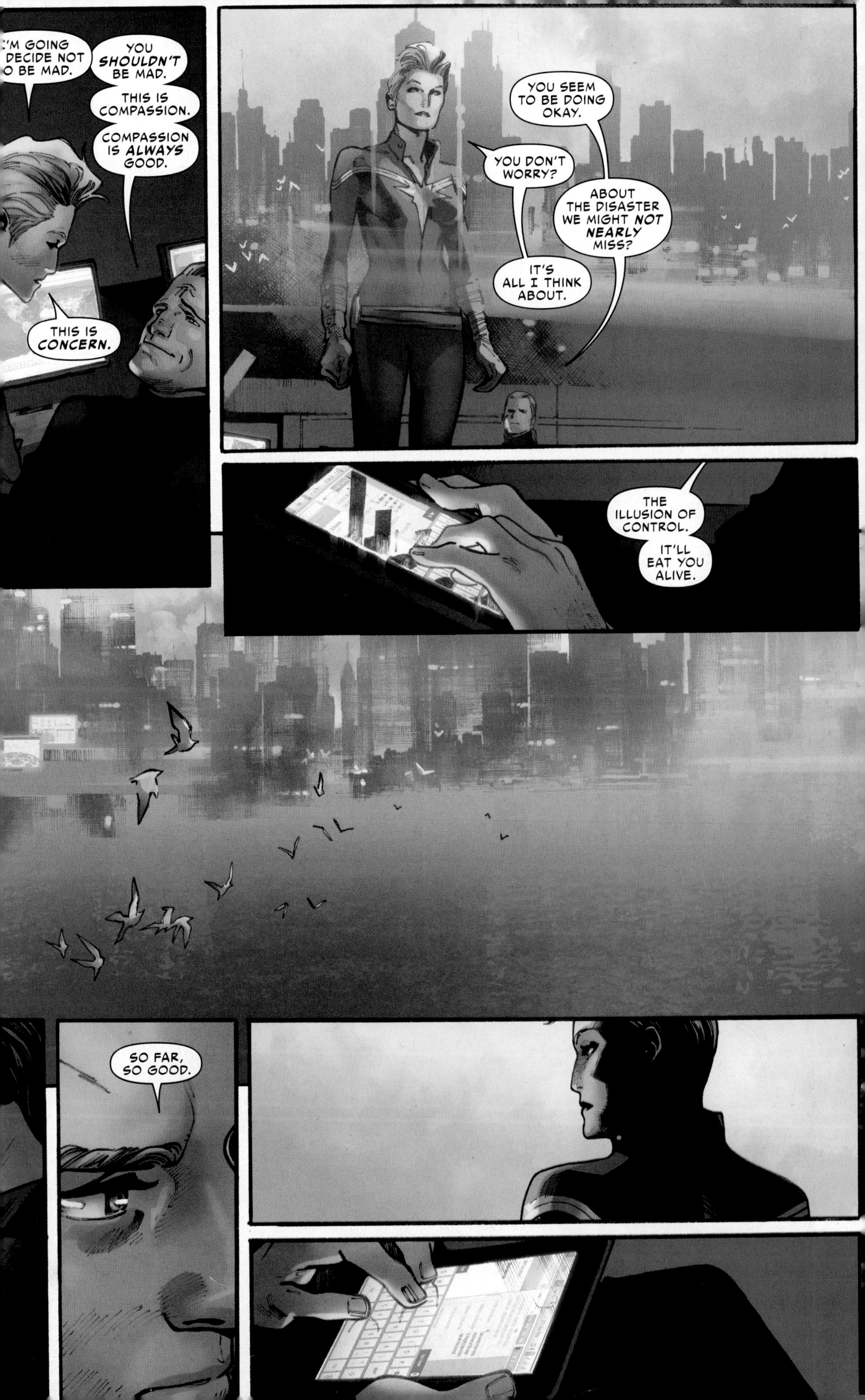

'M GOING
DECIDE NOT
O BE MAD.
YOU SHOULDN'T BE MAD.
THIS IS COMPASSION.
COMPASSION IS ALWAYS GOOD.
THIS IS CONCERN.
YOU SEEM TO BE DOING OKAY.
YOU DON'T WORRY?
ABOUT THE DISASTER WE MIGHT NOT NEARLY MISS?
IT'S ALL I THINK ABOUT.
THE ILLUSION OF CONTROL.
IT'LL EAT YOU ALIVE.
SO FAR, SO GOOD.

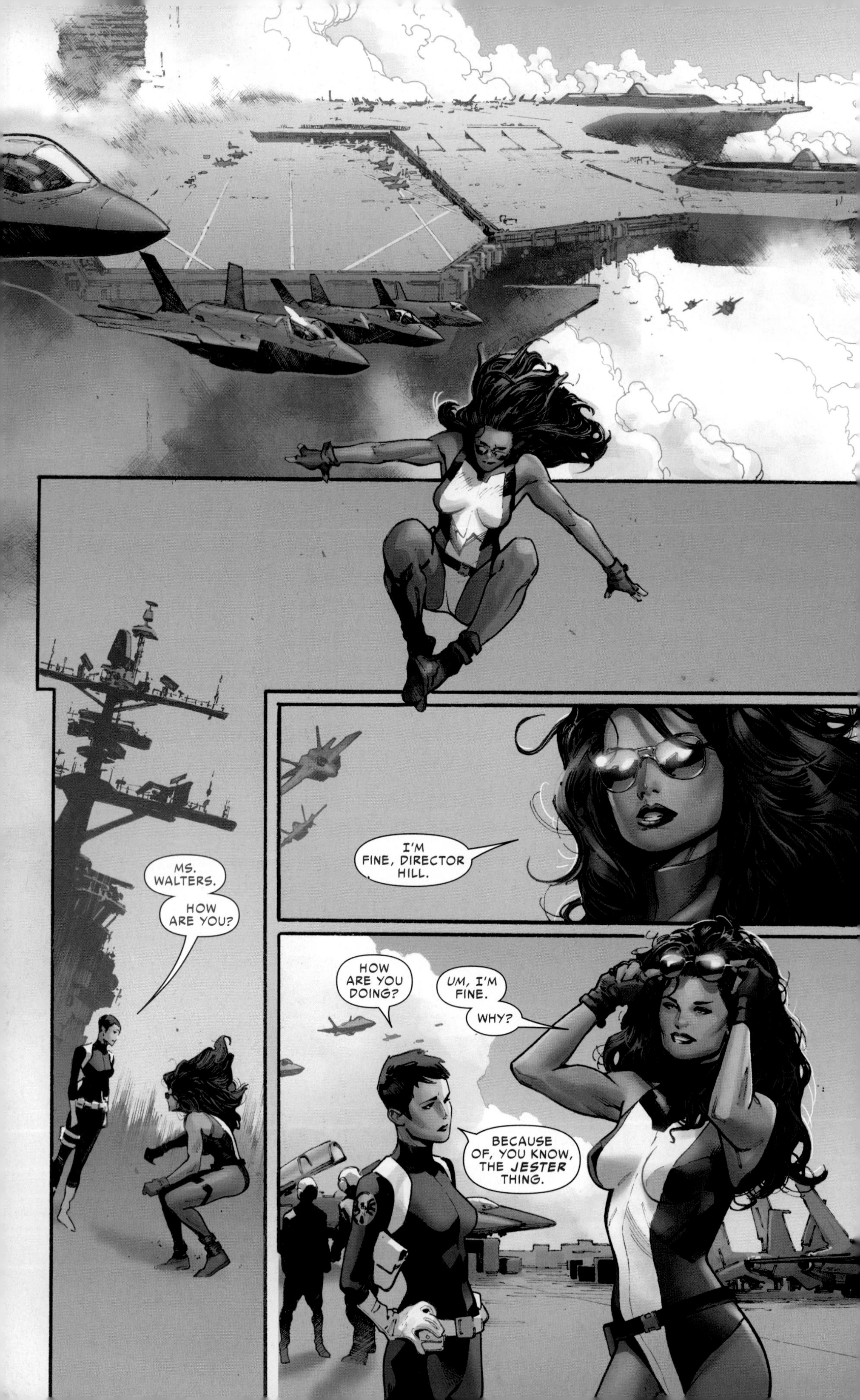
MS. WALTERS.
HOW ARE YOU?
I'M FINE, DIRECTOR HILL.
HOW ARE YOU DOING?
UM, I'M FINE.
WHY?
BECAUSE OF, YOU KNOW, THE JESTER THING.

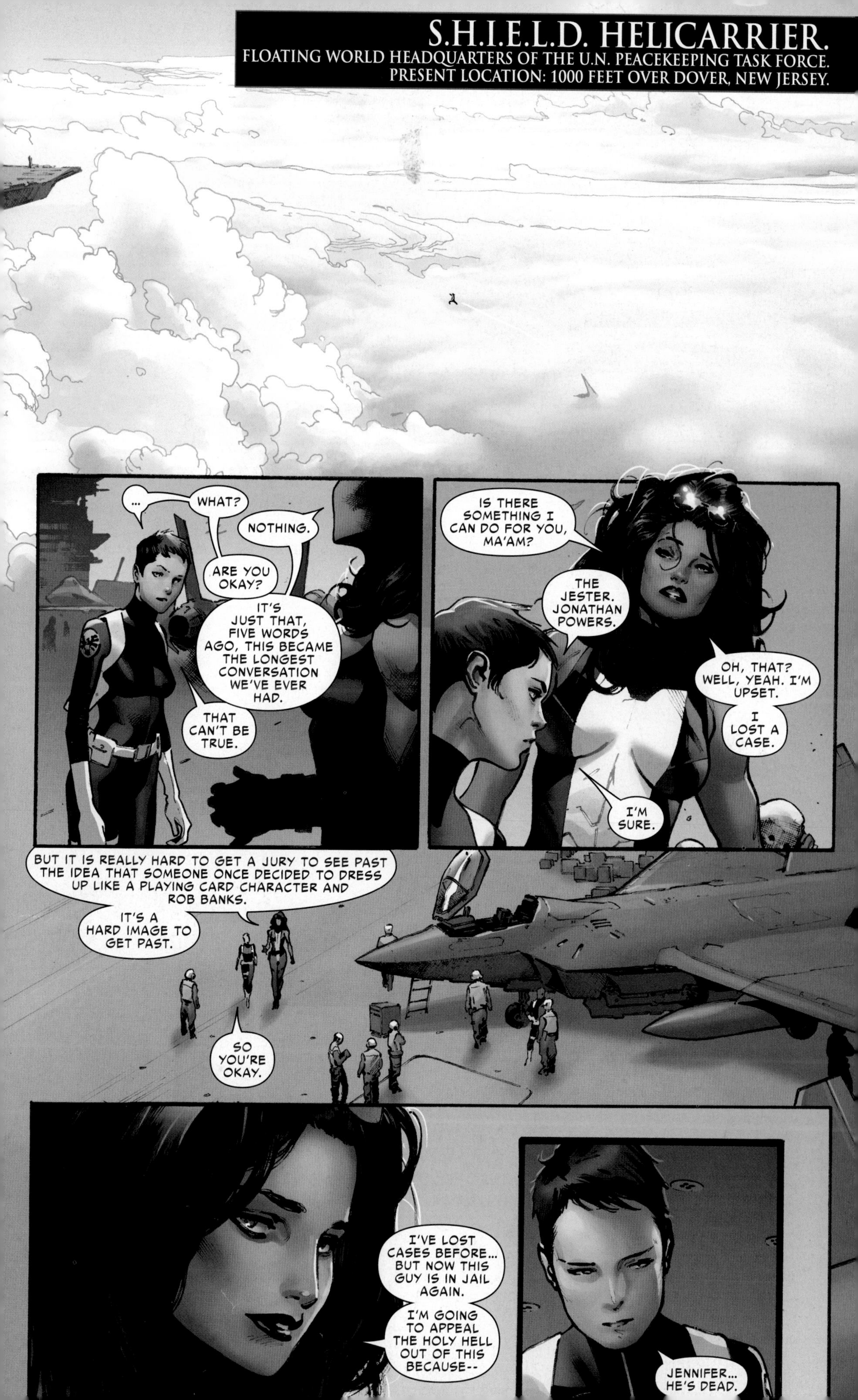
S.H.I.E.L.D. HELICARRIER.
FLOATING WORLD HEADQUARTERS OF THE U.N. PEACEKEEPING TASK FORCE.
PRESENT LOCATION: 1000 FEET OVER DOVER, NEW JERSEY.
...
WHAT?
NOTHING.
ARE YOU OKAY?
IT'S JUST THAT, FIVE WORDS AGO, THIS BECAME THE LONGEST CONVERSATION WE'VE EVER HAD.
THAT CAN'T BE TRUE.
IS THERE SOMETHING I CAN DO FOR YOU, MA'AM?
THE JESTER. JONATHAN POWERS.
OH, THAT? WELL, YEAH. I'M UPSET.
I LOST A CASE.
I'M SURE.
BUT IT IS REALLY HARD TO GET A JURY TO SEE PAST THE IDEA THAT SOMEONE ONCE DECIDED TO DRESS UP LIKE A PLAYING CARD CHARACTER AND ROB BANKS.
IT'S A HARD IMAGE TO GET PAST.
SO YOU'RE OKAY.
I'VE LOST CASES BEFORE... BUT NOW THIS GUY IS IN JAIL AGAIN.
I'M GOING TO APPEAL THE HOLY HELL OUT OF THIS BECAUSE--
JENNIFER... HE'S DEAD.

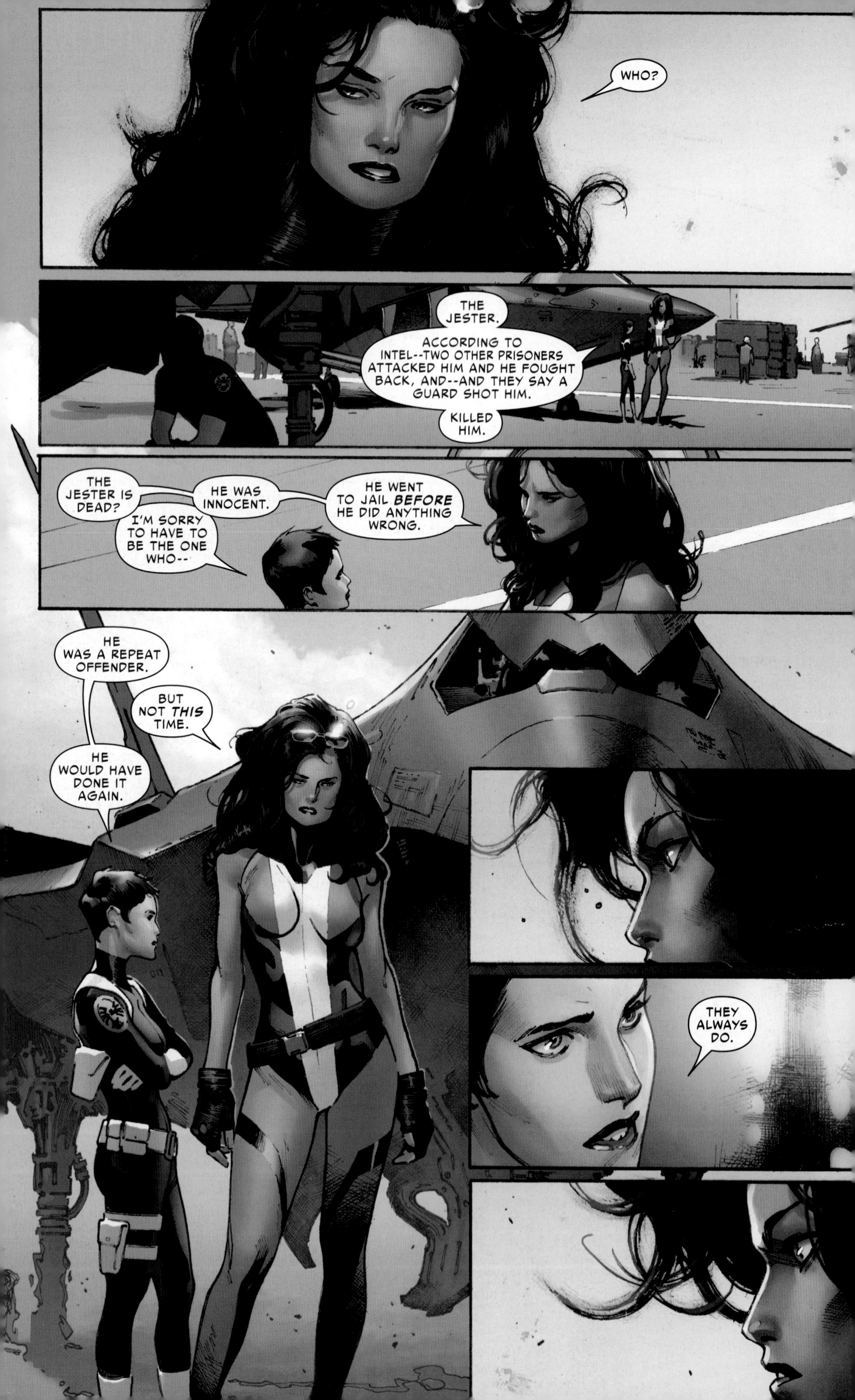
WHO?
THE JESTER.
ACCORDING TO INTEL--TWO OTHER PRISONERS ATTACKED HIM AND HE FOUGHT BACK, AND--AND THEY SAY A GUARD SHOT HIM.
KILLED HIM.
THE JESTER IS DEAD?
I'M SORRY TO HAVE TO BE THE ONE WHO--
HE WAS INNOCENT.
HE WENT TO JAIL *BEFORE* HE DID ANYTHING WRONG.
HE WAS A REPEAT OFFENDER.
BUT NOT *THIS* TIME.
HE WOULD HAVE DONE IT AGAIN.
THEY ALWAYS DO.

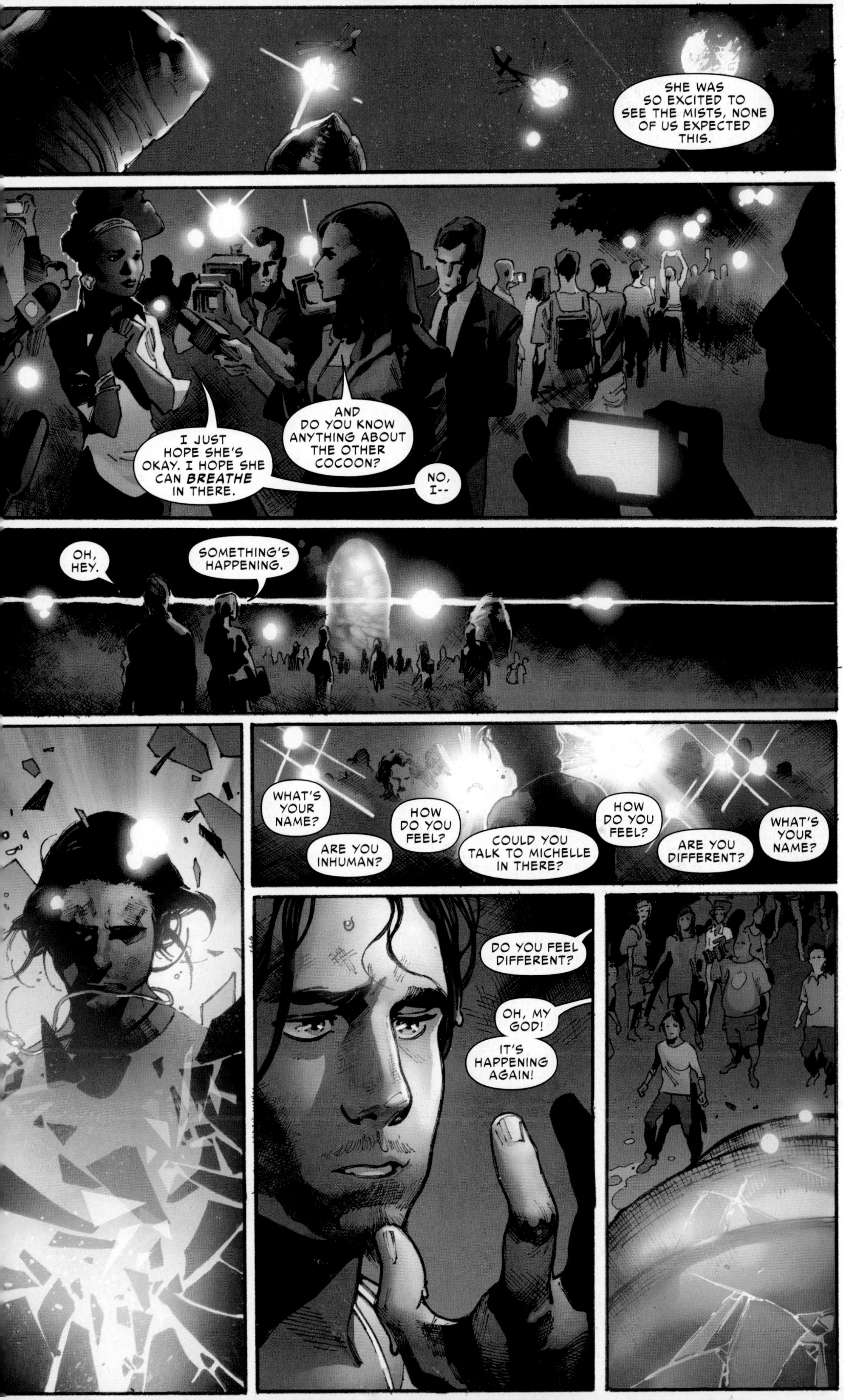
SHE WAS SO EXCITED TO SEE THE MISTS, NONE OF US EXPECTED THIS.
I JUST HOPE SHE'S OKAY. I HOPE SHE CAN *BREATHE* IN THERE.
AND DO YOU KNOW ANYTHING ABOUT THE OTHER COCOON?
NO, I--
OH, HEY.
SOMETHING'S HAPPENING.
WHAT'S YOUR NAME?
ARE YOU INHUMAN?
HOW DO YOU FEEL?
COULD YOU TALK TO MICHELLE IN THERE?
HOW DO YOU FEEL?
ARE YOU DIFFERENT?
WHAT'S YOUR NAME?
DO YOU FEEL DIFFERENT?
OH, MY GOD!
IT'S HAPPENING AGAIN!

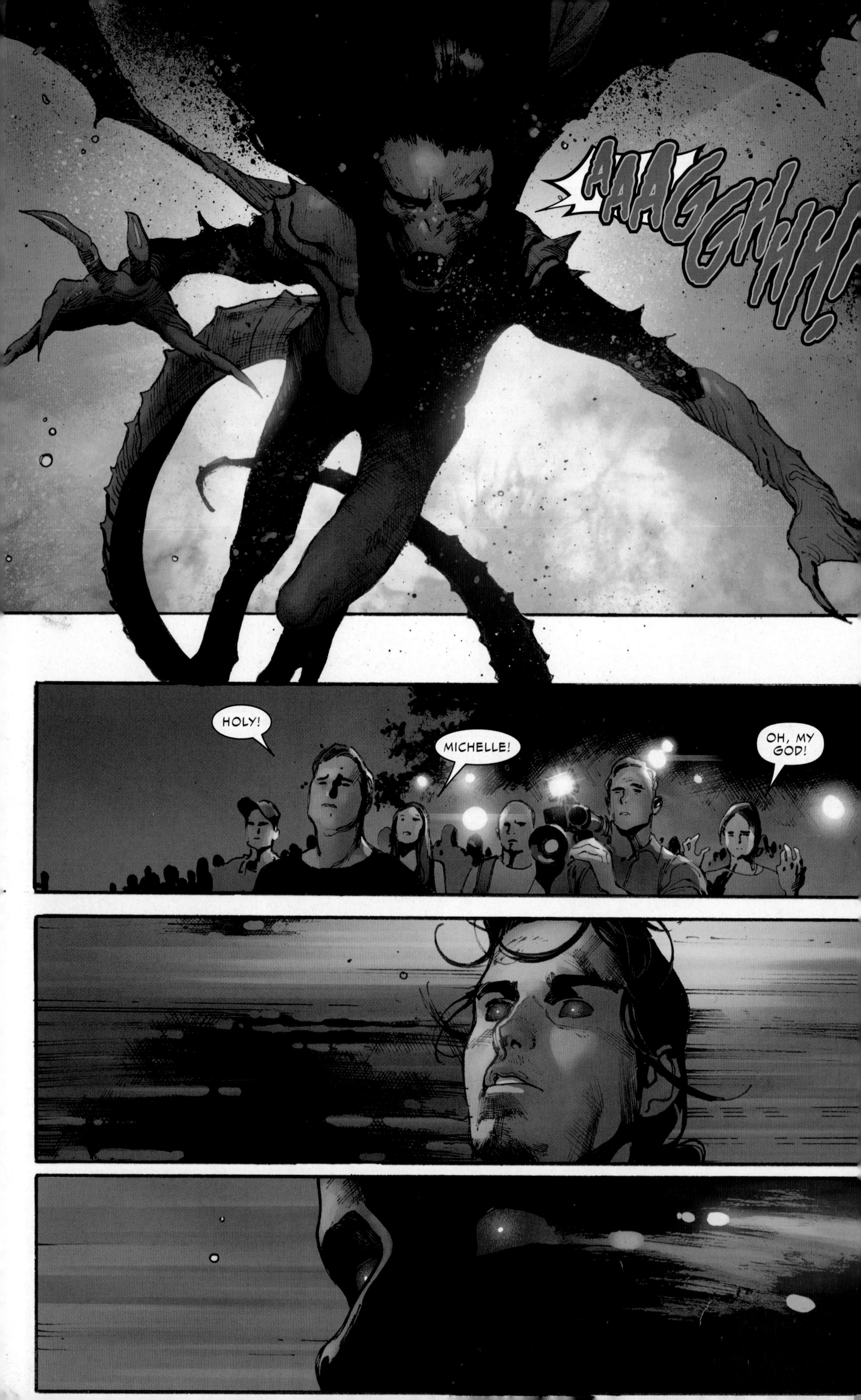
AAAGGHHH!
HOLY!
MICHELLE!
OH, MY GOD!

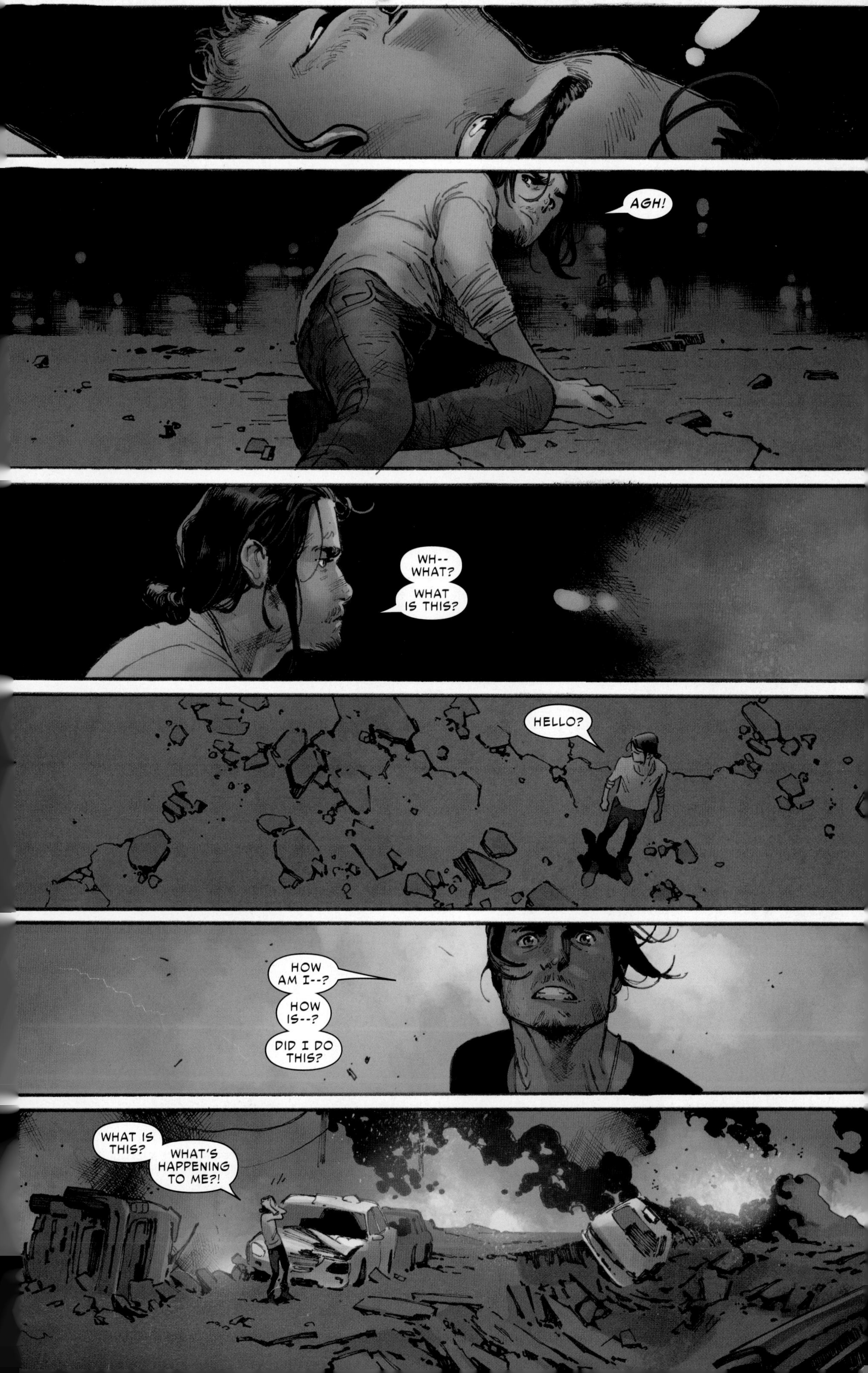
AGH!
WH-- WHAT?
WHAT IS THIS?
HELLO?
HOW AM I--?
HOW IS--?
DID I DO THIS?
WHAT IS THIS?
WHAT'S HAPPENING TO ME?!

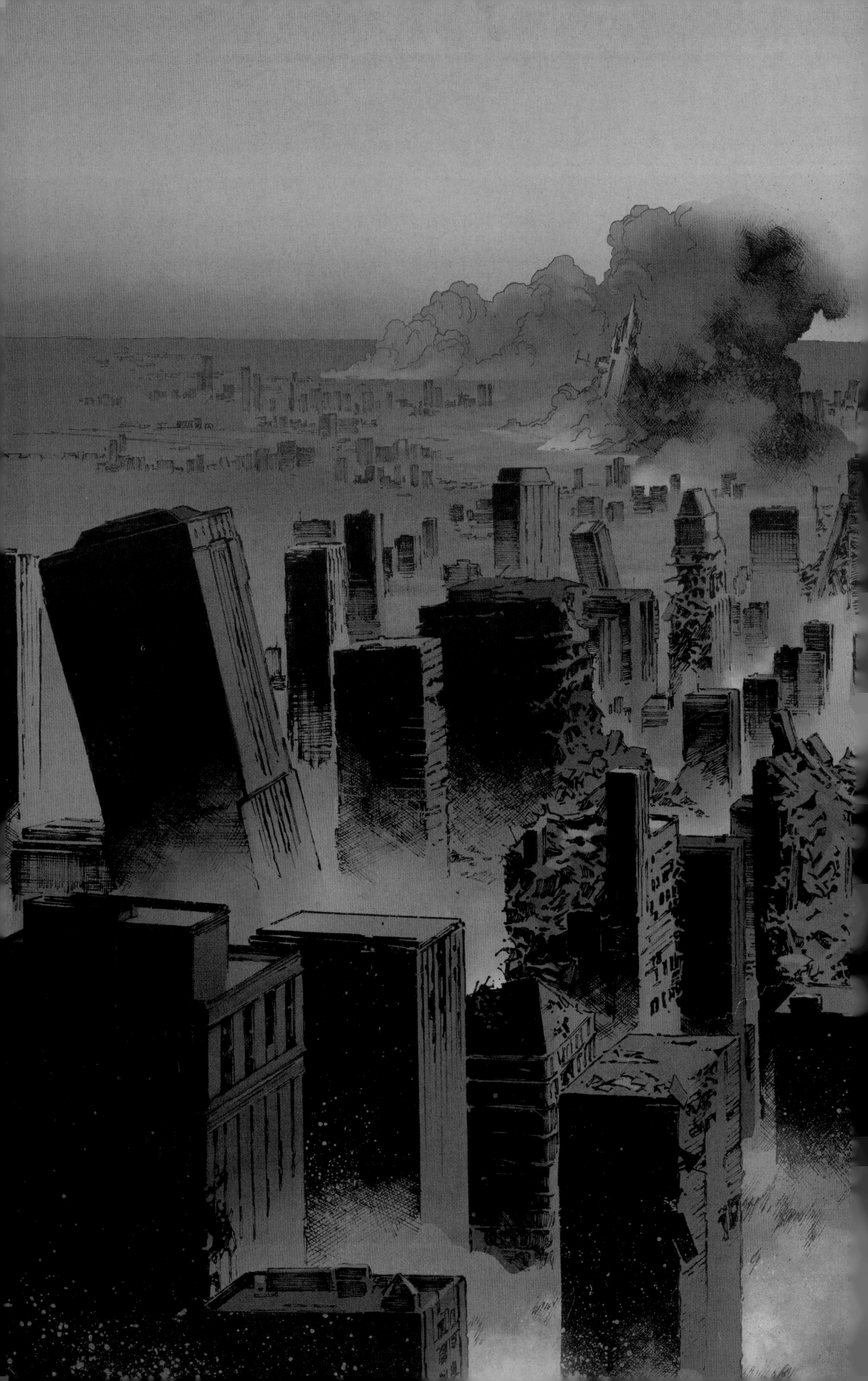

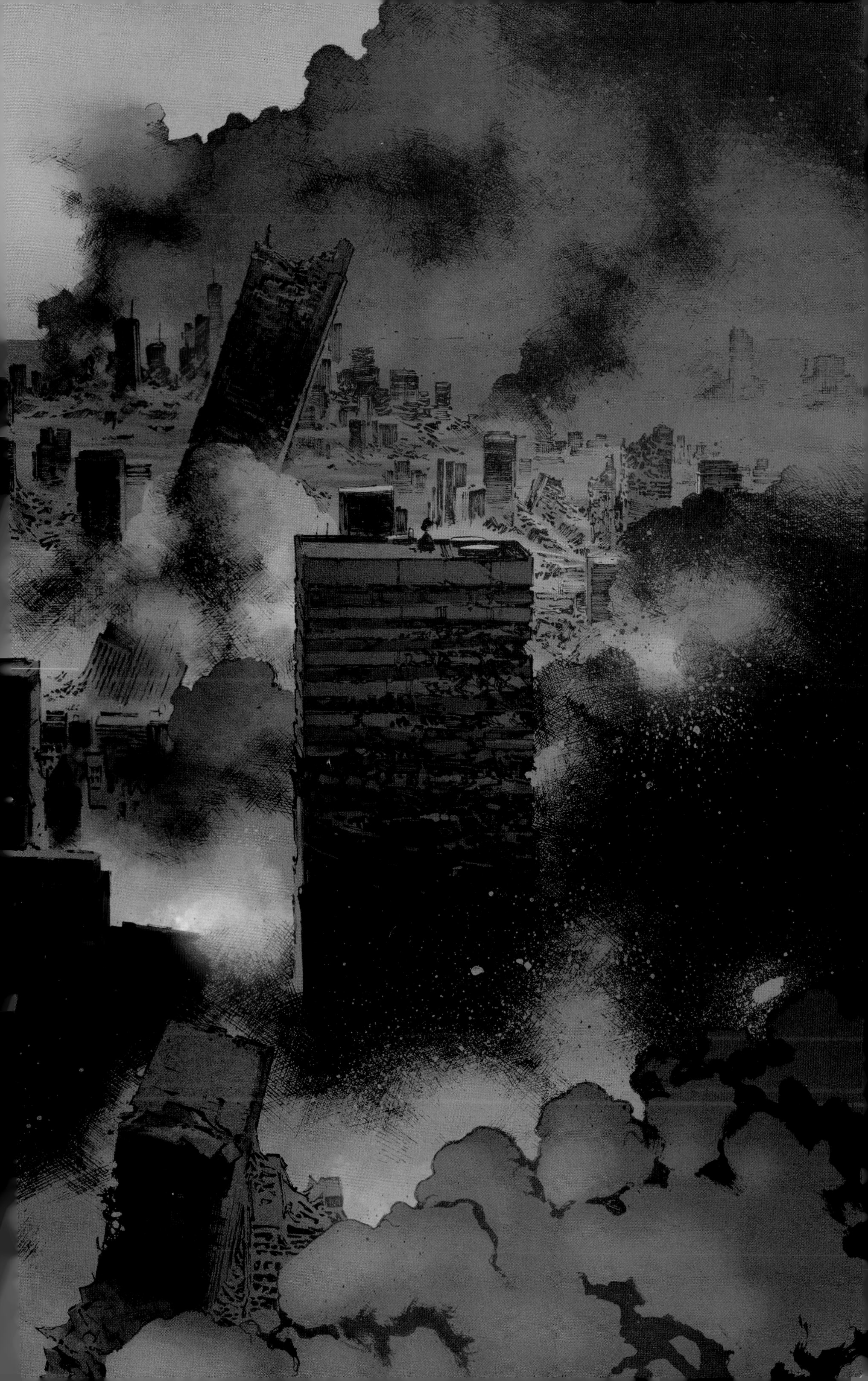

FREE COMIC BOOK DAY

CIVIL WAR II

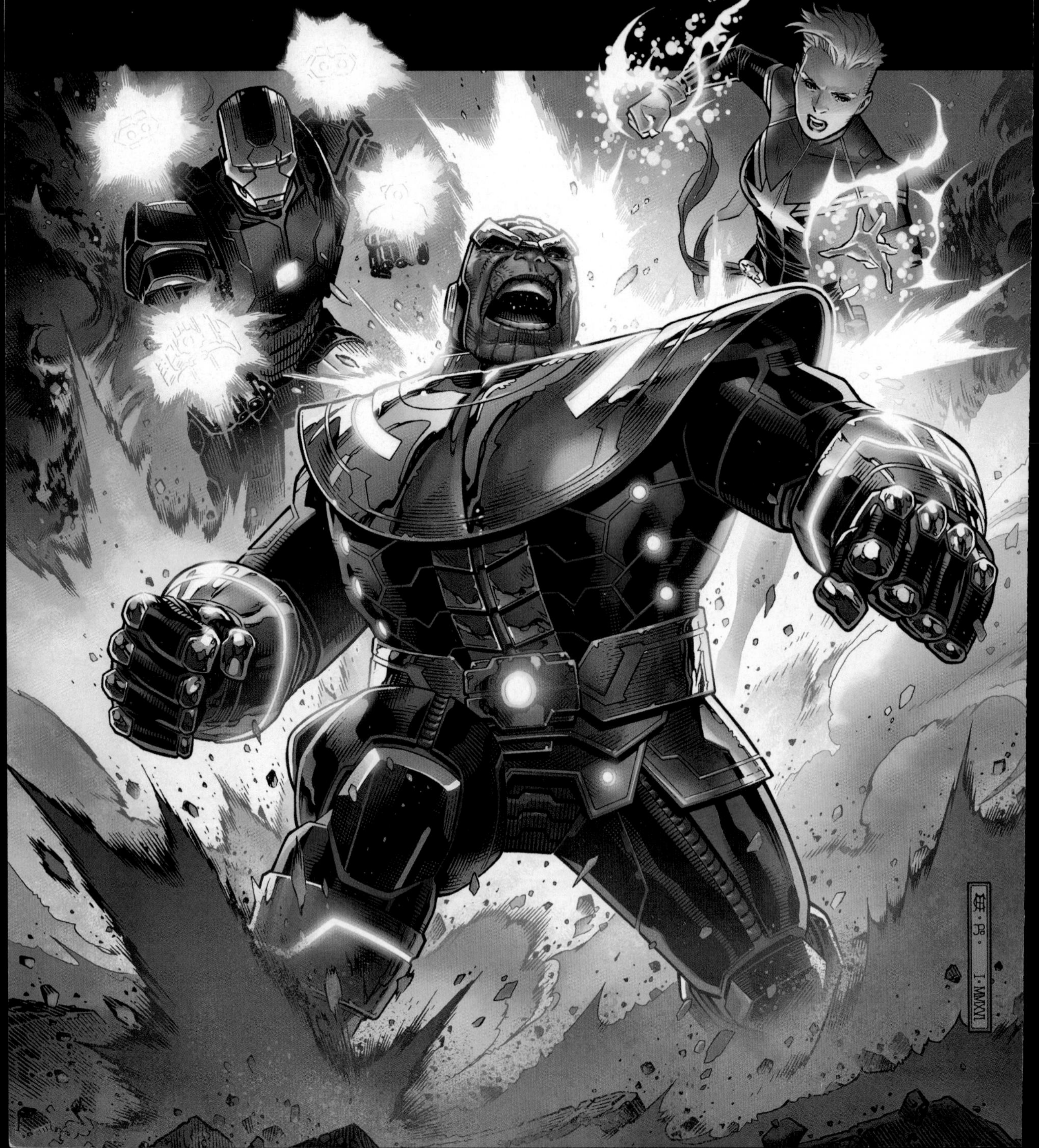

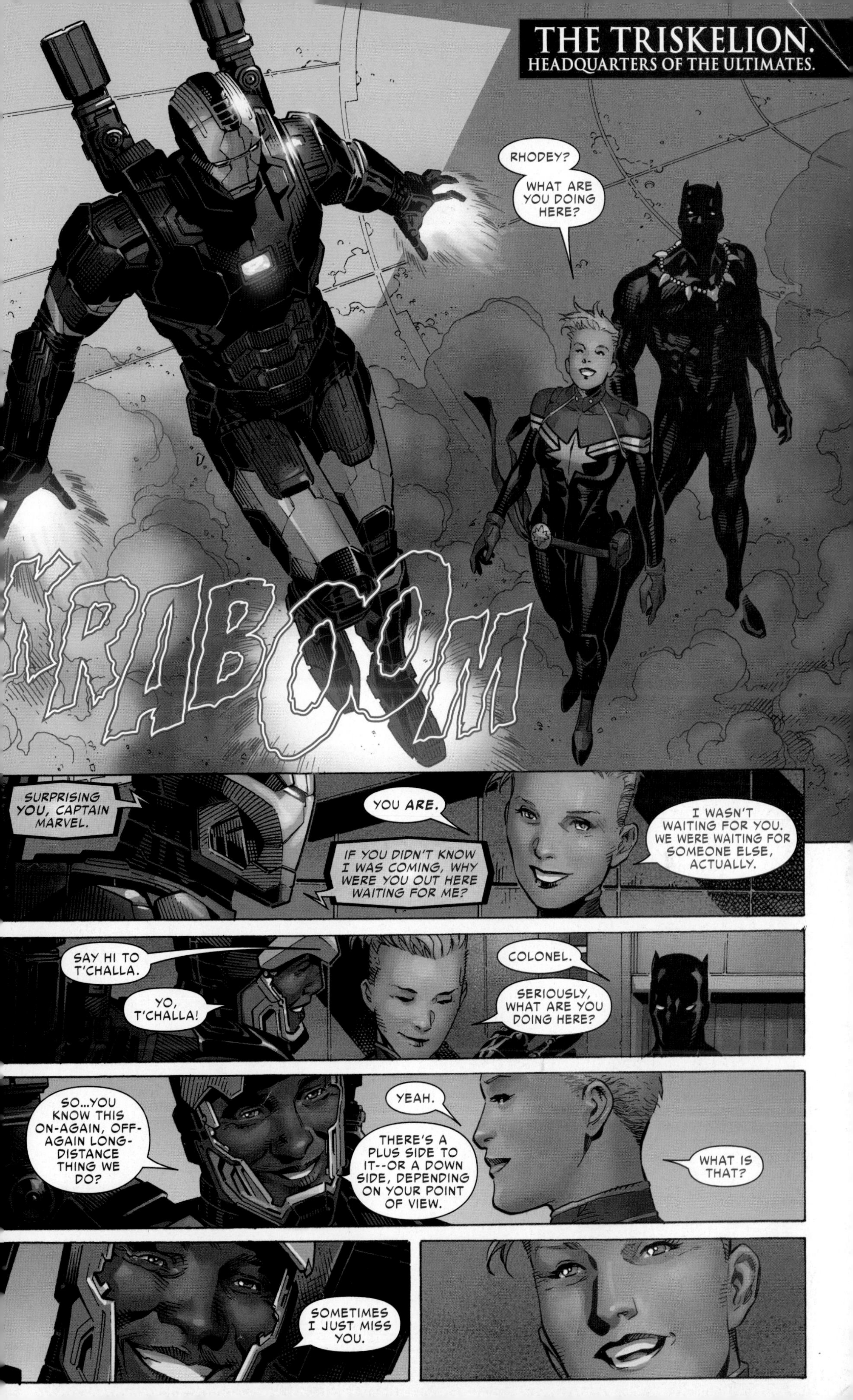
THE TRISKELION.
HEADQUARTERS OF THE ULTIMATES.
RHODEY?
WHAT ARE YOU DOING HERE?
KRABOOM
SURPRISING YOU, CAPTAIN MARVEL.
YOU ARE.
IF YOU DIDN'T KNOW I WAS COMING, WHY WERE YOU OUT HERE WAITING FOR ME?
I WASN'T WAITING FOR YOU. WE WERE WAITING FOR SOMEONE ELSE, ACTUALLY.
SAY HI TO T'CHALLA.
YO, T'CHALLA!
COLONEL.
SERIOUSLY, WHAT ARE YOU DOING HERE?
SO...YOU KNOW THIS ON-AGAIN, OFF-AGAIN LONG-DISTANCE THING WE DO?
YEAH.
THERE'S A PLUS SIDE TO IT--OR A DOWN SIDE, DEPENDING ON YOUR POINT OF VIEW.
WHAT IS THAT?
SOMETIMES I JUST MISS YOU.

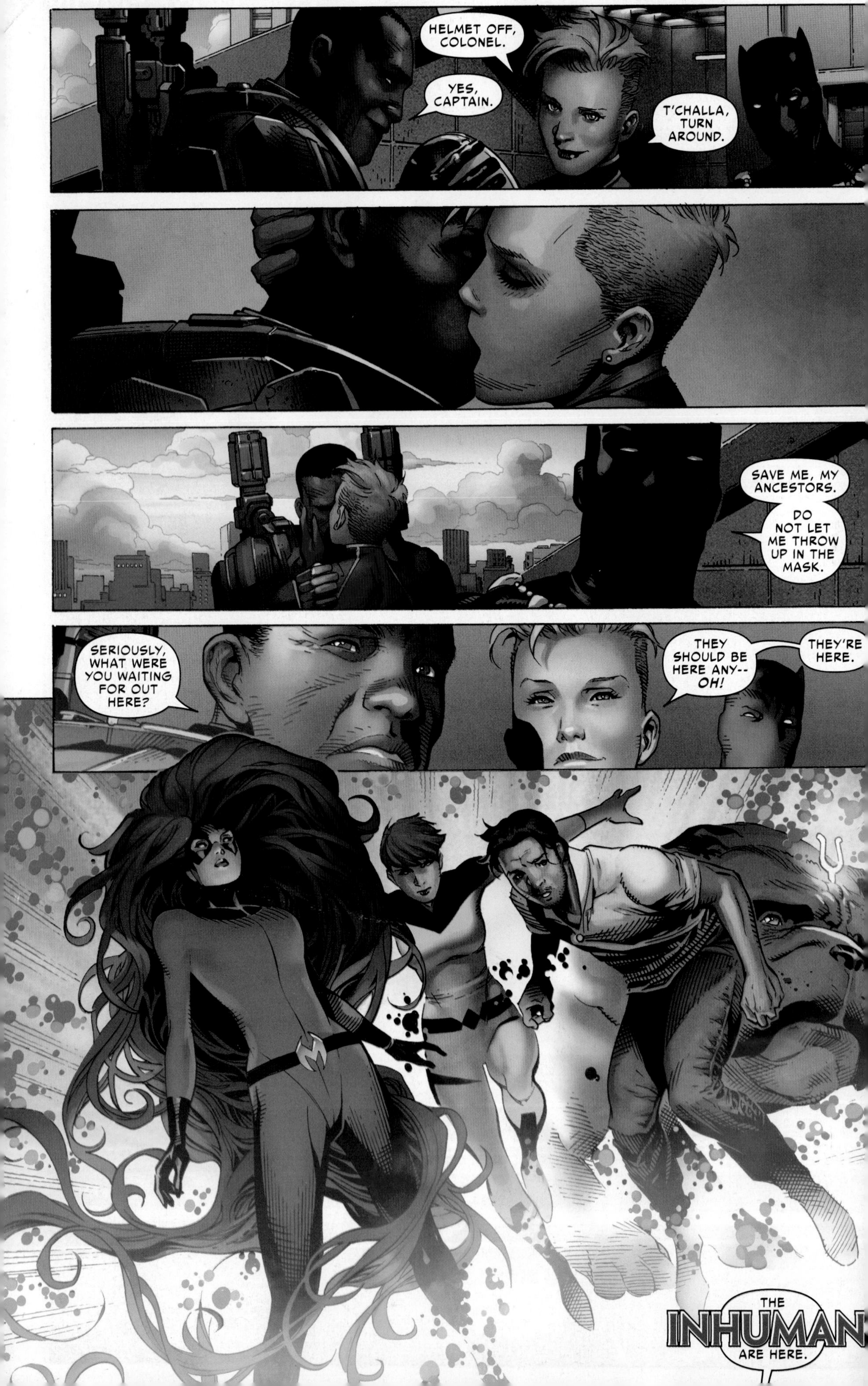
HELMET OFF, COLONEL.
YES, CAPTAIN.
T'CHALLA, TURN AROUND.
SAVE ME, MY ANCESTORS.
DO NOT LET ME THROW UP IN THE MASK.
SERIOUSLY, WHAT WERE YOU WAITING FOR OUT HERE?
THEY SHOULD BE HERE ANY-- OH!
THEY'RE HERE.
THE INHUMANS ARE HERE.

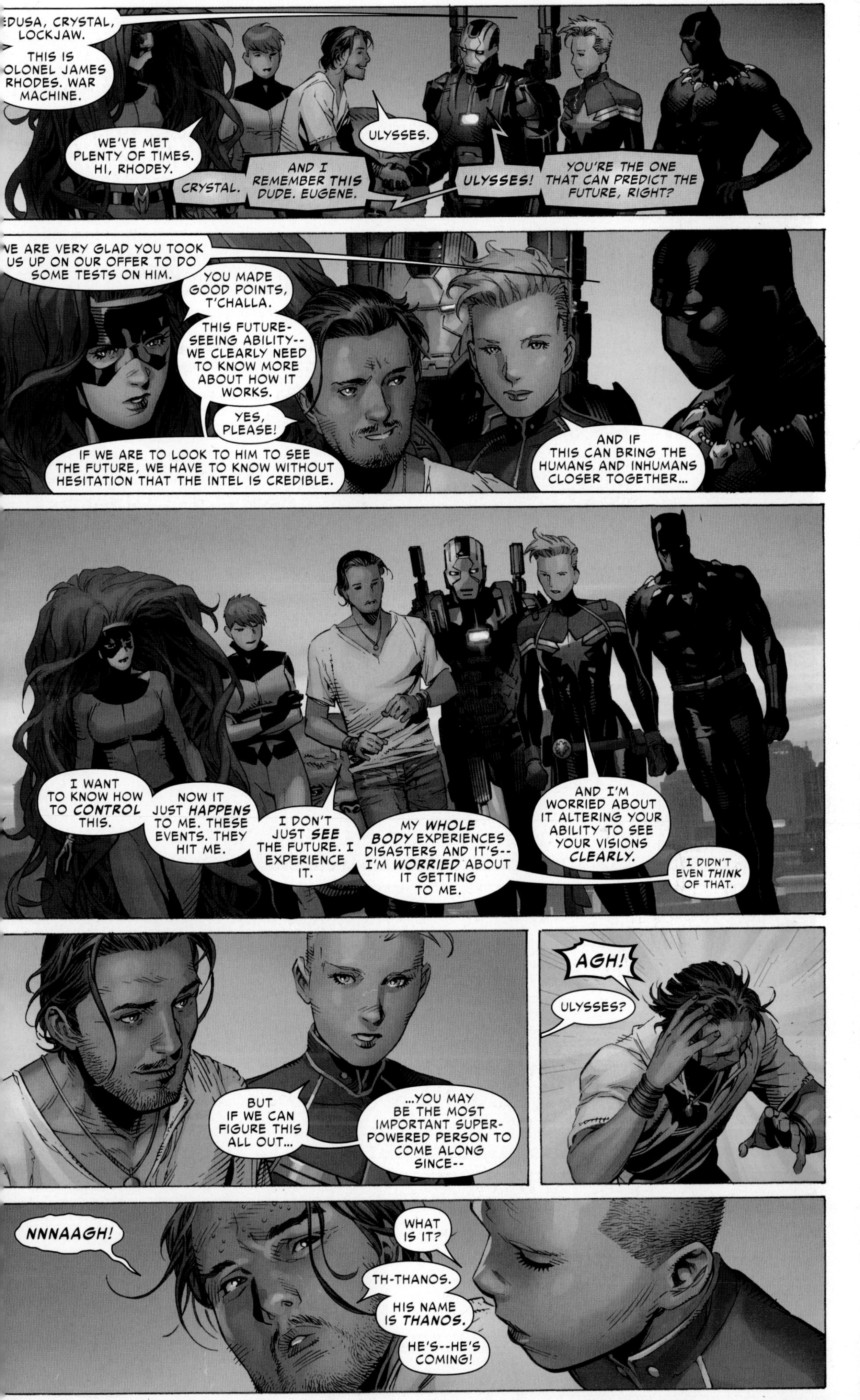

EDUSA, CRYSTAL, LOCKJAW.
THIS IS OLONEL JAMES RHODES. WAR MACHINE.
WE'VE MET PLENTY OF TIMES. HI, RHODEY.
CRYSTAL.
AND I REMEMBER THIS DUDE. EUGENE.
ULYSSES.
ULYSSES!
YOU'RE THE ONE THAT CAN PREDICT THE FUTURE, RIGHT?
WE ARE VERY GLAD YOU TOOK US UP ON OUR OFFER TO DO SOME TESTS ON HIM.
YOU MADE GOOD POINTS, T'CHALLA.
THIS FUTURE-SEEING ABILITY--WE CLEARLY NEED TO KNOW MORE ABOUT HOW IT WORKS.
YES, PLEASE!
IF WE ARE TO LOOK TO HIM TO SEE THE FUTURE, WE HAVE TO KNOW WITHOUT HESITATION THAT THE INTEL IS CREDIBLE.
AND IF THIS CAN BRING THE HUMANS AND INHUMANS CLOSER TOGETHER...
I WANT TO KNOW HOW TO CONTROL THIS.
NOW IT JUST HAPPENS TO ME. THESE EVENTS. THEY HIT ME.
I DON'T JUST SEE THE FUTURE. I EXPERIENCE IT.
MY WHOLE BODY EXPERIENCES DISASTERS AND IT'S--I'M WORRIED ABOUT IT GETTING TO ME.
AND I'M WORRIED ABOUT IT ALTERING YOUR ABILITY TO SEE YOUR VISIONS CLEARLY.
I DIDN'T EVEN THINK OF THAT.
BUT IF WE CAN FIGURE THIS ALL OUT...
...YOU MAY BE THE MOST IMPORTANT SUPER-POWERED PERSON TO COME ALONG SINCE--
AGH!
ULYSSES?
NNNAAGH!
WHAT IS IT?
TH-THANOS.
HIS NAME IS THANOS.
HE'S--HE'S COMING!

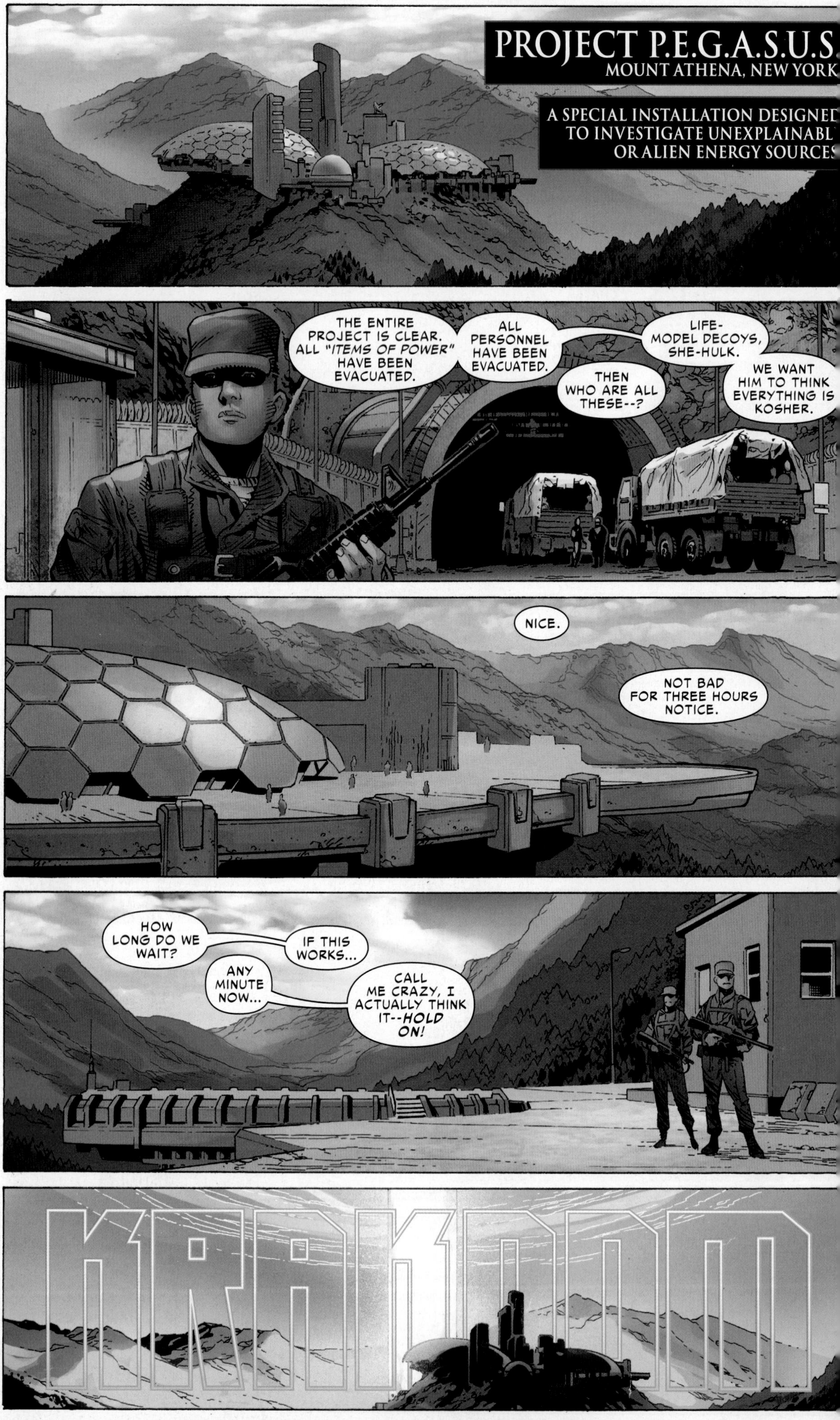
PROJECT P.E.G.A.S.U.S.
MOUNT ATHENA, NEW YORK
A SPECIAL INSTALLATION DESIGNED TO INVESTIGATE UNEXPLAINABLE OR ALIEN ENERGY SOURCES
THE ENTIRE PROJECT IS CLEAR. ALL "ITEMS OF POWER" HAVE BEEN EVACUATED.
ALL PERSONNEL HAVE BEEN EVACUATED.
THEN WHO ARE ALL THESE--?
LIFE-MODEL DECOYS, SHE-HULK.
WE WANT HIM TO THINK EVERYTHING IS KOSHER.
NICE.
NOT BAD FOR THREE HOURS NOTICE.
HOW LONG DO WE WAIT?
IF THIS WORKS...
ANY MINUTE NOW...
CALL ME CRAZY, I ACTUALLY THINK IT--HOLD ON!
KRAKOOM

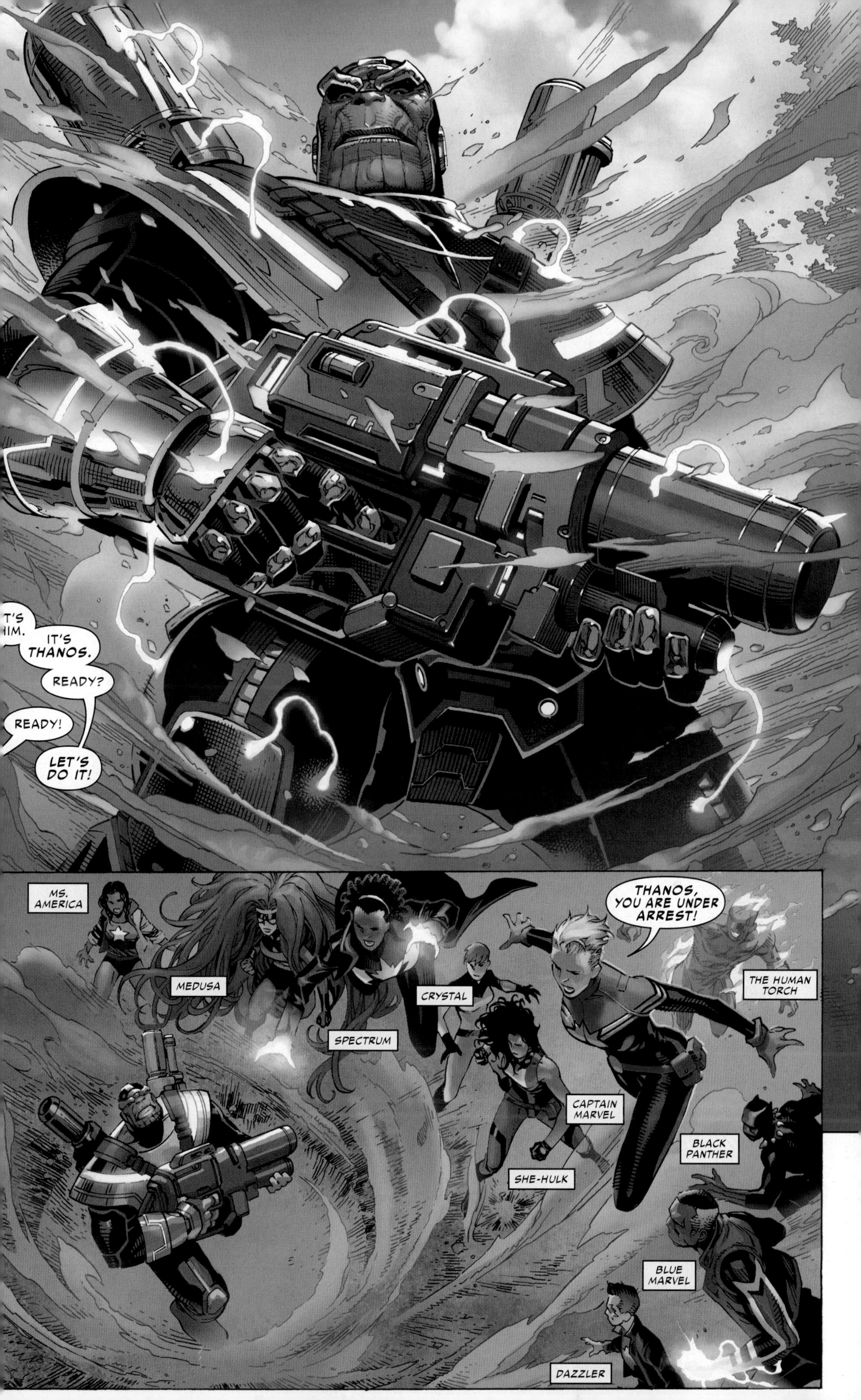
T'S
HIM.
IT'S
THANOS.
READY?
READY!
LET'S
DO IT!
MS.
AMERICA
MEDUSA
SPECTRUM
CRYSTAL
THANOS,
YOU ARE UNDER
ARREST!
THE HUMAN
TORCH
CAPTAIN
MARVEL
SHE-HULK
BLACK
PANTHER
BLUE
MARVEL
DAZZLER

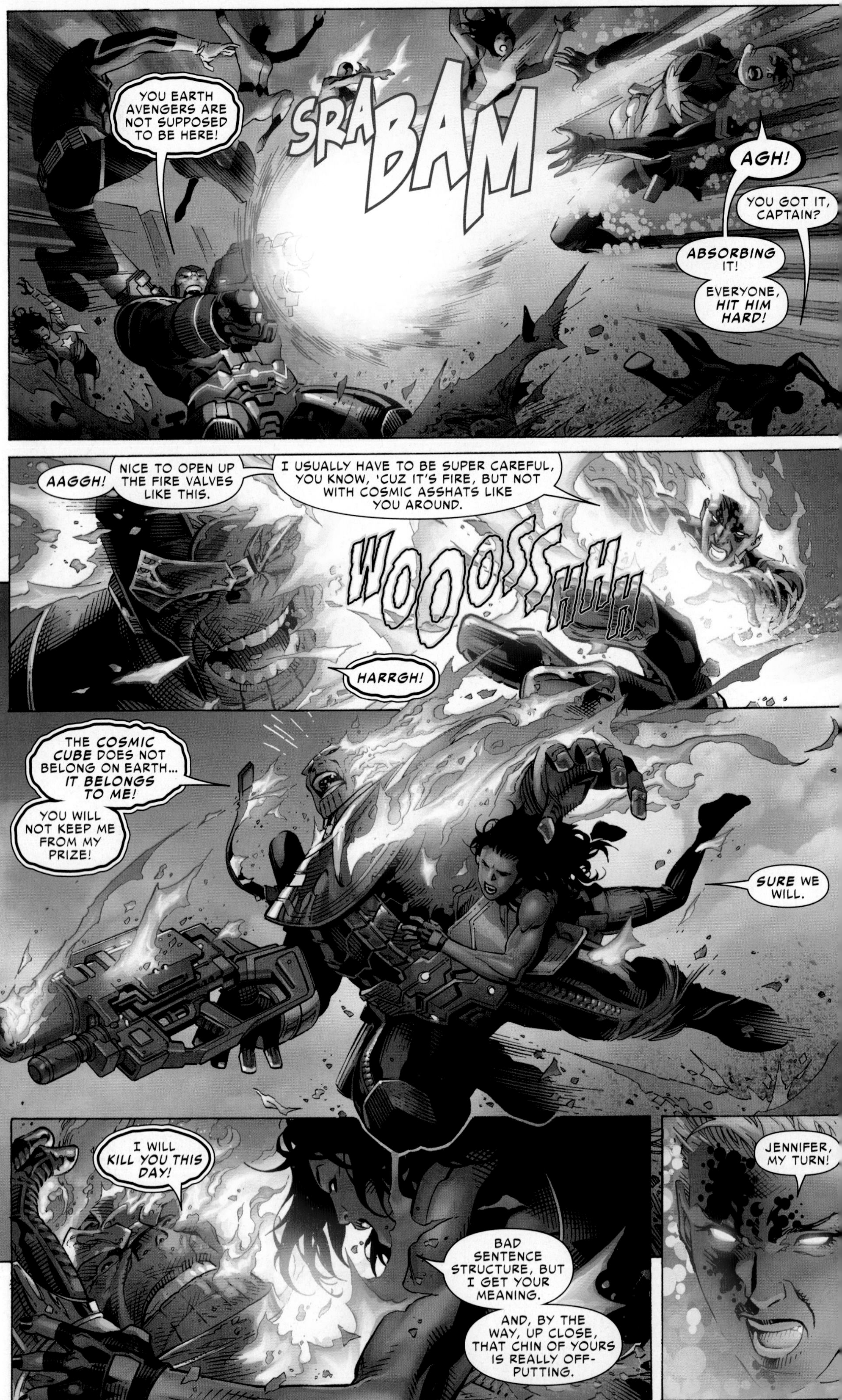

YOU EARTH AVENGERS ARE NOT SUPPOSED TO BE HERE!
SRABAM
AGH!
YOU GOT IT, CAPTAIN?
ABSORBING IT!
EVERYONE, HIT HIM HARD!
AAGGH!
NICE TO OPEN UP THE FIRE VALVES LIKE THIS.
I USUALLY HAVE TO BE SUPER CAREFUL, YOU KNOW, 'CUZ IT'S FIRE, BUT NOT WITH COSMIC ASSHATS LIKE YOU AROUND.
WOOOSSHHH
HARRGH!
THE COSMIC CUBE DOES NOT BELONG ON EARTH... IT BELONGS TO ME!
YOU WILL NOT KEEP ME FROM MY PRIZE!
SURE WE WILL.
I WILL KILL YOU THIS DAY!
BAD SENTENCE STRUCTURE, BUT I GET YOUR MEANING.
AND, BY THE WAY, UP CLOSE, THAT CHIN OF YOURS IS REALLY OFF-PUTTING.
JENNIFER, MY TURN!

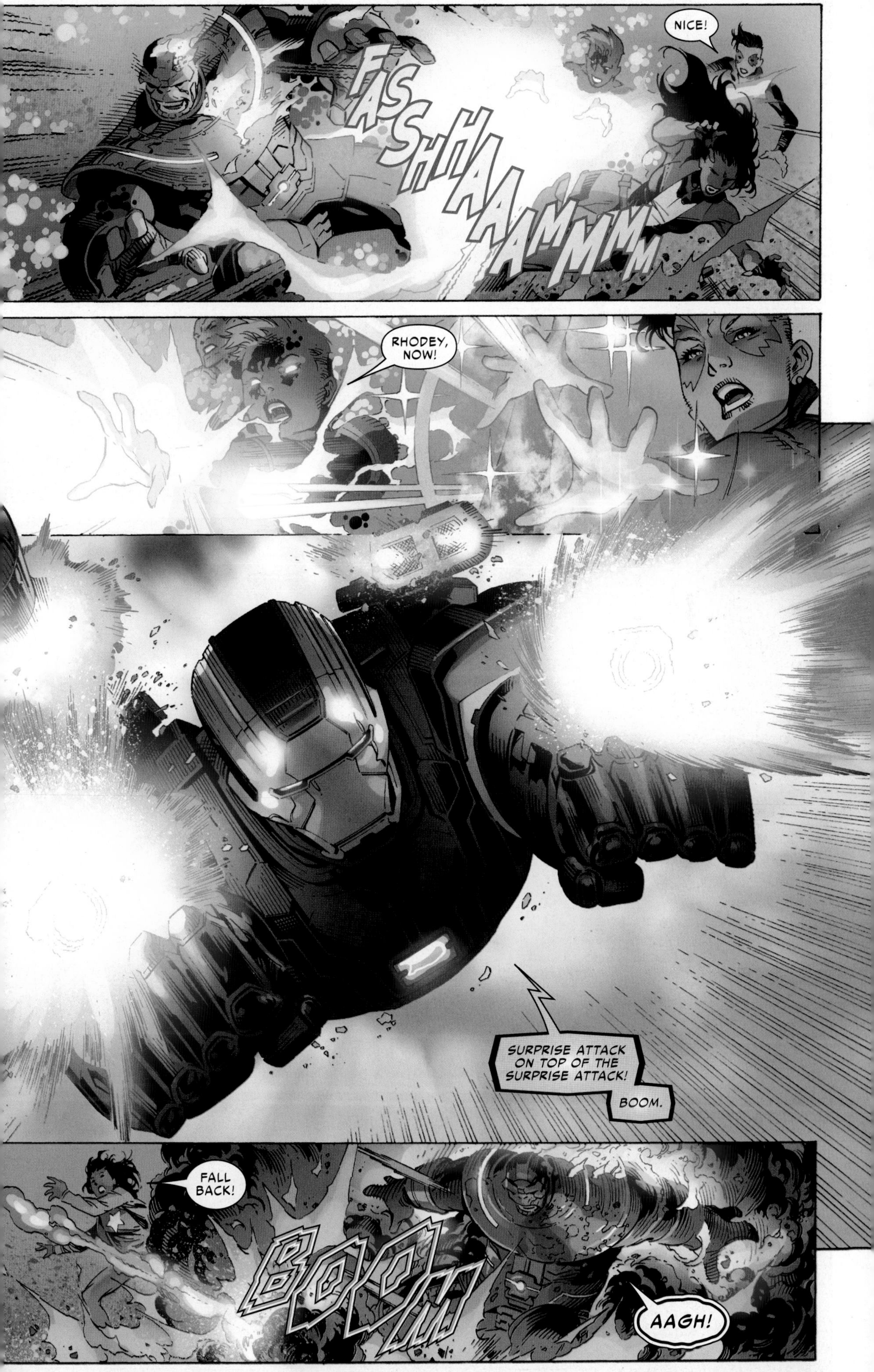
FASHHAAAMMMM
NICE!
RHODEY, NOW!
SURPRISE ATTACK ON TOP OF THE SURPRISE ATTACK!
BOOM.
FALL BACK!
BOOM
AAGH!

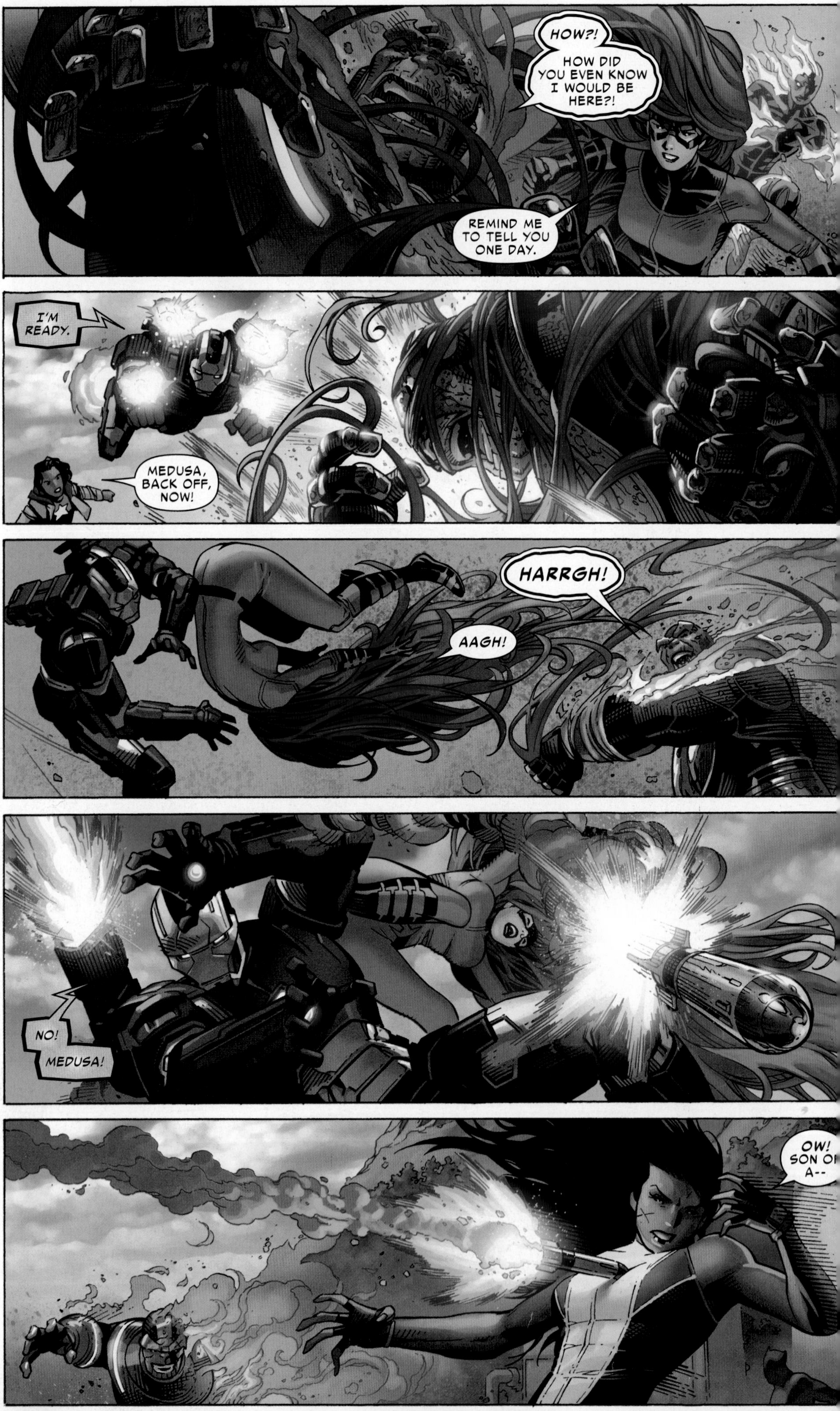

HOW?!
HOW DID YOU EVEN KNOW I WOULD BE HERE?!
REMIND ME TO TELL YOU ONE DAY.
I'M READY.
MEDUSA, BACK OFF, NOW!
HARRGH!
AAGH!
NO! MEDUSA!
OW! SON OF A--

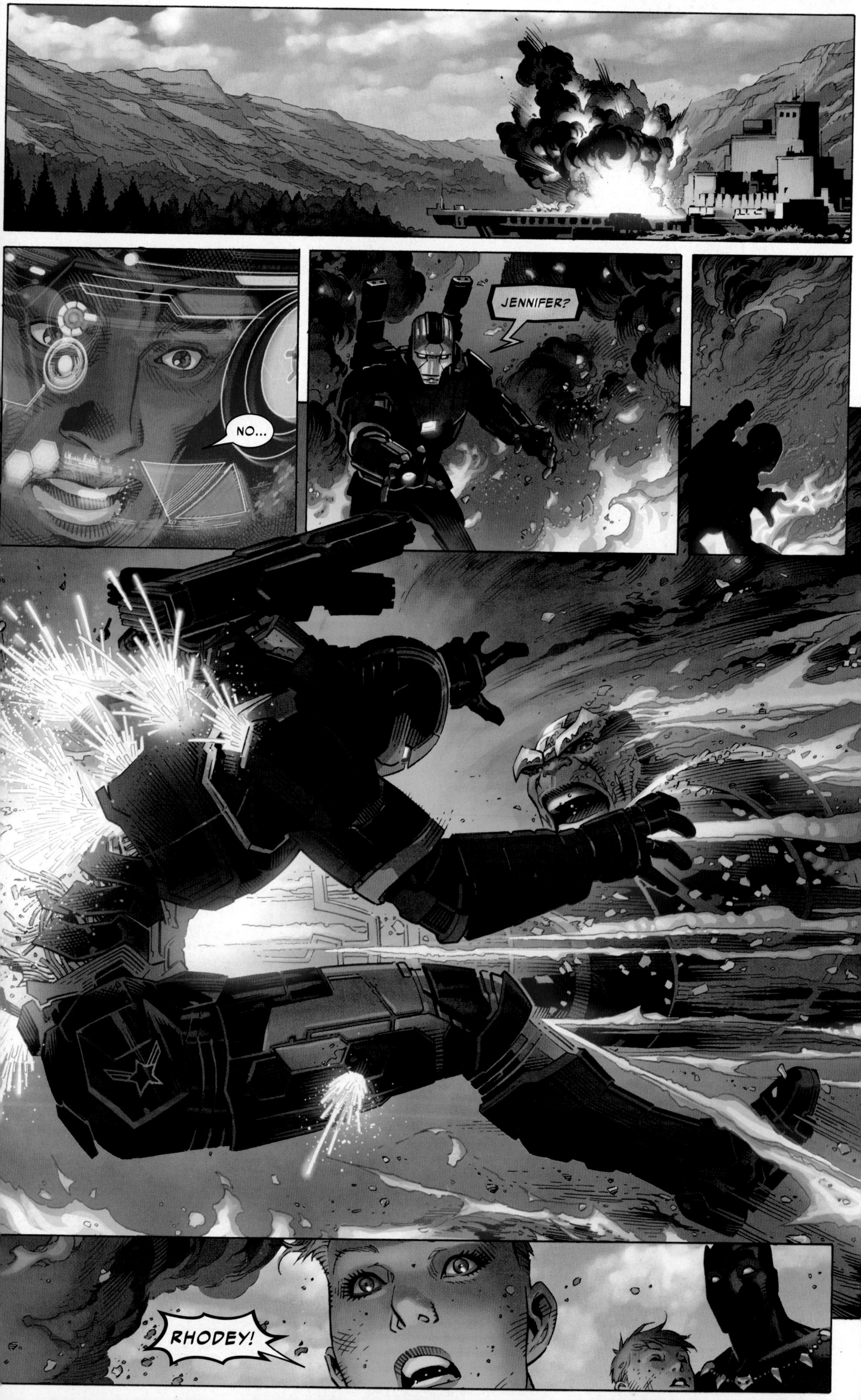
NO...
JENNIFER?
RHODEY!

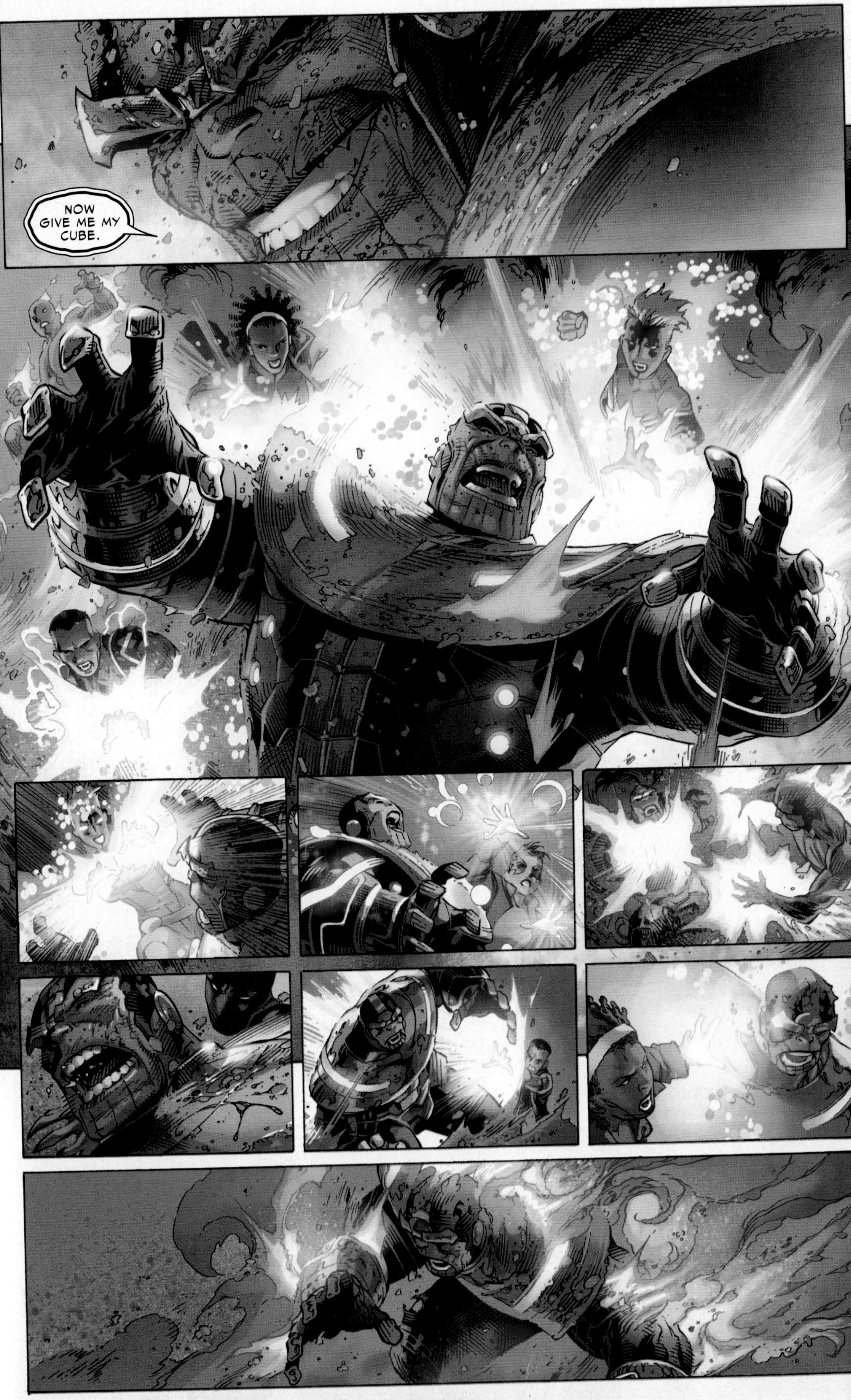
NOW GIVE ME MY CUBE.

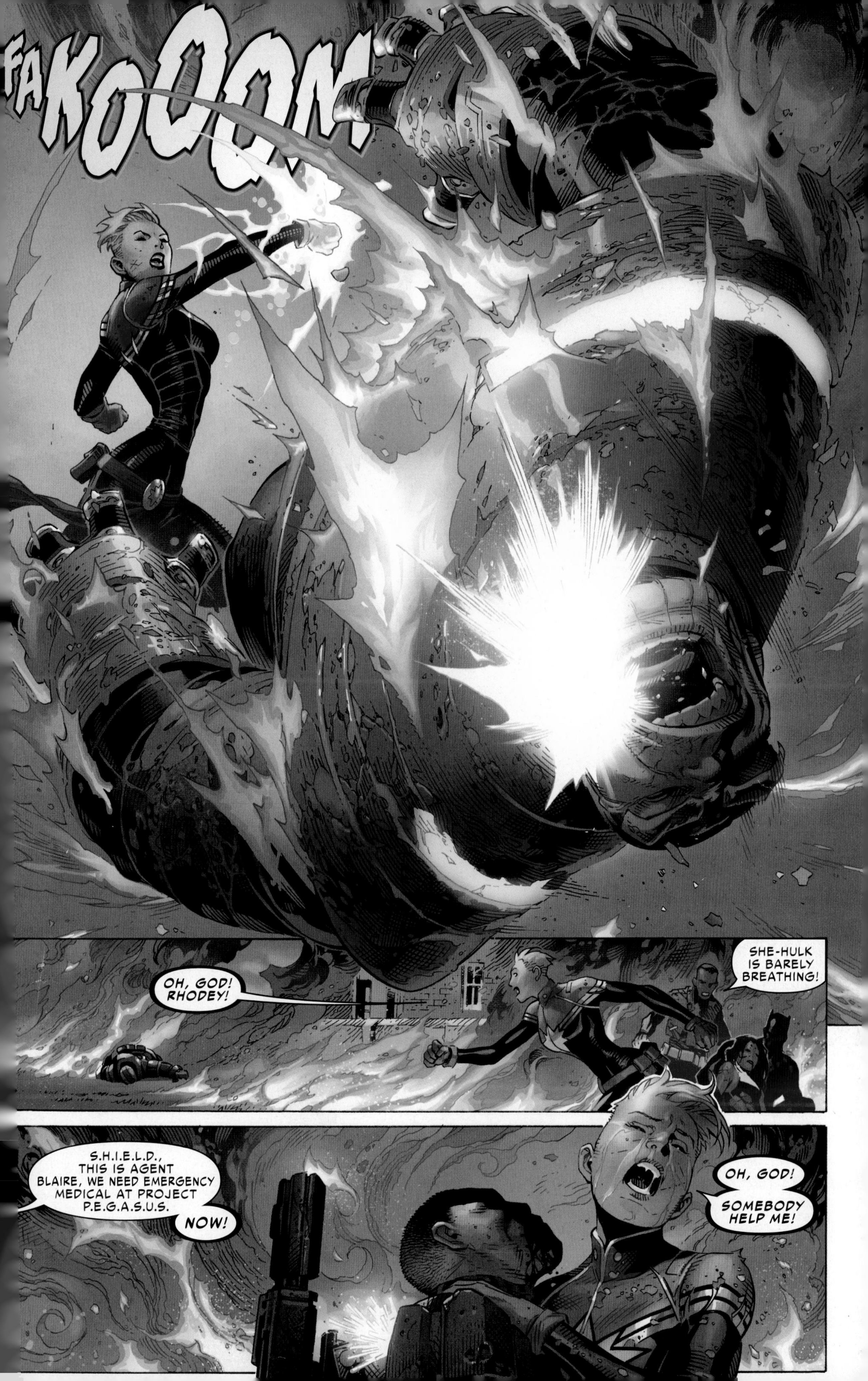
FAKOOOM
OH, GOD! RHODEY!
SHE-HULK IS BARELY BREATHING!
S.H.I.E.L.D., THIS IS AGENT BLAIRE, WE NEED EMERGENCY MEDICAL AT PROJECT P.E.G.A.S.U.S.
NOW!
OH, GOD!
SOMEBODY HELP ME!

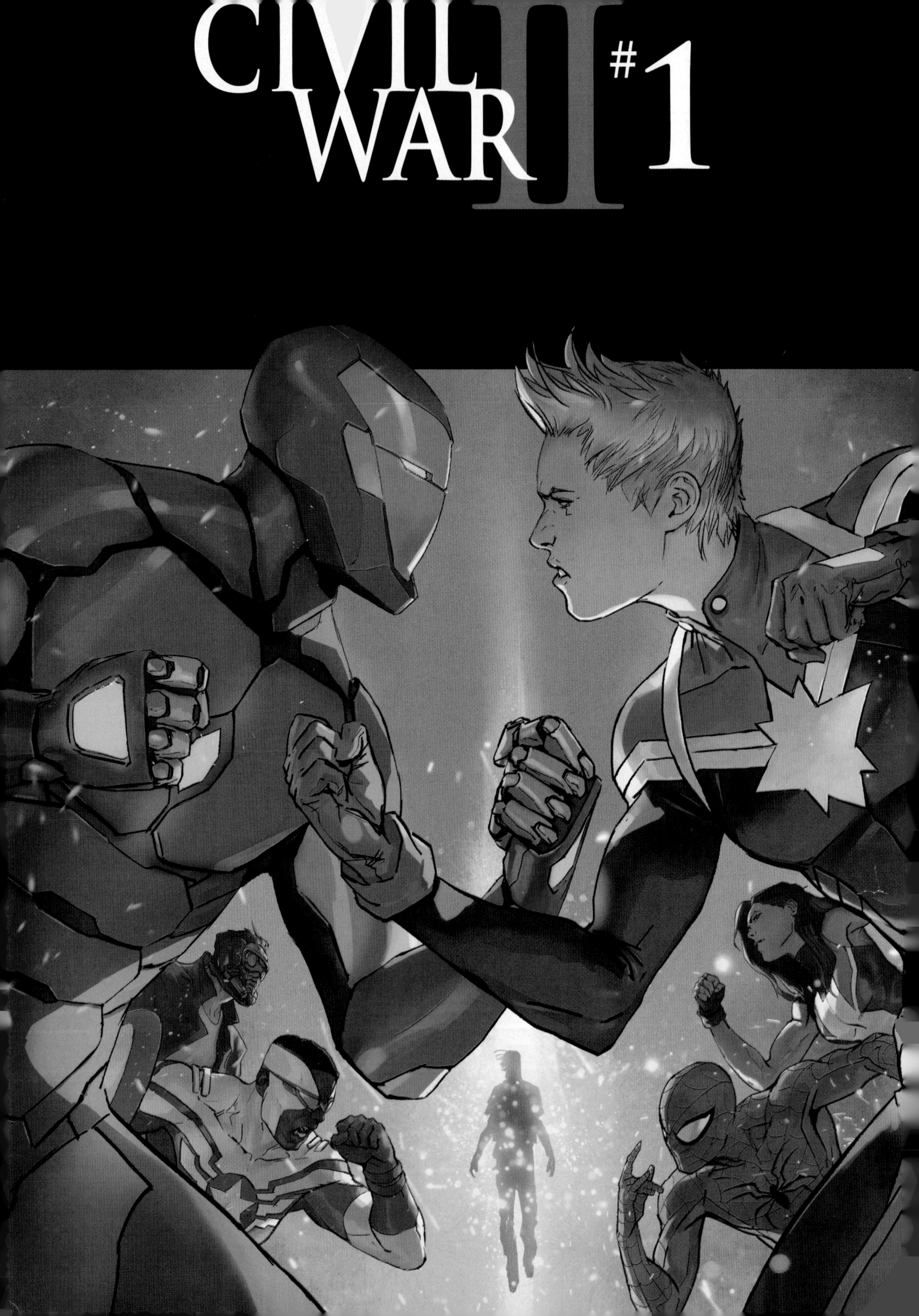
CIVIL WAR II
#1

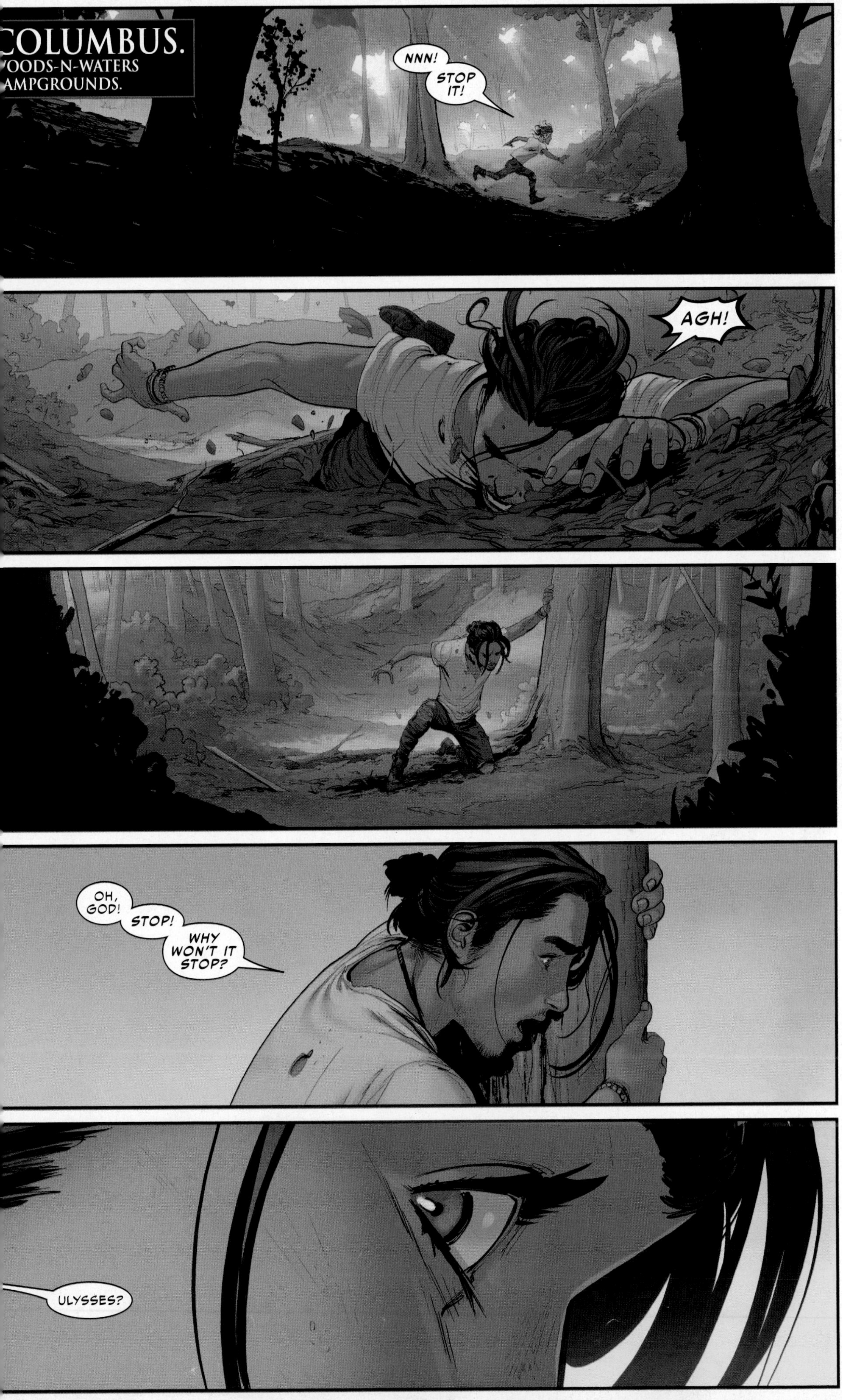
COLUMBUS.
OODS-N-WATERS
AMPGROUNDS.
NNN!
STOP IT!
AGH!
OH, GOD!
STOP!
WHY WON'T IT STOP?
ULYSSES?

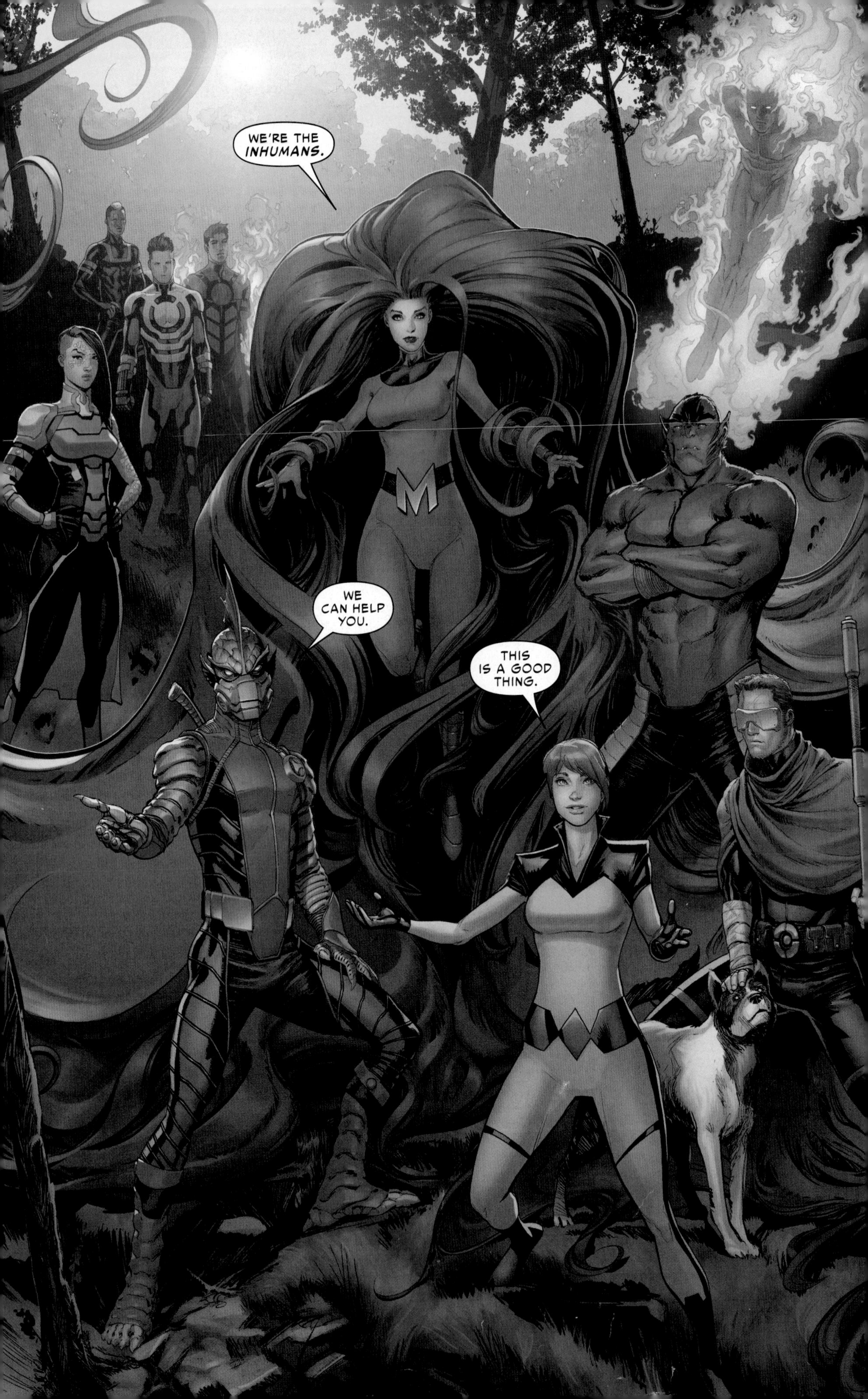
WE'RE THE INHUMANS.
WE CAN HELP YOU.
THIS IS A GOOD THING.

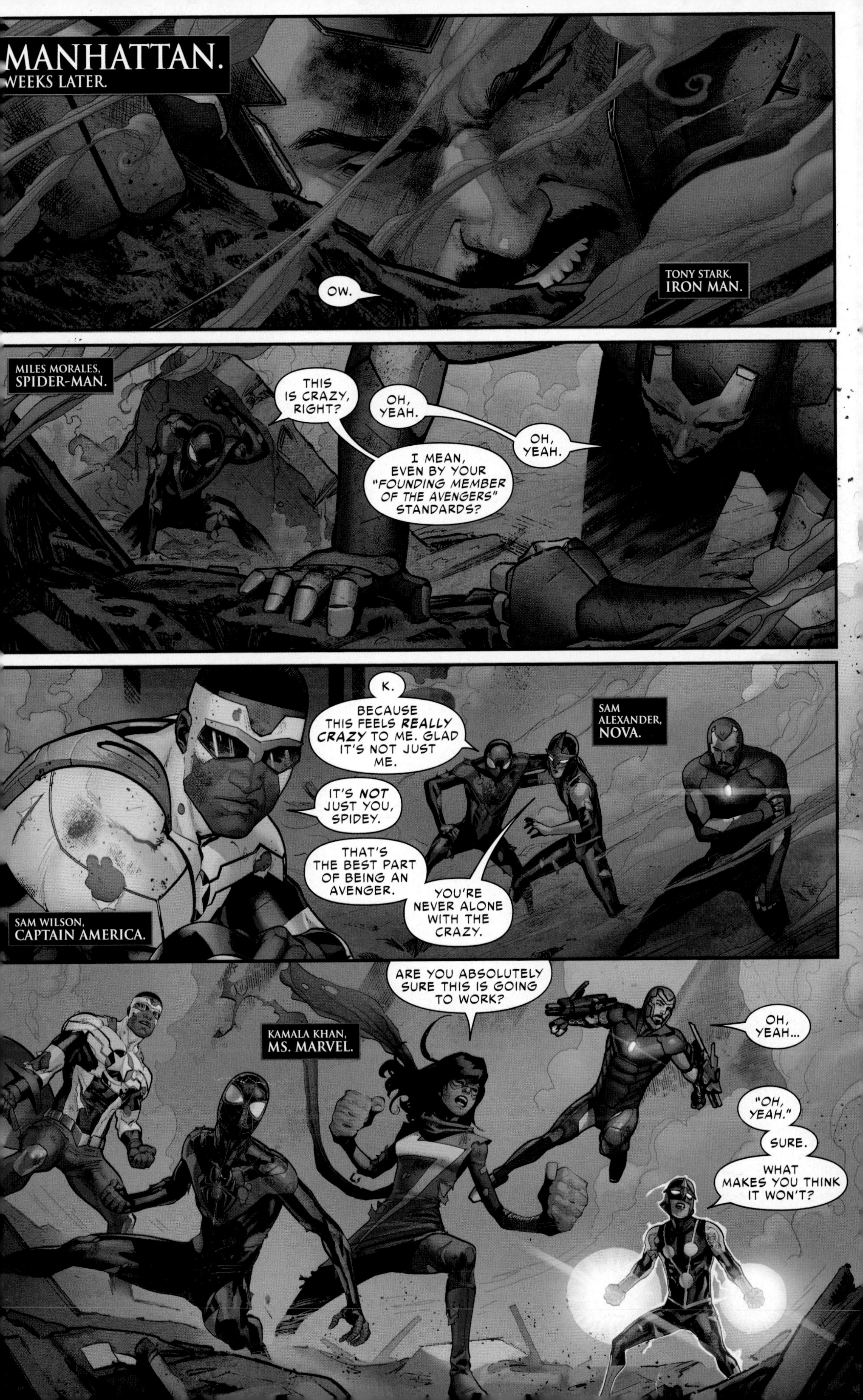
MANHATTAN.
WEEKS LATER.
TONY STARK,
IRON MAN.
OW.
MILES MORALES,
SPIDER-MAN.
THIS IS CRAZY, RIGHT?
OH, YEAH.
OH, YEAH.
I MEAN, EVEN BY YOUR "FOUNDING MEMBER OF THE AVENGERS" STANDARDS?
K.
BECAUSE THIS FEELS REALLY CRAZY TO ME. GLAD IT'S NOT JUST ME.
SAM ALEXANDER,
NOVA.
IT'S NOT JUST YOU, SPIDEY.
THAT'S THE BEST PART OF BEING AN AVENGER.
YOU'RE NEVER ALONE WITH THE CRAZY.
SAM WILSON,
CAPTAIN AMERICA.
ARE YOU ABSOLUTELY SURE THIS IS GOING TO WORK?
KAMALA KHAN,
MS. MARVEL.
OH, YEAH...
"OH, YEAH."
SURE.
WHAT MAKES YOU THINK IT WON'T?

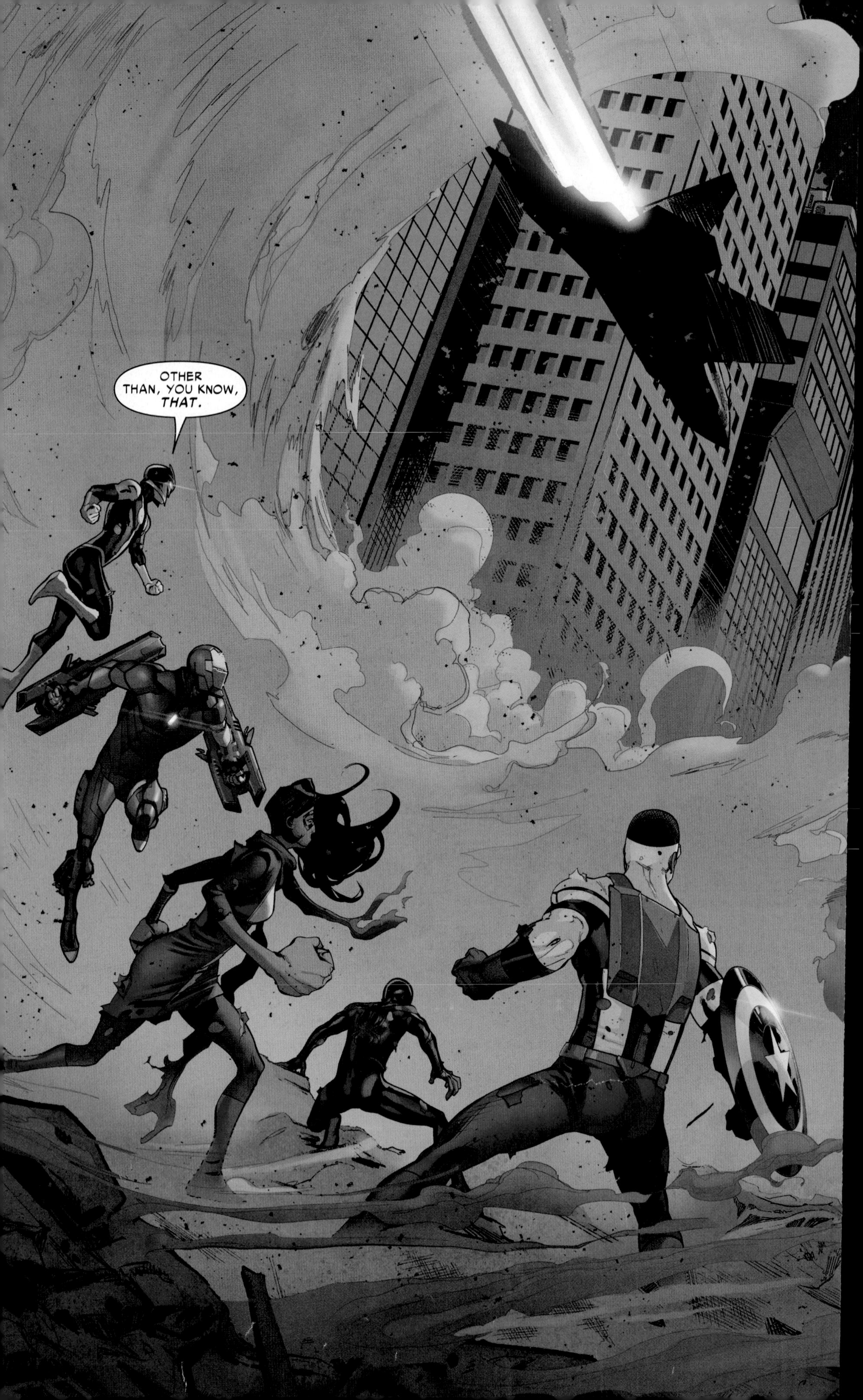
OTHER THAN, YOU KNOW, *THAT*.

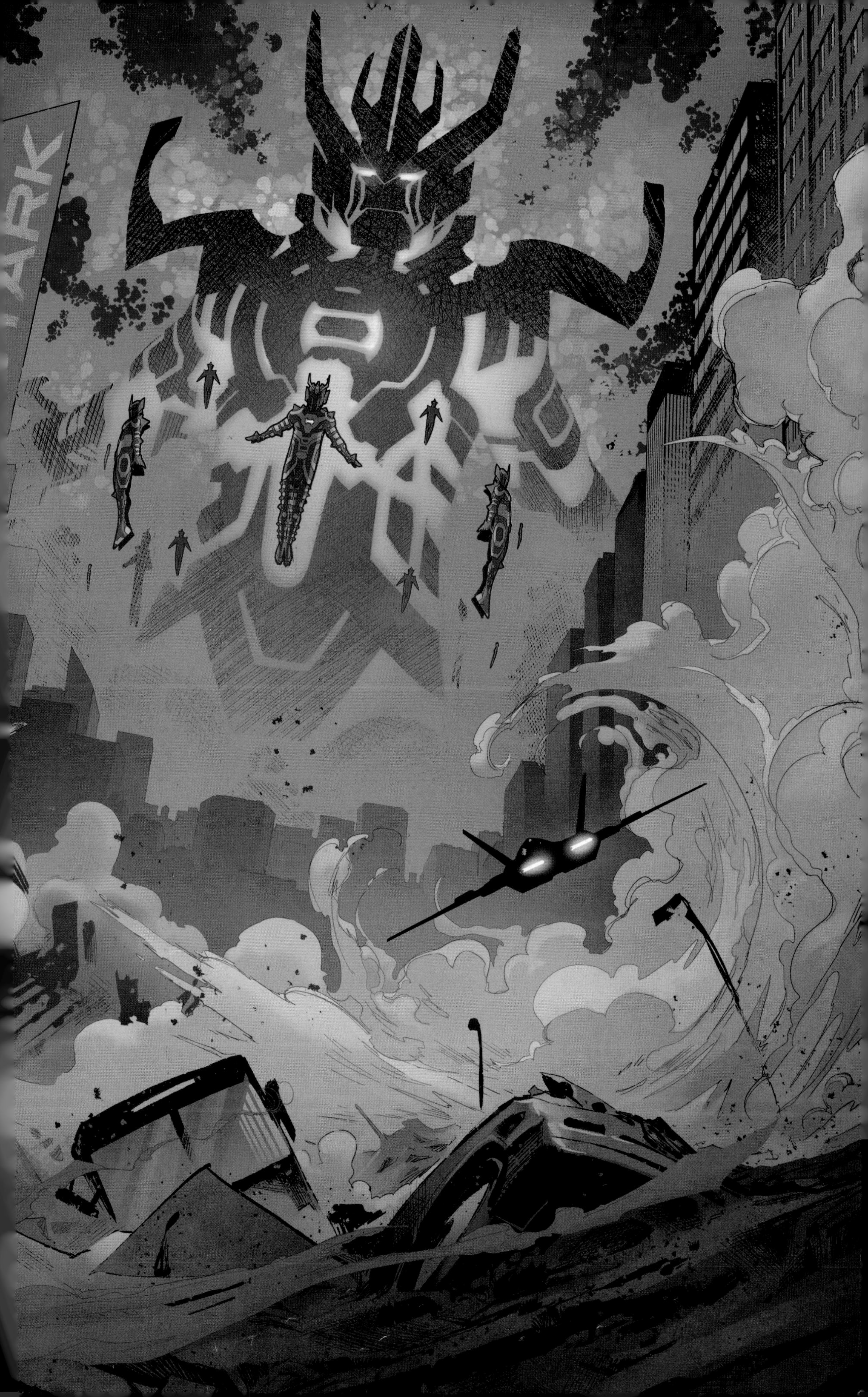
ARK

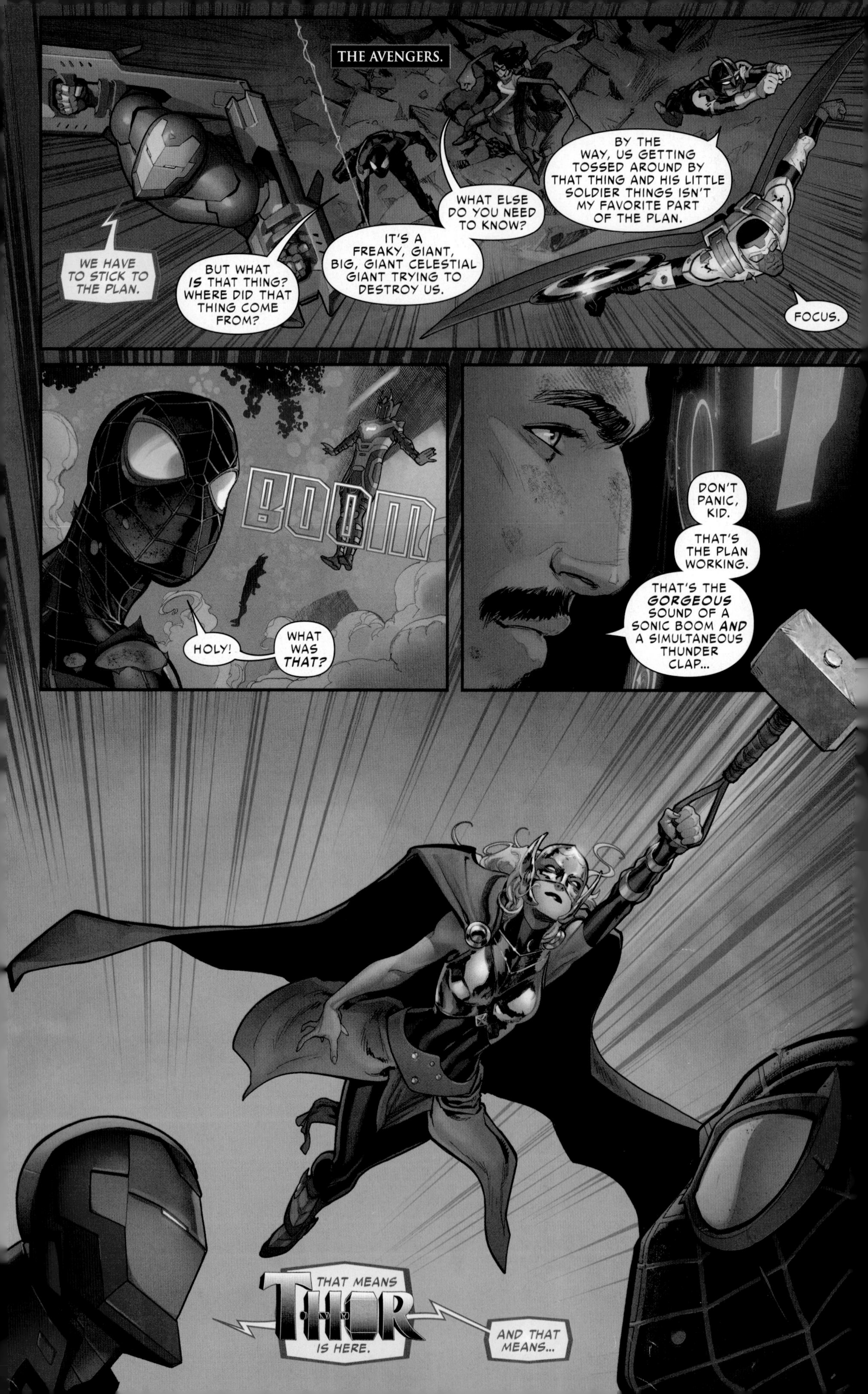
THE AVENGERS.
WE HAVE TO STICK TO THE PLAN.
BUT WHAT IS THAT THING? WHERE DID THAT THING COME FROM?
IT'S A FREAKY, GIANT, BIG, GIANT CELESTIAL GIANT TRYING TO DESTROY US.
WHAT ELSE DO YOU NEED TO KNOW?
BY THE WAY, US GETTING TOSSED AROUND BY THAT THING AND HIS LITTLE SOLDIER THINGS ISN'T MY FAVORITE PART OF THE PLAN.
FOCUS.
BOOM
HOLY!
WHAT WAS THAT?
DON'T PANIC, KID.
THAT'S THE PLAN WORKING.
THAT'S THE GORGEOUS SOUND OF A SONIC BOOM AND A SIMULTANEOUS THUNDER CLAP...
THAT MEANS THOR IS HERE.
AND THAT MEANS...

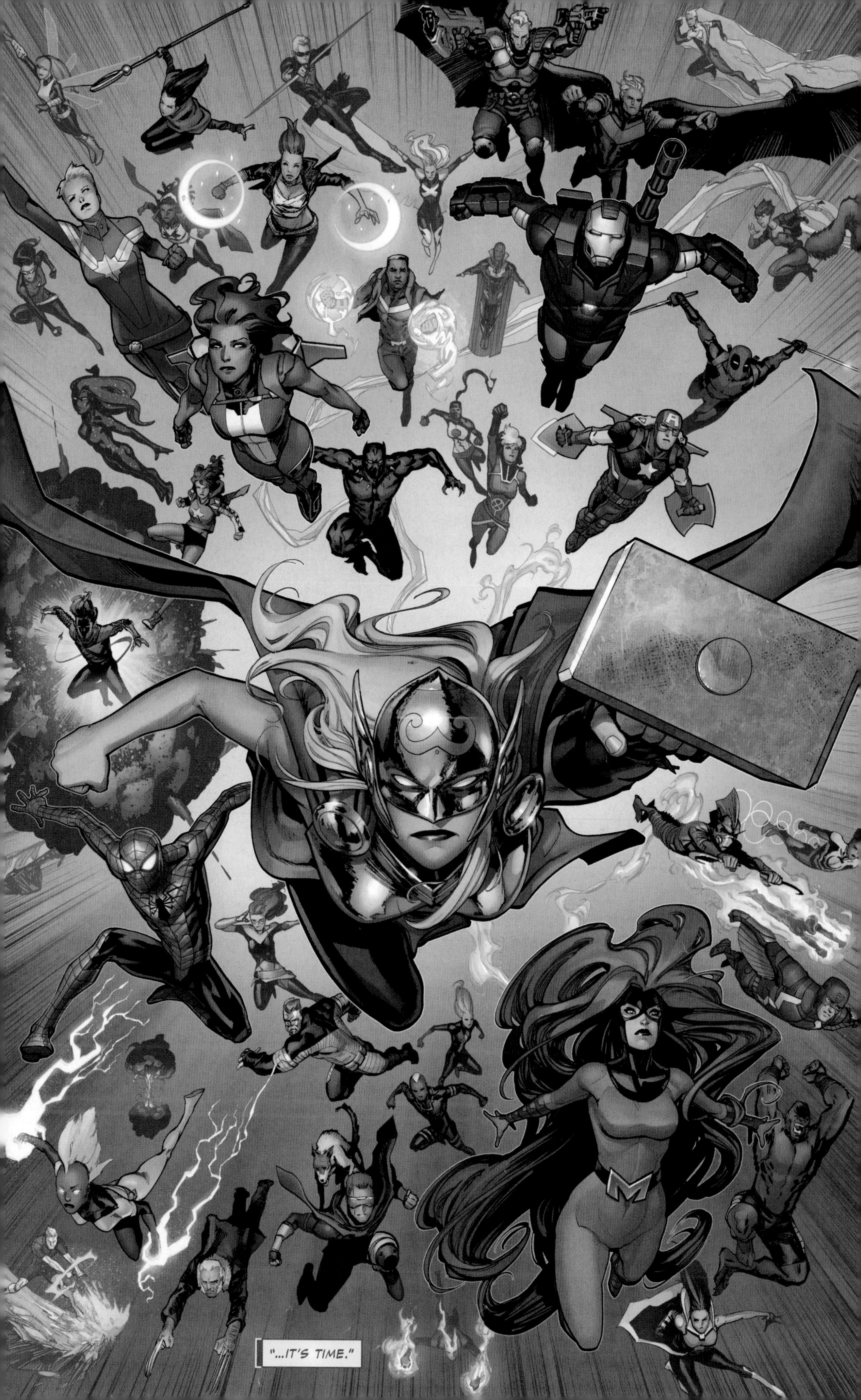
"...IT'S TIME."

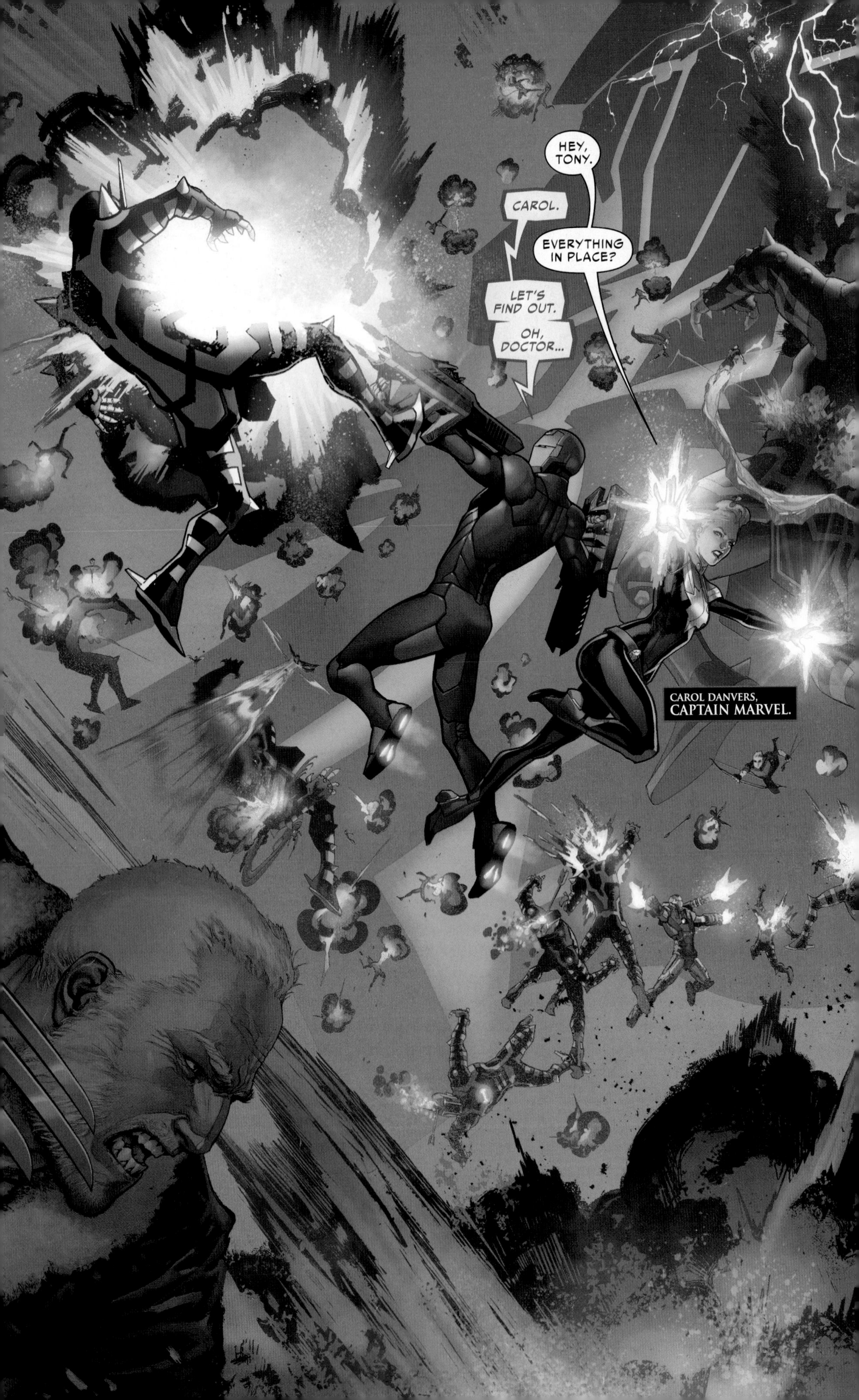

HEY, TONY.
CAROL.
EVERYTHING IN PLACE?
LET'S FIND OUT.
OH, DOCTOR...
CAROL DANVERS, CAPTAIN MARVEL.

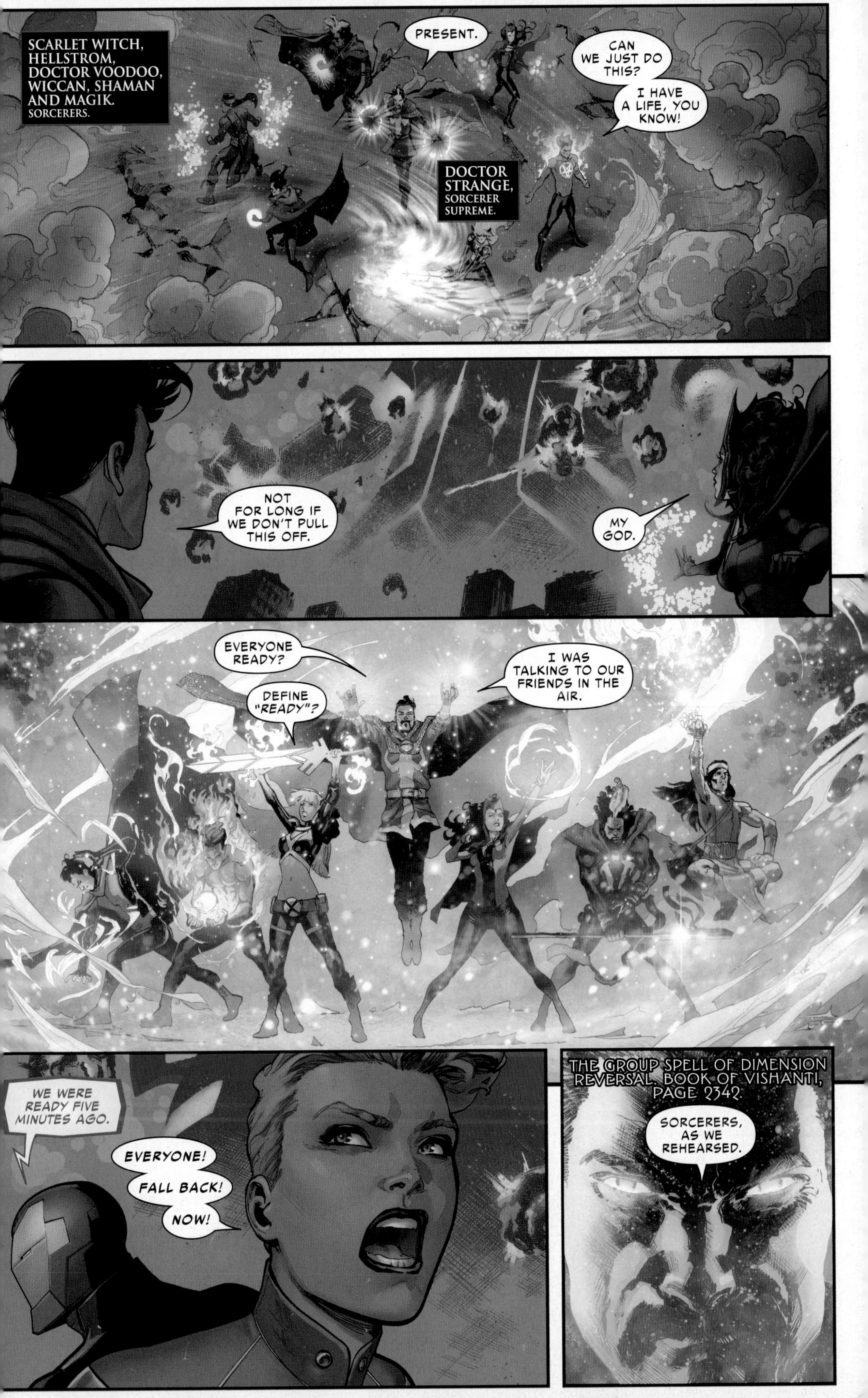

SCARLET WITCH, HELLSTROM, DOCTOR VOODOO, WICCAN, SHAMAN AND MAGIK. SORCERERS.
PRESENT.
CAN WE JUST DO THIS?
I HAVE A LIFE, YOU KNOW!
DOCTOR STRANGE, SORCERER SUPREME.
NOT FOR LONG IF WE DON'T PULL THIS OFF.
MY GOD.
EVERYONE READY?
DEFINE "READY"?
I WAS TALKING TO OUR FRIENDS IN THE AIR.
WE WERE READY FIVE MINUTES AGO.
EVERYONE!
FALL BACK!
NOW!
THE GROUP SPELL OF DIMENSION REVERSAL. BOOK OF VISHANTI, PAGE 2342.
SORCERERS, AS WE REHEARSED.

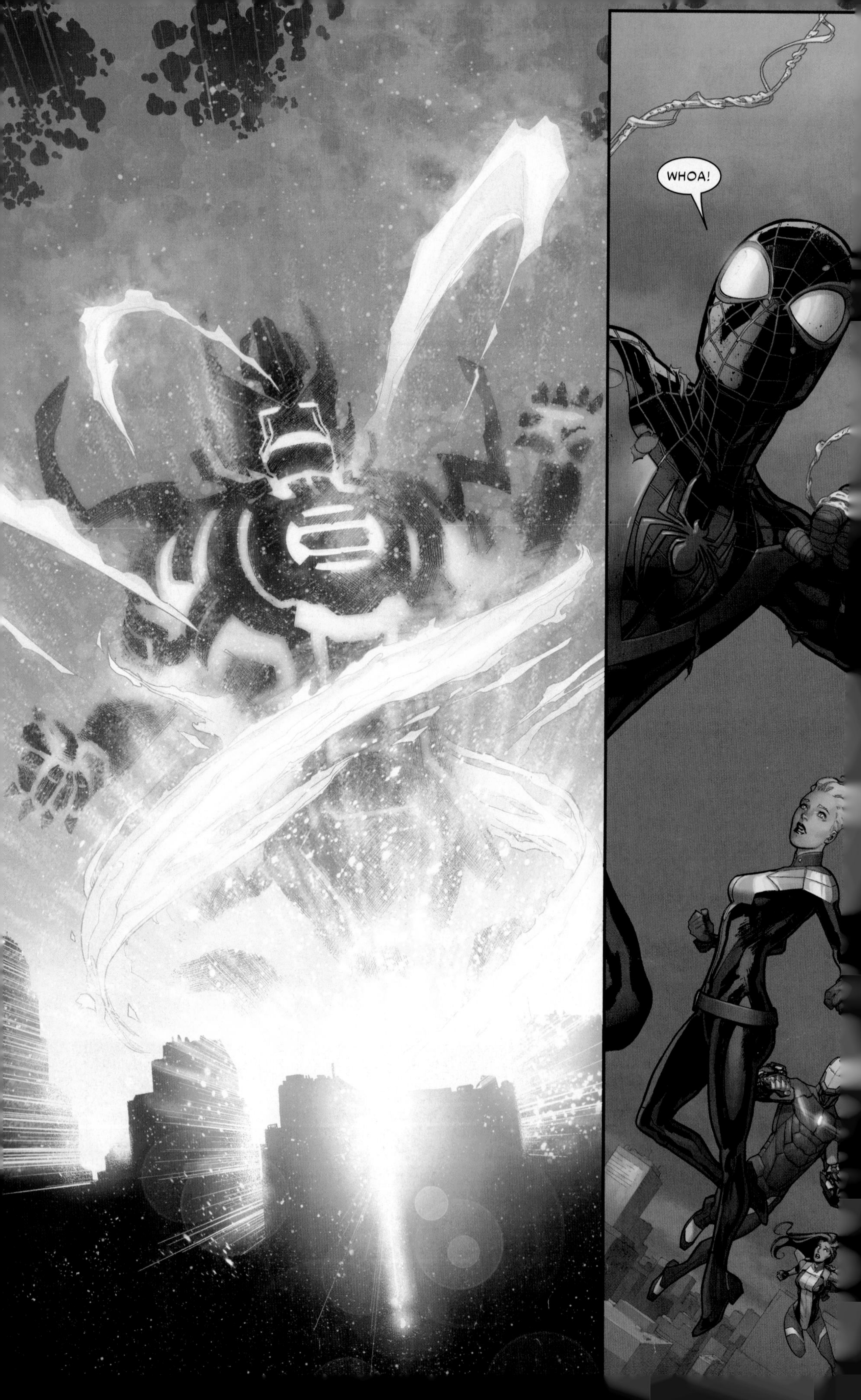
WHOA!

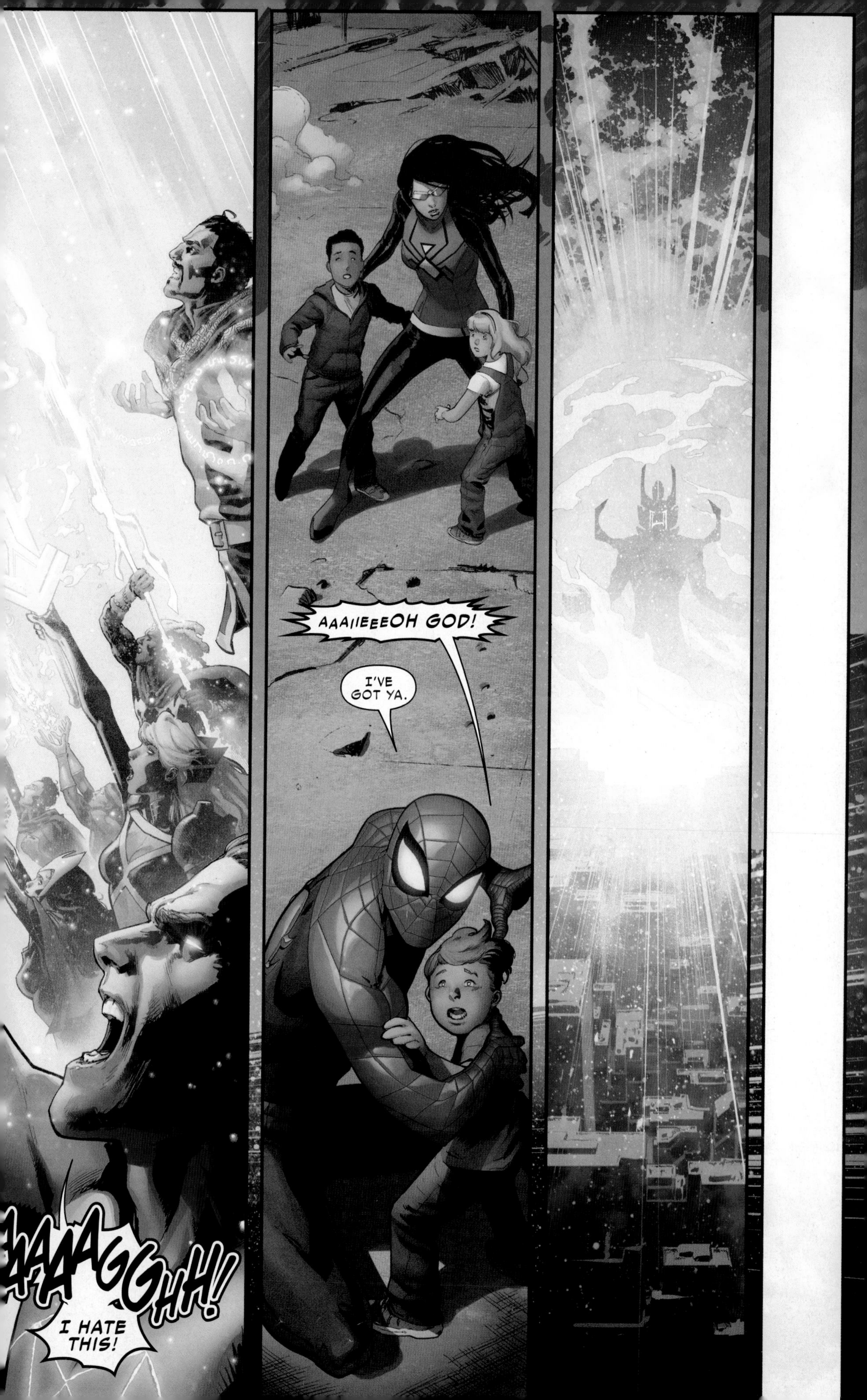
AAAIIEEEOH GOD!
I'VE GOT YA.
AAAAGGHH!!
I HATE THIS!

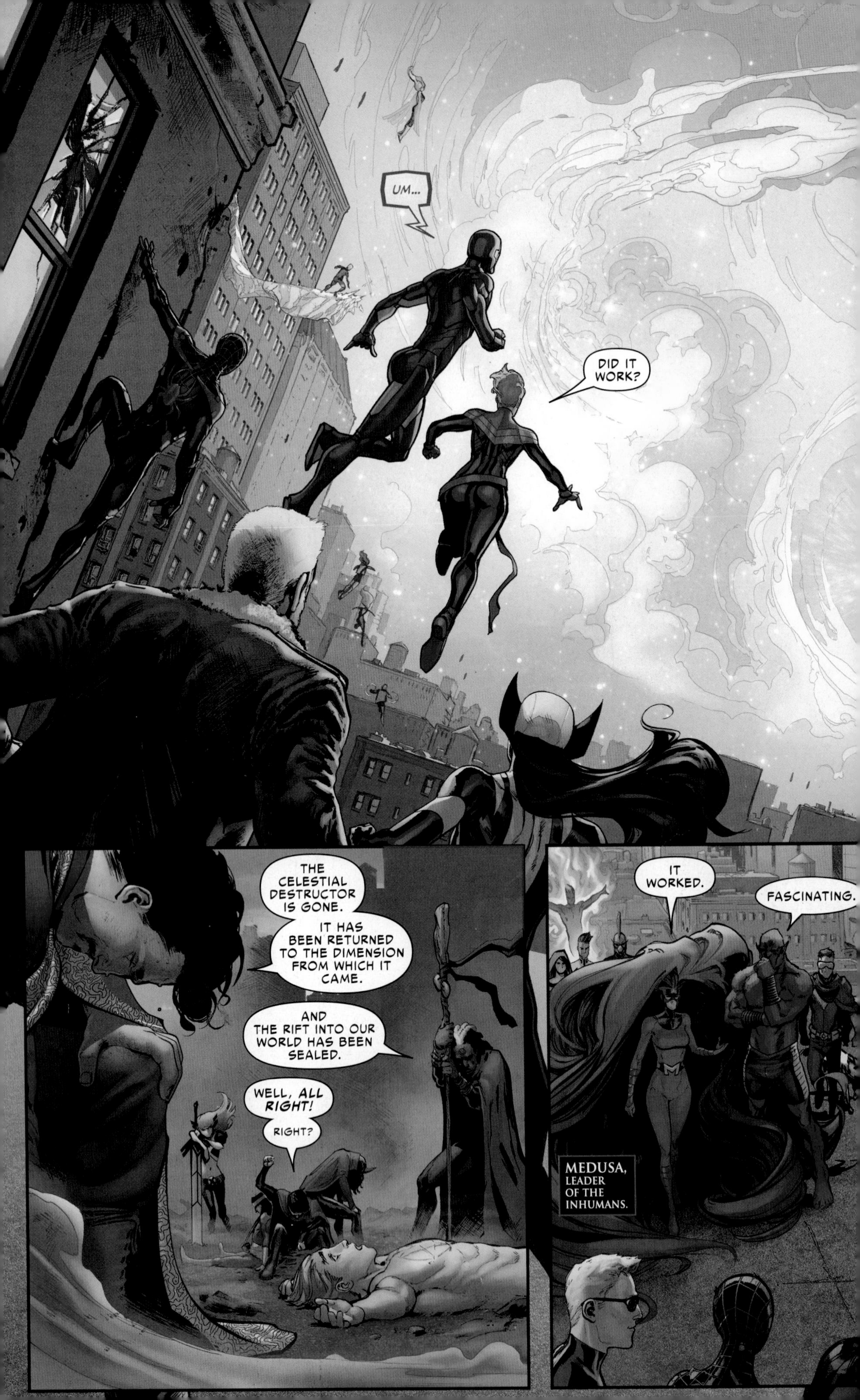
UM...
DID IT WORK?
THE CELESTIAL DESTRUCTOR IS GONE.
IT HAS BEEN RETURNED TO THE DIMENSION FROM WHICH IT CAME.
AND THE RIFT INTO OUR WORLD HAS BEEN SEALED.
WELL, ALL RIGHT!
RIGHT?
IT WORKED.
FASCINATING.
MEDUSA, LEADER OF THE INHUMANS.

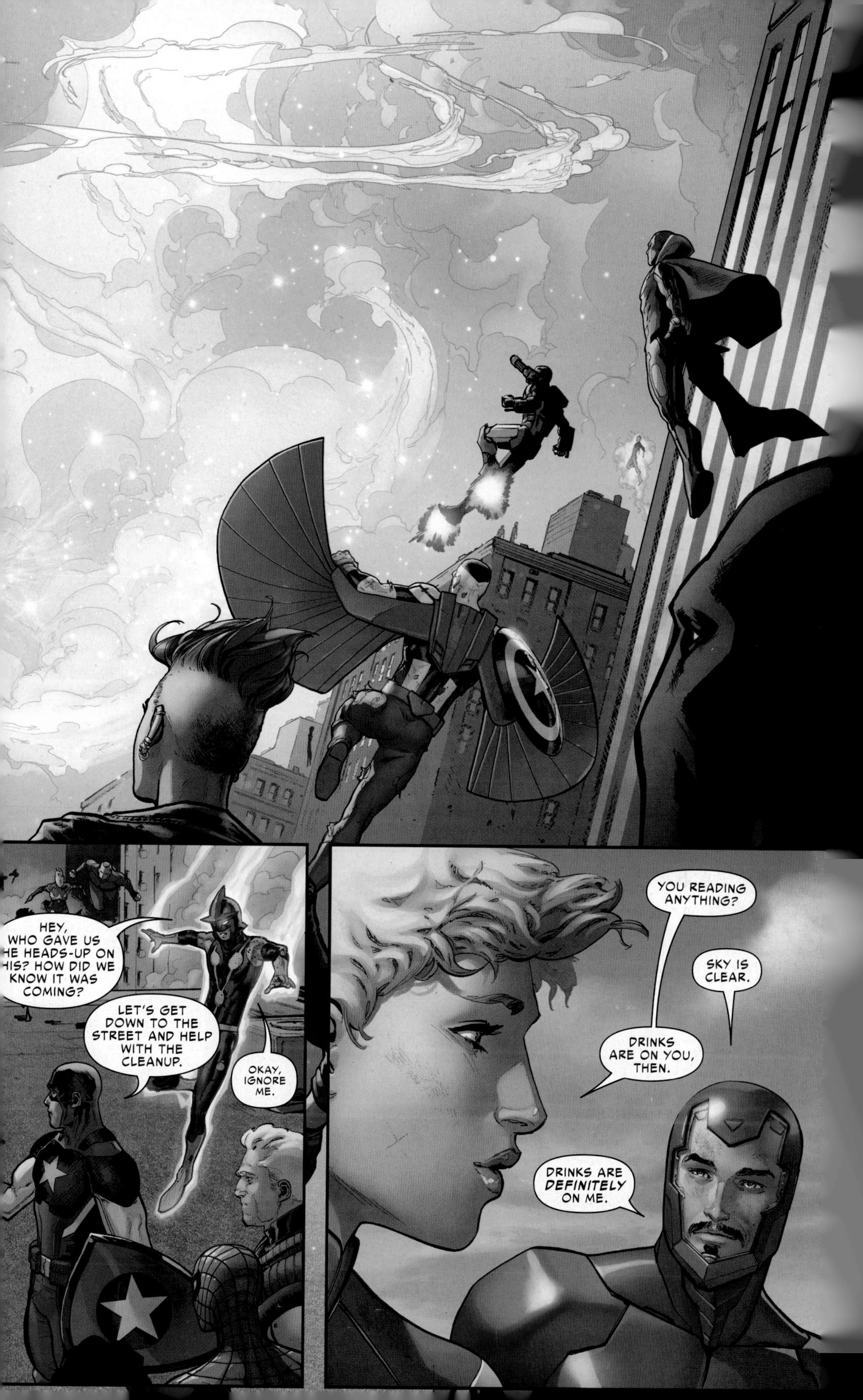
HEY, WHO GAVE US HE HEADS-UP ON HIS? HOW DID WE KNOW IT WAS COMING?
LET'S GET DOWN TO THE STREET AND HELP WITH THE CLEANUP.
OKAY, IGNORE ME.
YOU READING ANYTHING?
SKY IS CLEAR.
DRINKS ARE ON YOU, THEN.
DRINKS ARE *DEFINITELY* ON ME.

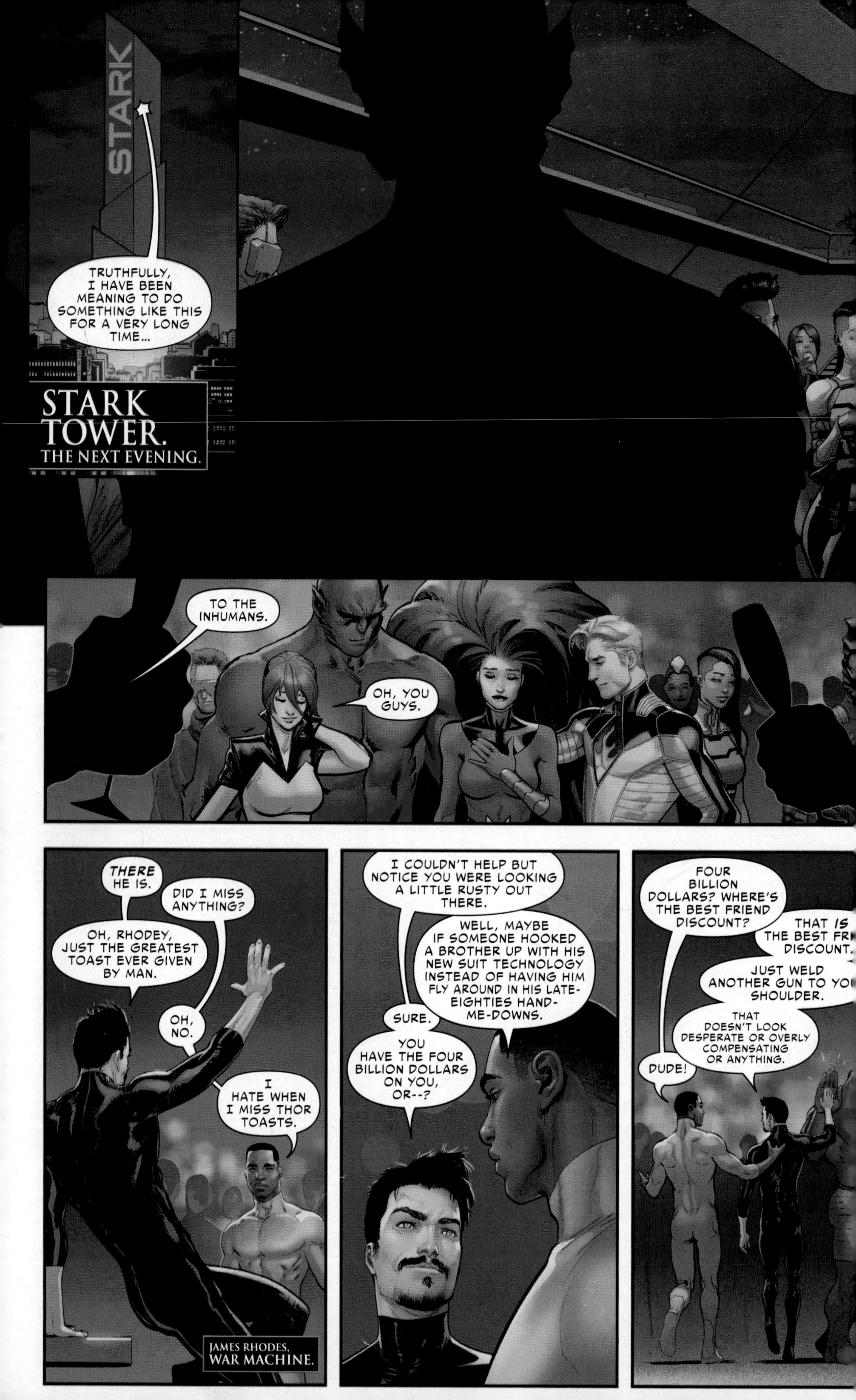
STARK
STARK TOWER. THE NEXT EVENING.
TRUTHFULLY, I HAVE BEEN MEANING TO DO SOMETHING LIKE THIS FOR A VERY LONG TIME...
TO THE INHUMANS.
OH, YOU GUYS.
THERE HE IS.
DID I MISS ANYTHING?
OH, RHODEY, JUST THE GREATEST TOAST EVER GIVEN BY MAN.
OH, NO.
I HATE WHEN I MISS THOR TOASTS.
JAMES RHODES, WAR MACHINE.
I COULDN'T HELP BUT NOTICE YOU WERE LOOKING A LITTLE RUSTY OUT THERE.
WELL, MAYBE IF SOMEONE HOOKED A BROTHER UP WITH HIS NEW SUIT TECHNOLOGY INSTEAD OF HAVING HIM FLY AROUND IN HIS LATE-EIGHTIES HAND-ME-DOWNS.
SURE.
YOU HAVE THE FOUR BILLION DOLLARS ON YOU, OR--?
FOUR BILLION DOLLARS? WHERE'S THE BEST FRIEND DISCOUNT?
THAT *IS* THE BEST FRI DISCOUNT.
JUST WELD ANOTHER GUN TO YO SHOULDER.
THAT DOESN'T LOOK DESPERATE OR OVERLY COMPENSATING OR ANYTHING.
DUDE!

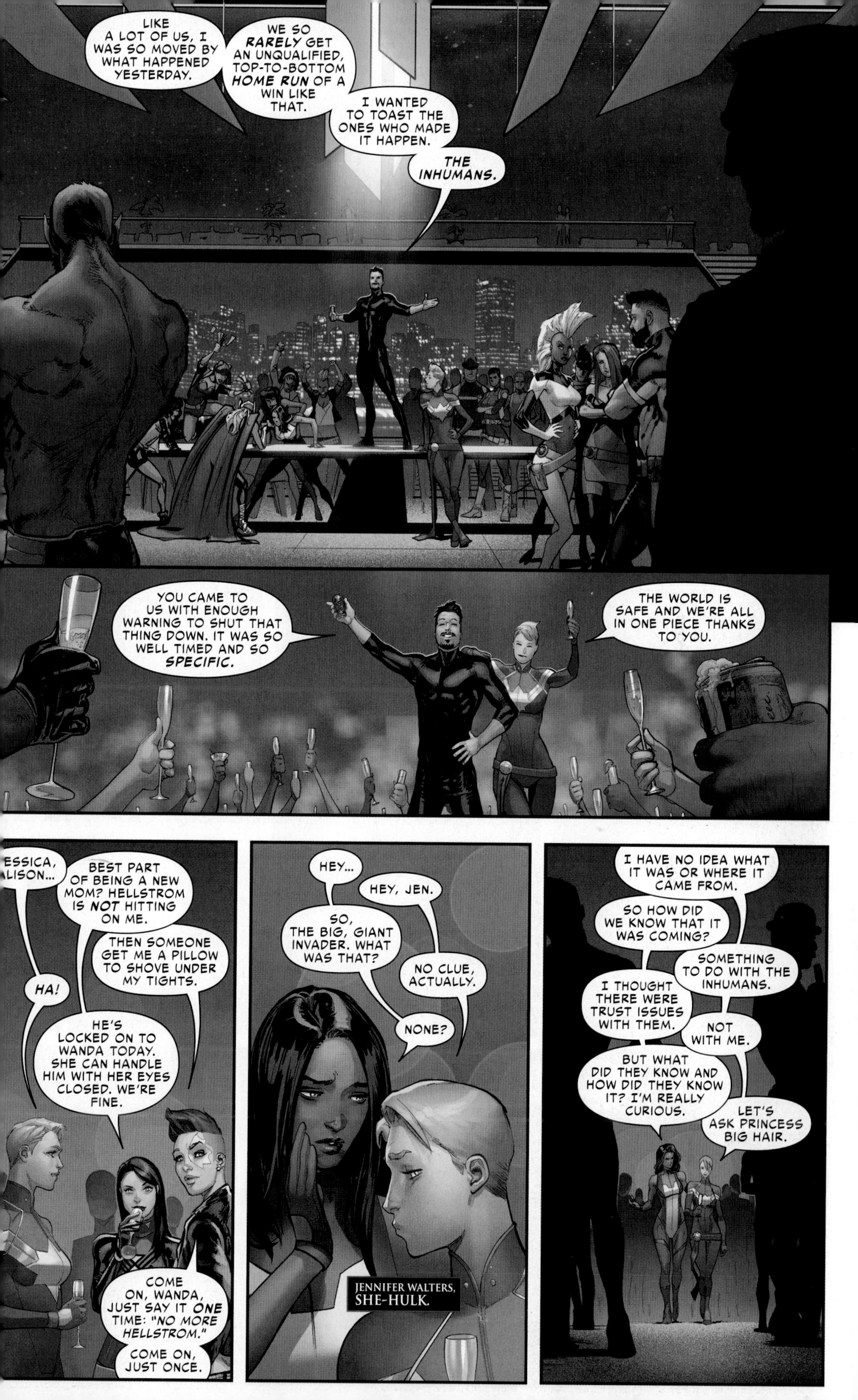
LIKE A LOT OF US, I WAS SO MOVED BY WHAT HAPPENED YESTERDAY.
WE SO RARELY GET AN UNQUALIFIED, TOP-TO-BOTTOM HOME RUN OF A WIN LIKE THAT.
I WANTED TO TOAST THE ONES WHO MADE IT HAPPEN.
THE INHUMANS.
YOU CAME TO US WITH ENOUGH WARNING TO SHUT THAT THING DOWN. IT WAS SO WELL TIMED AND SO SPECIFIC.
THE WORLD IS SAFE AND WE'RE ALL IN ONE PIECE THANKS TO YOU.
ESSICA, LISON...
BEST PART OF BEING A NEW MOM? HELLSTROM IS NOT HITTING ON ME.
THEN SOMEONE GET ME A PILLOW TO SHOVE UNDER MY TIGHTS.
HA!
HE'S LOCKED ON TO WANDA TODAY. SHE CAN HANDLE HIM WITH HER EYES CLOSED. WE'RE FINE.
COME ON, WANDA, JUST SAY IT ONE TIME: "NO MORE HELLSTROM."
COME ON, JUST ONCE.
HEY...
HEY, JEN.
SO, THE BIG, GIANT INVADER. WHAT WAS THAT?
NO CLUE, ACTUALLY.
NONE?
JENNIFER WALTERS, SHE-HULK.
I HAVE NO IDEA WHAT IT WAS OR WHERE IT CAME FROM.
SO HOW DID WE KNOW THAT IT WAS COMING?
SOMETHING TO DO WITH THE INHUMANS.
I THOUGHT THERE WERE TRUST ISSUES WITH THEM.
NOT WITH ME.
BUT WHAT DID THEY KNOW AND HOW DID THEY KNOW IT? I'M REALLY CURIOUS.
LET'S ASK PRINCESS BIG HAIR.

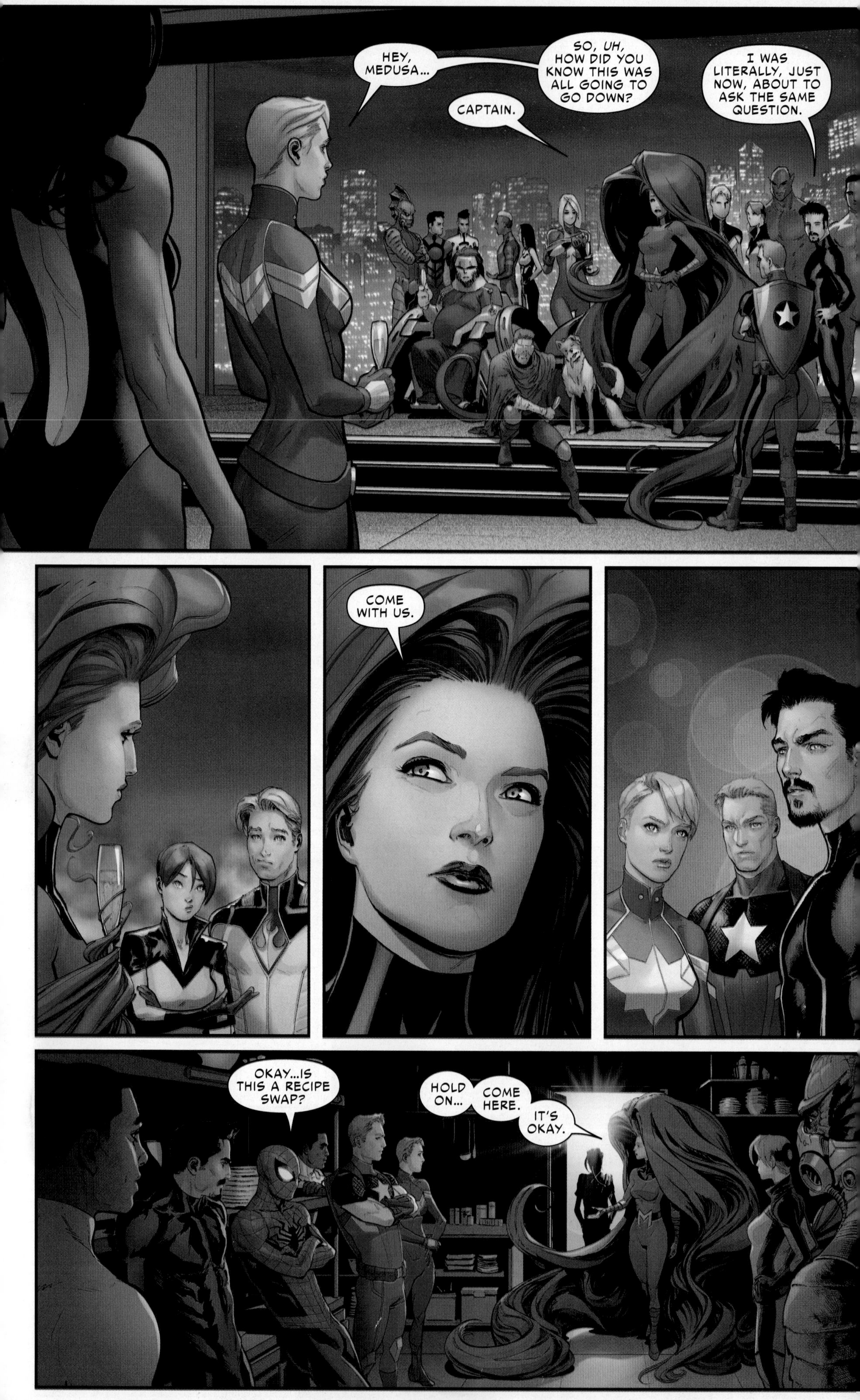
HEY, MEDUSA...
SO, UH, HOW DID YOU KNOW THIS WAS ALL GOING TO GO DOWN?
CAPTAIN.
I WAS LITERALLY, JUST NOW, ABOUT TO ASK THE SAME QUESTION.
COME WITH US.
OKAY...IS THIS A RECIPE SWAP?
HOLD ON...
COME HERE.
IT'S OKAY.

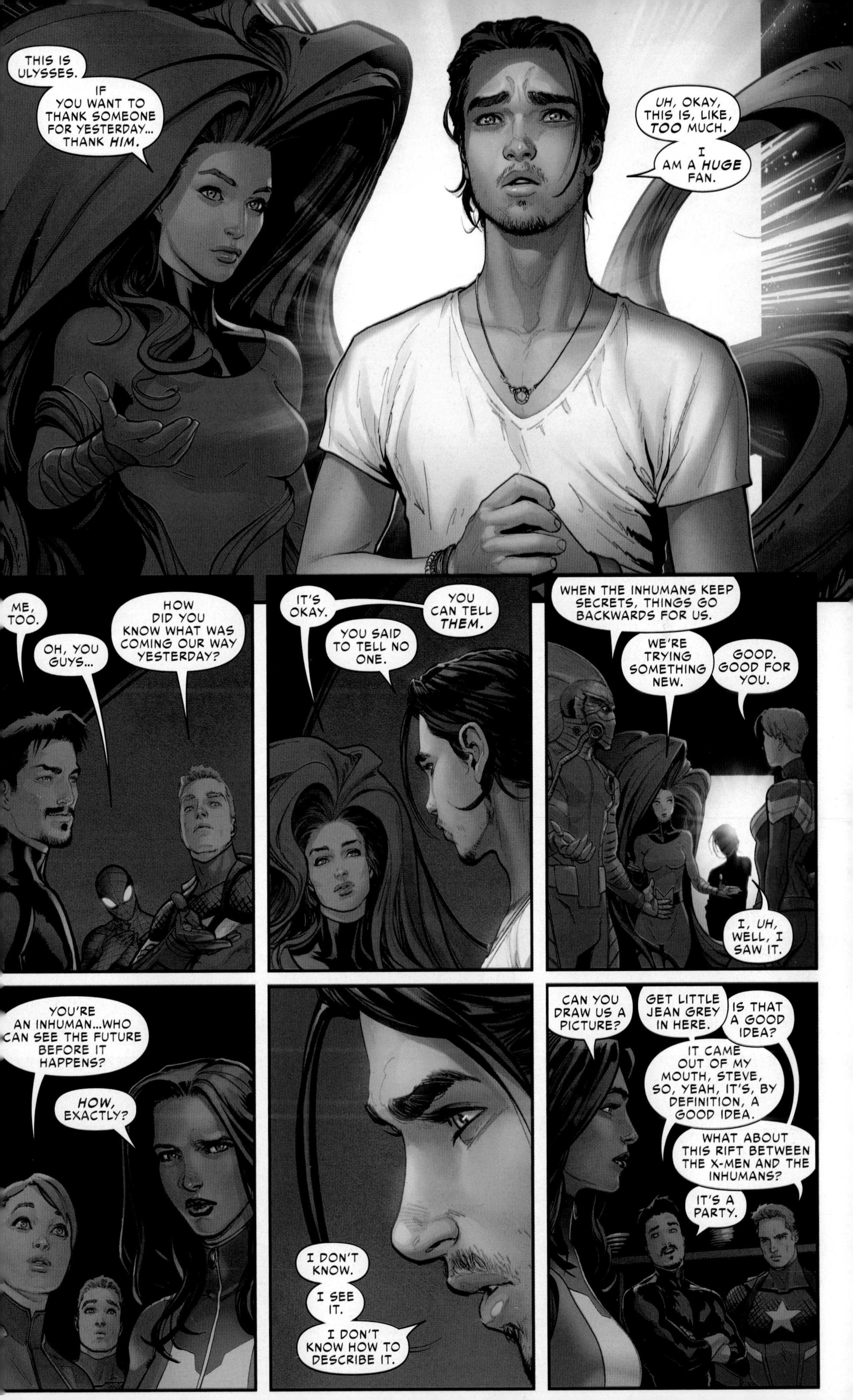

THIS IS ULYSSES.
IF YOU WANT TO THANK SOMEONE FOR YESTERDAY... THANK HIM.
UH, OKAY, THIS IS, LIKE, TOO MUCH.
I AM A HUGE FAN.
ME, TOO.
OH, YOU GUYS...
HOW DID YOU KNOW WHAT WAS COMING OUR WAY YESTERDAY?
IT'S OKAY.
YOU CAN TELL THEM.
YOU SAID TO TELL NO ONE.
WHEN THE INHUMANS KEEP SECRETS, THINGS GO BACKWARDS FOR US.
WE'RE TRYING SOMETHING NEW.
GOOD. GOOD FOR YOU.
I, UH, WELL, I SAW IT.
YOU'RE AN INHUMAN...WHO CAN SEE THE FUTURE BEFORE IT HAPPENS?
HOW, EXACTLY?
I DON'T KNOW.
I SEE IT.
I DON'T KNOW HOW TO DESCRIBE IT.
CAN YOU DRAW US A PICTURE?
GET LITTLE JEAN GREY IN HERE.
IS THAT A GOOD IDEA?
IT CAME OUT OF MY MOUTH, STEVE, SO, YEAH, IT'S, BY DEFINITION, A GOOD IDEA.
WHAT ABOUT THIS RIFT BETWEEN THE X-MEN AND THE INHUMANS?
IT'S A PARTY.

HI. I'M JEAN GREY.

I'M ONE OF THE X-MEN. I'M A PSYCHIC.

IS THIS REALLY NECESSARY?

LET'S SAY: YES.

RESPECTFULLY.

UH...

WHAT I'M GOING TO DO IS CREATE A LIMITED MIND HIVE BETWEEN *YOU* AND EVERYONE ELSE IN THIS KITCHEN.

THAT MEANS YOU CAN ACTUALLY *SHOW* THEM WHAT YOU SEE AND WHAT YOU DO...

UH...

UM--

...BUT YOU WON'T SHOW THEM EVERYTHING. YOU WON'T SHOW EVERY WEIRD THOUGHT YOU HAVE IN YOUR HEAD.

I DON'T HAVE ANY WEIRD THOUGHTS IN MY HEAD.

EVERYBODY DOES.

YOU SHOULD SEE WHAT SHE-HULK IS THINKING ABOUT RIGHT NOW.

HEY.

NOT COOL.

WHAT DO I DO?

JUST RELAX.

AND TELL US YOUR STORY.

AND I'LL SHOW THEM WHAT YOU SEE WHEN YOU SEE WHAT YOU SEE...

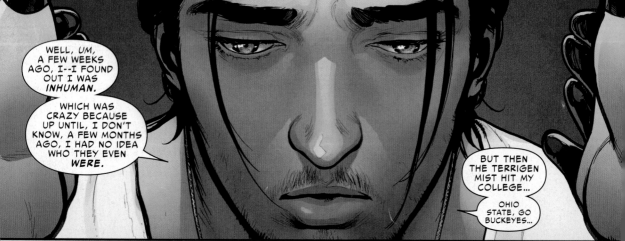

WELL, UM, A FEW WEEKS AGO, I--I FOUND OUT I WAS *INHUMAN.*

WHICH WAS CRAZY BECAUSE UP UNTIL, I DON'T KNOW, A FEW MONTHS AGO, I HAD NO IDEA WHO THEY EVEN *WERE.*

BUT THEN THE TERRIGEN MIST HIT MY COLLEGE...

OHIO STATE, GO BUCKEYES...

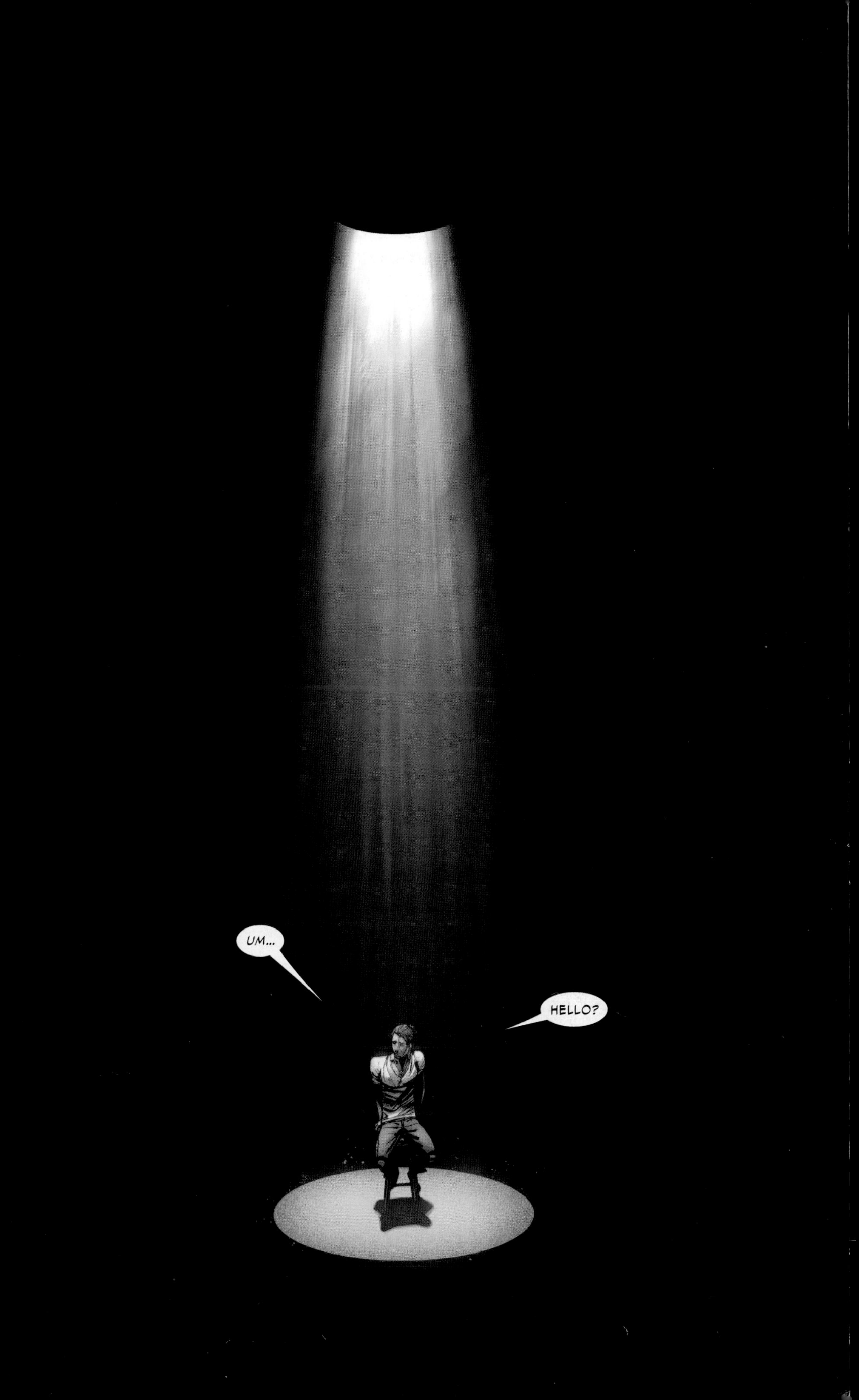
UM...
HELLO?

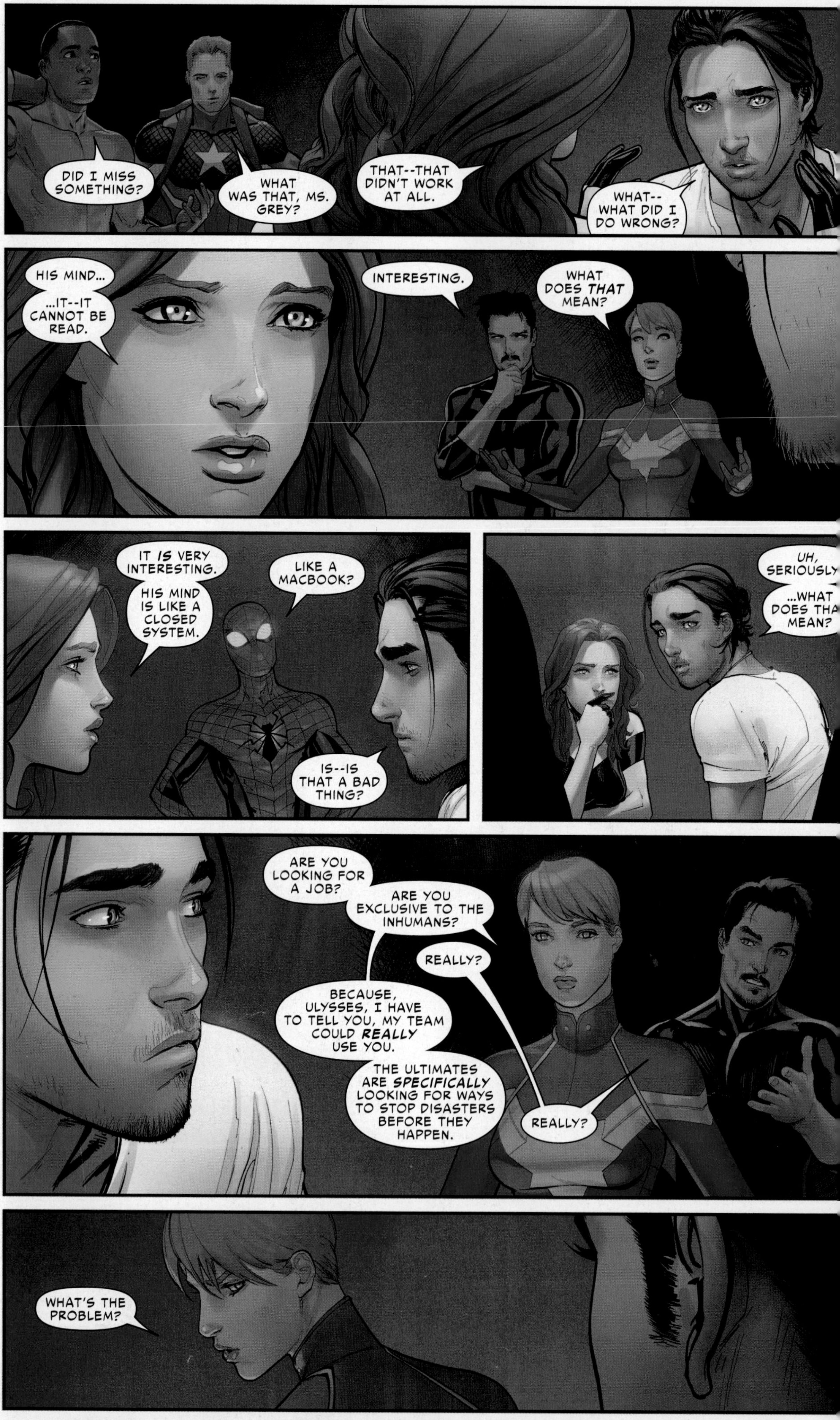

DID I MISS SOMETHING?
WHAT WAS THAT, MS. GREY?
THAT--THAT DIDN'T WORK AT ALL.
WHAT-- WHAT DID I DO WRONG?
HIS MIND...
...IT--IT CANNOT BE READ.
INTERESTING.
WHAT DOES *THAT* MEAN?
IT *IS* VERY INTERESTING.
HIS MIND IS LIKE A CLOSED SYSTEM.
LIKE A MACBOOK?
IS--IS THAT A BAD THING?
UH, SERIOUSLY
...WHAT DOES THA MEAN?
ARE YOU LOOKING FOR A JOB?
ARE YOU EXCLUSIVE TO THE INHUMANS?
REALLY?
BECAUSE, ULYSSES, I HAVE TO TELL YOU, MY TEAM COULD *REALLY* USE YOU.
THE ULTIMATES ARE *SPECIFICALLY* LOOKING FOR WAYS TO STOP DISASTERS BEFORE THEY HAPPEN.
REALLY?
WHAT'S THE PROBLEM?

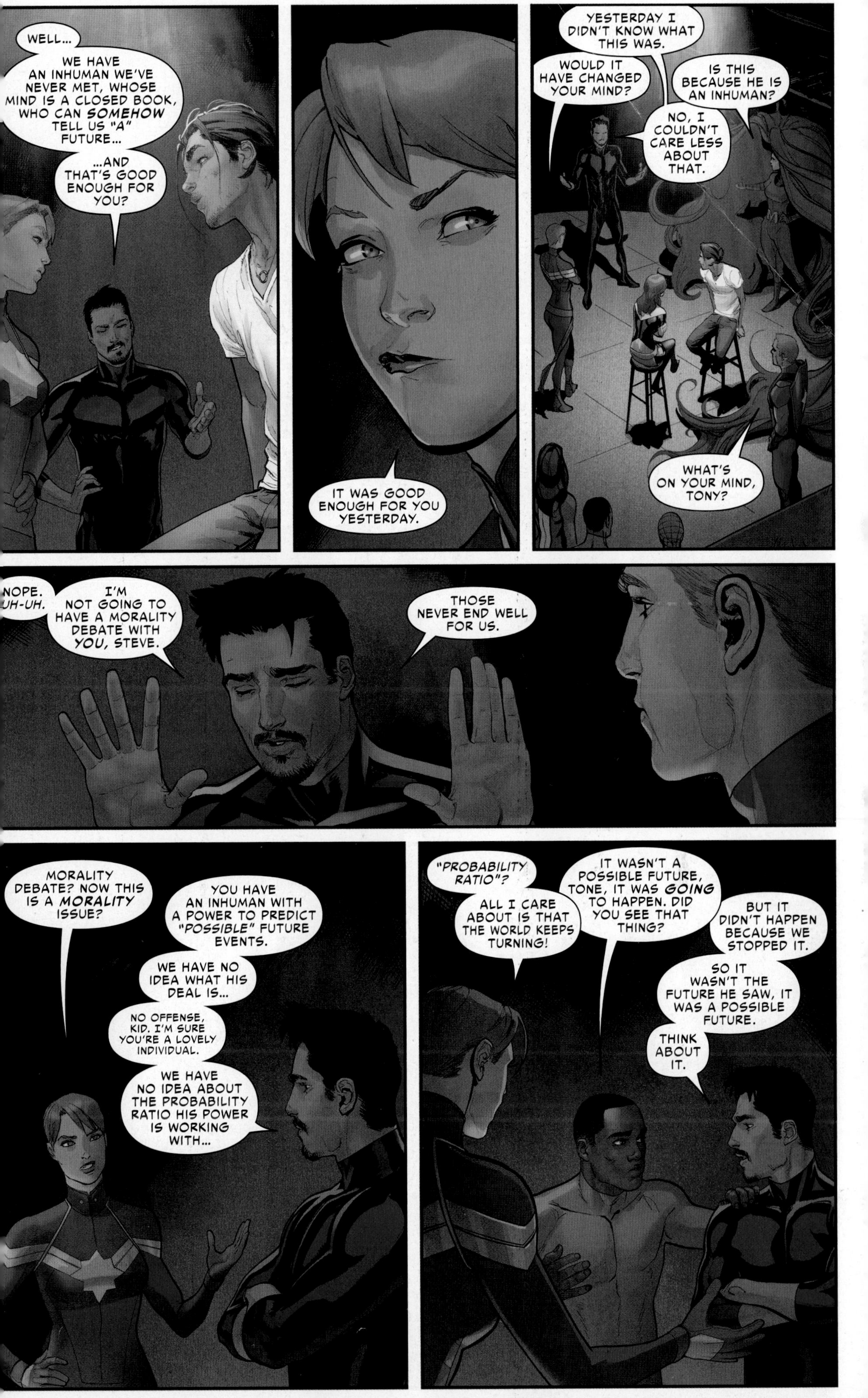
WELL...
WE HAVE AN INHUMAN WE'VE NEVER MET, WHOSE MIND IS A CLOSED BOOK, WHO CAN *SOMEHOW* TELL US "A" FUTURE...
...AND THAT'S GOOD ENOUGH FOR YOU?
IT WAS GOOD ENOUGH FOR YOU YESTERDAY.
YESTERDAY I DIDN'T KNOW WHAT THIS WAS.
WOULD IT HAVE CHANGED YOUR MIND?
IS THIS BECAUSE HE IS AN INHUMAN?
NO, I COULDN'T CARE LESS ABOUT THAT.
WHAT'S ON YOUR MIND, TONY?
NOPE. *UH-UH.*
I'M NOT GOING TO HAVE A MORALITY DEBATE WITH *YOU,* STEVE.
THOSE NEVER END WELL FOR US.
MORALITY DEBATE? NOW THIS IS A *MORALITY* ISSUE?
YOU HAVE AN INHUMAN WITH A POWER TO PREDICT *"POSSIBLE"* FUTURE EVENTS.
WE HAVE NO IDEA WHAT HIS DEAL IS...
NO OFFENSE, KID. I'M SURE YOU'RE A LOVELY INDIVIDUAL.
WE HAVE NO IDEA ABOUT THE PROBABILITY RATIO HIS POWER IS WORKING WITH...
"PROBABILITY RATIO"?
ALL I CARE ABOUT IS THAT THE WORLD KEEPS TURNING!
IT WASN'T A POSSIBLE FUTURE, TONE, IT WAS *GOING* TO HAPPEN. DID YOU SEE THAT THING?
BUT IT DIDN'T HAPPEN BECAUSE WE STOPPED IT.
SO IT WASN'T THE FUTURE HE SAW, IT WAS A POSSIBLE FUTURE.
THINK ABOUT IT.

IF EVERYONE'S ALIVE AT THE END OF THE DAY...

...IT WAS THE RIGHT THING TO DO.

TELL US YOUR STORY, KID...

...TELL US MORE ABOUT YOUR--HOW YOU GOT YOUR POWERS...

WELL, UM, OKAY. A FEW WEEKS AGO, I--I FOUND OUT I WAS INHUMAN.

GREAT.

SO, YOU ALL PROBABLY KNOW MORE ABOUT ALL THAT THAN I DO, BUT THIS TERRIGEN MIST CRAWLS AROUND THE PLANET AND TURNS ANYONE WHO HAS SOME INHUMAN DNA IN THEM INTO INHUMANS.

SURE, SURE...

AND I WAS ONE OF "THE LUCKY ONES."

AND I HAD NO IDEA WHAT WAS DIFFERENT ABOUT ME.

I LOOKED OKAY. I MEAN, THE SAME...

AND THEN--

--THEN IT HAPPENED.

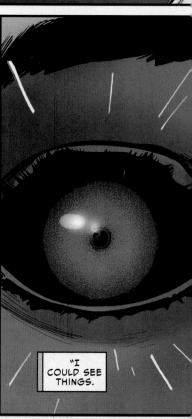

"I COULD SEE THINGS."

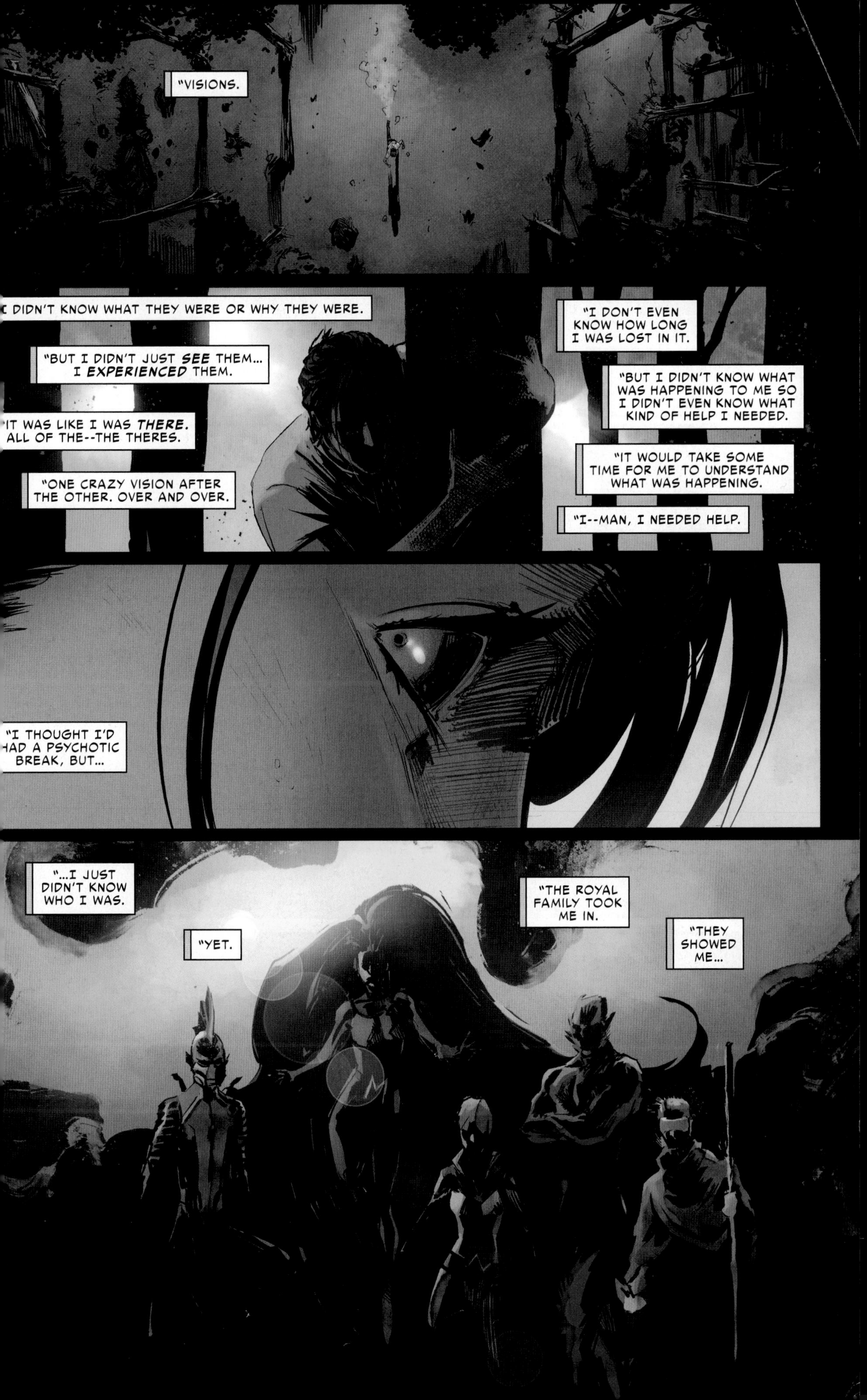
"VISIONS.
I DIDN'T KNOW WHAT THEY WERE OR WHY THEY WERE.
"BUT I DIDN'T JUST SEE THEM... I EXPERIENCED THEM.
"IT WAS LIKE I WAS THERE. ALL OF THE--THE THERES.
"ONE CRAZY VISION AFTER THE OTHER. OVER AND OVER.
"I DON'T EVEN KNOW HOW LONG I WAS LOST IN IT.
"BUT I DIDN'T KNOW WHAT WAS HAPPENING TO ME SO I DIDN'T EVEN KNOW WHAT KIND OF HELP I NEEDED.
"IT WOULD TAKE SOME TIME FOR ME TO UNDERSTAND WHAT WAS HAPPENING.
"I--MAN, I NEEDED HELP.
"I THOUGHT I'D HAD A PSYCHOTIC BREAK, BUT...
"...I JUST DIDN'T KNOW WHO I WAS.
"YET.
"THE ROYAL FAMILY TOOK ME IN.
"THEY SHOWED ME...

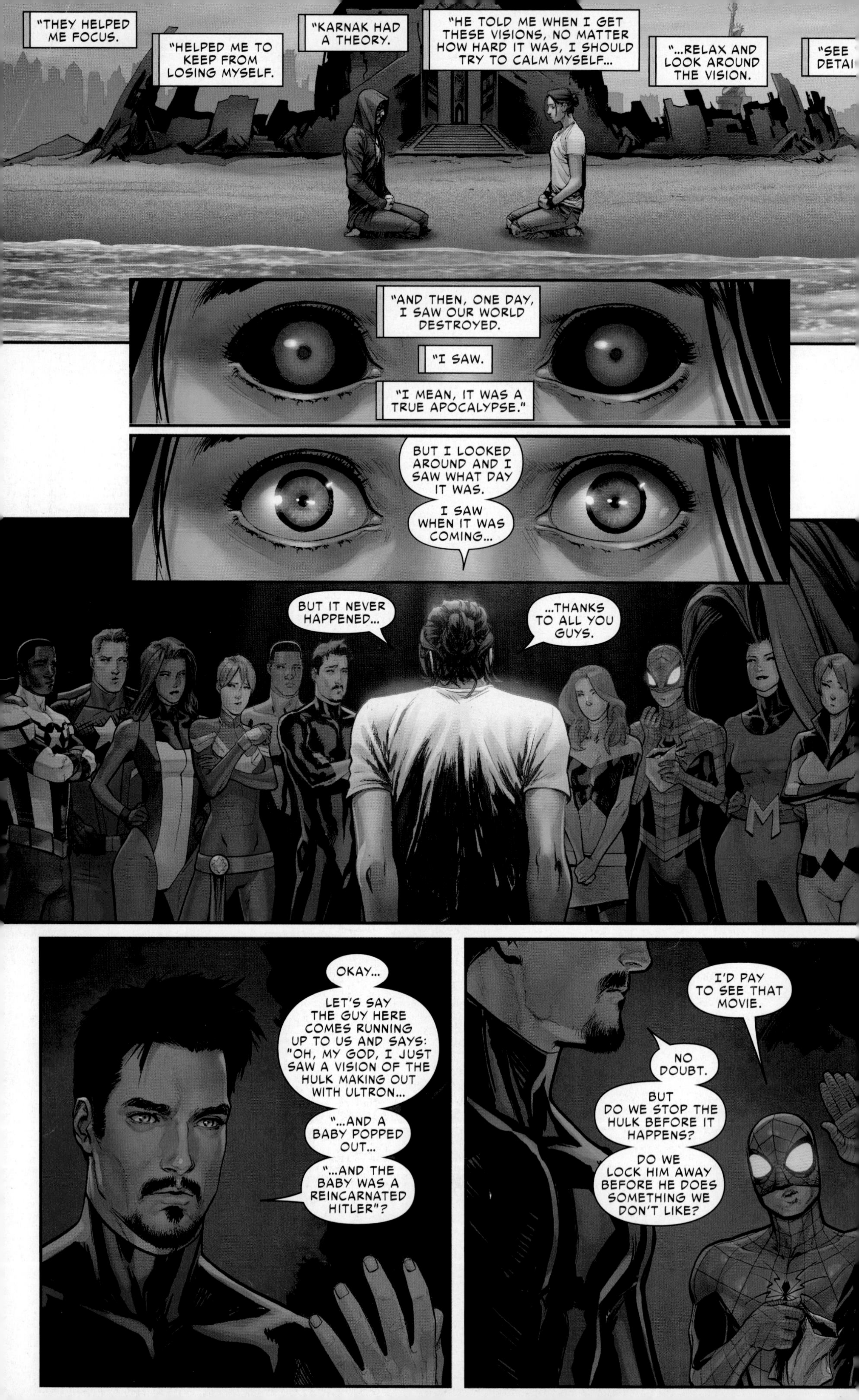
"THEY HELPED ME FOCUS.
"HELPED ME TO KEEP FROM LOSING MYSELF.
"KARNAK HAD A THEORY.
"HE TOLD ME WHEN I GET THESE VISIONS, NO MATTER HOW HARD IT WAS, I SHOULD TRY TO CALM MYSELF...
"...RELAX AND LOOK AROUND THE VISION.
"SEE
DETAI
"AND THEN, ONE DAY, I SAW OUR WORLD DESTROYED.
"I SAW.
"I MEAN, IT WAS A TRUE APOCALYPSE."
BUT I LOOKED AROUND AND I SAW WHAT DAY IT WAS.
I SAW WHEN IT WAS COMING...
BUT IT NEVER HAPPENED...
...THANKS TO ALL YOU GUYS.
OKAY...
LET'S SAY THE GUY HERE COMES RUNNING UP TO US AND SAYS: "OH, MY GOD, I JUST SAW A VISION OF THE HULK MAKING OUT WITH ULTRON...
"...AND A BABY POPPED OUT...
"...AND THE BABY WAS A REINCARNATED HITLER"?
I'D PAY TO SEE THAT MOVIE.
NO DOUBT.
BUT DO WE STOP THE HULK BEFORE IT HAPPENS?
DO WE LOCK HIM AWAY BEFORE HE DOES SOMETHING WE DON'T LIKE?

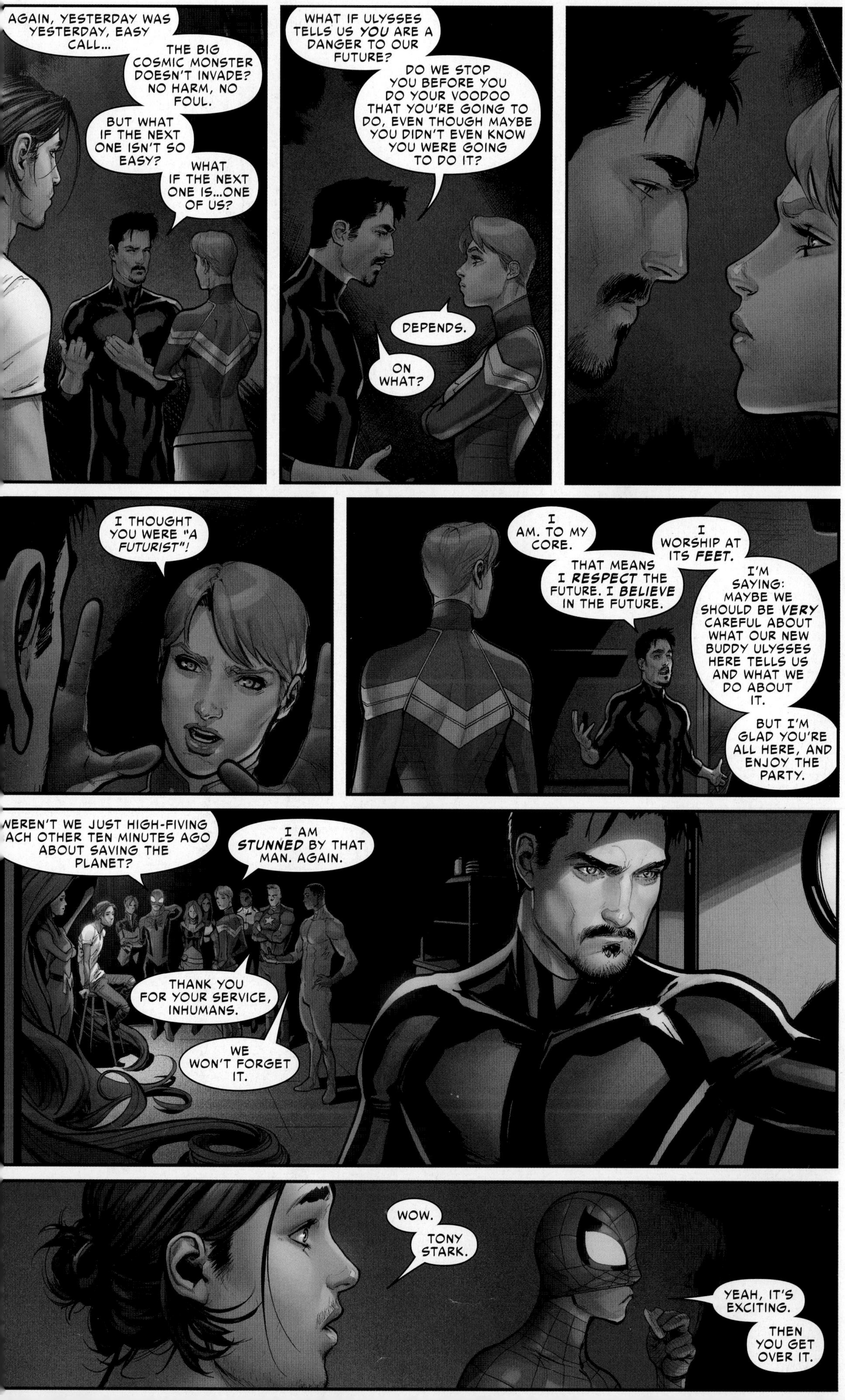
AGAIN, YESTERDAY WAS YESTERDAY, EASY CALL...
THE BIG COSMIC MONSTER DOESN'T INVADE? NO HARM, NO FOUL.
BUT WHAT IF THE NEXT ONE ISN'T SO EASY?
WHAT IF THE NEXT ONE IS...ONE OF US?
WHAT IF ULYSSES TELLS US YOU ARE A DANGER TO OUR FUTURE?
DO WE STOP YOU BEFORE YOU DO YOUR VOODOO THAT YOU'RE GOING TO DO, EVEN THOUGH MAYBE YOU DIDN'T EVEN KNOW YOU WERE GOING TO DO IT?
DEPENDS.
ON WHAT?
I THOUGHT YOU WERE "A FUTURIST"!
I AM. TO MY CORE.
THAT MEANS I RESPECT THE FUTURE. I BELIEVE IN THE FUTURE.
I WORSHIP AT ITS FEET.
I'M SAYING: MAYBE WE SHOULD BE VERY CAREFUL ABOUT WHAT OUR NEW BUDDY ULYSSES HERE TELLS US AND WHAT WE DO ABOUT IT.
BUT I'M GLAD YOU'RE ALL HERE, AND ENJOY THE PARTY.
WEREN'T WE JUST HIGH-FIVING ACH OTHER TEN MINUTES AGO ABOUT SAVING THE PLANET?
I AM STUNNED BY THAT MAN. AGAIN.
THANK YOU FOR YOUR SERVICE, INHUMANS.
WE WON'T FORGET IT.
WOW.
TONY STARK.
YEAH, IT'S EXCITING.
THEN YOU GET OVER IT.

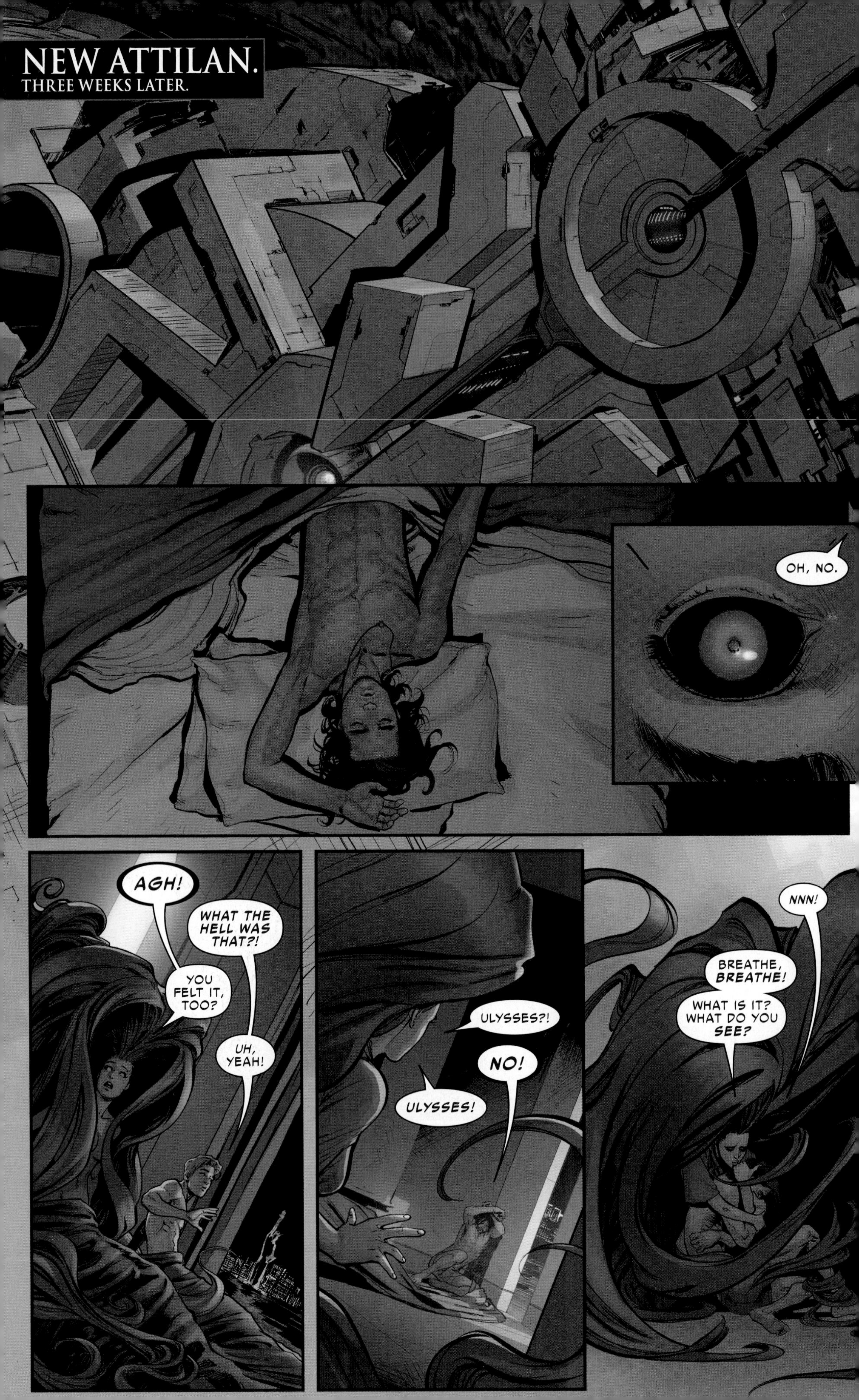
NEW ATTILAN.
THREE WEEKS LATER.
OH, NO.
AGH!
WHAT THE HELL WAS THAT?!
YOU FELT IT, TOO?
UH, YEAH!
ULYSSES?!
NO!
ULYSSES!
NNN!
BREATHE, BREATHE!
WHAT IS IT? WHAT DO YOU SEE?

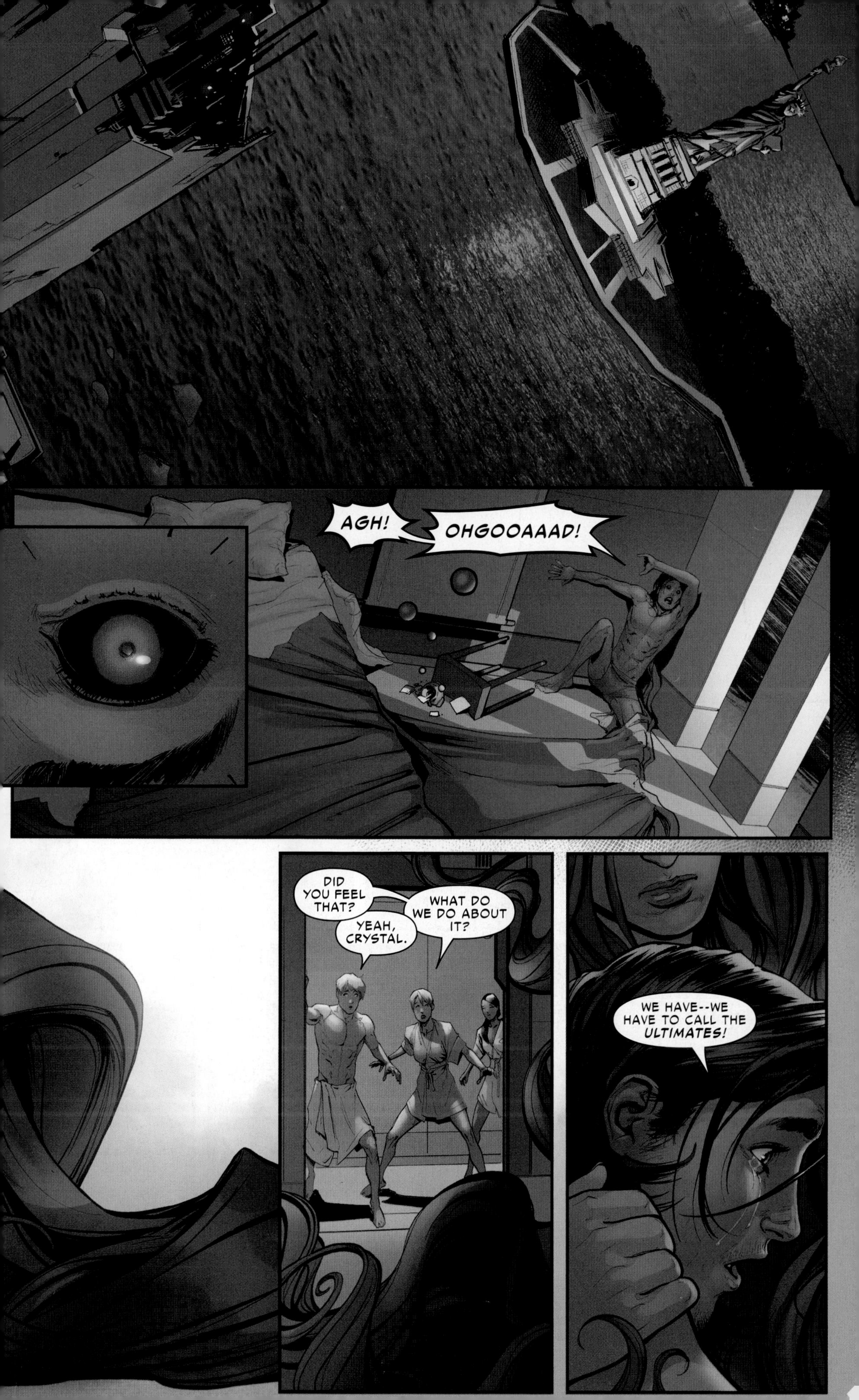
AGH!
OHGOOAAAD!
DID YOU FEEL THAT?
YEAH, CRYSTAL.
WHAT DO WE DO ABOUT IT?
WE HAVE--WE HAVE TO CALL THE *ULTIMATES!*

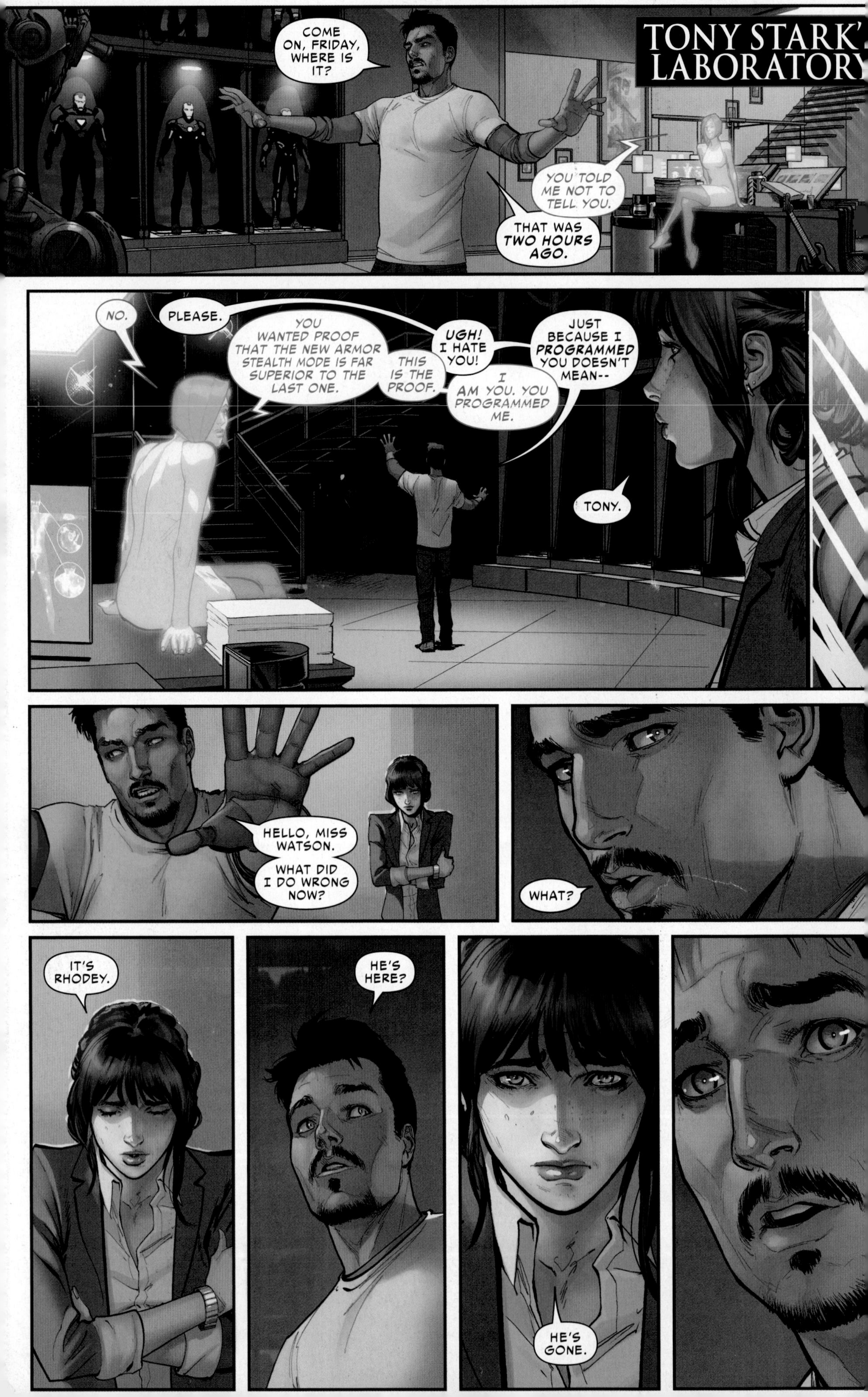
TONY STARK'S LABORATORY
COME ON, FRIDAY, WHERE IS IT?
YOU TOLD ME NOT TO TELL YOU.
THAT WAS TWO HOURS AGO.
NO.
PLEASE.
YOU WANTED PROOF THAT THE NEW ARMOR STEALTH MODE IS FAR SUPERIOR TO THE LAST ONE.
THIS IS THE PROOF.
UGH! I HATE YOU!
JUST BECAUSE I PROGRAMMED YOU DOESN'T MEAN--
I AM YOU. YOU PROGRAMMED ME.
TONY.
HELLO, MISS WATSON.
WHAT DID I DO WRONG NOW?
WHAT?
IT'S RHODEY.
HE'S HERE?
HE'S GONE.

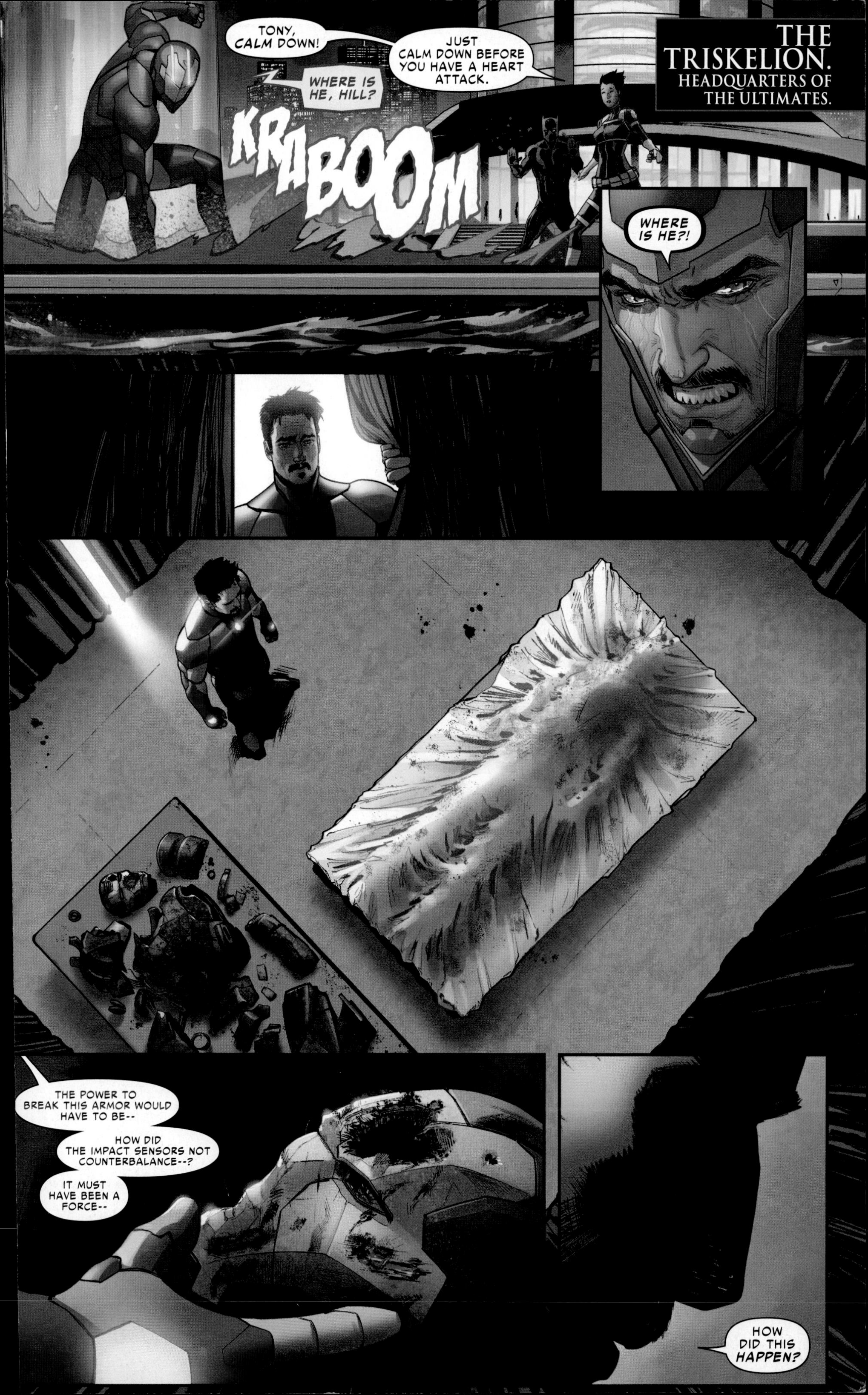
THE TRISKELION. HEADQUARTERS OF THE ULTIMATES.
TONY, CALM DOWN!
JUST CALM DOWN BEFORE YOU HAVE A HEART ATTACK.
WHERE IS HE, HILL?
KRABOOM
WHERE IS HE?!
THE POWER TO BREAK THIS ARMOR WOULD HAVE TO BE--
HOW DID THE IMPACT SENSORS NOT COUNTERBALANCE--?
IT MUST HAVE BEEN A FORCE--
HOW DID THIS HAPPEN?

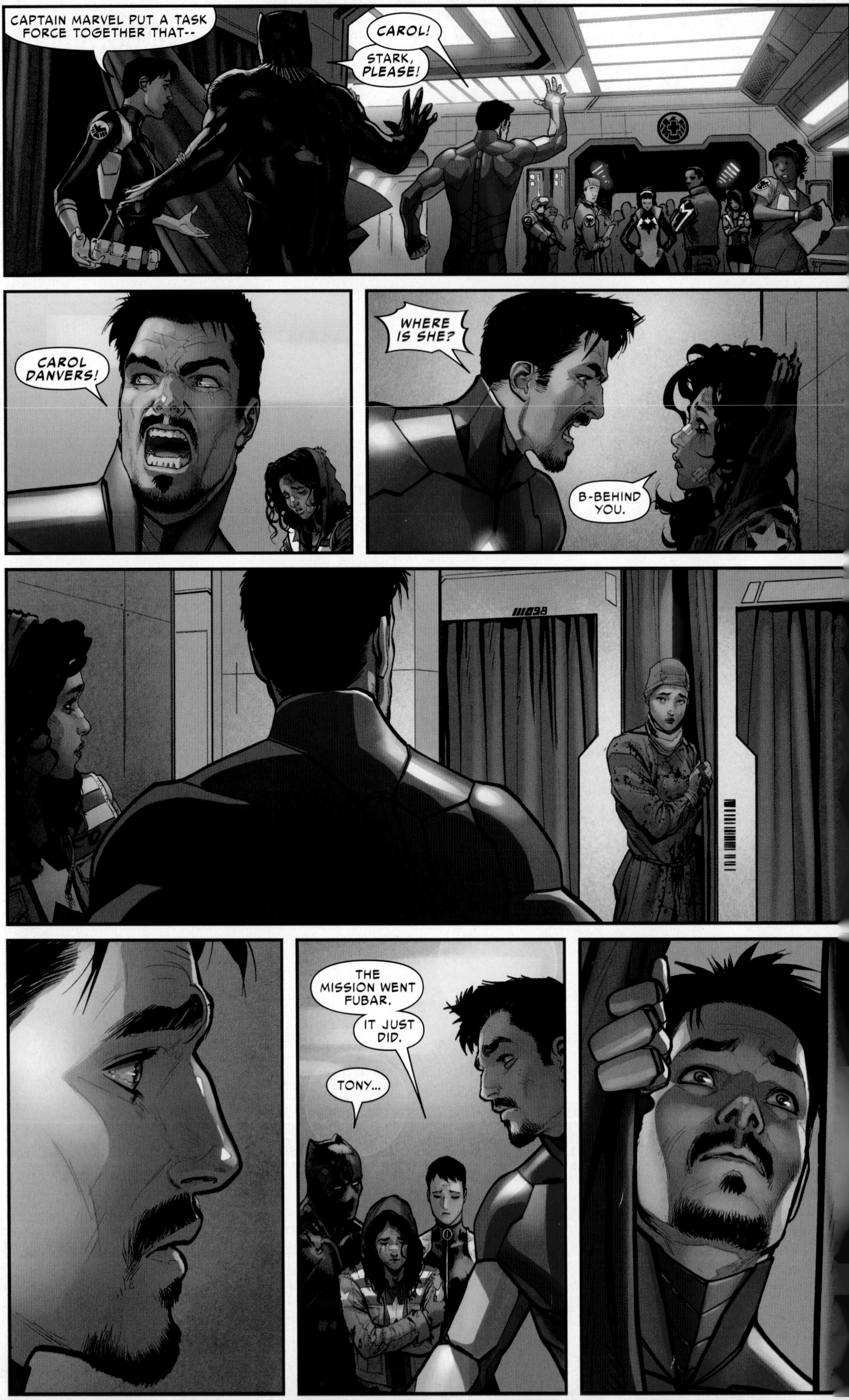
CAPTAIN MARVEL PUT A TASK FORCE TOGETHER THAT--
CAROL!
STARK, PLEASE!
CAROL DANVERS!
WHERE IS SHE?
B-BEHIND YOU.
THE MISSION WENT FUBAR.
IT JUST DID.
TONY...

IS SHE-HULK--?

IS--IS SHE--?

SHE'S ALIVE.

BUT THEY'RE NOT SURE IF SHE'LL EVER WAKE UP.

OR IF SHE WILL EVER *WALK* AGAIN.

HER BIOLOGY IS SO SPECIFIC. SO UNIQUE.

THEY JUST DON'T KNOW. THEY NEED A GAMMA SPECIALIST. WE NEED BRUCE BANNER.

WHAT HAPPENED?

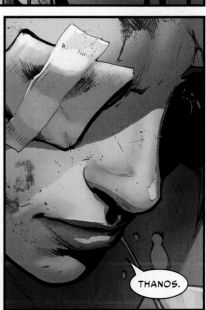

THANOS.

THANOS WAS BACK ON EARTH?

HE--HE ATTACKED YOU?

NOT EXACTLY.

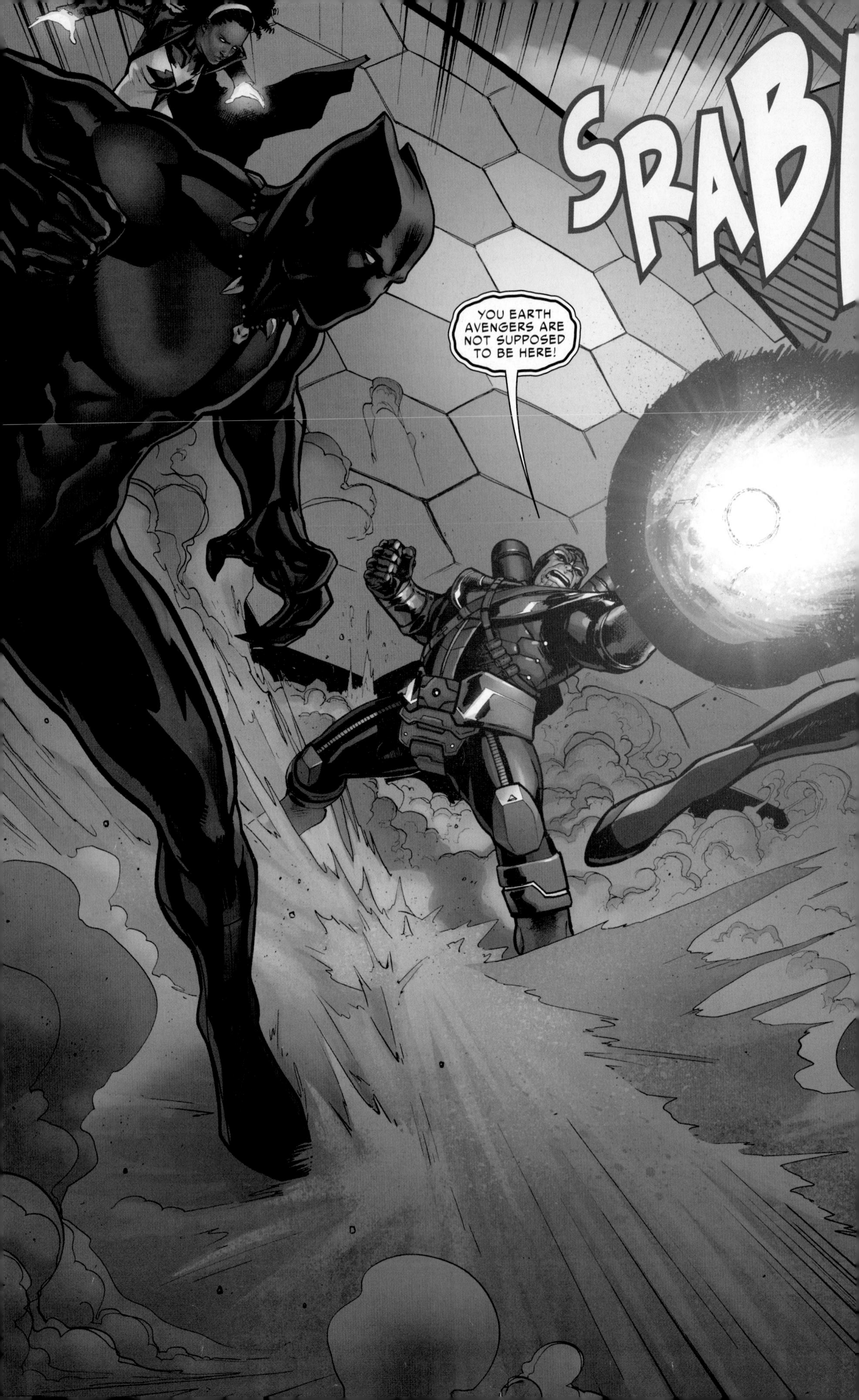
SRAB
YOU EARTH AVENGERS ARE NOT SUPPOSED TO BE HERE!

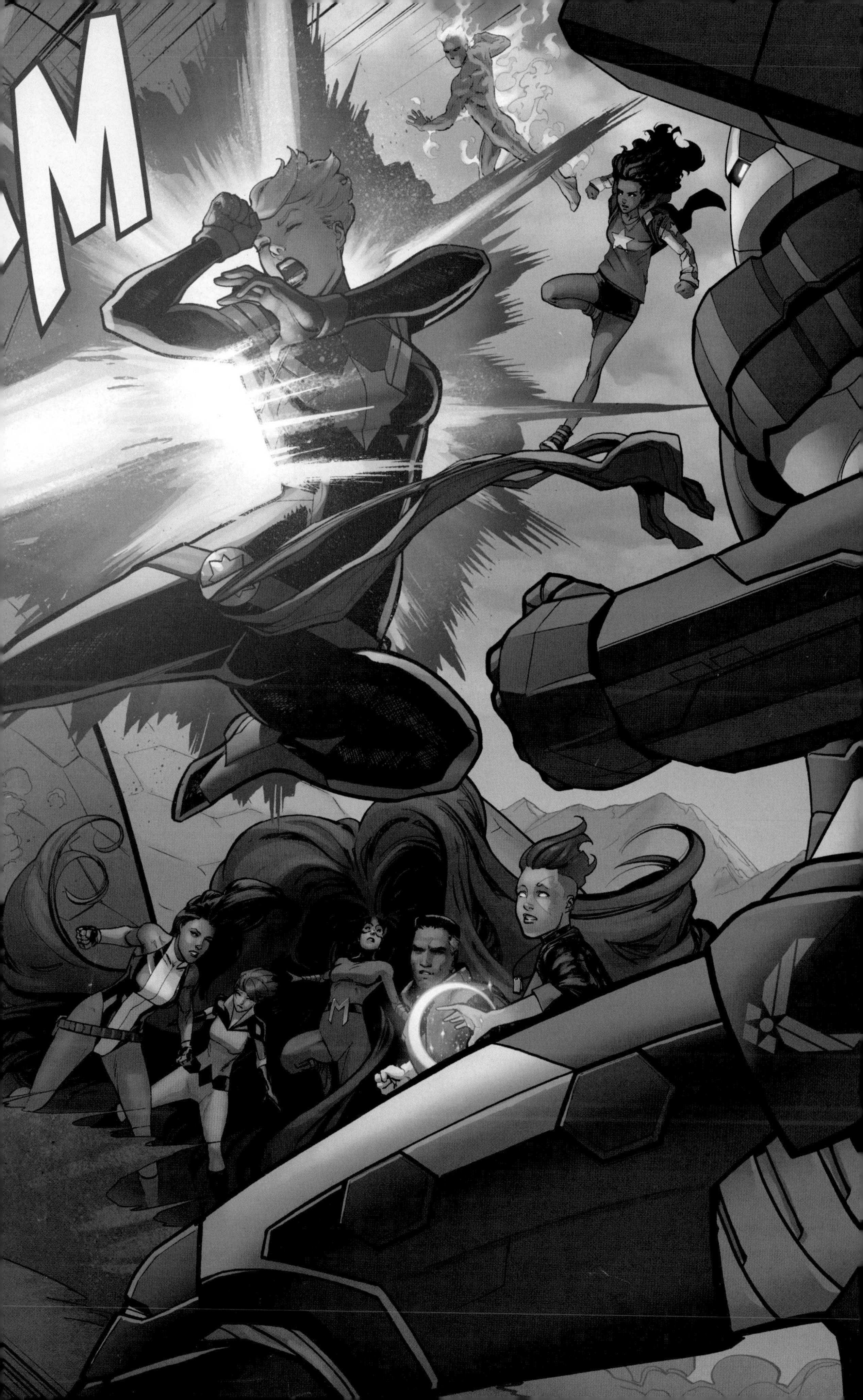
M

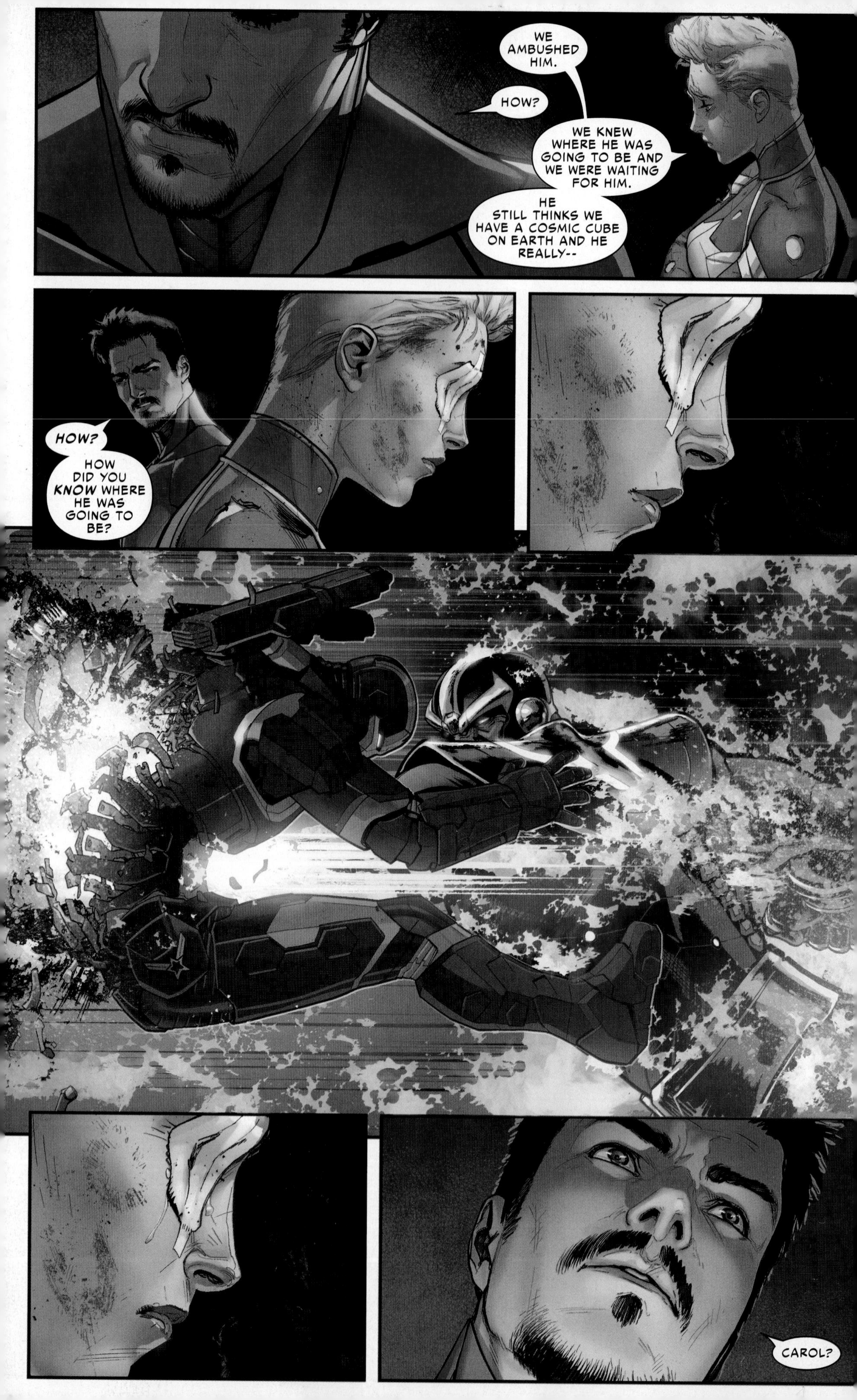
WE AMBUSHED HIM.
HOW?
WE KNEW WHERE HE WAS GOING TO BE AND WE WERE WAITING FOR HIM.
HE STILL THINKS WE HAVE A COSMIC CUBE ON EARTH AND HE REALLY--
HOW?
HOW DID YOU KNOW WHERE HE WAS GOING TO BE?
CAROL?

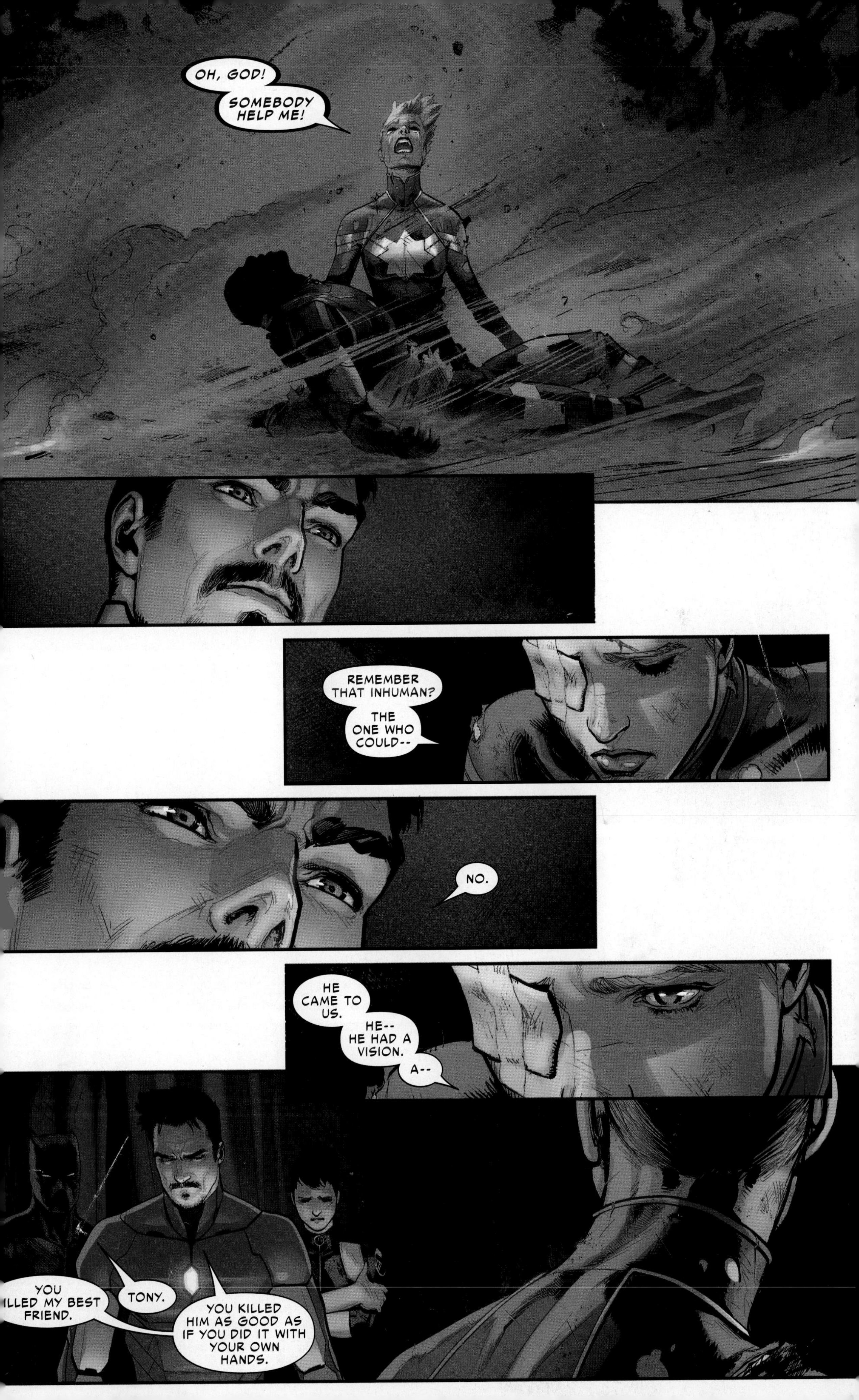

OH, GOD!
SOMEBODY HELP ME!
REMEMBER THAT INHUMAN?
THE ONE WHO COULD--
NO.
HE CAME TO US.
HE-- HE HAD A VISION.
A--
TONY.
YOU ILLED MY BEST FRIEND.
YOU KILLED HIM AS GOOD AS IF YOU DID IT WITH YOUR OWN HANDS.

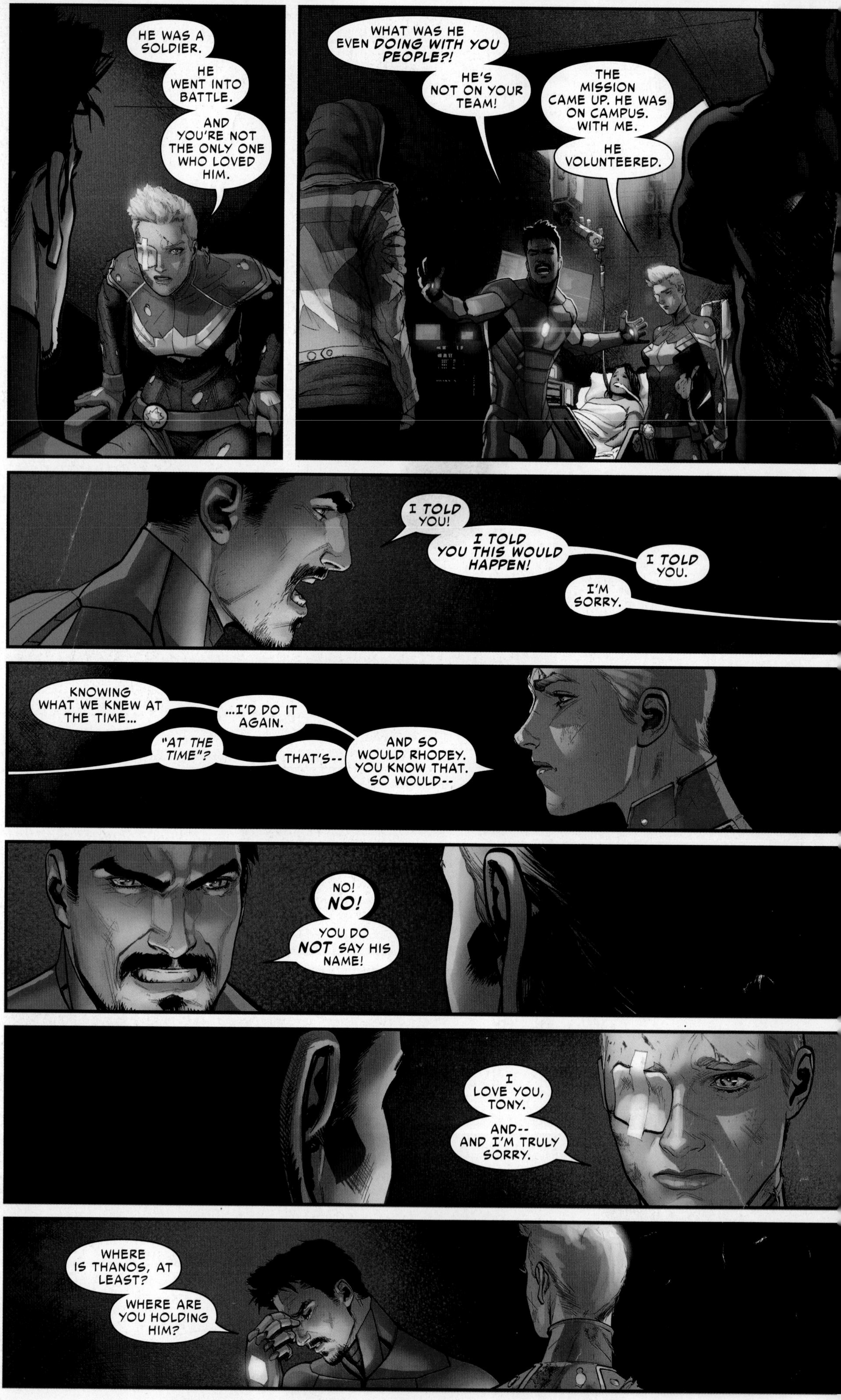
HE WAS A SOLDIER.
HE WENT INTO BATTLE.
AND YOU'RE NOT THE ONLY ONE WHO LOVED HIM.
WHAT WAS HE EVEN *DOING WITH YOU PEOPLE?!*
HE'S NOT ON YOUR TEAM!
THE MISSION CAME UP. HE WAS ON CAMPUS. WITH ME.
HE VOLUNTEERED.
I *TOLD* YOU!
I TOLD YOU THIS WOULD HAPPEN!
I *TOLD* YOU.
I'M SORRY.
KNOWING WHAT WE KNEW AT THE TIME...
...I'D DO IT AGAIN.
AND SO WOULD RHODEY. YOU KNOW THAT. SO WOULD--
"AT THE TIME"?
THAT'S--
NO! ***NO!***
YOU DO ***NOT*** SAY HIS NAME!
I LOVE YOU, TONY.
AND-- AND I'M TRULY SORRY.
WHERE IS THANOS, AT LEAST?
WHERE ARE YOU HOLDING HIM?

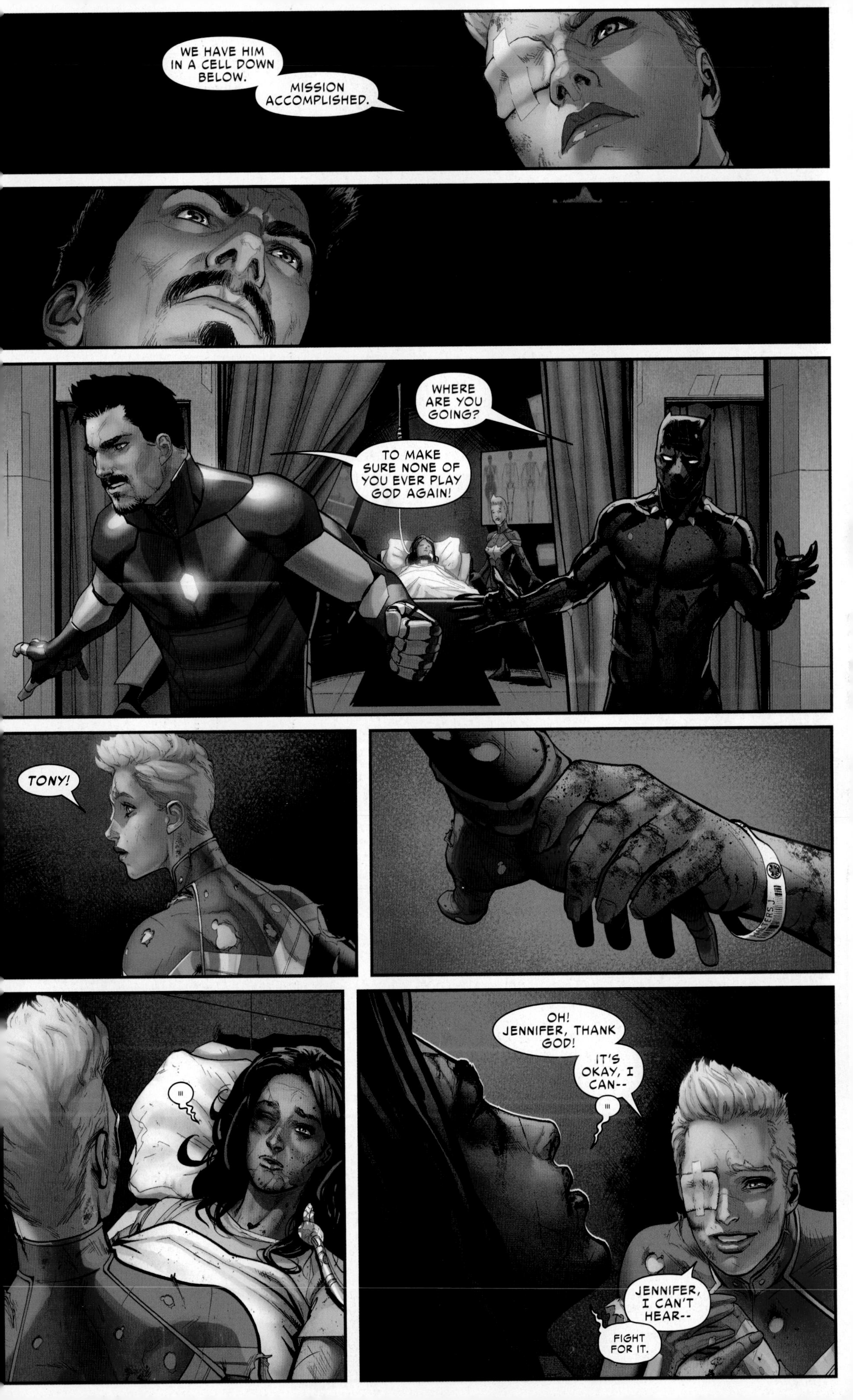

WE HAVE HIM IN A CELL DOWN BELOW.
MISSION ACCOMPLISHED.
WHERE ARE YOU GOING?
TO MAKE SURE NONE OF YOU EVER PLAY GOD AGAIN!
TONY!
OH! JENNIFER, THANK GOD!
IT'S OKAY, I CAN--
JENNIFER, I CAN'T HEAR--
FIGHT FOR IT.

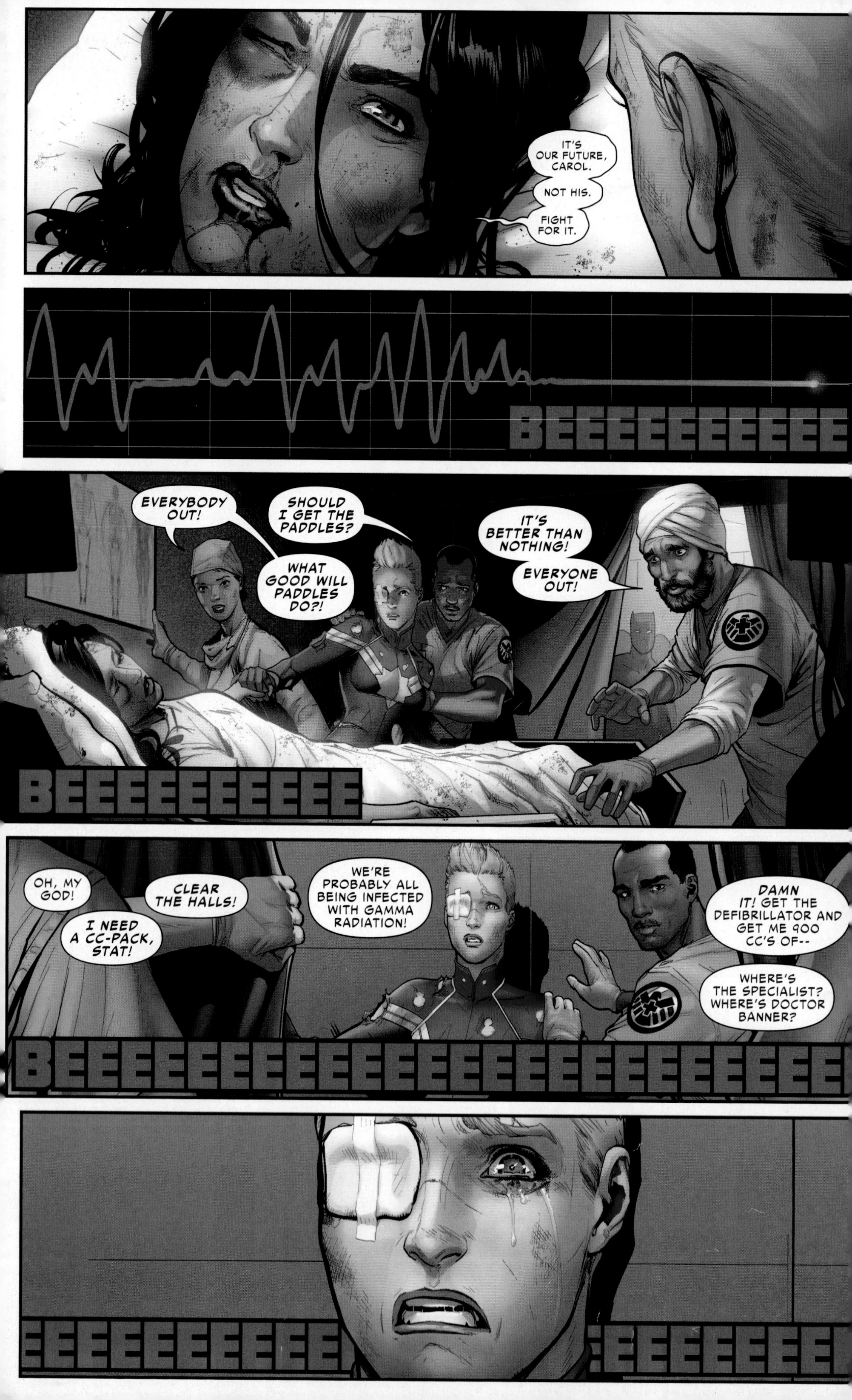

IT'S OUR FUTURE, CAROL.
NOT HIS.
FIGHT FOR IT.
BEEEEEEEEEEE
EVERYBODY OUT!
SHOULD I GET THE PADDLES?
WHAT GOOD WILL PADDLES DO?!
IT'S BETTER THAN NOTHING!
EVERYONE OUT!
BEEEEEEEEEEE
OH, MY GOD!
I NEED A CC-PACK, STAT!
CLEAR THE HALLS!
WE'RE PROBABLY ALL BEING INFECTED WITH GAMMA RADIATION!
DAMN IT! GET THE DEFIBRILLATOR AND GET ME 900 CC'S OF--
WHERE'S THE SPECIALIST? WHERE'S DOCTOR BANNER?
BEEEEEEEEEEEEEEEEEEEEEEEE
EEEEEEEEEEE
EEEEEEEEE

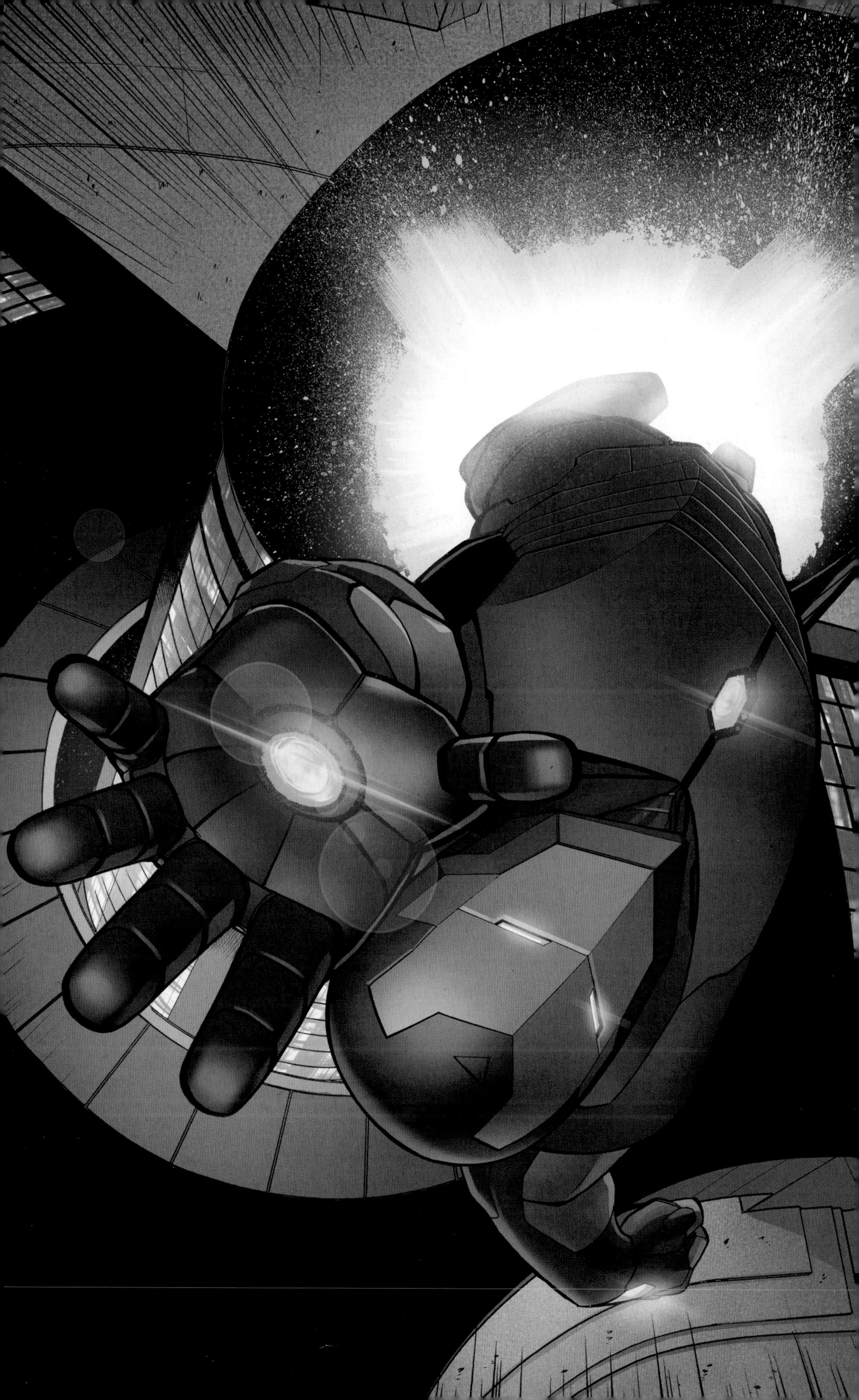

CIVIL WAR II #2

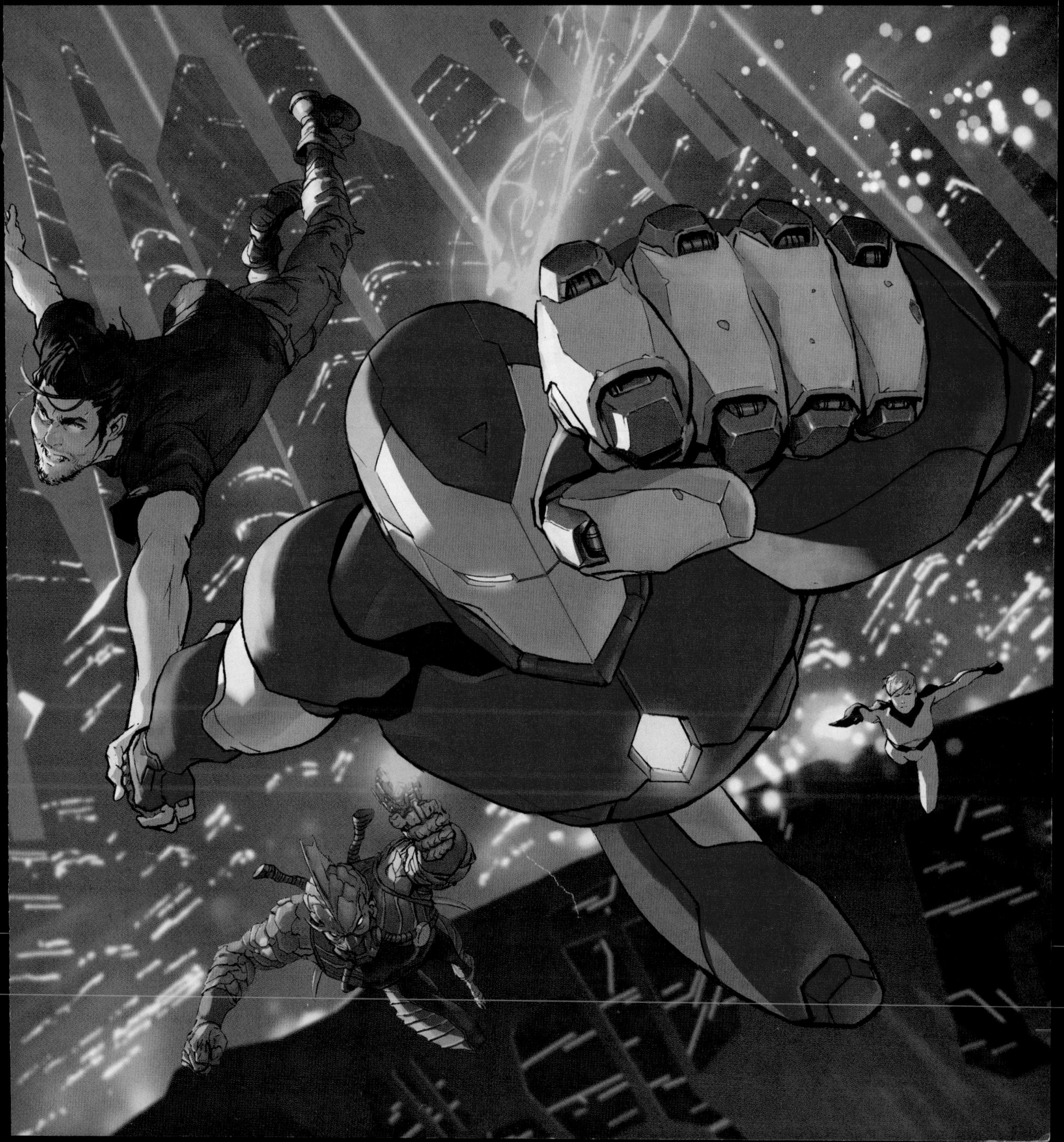

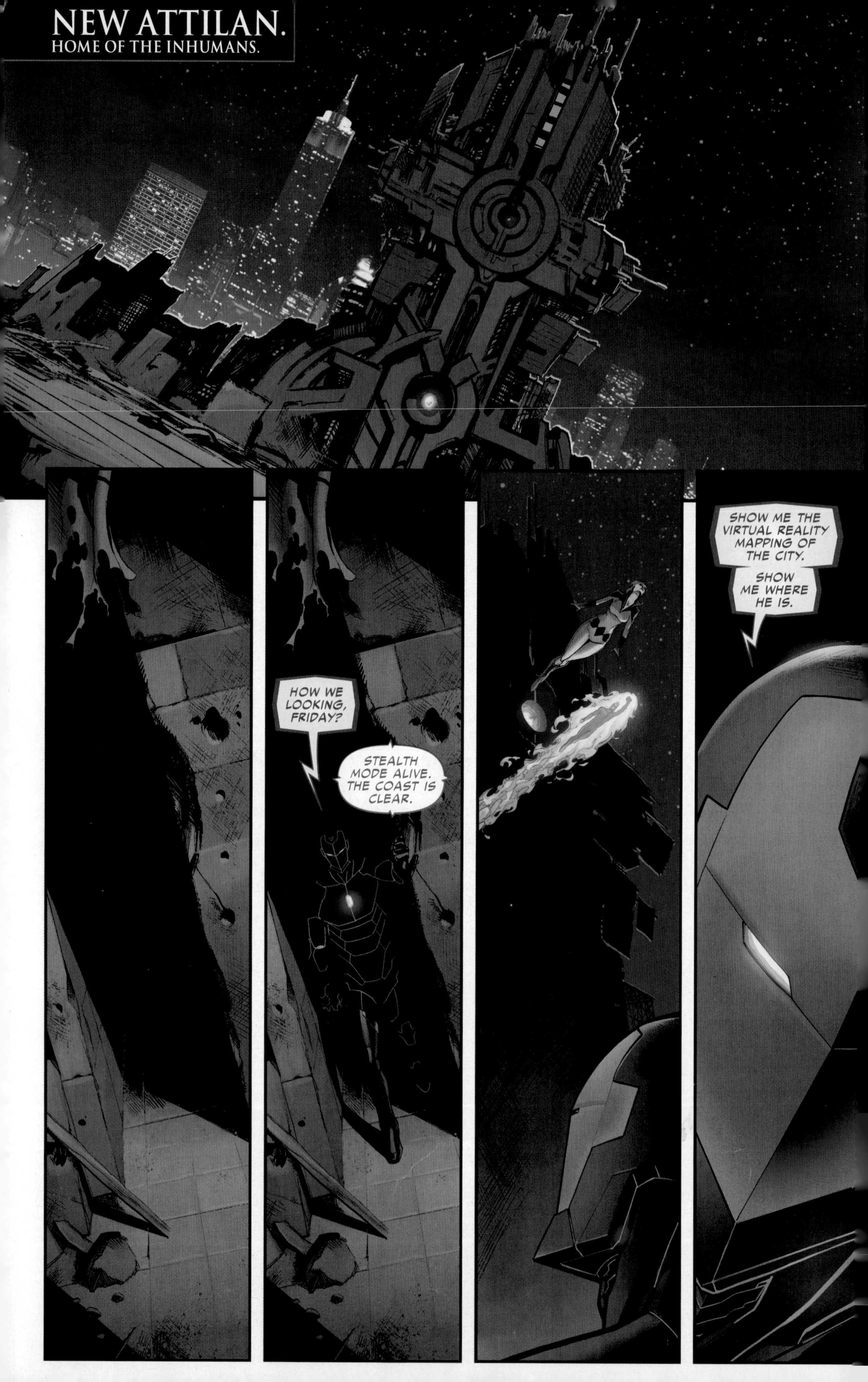
NEW ATTILAN.
HOME OF THE INHUMANS.
HOW WE LOOKING, FRIDAY?
STEALTH MODE ALIVE. THE COAST IS CLEAR.
SHOW ME THE VIRTUAL REALITY MAPPING OF THE CITY.
SHOW ME WHERE HE IS.

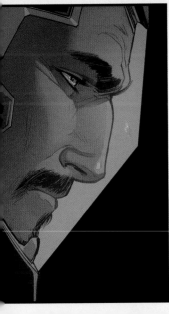

DON'T DO THIS, TONY.

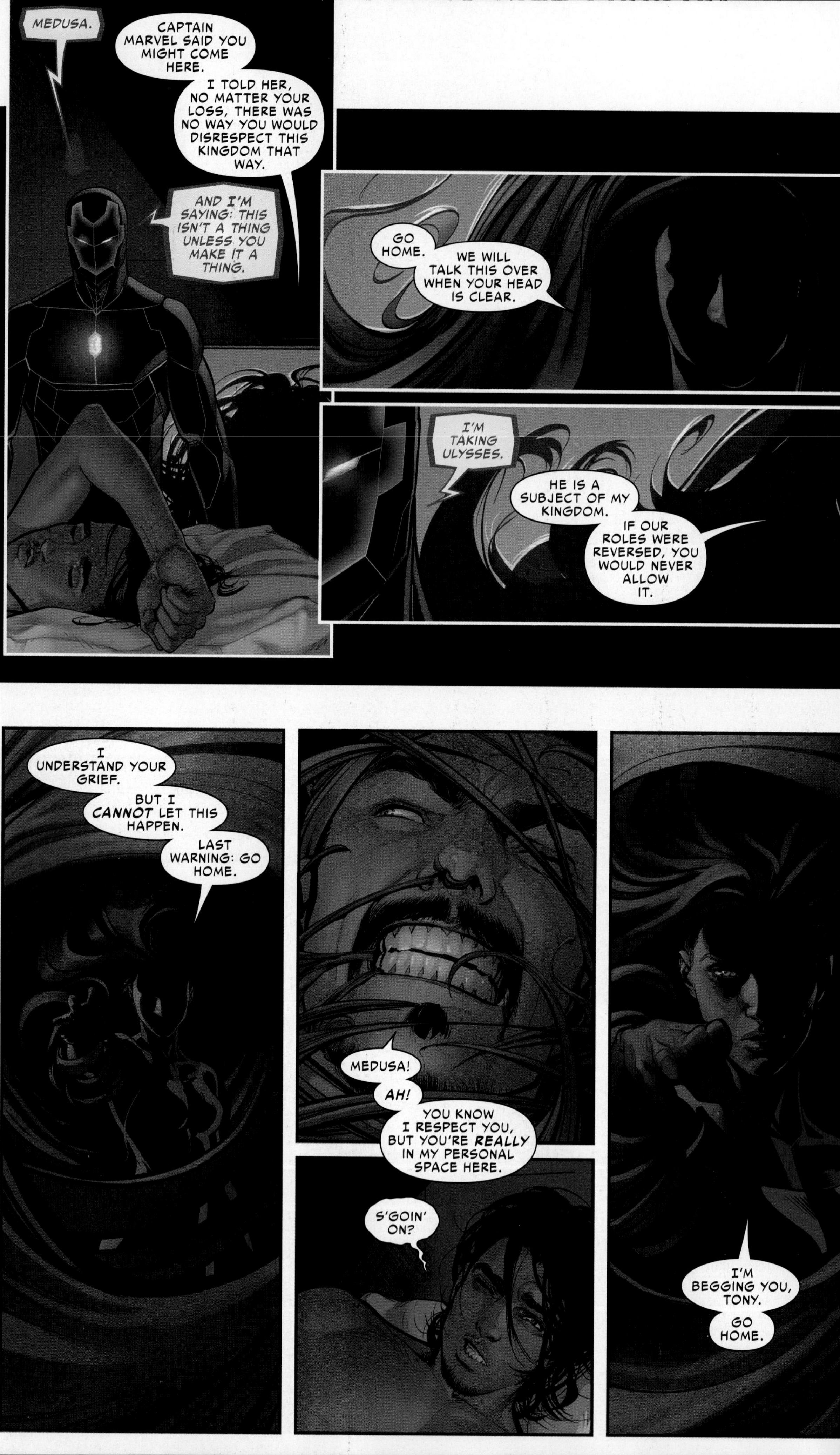
MEDUSA.
CAPTAIN MARVEL SAID YOU MIGHT COME HERE.
I TOLD HER, NO MATTER YOUR LOSS, THERE WAS NO WAY YOU WOULD DISRESPECT THIS KINGDOM THAT WAY.
AND I'M SAYING: THIS ISN'T A THING UNLESS YOU MAKE IT A THING.
GO HOME.
WE WILL TALK THIS OVER WHEN YOUR HEAD IS CLEAR.
I'M TAKING ULYSSES.
HE IS A SUBJECT OF MY KINGDOM.
IF OUR ROLES WERE REVERSED, YOU WOULD NEVER ALLOW IT.
I UNDERSTAND YOUR GRIEF.
BUT I CANNOT LET THIS HAPPEN.
LAST WARNING: GO HOME.
MEDUSA!
AH!
YOU KNOW I RESPECT YOU, BUT YOU'RE REALLY IN MY PERSONAL SPACE HERE.
S'GOIN' ON?
I'M BEGGING YOU, TONY.
GO HOME.

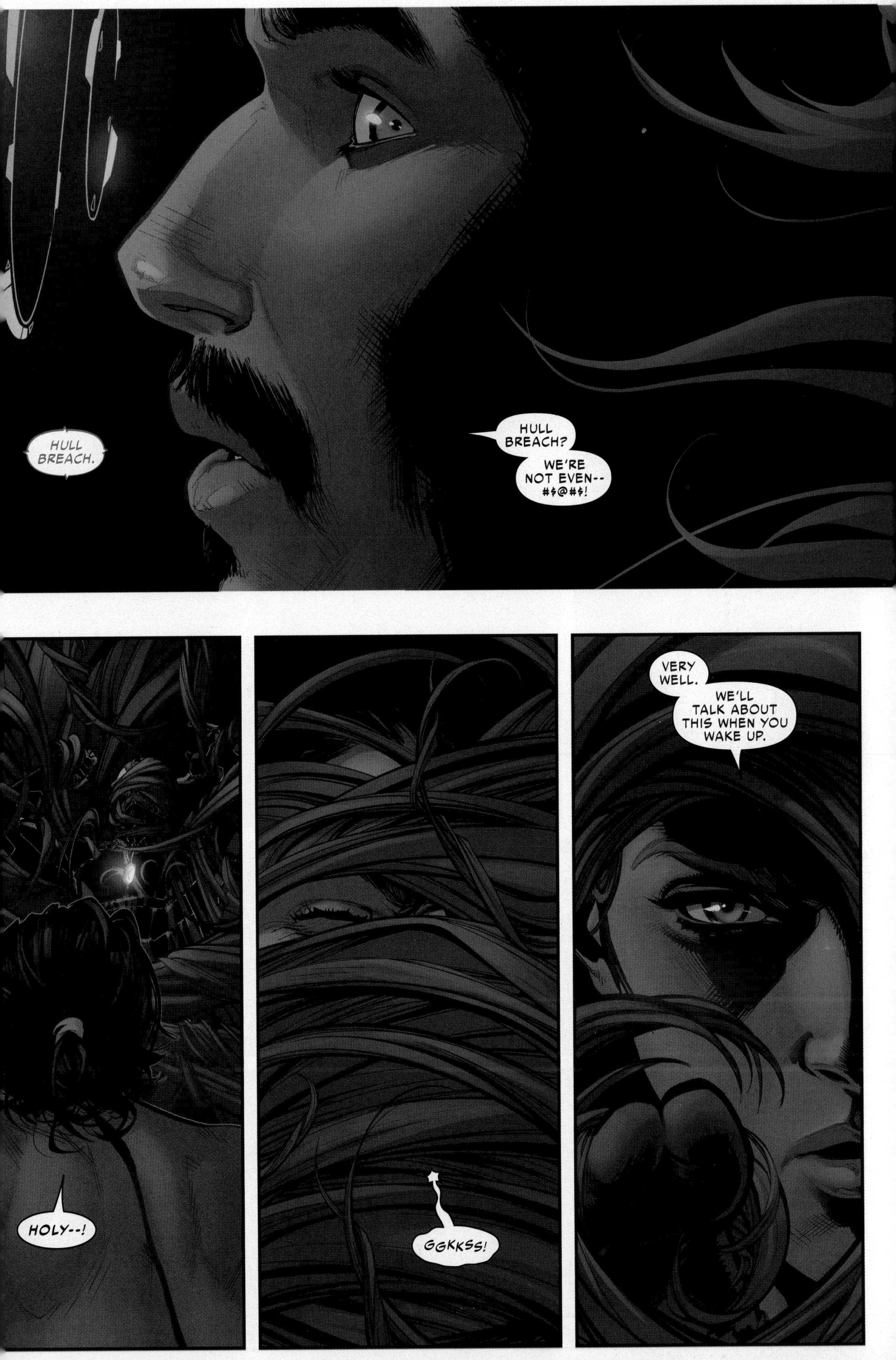
HULL BREACH.
HULL BREACH?
WE'RE NOT EVEN-- #$@#$!
HOLY--!
GGKKSS!
VERY WELL.
WE'LL TALK ABOUT THIS WHEN YOU WAKE UP.

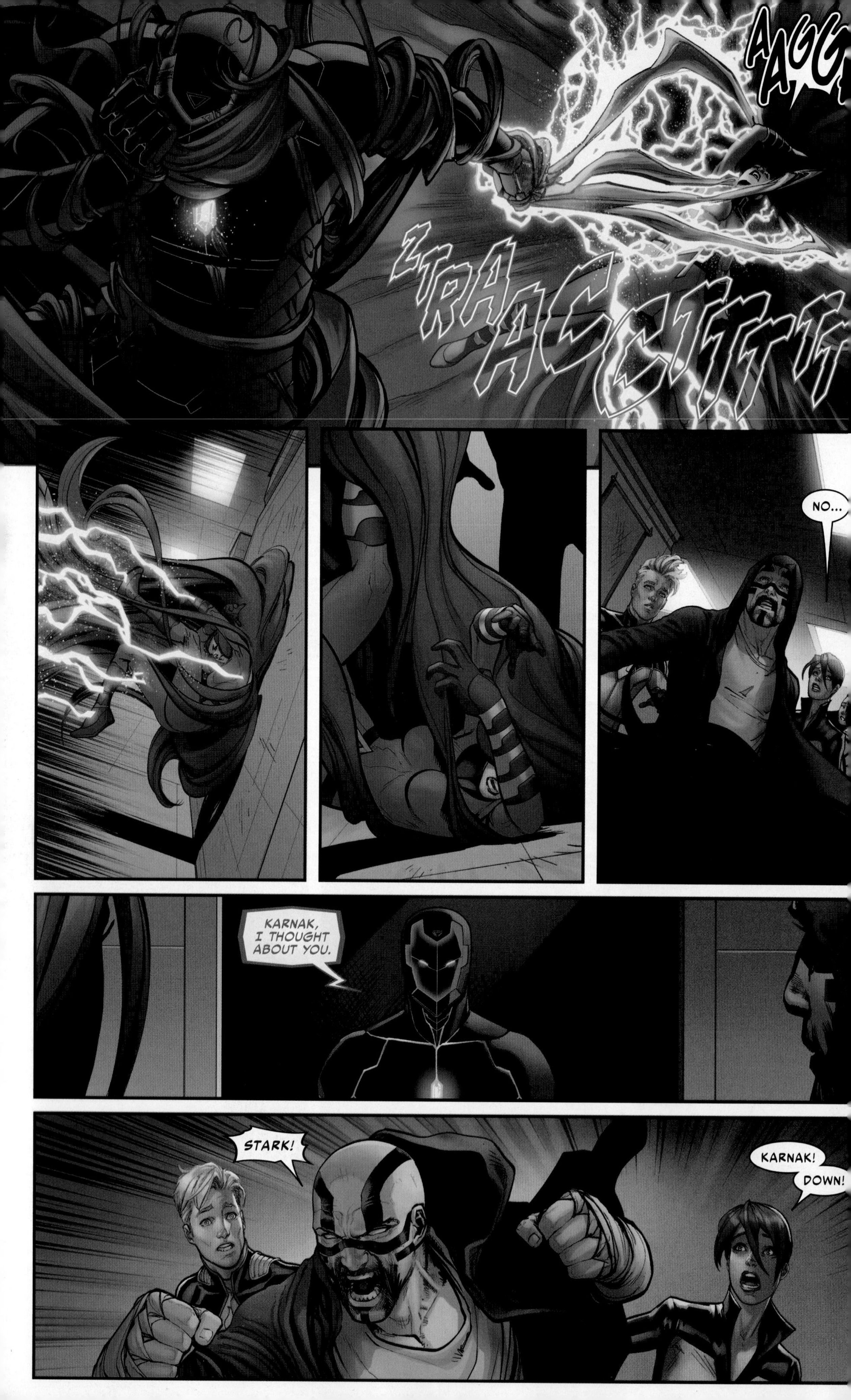
AAGG
ZTRAACCTTTT
NO...
KARNAK, I THOUGHT ABOUT YOU.
STARK!
KARNAK!
DOWN!

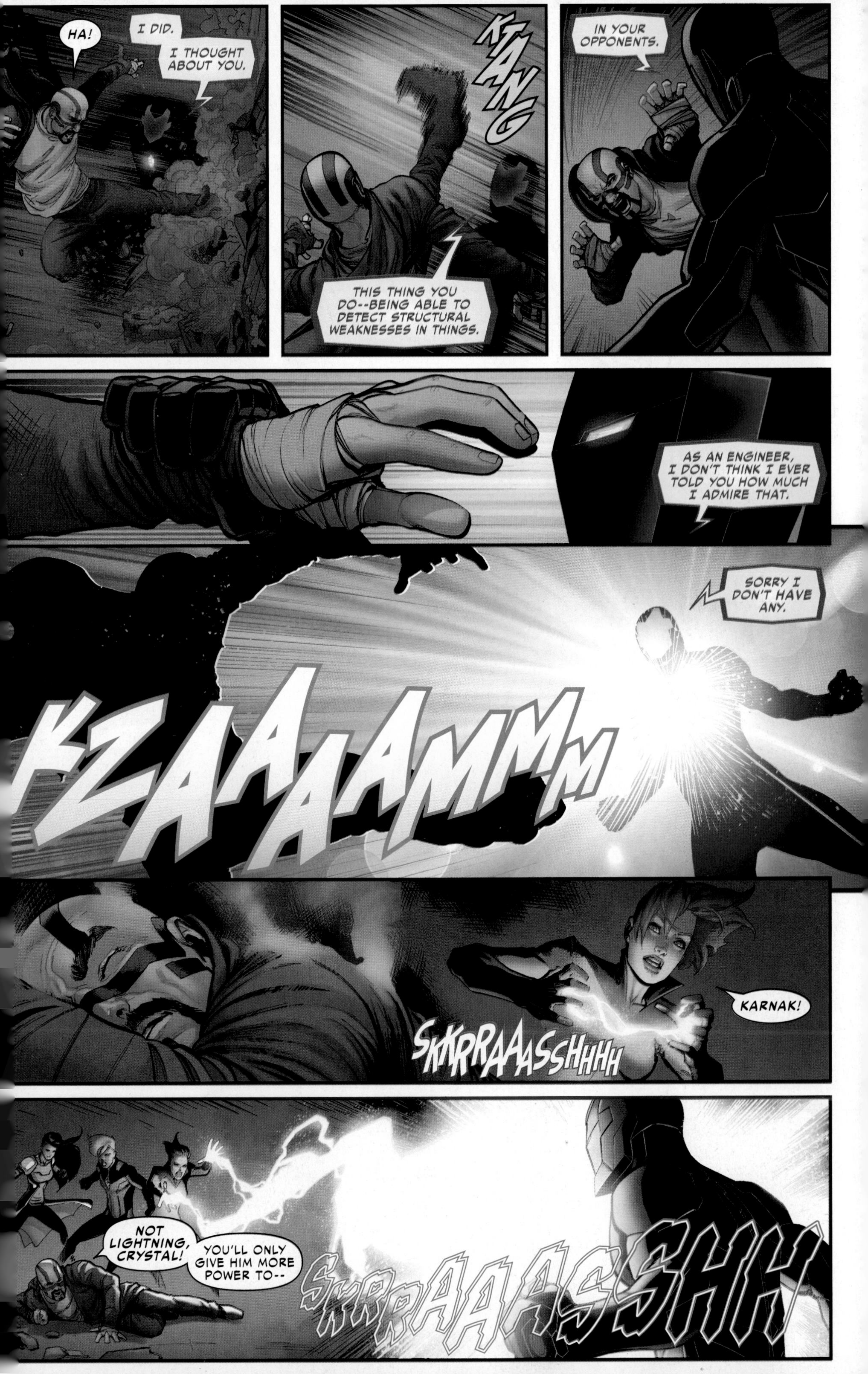
HA!
I DID.
I THOUGHT ABOUT YOU.
KTANG
THIS THING YOU DO--BEING ABLE TO DETECT STRUCTURAL WEAKNESSES IN THINGS.
IN YOUR OPPONENTS.
AS AN ENGINEER, I DON'T THINK I EVER TOLD YOU HOW MUCH I ADMIRE THAT.
SORRY I DON'T HAVE ANY.
KZAAAAMMM
KARNAK!
SKKRRAAASSHHHH
NOT LIGHTNING, CRYSTAL!
YOU'LL ONLY GIVE HIM MORE POWER TO--
SKRRAAASSHH

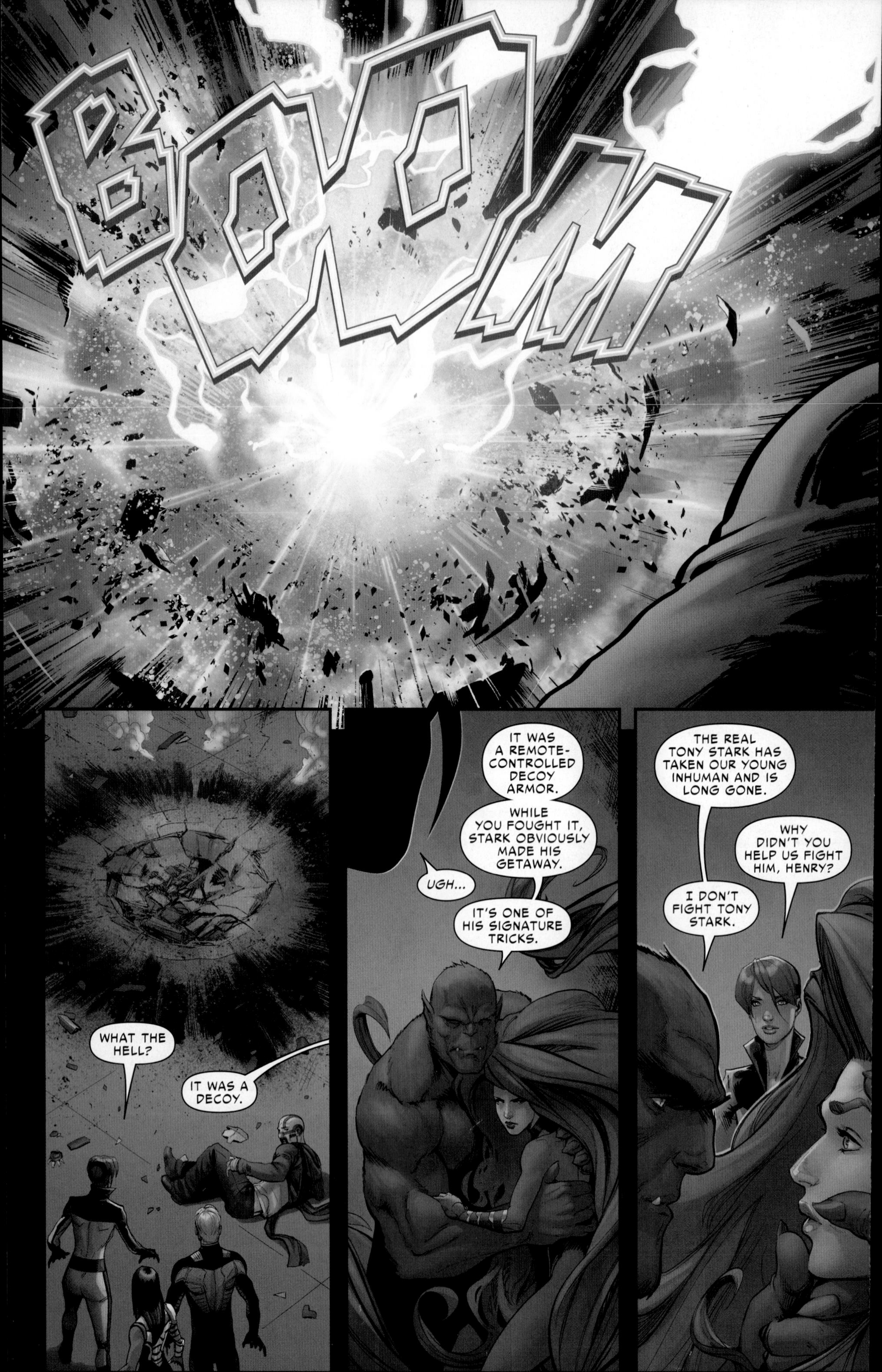
BOOOM
WHAT THE HELL?
IT WAS A DECOY.
IT WAS A REMOTE-CONTROLLED DECOY ARMOR.
WHILE YOU FOUGHT IT, STARK OBVIOUSLY MADE HIS GETAWAY.
UGH...
IT'S ONE OF HIS SIGNATURE TRICKS.
THE REAL TONY STARK HAS TAKEN OUR YOUNG INHUMAN AND IS LONG GONE.
WHY DIDN'T YOU HELP US FIGHT HIM, HENRY?
I DON'T FIGHT TONY STARK.

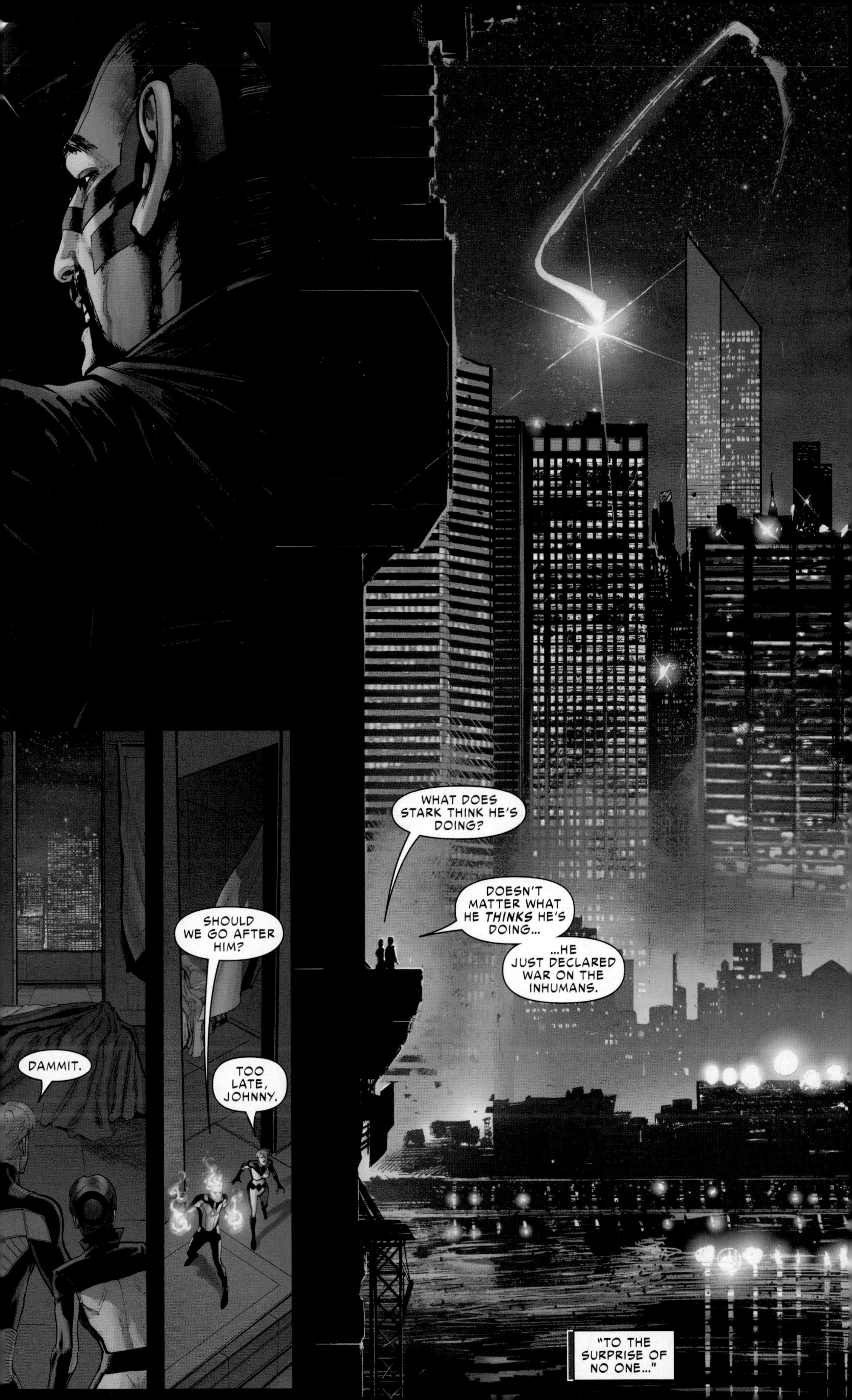
WHAT DOES STARK THINK HE'S DOING?
DOESN'T MATTER WHAT HE THINKS HE'S DOING...
...HE JUST DECLARED WAR ON THE INHUMANS.
SHOULD WE GO AFTER HIM?
DAMMIT.
TOO LATE, JOHNNY.
"TO THE SURPRISE OF NO ONE..."

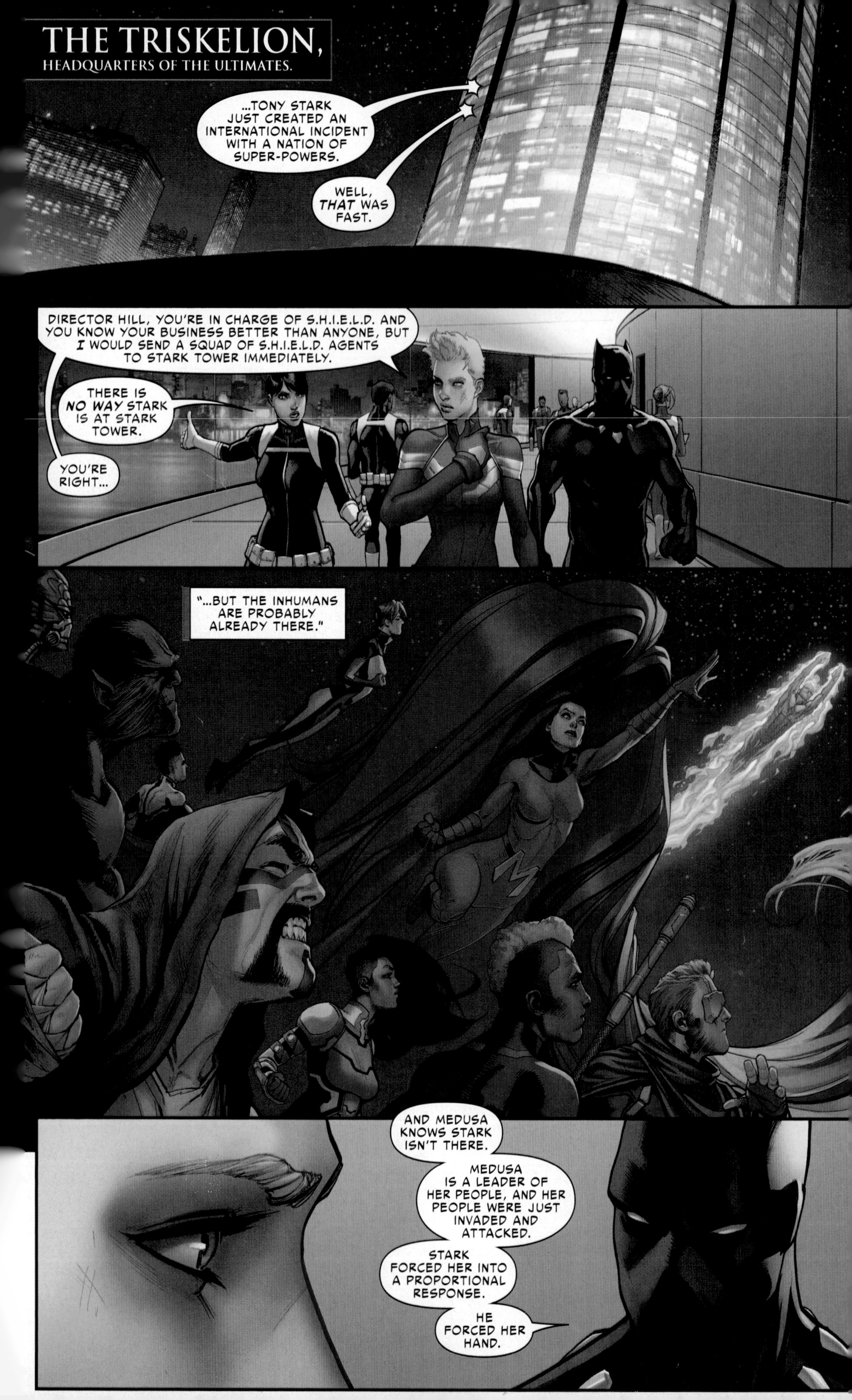
THE TRISKELION,
HEADQUARTERS OF THE ULTIMATES.
...TONY STARK JUST CREATED AN INTERNATIONAL INCIDENT WITH A NATION OF SUPER-POWERS.
WELL, THAT WAS FAST.
DIRECTOR HILL, YOU'RE IN CHARGE OF S.H.I.E.L.D. AND YOU KNOW YOUR BUSINESS BETTER THAN ANYONE, BUT I WOULD SEND A SQUAD OF S.H.I.E.L.D. AGENTS TO STARK TOWER IMMEDIATELY.
THERE IS NO WAY STARK IS AT STARK TOWER.
YOU'RE RIGHT...
"...BUT THE INHUMANS ARE PROBABLY ALREADY THERE."
AND MEDUSA KNOWS STARK ISN'T THERE.
MEDUSA IS A LEADER OF HER PEOPLE, AND HER PEOPLE WERE JUST INVADED AND ATTACKED.
STARK FORCED HER INTO A PROPORTIONAL RESPONSE.
HE FORCED HER HAND.

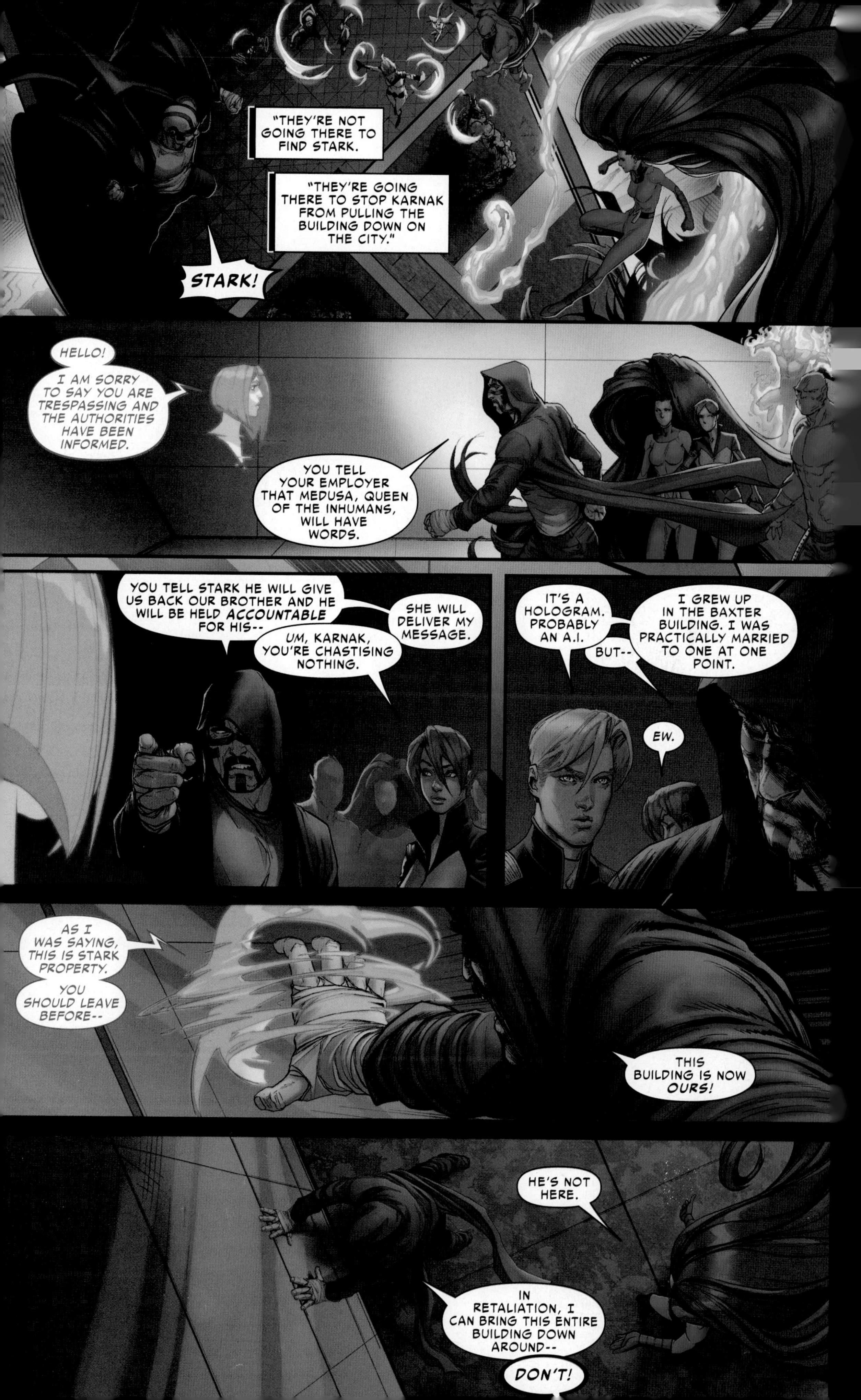
"THEY'RE NOT GOING THERE TO FIND STARK.
"THEY'RE GOING THERE TO STOP KARNAK FROM PULLING THE BUILDING DOWN ON THE CITY."
STARK!
HELLO!
I AM SORRY TO SAY YOU ARE TRESPASSING AND THE AUTHORITIES HAVE BEEN INFORMED.
YOU TELL YOUR EMPLOYER THAT MEDUSA, QUEEN OF THE INHUMANS, WILL HAVE WORDS.
YOU TELL STARK HE WILL GIVE US BACK OUR BROTHER AND HE WILL BE HELD ACCOUNTABLE FOR HIS--
SHE WILL DELIVER MY MESSAGE.
UM, KARNAK, YOU'RE CHASTISING NOTHING.
IT'S A HOLOGRAM. PROBABLY AN A.I.
BUT--
I GREW UP IN THE BAXTER BUILDING. I WAS PRACTICALLY MARRIED TO ONE AT ONE POINT.
EW.
AS I WAS SAYING, THIS IS STARK PROPERTY.
YOU SHOULD LEAVE BEFORE--
THIS BUILDING IS NOW OURS!
HE'S NOT HERE.
IN RETALIATION, I CAN BRING THIS ENTIRE BUILDING DOWN AROUND--
DON'T!

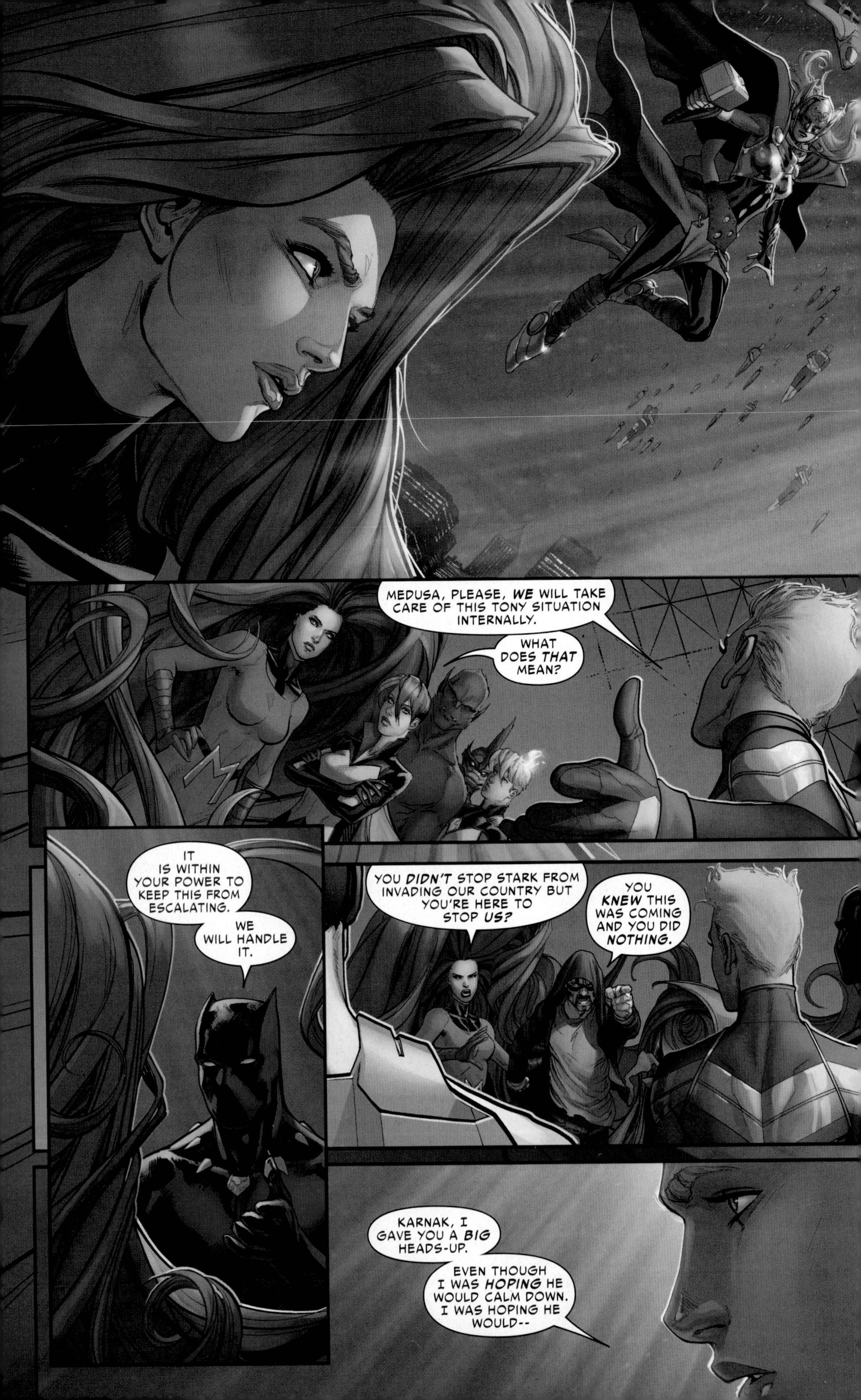
MEDUSA, PLEASE, WE WILL TAKE CARE OF THIS TONY SITUATION INTERNALLY.
WHAT DOES THAT MEAN?
IT IS WITHIN YOUR POWER TO KEEP THIS FROM ESCALATING.
WE WILL HANDLE IT.
YOU DIDN'T STOP STARK FROM INVADING OUR COUNTRY BUT YOU'RE HERE TO STOP US?
YOU KNEW THIS WAS COMING AND YOU DID NOTHING.
KARNAK, I GAVE YOU A BIG HEADS-UP.
EVEN THOUGH I WAS HOPING HE WOULD CALM DOWN. I WAS HOPING HE WOULD--

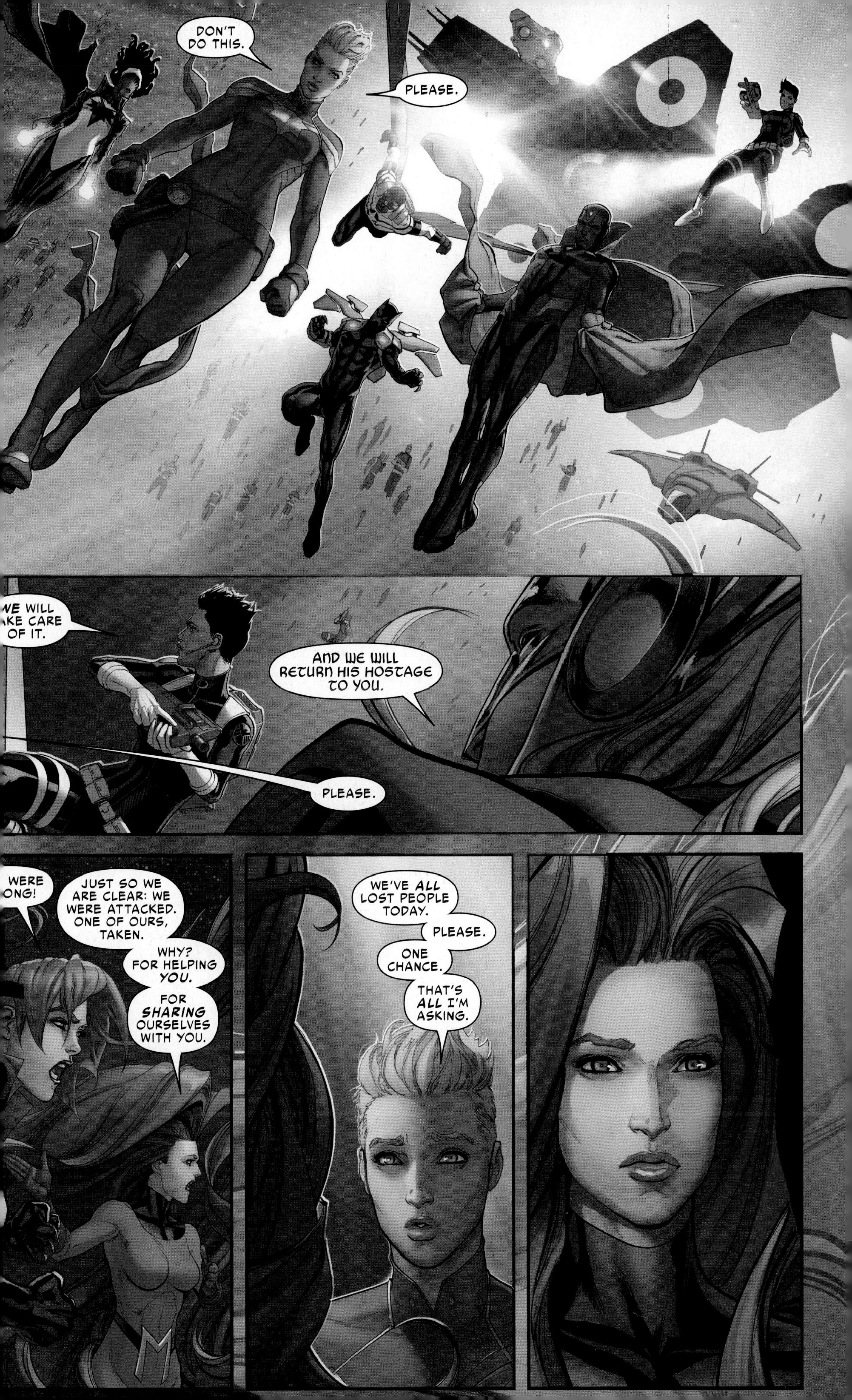

DON'T DO THIS.
PLEASE.
WE WILL AKE CARE OF IT.
AND WE WILL RETURN HIS HOSTAGE TO YOU.
PLEASE.
WERE ONG!
JUST SO WE ARE CLEAR: WE WERE ATTACKED. ONE OF OURS, TAKEN.
WHY? FOR HELPING *YOU*.
FOR *SHARING* OURSELVES WITH YOU.
WE'VE *ALL* LOST PEOPLE TODAY.
PLEASE.
ONE CHANCE.
THAT'S *ALL* I'M ASKING.

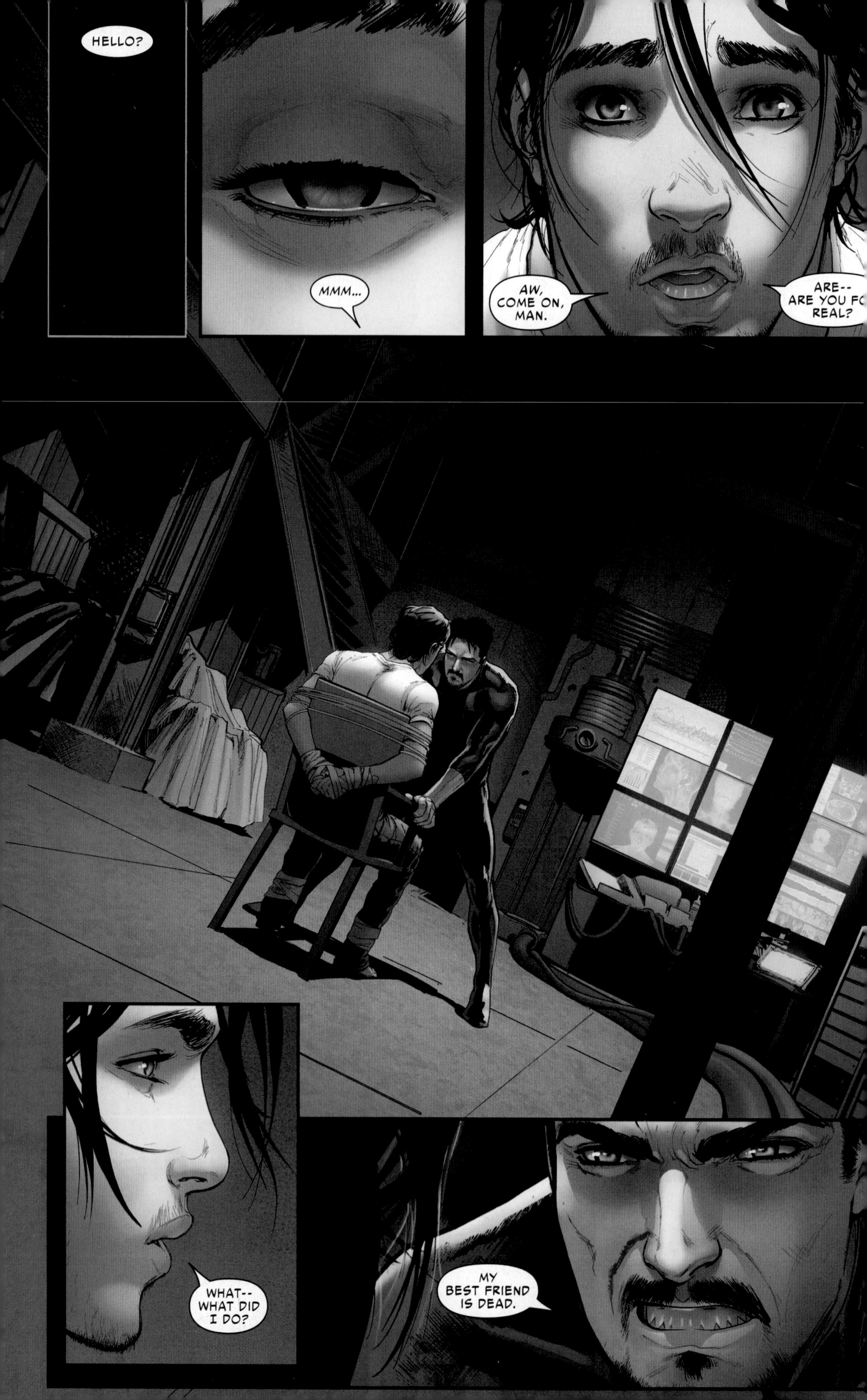

HELLO?
MMM...
AW, COME ON, MAN.
ARE-- ARE YOU FO REAL?
WHAT-- WHAT DID I DO?
MY BEST FRIEND IS DEAD.

I'M SORRY.

YOU'RE "SORRY." THANK YOU. I FEEL SO MUCH BETTER NOW.

I'M STILL NOT SURE WHAT I DID. I DON'T EVEN KNOW WHO WE'RE TALKING ABOUT.

COLONEL JAMES RHODES. AN HONEST-TO-GOD AMERICAN HERO. THE MISSION YOU SENT HIM ON COST HIM HIS LIFE.

M-ME? I DIDN'T SEND ANYBODY ANYWHERE.

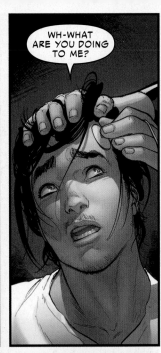

WH-WHAT ARE YOU DOING TO ME?

ARE--ARE YOU GOING TO HURT ME? ARE YOU GOING TO KILL ME?

I'M IRON MAN. I'M ONE OF THE GOOD GUYS. I--I KNOW. I'M A BIG FAN. SHUT UP. WAS.

I--I DIDN'T KILL YOUR FRIEND. SHOW ME HOW YOUR POWERS WORK. WHAT?

THESE VISIONS THAT YOU HAVE. HAVE ONE. SHOW ME.

I DON'T JUST MAKE THEM. THEY--THEY KIND OF JUST HAPPEN. I CAN'T CONTROL WHEN.

OW!

ANYTHING, FRIDAY?

WHY DID YOU D THAT?

BRAIN-WAVE ENTRAINMENT.

I WANTED TO SEE HOW OUTSIDE STIMULUS AFFECTED YOUR ABILITY TO SEE ONE OF YOUR VISIONS OR IF IT WOULD STIMULATE ONE.

OW.

NEXT TIME I'LL TICKLE YOU.

LET ME GO!

LESS TALKING, MORE VISION.

LET ME GO!

FRIDAY?

THERE'RE DEFINITELY SOME INTERESTING NEURAL SIGNAL ENERGY PATTERNS MOVING AROUND HIS FRONTAL LOBE.

"INTERESTING" AS IN--?

I NEED MORE DATA. HIT HIM AGAIN.

NO! HEY!

NEVER MIND. THERE YOU GO. FEAR WORKS, TOO.

WHAT DO YOU HA FRIDAY?

A SPIKE.

A SPIKE?

A SURGE IN ALPHA BRAIN-WAVE ACTIVITY THAT IS NOT IN THE NORMAL REGISTER.

WHAT DO YOU WANT FROM ME?

I'LL TELL YOU...

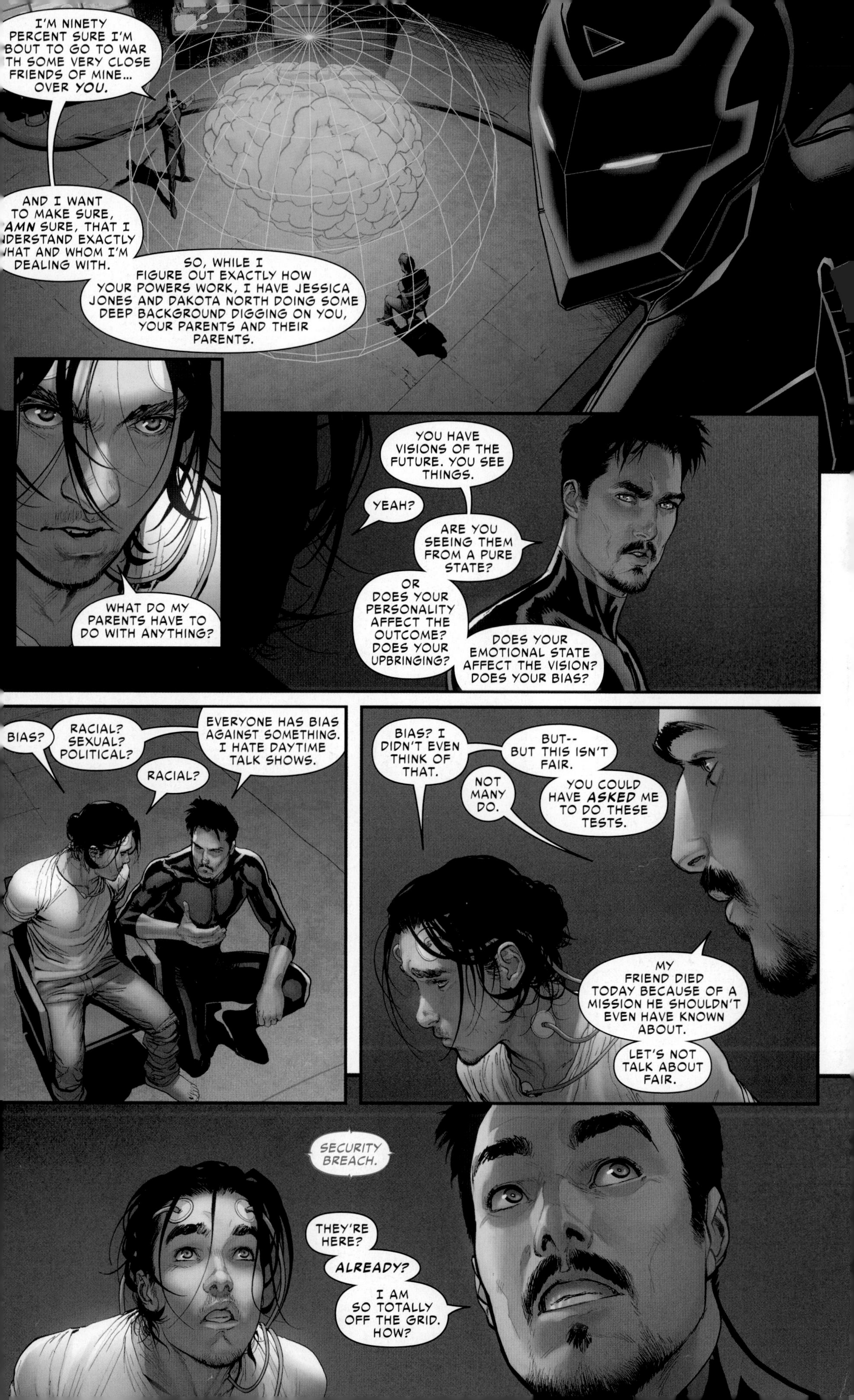

I'M NINETY PERCENT SURE I'M BOUT TO GO TO WAR TH SOME VERY CLOSE FRIENDS OF MINE... OVER *YOU.*
AND I WANT TO MAKE SURE, *AMN* SURE, THAT I NDERSTAND EXACTLY HAT AND WHOM I'M DEALING WITH.
SO, WHILE I FIGURE OUT EXACTLY HOW YOUR POWERS WORK, I HAVE JESSICA JONES AND DAKOTA NORTH DOING SOME DEEP BACKGROUND DIGGING ON YOU, YOUR PARENTS AND THEIR PARENTS.
WHAT DO MY PARENTS HAVE TO DO WITH ANYTHING?
YOU HAVE VISIONS OF THE FUTURE. YOU SEE THINGS.
YEAH?
ARE YOU SEEING THEM FROM A PURE STATE?
OR DOES YOUR PERSONALITY AFFECT THE OUTCOME? DOES YOUR UPBRINGING?
DOES YOUR EMOTIONAL STATE AFFECT THE VISION? DOES YOUR BIAS?
BIAS?
RACIAL? SEXUAL? POLITICAL?
EVERYONE HAS BIAS AGAINST SOMETHING. I HATE DAYTIME TALK SHOWS.
RACIAL?
BIAS? I DIDN'T EVEN THINK OF THAT.
NOT MANY DO.
BUT-- BUT THIS ISN'T FAIR.
YOU COULD HAVE *ASKED* ME TO DO THESE TESTS.
MY FRIEND DIED TODAY BECAUSE OF A MISSION HE SHOULDN'T EVEN HAVE KNOWN ABOUT.
LET'S NOT TALK ABOUT FAIR.
SECURITY BREACH.
THEY'RE HERE?
ALREADY?
I AM SO TOTALLY OFF THE GRID. HOW?

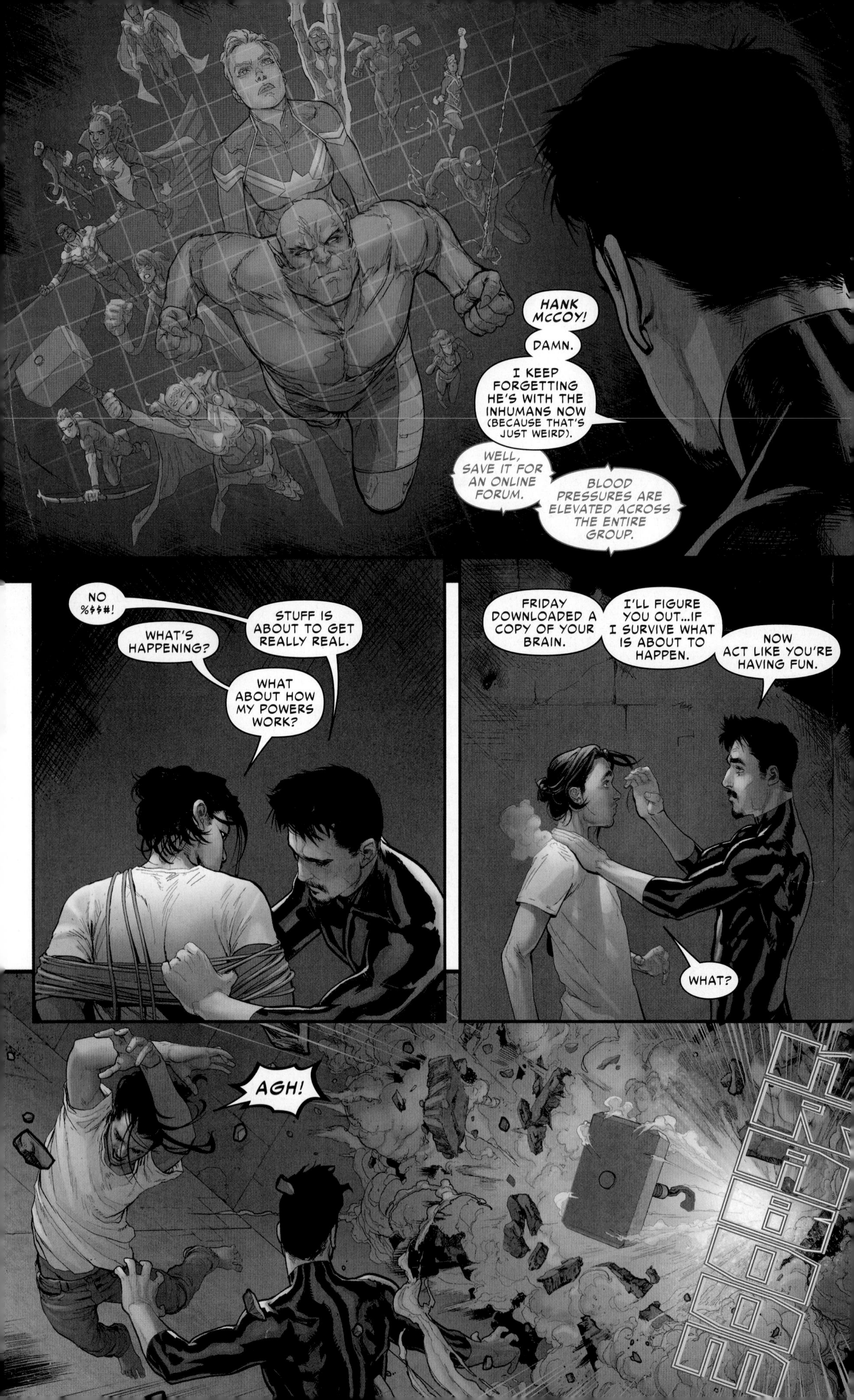
HANK McCOY!
DAMN.
I KEEP FORGETTING HE'S WITH THE INHUMANS NOW (BECAUSE THAT'S JUST WEIRD).
WELL, SAVE IT FOR AN ONLINE FORUM.
BLOOD PRESSURES ARE ELEVATED ACROSS THE ENTIRE GROUP.
NO %$$#!
STUFF IS ABOUT TO GET REALLY REAL.
WHAT'S HAPPENING?
WHAT ABOUT HOW MY POWERS WORK?
FRIDAY DOWNLOADED A COPY OF YOUR BRAIN.
I'LL FIGURE YOU OUT...IF I SURVIVE WHAT IS ABOUT TO HAPPEN.
NOW ACT LIKE YOU'RE HAVING FUN.
WHAT?
AGH!

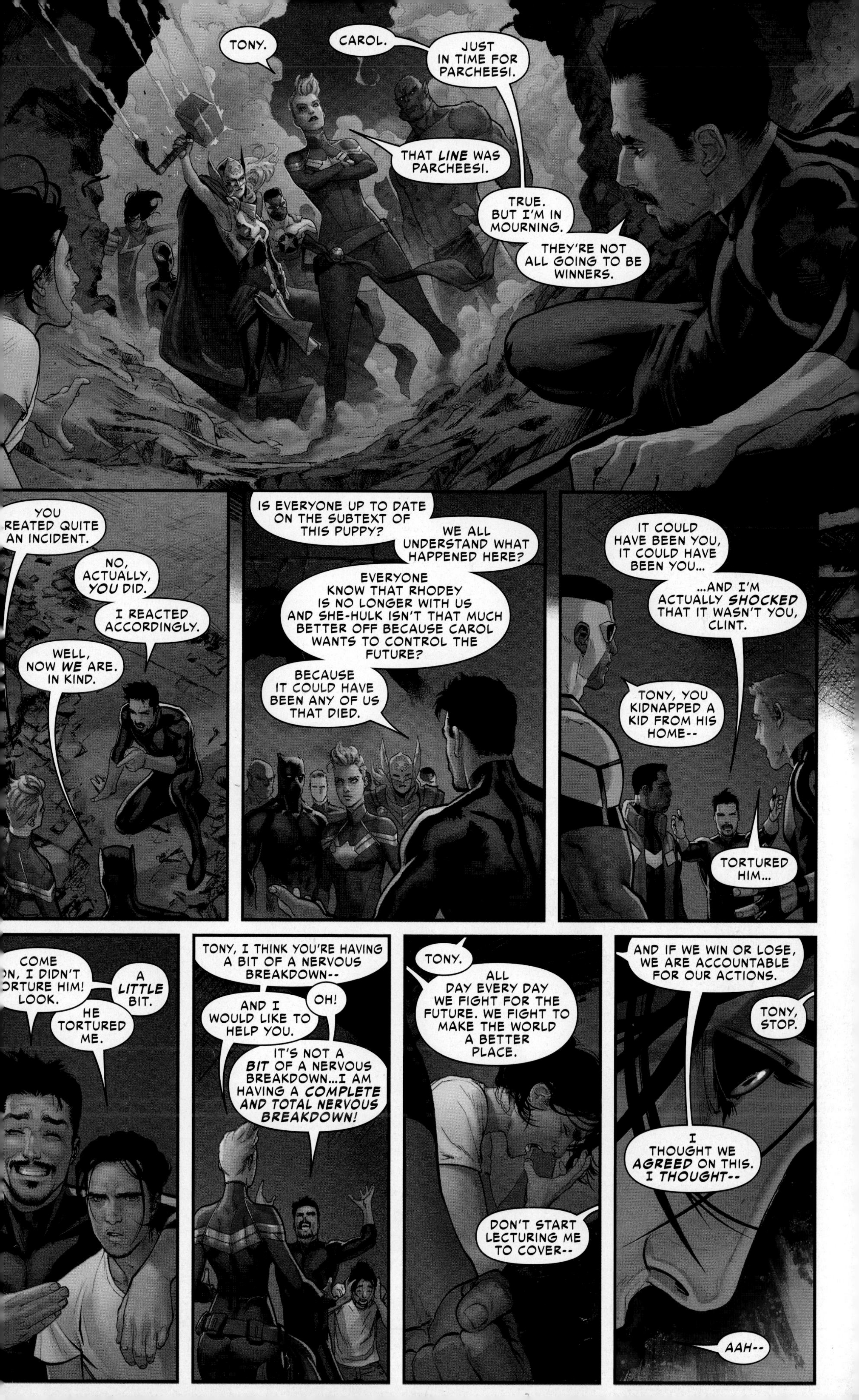
TONY.
CAROL.
JUST IN TIME FOR PARCHEESI.
THAT LINE WAS PARCHEESI.
TRUE. BUT I'M IN MOURNING.
THEY'RE NOT ALL GOING TO BE WINNERS.
YOU REATED QUITE AN INCIDENT.
NO, ACTUALLY, YOU DID.
I REACTED ACCORDINGLY.
WELL, NOW WE ARE. IN KIND.
IS EVERYONE UP TO DATE ON THE SUBTEXT OF THIS PUPPY?
WE ALL UNDERSTAND WHAT HAPPENED HERE?
EVERYONE KNOW THAT RHODEY IS NO LONGER WITH US AND SHE-HULK ISN'T THAT MUCH BETTER OFF BECAUSE CAROL WANTS TO CONTROL THE FUTURE?
BECAUSE IT COULD HAVE BEEN ANY OF US THAT DIED.
IT COULD HAVE BEEN YOU, IT COULD HAVE BEEN YOU...
...AND I'M ACTUALLY SHOCKED THAT IT WASN'T YOU, CLINT.
TONY, YOU KIDNAPPED A KID FROM HIS HOME--
TORTURED HIM...
COME ON, I DIDN'T ORTURE HIM! LOOK.
A LITTLE BIT.
HE TORTURED ME.
TONY, I THINK YOU'RE HAVING A BIT OF A NERVOUS BREAKDOWN--
AND I WOULD LIKE TO HELP YOU.
OH!
IT'S NOT A BIT OF A NERVOUS BREAKDOWN...I AM HAVING A COMPLETE AND TOTAL NERVOUS BREAKDOWN!
TONY.
ALL DAY EVERY DAY WE FIGHT FOR THE FUTURE. WE FIGHT TO MAKE THE WORLD A BETTER PLACE.
DON'T START LECTURING ME TO COVER--
AND IF WE WIN OR LOSE, WE ARE ACCOUNTABLE FOR OUR ACTIONS.
TONY, STOP.
I THOUGHT WE AGREED ON THIS. I THOUGHT--
AAH--

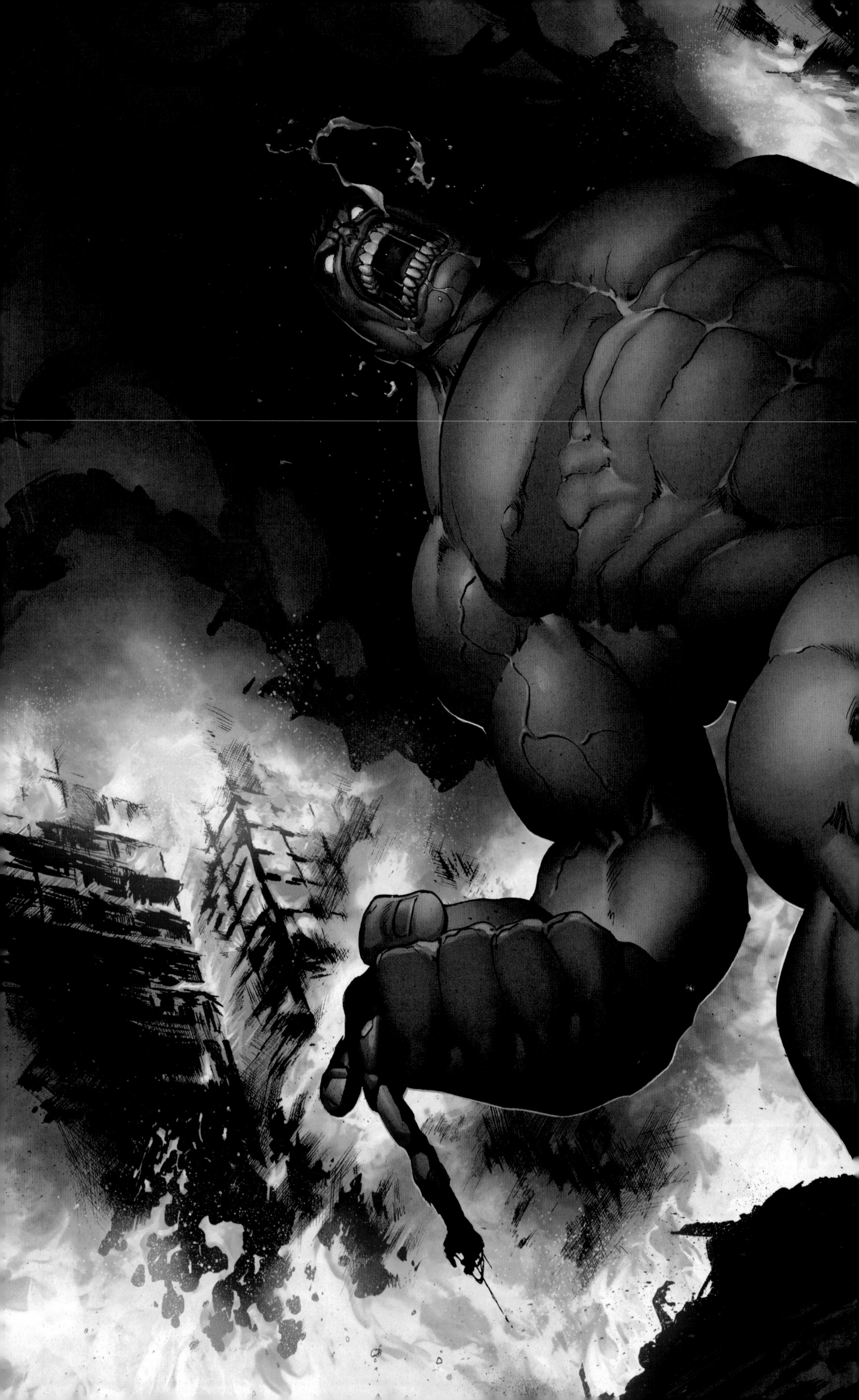

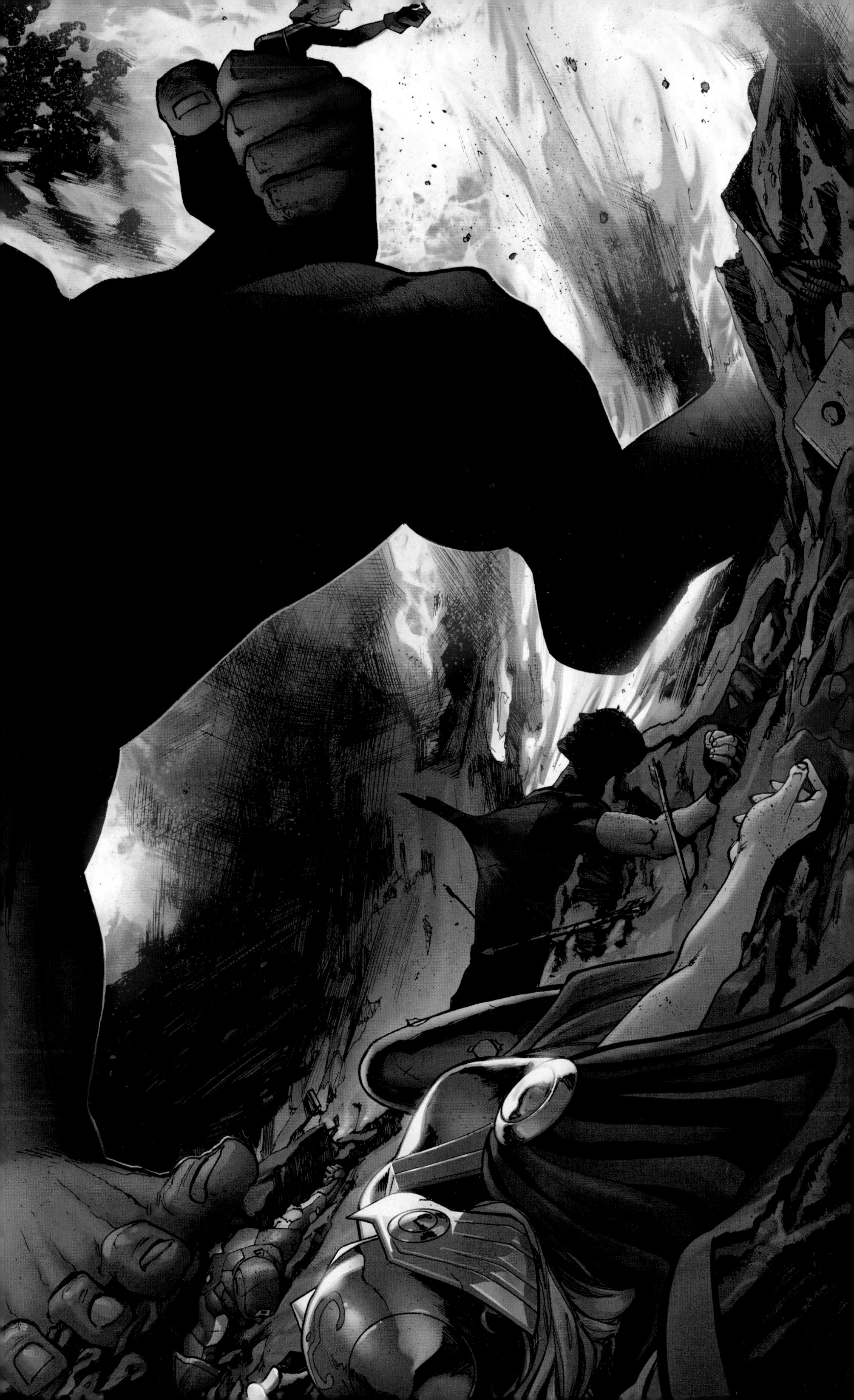

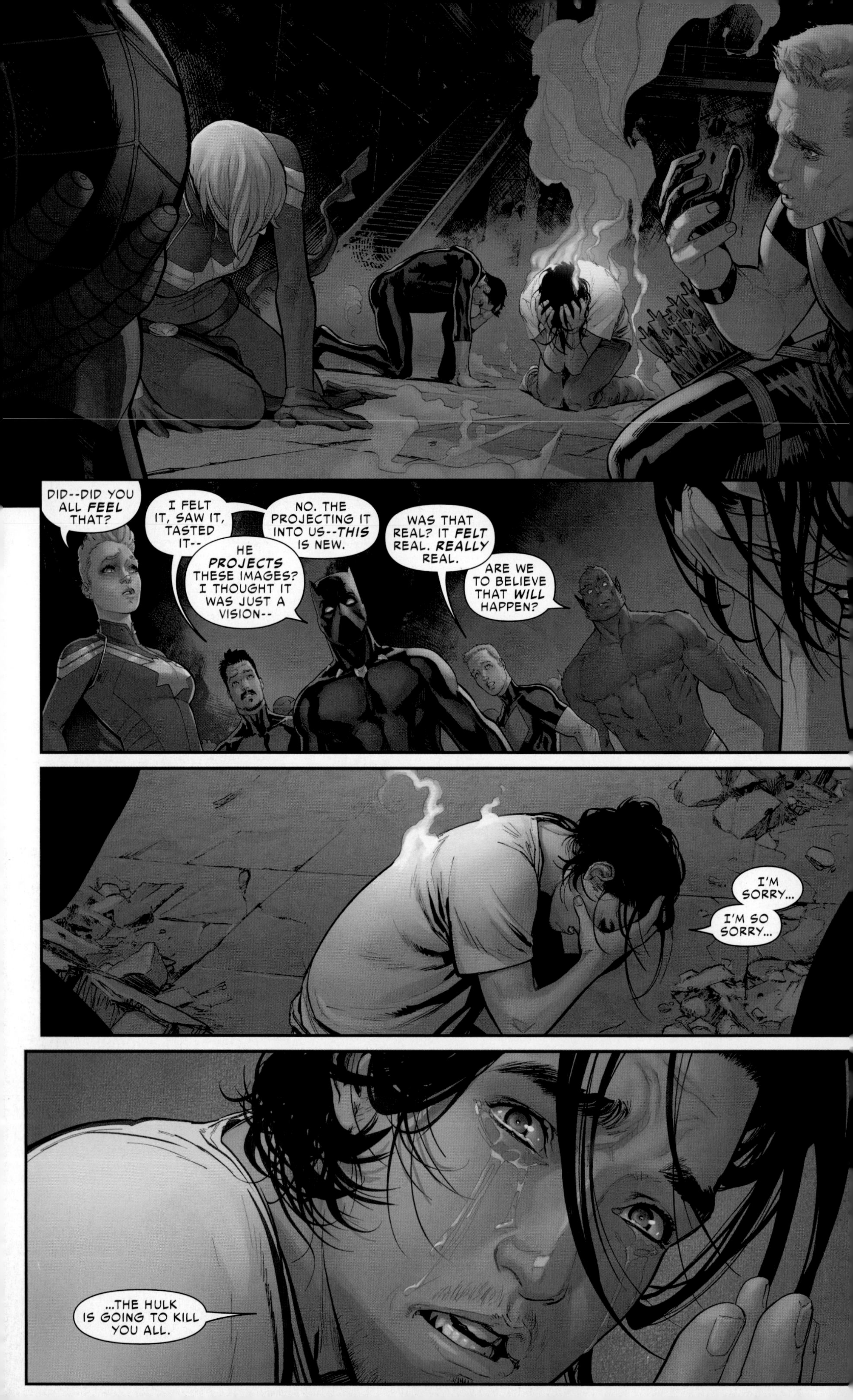
DID--DID YOU ALL FEEL THAT?
I FELT IT, SAW IT, TASTED IT--
HE PROJECTS THESE IMAGES? I THOUGHT IT WAS JUST A VISION--
NO. THE PROJECTING IT INTO US--THIS IS NEW.
WAS THAT REAL? IT FELT REAL. REALLY REAL.
ARE WE TO BELIEVE THAT WILL HAPPEN?
I'M SORRY...
I'M SO SORRY...
...THE HULK IS GOING TO KILL YOU ALL.

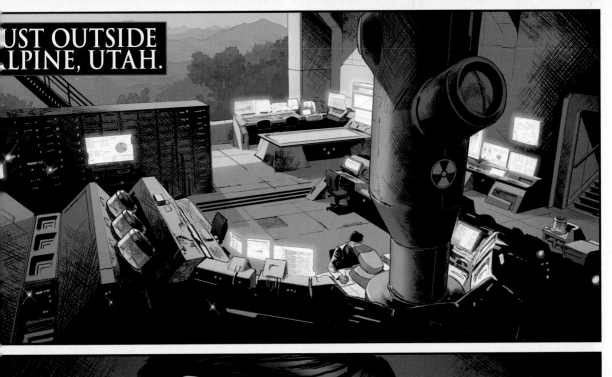

DOCTOR BANNER?

OH, COLONEL DANVERS.

WHAT A PLEASANT SURPRISE.

WHAT CAN I DO FOR YOU?

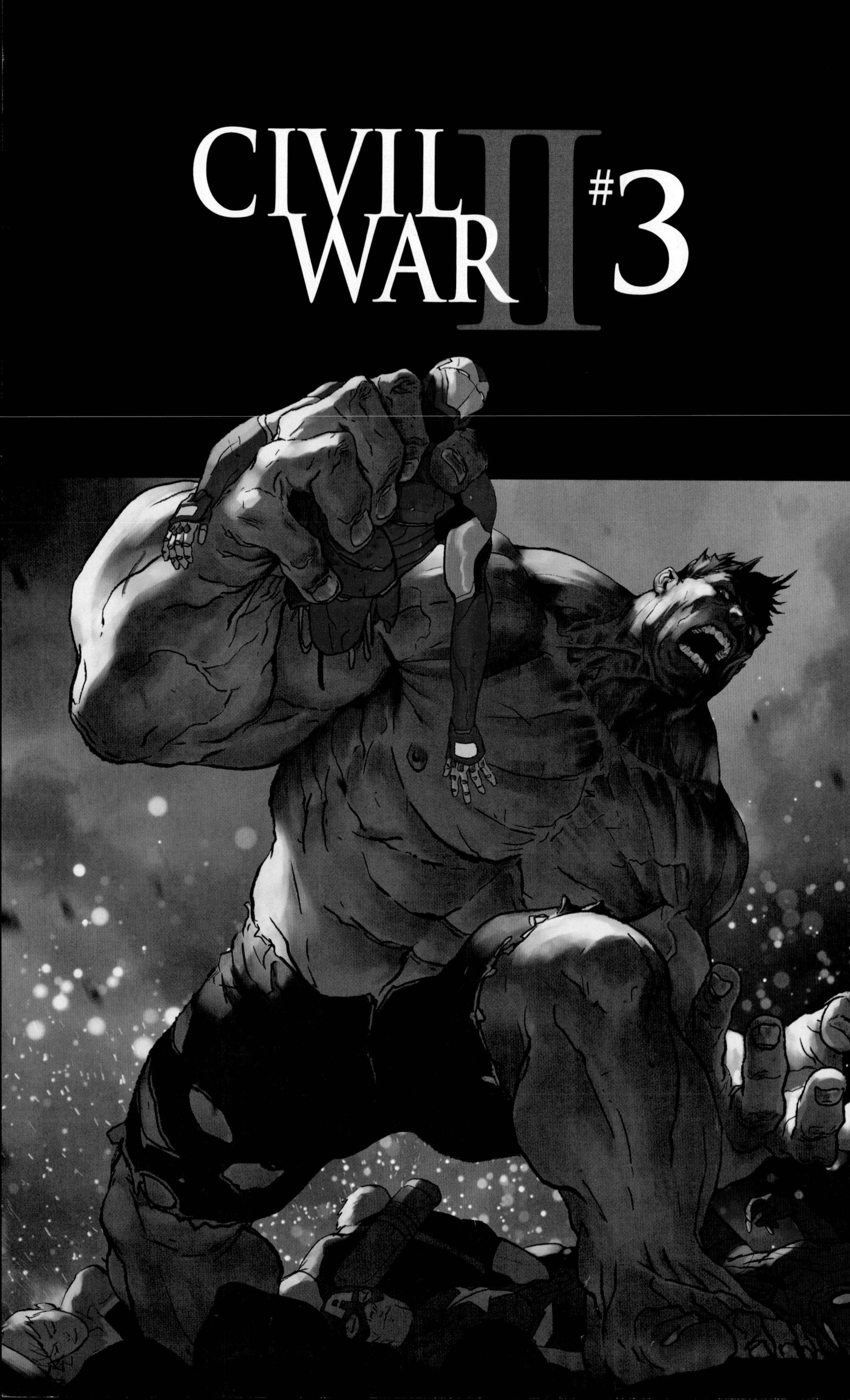
CIVIL WAR II
#3

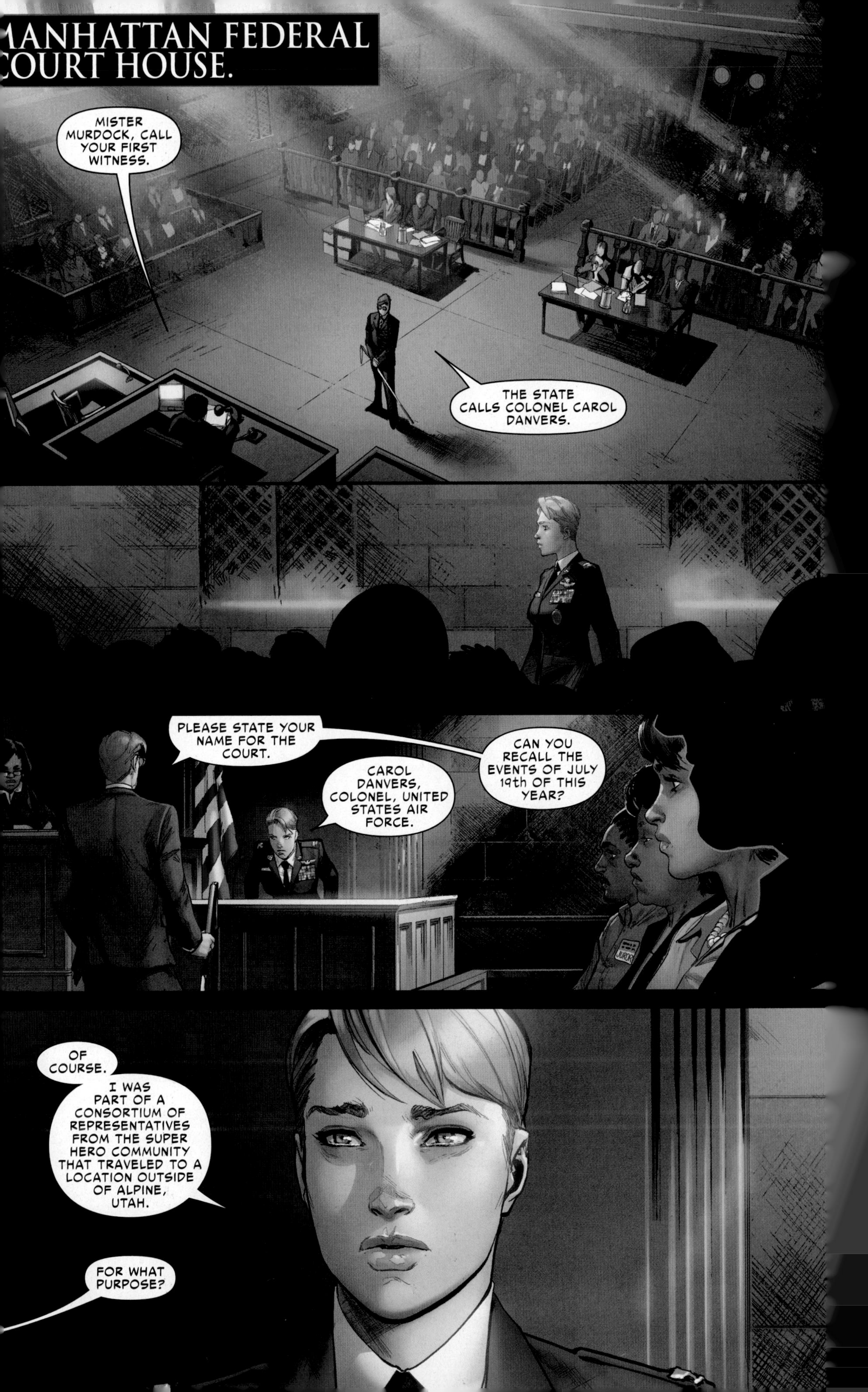
MANHATTAN FEDERAL COURT HOUSE.
MISTER MURDOCK, CALL YOUR FIRST WITNESS.
THE STATE CALLS COLONEL CAROL DANVERS.
PLEASE STATE YOUR NAME FOR THE COURT.
CAROL DANVERS, COLONEL, UNITED STATES AIR FORCE.
CAN YOU RECALL THE EVENTS OF JULY 19th OF THIS YEAR?
OF COURSE.
I WAS PART OF A CONSORTIUM OF REPRESENTATIVES FROM THE SUPER HERO COMMUNITY THAT TRAVELED TO A LOCATION OUTSIDE OF ALPINE, UTAH.
FOR WHAT PURPOSE?

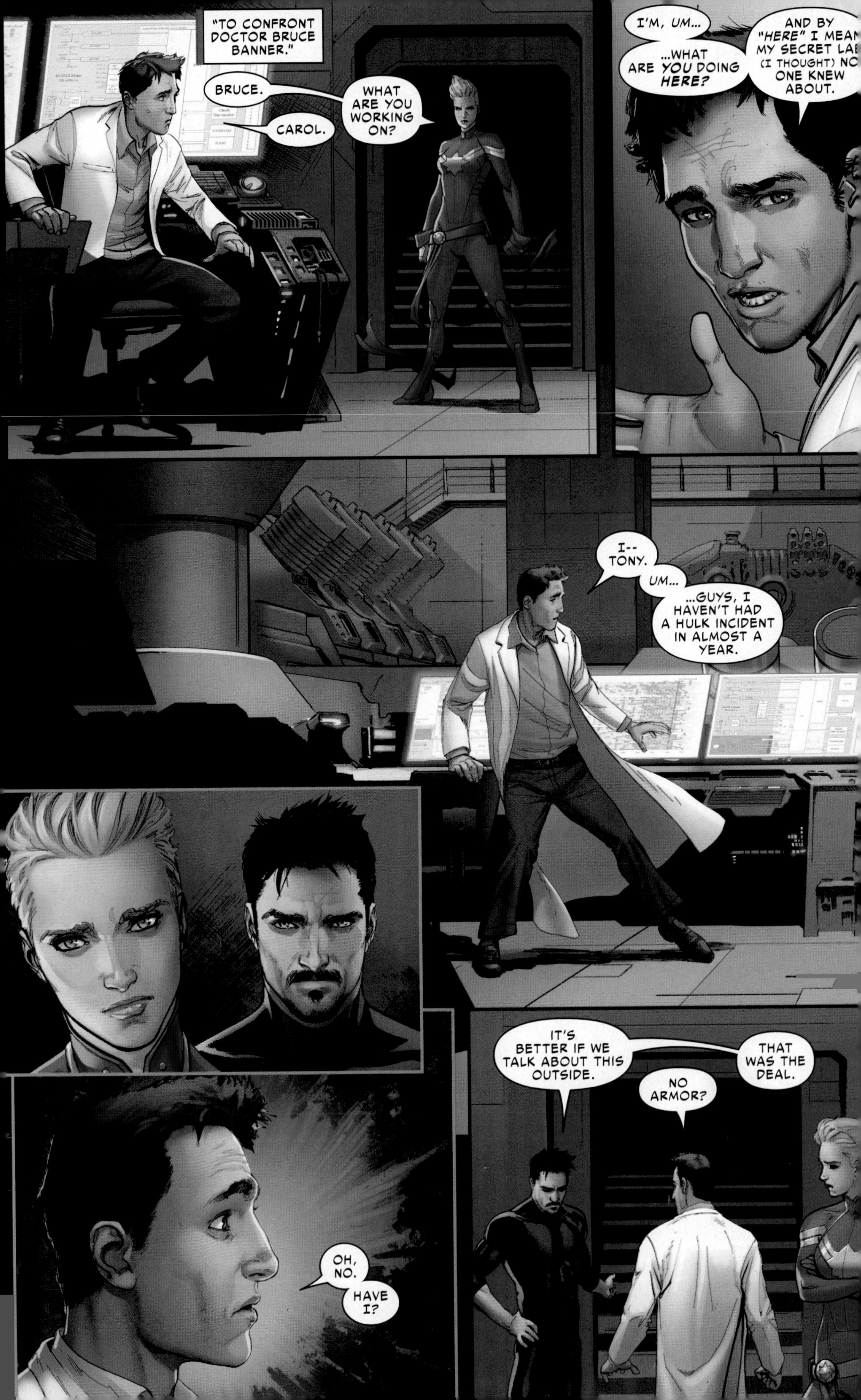
"TO CONFRONT DOCTOR BRUCE BANNER."
BRUCE.
CAROL.
WHAT ARE YOU WORKING ON?
I'M, UM...
...WHAT ARE YOU DOING HERE?
AND BY "HERE" I MEAN MY SECRET LAB (I THOUGHT) NO ONE KNEW ABOUT.
I-- TONY.
UM...
...GUYS, I HAVEN'T HAD A HULK INCIDENT IN ALMOST A YEAR.
OH, NO.
HAVE I?
IT'S BETTER IF WE TALK ABOUT THIS OUTSIDE.
NO ARMOR?
THAT WAS THE DEAL.

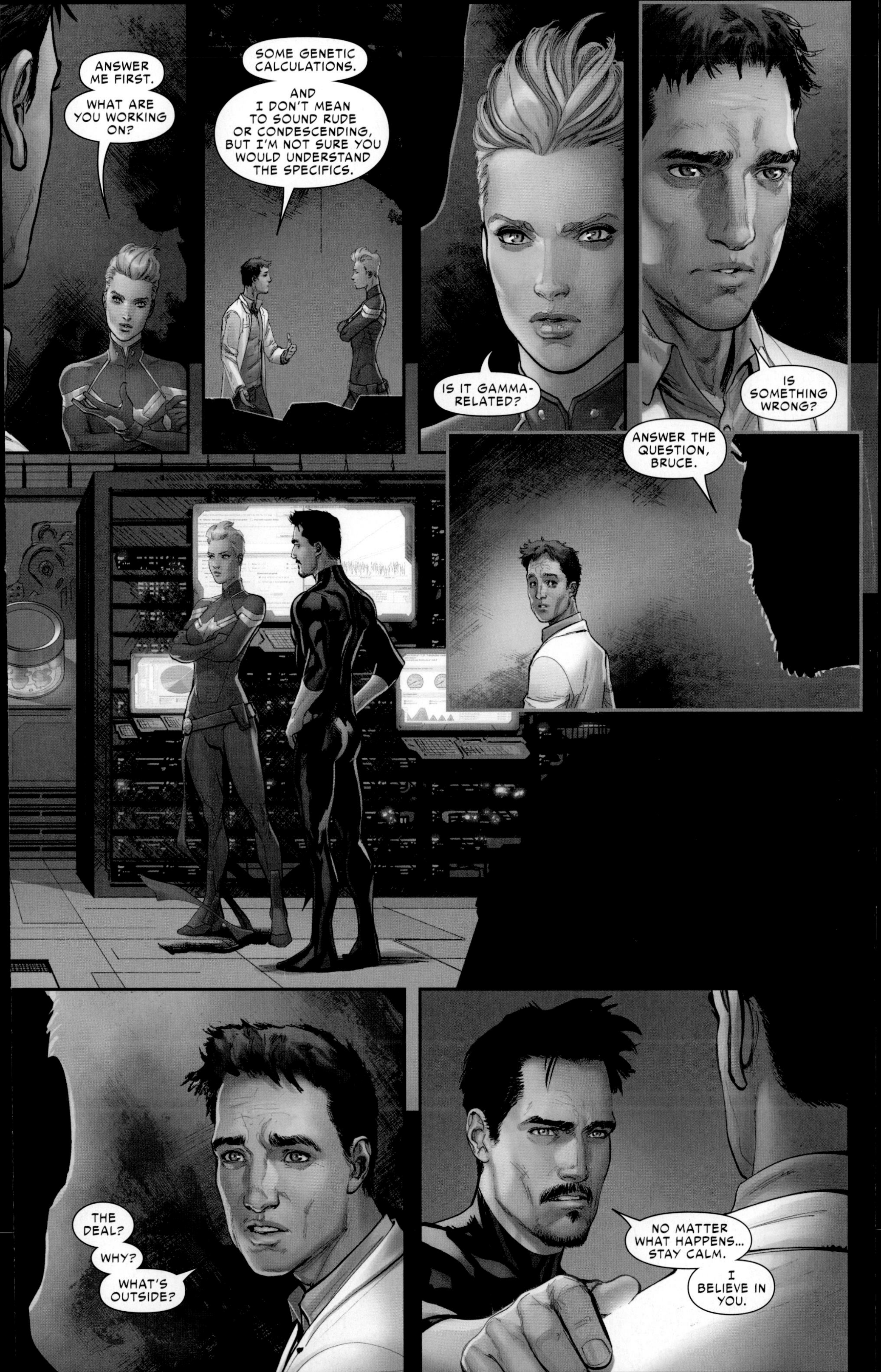
ANSWER ME FIRST.
WHAT ARE YOU WORKING ON?
SOME GENETIC CALCULATIONS.
AND I DON'T MEAN TO SOUND RUDE OR CONDESCENDING, BUT I'M NOT SURE YOU WOULD UNDERSTAND THE SPECIFICS.
IS IT GAMMA-RELATED?
IS SOMETHING WRONG?
ANSWER THE QUESTION, BRUCE.
THE DEAL?
WHY?
WHAT'S OUTSIDE?
NO MATTER WHAT HAPPENS... STAY CALM.
I BELIEVE IN YOU.

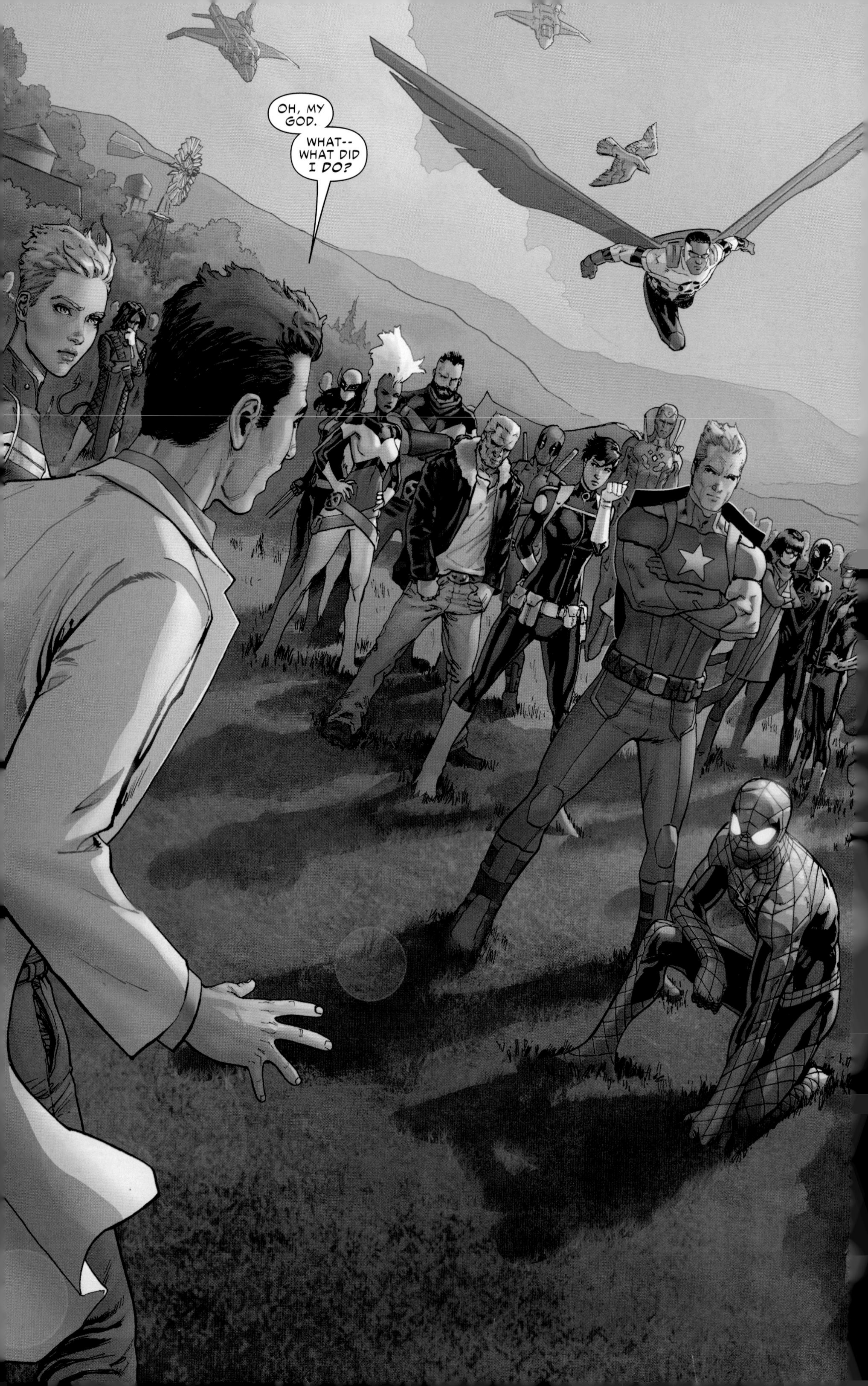
OH, MY GOD.
WHAT-- WHAT DID I DO?

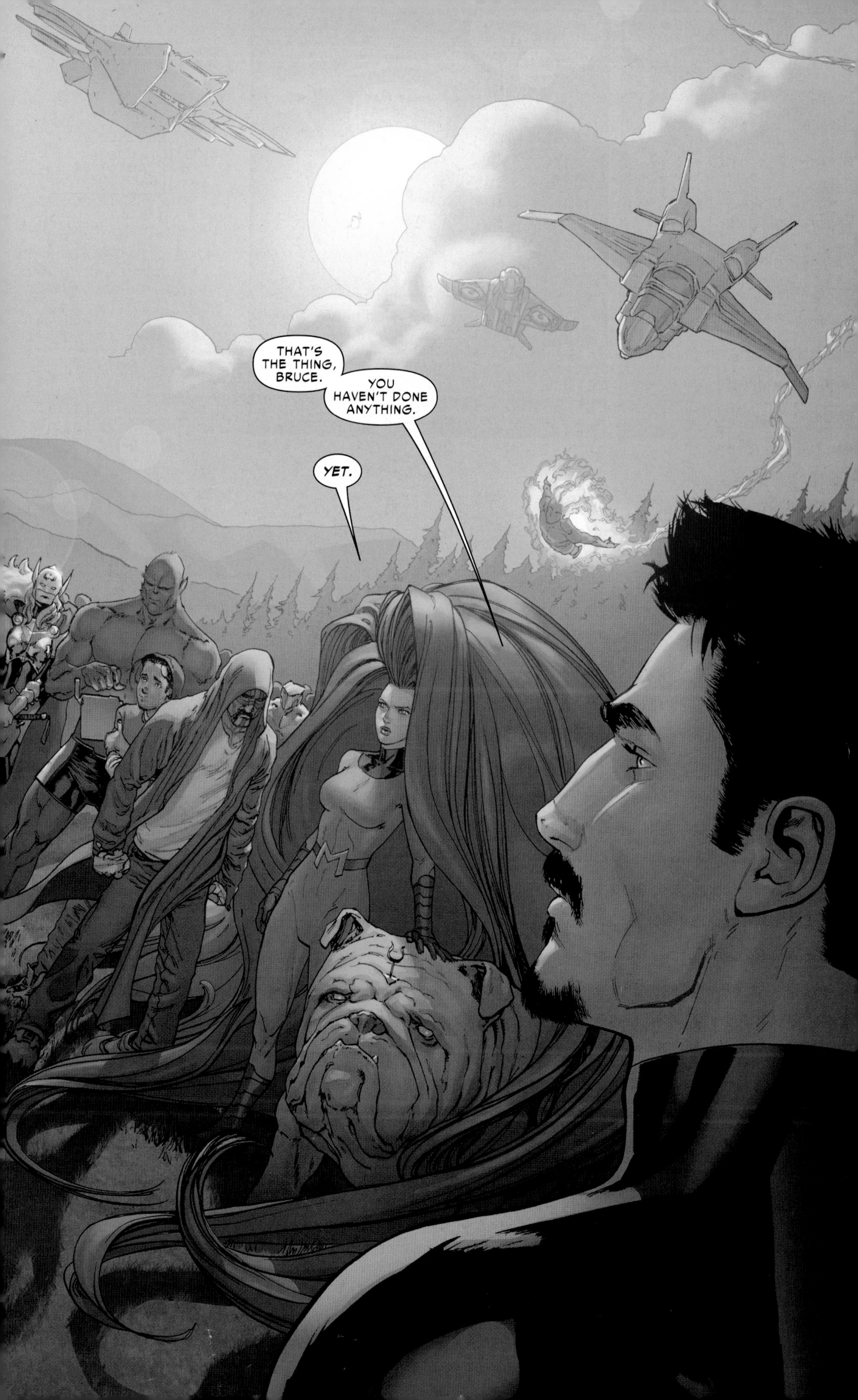
THAT'S THE THING, BRUCE.
YOU HAVEN'T DONE ANYTHING.
YET.

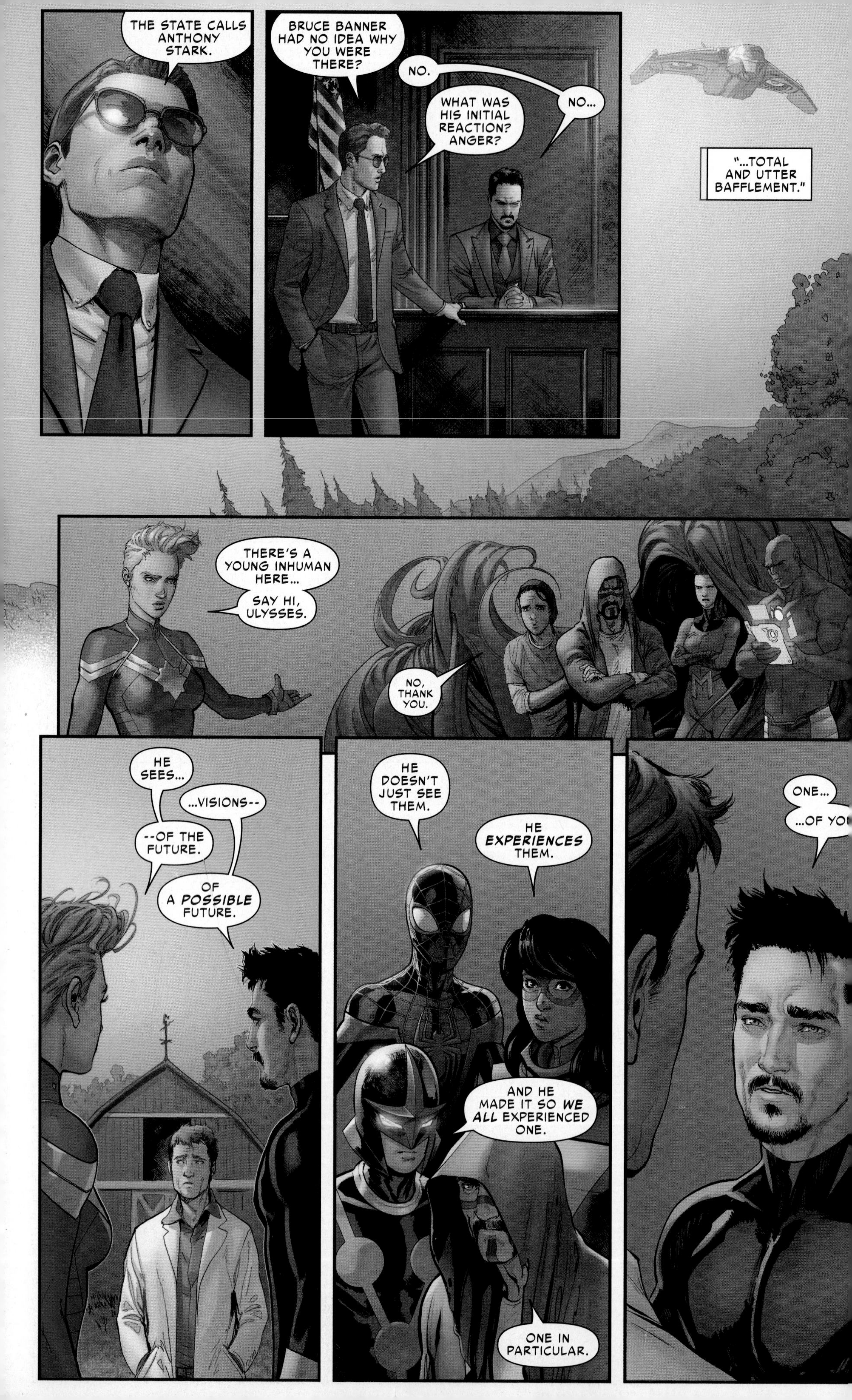
THE STATE CALLS ANTHONY STARK.
BRUCE BANNER HAD NO IDEA WHY YOU WERE THERE?
NO.
WHAT WAS HIS INITIAL REACTION? ANGER?
NO...
"...TOTAL AND UTTER BAFFLEMENT."
THERE'S A YOUNG INHUMAN HERE...
SAY HI, ULYSSES.
NO, THANK YOU.
HE SEES...
...VISIONS--
--OF THE FUTURE.
OF A POSSIBLE FUTURE.
HE DOESN'T JUST SEE THEM.
HE EXPERIENCES THEM.
AND HE MADE IT SO WE ALL EXPERIENCED ONE.
ONE IN PARTICULAR.
ONE...
...OF YO

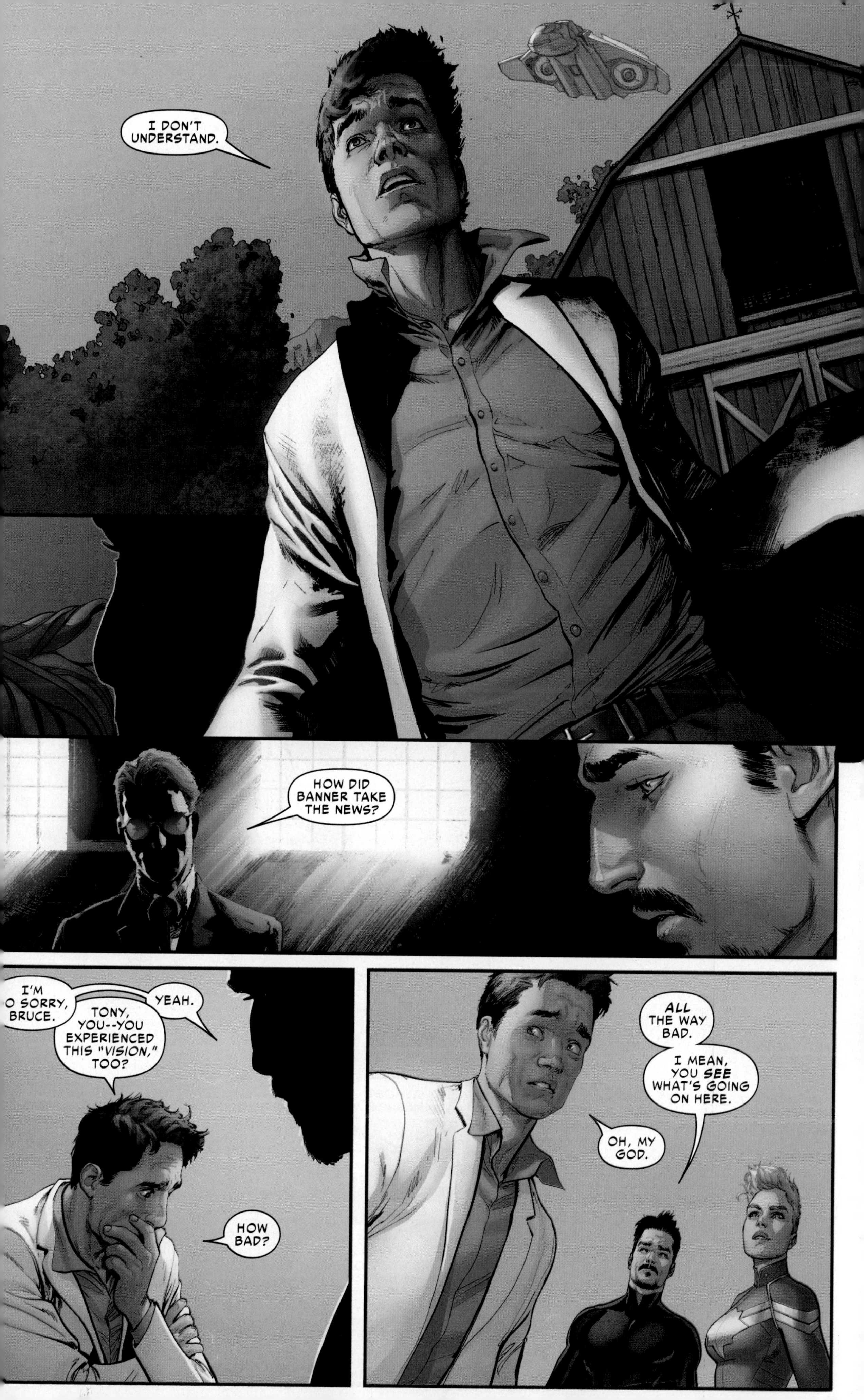
I DON'T UNDERSTAND.
HOW DID BANNER TAKE THE NEWS?
I'M O SORRY, BRUCE.
TONY, YOU--YOU EXPERIENCED THIS "VISION," TOO?
YEAH.
HOW BAD?
ALL THE WAY BAD.
I MEAN, YOU SEE WHAT'S GOING ON HERE.
OH, MY GOD.

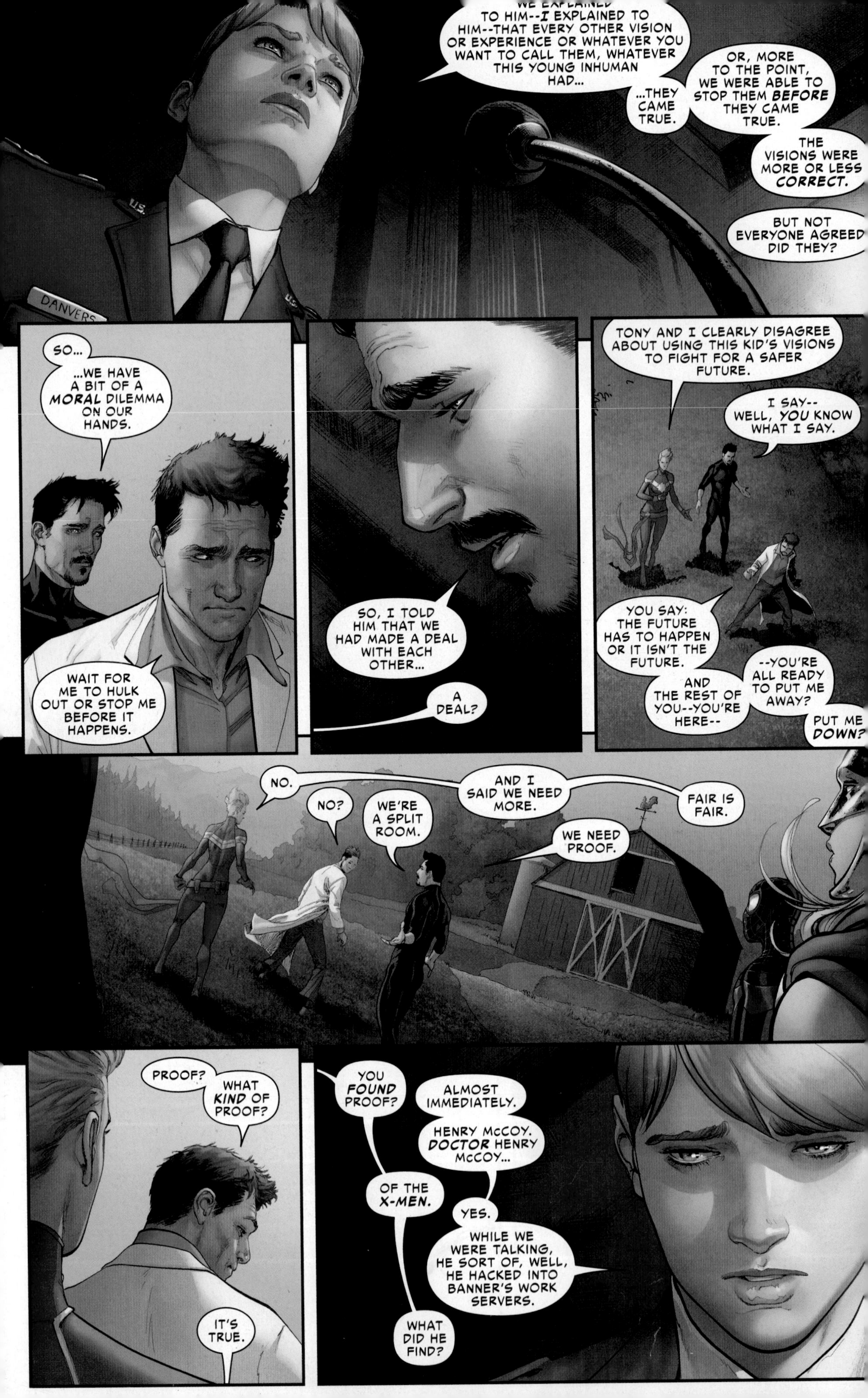
WE EXPLAINED TO HIM--I EXPLAINED TO HIM--THAT EVERY OTHER VISION OR EXPERIENCE OR WHATEVER YOU WANT TO CALL THEM, WHATEVER THIS YOUNG INHUMAN HAD...
...THEY CAME TRUE.
OR, MORE TO THE POINT, WE WERE ABLE TO STOP THEM BEFORE THEY CAME TRUE.
THE VISIONS WERE MORE OR LESS CORRECT.
BUT NOT EVERYONE AGREED DID THEY?
DANVERS
SO...
...WE HAVE A BIT OF A MORAL DILEMMA ON OUR HANDS.
WAIT FOR ME TO HULK OUT OR STOP ME BEFORE IT HAPPENS.
SO, I TOLD HIM THAT WE HAD MADE A DEAL WITH EACH OTHER...
A DEAL?
TONY AND I CLEARLY DISAGREE ABOUT USING THIS KID'S VISIONS TO FIGHT FOR A SAFER FUTURE.
I SAY-- WELL, YOU KNOW WHAT I SAY.
YOU SAY: THE FUTURE HAS TO HAPPEN OR IT ISN'T THE FUTURE.
AND THE REST OF YOU--YOU'RE HERE--
--YOU'RE ALL READY TO PUT ME AWAY?
PUT ME DOWN?
NO.
NO?
WE'RE A SPLIT ROOM.
AND I SAID WE NEED MORE.
FAIR IS FAIR.
WE NEED PROOF.
PROOF?
WHAT KIND OF PROOF?
IT'S TRUE.
YOU FOUND PROOF?
ALMOST IMMEDIATELY.
HENRY McCOY. DOCTOR HENRY McCOY...
OF THE X-MEN.
YES.
WHILE WE WERE TALKING, HE SORT OF, WELL, HE HACKED INTO BANNER'S WORK SERVERS.
WHAT DID HE FIND?

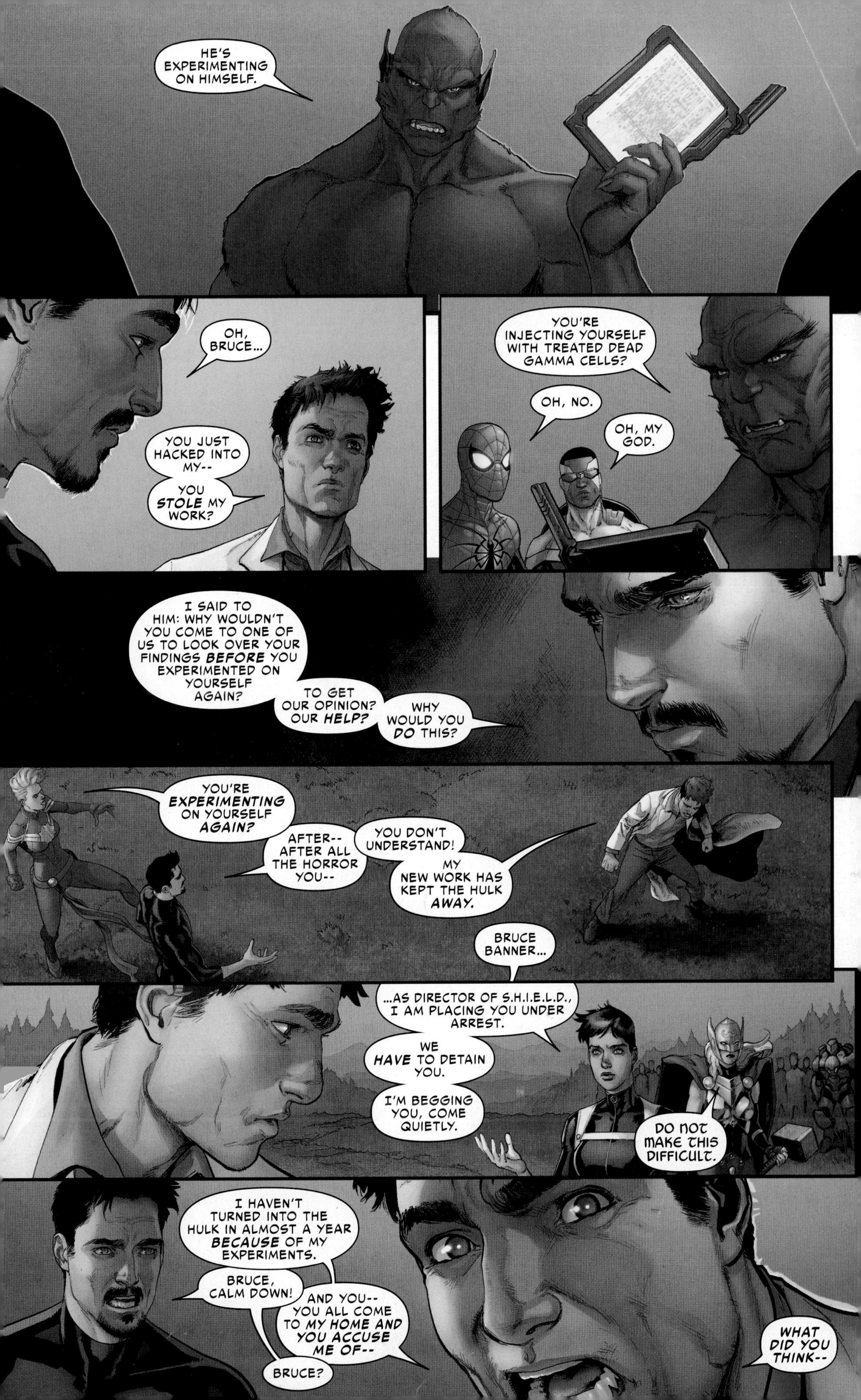
HE'S EXPERIMENTING ON HIMSELF.
OH, BRUCE...
YOU JUST HACKED INTO MY--
YOU STOLE MY WORK?
YOU'RE INJECTING YOURSELF WITH TREATED DEAD GAMMA CELLS?
OH, NO.
OH, MY GOD.
I SAID TO HIM: WHY WOULDN'T YOU COME TO ONE OF US TO LOOK OVER YOUR FINDINGS BEFORE YOU EXPERIMENTED ON YOURSELF AGAIN?
TO GET OUR OPINION? OUR HELP?
WHY WOULD YOU DO THIS?
YOU'RE EXPERIMENTING ON YOURSELF AGAIN?
AFTER-- AFTER ALL THE HORROR YOU--
YOU DON'T UNDERSTAND!
MY NEW WORK HAS KEPT THE HULK AWAY.
BRUCE BANNER...
...AS DIRECTOR OF S.H.I.E.L.D., I AM PLACING YOU UNDER ARREST.
WE HAVE TO DETAIN YOU.
I'M BEGGING YOU, COME QUIETLY.
DO NOT MAKE THIS DIFFICULT.
I HAVEN'T TURNED INTO THE HULK IN ALMOST A YEAR BECAUSE OF MY EXPERIMENTS.
BRUCE, CALM DOWN!
AND YOU-- YOU ALL COME TO MY HOME AND YOU ACCUSE ME OF--
BRUCE?
WHAT DID YOU THINK--

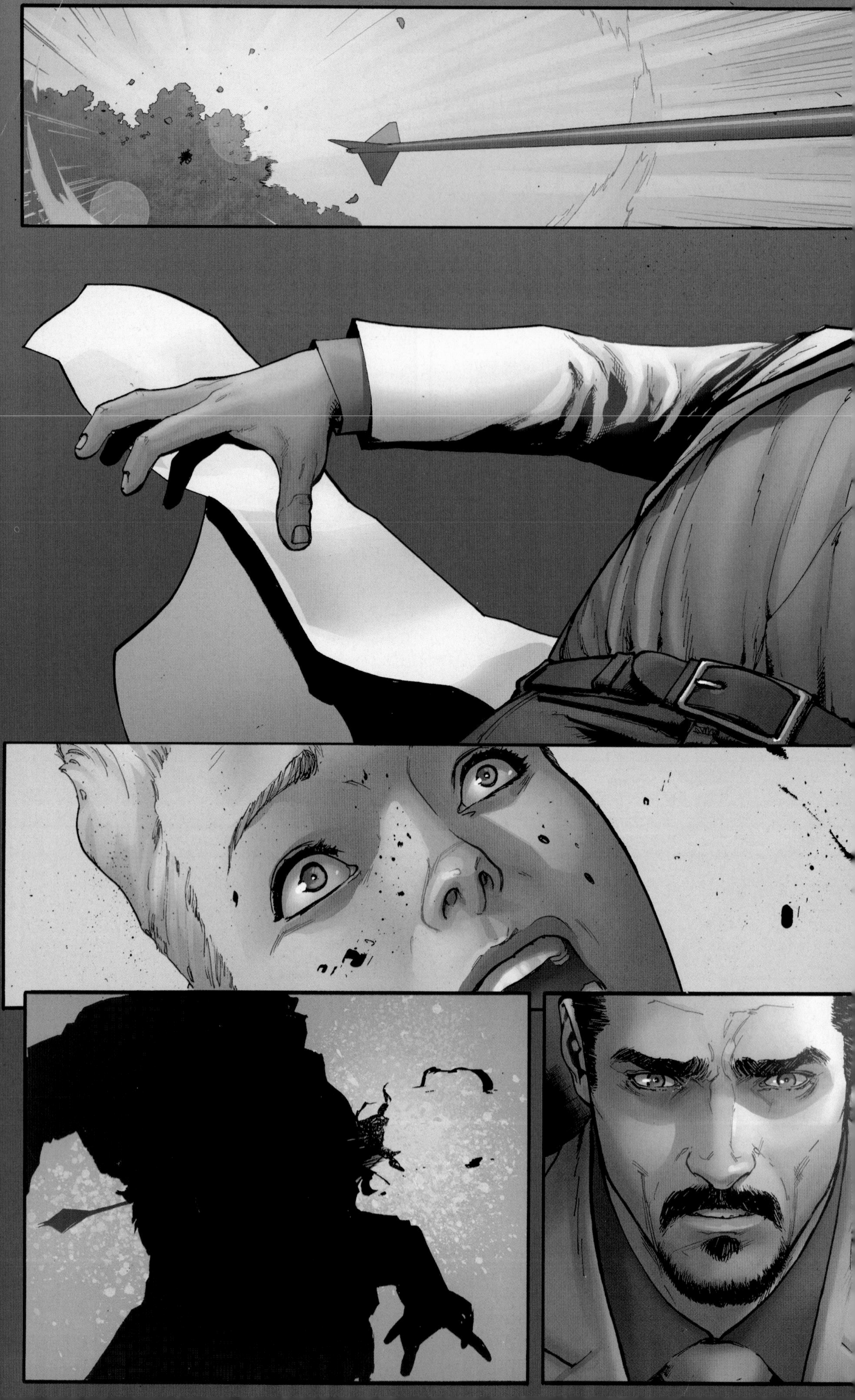

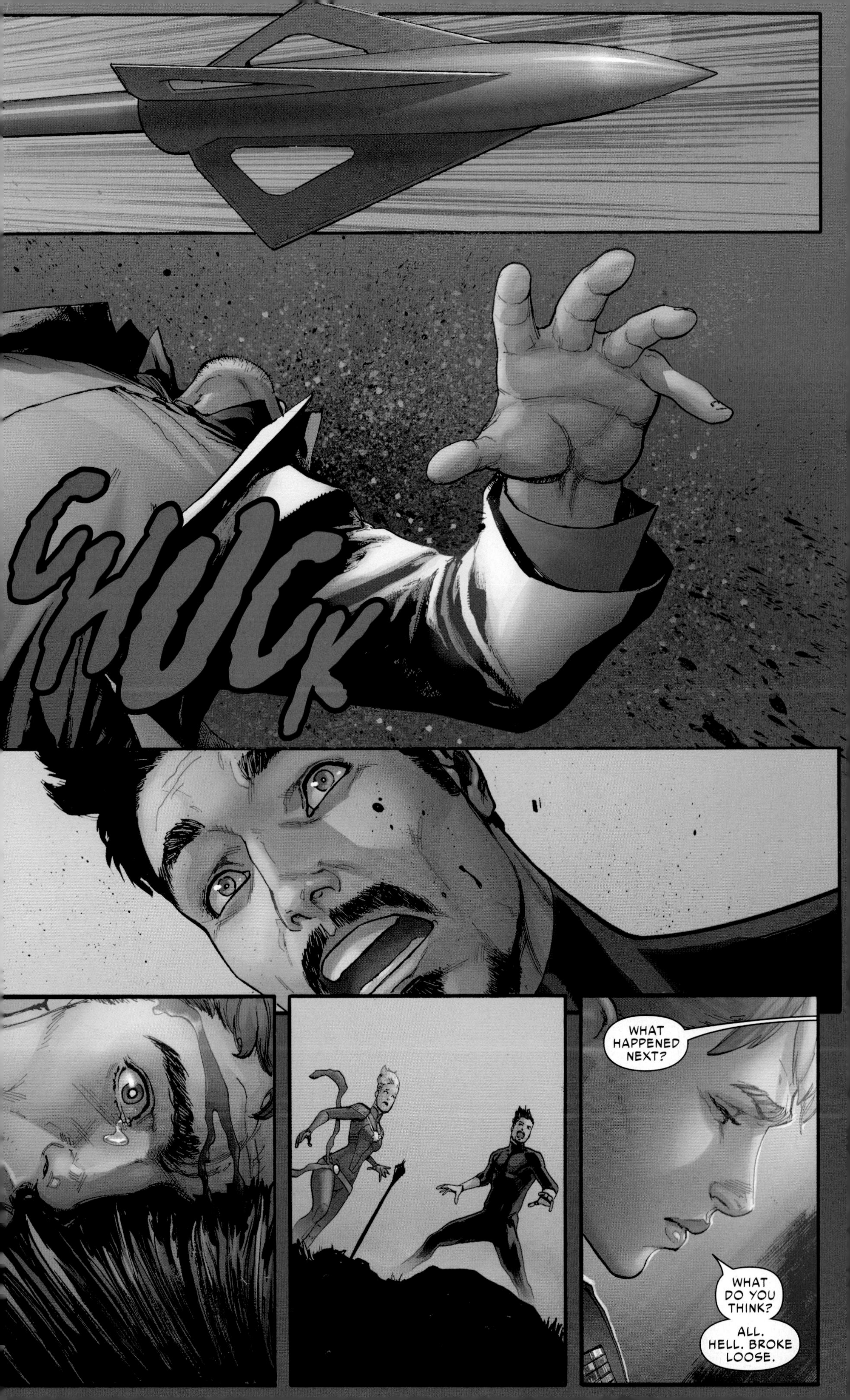
CHUCK
WHAT HAPPENED NEXT?
WHAT DO YOU THINK?
ALL. HELL. BROKE LOOSE.

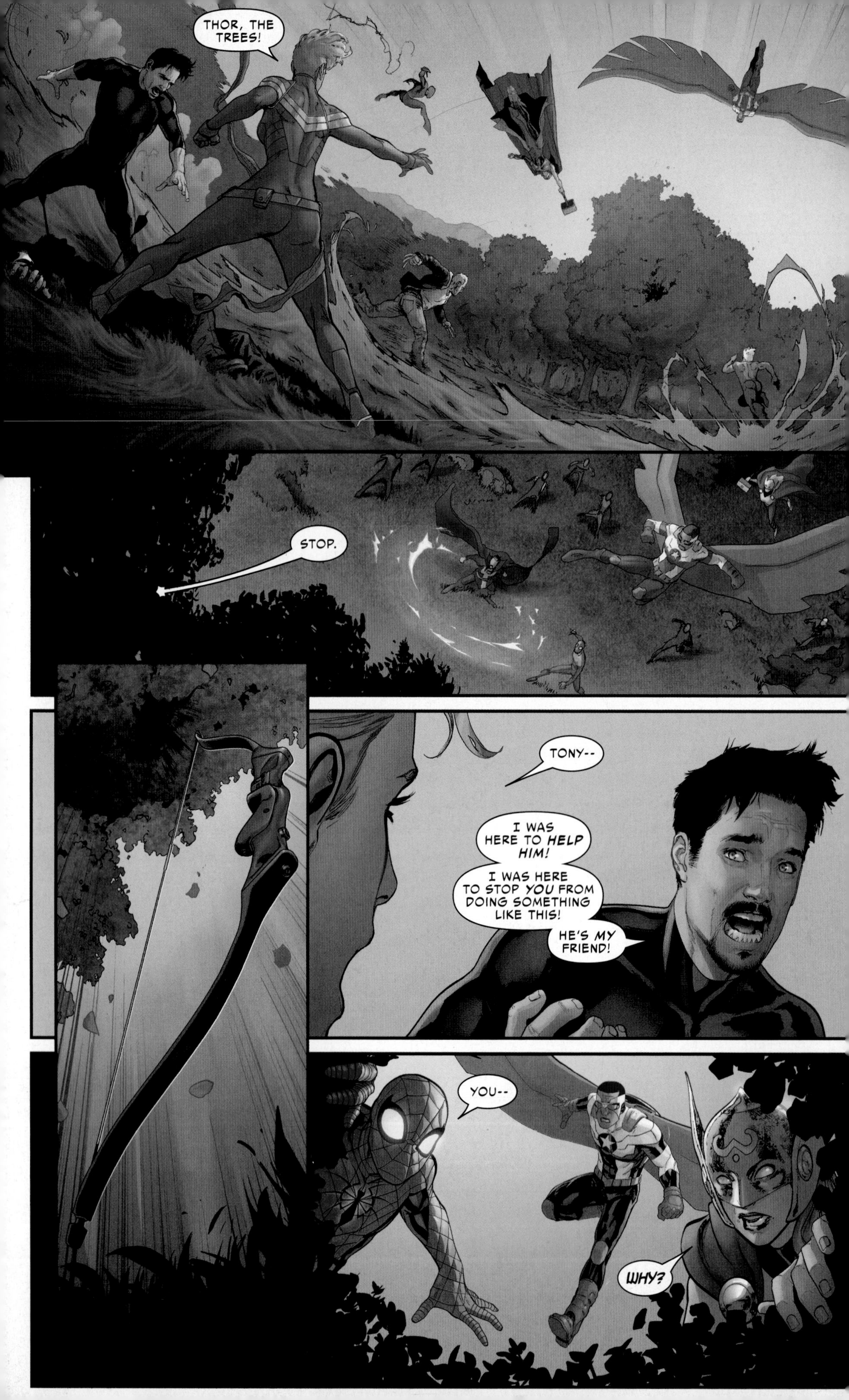
THOR, THE TREES!
STOP.
TONY--
I WAS HERE TO HELP HIM!
I WAS HERE TO STOP YOU FROM DOING SOMETHING LIKE THIS!
HE'S MY FRIEND!
YOU--
WHY?

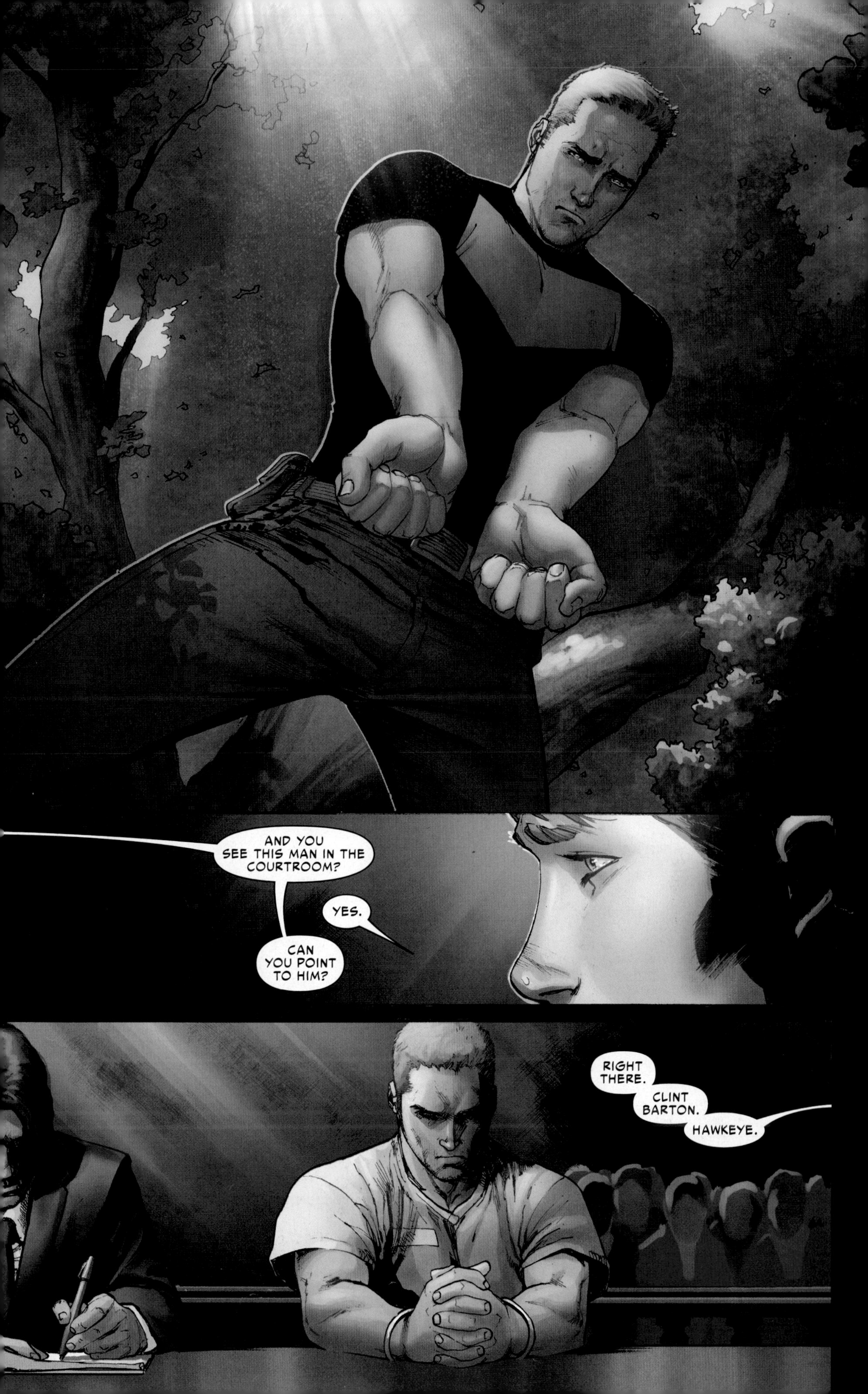
AND YOU SEE THIS MAN IN THE COURTROOM?
YES.
CAN YOU POINT TO HIM?
RIGHT THERE.
CLINT BARTON.
HAWKEYE.

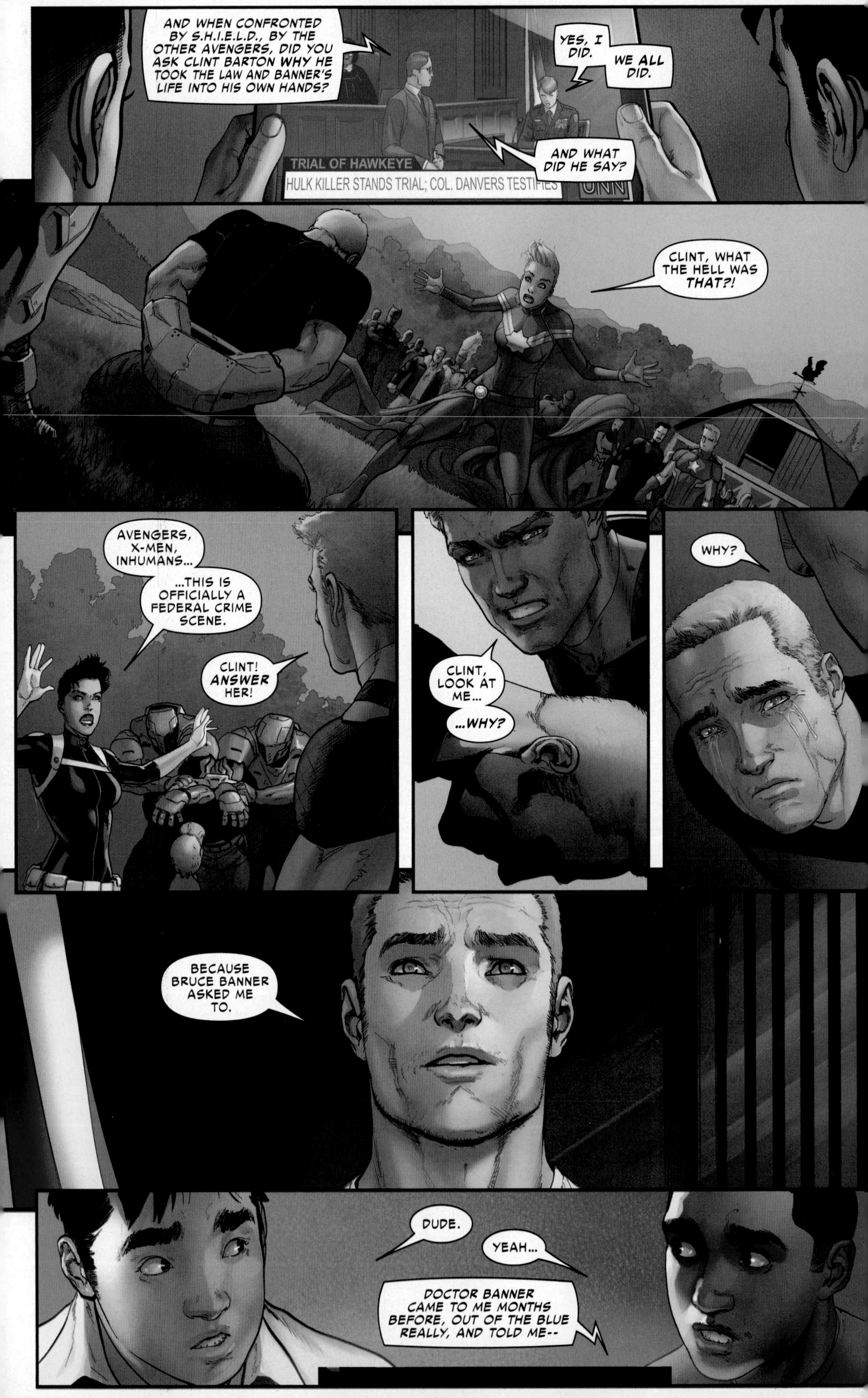
AND WHEN CONFRONTED BY S.H.I.E.L.D., BY THE OTHER AVENGERS, DID YOU ASK CLINT BARTON WHY HE TOOK THE LAW AND BANNER'S LIFE INTO HIS OWN HANDS?
YES, I DID.
WE ALL DID.
AND WHAT DID HE SAY?
TRIAL OF HAWKEYE
HULK KILLER STANDS TRIAL; COL. DANVERS TESTIFIES
CLINT, WHAT THE HELL WAS THAT?!
AVENGERS, X-MEN, INHUMANS...
...THIS IS OFFICIALLY A FEDERAL CRIME SCENE.
CLINT! ANSWER HER!
CLINT, LOOK AT ME...
...WHY?
WHY?
BECAUSE BRUCE BANNER ASKED ME TO.
DUDE.
YEAH...
DOCTOR BANNER CAME TO ME MONTHS BEFORE, OUT OF THE BLUE REALLY, AND TOLD ME--

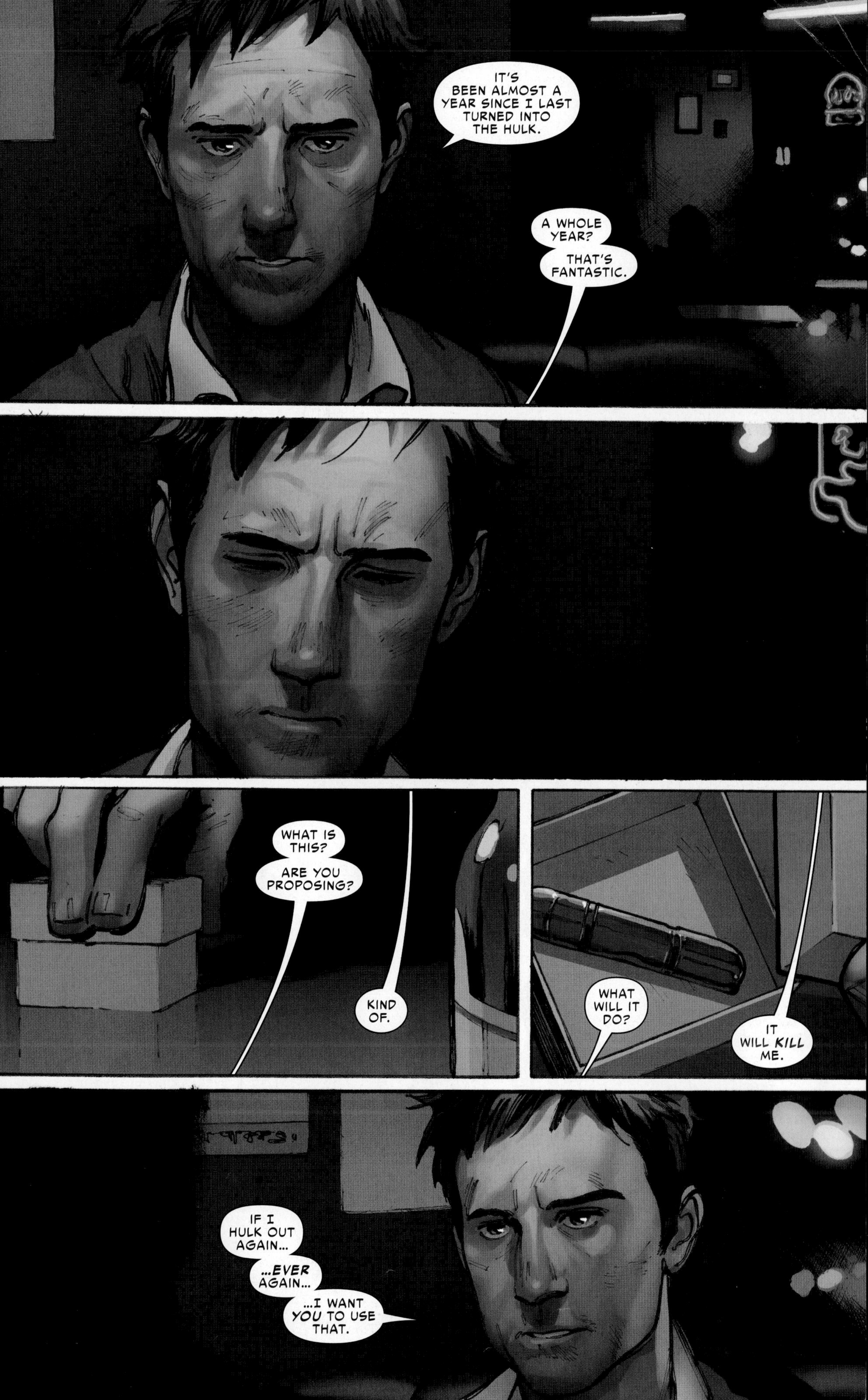
IT'S BEEN ALMOST A YEAR SINCE I LAST TURNED INTO THE HULK.
A WHOLE YEAR?
THAT'S FANTASTIC.
WHAT IS THIS?
ARE YOU PROPOSING?
KIND OF.
WHAT WILL IT DO?
IT WILL KILL ME.
IF I HULK OUT AGAIN...
...EVER AGAIN...
...I WANT YOU TO USE THAT.

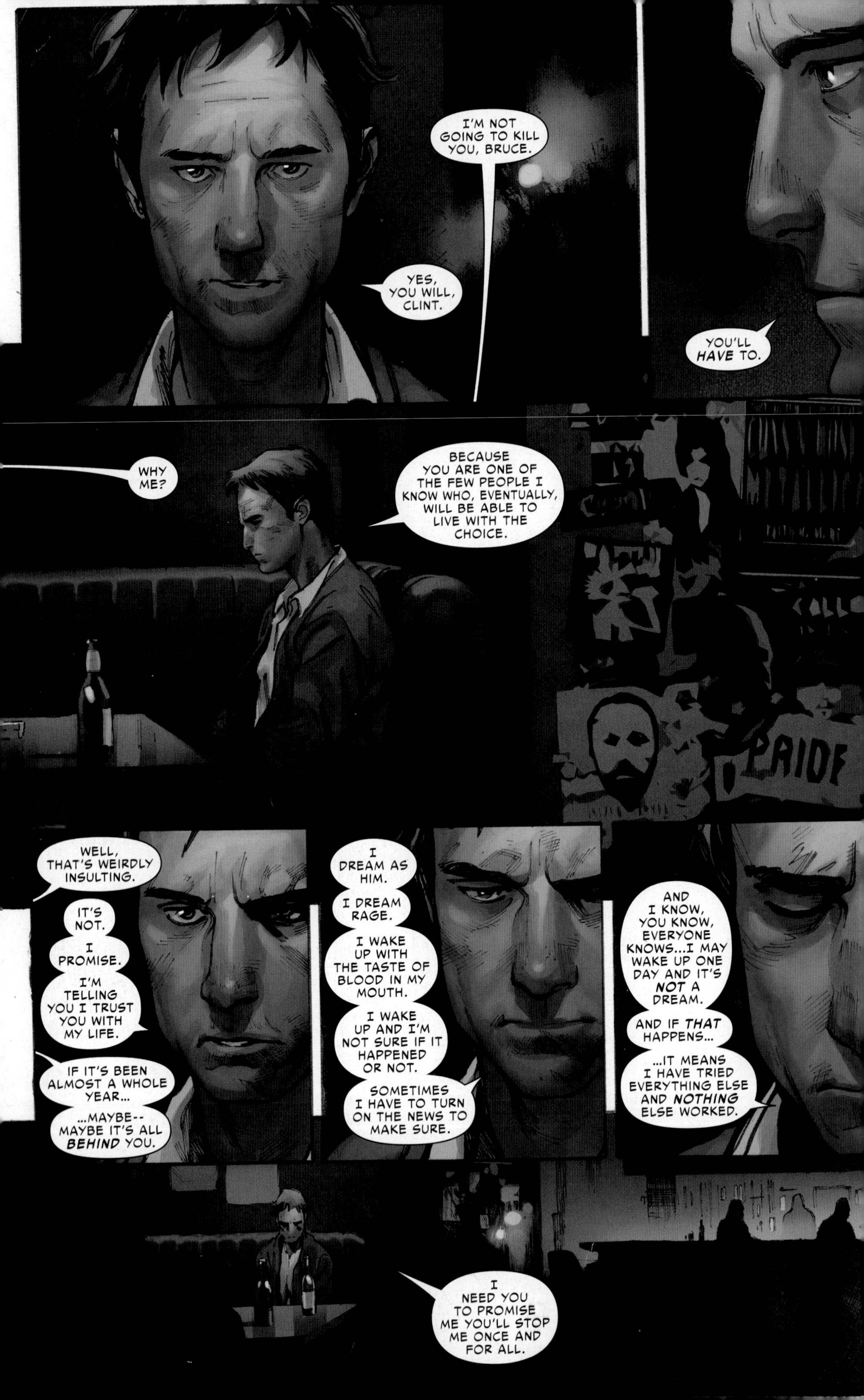
I'M NOT GOING TO KILL YOU, BRUCE.
YES, YOU WILL, CLINT.
YOU'LL HAVE TO.
WHY ME?
BECAUSE YOU ARE ONE OF THE FEW PEOPLE I KNOW WHO, EVENTUALLY, WILL BE ABLE TO LIVE WITH THE CHOICE.
PRIDE
WELL, THAT'S WEIRDLY INSULTING.
IT'S NOT.
I PROMISE.
I'M TELLING YOU I TRUST YOU WITH MY LIFE.
IF IT'S BEEN ALMOST A WHOLE YEAR...
...MAYBE-- MAYBE IT'S ALL BEHIND YOU.
I DREAM AS HIM.
I DREAM RAGE.
I WAKE UP WITH THE TASTE OF BLOOD IN MY MOUTH.
I WAKE UP AND I'M NOT SURE IF IT HAPPENED OR NOT.
SOMETIMES I HAVE TO TURN ON THE NEWS TO MAKE SURE.
AND I KNOW, YOU KNOW, EVERYONE KNOWS...I MAY WAKE UP ONE DAY AND IT'S NOT A DREAM.
AND IF THAT HAPPENS...
...IT MEANS I HAVE TRIED EVERYTHING ELSE AND NOTHING ELSE WORKED.
I NEED YOU TO PROMISE ME YOU'LL STOP ME ONCE AND FOR ALL.

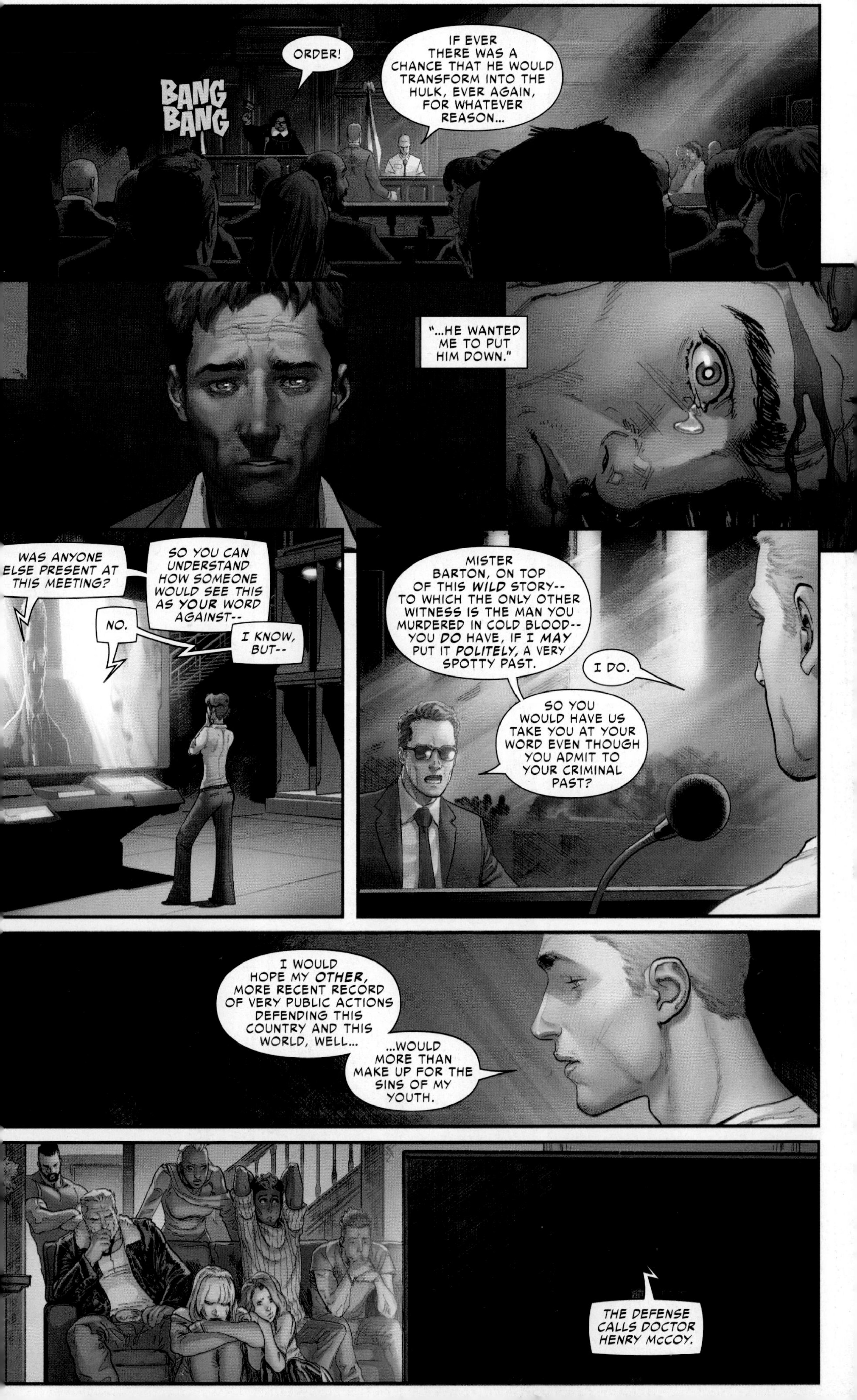
BANG BANG
ORDER!
IF EVER THERE WAS A CHANCE THAT HE WOULD TRANSFORM INTO THE HULK, EVER AGAIN, FOR WHATEVER REASON...
"...HE WANTED ME TO PUT HIM DOWN."
WAS ANYONE ELSE PRESENT AT THIS MEETING?
NO.
SO YOU CAN UNDERSTAND HOW SOMEONE WOULD SEE THIS AS YOUR WORD AGAINST--
I KNOW, BUT--
MISTER BARTON, ON TOP OF THIS WILD STORY-- TO WHICH THE ONLY OTHER WITNESS IS THE MAN YOU MURDERED IN COLD BLOOD-- YOU DO HAVE, IF I MAY PUT IT POLITELY, A VERY SPOTTY PAST.
I DO.
SO YOU WOULD HAVE US TAKE YOU AT YOUR WORD EVEN THOUGH YOU ADMIT TO YOUR CRIMINAL PAST?
I WOULD HOPE MY OTHER, MORE RECENT RECORD OF VERY PUBLIC ACTIONS DEFENDING THIS COUNTRY AND THIS WORLD, WELL...
...WOULD MORE THAN MAKE UP FOR THE SINS OF MY YOUTH.
THE DEFENSE CALLS DOCTOR HENRY McCOY.

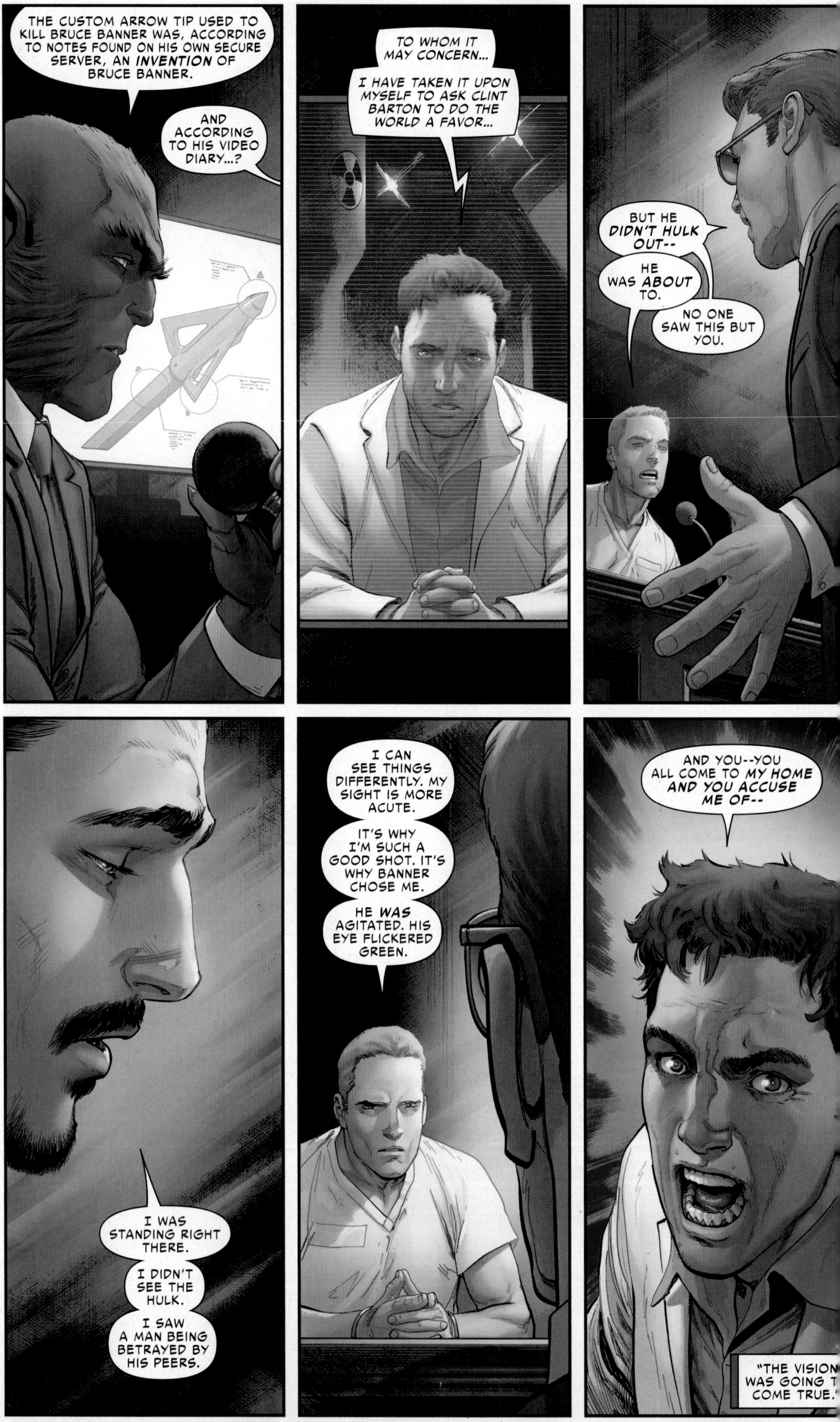
THE CUSTOM ARROW TIP USED TO KILL BRUCE BANNER WAS, ACCORDING TO NOTES FOUND ON HIS OWN SECURE SERVER, AN INVENTION OF BRUCE BANNER.
AND ACCORDING TO HIS VIDEO DIARY...?
TO WHOM IT MAY CONCERN...
I HAVE TAKEN IT UPON MYSELF TO ASK CLINT BARTON TO DO THE WORLD A FAVOR...
BUT HE DIDN'T HULK OUT--
HE WAS ABOUT TO.
NO ONE SAW THIS BUT YOU.
I WAS STANDING RIGHT THERE.
I DIDN'T SEE THE HULK.
I SAW A MAN BEING BETRAYED BY HIS PEERS.
I CAN SEE THINGS DIFFERENTLY. MY SIGHT IS MORE ACUTE.
IT'S WHY I'M SUCH A GOOD SHOT. IT'S WHY BANNER CHOSE ME.
HE WAS AGITATED. HIS EYE FLICKERED GREEN.
AND YOU--YOU ALL COME TO MY HOME AND YOU ACCUSE ME OF--
"THE VISION WAS GOING T COME TRUE.

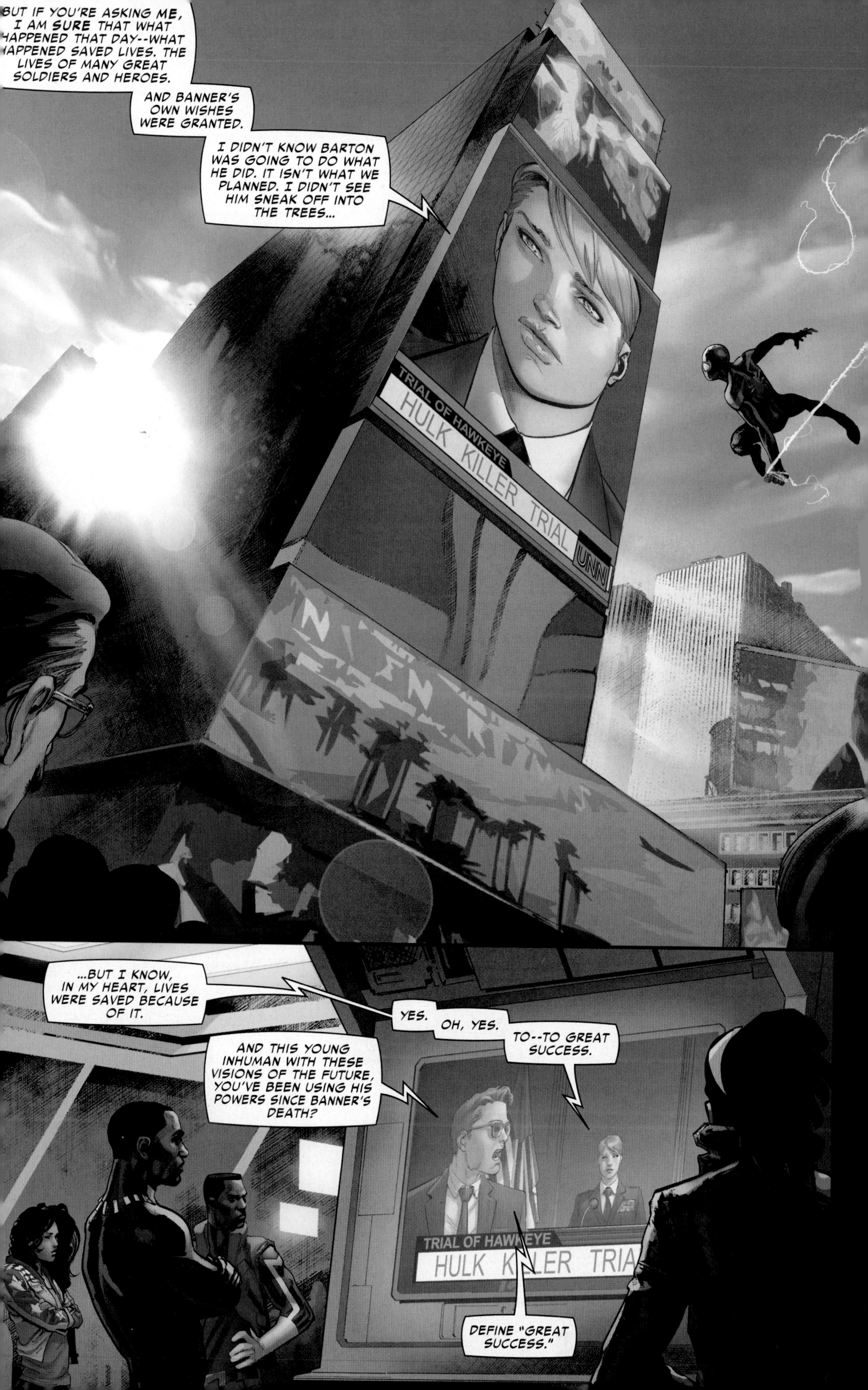
BUT IF YOU'RE ASKING ME, I AM SURE THAT WHAT HAPPENED THAT DAY--WHAT HAPPENED SAVED LIVES. THE LIVES OF MANY GREAT SOLDIERS AND HEROES.
AND BANNER'S OWN WISHES WERE GRANTED.
I DIDN'T KNOW BARTON WAS GOING TO DO WHAT HE DID. IT ISN'T WHAT WE PLANNED. I DIDN'T SEE HIM SNEAK OFF INTO THE TREES...
TRIAL OF HAWKEYE
HULK KILLER TRIAL
UNN
...BUT I KNOW, IN MY HEART, LIVES WERE SAVED BECAUSE OF IT.
YES.
OH, YES.
TO--TO GREAT SUCCESS.
AND THIS YOUNG INHUMAN WITH THESE VISIONS OF THE FUTURE, YOU'VE BEEN USING HIS POWERS SINCE BANNER'S DEATH?
TRIAL OF HAWKEYE
DEFINE "GREAT SUCCESS."

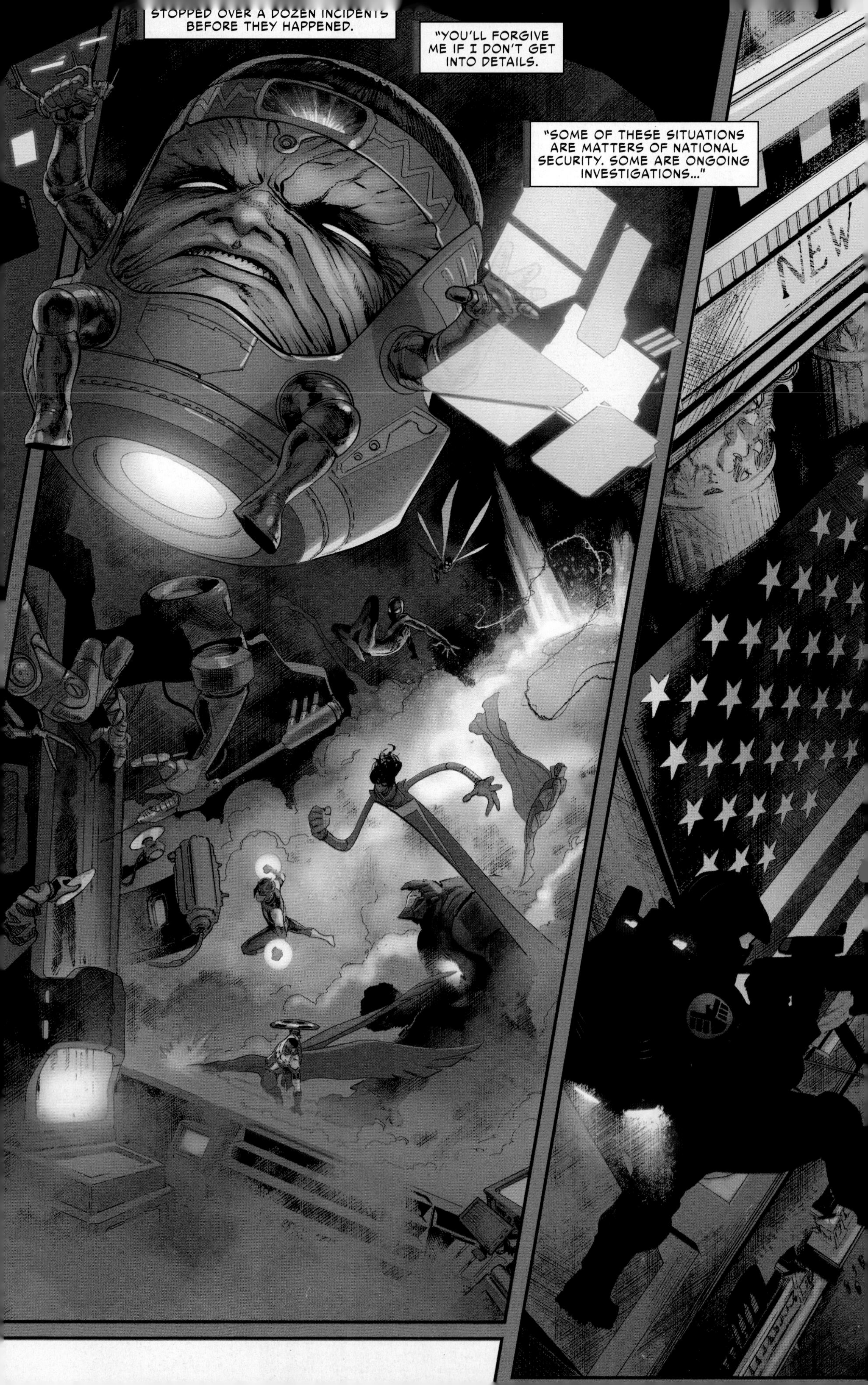
STOPPED OVER A DOZEN INCIDENTS BEFORE THEY HAPPENED.
"YOU'LL FORGIVE ME IF I DON'T GET INTO DETAILS.
"SOME OF THESE SITUATIONS ARE MATTERS OF NATIONAL SECURITY. SOME ARE ONGOING INVESTIGATIONS..."
NEW

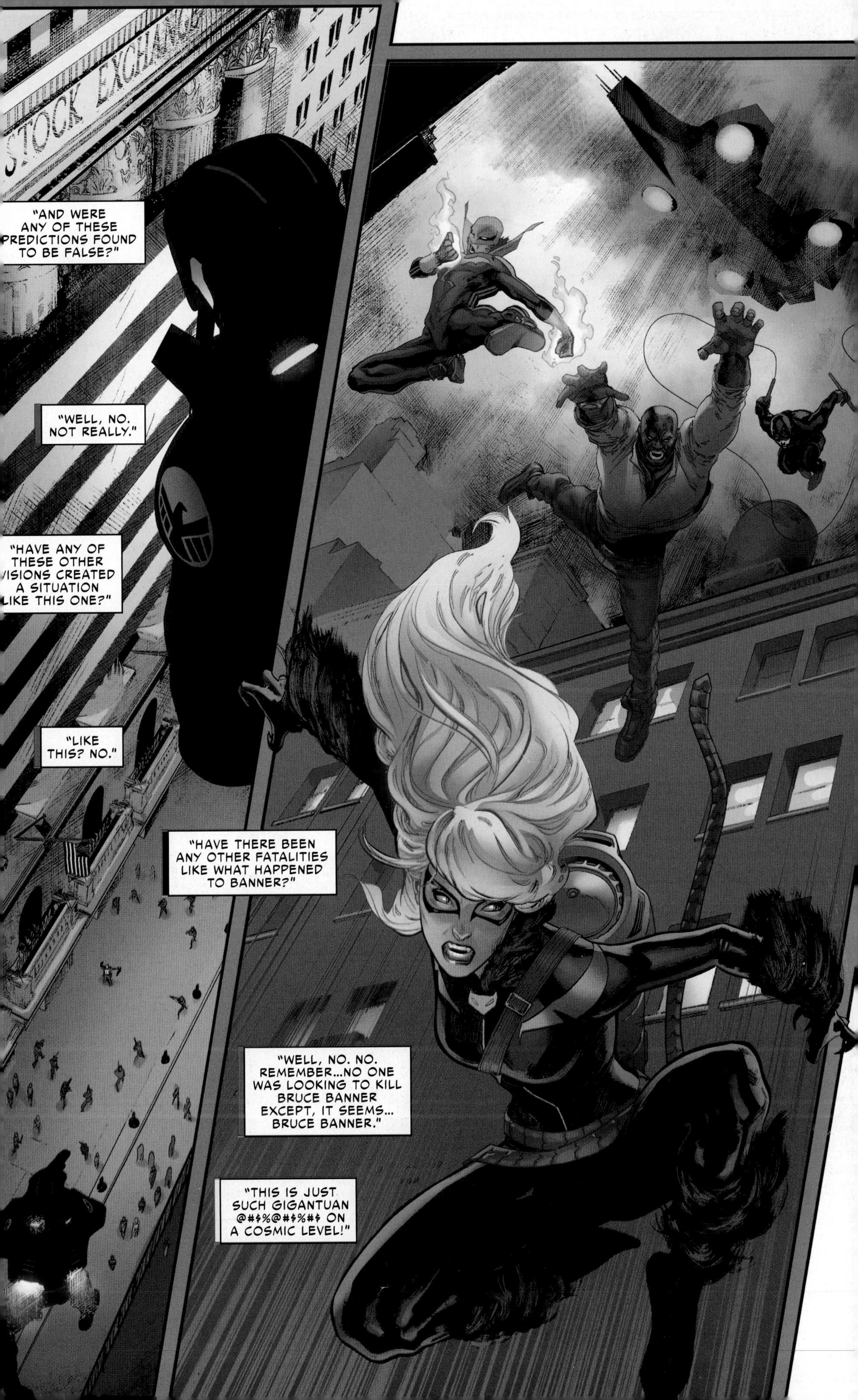

STOCK EXCHAN
"AND WERE ANY OF THESE PREDICTIONS FOUND TO BE FALSE?"
"WELL, NO. NOT REALLY."
"HAVE ANY OF THESE OTHER ISIONS CREATED A SITUATION LIKE THIS ONE?"
"LIKE THIS? NO."
"HAVE THERE BEEN ANY OTHER FATALITIES LIKE WHAT HAPPENED TO BANNER?"
"WELL, NO. NO. REMEMBER...NO ONE WAS LOOKING TO KILL BRUCE BANNER EXCEPT, IT SEEMS... BRUCE BANNER."
"THIS IS JUST SUCH GIGANTUAN @#$%@#$%#$ ON A COSMIC LEVEL!"

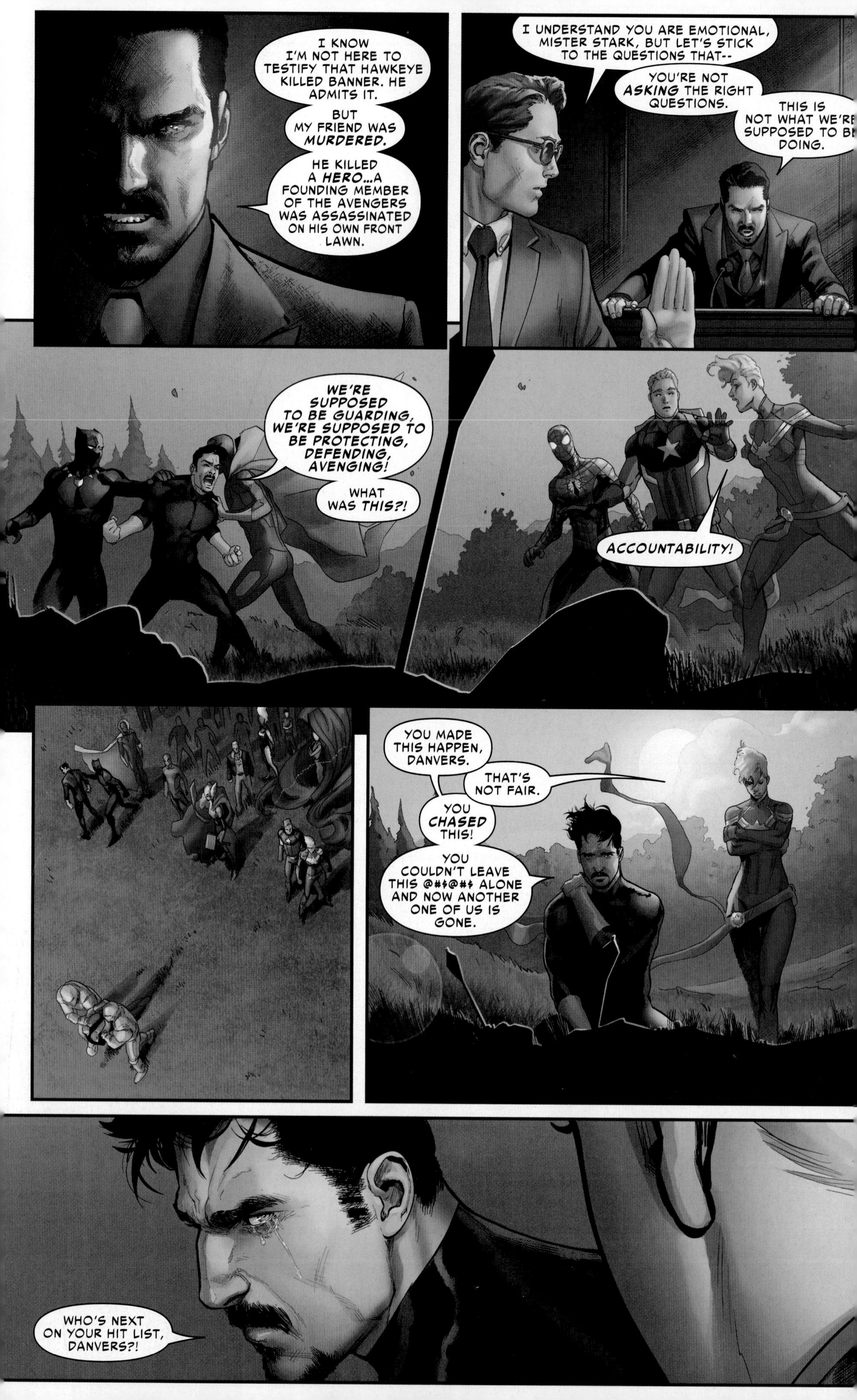
I KNOW I'M NOT HERE TO TESTIFY THAT HAWKEYE KILLED BANNER. HE ADMITS IT.
BUT MY FRIEND WAS *MURDERED.*
HE KILLED A *HERO*...A FOUNDING MEMBER OF THE AVENGERS WAS ASSASSINATED ON HIS OWN FRONT LAWN.
I UNDERSTAND YOU ARE EMOTIONAL, MISTER STARK, BUT LET'S STICK TO THE QUESTIONS THAT--
YOU'RE NOT *ASKING* THE RIGHT QUESTIONS.
THIS IS NOT WHAT WE'RE SUPPOSED TO BE DOING.
WE'RE SUPPOSED TO BE GUARDING, WE'RE SUPPOSED TO BE PROTECTING, DEFENDING, AVENGING!
WHAT WAS *THIS?!*
ACCOUNTABILITY!
YOU MADE THIS HAPPEN, DANVERS.
THAT'S NOT FAIR.
YOU *CHASED* THIS!
YOU COULDN'T LEAVE THIS @#$@#$ ALONE AND NOW ANOTHER ONE OF US IS GONE.
WHO'S NEXT ON YOUR HIT LIST, DANVERS?!

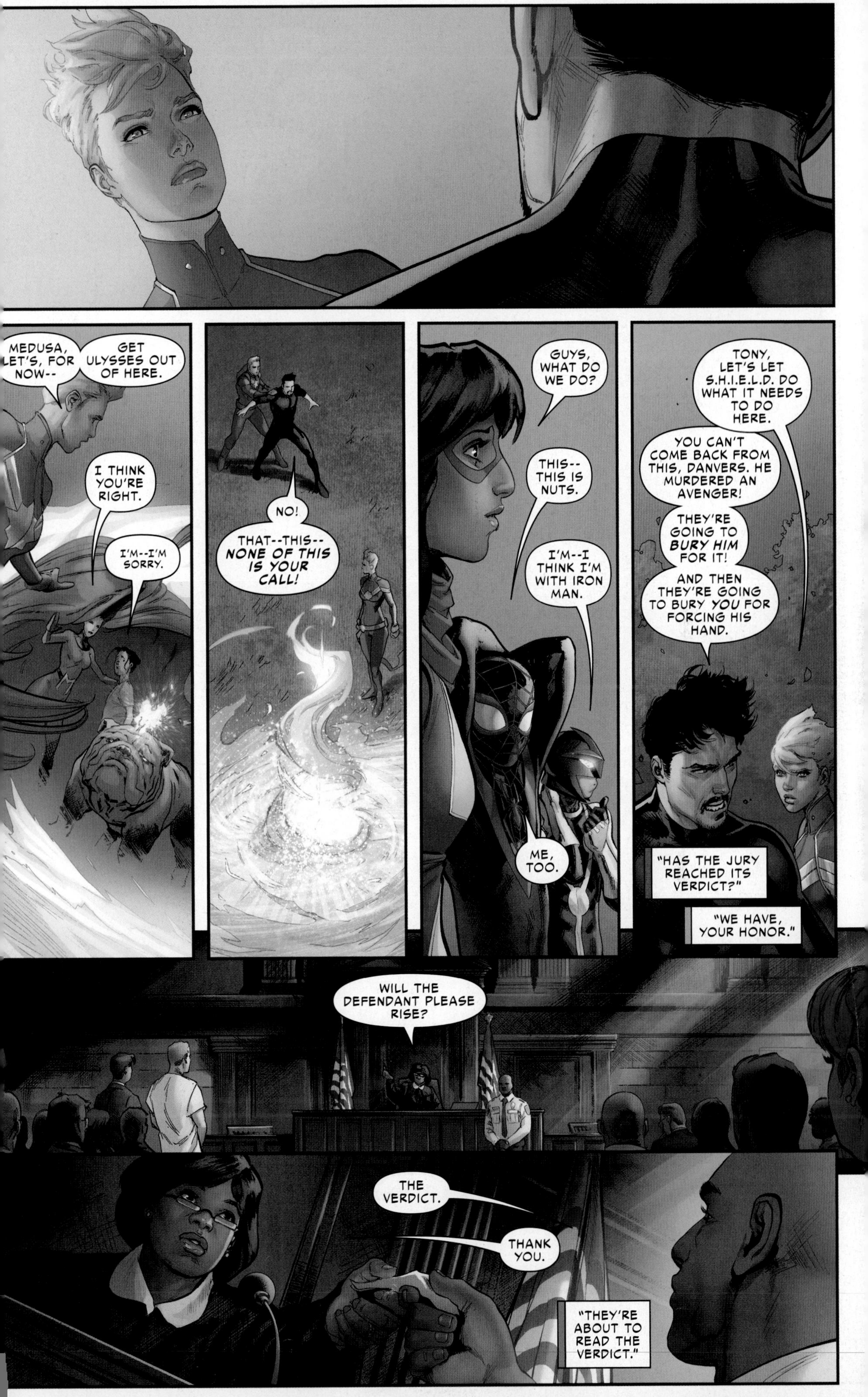
MEDUSA, LET'S, FOR NOW--
GET ULYSSES OUT OF HERE.
I THINK YOU'RE RIGHT.
I'M--I'M SORRY.
NO!
THAT--THIS-- NONE OF THIS IS YOUR CALL!
GUYS, WHAT DO WE DO?
THIS-- THIS IS NUTS.
I'M--I THINK I'M WITH IRON MAN.
ME, TOO.
TONY, LET'S LET S.H.I.E.L.D. DO WHAT IT NEEDS TO DO HERE.
YOU CAN'T COME BACK FROM THIS, DANVERS. HE MURDERED AN AVENGER!
THEY'RE GOING TO BURY HIM FOR IT!
AND THEN THEY'RE GOING TO BURY YOU FOR FORCING HIS HAND.
"HAS THE JURY REACHED ITS VERDICT?"
"WE HAVE, YOUR HONOR."
WILL THE DEFENDANT PLEASE RISE?
THE VERDICT.
THANK YOU.
"THEY'RE ABOUT TO READ THE VERDICT."

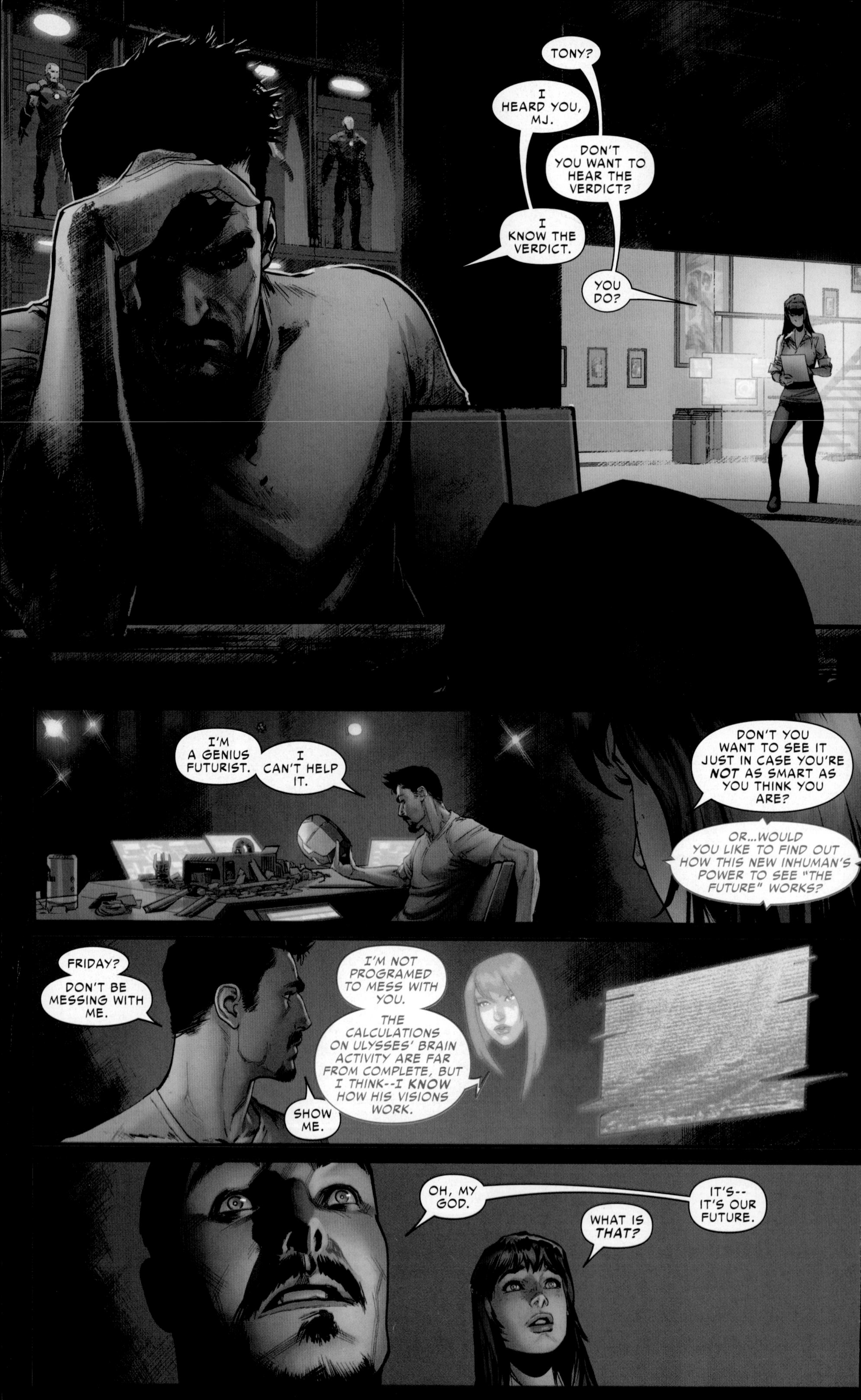
TONY?
I HEARD YOU, MJ.
DON'T YOU WANT TO HEAR THE VERDICT?
I KNOW THE VERDICT.
YOU DO?
I'M A GENIUS FUTURIST.
I CAN'T HELP IT.
DON'T YOU WANT TO SEE IT JUST IN CASE YOU'RE NOT AS SMART AS YOU THINK YOU ARE?
OR...WOULD YOU LIKE TO FIND OUT HOW THIS NEW INHUMAN'S POWER TO SEE "THE FUTURE" WORKS?
FRIDAY?
DON'T BE MESSING WITH ME.
I'M NOT PROGRAMED TO MESS WITH YOU.
THE CALCULATIONS ON ULYSSES' BRAIN ACTIVITY ARE FAR FROM COMPLETE, BUT I THINK--I KNOW HOW HIS VISIONS WORK.
SHOW ME.
OH, MY GOD.
WHAT IS THAT?
IT'S-- IT'S OUR FUTURE.

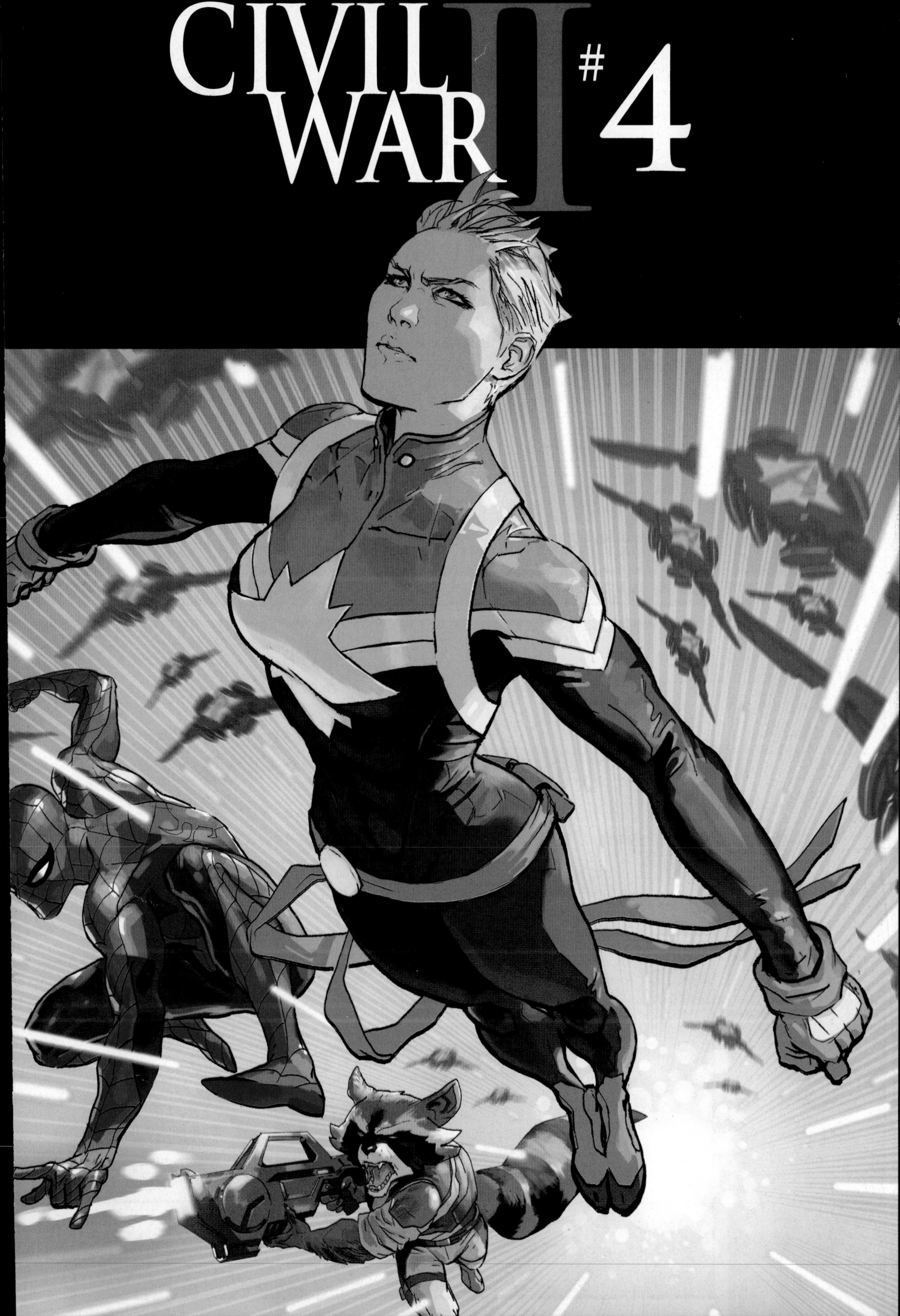
CIVIL WAR II
#4

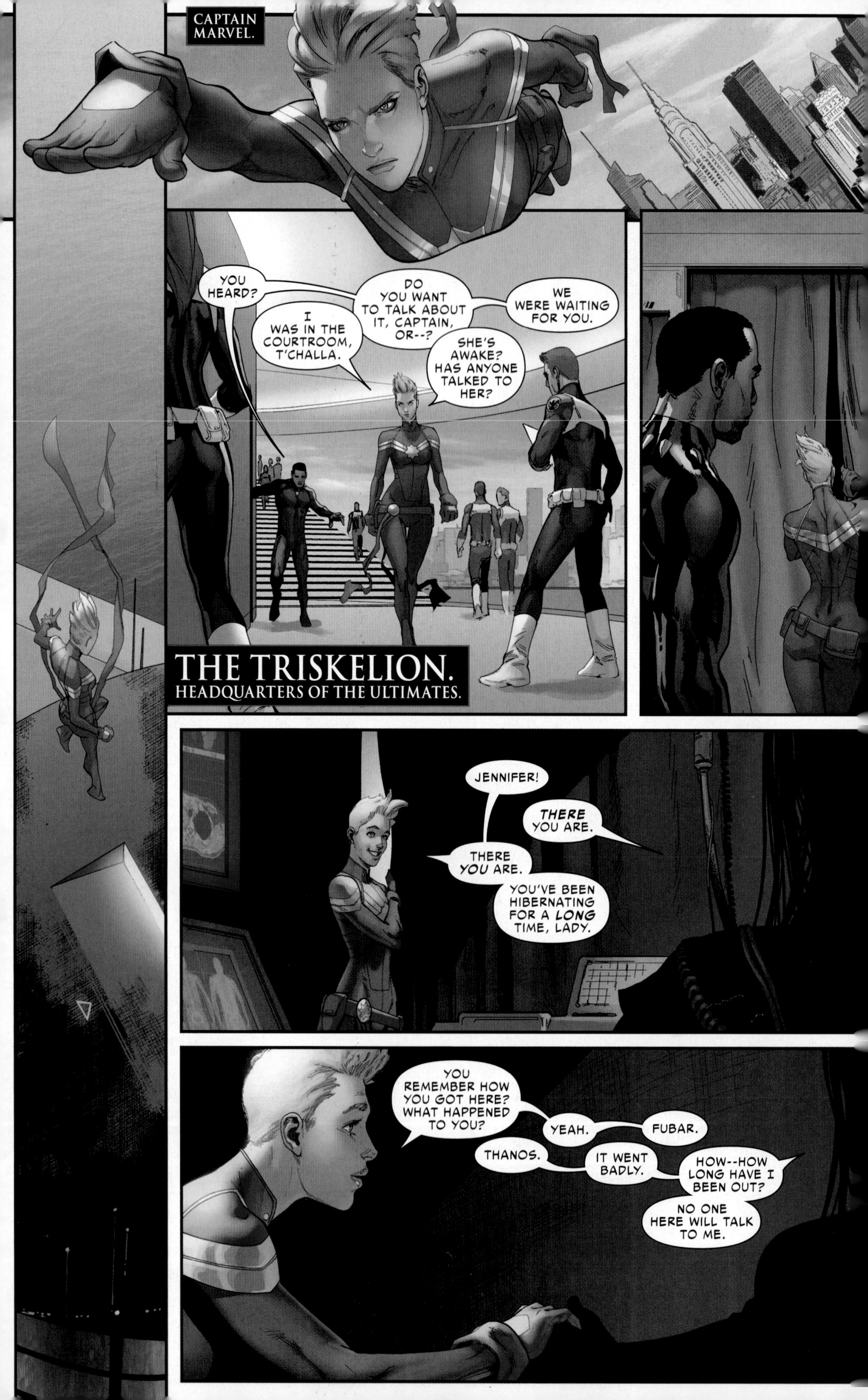
CAPTAIN MARVEL.
YOU HEARD?
DO YOU WANT TO TALK ABOUT IT, CAPTAIN, OR--?
WE WERE WAITING FOR YOU.
I WAS IN THE COURTROOM, T'CHALLA.
SHE'S AWAKE? HAS ANYONE TALKED TO HER?
THE TRISKELION.
HEADQUARTERS OF THE ULTIMATES.
JENNIFER!
THERE YOU ARE.
THERE YOU ARE.
YOU'VE BEEN HIBERNATING FOR A LONG TIME, LADY.
YOU REMEMBER HOW YOU GOT HERE? WHAT HAPPENED TO YOU?
YEAH.
FUBAR.
THANOS.
IT WENT BADLY.
HOW--HOW LONG HAVE I BEEN OUT?
NO ONE HERE WILL TALK TO ME.

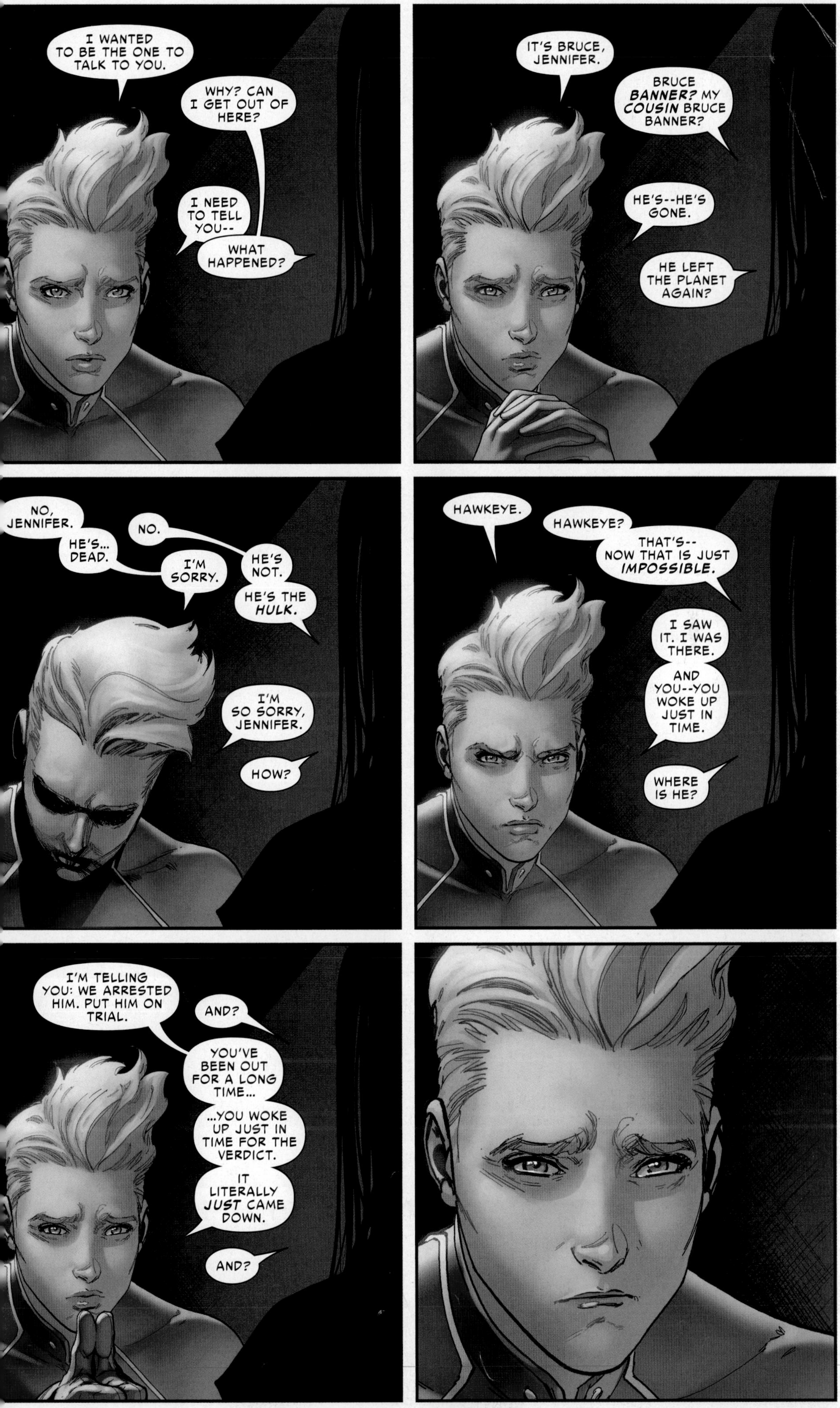
I WANTED TO BE THE ONE TO TALK TO YOU.
WHY? CAN I GET OUT OF HERE?
I NEED TO TELL YOU--
WHAT HAPPENED?
IT'S BRUCE, JENNIFER.
BRUCE BANNER? MY COUSIN BRUCE BANNER?
HE'S--HE'S GONE.
HE LEFT THE PLANET AGAIN?
NO, JENNIFER.
HE'S... DEAD.
NO.
HE'S NOT.
I'M SORRY.
HE'S THE HULK.
I'M SO SORRY, JENNIFER.
HOW?
HAWKEYE.
HAWKEYE?
THAT'S-- NOW THAT IS JUST IMPOSSIBLE.
I SAW IT. I WAS THERE.
AND YOU--YOU WOKE UP JUST IN TIME.
WHERE IS HE?
I'M TELLING YOU: WE ARRESTED HIM. PUT HIM ON TRIAL.
AND?
YOU'VE BEEN OUT FOR A LONG TIME...
...YOU WOKE UP JUST IN TIME FOR THE VERDICT.
IT LITERALLY JUST CAME DOWN.
AND?

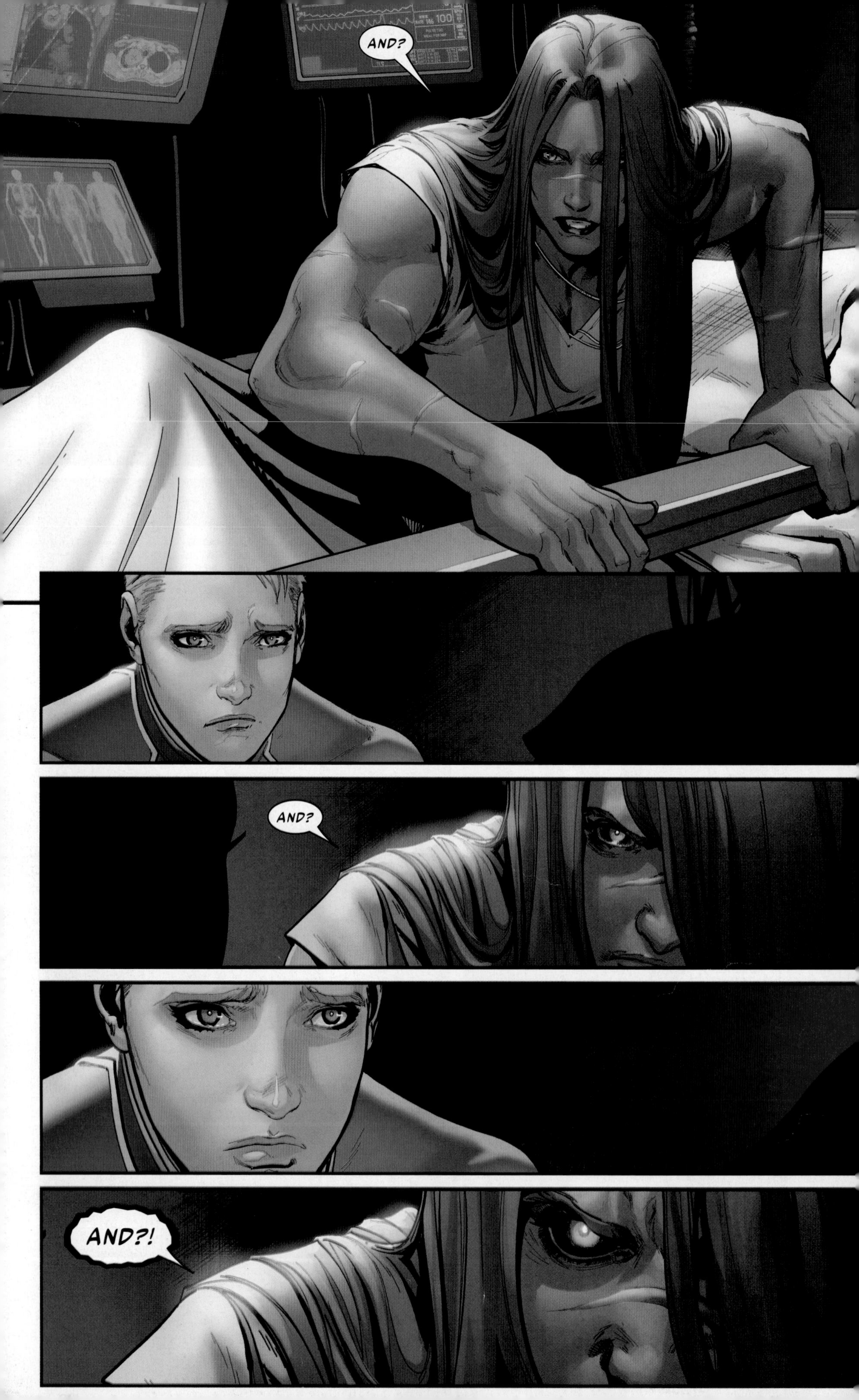
AND?
AND?
AND?!

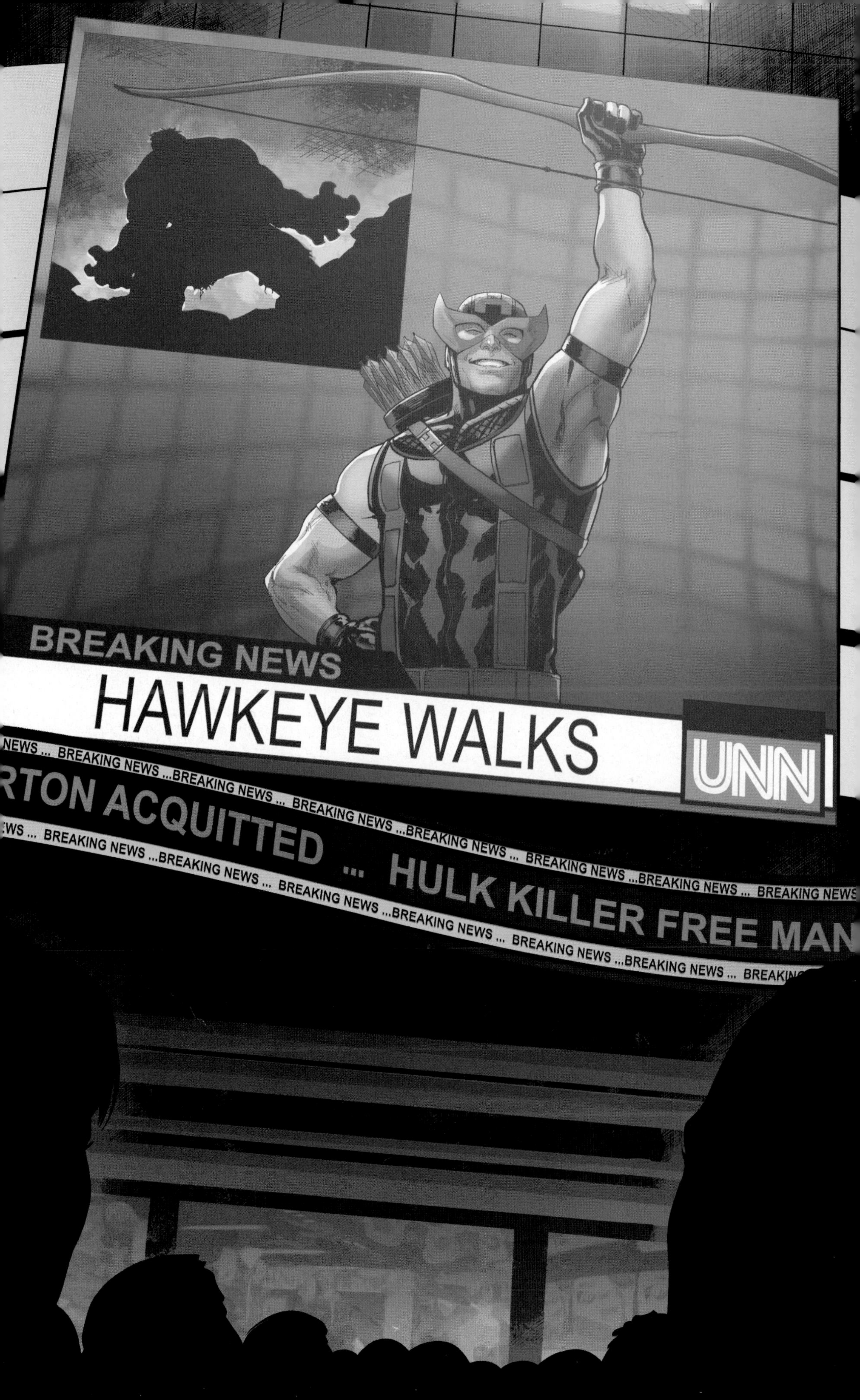
BREAKING NEWS
HAWKEYE WALKS
UNN
RTON ACQUITTED ... HULK KILLER FREE MAN

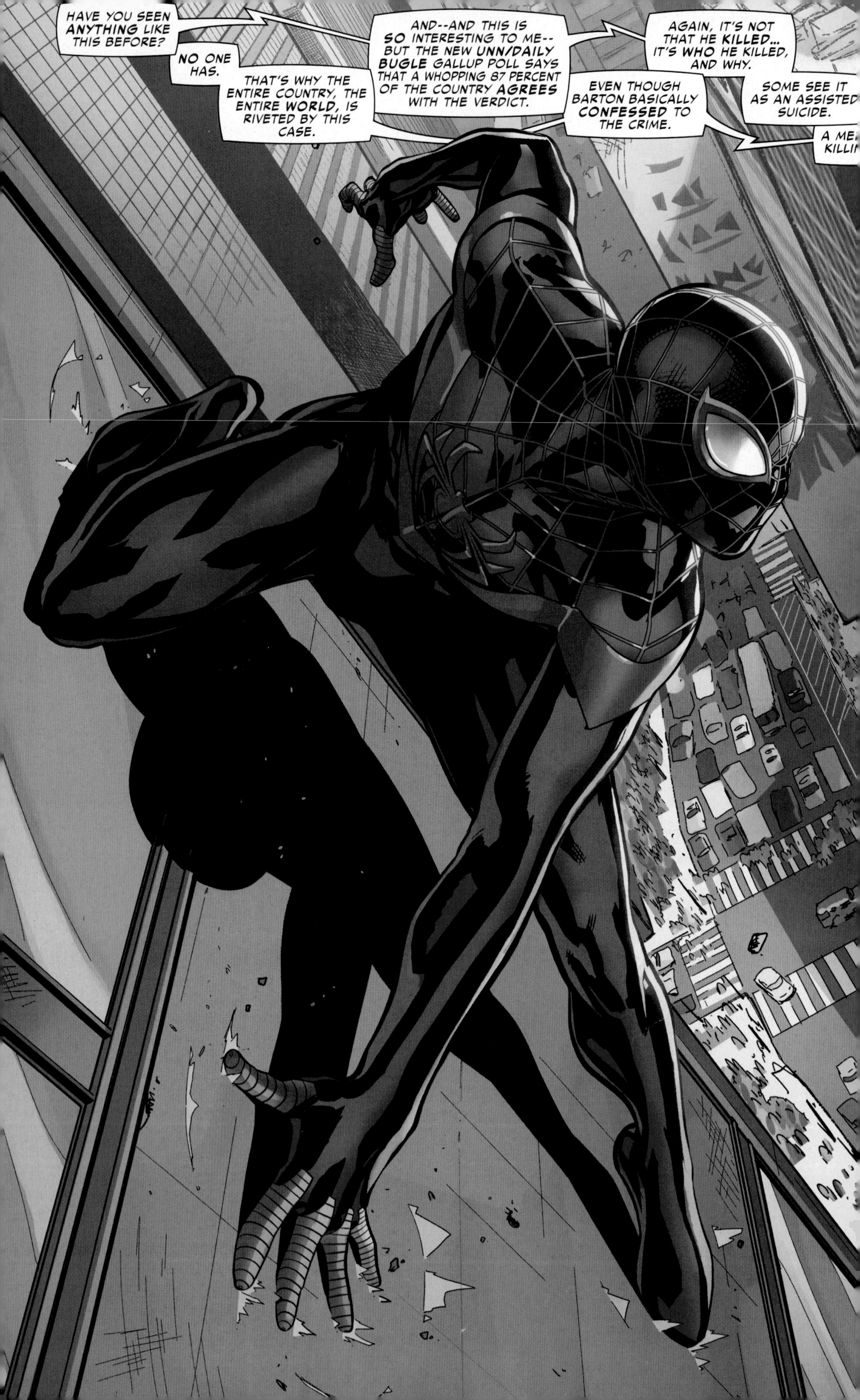
HAVE YOU SEEN ANYTHING LIKE THIS BEFORE?
NO ONE HAS.
THAT'S WHY THE ENTIRE COUNTRY, THE ENTIRE WORLD, IS RIVETED BY THIS CASE.
AND--AND THIS IS SO INTERESTING TO ME-- BUT THE NEW UNN/DAILY BUGLE GALLUP POLL SAYS THAT A WHOPPING 87 PERCENT OF THE COUNTRY AGREES WITH THE VERDICT.
EVEN THOUGH BARTON BASICALLY CONFESSED TO THE CRIME.
AGAIN, IT'S NOT THAT HE KILLED... IT'S WHO HE KILLED, AND WHY.
SOME SEE IT AS AN ASSISTED SUICIDE.

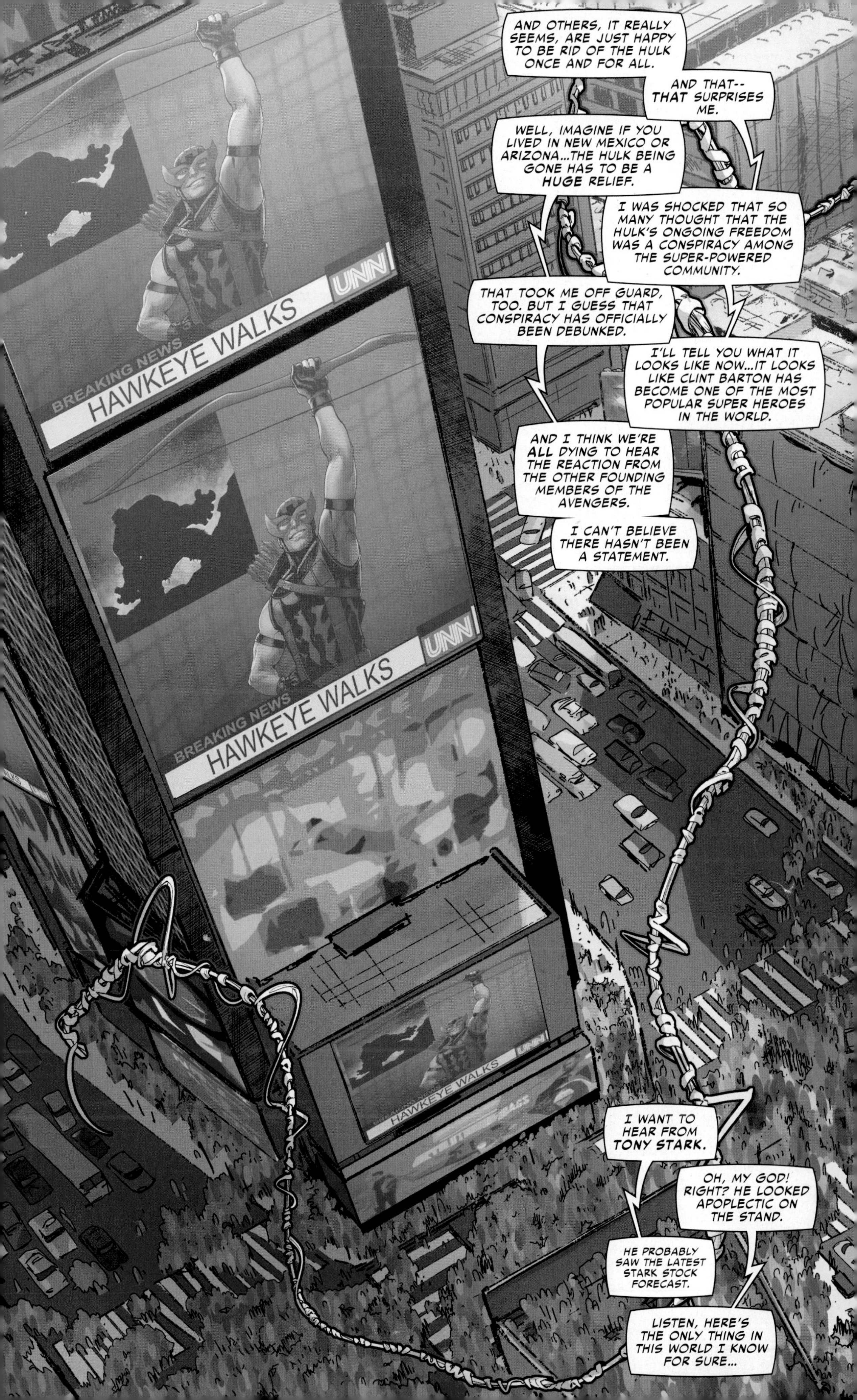

AND OTHERS, IT REALLY SEEMS, ARE JUST HAPPY TO BE RID OF THE HULK ONCE AND FOR ALL.
AND THAT-- THAT SURPRISES ME.
WELL, IMAGINE IF YOU LIVED IN NEW MEXICO OR ARIZONA...THE HULK BEING GONE HAS TO BE A HUGE RELIEF.
I WAS SHOCKED THAT SO MANY THOUGHT THAT THE HULK'S ONGOING FREEDOM WAS A CONSPIRACY AMONG THE SUPER-POWERED COMMUNITY.
THAT TOOK ME OFF GUARD, TOO. BUT I GUESS THAT CONSPIRACY HAS OFFICIALLY BEEN DEBUNKED.
I'LL TELL YOU WHAT IT LOOKS LIKE NOW...IT LOOKS LIKE CLINT BARTON HAS BECOME ONE OF THE MOST POPULAR SUPER HEROES IN THE WORLD.
AND I THINK WE'RE ALL DYING TO HEAR THE REACTION FROM THE OTHER FOUNDING MEMBERS OF THE AVENGERS.
I CAN'T BELIEVE THERE HASN'T BEEN A STATEMENT.
UNN
BREAKING NEWS
HAWKEYE WALKS
UNN
BREAKING NEWS
HAWKEYE WALKS
UNN
HAWKEYE WALKS
I WANT TO HEAR FROM TONY STARK.
OH, MY GOD! RIGHT? HE LOOKED APOPLECTIC ON THE STAND.
HE PROBABLY SAW THE LATEST STARK STOCK FORECAST.
LISTEN, HERE'S THE ONLY THING IN THIS WORLD I KNOW FOR SURE...

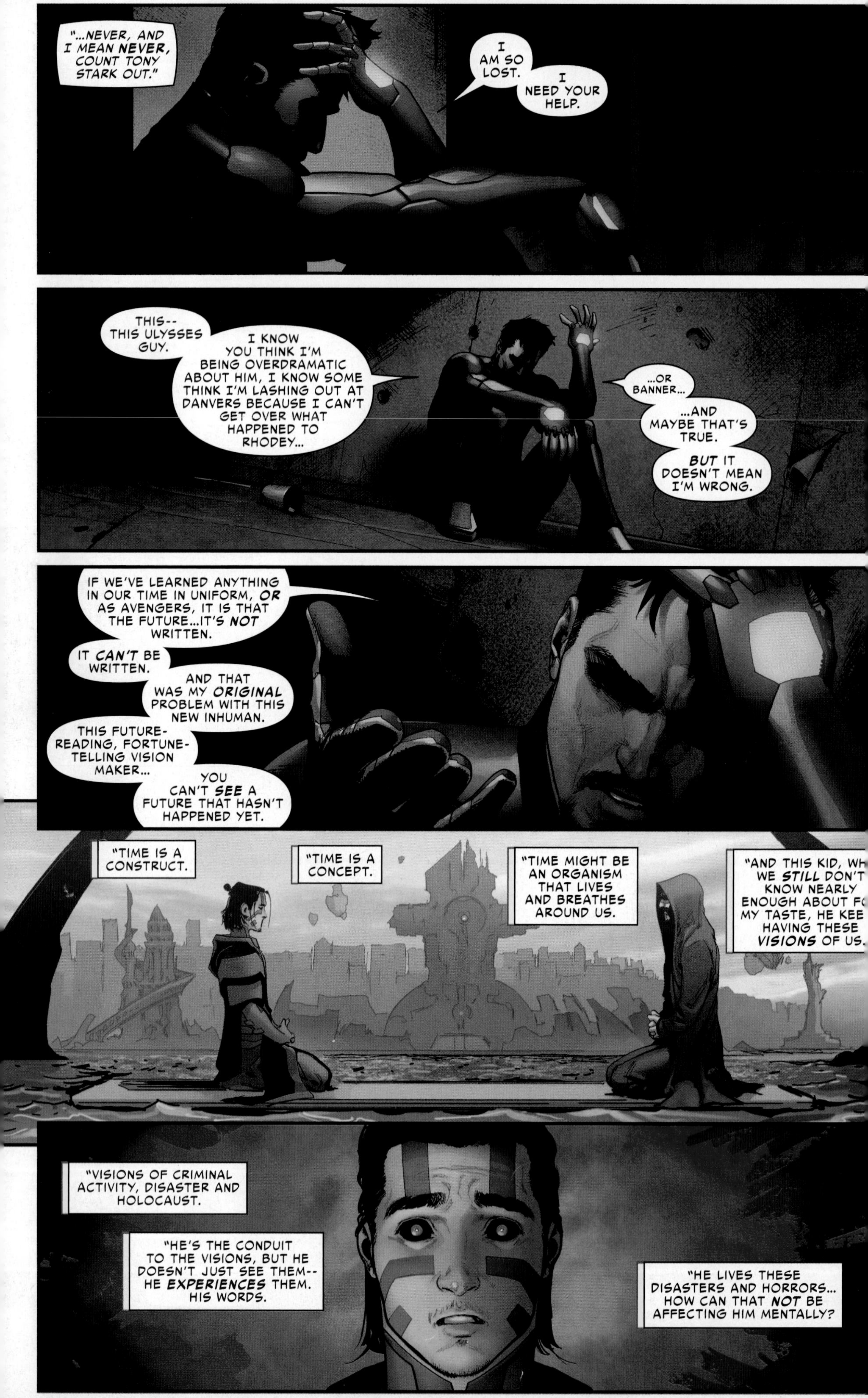
"...NEVER, AND I MEAN NEVER, COUNT TONY STARK OUT."
I AM SO LOST.
I NEED YOUR HELP.
THIS-- THIS ULYSSES GUY.
I KNOW YOU THINK I'M BEING OVERDRAMATIC ABOUT HIM, I KNOW SOME THINK I'M LASHING OUT AT DANVERS BECAUSE I CAN'T GET OVER WHAT HAPPENED TO RHODEY...
...OR BANNER...
...AND MAYBE THAT'S TRUE.
BUT IT DOESN'T MEAN I'M WRONG.
IF WE'VE LEARNED ANYTHING IN OUR TIME IN UNIFORM, OR AS AVENGERS, IT IS THAT THE FUTURE...IT'S NOT WRITTEN.
IT CAN'T BE WRITTEN.
AND THAT WAS MY ORIGINAL PROBLEM WITH THIS NEW INHUMAN.
THIS FUTURE-READING, FORTUNE-TELLING VISION MAKER...
YOU CAN'T SEE A FUTURE THAT HASN'T HAPPENED YET.
"TIME IS A CONSTRUCT.
"TIME IS A CONCEPT.
"TIME MIGHT BE AN ORGANISM THAT LIVES AND BREATHES AROUND US.
"AND THIS KID, WH
WE STILL DON'T
KNOW NEARLY
ENOUGH ABOUT F
MY TASTE, HE KEE
HAVING THESE
VISIONS OF US.
"VISIONS OF CRIMINAL ACTIVITY, DISASTER AND HOLOCAUST.
"HE'S THE CONDUIT TO THE VISIONS, BUT HE DOESN'T JUST SEE THEM-- HE EXPERIENCES THEM. HIS WORDS.
"HE LIVES THESE DISASTERS AND HORRORS... HOW CAN THAT NOT BE AFFECTING HIM MENTALLY?

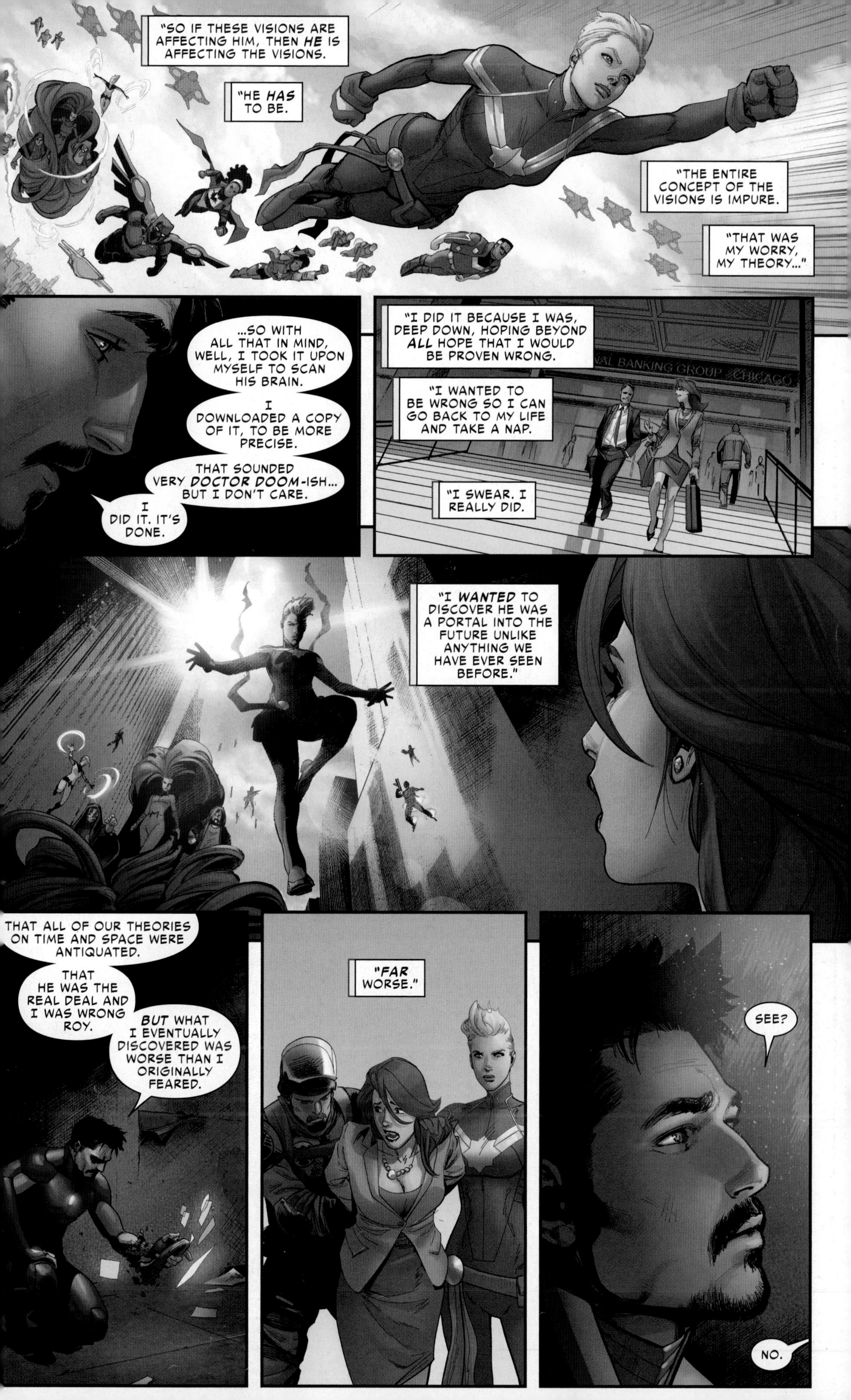
"SO IF THESE VISIONS ARE AFFECTING HIM, THEN HE IS AFFECTING THE VISIONS.
"HE HAS TO BE.
"THE ENTIRE CONCEPT OF THE VISIONS IS IMPURE.
"THAT WAS MY WORRY, MY THEORY..."
...SO WITH ALL THAT IN MIND, WELL, I TOOK IT UPON MYSELF TO SCAN HIS BRAIN.
I DOWNLOADED A COPY OF IT, TO BE MORE PRECISE.
THAT SOUNDED VERY DOCTOR DOOM-ISH... BUT I DON'T CARE.
I DID IT. IT'S DONE.
"I DID IT BECAUSE I WAS, DEEP DOWN, HOPING BEYOND ALL HOPE THAT I WOULD BE PROVEN WRONG.
"I WANTED TO BE WRONG SO I CAN GO BACK TO MY LIFE AND TAKE A NAP.
"I SWEAR. I REALLY DID.
"I WANTED TO DISCOVER HE WAS A PORTAL INTO THE FUTURE UNLIKE ANYTHING WE HAVE EVER SEEN BEFORE."
THAT ALL OF OUR THEORIES ON TIME AND SPACE WERE ANTIQUATED.
THAT HE WAS THE REAL DEAL AND I WAS WRONG ROY.
BUT WHAT I EVENTUALLY DISCOVERED WAS WORSE THAN I ORIGINALLY FEARED.
"FAR WORSE."
SEE?
NO.

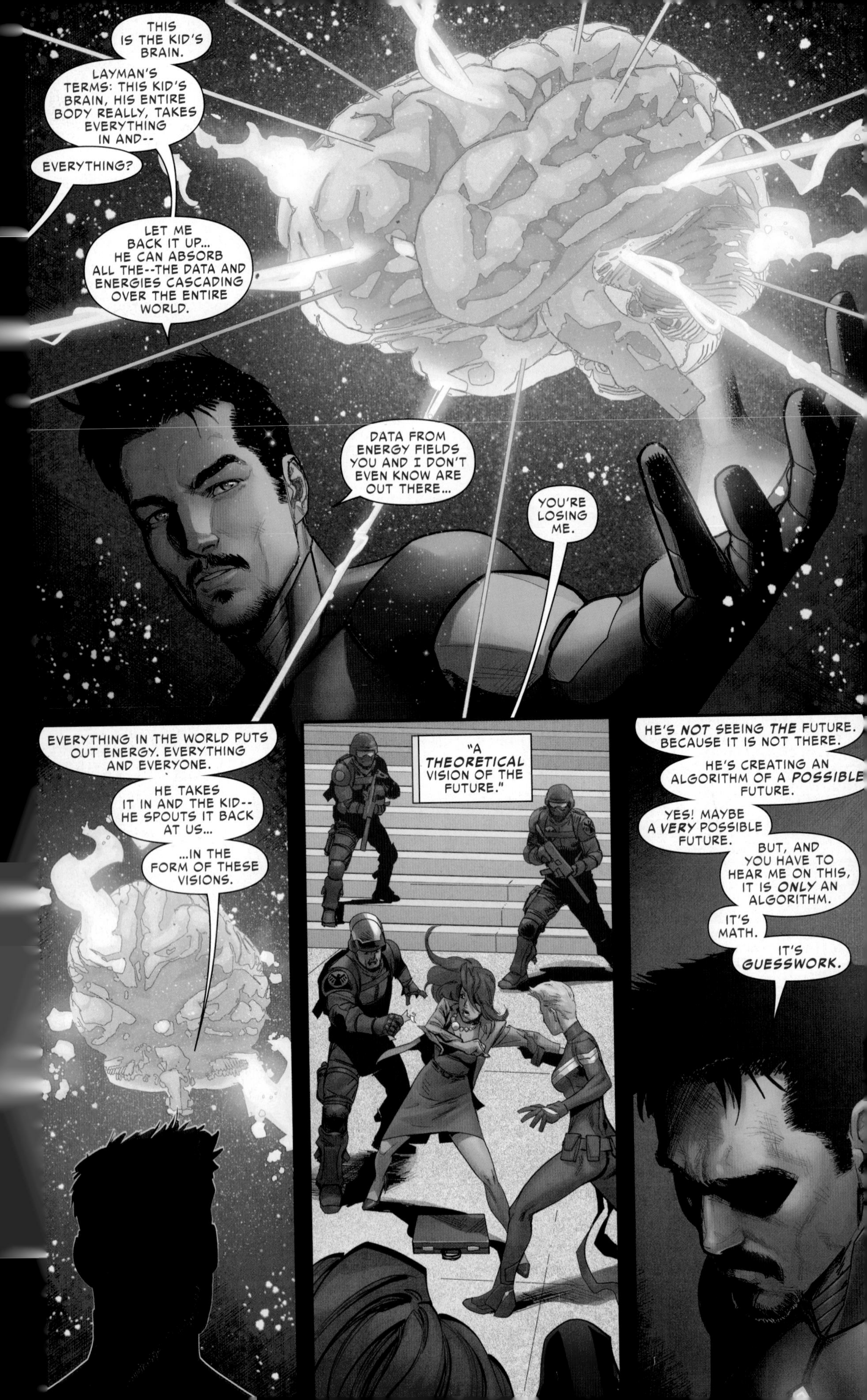
THIS IS THE KID'S BRAIN.
LAYMAN'S TERMS: THIS KID'S BRAIN, HIS ENTIRE BODY REALLY, TAKES EVERYTHING IN AND--
EVERYTHING?
LET ME BACK IT UP... HE CAN ABSORB ALL THE--THE DATA AND ENERGIES CASCADING OVER THE ENTIRE WORLD.
DATA FROM ENERGY FIELDS YOU AND I DON'T EVEN KNOW ARE OUT THERE...
YOU'RE LOSING ME.
EVERYTHING IN THE WORLD PUTS OUT ENERGY. EVERYTHING AND EVERYONE.
HE TAKES IT IN AND THE KID-- HE SPOUTS IT BACK AT US...
...IN THE FORM OF THESE VISIONS.
"A *THEORETICAL* VISION OF THE FUTURE."
HE'S *NOT* SEEING *THE* FUTURE. BECAUSE IT IS NOT THERE.
HE'S CREATING AN ALGORITHM OF A *POSSIBLE* FUTURE.
YES! MAYBE A *VERY* POSSIBLE FUTURE.
BUT, AND YOU HAVE TO HEAR ME ON THIS, IT IS *ONLY* AN ALGORITHM.
IT'S MATH.
IT'S *GUESSWORK.*

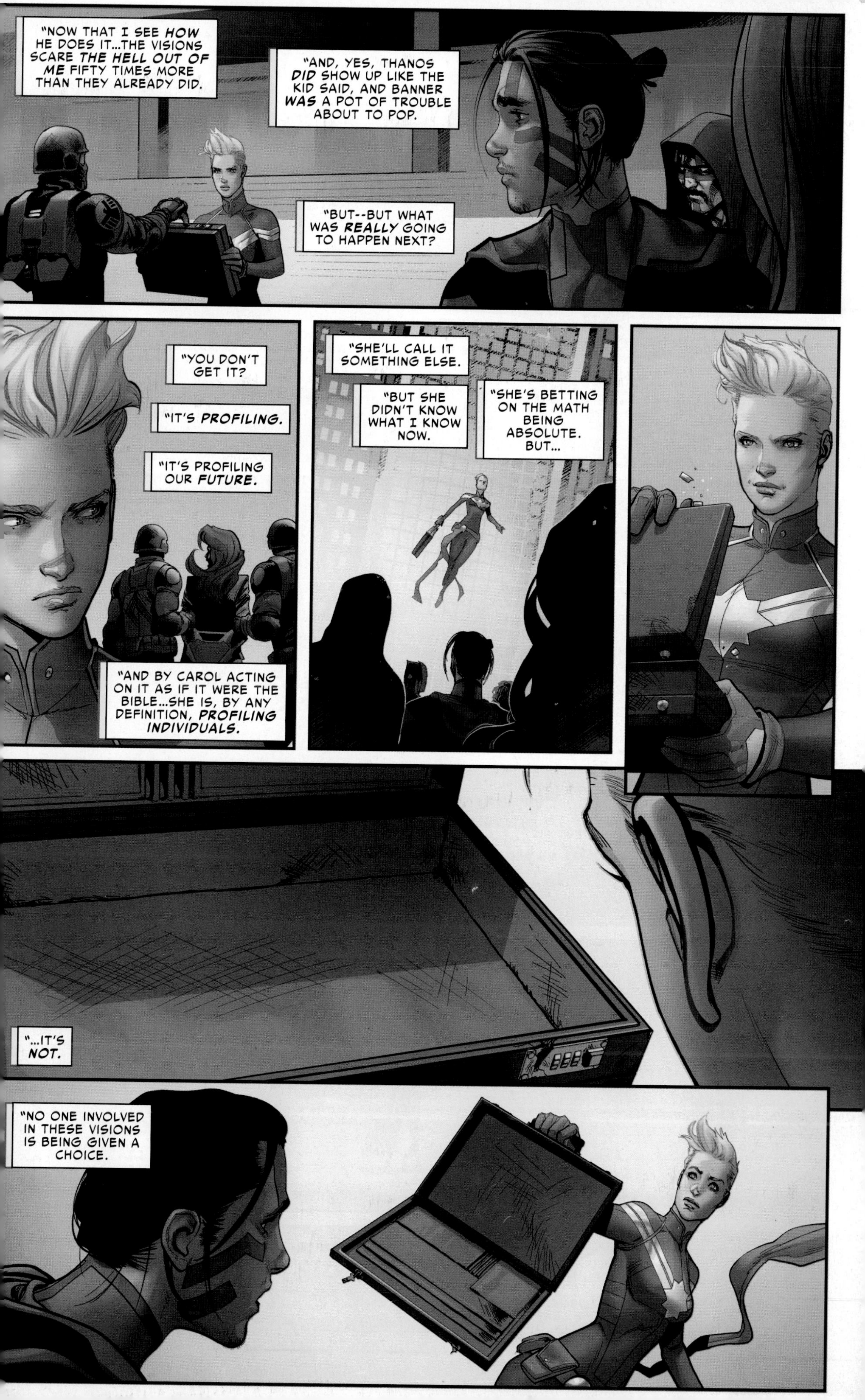
"NOW THAT I SEE HOW HE DOES IT...THE VISIONS SCARE THE HELL OUT OF ME FIFTY TIMES MORE THAN THEY ALREADY DID.
"AND, YES, THANOS DID SHOW UP LIKE THE KID SAID, AND BANNER WAS A POT OF TROUBLE ABOUT TO POP.
"BUT--BUT WHAT WAS REALLY GOING TO HAPPEN NEXT?
"YOU DON'T GET IT?
"IT'S PROFILING.
"IT'S PROFILING OUR FUTURE.
"AND BY CAROL ACTING ON IT AS IF IT WERE THE BIBLE...SHE IS, BY ANY DEFINITION, PROFILING INDIVIDUALS.
"SHE'LL CALL IT SOMETHING ELSE.
"BUT SHE DIDN'T KNOW WHAT I KNOW NOW.
"SHE'S BETTING ON THE MATH BEING ABSOLUTE. BUT...
"...IT'S NOT.
"NO ONE INVOLVED IN THESE VISIONS IS BEING GIVEN A CHOICE.

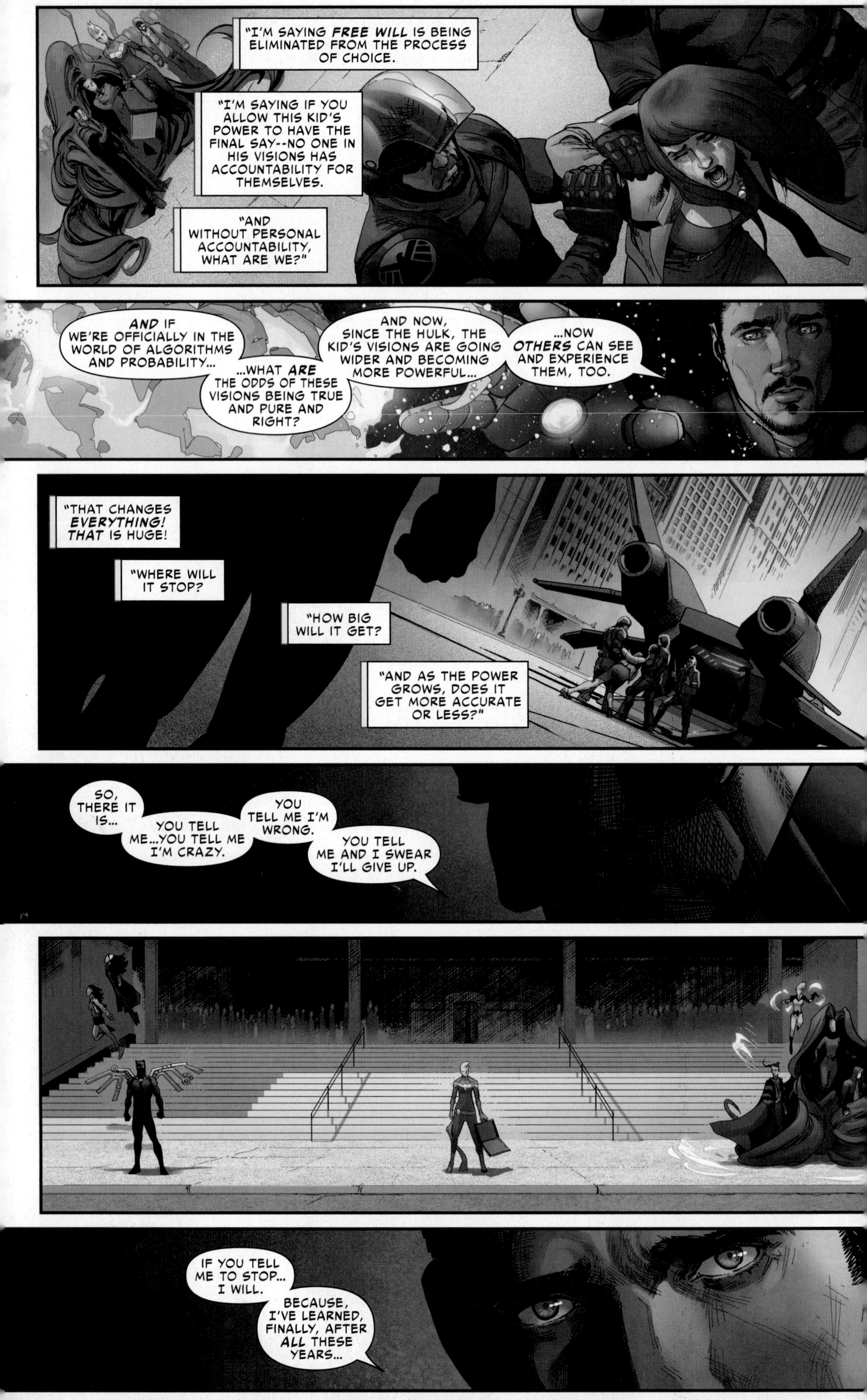
"I'M SAYING FREE WILL IS BEING ELIMINATED FROM THE PROCESS OF CHOICE.
"I'M SAYING IF YOU ALLOW THIS KID'S POWER TO HAVE THE FINAL SAY--NO ONE IN HIS VISIONS HAS ACCOUNTABILITY FOR THEMSELVES.
"AND WITHOUT PERSONAL ACCOUNTABILITY, WHAT ARE WE?"
AND IF WE'RE OFFICIALLY IN THE WORLD OF ALGORITHMS AND PROBABILITY...
...WHAT ARE THE ODDS OF THESE VISIONS BEING TRUE AND PURE AND RIGHT?
AND NOW, SINCE THE HULK, THE KID'S VISIONS ARE GOING WIDER AND BECOMING MORE POWERFUL...
...NOW OTHERS CAN SEE AND EXPERIENCE THEM, TOO.
"THAT CHANGES EVERYTHING! THAT IS HUGE!
"WHERE WILL IT STOP?
"HOW BIG WILL IT GET?
"AND AS THE POWER GROWS, DOES IT GET MORE ACCURATE OR LESS?"
SO, THERE IT IS...
YOU TELL ME...YOU TELL ME I'M CRAZY.
YOU TELL ME I'M WRONG.
YOU TELL ME AND I SWEAR I'LL GIVE UP.
IF YOU TELL ME TO STOP... I WILL.
BECAUSE, I'VE LEARNED, FINALLY, AFTER ALL THESE YEARS...

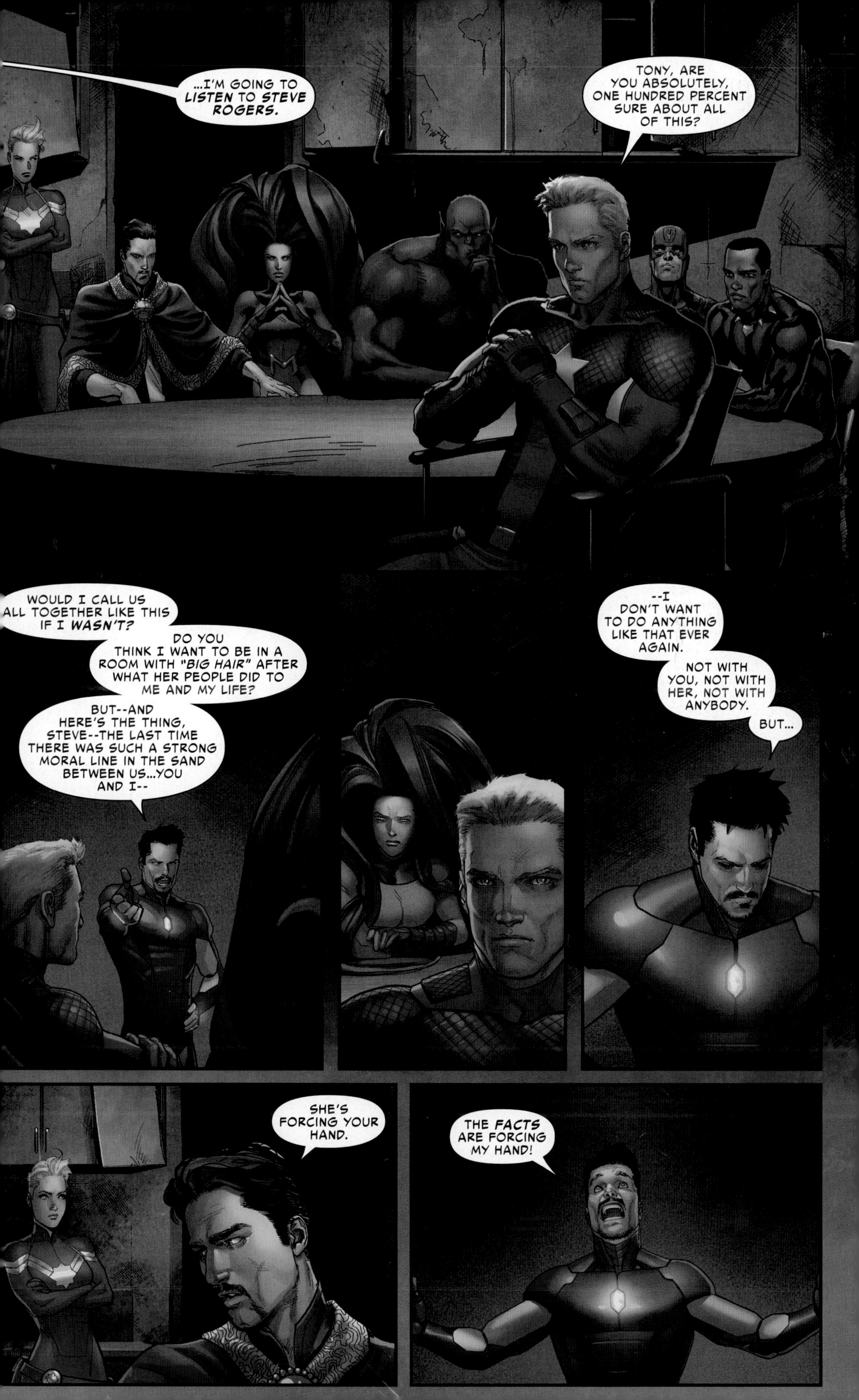
...I'M GOING TO LISTEN TO STEVE ROGERS.
TONY, ARE YOU ABSOLUTELY, ONE HUNDRED PERCENT SURE ABOUT ALL OF THIS?
WOULD I CALL US ALL TOGETHER LIKE THIS IF I WASN'T?
DO YOU THINK I WANT TO BE IN A ROOM WITH "BIG HAIR" AFTER WHAT HER PEOPLE DID TO ME AND MY LIFE?
BUT--AND HERE'S THE THING, STEVE--THE LAST TIME THERE WAS SUCH A STRONG MORAL LINE IN THE SAND BETWEEN US...YOU AND I--
--I DON'T WANT TO DO ANYTHING LIKE THAT EVER AGAIN.
NOT WITH YOU, NOT WITH HER, NOT WITH ANYBODY.
BUT...
SHE'S FORCING YOUR HAND.
THE FACTS ARE FORCING MY HAND!

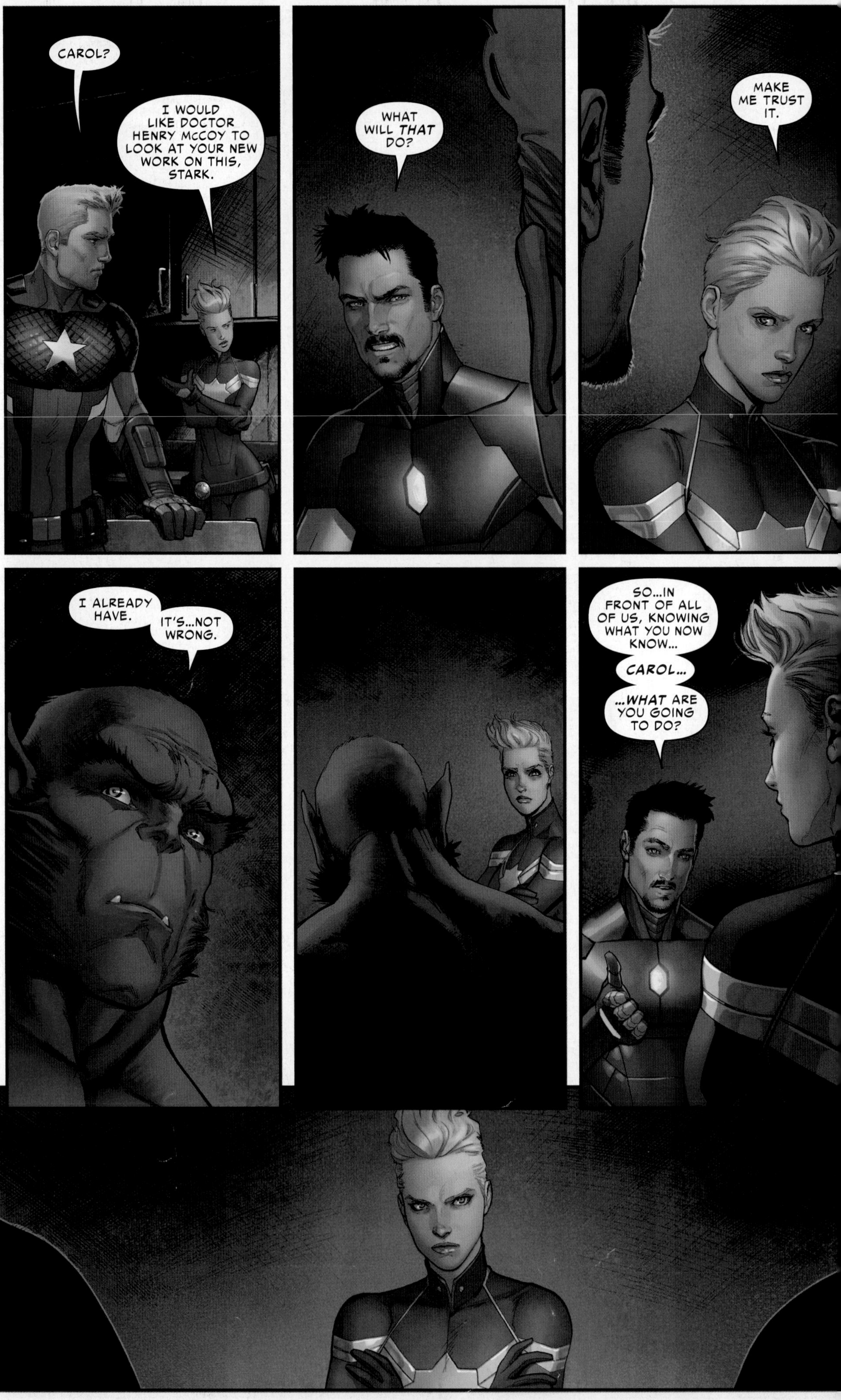
CAROL?
I WOULD LIKE DOCTOR HENRY McCOY TO LOOK AT YOUR NEW WORK ON THIS, STARK.
WHAT WILL *THAT* DO?
MAKE ME TRUST IT.
I ALREADY HAVE.
IT'S...NOT WRONG.
SO...IN FRONT OF ALL OF US, KNOWING WHAT YOU NOW KNOW...
CAROL...
...*WHAT* ARE YOU GOING TO DO?

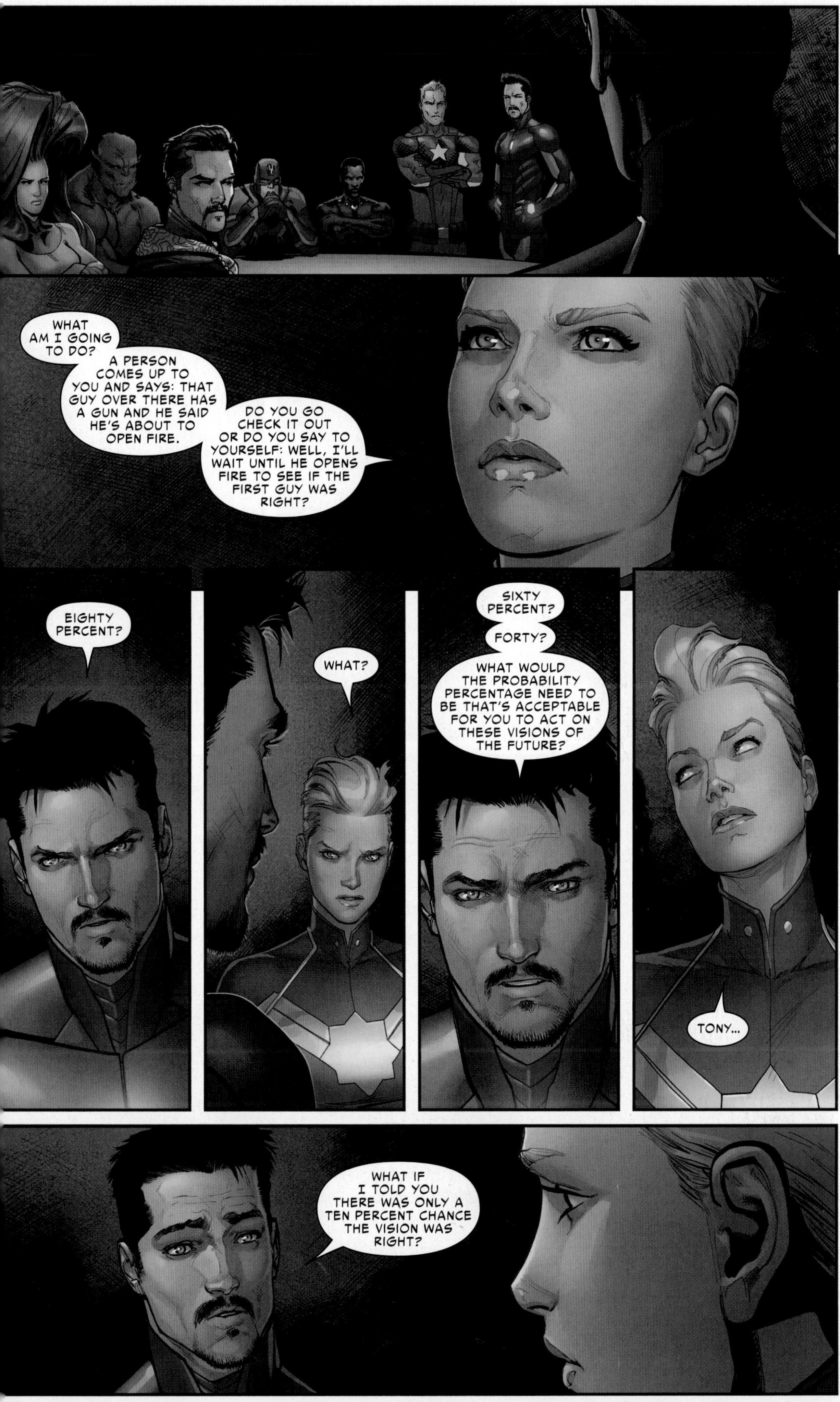

WHAT AM I GOING TO DO?
A PERSON COMES UP TO YOU AND SAYS: THAT GUY OVER THERE HAS A GUN AND HE SAID HE'S ABOUT TO OPEN FIRE.
DO YOU GO CHECK IT OUT OR DO YOU SAY TO YOURSELF: WELL, I'LL WAIT UNTIL HE OPENS FIRE TO SEE IF THE FIRST GUY WAS RIGHT?
EIGHTY PERCENT?
WHAT?
SIXTY PERCENT?
FORTY?
WHAT WOULD THE PROBABILITY PERCENTAGE NEED TO BE THAT'S ACCEPTABLE FOR YOU TO ACT ON THESE VISIONS OF THE FUTURE?
TONY...
WHAT IF I TOLD YOU THERE WAS ONLY A TEN PERCENT CHANCE THE VISION WAS RIGHT?

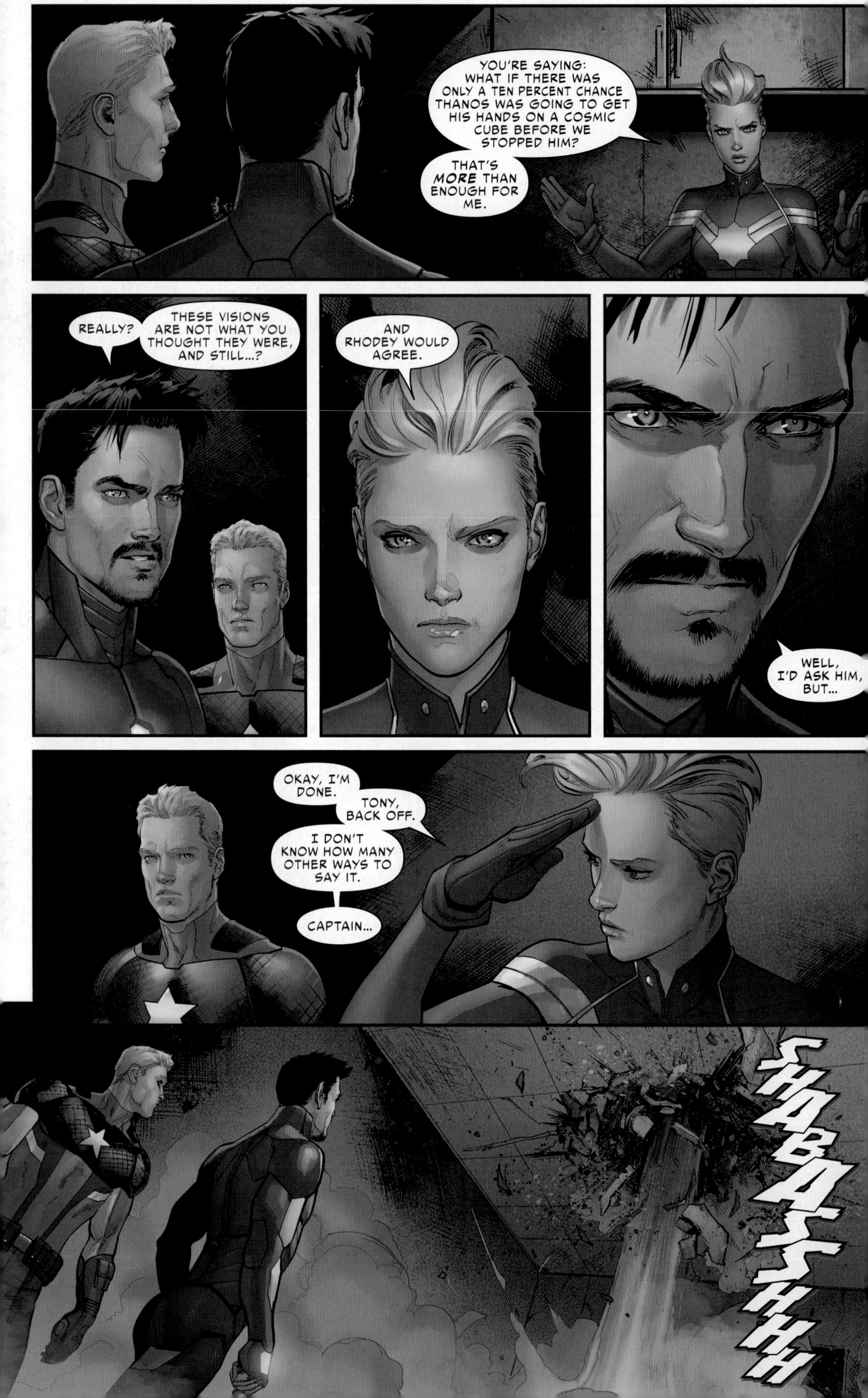
YOU'RE SAYING: WHAT IF THERE WAS ONLY A TEN PERCENT CHANCE THANOS WAS GOING TO GET HIS HANDS ON A COSMIC CUBE BEFORE WE STOPPED HIM?
THAT'S *MORE* THAN ENOUGH FOR ME.
REALLY?
THESE VISIONS ARE NOT WHAT YOU THOUGHT THEY WERE, AND STILL...?
AND RHODEY WOULD AGREE.
WELL, I'D ASK HIM, BUT...
OKAY, I'M DONE.
TONY, BACK OFF.
I DON'T KNOW HOW MANY OTHER WAYS TO SAY IT.
CAPTAIN...
SHABASSHHH

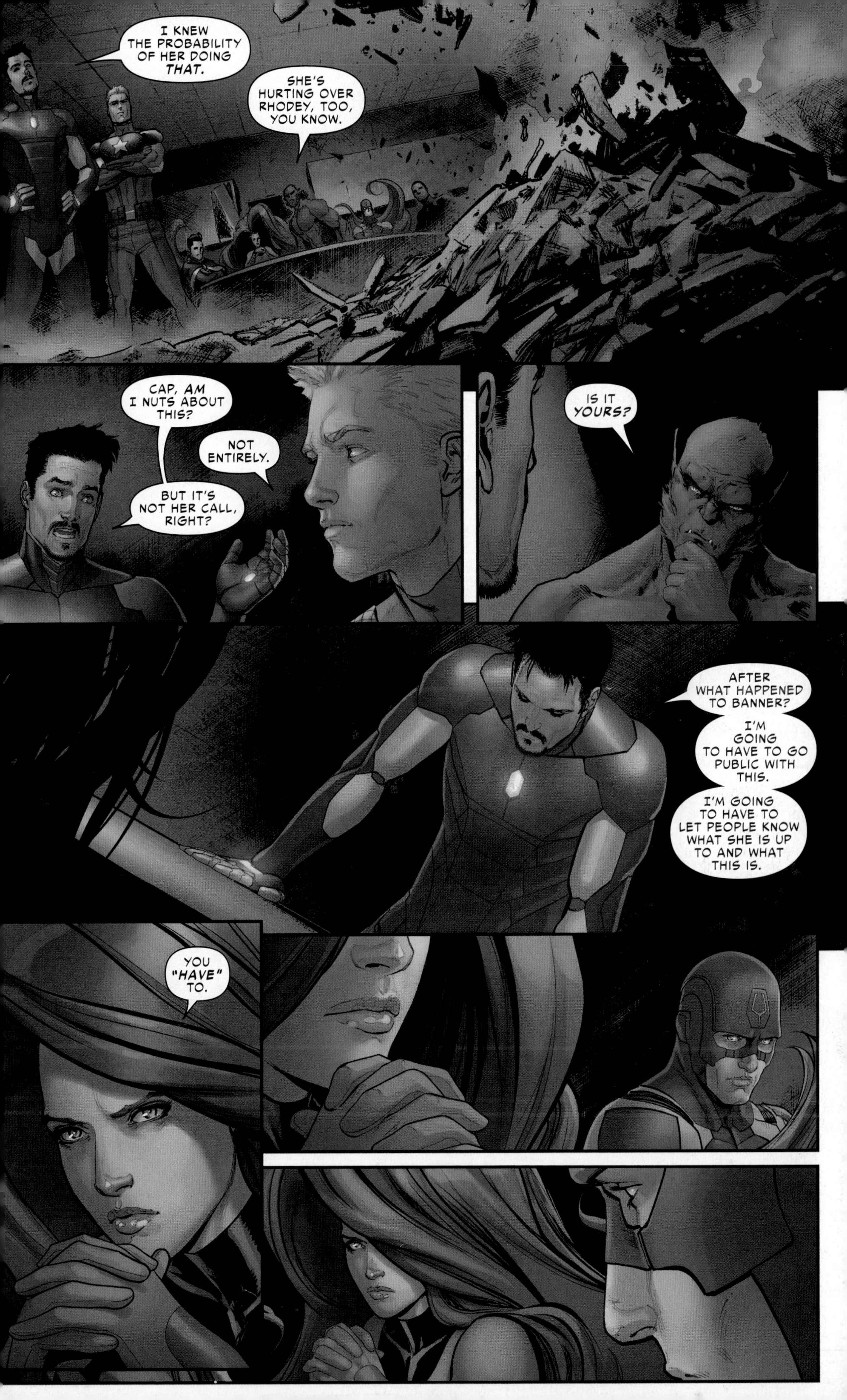
I KNEW THE PROBABILITY OF HER DOING *THAT.*
SHE'S HURTING OVER RHODEY, TOO, YOU KNOW.
CAP, *AM* I NUTS ABOUT THIS?
NOT ENTIRELY.
BUT IT'S NOT HER CALL, RIGHT?
IS IT *YOURS?*
AFTER WHAT HAPPENED TO BANNER?
I'M GOING TO HAVE TO GO PUBLIC WITH THIS.
I'M GOING TO HAVE TO LET PEOPLE KNOW WHAT SHE IS UP TO AND WHAT THIS IS.
YOU *"HAVE"* TO.

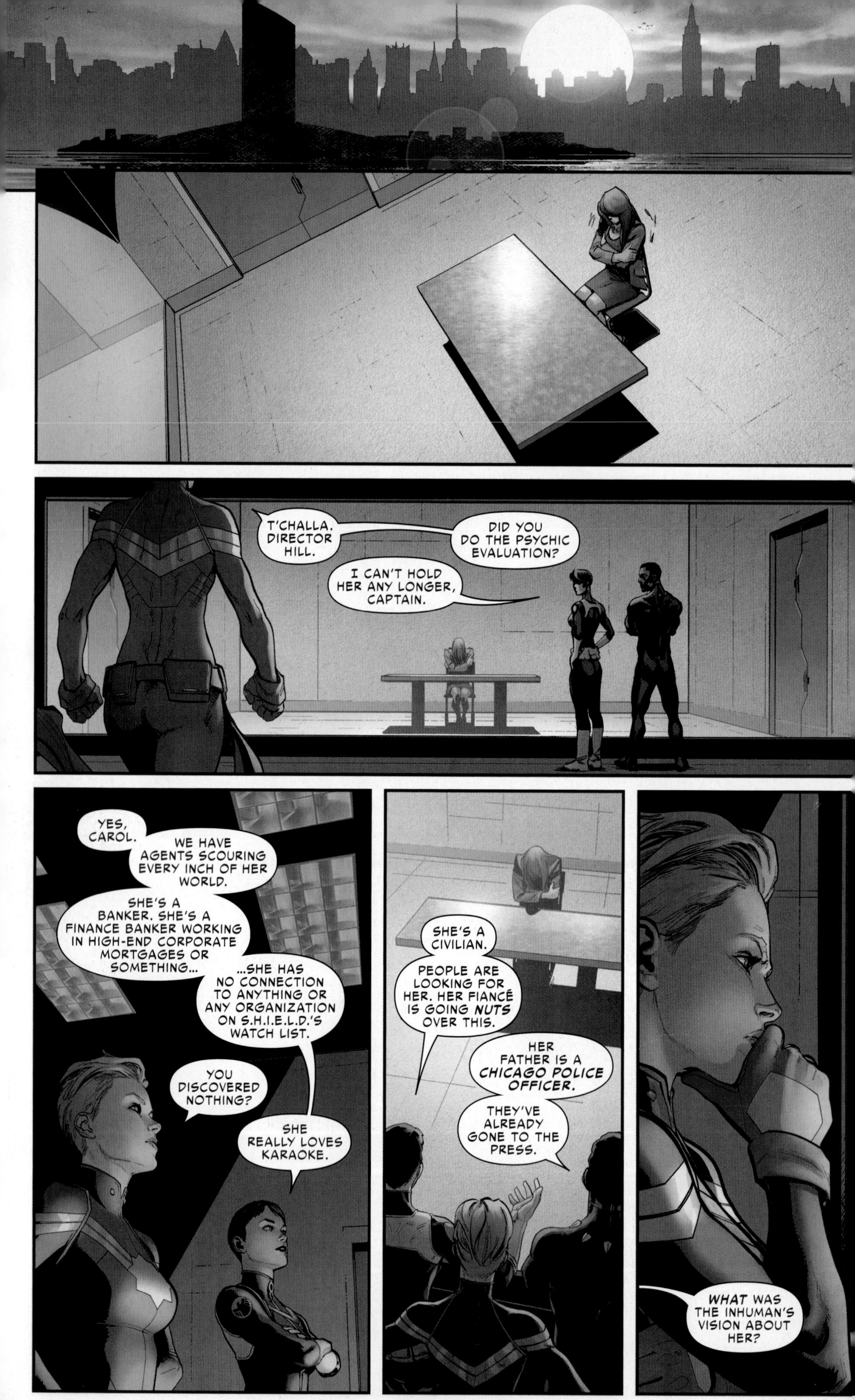
T'CHALLA. DIRECTOR HILL.
DID YOU DO THE PSYCHIC EVALUATION?
I CAN'T HOLD HER ANY LONGER, CAPTAIN.
YES, CAROL.
WE HAVE AGENTS SCOURING EVERY INCH OF HER WORLD.
SHE'S A BANKER. SHE'S A FINANCE BANKER WORKING IN HIGH-END CORPORATE MORTGAGES OR SOMETHING...
...SHE HAS NO CONNECTION TO ANYTHING OR ANY ORGANIZATION ON S.H.I.E.L.D.'S WATCH LIST.
YOU DISCOVERED NOTHING?
SHE REALLY LOVES KARAOKE.
SHE'S A CIVILIAN.
PEOPLE ARE LOOKING FOR HER. HER FIANCÉ IS GOING *NUTS* OVER THIS.
HER FATHER IS A *CHICAGO POLICE OFFICER.*
THEY'VE ALREADY GONE TO THE PRESS.
WHAT WAS THE INHUMAN'S VISION ABOUT HER?

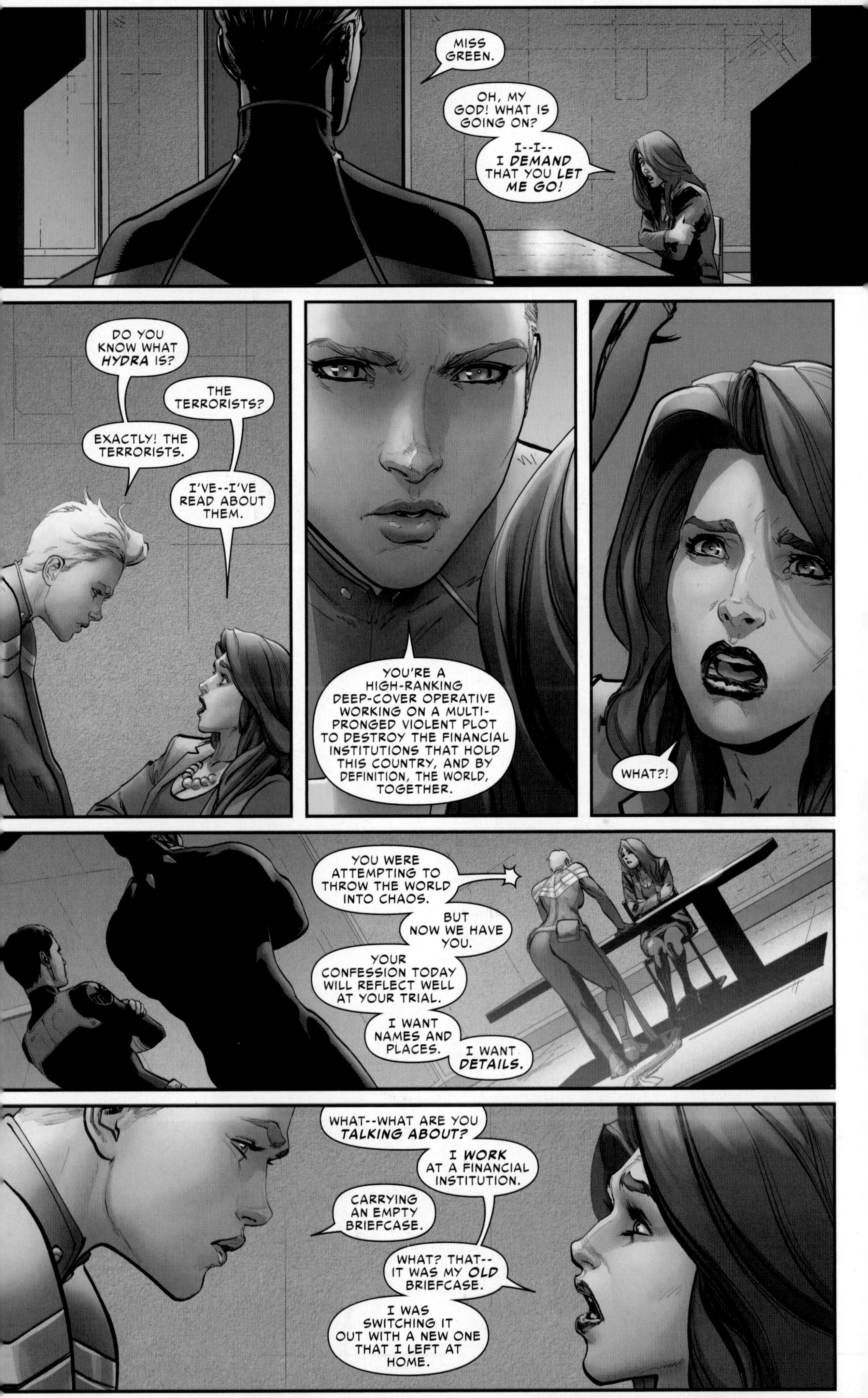
MISS GREEN.
OH, MY GOD! WHAT IS GOING ON?
I--I-- I DEMAND THAT YOU LET ME GO!
DO YOU KNOW WHAT HYDRA IS?
THE TERRORISTS?
EXACTLY! THE TERRORISTS.
I'VE--I'VE READ ABOUT THEM.
YOU'RE A HIGH-RANKING DEEP-COVER OPERATIVE WORKING ON A MULTI-PRONGED VIOLENT PLOT TO DESTROY THE FINANCIAL INSTITUTIONS THAT HOLD THIS COUNTRY, AND BY DEFINITION, THE WORLD, TOGETHER.
WHAT?!
YOU WERE ATTEMPTING TO THROW THE WORLD INTO CHAOS.
BUT NOW WE HAVE YOU.
YOUR CONFESSION TODAY WILL REFLECT WELL AT YOUR TRIAL.
I WANT NAMES AND PLACES.
I WANT DETAILS.
WHAT--WHAT ARE YOU TALKING ABOUT?
I WORK AT A FINANCIAL INSTITUTION.
CARRYING AN EMPTY BRIEFCASE.
WHAT? THAT-- IT WAS MY OLD BRIEFCASE.
I WAS SWITCHING IT OUT WITH A NEW ONE THAT I LEFT AT HOME.

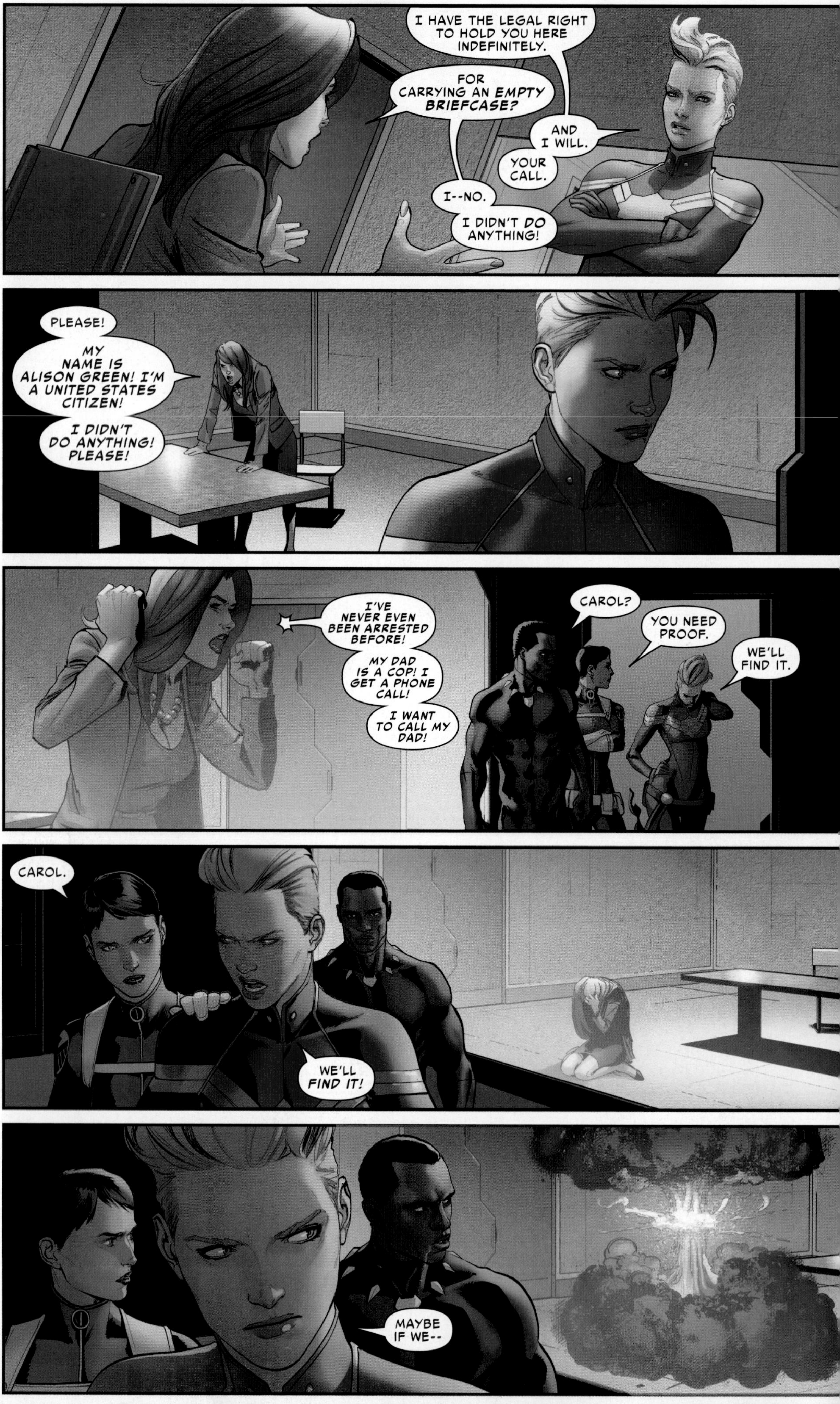

I HAVE THE LEGAL RIGHT TO HOLD YOU HERE INDEFINITELY.
FOR CARRYING AN EMPTY BRIEFCASE?
AND I WILL.
YOUR CALL.
I--NO.
I DIDN'T DO ANYTHING!
PLEASE!
MY NAME IS ALISON GREEN! I'M A UNITED STATES CITIZEN!
I DIDN'T DO ANYTHING! PLEASE!
I'VE NEVER EVEN BEEN ARRESTED BEFORE!
MY DAD IS A COP! I GET A PHONE CALL!
I WANT TO CALL MY DAD!
CAROL?
YOU NEED PROOF.
WE'LL FIND IT.
CAROL.
WE'LL FIND IT!
MAYBE IF WE--

UH-OH.

BRIMSTONE SMOKE.

IT WAS NIGHTCRAWLER.

THE X-MAN?

HE TELEPORTED HER OUT OF-- DAMN IT, TONY!

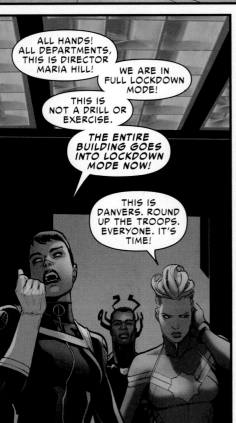

ALL HANDS! ALL DEPARTMENTS, THIS IS DIRECTOR MARIA HILL!

WE ARE IN FULL LOCKDOWN MODE!

THIS IS NOT A DRILL OR EXERCISE.

THE ENTIRE BUILDING GOES INTO LOCKDOWN MODE NOW!

THIS IS DANVERS. ROUND UP THE TROOPS. EVERYONE. IT'S TIME!

I'M ARRESTING TONY STARK.

YOU'LL NEED TO FIND HIM FIRST.

UM...

...NO, YOU WON'T.

HE'S HERE?

ROOFTOP.

WELL, WE WERE READY FOR THIS.

NOT FOR THIS.

TONY, YOU %¢#&! THIS IS NOT HAPPENING!

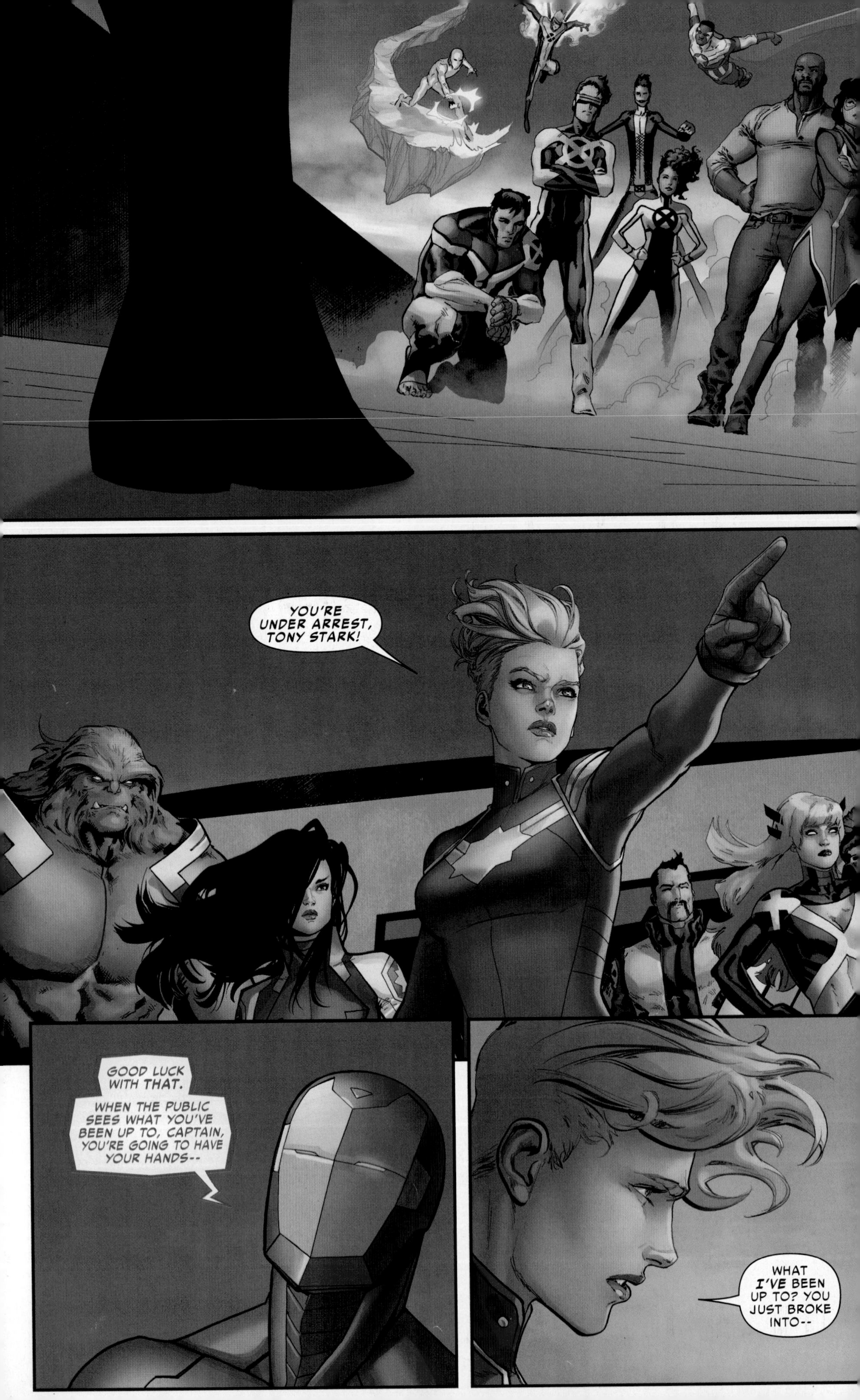
YOU'RE UNDER ARREST, TONY STARK!
GOOD LUCK WITH THAT.
WHEN THE PUBLIC SEES WHAT YOU'VE BEEN UP TO, CAPTAIN, YOU'RE GOING TO HAVE YOUR HANDS--
WHAT I'VE BEEN UP TO? YOU JUST BROKE INTO--

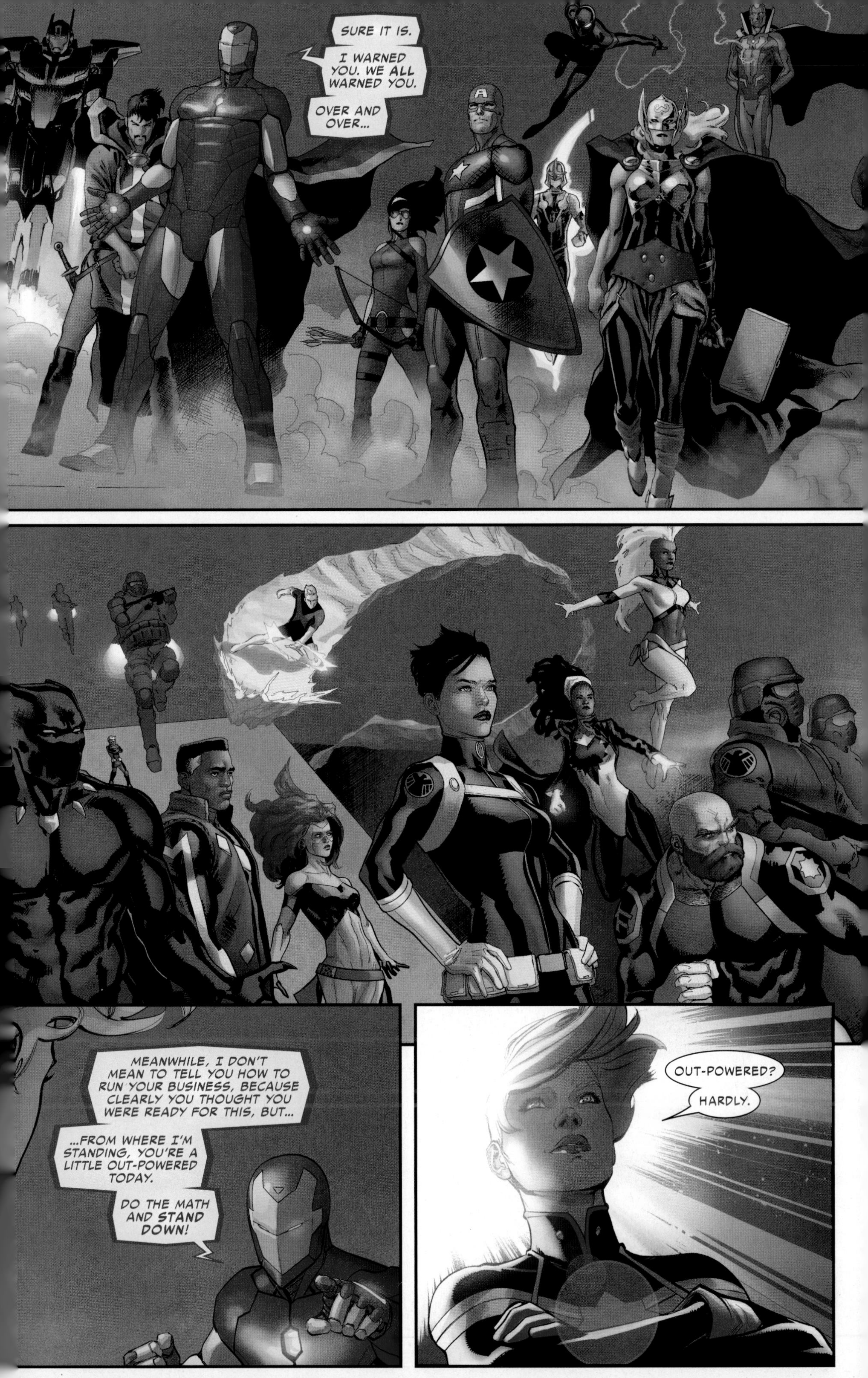
SURE IT IS.
I WARNED YOU. WE ALL WARNED YOU.
OVER AND OVER...
MEANWHILE, I DON'T MEAN TO TELL YOU HOW TO RUN YOUR BUSINESS, BECAUSE CLEARLY YOU THOUGHT YOU WERE READY FOR THIS, BUT...
...FROM WHERE I'M STANDING, YOU'RE A LITTLE OUT-POWERED TODAY.
DO THE MATH AND STAND DOWN!
OUT-POWERED?
HARDLY.

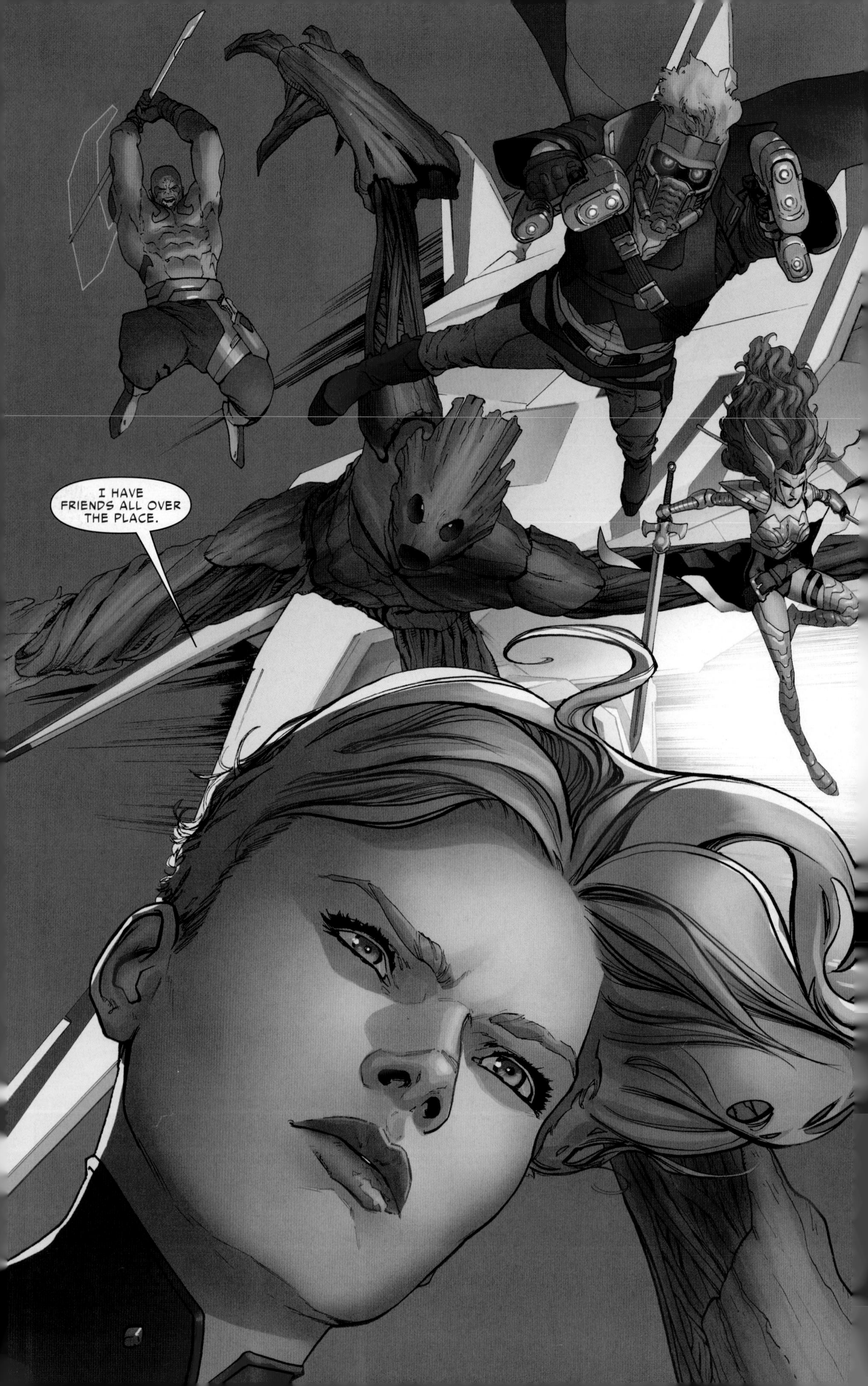
I HAVE FRIENDS ALL OVER THE PLACE.

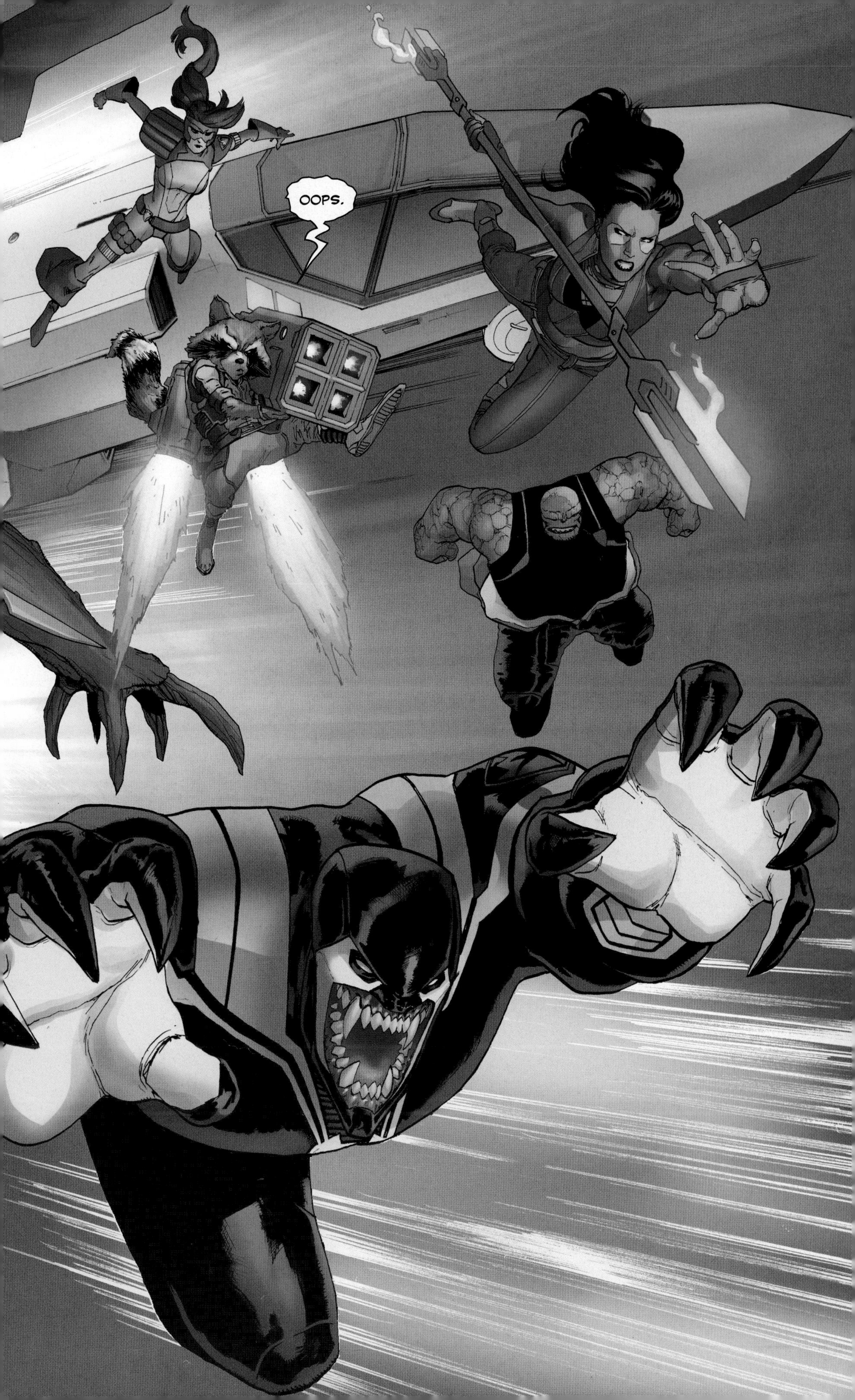
OOPS.

CIVIL WAR II #5

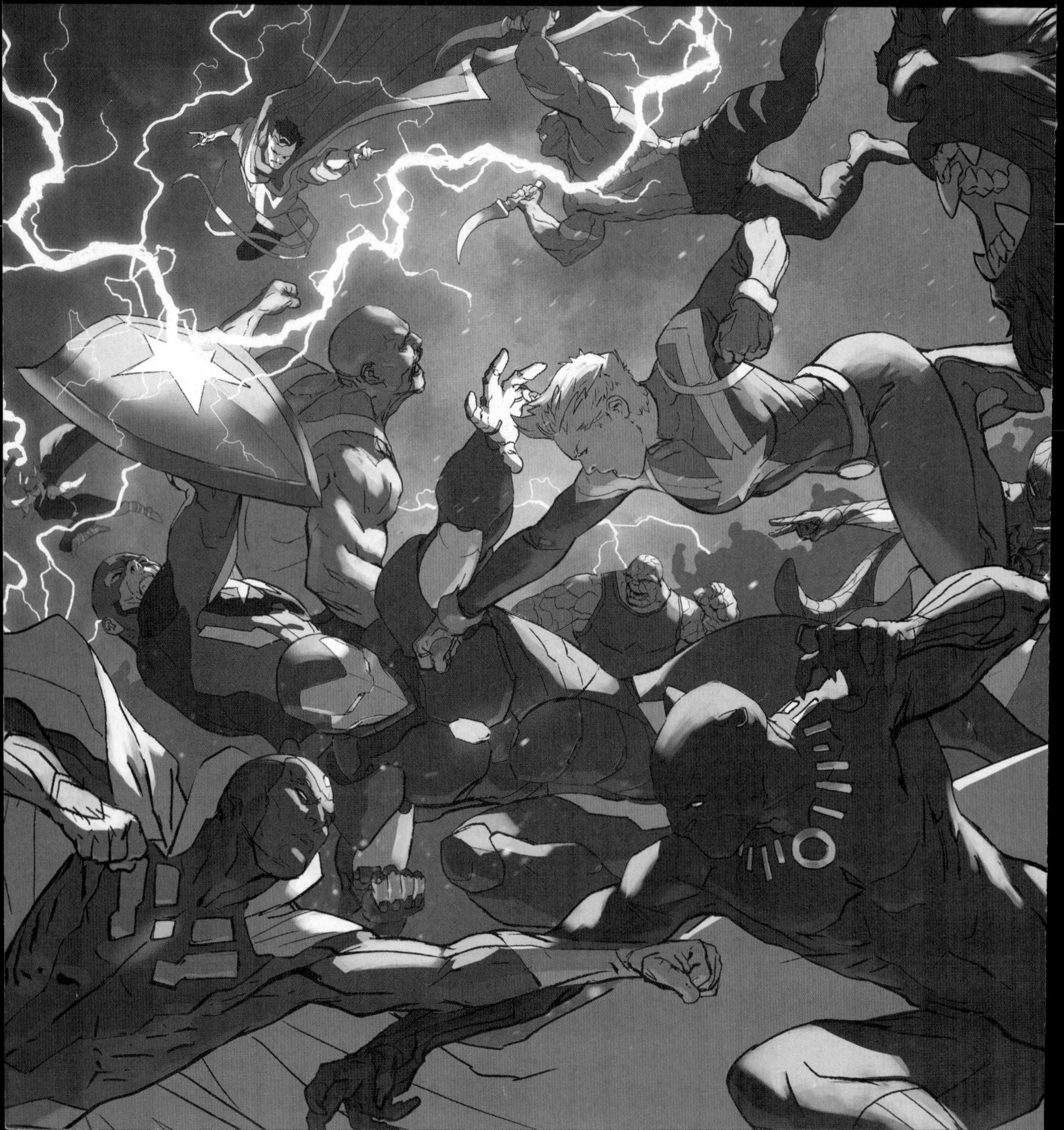

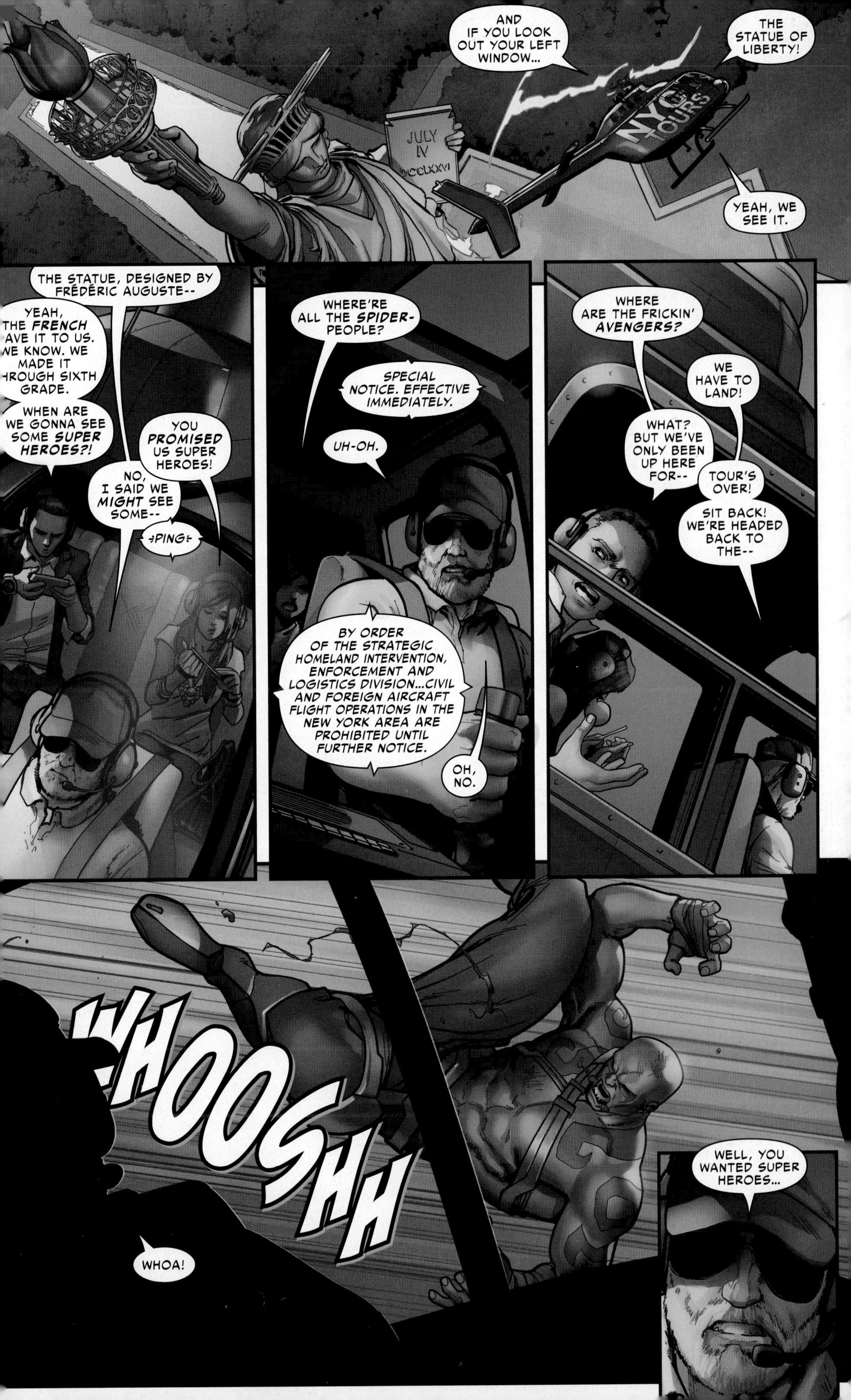
AND IF YOU LOOK OUT YOUR LEFT WINDOW...
THE STATUE OF LIBERTY!
YEAH, WE SEE IT.
NYC TOURS
JULY IV
THE STATUE, DESIGNED BY FRÉDÉRIC AUGUSTE--
YEAH, THE FRENCH AVE IT TO US. WE KNOW. WE MADE IT HROUGH SIXTH GRADE.
WHEN ARE WE GONNA SEE SOME SUPER HEROES?!
YOU PROMISED US SUPER HEROES!
NO, I SAID WE MIGHT SEE SOME--
PING
WHERE'RE ALL THE SPIDER-PEOPLE?
SPECIAL NOTICE. EFFECTIVE IMMEDIATELY.
UH-OH.
BY ORDER OF THE STRATEGIC HOMELAND INTERVENTION, ENFORCEMENT AND LOGISTICS DIVISION...CIVIL AND FOREIGN AIRCRAFT FLIGHT OPERATIONS IN THE NEW YORK AREA ARE PROHIBITED UNTIL FURTHER NOTICE.
OH, NO.
WHERE ARE THE FRICKIN' AVENGERS?
WE HAVE TO LAND!
WHAT? BUT WE'VE ONLY BEEN UP HERE FOR--
TOUR'S OVER!
SIT BACK! WE'RE HEADED BACK TO THE--
WHOOSHH
WHOA!
WELL, YOU WANTED SUPER HEROES...

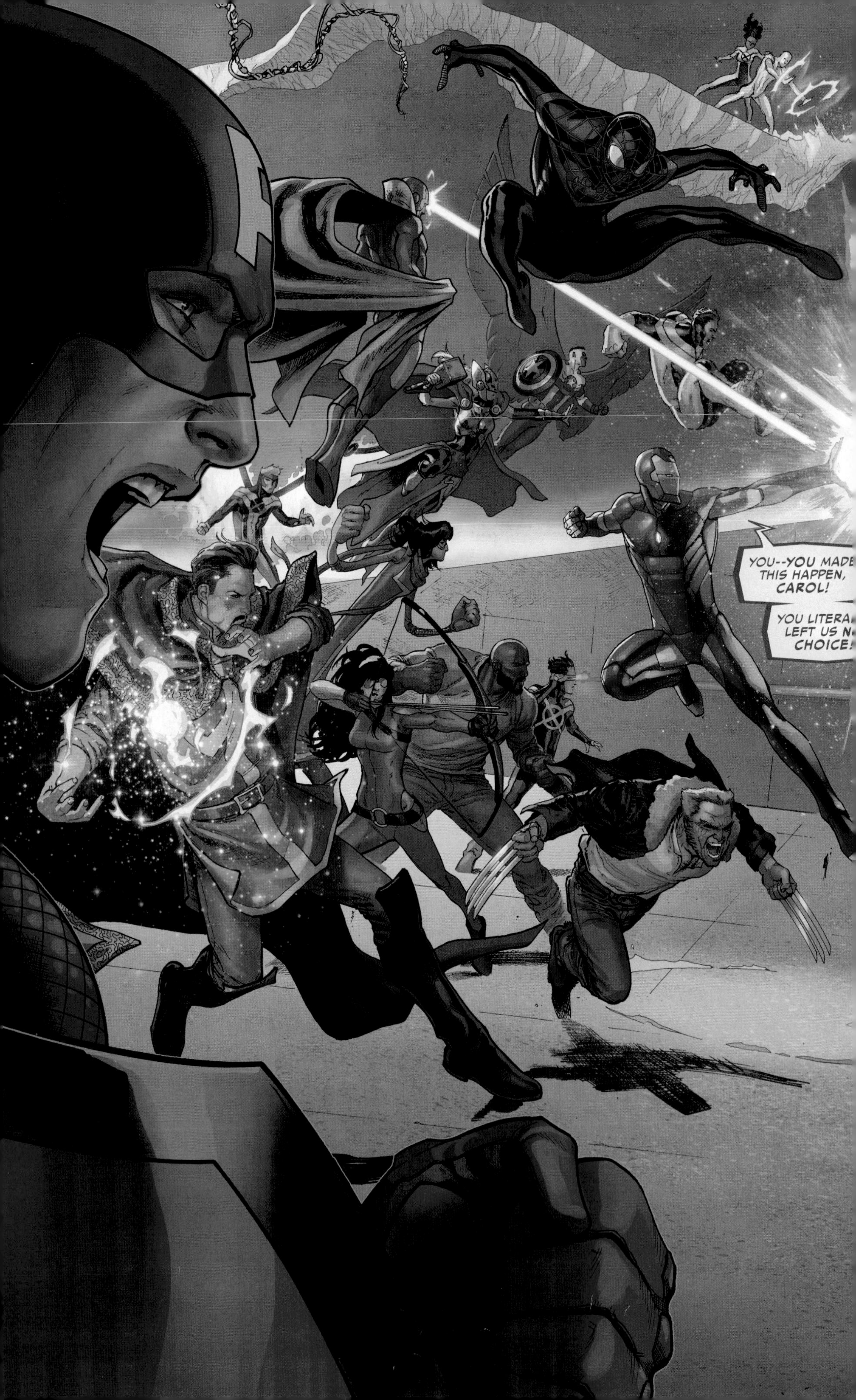
YOU--YOU MADE THIS HAPPEN, CAROL!
YOU LITERA LEFT US N CHOICE!

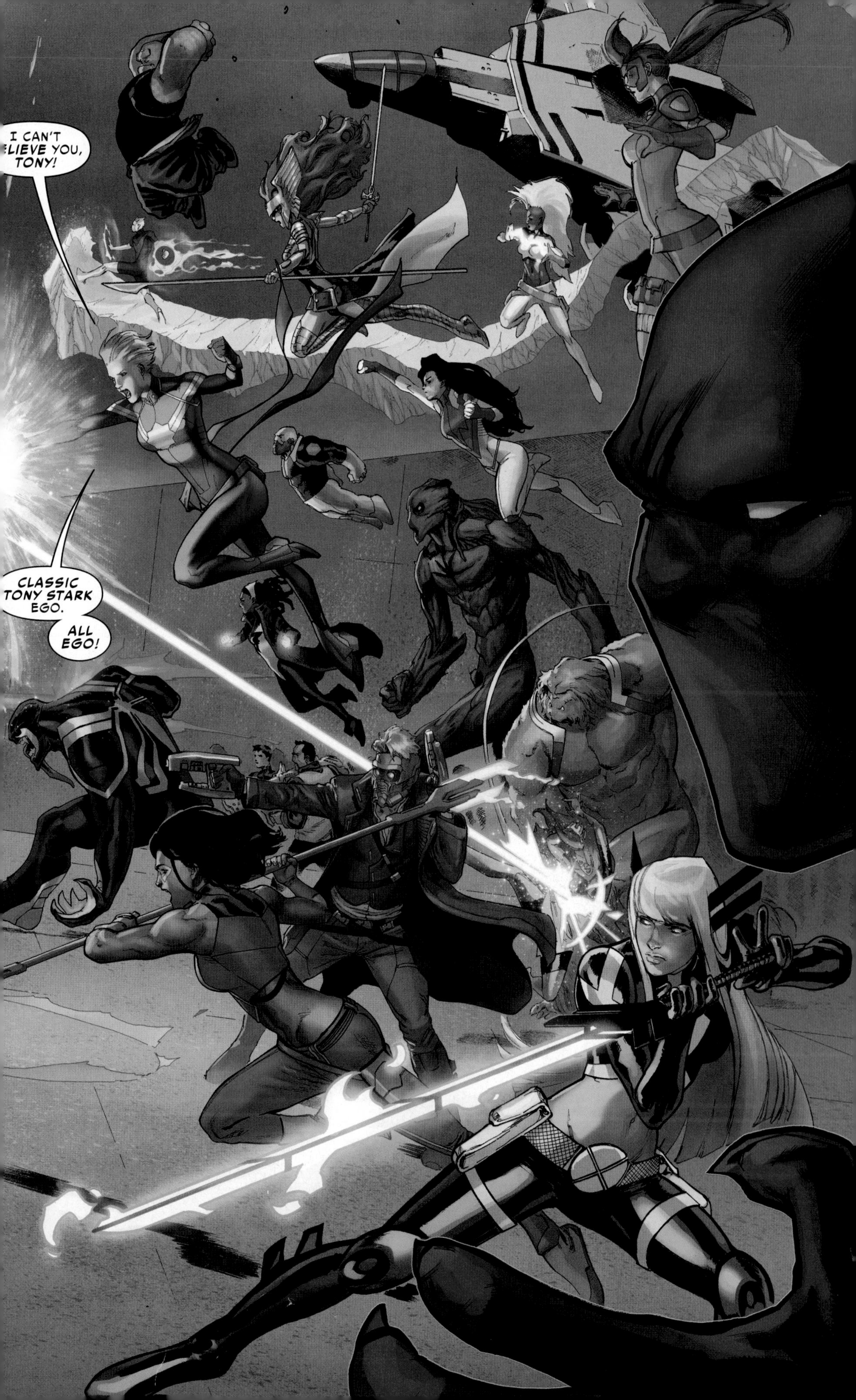
I CAN'T ELIEVE YOU, TONY!
CLASSIC TONY STARK EGO.
ALL EGO!

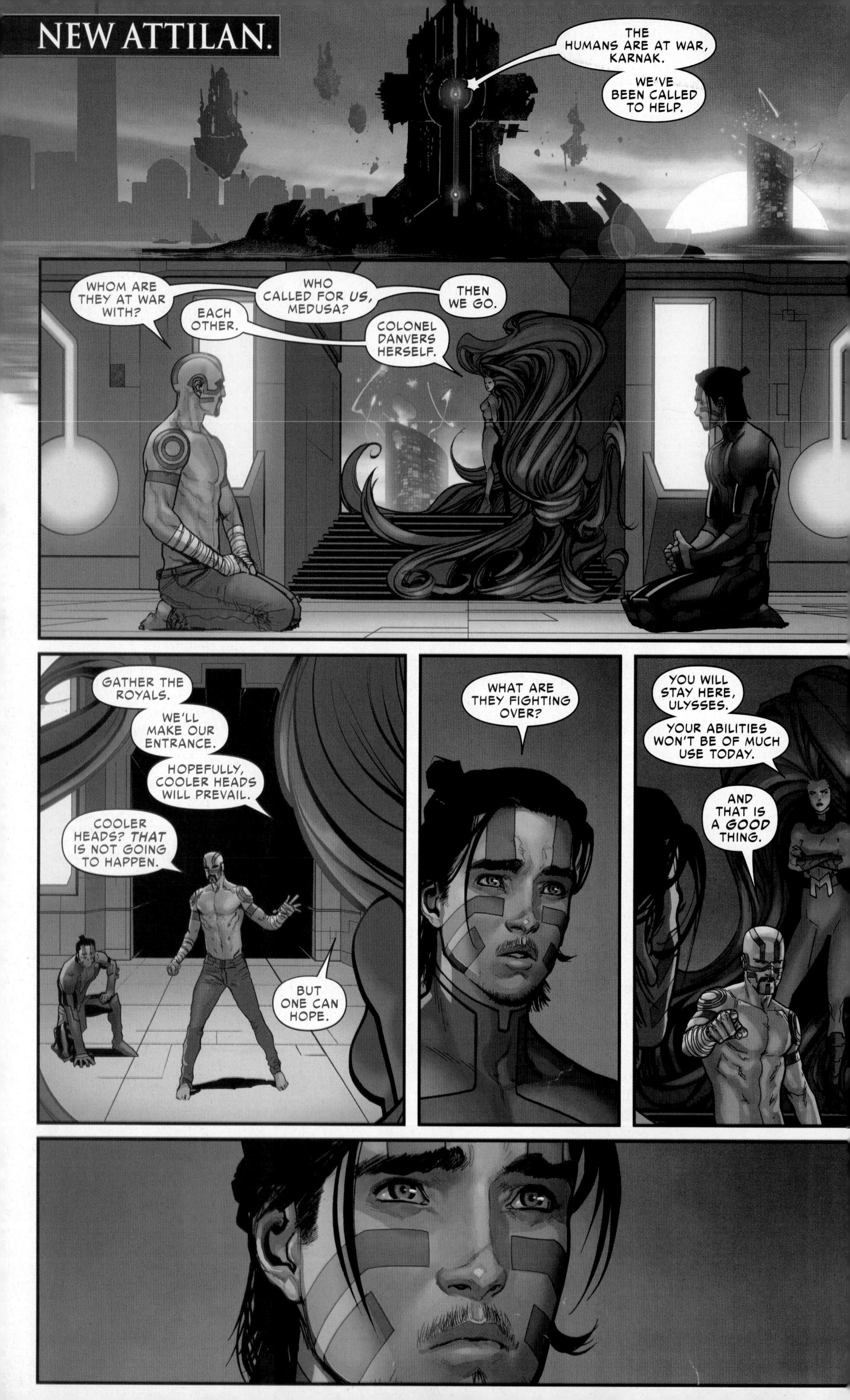
NEW ATTILAN.
THE HUMANS ARE AT WAR, KARNAK.
WE'VE BEEN CALLED TO HELP.
WHOM ARE THEY AT WAR WITH?
EACH OTHER.
WHO CALLED FOR *US*, MEDUSA?
COLONEL DANVERS HERSELF.
THEN WE GO.
GATHER THE ROYALS.
WE'LL MAKE OUR ENTRANCE.
HOPEFULLY, COOLER HEADS WILL PREVAIL.
COOLER HEADS? *THAT* IS NOT GOING TO HAPPEN.
BUT ONE CAN HOPE.
WHAT ARE THEY FIGHTING OVER?
YOU WILL STAY HERE, ULYSSES.
YOUR ABILITIES WON'T BE OF MUCH USE TODAY.
AND THAT IS A *GOOD* THING.

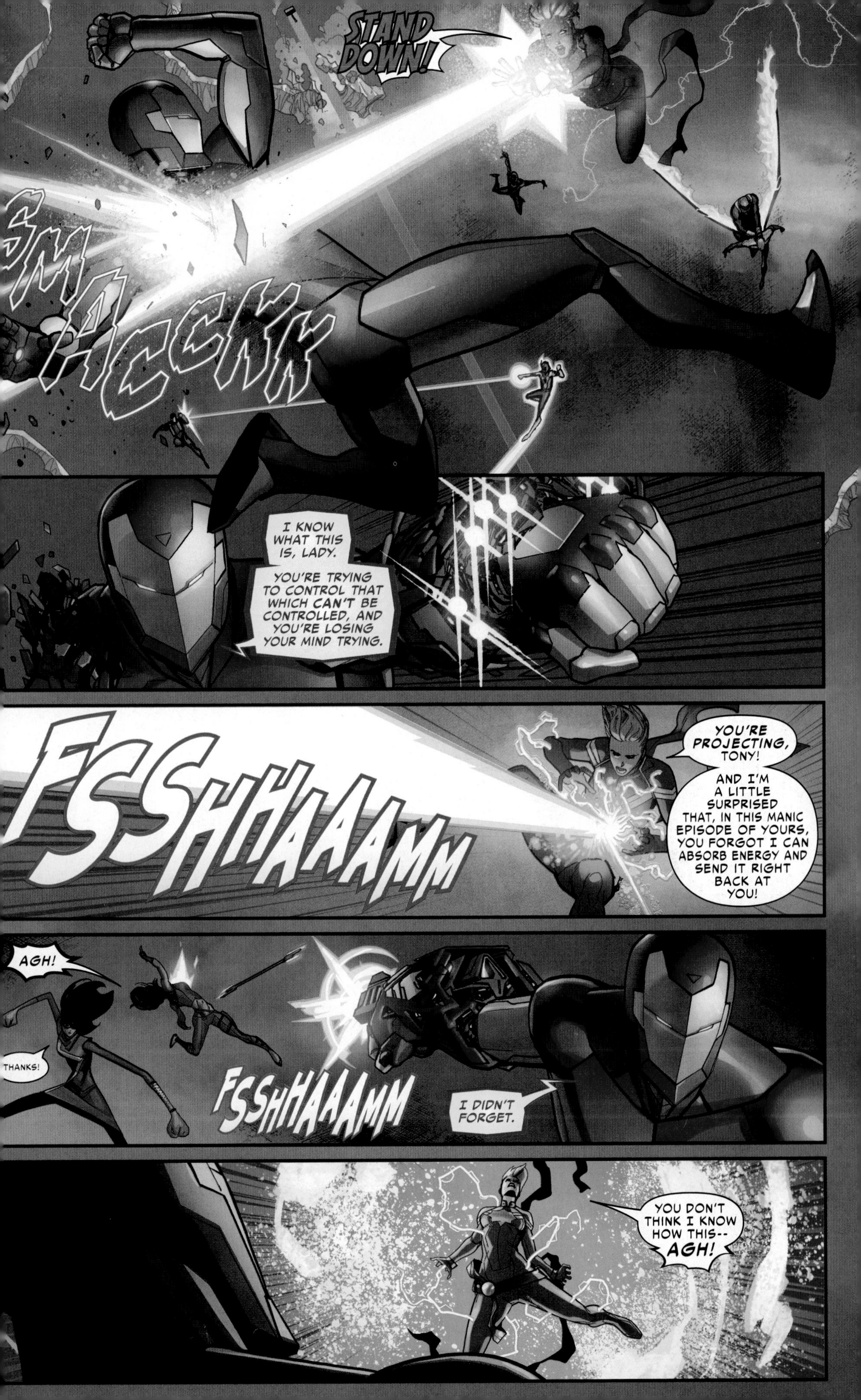
STAND DOWN!
SMACCKK
I KNOW WHAT THIS IS, LADY.
YOU'RE TRYING TO CONTROL THAT WHICH CAN'T BE CONTROLLED, AND YOU'RE LOSING YOUR MIND TRYING.
FSSHHAAAMM
YOU'RE PROJECTING, TONY!
AND I'M A LITTLE SURPRISED THAT, IN THIS MANIC EPISODE OF YOURS, YOU FORGOT I CAN ABSORB ENERGY AND SEND IT RIGHT BACK AT YOU!
AGH!
THANKS!
FSSHHAAAMM
I DIDN'T FORGET.
YOU DON'T THINK I KNOW HOW THIS-- AGH!

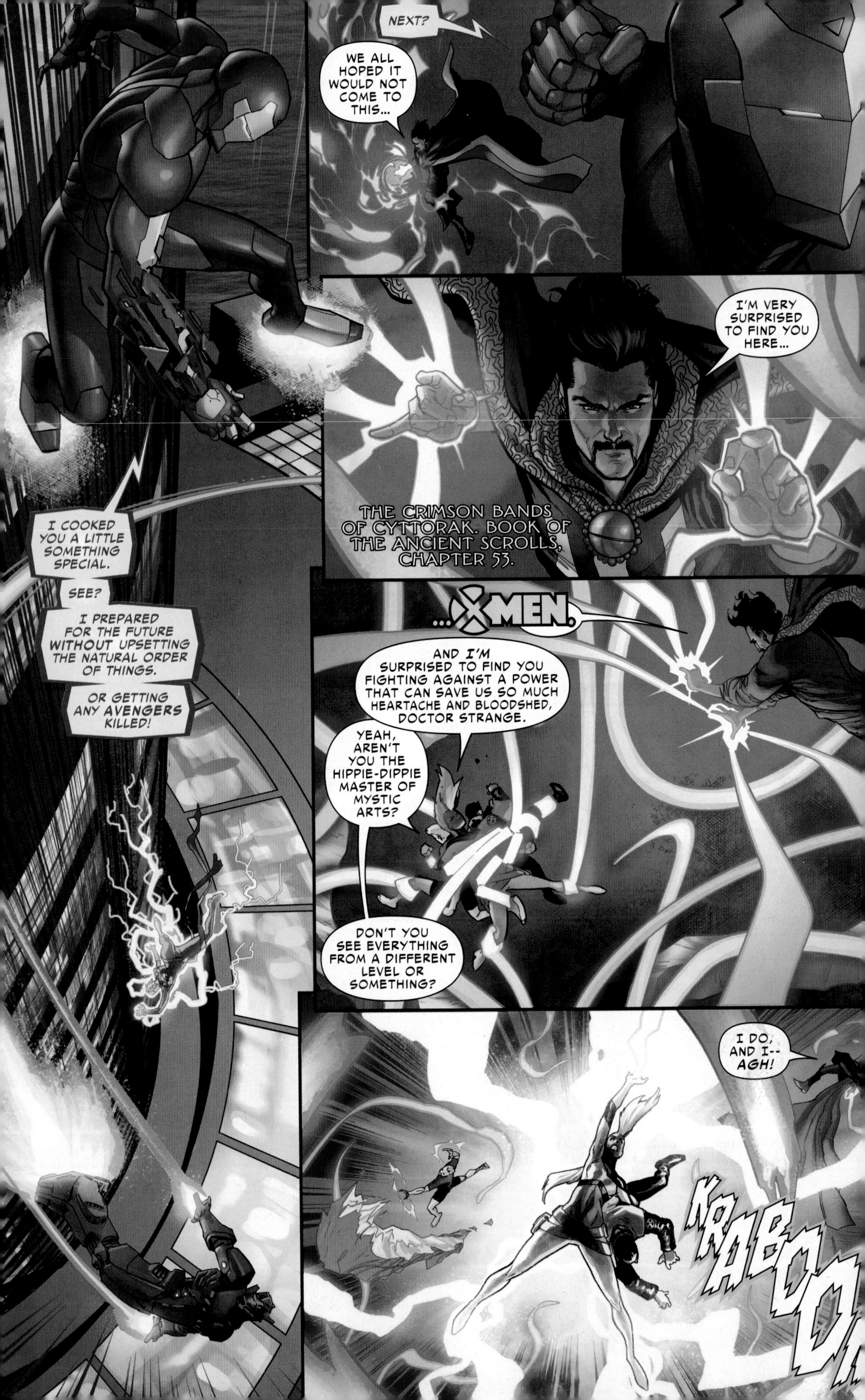

NEXT?
WE ALL HOPED IT WOULD NOT COME TO THIS...
I'M VERY SURPRISED TO FIND YOU HERE...
THE CRIMSON BANDS OF CYTTORAK. BOOK OF THE ANCIENT SCROLLS, CHAPTER 53.
I COOKED YOU A LITTLE SOMETHING SPECIAL.
SEE?
I PREPARED FOR THE FUTURE WITHOUT UPSETTING THE NATURAL ORDER OF THINGS.
OR GETTING ANY AVENGERS KILLED!
...X-MEN.
AND I'M SURPRISED TO FIND YOU FIGHTING AGAINST A POWER THAT CAN SAVE US SO MUCH HEARTACHE AND BLOODSHED, DOCTOR STRANGE.
YEAH, AREN'T YOU THE HIPPIE-DIPPIE MASTER OF MYSTIC ARTS?
DON'T YOU SEE EVERYTHING FROM A DIFFERENT LEVEL OR SOMETHING?
I DO, AND I-- AGH!
KRABOOM

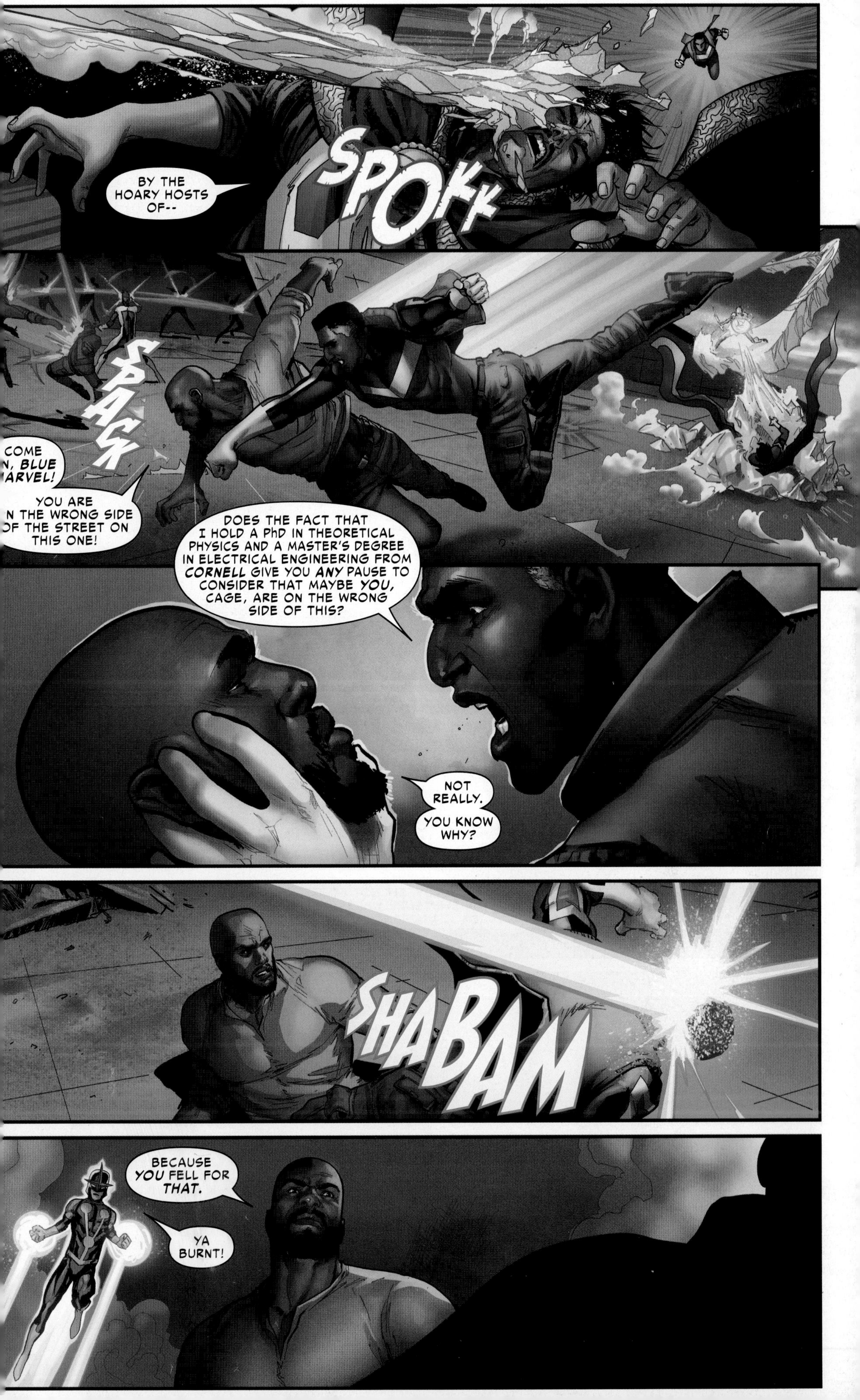
BY THE HOARY HOSTS OF--
SPOKK
SPACK
COME N, BLUE ARVEL!
YOU ARE N THE WRONG SIDE OF THE STREET ON THIS ONE!
DOES THE FACT THAT I HOLD A PhD IN THEORETICAL PHYSICS AND A MASTER'S DEGREE IN ELECTRICAL ENGINEERING FROM CORNELL GIVE YOU ANY PAUSE TO CONSIDER THAT MAYBE YOU, CAGE, ARE ON THE WRONG SIDE OF THIS?
NOT REALLY.
YOU KNOW WHY?
SHABAM
BECAUSE YOU FELL FOR THAT.
YA BURNT!

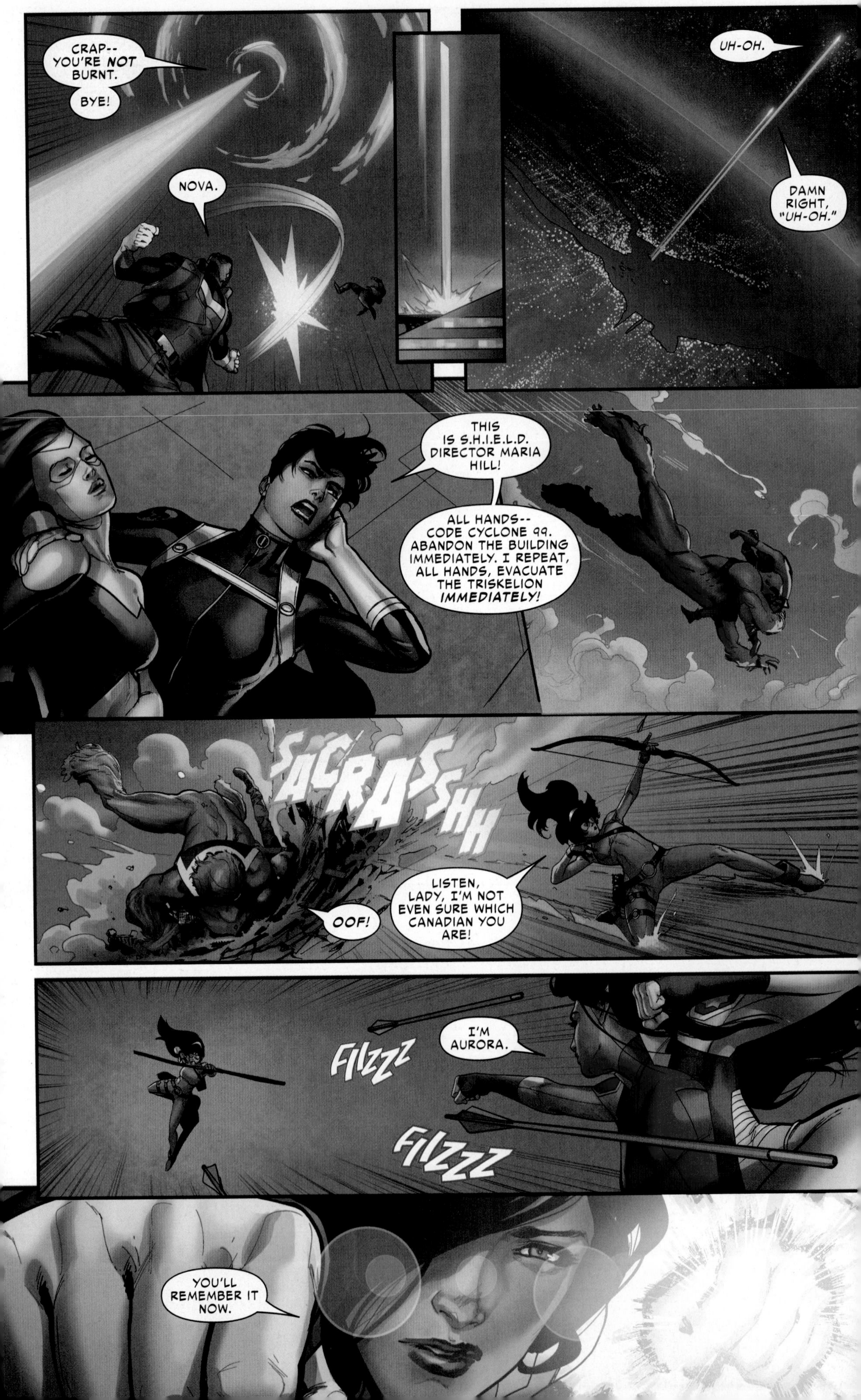
CRAP-- YOU'RE *NOT* BURNT.
BYE!
NOVA.
UH-OH.
DAMN RIGHT, "*UH-OH.*"
THIS IS S.H.I.E.L.D. DIRECTOR MARIA HILL!
ALL HANDS-- CODE CYCLONE 99. ABANDON THE BUILDING IMMEDIATELY. I REPEAT, ALL HANDS, EVACUATE THE TRISKELION *IMMEDIATELY!*
SACRASSHH
OOF!
LISTEN, LADY, I'M NOT EVEN SURE WHICH CANADIAN YOU ARE!
FIZZZ
I'M AURORA.
FIZZZZ
YOU'LL REMEMBER IT NOW.

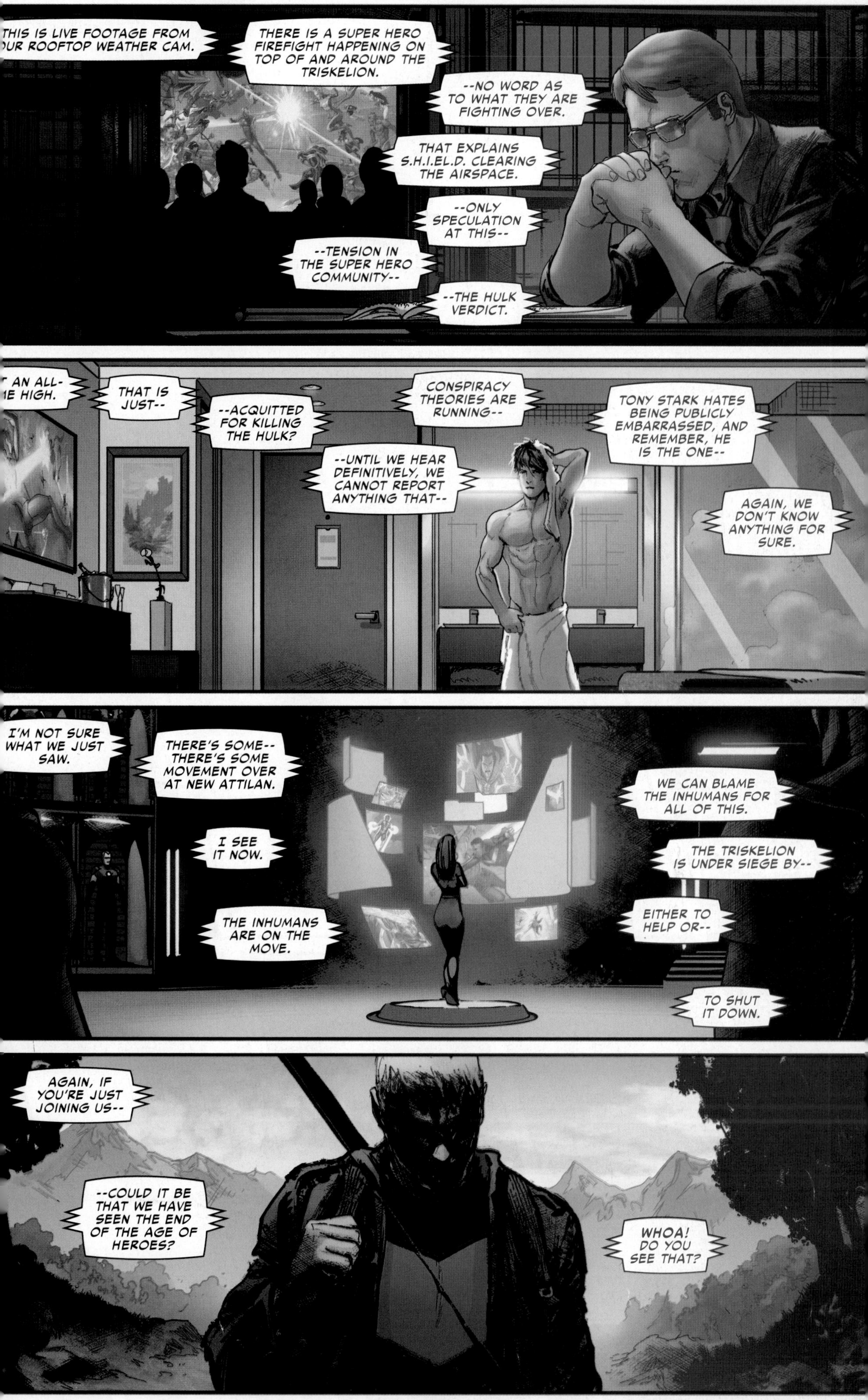
THIS IS LIVE FOOTAGE FROM OUR ROOFTOP WEATHER CAM.
THERE IS A SUPER HERO FIREFIGHT HAPPENING ON TOP OF AND AROUND THE TRISKELION.
--NO WORD AS TO WHAT THEY ARE FIGHTING OVER.
THAT EXPLAINS S.H.I.E.L.D. CLEARING THE AIRSPACE.
--ONLY SPECULATION AT THIS--
--TENSION IN THE SUPER HERO COMMUNITY--
--THE HULK VERDICT.
AN ALL-
HIGH.
THAT IS JUST--
--ACQUITTED FOR KILLING THE HULK?
CONSPIRACY THEORIES ARE RUNNING--
--UNTIL WE HEAR DEFINITIVELY, WE CANNOT REPORT ANYTHING THAT--
TONY STARK HATES BEING PUBLICLY EMBARRASSED, AND REMEMBER, HE IS THE ONE--
AGAIN, WE DON'T KNOW ANYTHING FOR SURE.
I'M NOT SURE WHAT WE JUST SAW.
THERE'S SOME-- THERE'S SOME MOVEMENT OVER AT NEW ATTILAN.
I SEE IT NOW.
THE INHUMANS ARE ON THE MOVE.
WE CAN BLAME THE INHUMANS FOR ALL OF THIS.
THE TRISKELION IS UNDER SIEGE BY--
EITHER TO HELP OR--
TO SHUT IT DOWN.
AGAIN, IF YOU'RE JUST JOINING US--
--COULD IT BE THAT WE HAVE SEEN THE END OF THE AGE OF HEROES?
WHOA! DO YOU SEE THAT?

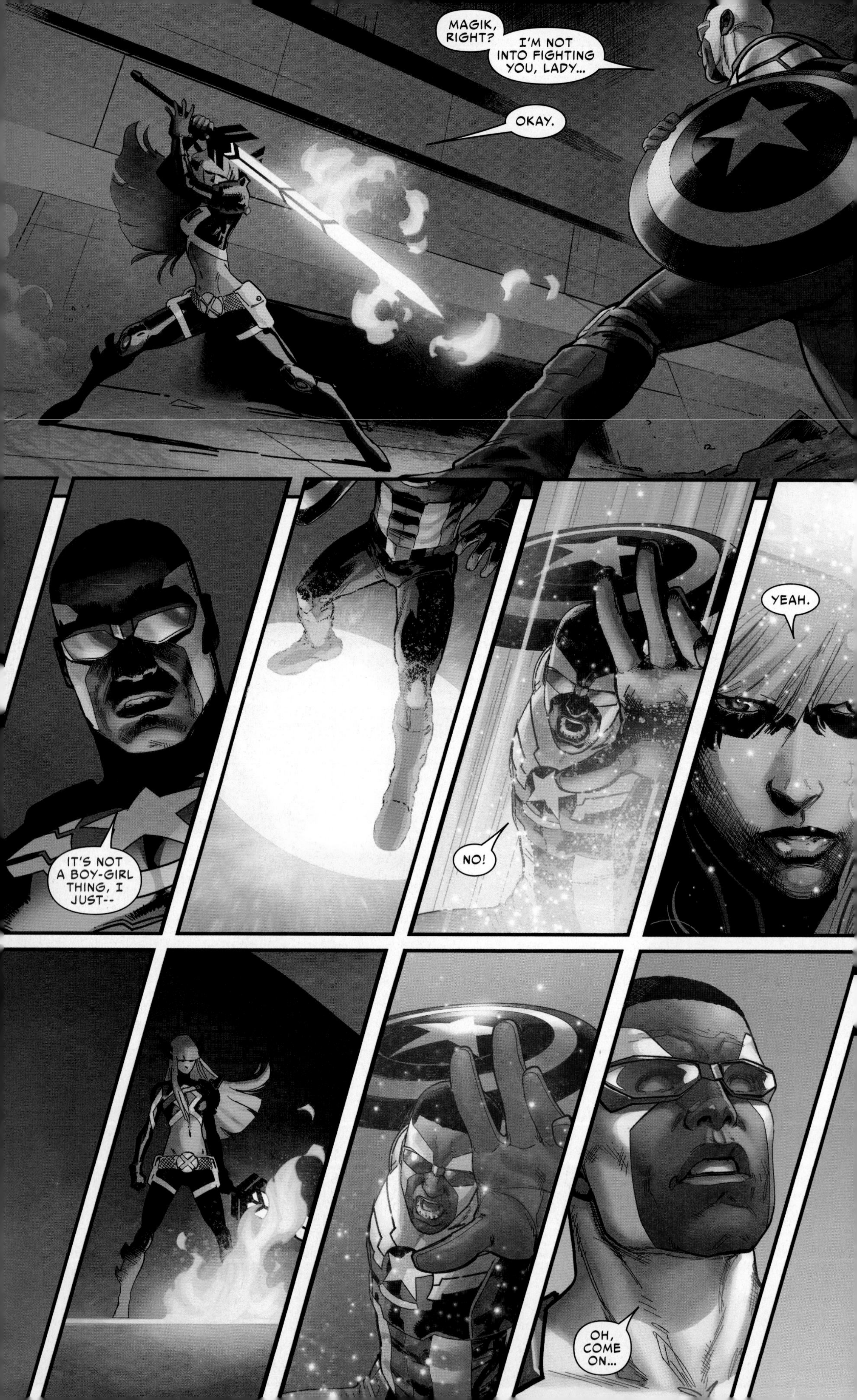
MAGIK, RIGHT?
I'M NOT INTO FIGHTING YOU, LADY...
OKAY.
IT'S NOT A BOY-GIRL THING, I JUST--
NO!
YEAH.
OH, COME ON...

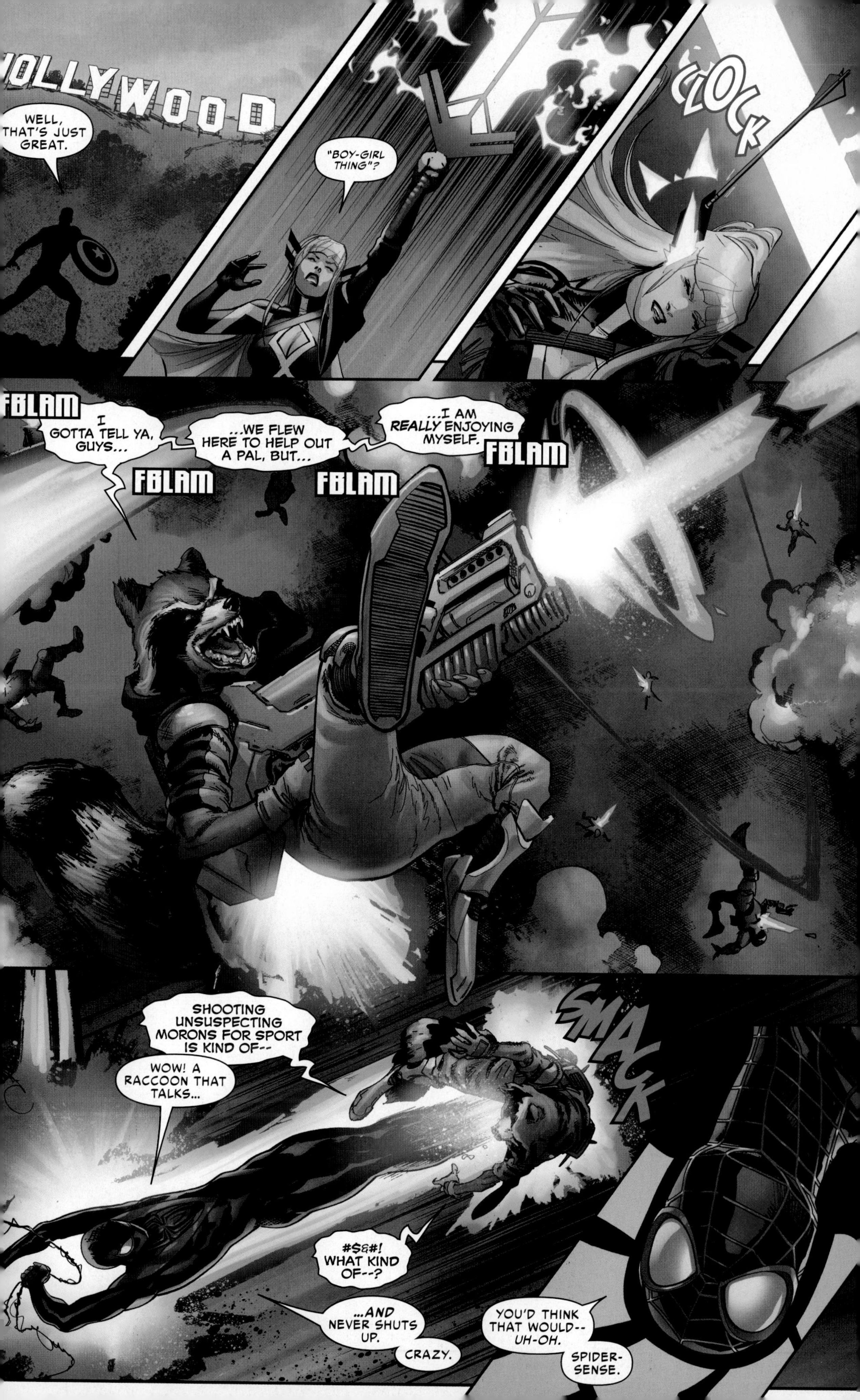

HOLLYWOOD
WELL, THAT'S JUST GREAT.
"BOY-GIRL THING"?
CLOCK
FBLAM
I GOTTA TELL YA, GUYS...
...WE FLEW HERE TO HELP OUT A PAL, BUT...
...I AM REALLY ENJOYING MYSELF.
FBLAM
FBLAM
FBLAM
SHOOTING UNSUSPECTING MORONS FOR SPORT IS KIND OF--
WOW! A RACCOON THAT TALKS...
SMACK
#$&#! WHAT KIND OF--?
...AND NEVER SHUTS UP.
CRAZY.
YOU'D THINK THAT WOULD-- UH-OH.
SPIDER-SENSE.

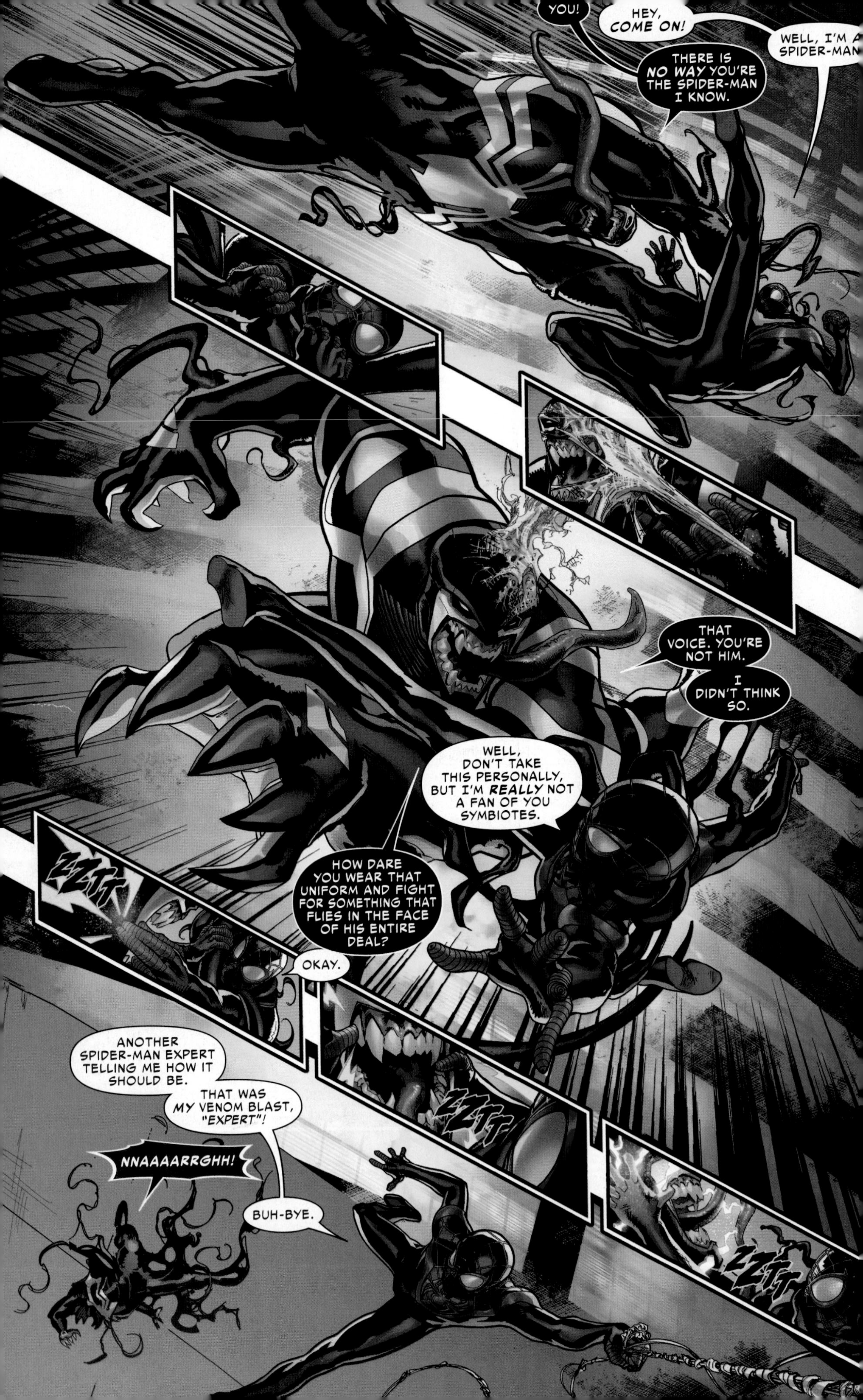
YOU!
HEY, COME ON!
THERE IS NO WAY YOU'RE THE SPIDER-MAN I KNOW.
WELL, I'M A SPIDER-MAN
THAT VOICE. YOU'RE NOT HIM.
I DIDN'T THINK SO.
WELL, DON'T TAKE THIS PERSONALLY, BUT I'M REALLY NOT A FAN OF YOU SYMBIOTES.
HOW DARE YOU WEAR THAT UNIFORM AND FIGHT FOR SOMETHING THAT FLIES IN THE FACE OF HIS ENTIRE DEAL?
ZZTT
OKAY.
ANOTHER SPIDER-MAN EXPERT TELLING ME HOW IT SHOULD BE.
ZZTT
THAT WAS MY VENOM BLAST, "EXPERT"!
NNAAAARRGHH!
BUH-BYE.
ZZTT

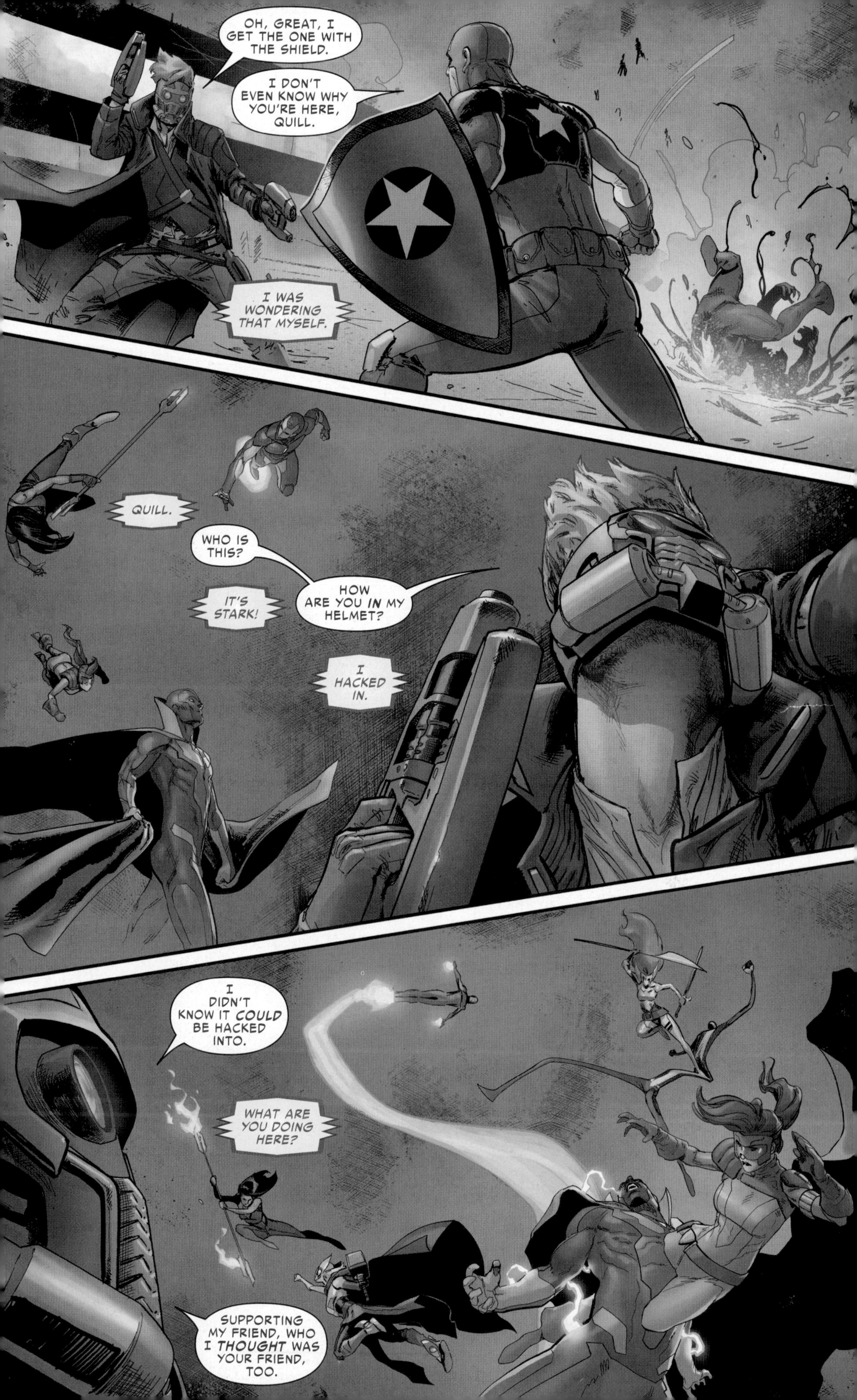
OH, GREAT, I GET THE ONE WITH THE SHIELD.
I DON'T EVEN KNOW WHY YOU'RE HERE, QUILL.
I WAS WONDERING THAT MYSELF.
QUILL.
WHO IS THIS?
HOW ARE YOU IN MY HELMET?
IT'S STARK!
I HACKED IN.
I DIDN'T KNOW IT COULD BE HACKED INTO.
WHAT ARE YOU DOING HERE?
SUPPORTING MY FRIEND, WHO I THOUGHT WAS YOUR FRIEND, TOO.

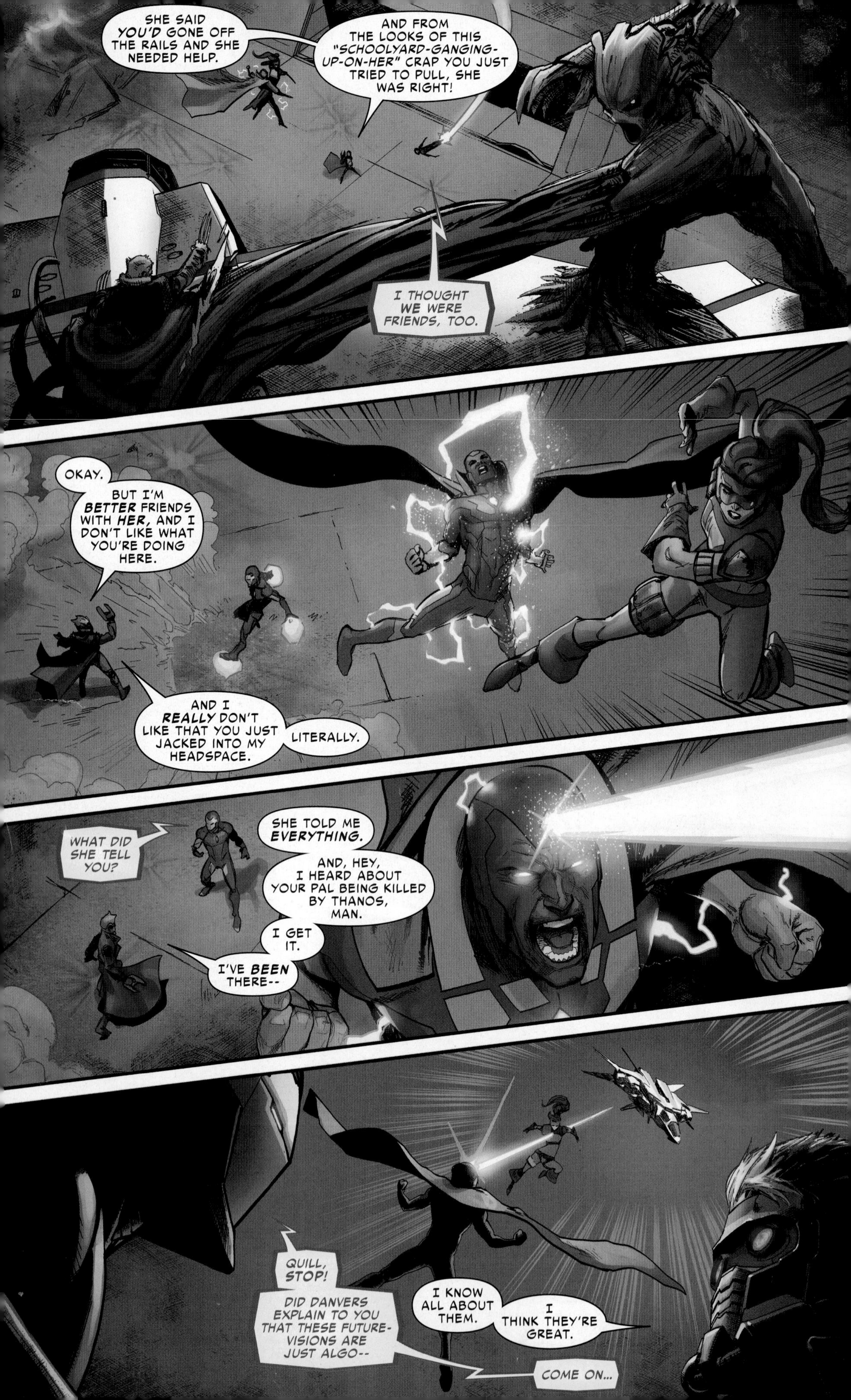
SHE SAID YOU'D GONE OFF THE RAILS AND SHE NEEDED HELP.
AND FROM THE LOOKS OF THIS "SCHOOLYARD-GANGING-UP-ON-HER" CRAP YOU JUST TRIED TO PULL, SHE WAS RIGHT!
I THOUGHT WE WERE FRIENDS, TOO.
OKAY.
BUT I'M BETTER FRIENDS WITH HER, AND I DON'T LIKE WHAT YOU'RE DOING HERE.
AND I REALLY DON'T LIKE THAT YOU JUST JACKED INTO MY HEADSPACE.
LITERALLY.
WHAT DID SHE TELL YOU?
SHE TOLD ME EVERYTHING.
AND, HEY, I HEARD ABOUT YOUR PAL BEING KILLED BY THANOS, MAN.
I GET IT.
I'VE BEEN THERE--
QUILL, STOP!
DID DANVERS EXPLAIN TO YOU THAT THESE FUTURE-VISIONS ARE JUST ALGO--
I KNOW ALL ABOUT THEM.
I THINK THEY'RE GREAT.
COME ON...

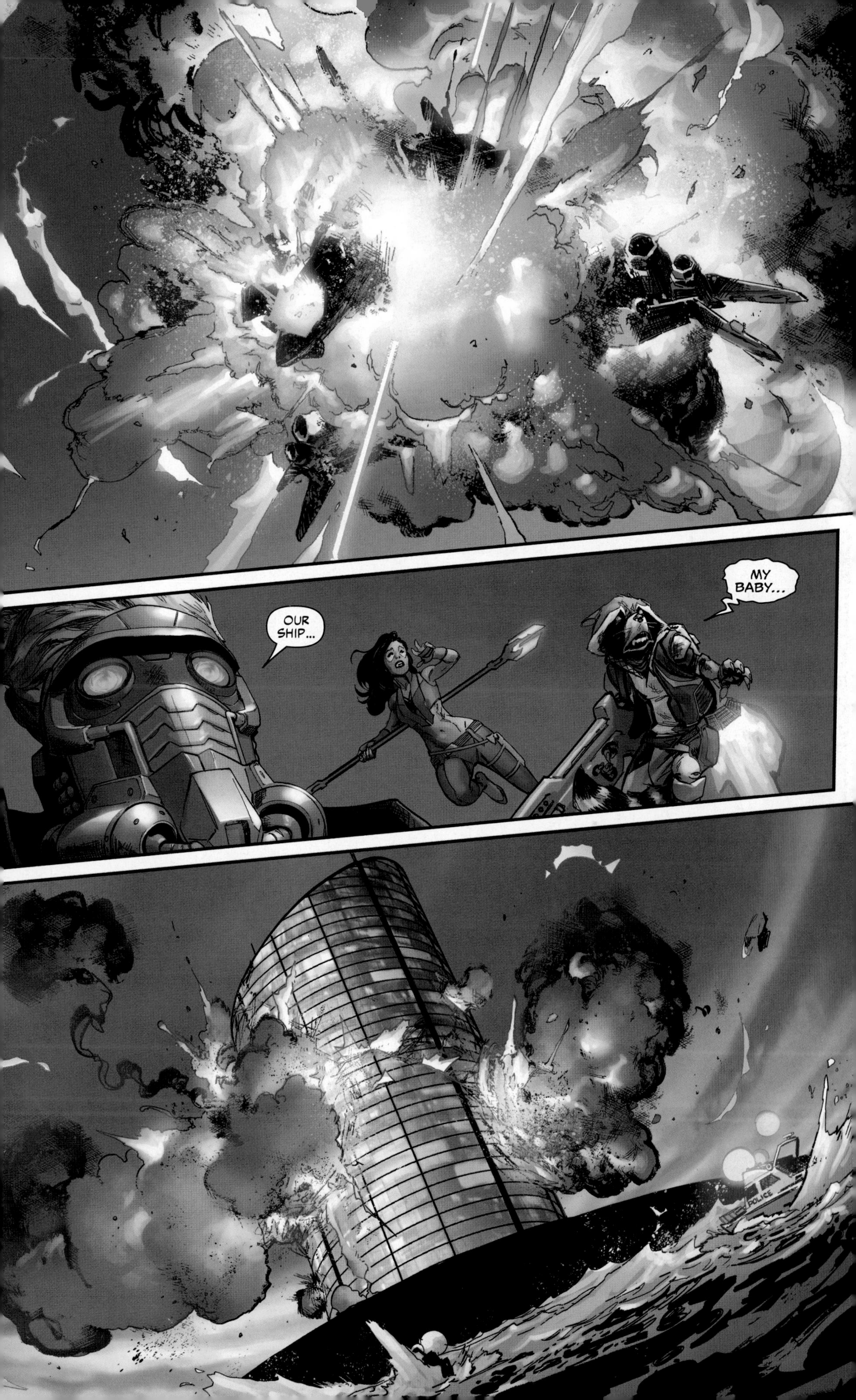
OUR SHIP...
MY BABY...
POLICE

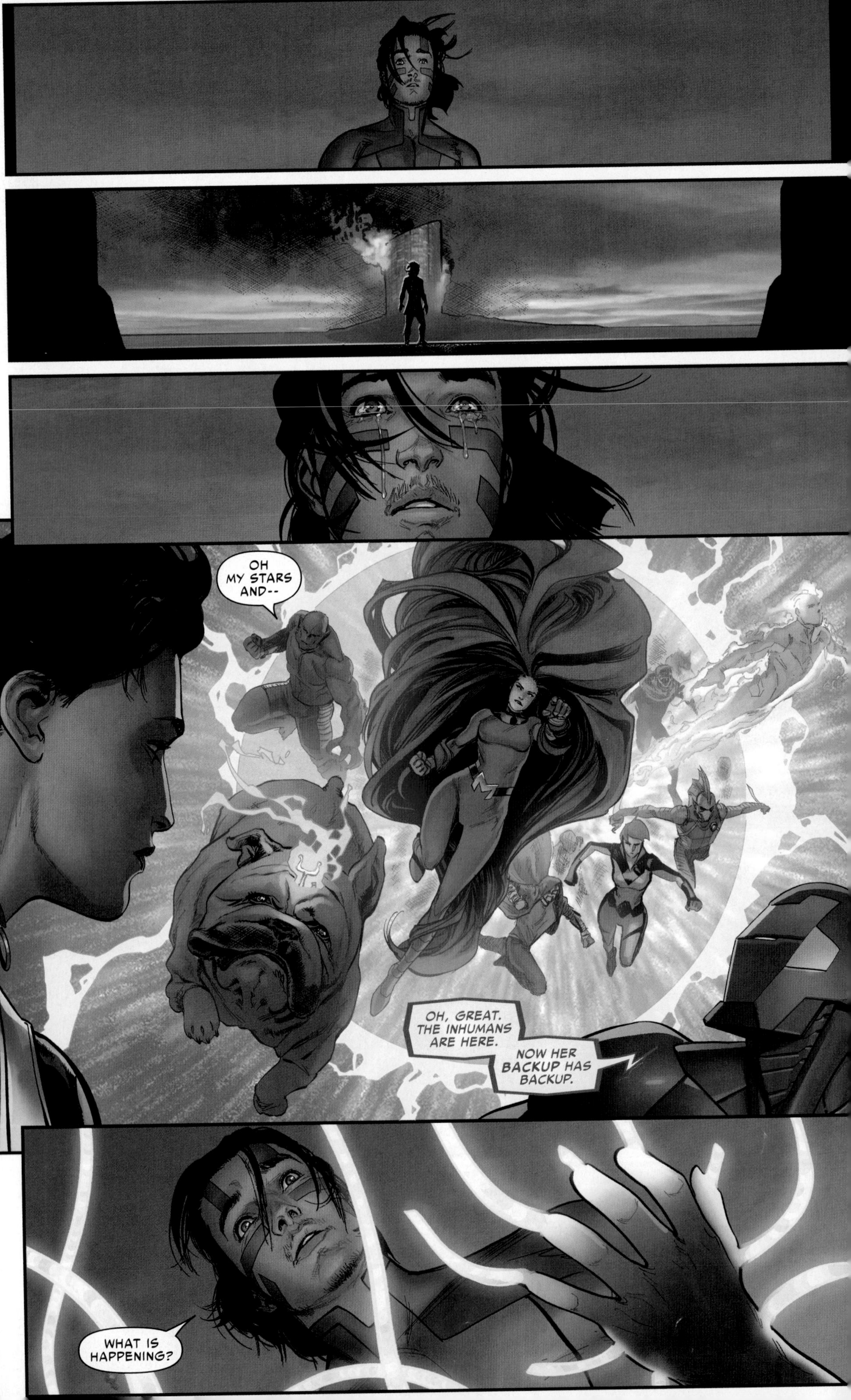
OH MY STARS AND--
OH, GREAT. THE INHUMANS ARE HERE.
NOW HER BACKUP HAS BACKUP.
WHAT IS HAPPENING?

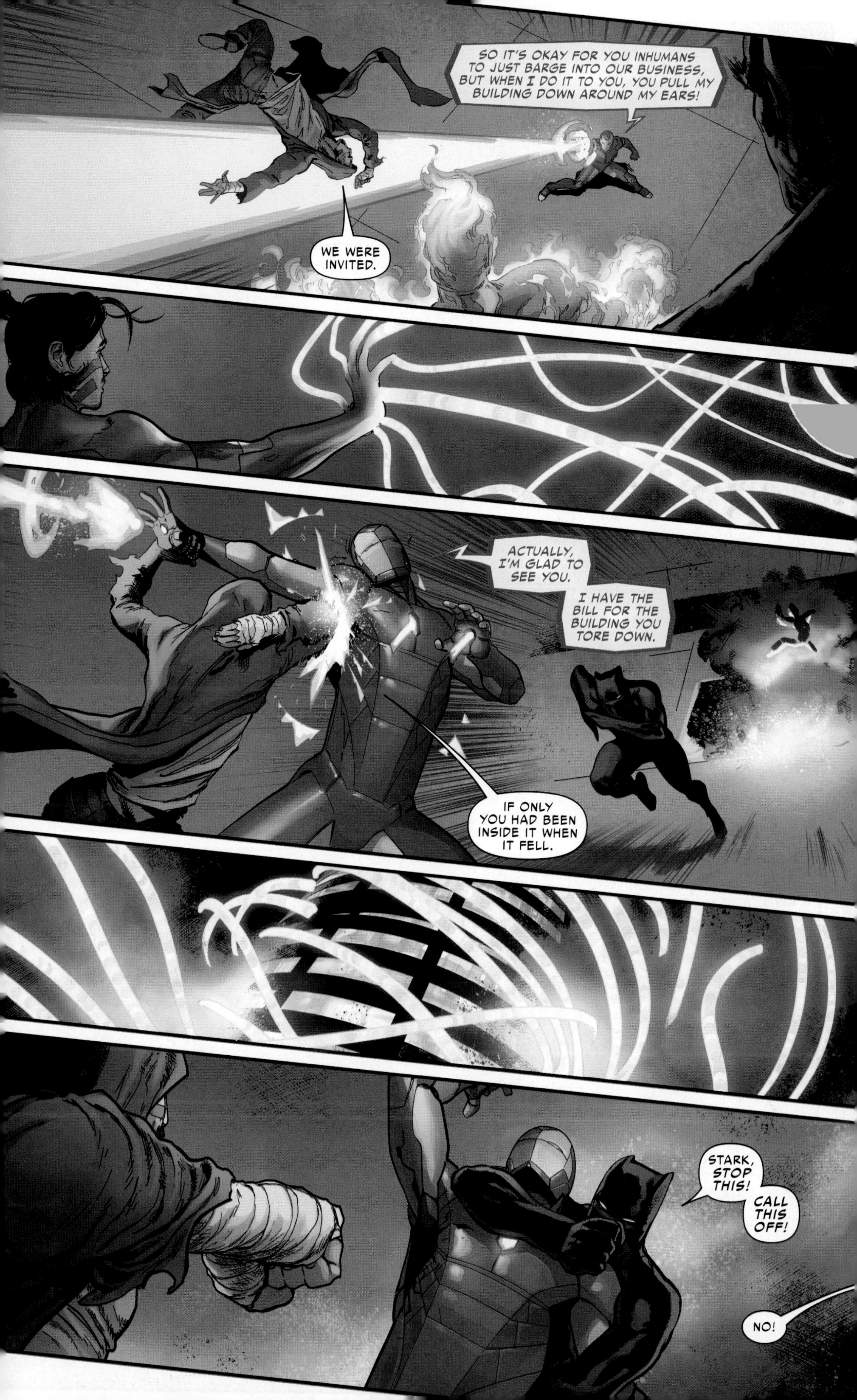
SO IT'S OKAY FOR YOU INHUMANS TO JUST BARGE INTO OUR BUSINESS, BUT WHEN I DO IT TO YOU, YOU PULL MY BUILDING DOWN AROUND MY EARS!
WE WERE INVITED.
ACTUALLY, I'M GLAD TO SEE YOU.
I HAVE THE BILL FOR THE BUILDING YOU TORE DOWN.
IF ONLY YOU HAD BEEN INSIDE IT WHEN IT FELL.
STARK, STOP THIS!
CALL THIS OFF!
NO!

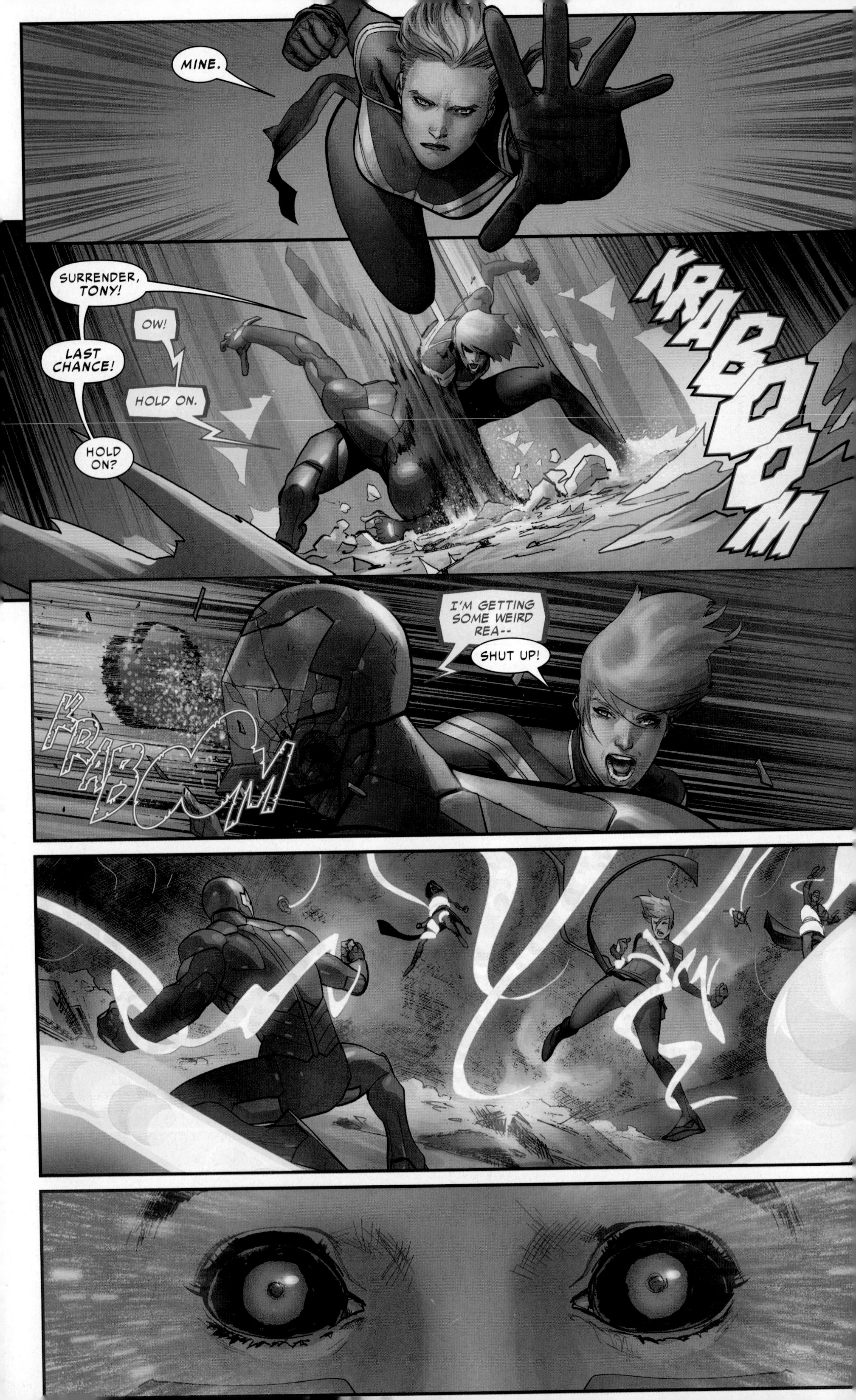
MINE.
SURRENDER, TONY!
OW!
LAST CHANCE!
HOLD ON.
HOLD ON?
KRABOOM
I'M GETTING SOME WEIRD REA--
SHUT UP!
KRABOOM

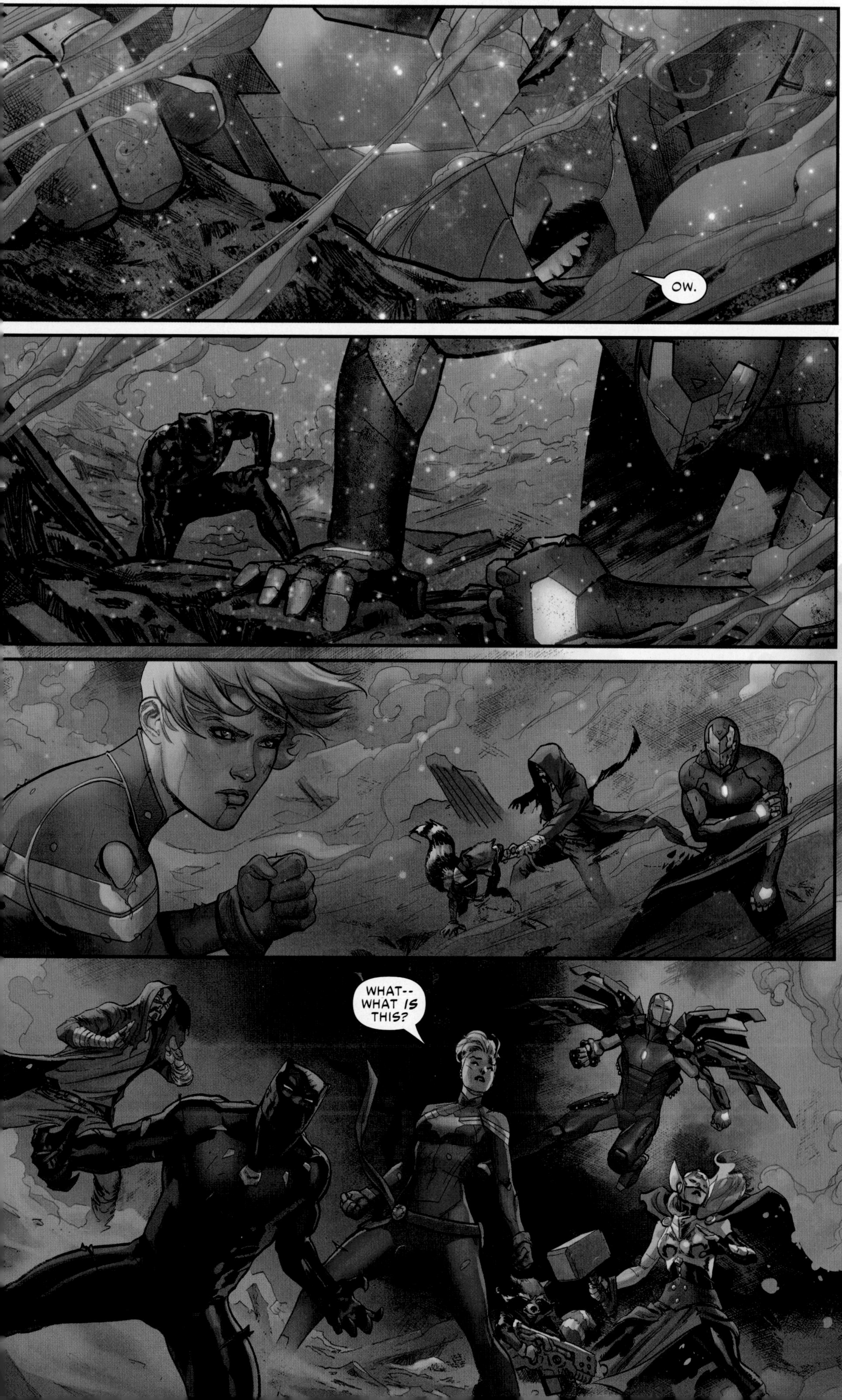
OW.
WHAT--
WHAT IS
THIS?

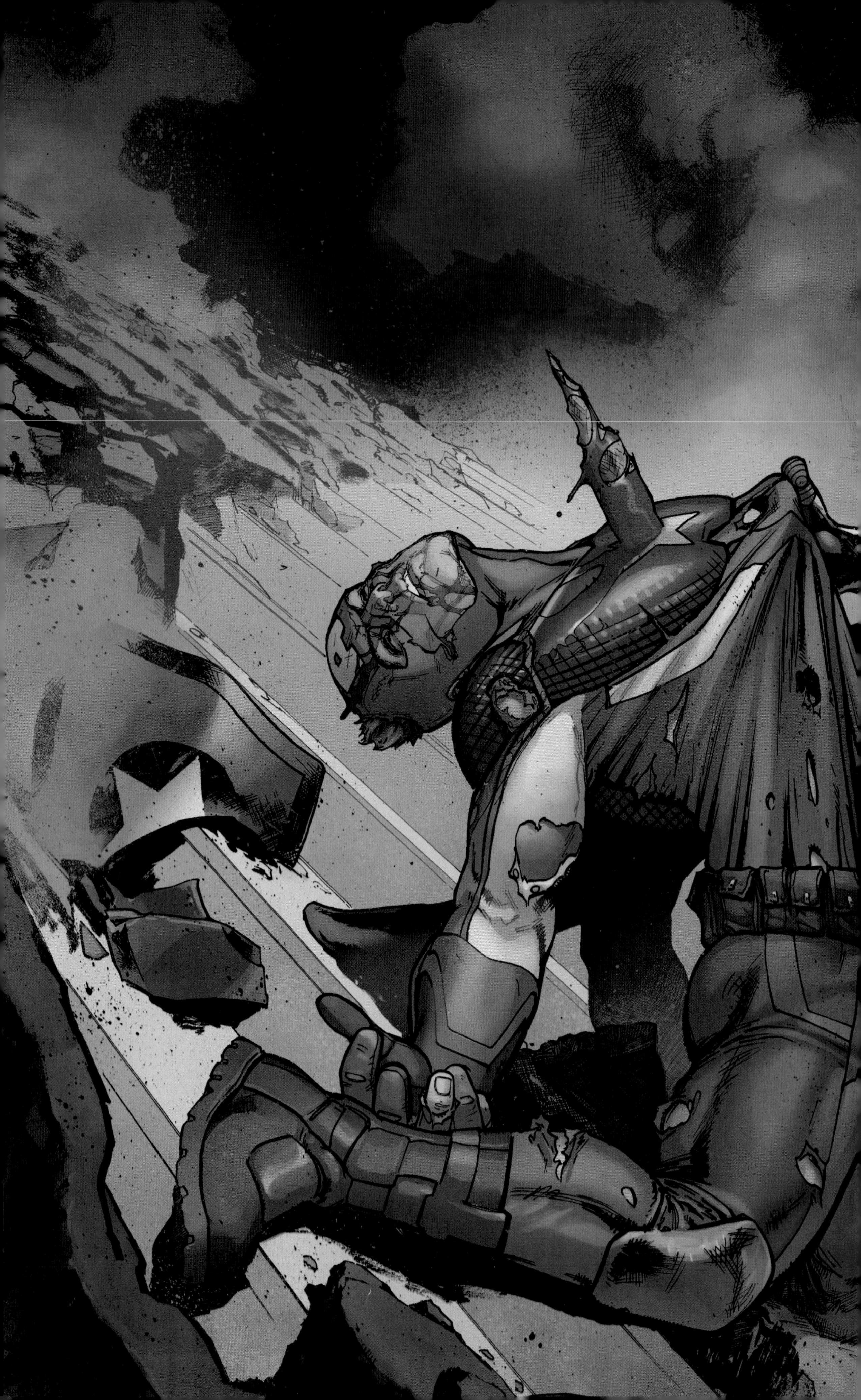

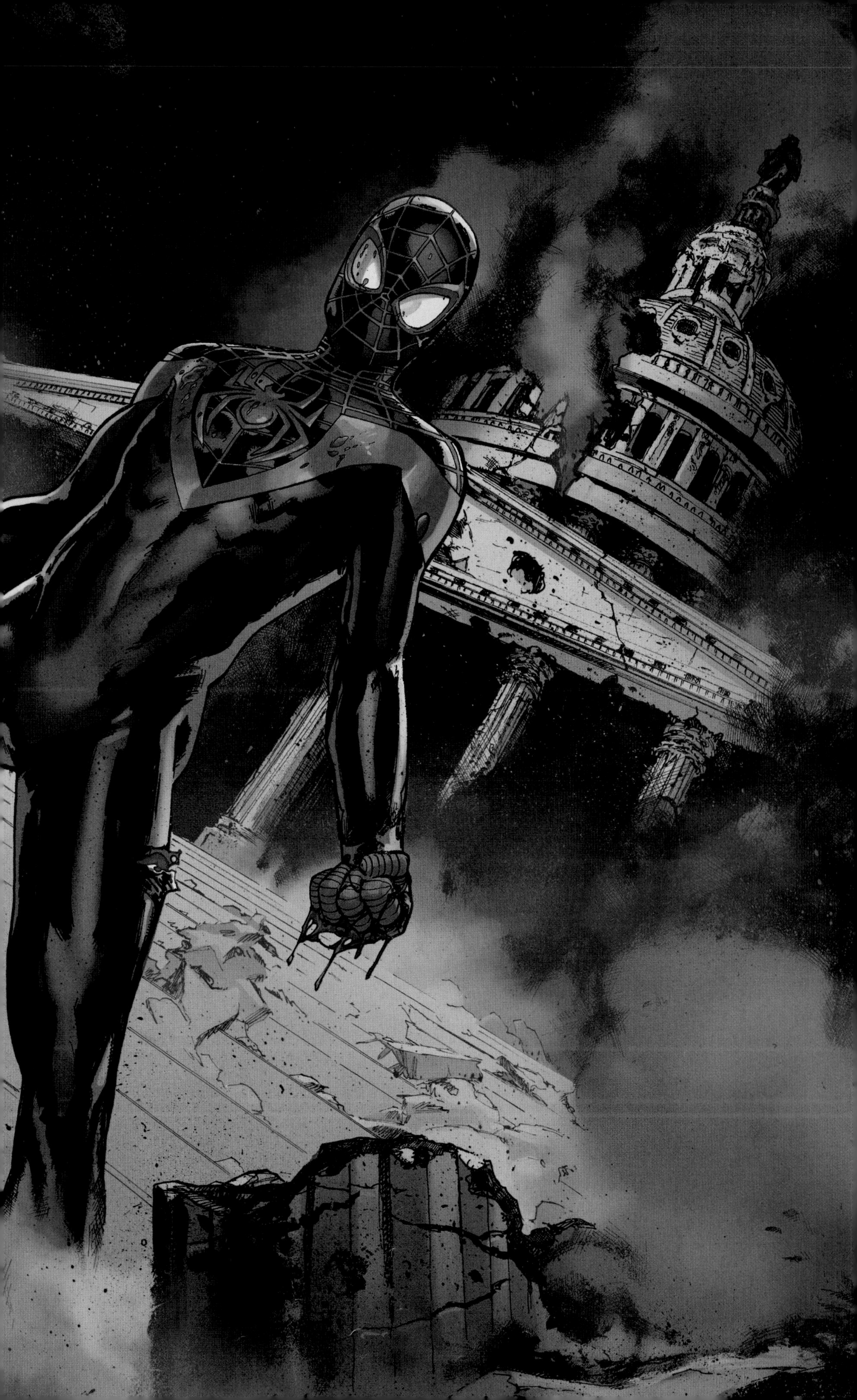

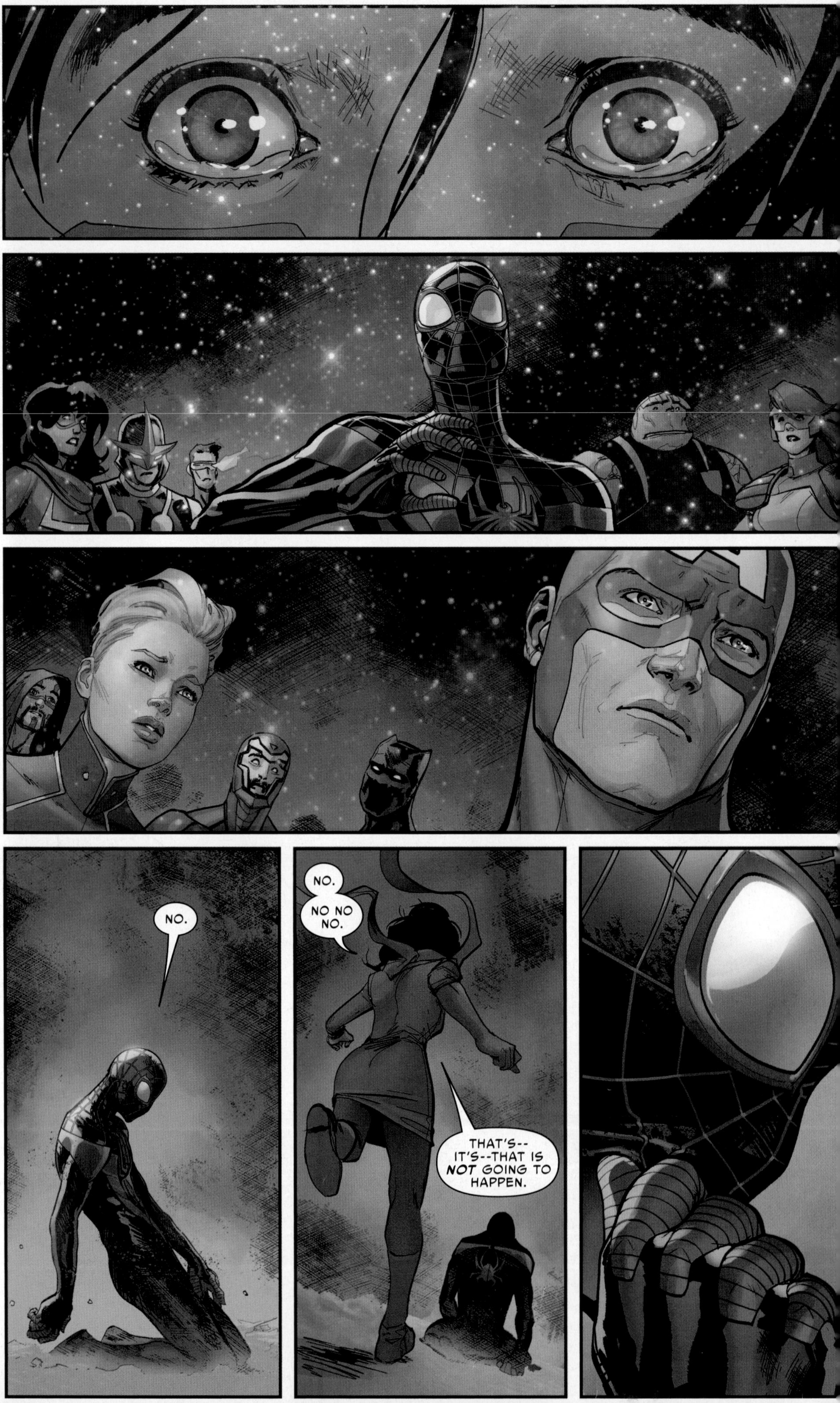
NO.
NO.
NO NO NO.
THAT'S--IT'S--THAT IS *NOT* GOING TO HAPPEN.

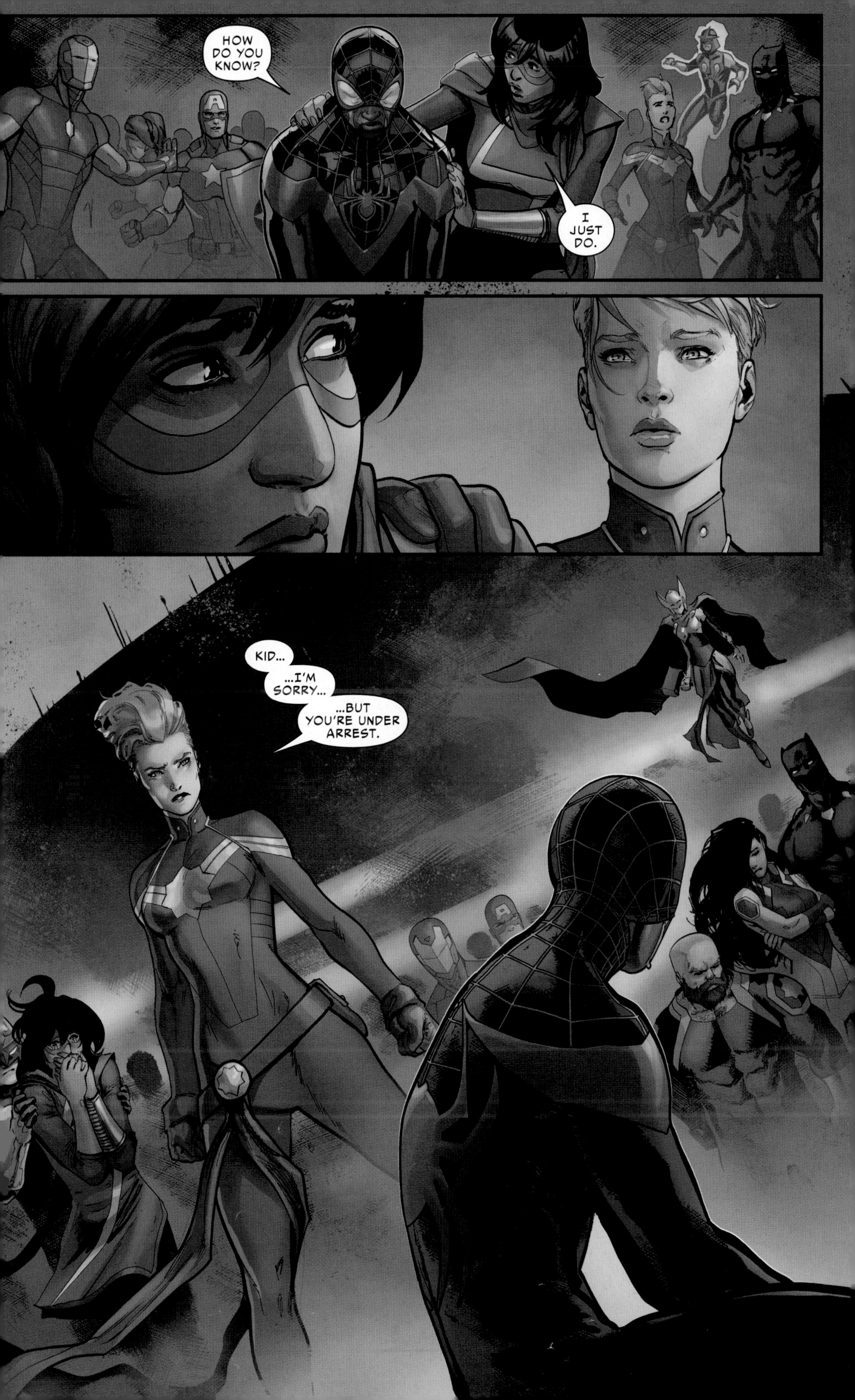
HOW DO YOU KNOW?
I JUST DO.
KID...
...I'M SORRY...
...BUT YOU'RE UNDER ARREST.

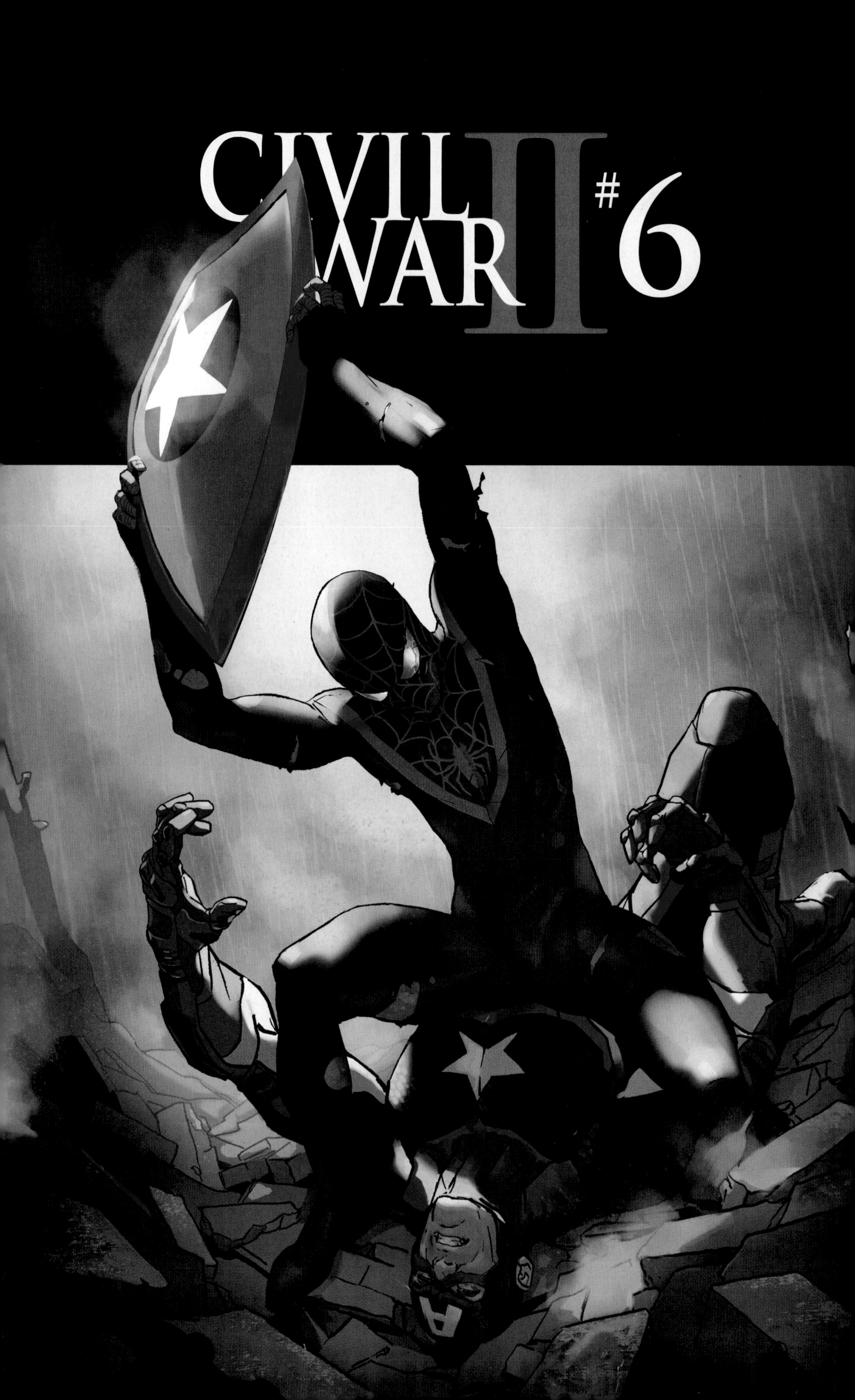
CIVIL WAR II
#6

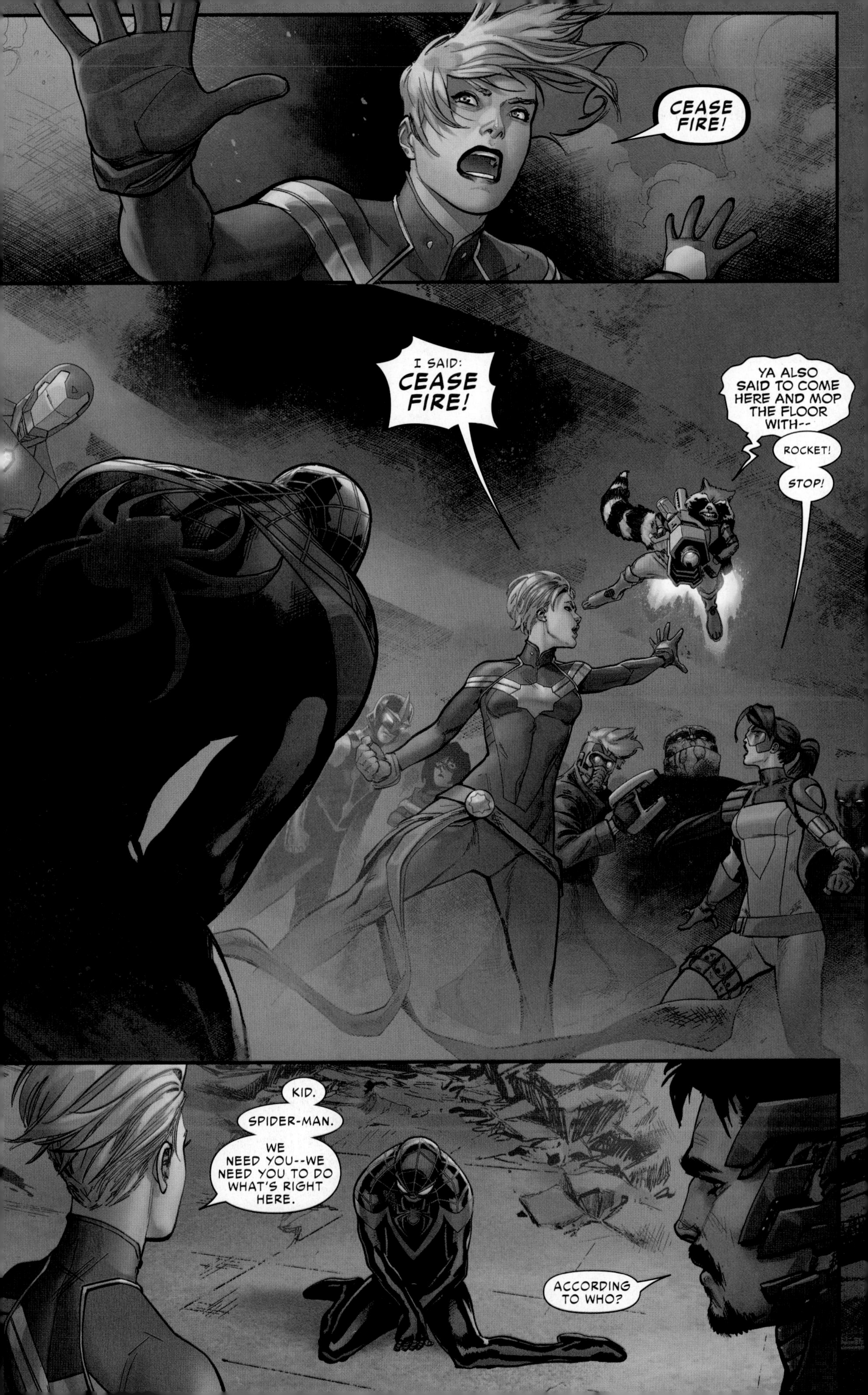
CEASE FIRE!
I SAID: CEASE FIRE!
YA ALSO SAID TO COME HERE AND MOP THE FLOOR WITH--
ROCKET!
STOP!
KID.
SPIDER-MAN.
WE NEED YOU--WE NEED YOU TO DO WHAT'S RIGHT HERE.
ACCORDING TO WHO?

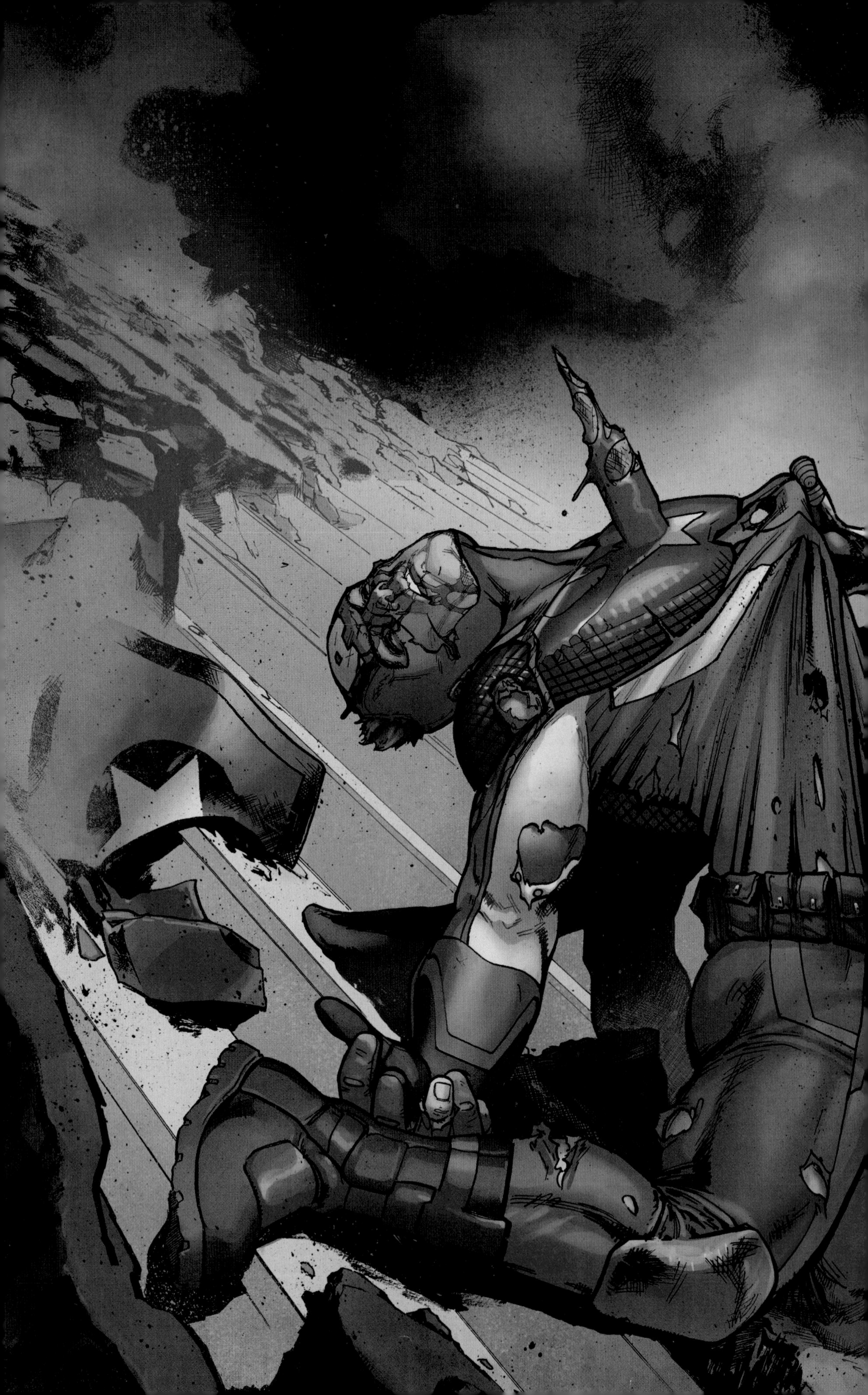

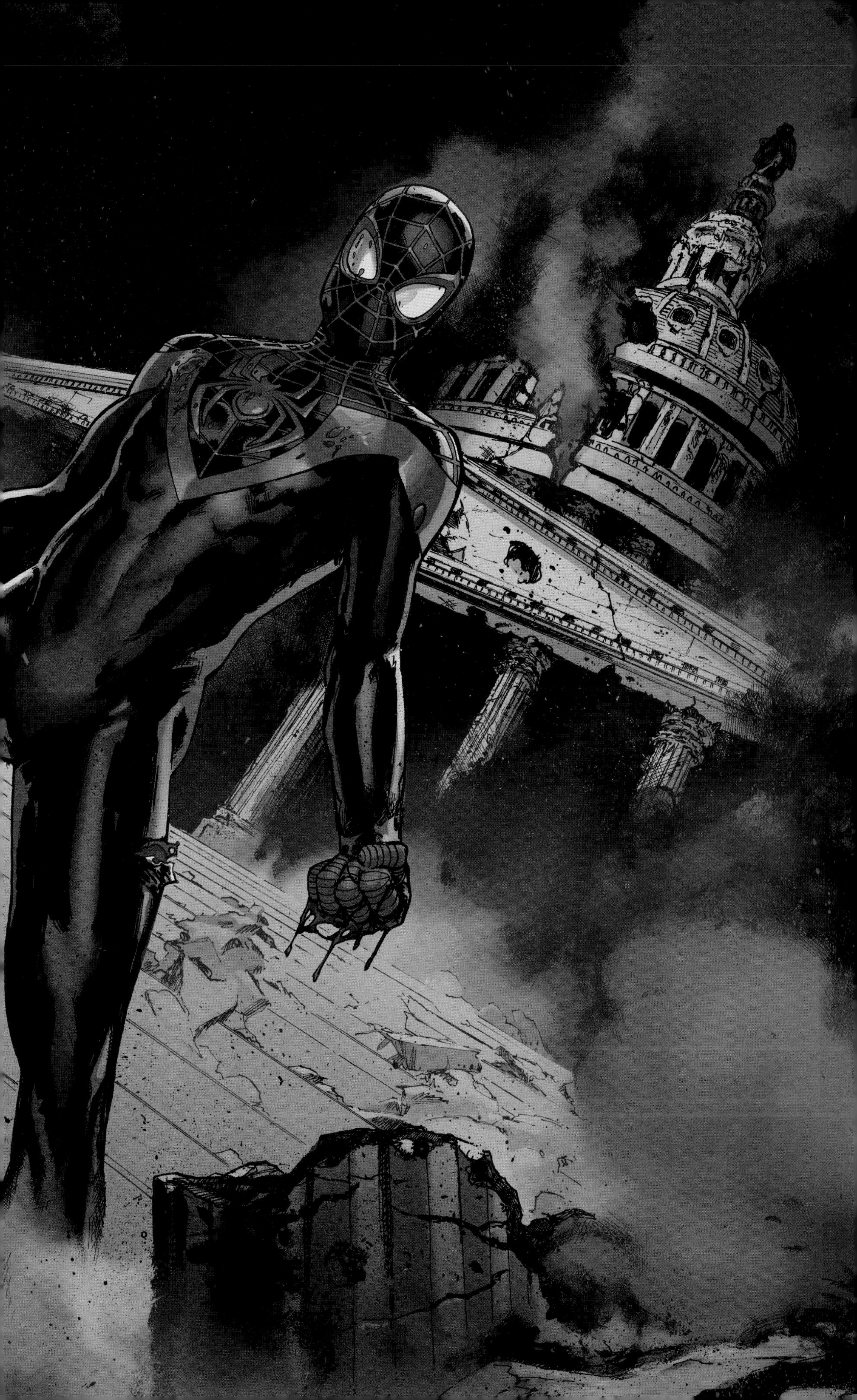

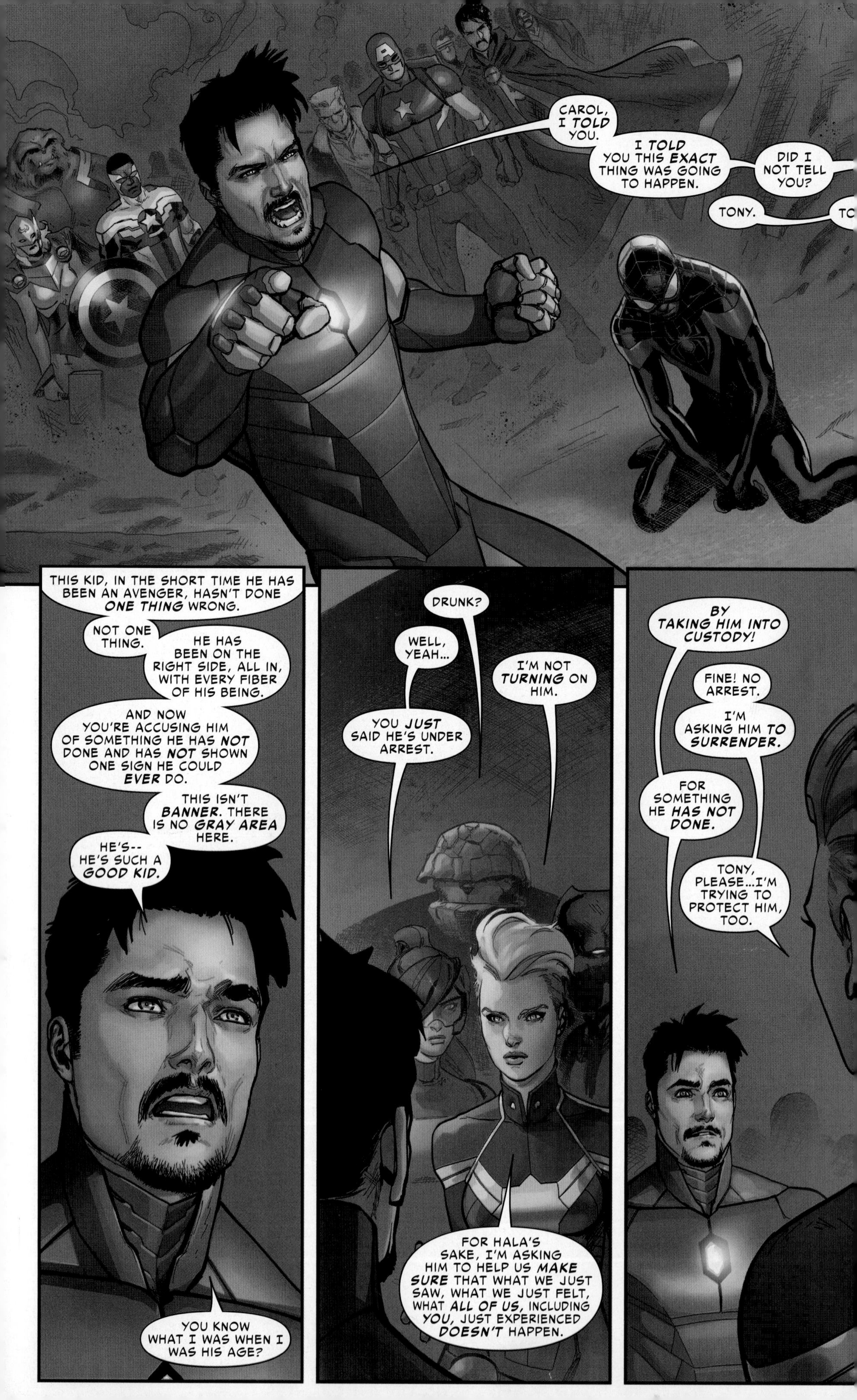

CAROL, I TOLD YOU.
I TOLD YOU THIS EXACT THING WAS GOING TO HAPPEN.
DID I NOT TELL YOU?
TONY.
THIS KID, IN THE SHORT TIME HE HAS BEEN AN AVENGER, HASN'T DONE ONE THING WRONG.
NOT ONE THING.
HE HAS BEEN ON THE RIGHT SIDE, ALL IN, WITH EVERY FIBER OF HIS BEING.
AND NOW YOU'RE ACCUSING HIM OF SOMETHING HE HAS NOT DONE AND HAS NOT SHOWN ONE SIGN HE COULD EVER DO.
THIS ISN'T BANNER. THERE IS NO GRAY AREA HERE.
HE'S-- HE'S SUCH A GOOD KID.
YOU KNOW WHAT I WAS WHEN I WAS HIS AGE?
DRUNK?
WELL, YEAH...
YOU JUST SAID HE'S UNDER ARREST.
I'M NOT TURNING ON HIM.
FOR HALA'S SAKE, I'M ASKING HIM TO HELP US MAKE SURE THAT WHAT WE JUST SAW, WHAT WE JUST FELT, WHAT ALL OF US, INCLUDING YOU, JUST EXPERIENCED DOESN'T HAPPEN.
BY TAKING HIM INTO CUSTODY!
FINE! NO ARREST.
I'M ASKING HIM TO SURRENDER.
FOR SOMETHING HE HAS NOT DONE.
TONY, PLEASE...I'M TRYING TO PROTECT HIM, TOO.

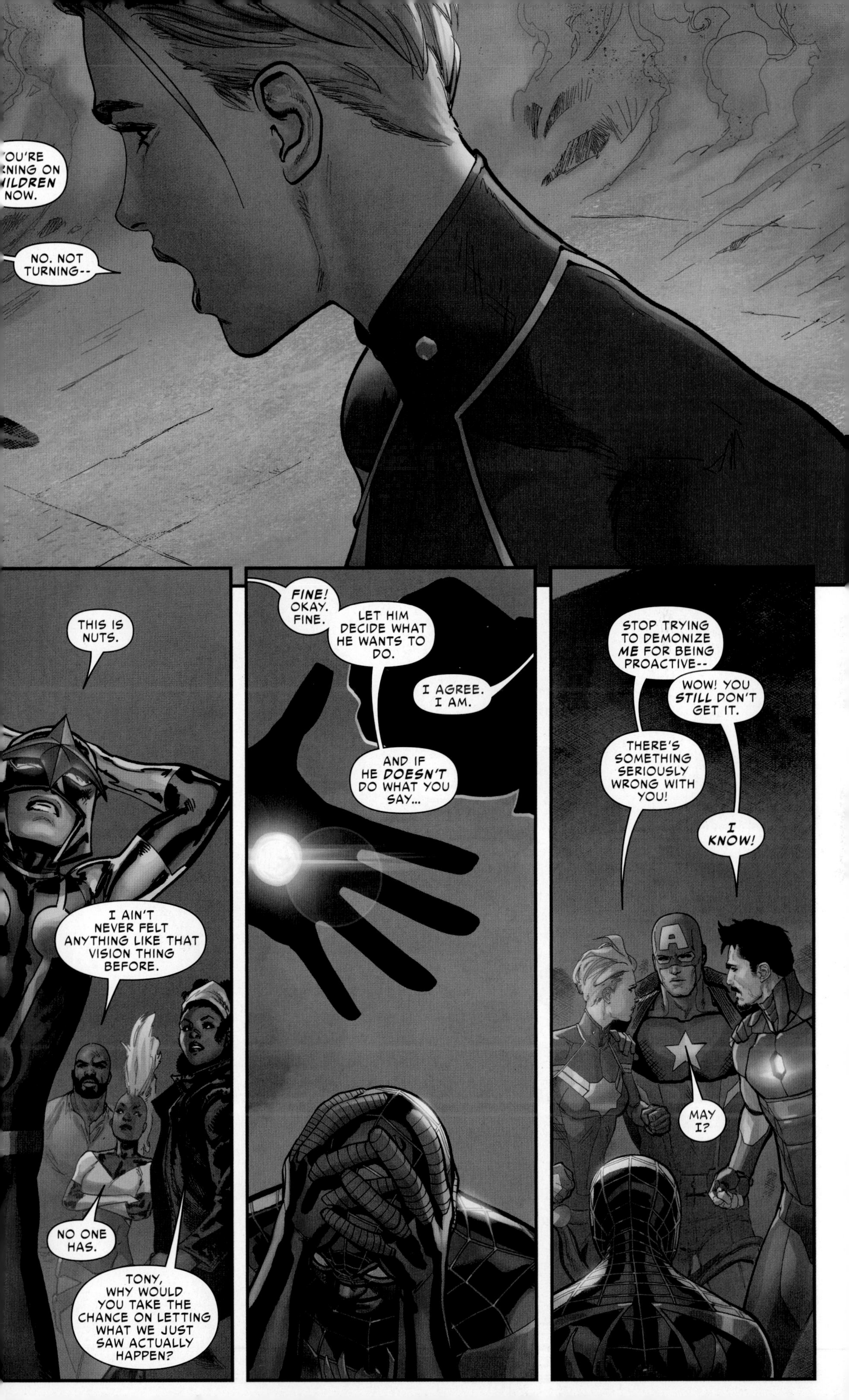

OU'RE
NING ON
HILDREN
NOW.
NO. NOT TURNING--
THIS IS NUTS.
I AIN'T NEVER FELT ANYTHING LIKE THAT VISION THING BEFORE.
NO ONE HAS.
TONY, WHY WOULD YOU TAKE THE CHANCE ON LETTING WHAT WE JUST SAW ACTUALLY HAPPEN?
FINE! OKAY. FINE.
LET HIM DECIDE WHAT HE WANTS TO DO.
I AGREE. I AM.
AND IF HE DOESN'T DO WHAT YOU SAY...
STOP TRYING TO DEMONIZE ME FOR BEING PROACTIVE--
WOW! YOU STILL DON'T GET IT.
THERE'S SOMETHING SERIOUSLY WRONG WITH YOU!
I KNOW!
MAY I?

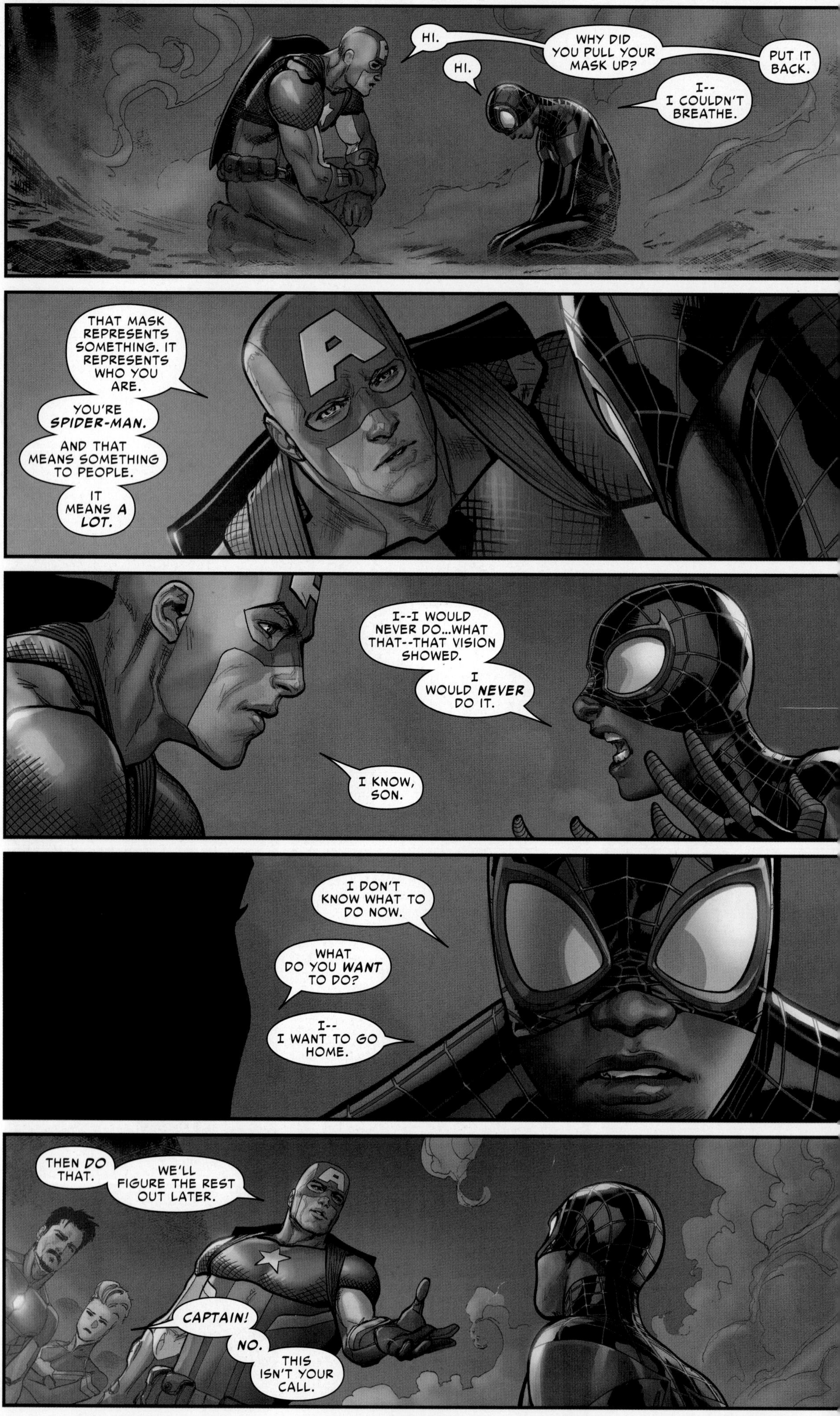
HI.
HI.
WHY DID YOU PULL YOUR MASK UP?
PUT IT BACK.
I-- I COULDN'T BREATHE.
THAT MASK REPRESENTS SOMETHING. IT REPRESENTS WHO YOU ARE.
YOU'RE SPIDER-MAN.
AND THAT MEANS SOMETHING TO PEOPLE.
IT MEANS A LOT.
I--I WOULD NEVER DO...WHAT THAT--THAT VISION SHOWED.
I WOULD NEVER DO IT.
I KNOW, SON.
I DON'T KNOW WHAT TO DO NOW.
WHAT DO YOU WANT TO DO?
I-- I WANT TO GO HOME.
THEN DO THAT.
WE'LL FIGURE THE REST OUT LATER.
CAPTAIN!
NO.
THIS ISN'T YOUR CALL.

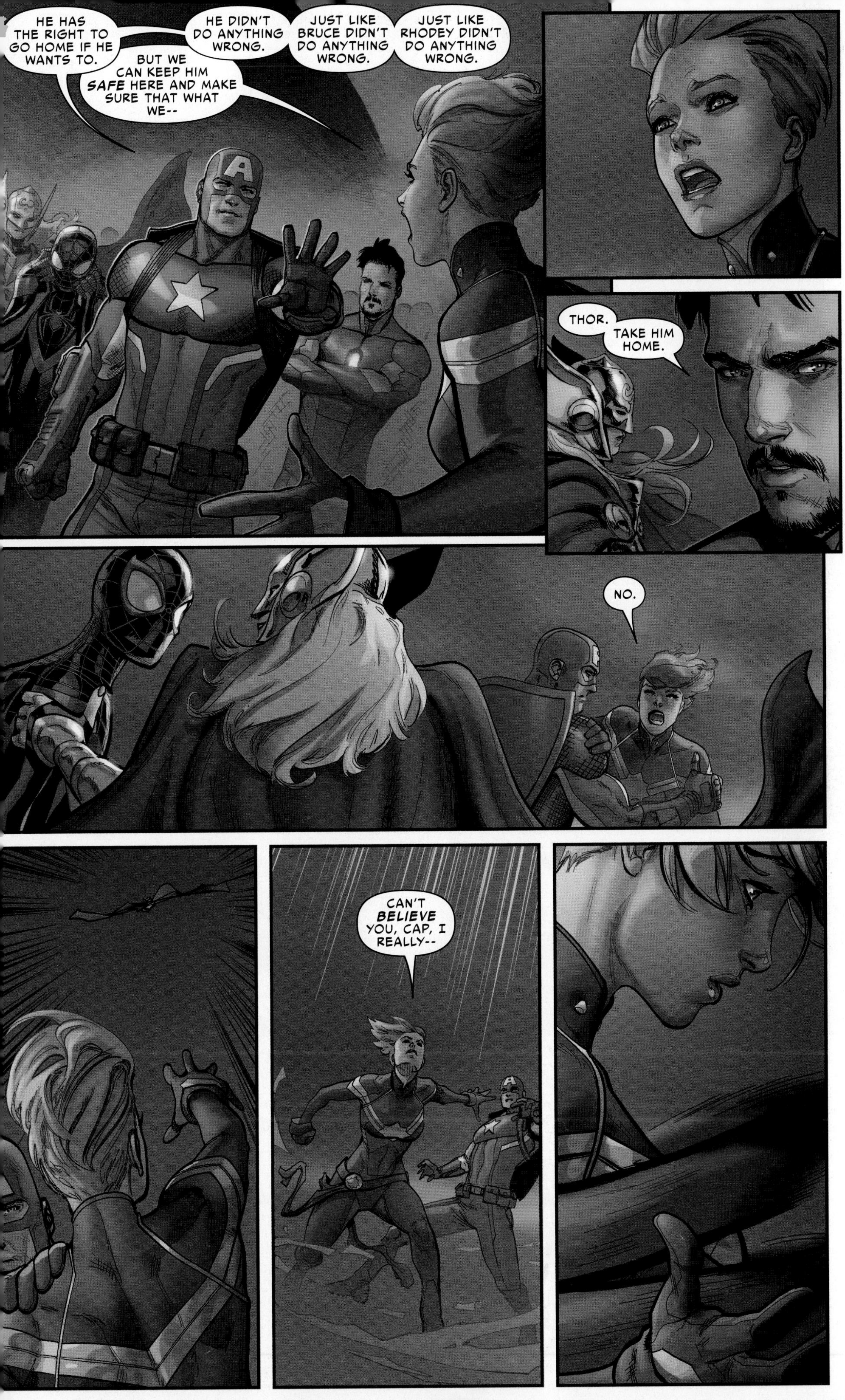
HE HAS THE RIGHT TO GO HOME IF HE WANTS TO.
BUT WE CAN KEEP HIM SAFE HERE AND MAKE SURE THAT WHAT WE--
HE DIDN'T DO ANYTHING WRONG.
JUST LIKE BRUCE DIDN'T DO ANYTHING WRONG.
JUST LIKE RHODEY DIDN'T DO ANYTHING WRONG.
THOR.
TAKE HIM HOME.
NO.
CAN'T BELIEVE YOU, CAP, I REALLY--

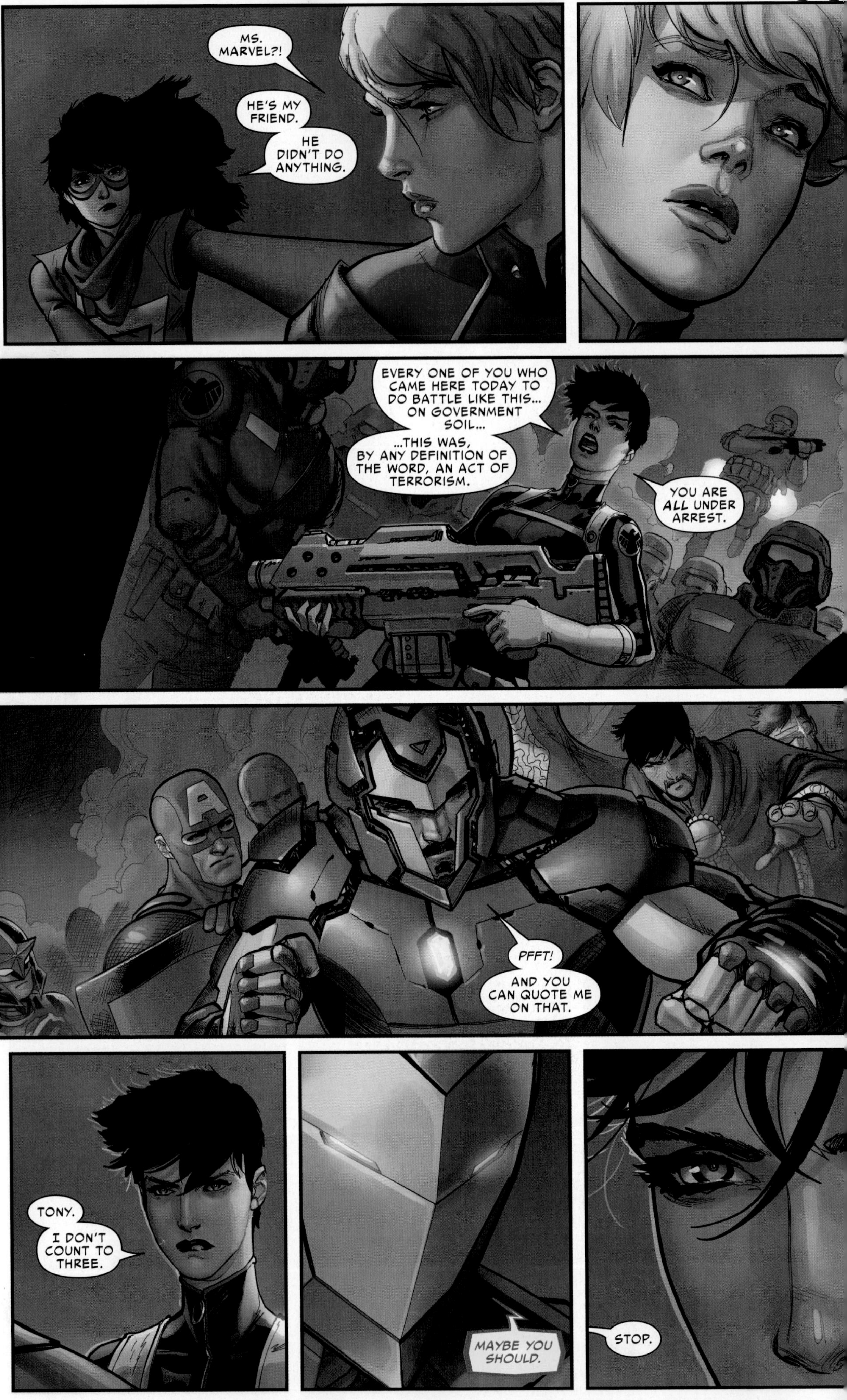
MS. MARVEL?!
HE'S MY FRIEND.
HE DIDN'T DO ANYTHING.
EVERY ONE OF YOU WHO CAME HERE TODAY TO DO BATTLE LIKE THIS... ON GOVERNMENT SOIL...
...THIS WAS, BY ANY DEFINITION OF THE WORD, AN ACT OF TERRORISM.
YOU ARE ALL UNDER ARREST.
PFFT!
AND YOU CAN QUOTE ME ON THAT.
TONY.
I DON'T COUNT TO THREE.
MAYBE YOU SHOULD.
STOP.

IF YOU FIRE ON THEM, YOU HAVE TO GO THROUGH ME.

T'CHALLA.

I HAVE SEEN TOO MUCH, CAPTAIN MARVEL.

I CAN NO LONGER DEFEND ANY OF THIS.

AT THE BEGINNING I COULD.

I COULD.

BUT I HAVE GROWN MORE AND MORE UNCOMFORTABLE WITH MY PART IN THIS.

AND LONG, LONG AGO I LEARNED THAT IF YOU ARE ON CAPTAIN AMERICA'S SIDE...YOU CAN REST EASY KNOWING YOU ARE ON THE RIGHT SIDE.

AND IF HE, EVEN AFTER WHAT WE HAVE ALL EXPERIENCED, WOULD CHOOSE TO PROTECT THAT CHILD AVENGER'S RIGHT TO BE...

...THEN THAT IS WHAT I SHOULD HAVE BEEN DOING THIS ENTIRE TIME.

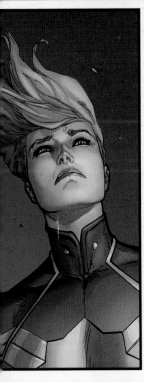

IF YOU ATTACK ME...

...YOU ATTACK THE KINGDOM OF WAKANDA.

OH, NO! NO NO NO...

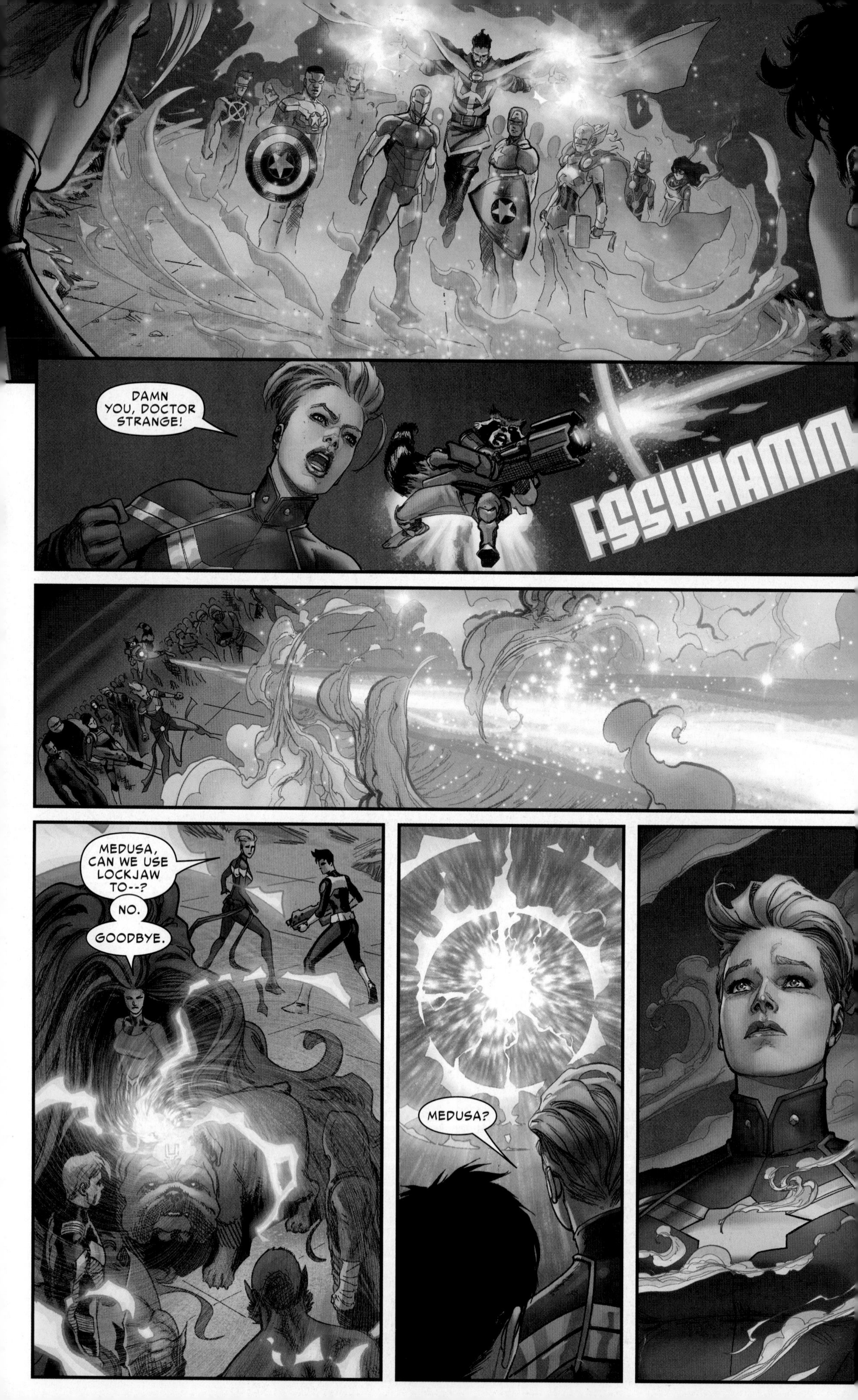
DAMN YOU, DOCTOR STRANGE!
FSSHHAMM
MEDUSA, CAN WE USE LOCKJAW TO--?
NO.
GOODBYE.
MEDUSA?

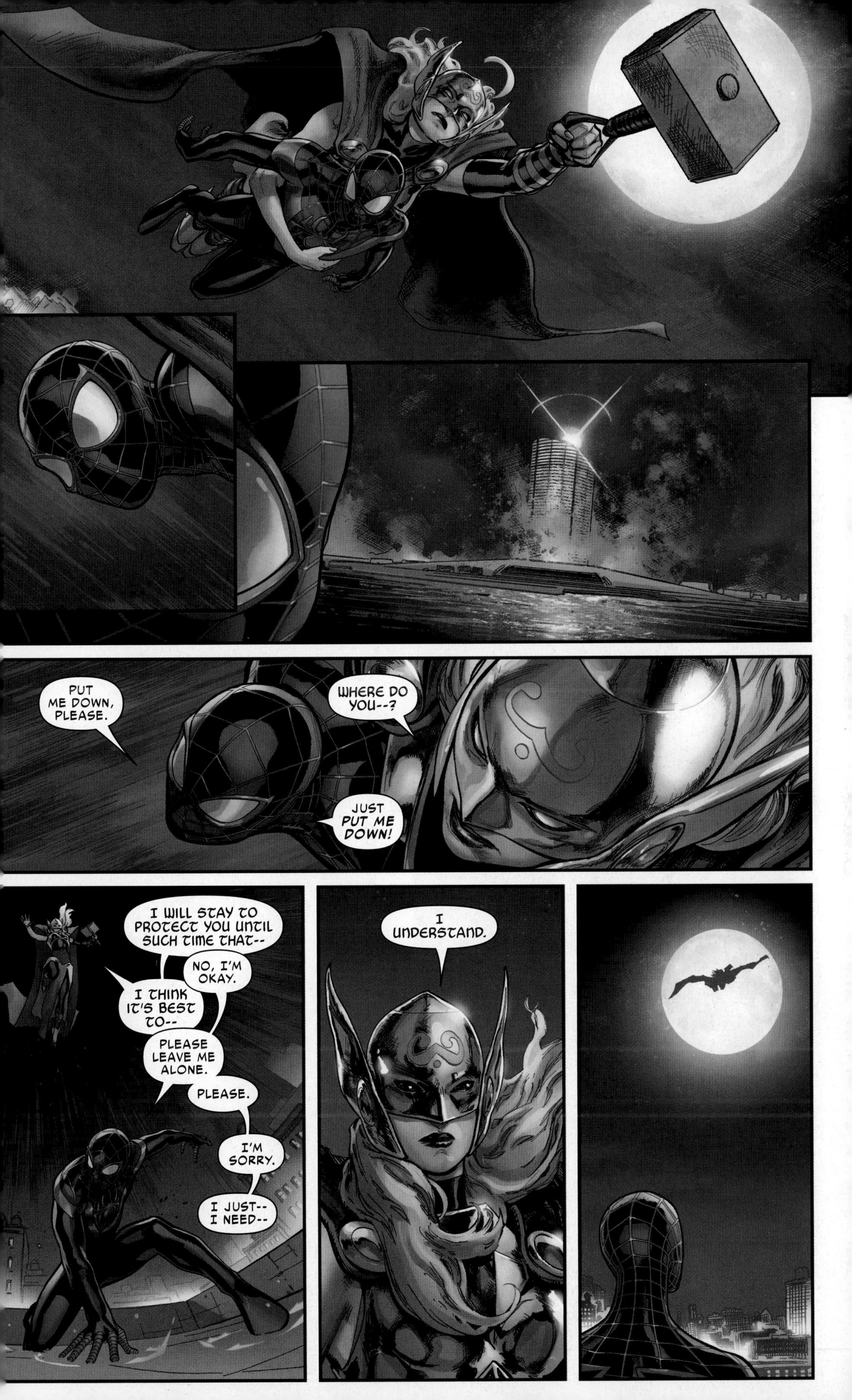
PUT ME DOWN, PLEASE.
WHERE DO YOU--?
JUST PUT ME DOWN!
I WILL STAY TO PROTECT YOU UNTIL SUCH TIME THAT--
NO, I'M OKAY.
I THINK IT'S BEST TO--
PLEASE LEAVE ME ALONE.
PLEASE.
I'M SORRY.
I JUST-- I NEED--
I UNDERSTAND.

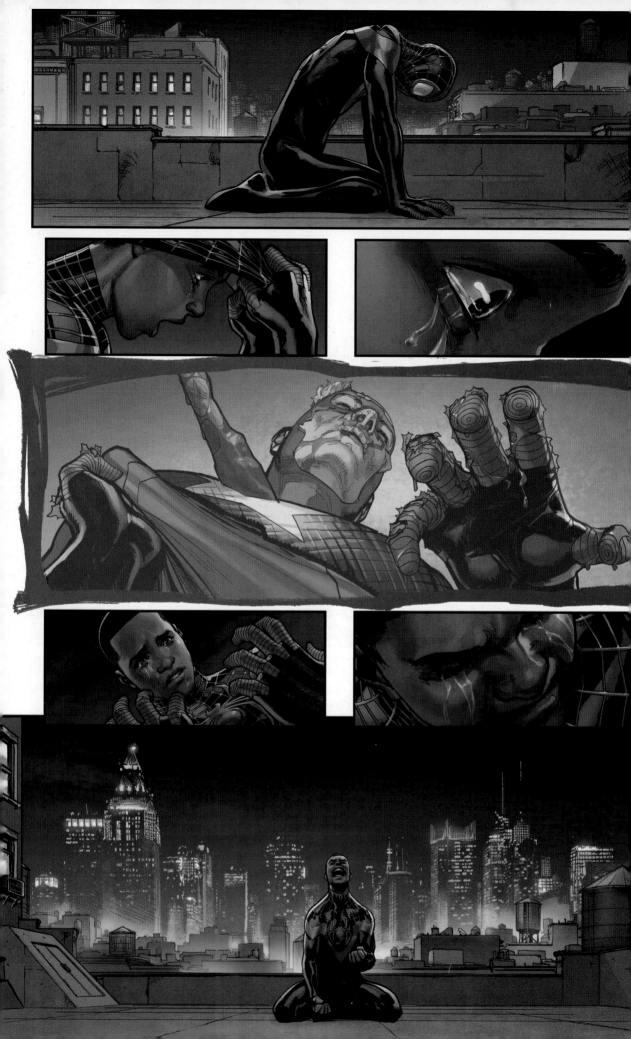

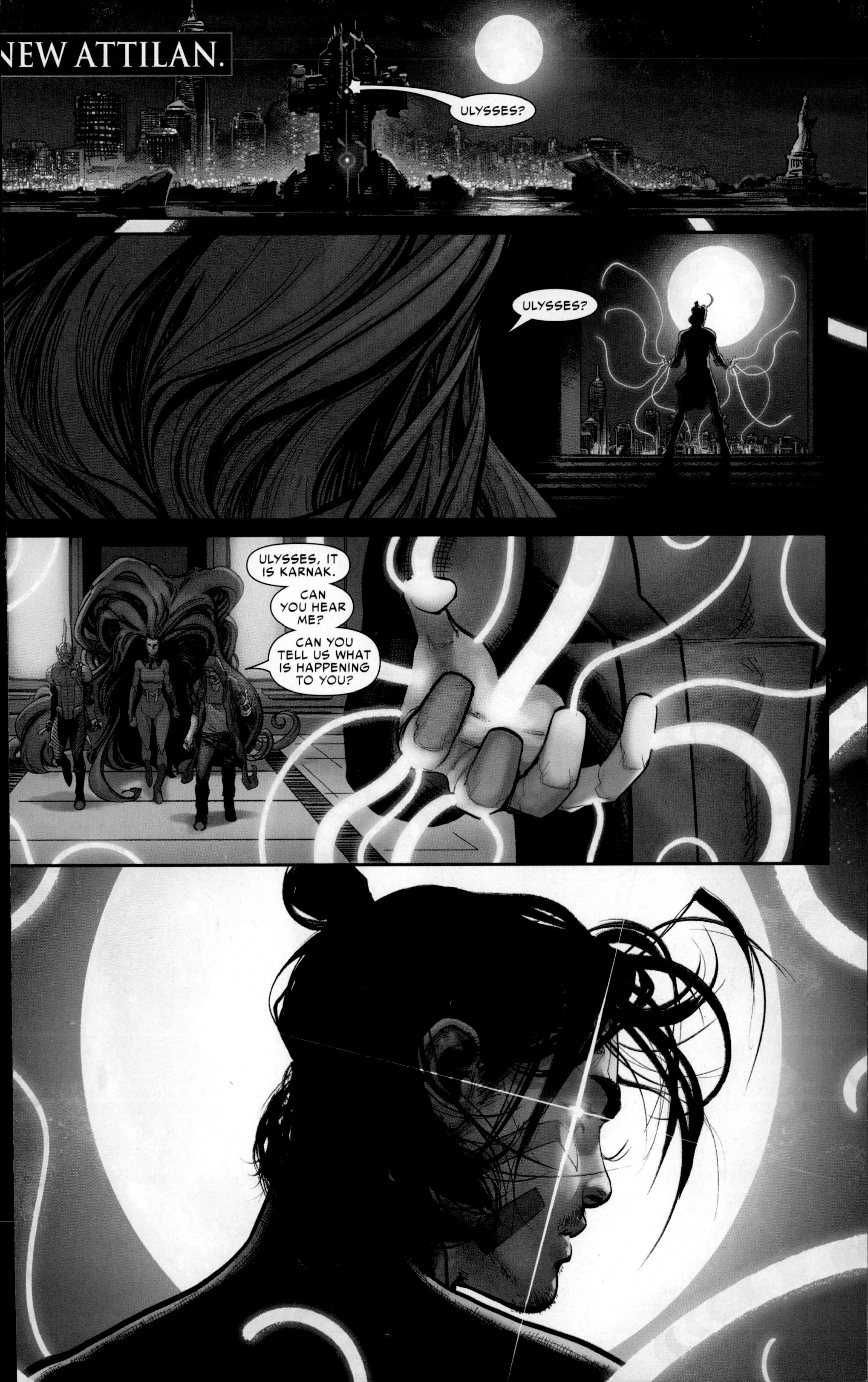

NEW ATTILAN.
ULYSSES?
ULYSSES?
ULYSSES, IT IS KARNAK.
CAN YOU HEAR ME?
CAN YOU TELL US WHAT IS HAPPENING TO YOU?

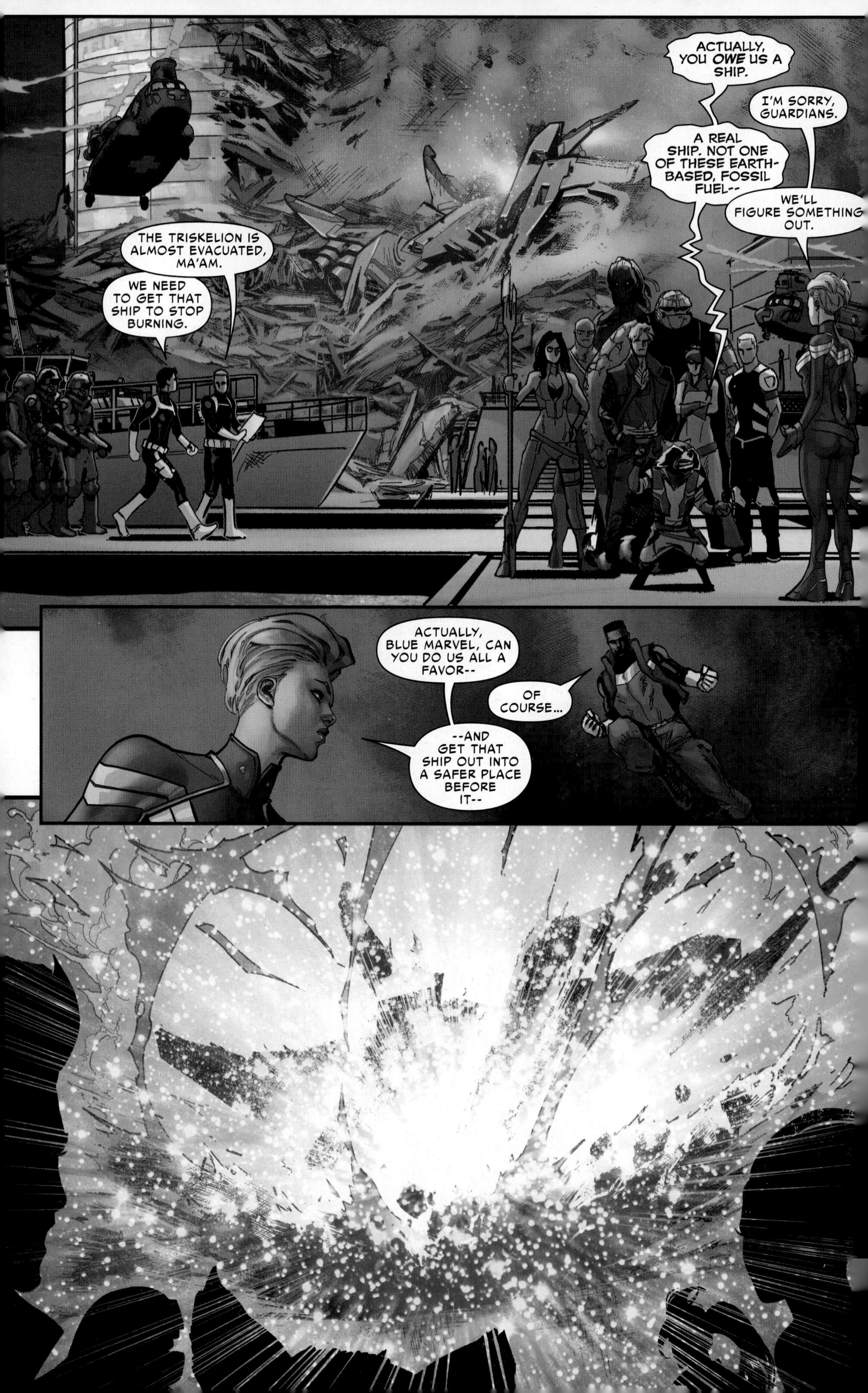
THE TRISKELION IS ALMOST EVACUATED, MA'AM.
WE NEED TO GET THAT SHIP TO STOP BURNING.
ACTUALLY, YOU *OWE* US A SHIP.
A REAL SHIP. NOT ONE OF THESE EARTH-BASED, FOSSIL FUEL--
I'M SORRY, GUARDIANS.
WE'LL FIGURE SOMETHING OUT.
ACTUALLY, BLUE MARVEL, CAN YOU DO US ALL A FAVOR--
OF COURSE...
--AND GET THAT SHIP OUT INTO A SAFER PLACE BEFORE IT--

WELL, WE'RE ALL CRASHING WITH *YOU* 'TIL YOU COUGH UP A NEW SHIP.

I HAVE TO TELL YOU...

PLEASE DON'T LECTURE ME, PETER QUILL. PLEASE.

ACTUALLY, NO.

I WAS GOING TO TELL YOU YOU'RE RIGHT.

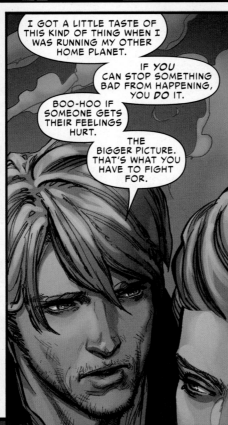

I GOT A LITTLE TASTE OF THIS KIND OF THING WHEN I WAS RUNNING MY OTHER HOME PLANET.

IF *YOU* CAN STOP SOMETHING BAD FROM HAPPENING, YOU *DO* IT.

BOO-HOO IF SOMEONE GETS THEIR FEELINGS HURT.

THE BIGGER PICTURE. THAT'S WHAT YOU HAVE TO FIGHT FOR.

I AM GROOT.

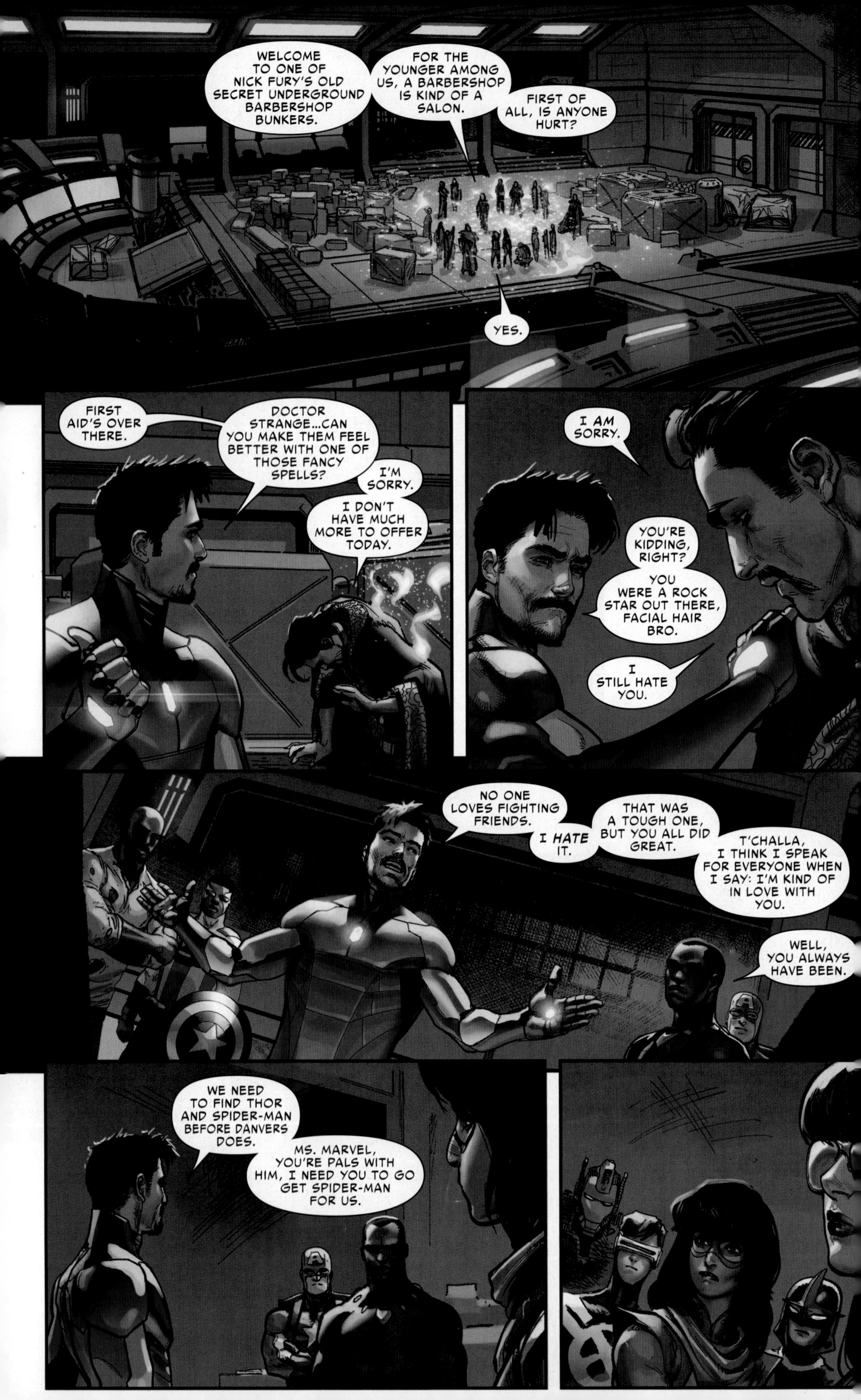
WELCOME TO ONE OF NICK FURY'S OLD SECRET UNDERGROUND BARBERSHOP BUNKERS.
FOR THE YOUNGER AMONG US, A BARBERSHOP IS KIND OF A SALON.
FIRST OF ALL, IS ANYONE HURT?
YES.
FIRST AID'S OVER THERE.
DOCTOR STRANGE...CAN YOU MAKE THEM FEEL BETTER WITH ONE OF THOSE FANCY SPELLS?
I'M SORRY.
I DON'T HAVE MUCH MORE TO OFFER TODAY.
I *AM* SORRY.
YOU'RE KIDDING, RIGHT?
YOU WERE A ROCK STAR OUT THERE, FACIAL HAIR BRO.
I STILL HATE YOU.
NO ONE LOVES FIGHTING FRIENDS.
I *HATE* IT.
THAT WAS A TOUGH ONE, BUT YOU ALL DID GREAT.
T'CHALLA, I THINK I SPEAK FOR EVERYONE WHEN I SAY: I'M KIND OF IN LOVE WITH YOU.
WELL, YOU ALWAYS HAVE BEEN.
WE NEED TO FIND THOR AND SPIDER-MAN BEFORE DANVERS DOES.
MS. MARVEL, YOU'RE PALS WITH HIM, I NEED YOU TO GO GET SPIDER-MAN FOR US.

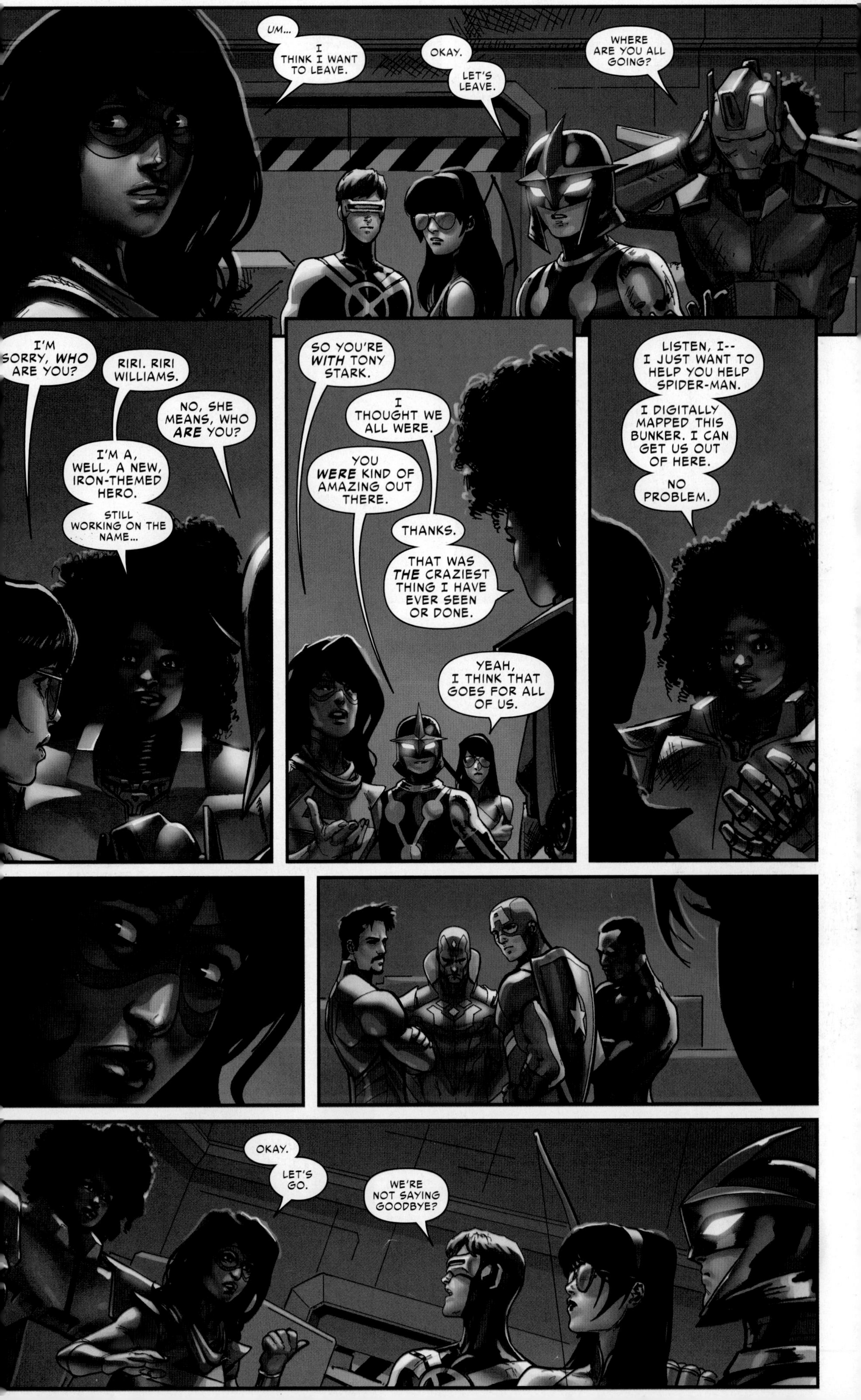
UM...
I THINK I WANT TO LEAVE.
OKAY.
LET'S LEAVE.
WHERE ARE YOU ALL GOING?
I'M SORRY, WHO ARE YOU?
RIRI. RIRI WILLIAMS.
NO, SHE MEANS, WHO ARE YOU?
I'M A, WELL, A NEW, IRON-THEMED HERO.
STILL WORKING ON THE NAME...
SO YOU'RE WITH TONY STARK.
I THOUGHT WE ALL WERE.
YOU WERE KIND OF AMAZING OUT THERE.
THANKS.
THAT WAS THE CRAZIEST THING I HAVE EVER SEEN OR DONE.
YEAH, I THINK THAT GOES FOR ALL OF US.
LISTEN, I-- I JUST WANT TO HELP YOU HELP SPIDER-MAN.
I DIGITALLY MAPPED THIS BUNKER. I CAN GET US OUT OF HERE.
NO PROBLEM.
OKAY.
LET'S GO.
WE'RE NOT SAYING GOODBYE?

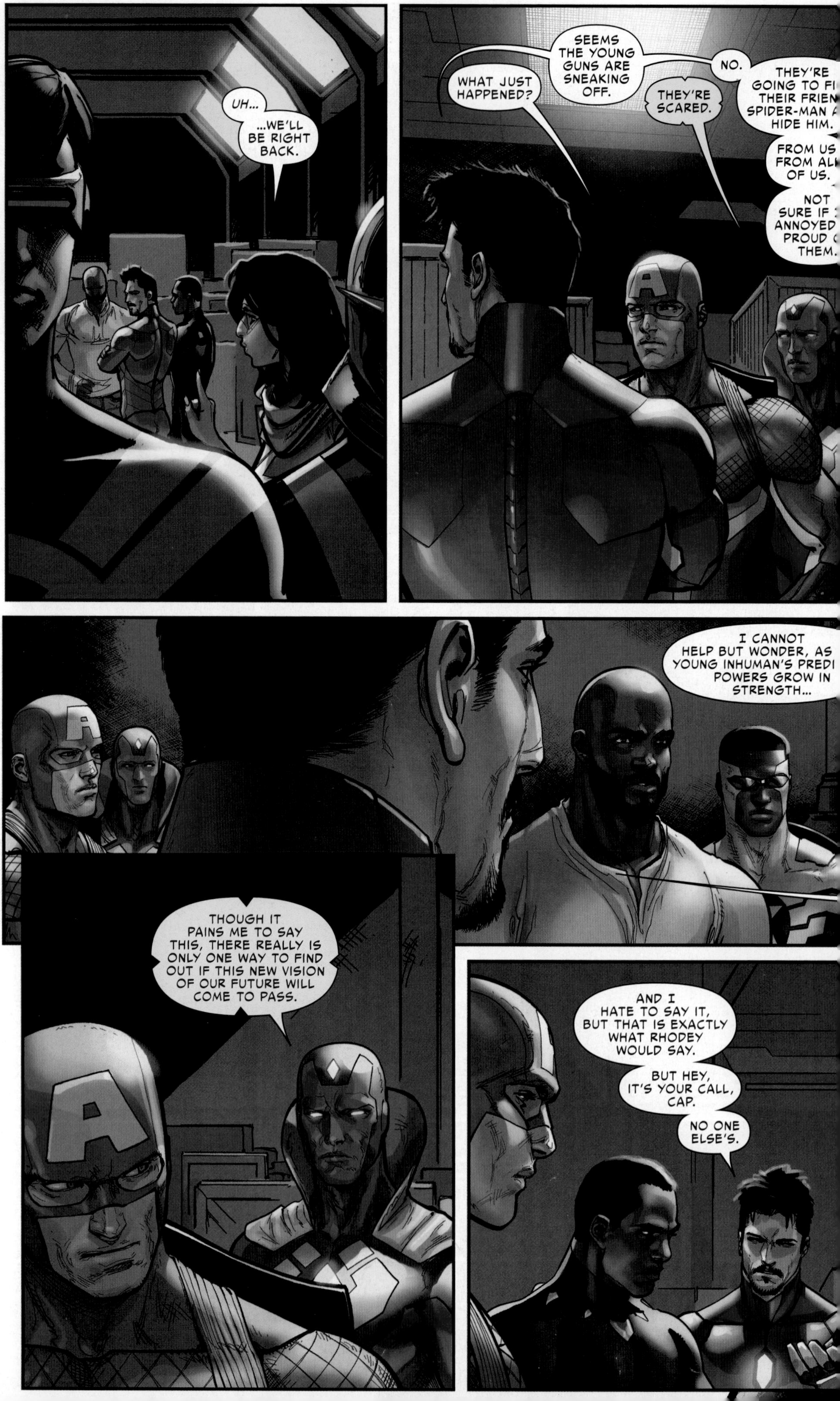

UH... ...WE'LL BE RIGHT BACK.
WHAT JUST HAPPENED?
SEEMS THE YOUNG GUNS ARE SNEAKING OFF.
THEY'RE SCARED.
NO.
THEY'RE GOING TO FI THEIR FRIEN SPIDER-MAN A HIDE HIM.
FROM US FROM AL OF US.
NOT SURE IF ANNOYED PROUD THEM.
I CANNOT HELP BUT WONDER, AS YOUNG INHUMAN'S PREDI POWERS GROW IN STRENGTH...
THOUGH IT PAINS ME TO SAY THIS, THERE REALLY IS ONLY ONE WAY TO FIND OUT IF THIS NEW VISION OF OUR FUTURE WILL COME TO PASS.
AND I HATE TO SAY IT, BUT THAT IS EXACTLY WHAT RHODEY WOULD SAY.
BUT HEY, IT'S YOUR CALL, CAP.
NO ONE ELSE'S.

HEY, YOU AND THAT *NEW* SPIDER-MAN DON'T HAVE ANY BAGGAGE I DON'T KNOW ABOUT, DO YOU?

NO! I BARELY KNOW HIM.

JUST MAKING SURE.

THE REASON I AM HERE WITH YOU NOW--

--IS THAT THERE *HAVE* BEEN OTHER VISIONS THAT HAVEN'T BEEN ACCURATE.

YES.

I KNEW IT!

BUT MANY WERE.

BUT NOW? WITH THIS ONE?

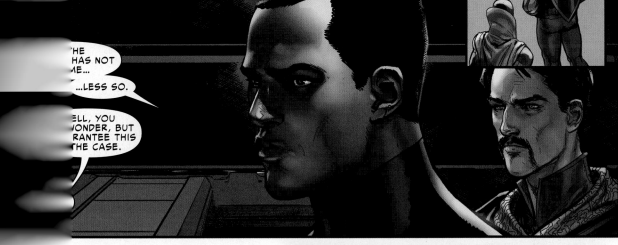

HE HAS NOT ME...

...LESS SO.

ELL, YOU ONDER, BUT RANTEE THIS HE CASE.

WELL, *AND* SPIDER-MAN'S...

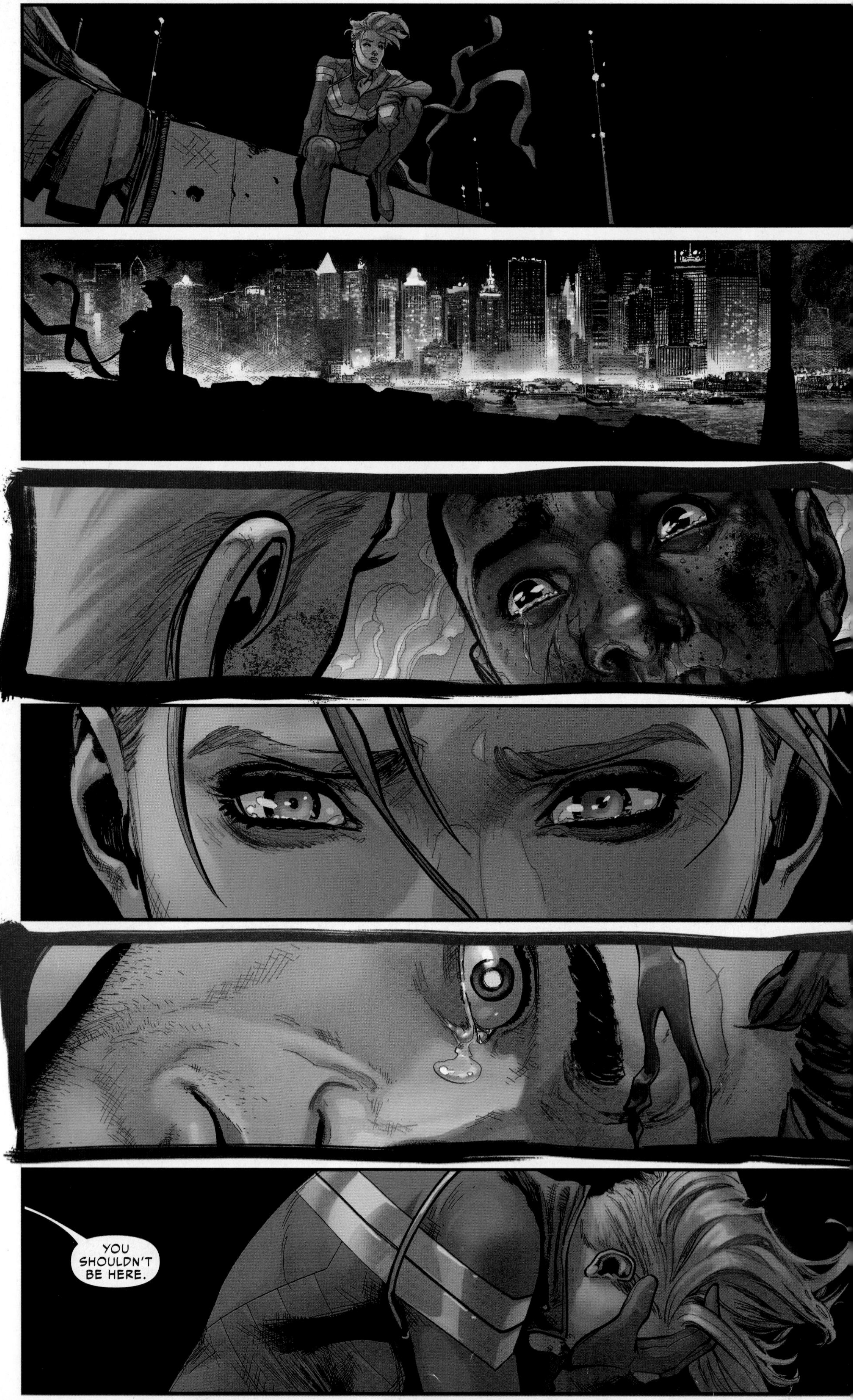
YOU SHOULDN'T BE HERE.

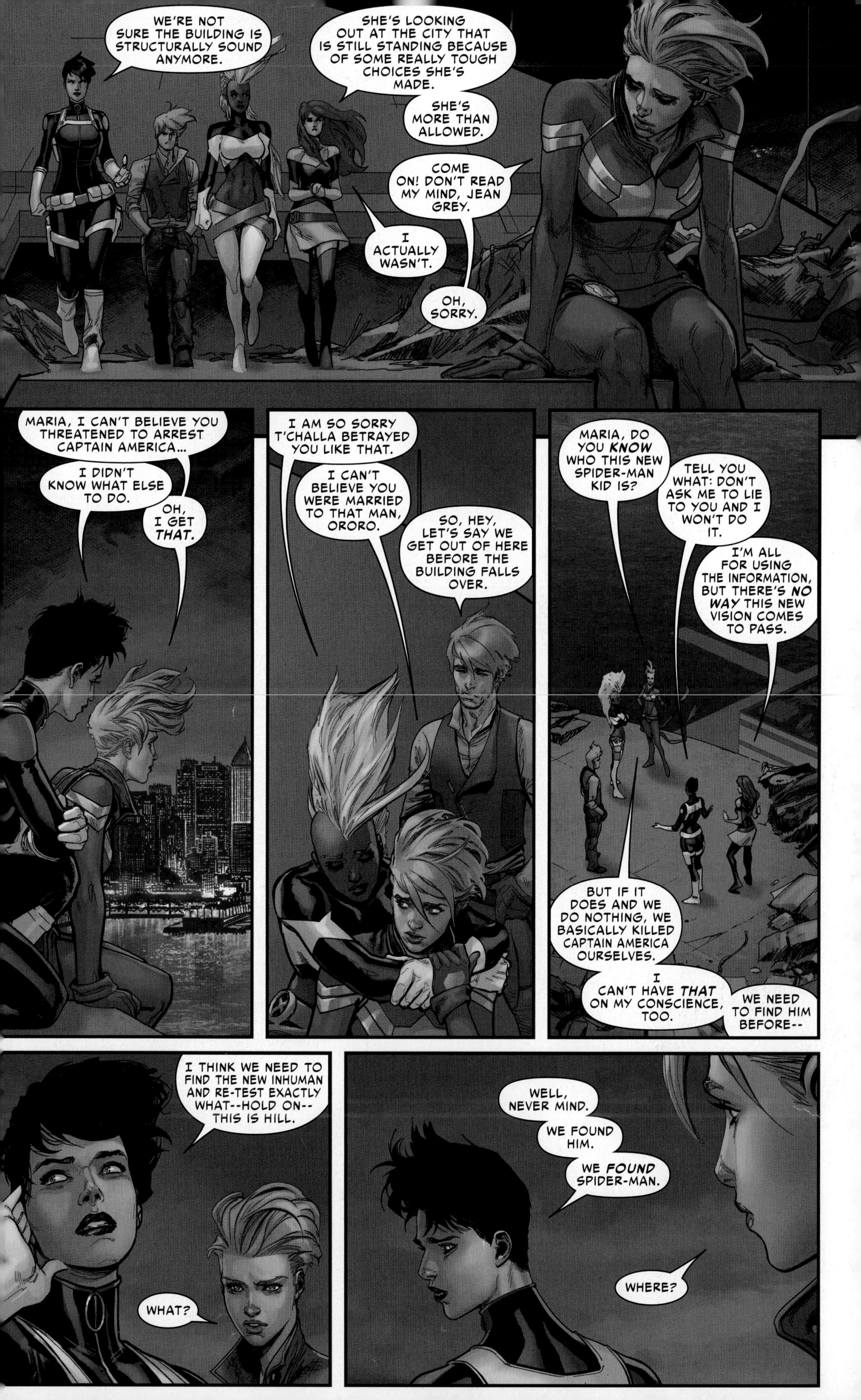
WE'RE NOT SURE THE BUILDING IS STRUCTURALLY SOUND ANYMORE.
SHE'S LOOKING OUT AT THE CITY THAT IS STILL STANDING BECAUSE OF SOME REALLY TOUGH CHOICES SHE'S MADE.
SHE'S MORE THAN ALLOWED.
COME ON! DON'T READ MY MIND, JEAN GREY.
I ACTUALLY WASN'T.
OH, SORRY.
MARIA, I CAN'T BELIEVE YOU THREATENED TO ARREST CAPTAIN AMERICA...
I DIDN'T KNOW WHAT ELSE TO DO.
OH, I GET *THAT.*
I AM SO SORRY T'CHALLA BETRAYED YOU LIKE THAT.
I CAN'T BELIEVE YOU WERE MARRIED TO THAT MAN, ORORO.
SO, HEY, LET'S SAY WE GET OUT OF HERE BEFORE THE BUILDING FALLS OVER.
MARIA, DO YOU *KNOW* WHO THIS NEW SPIDER-MAN KID IS?
TELL YOU WHAT: DON'T ASK ME TO LIE TO YOU AND I WON'T DO IT.
I'M ALL FOR USING THE INFORMATION, BUT THERE'S *NO WAY* THIS NEW VISION COMES TO PASS.
BUT IF IT DOES AND WE DO NOTHING, WE BASICALLY KILLED CAPTAIN AMERICA OURSELVES.
I CAN'T HAVE *THAT* ON MY CONSCIENCE, TOO.
WE NEED TO FIND HIM BEFORE--
I THINK WE NEED TO FIND THE NEW INHUMAN AND RE-TEST EXACTLY WHAT--HOLD ON-- THIS IS HILL.
WHAT?
WELL, NEVER MIND.
WE FOUND HIM.
WE *FOUND* SPIDER-MAN.
WHERE?

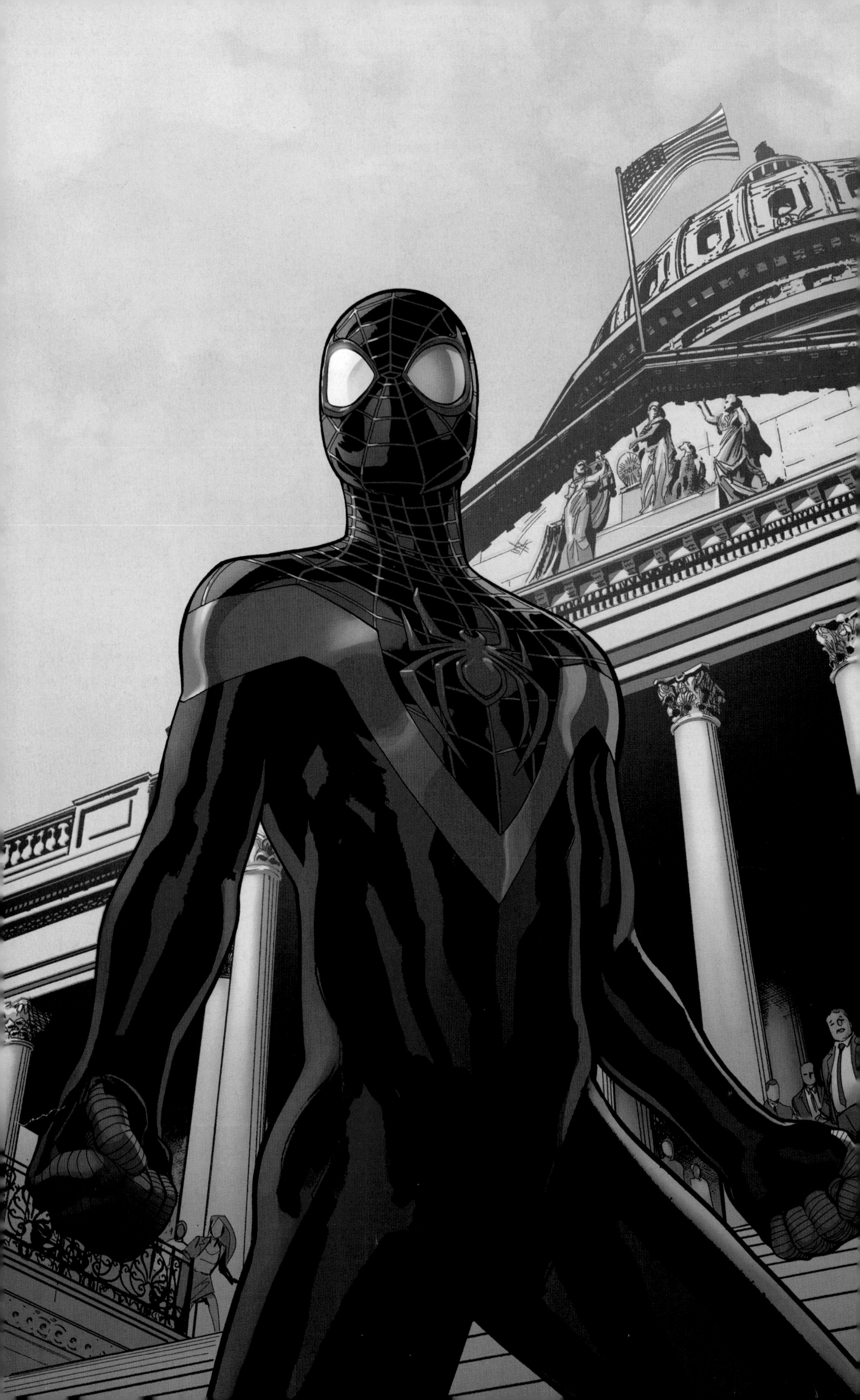

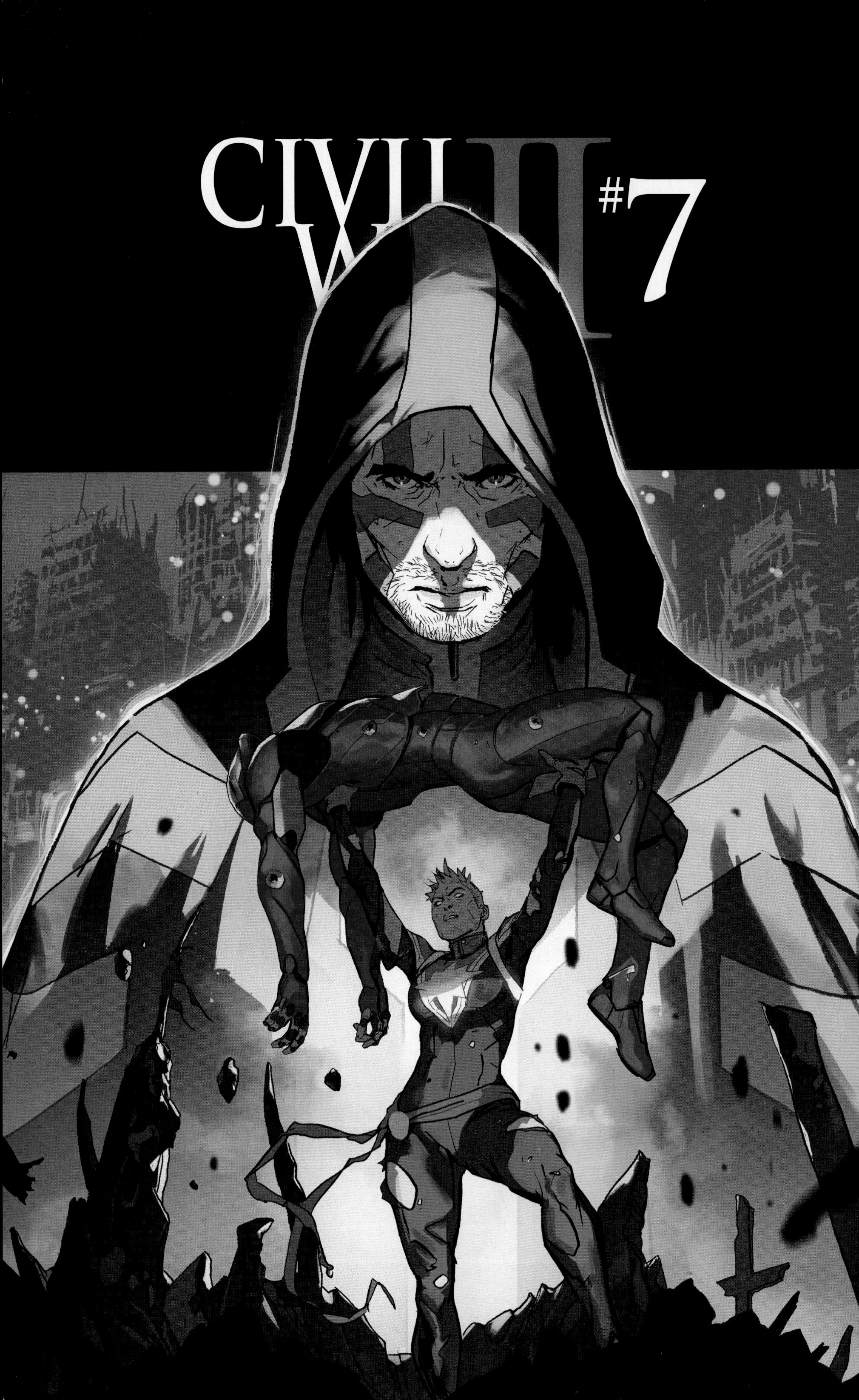
CIVIL WAR II
#7

...SSES?

NEW ATTILAN.

ULYSSES? CAN YOU HEAR ME?

FOCUS, INHUMAN!

WE NEED TO SPEAK WITH YOU.

WE WANT TO HELP YOU, BUT WE NEED TO--

YOUR BIRTHRIGHT, YOUR INHUMAN ABILITIES, SEEM TO BE EVOLVING EVEN FASTER THAN WE HAD GUESSED THEY WOULD.

YOUR VISIONS ARE MORE POTENT, AND THE VISIONS THEMSELVES ARE MORE--ARE MORE--

OFF-PUTTING.

--ERRATIC.

THE ULTIMATES WOULD LIKE TO BRING YOU IN FOR MORE STUDY.

BUT--BUT WE'LL ONLY AGREE TO IT IF YOU AGREE TO IT.

IT'S IMPORTANT TO ME, AS THE LEADER OF OUR FAMILY, THAT YOU CHOOSE TO SEEK HELP.

THAT YOU SEE THE NEED.

ANSWER YOUR QUEEN, ULYSSES.

I SEE YOU SLIPPING FROM US.

I SEE YOU--

CAN HE HEAR ME?

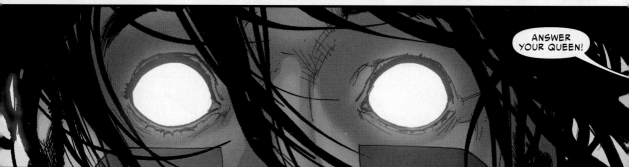

ANSWER YOUR QUEEN!

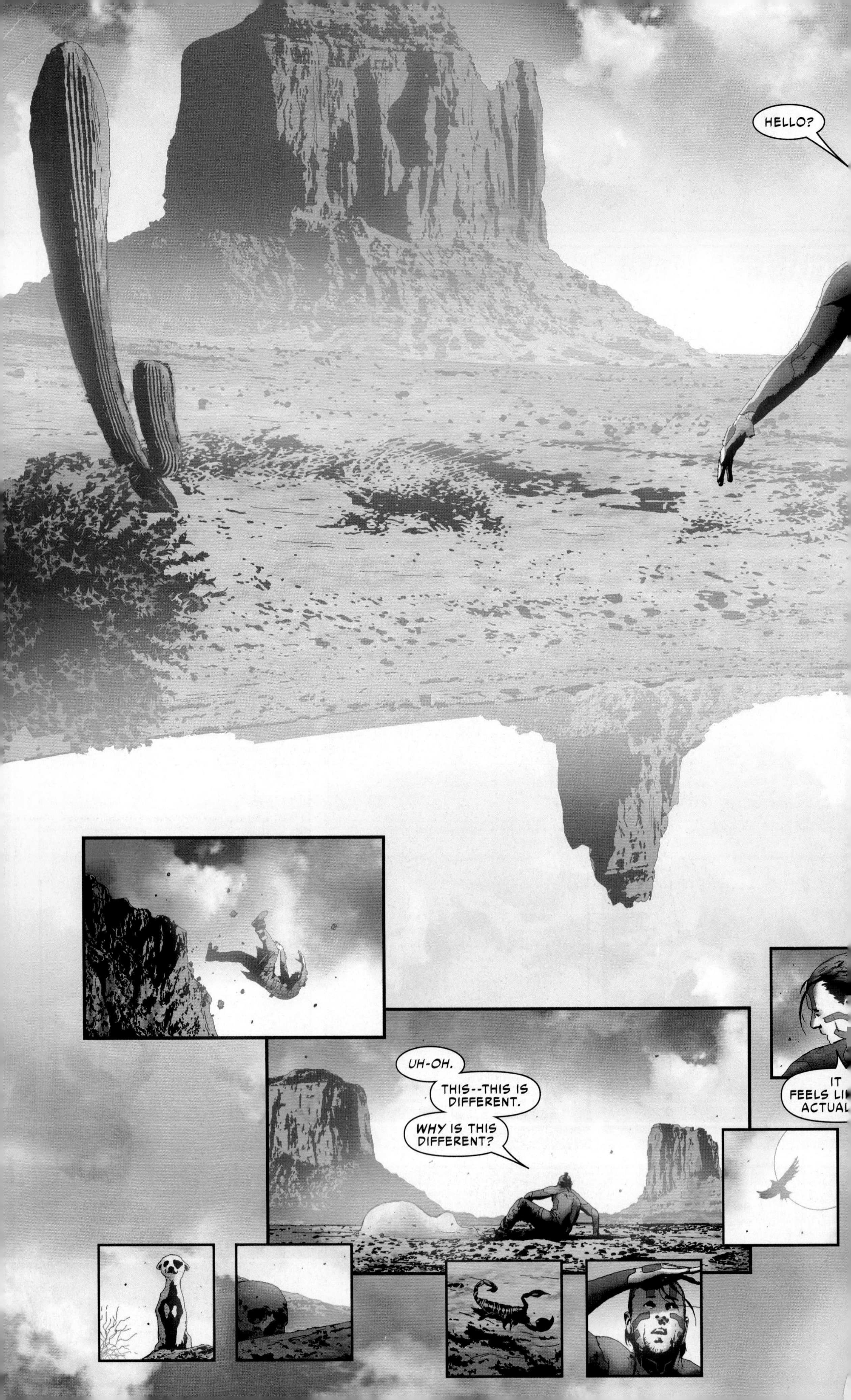
HELLO?
UH-OH.
THIS--THIS IS DIFFERENT.
WHY IS THIS DIFFERENT?
IT FEELS LI
ACTUAL

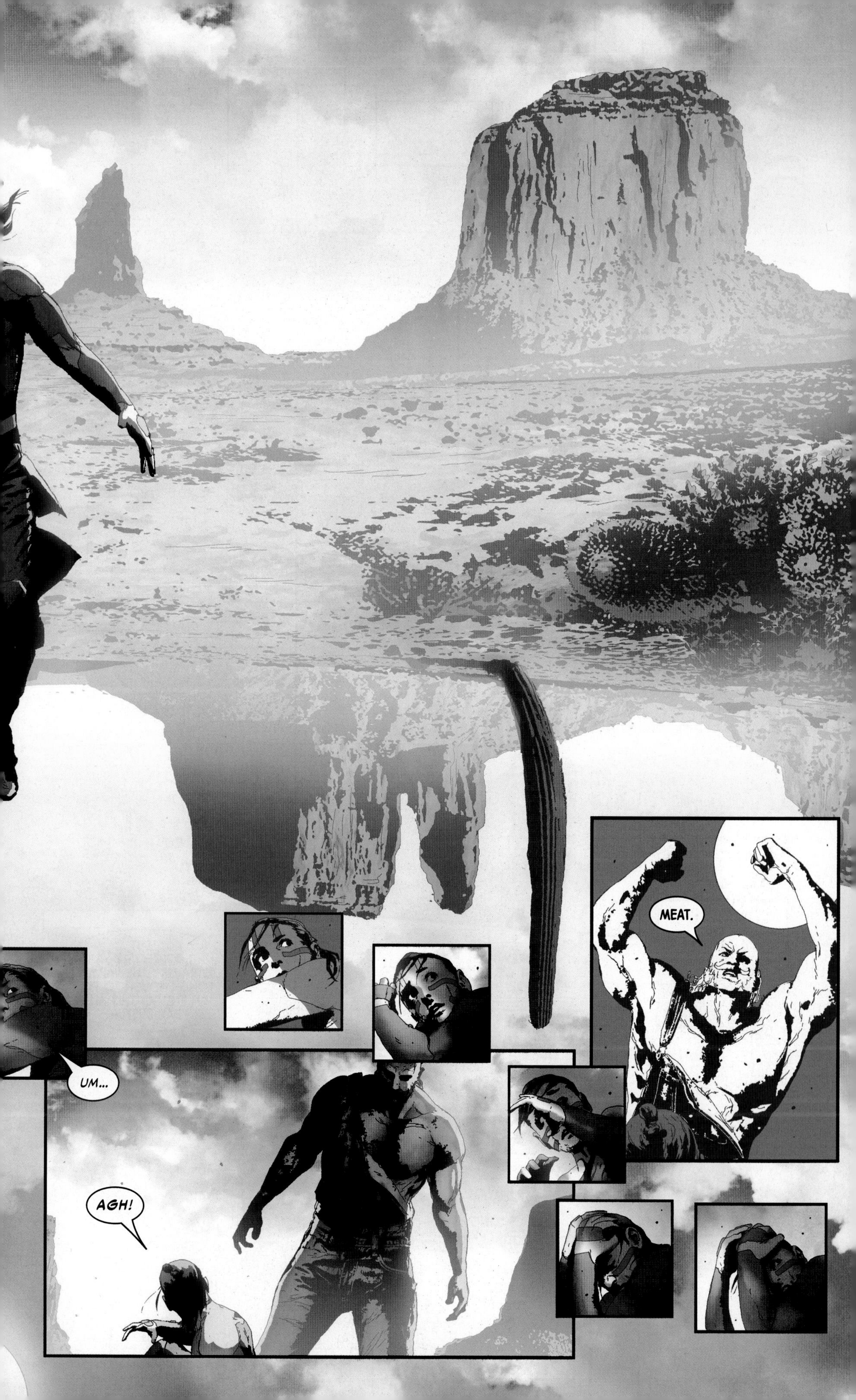
MEAT.
UM...
AGH!

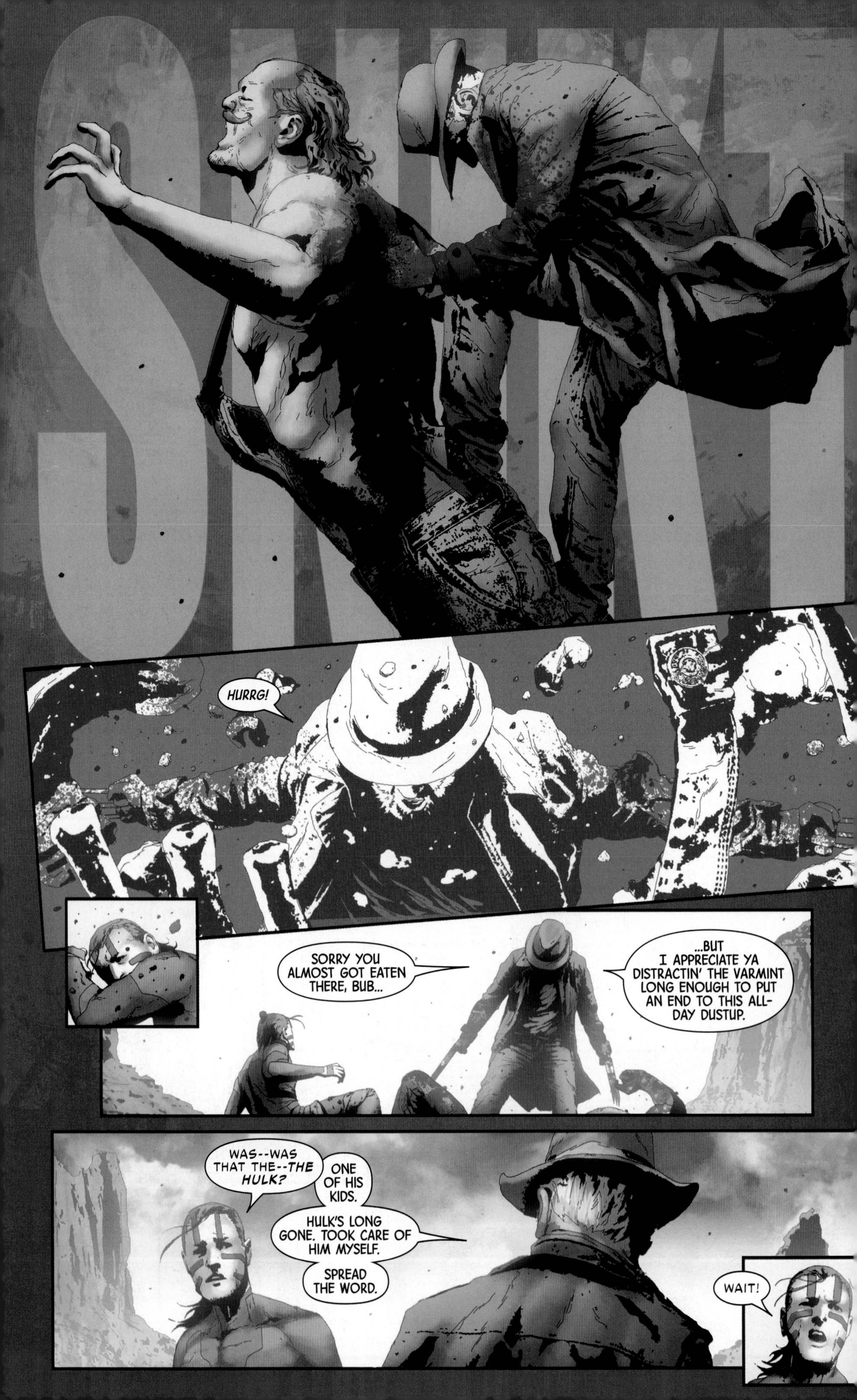
HURRG!
SORRY YOU ALMOST GOT EATEN THERE, BUB...
...BUT I APPRECIATE YA DISTRACTIN' THE VARMINT LONG ENOUGH TO PUT AN END TO THIS ALL-DAY DUSTUP.
WAS--WAS THAT THE--THE HULK?
ONE OF HIS KIDS.
HULK'S LONG GONE. TOOK CARE OF HIM MYSELF.
SPREAD THE WORD.
WAIT!

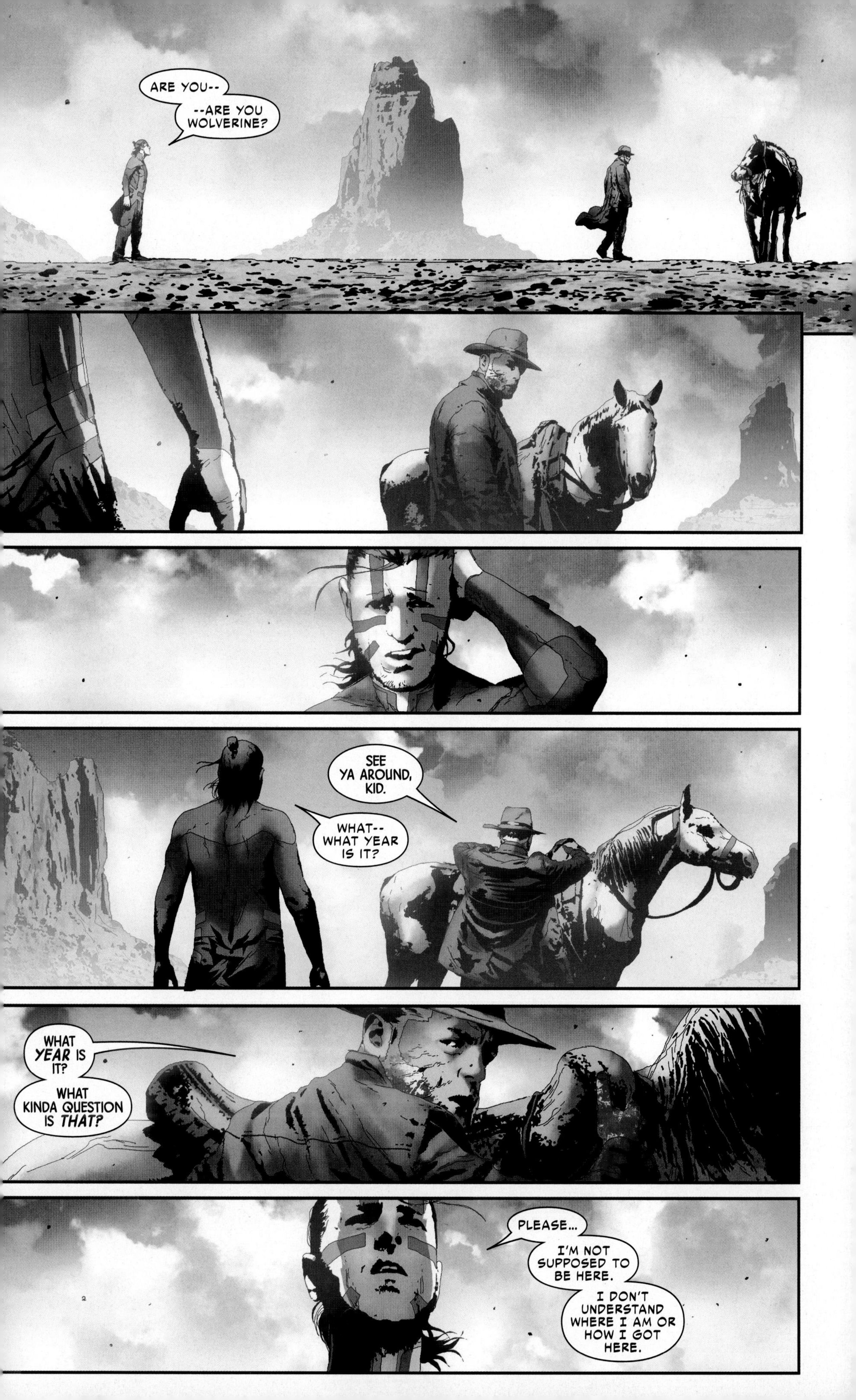
ARE YOU--
--ARE YOU WOLVERINE?
SEE YA AROUND, KID.
WHAT--WHAT YEAR IS IT?
WHAT *YEAR* IS IT?
WHAT KINDA QUESTION IS *THAT?*
PLEASE...
I'M NOT SUPPOSED TO BE HERE.
I DON'T UNDERSTAND WHERE I AM OR HOW I GOT HERE.

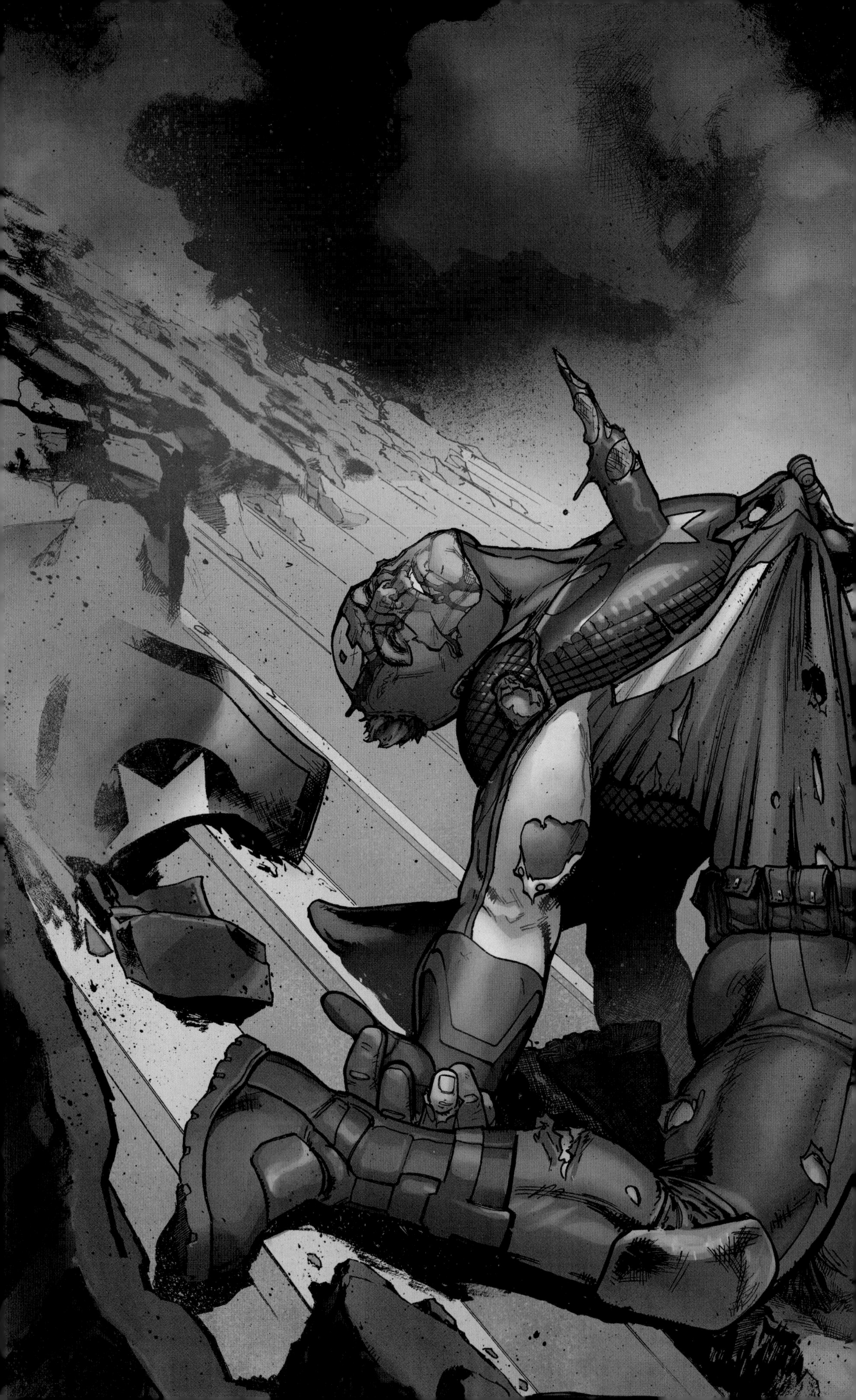

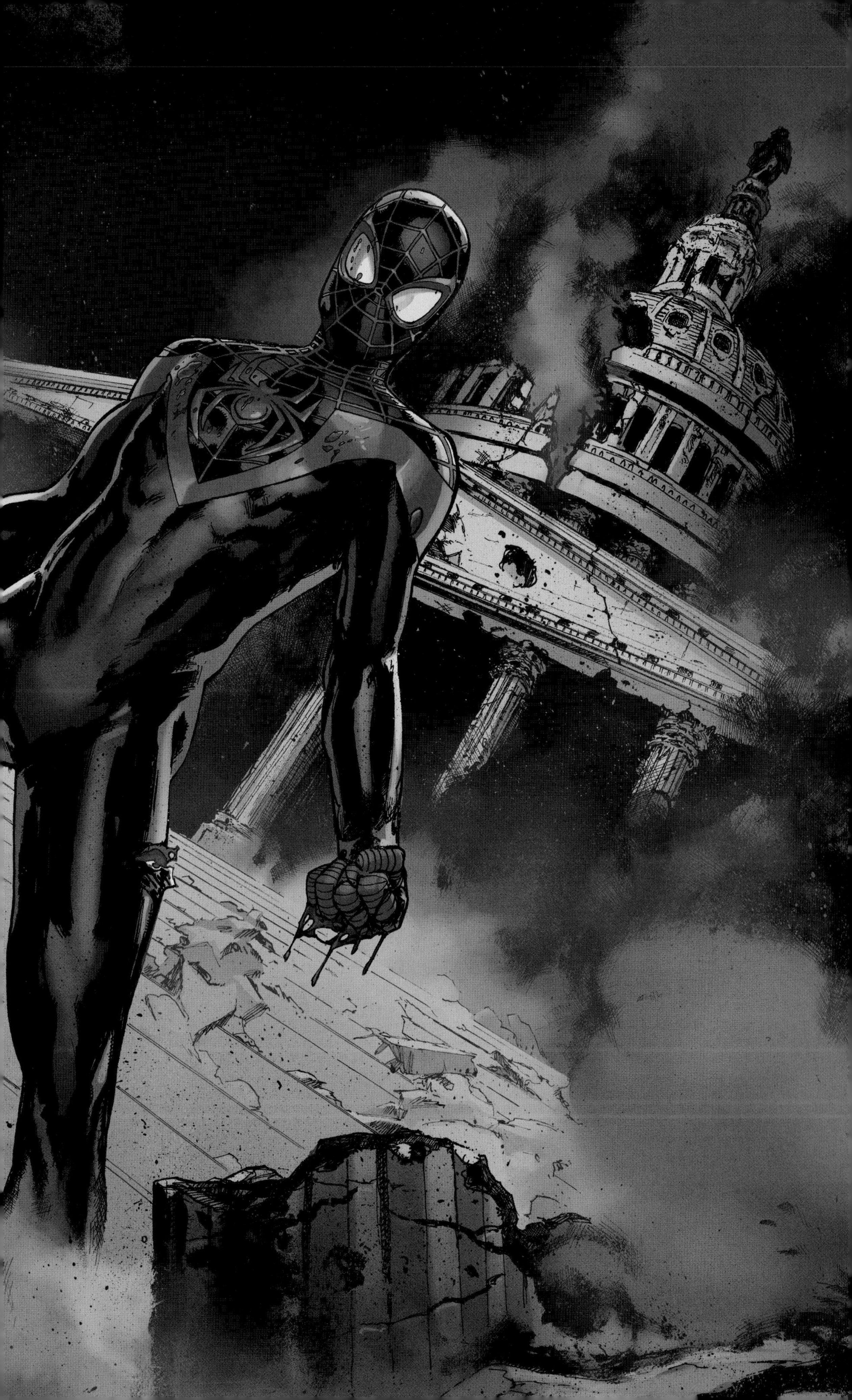

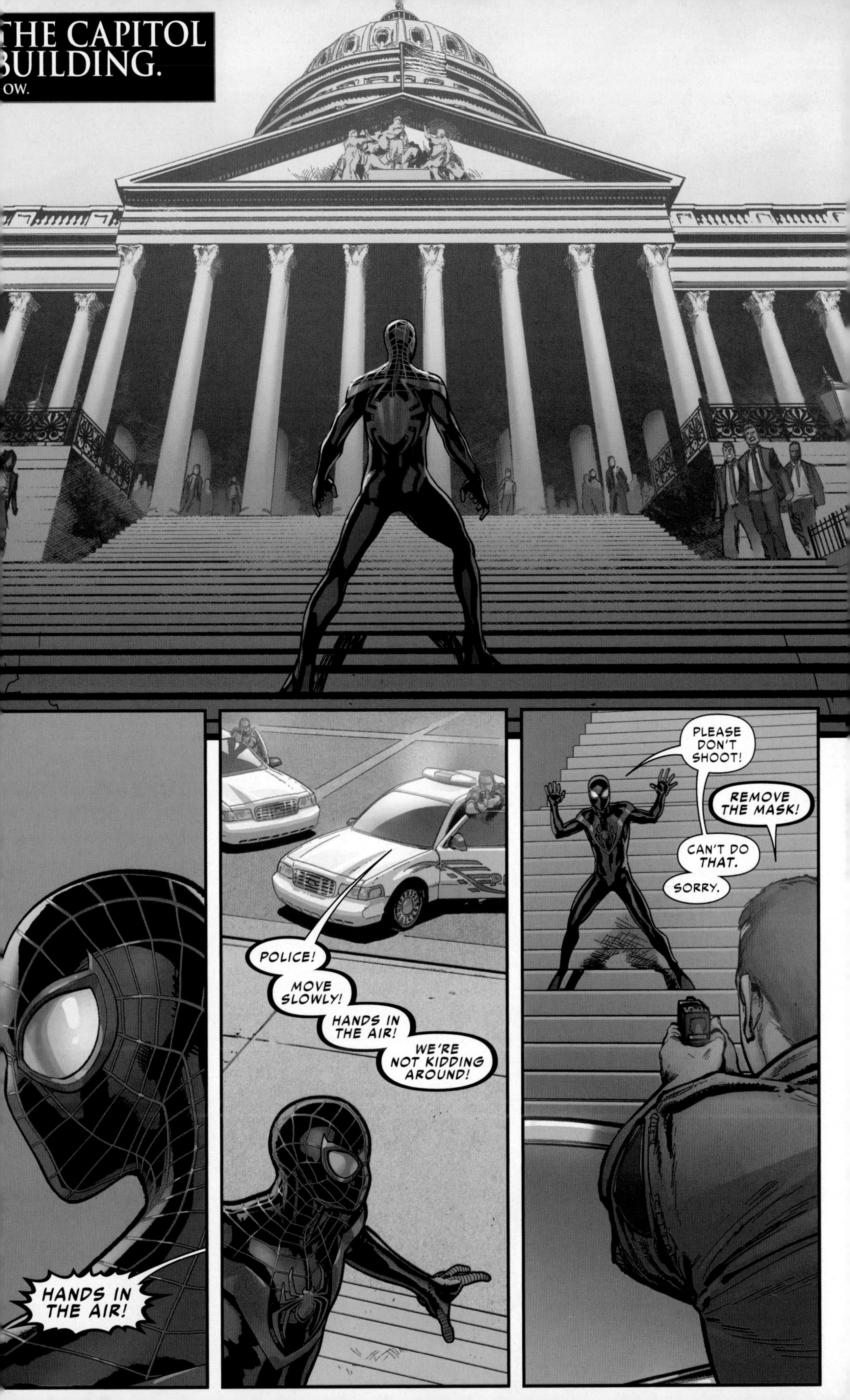
THE CAPITOL
BUILDING.
OW.
HANDS IN THE AIR!
POLICE!
MOVE SLOWLY!
HANDS IN THE AIR!
WE'RE NOT KIDDING AROUND!
PLEASE DON'T SHOOT!
REMOVE THE MASK!
CAN'T DO THAT.
SORRY.

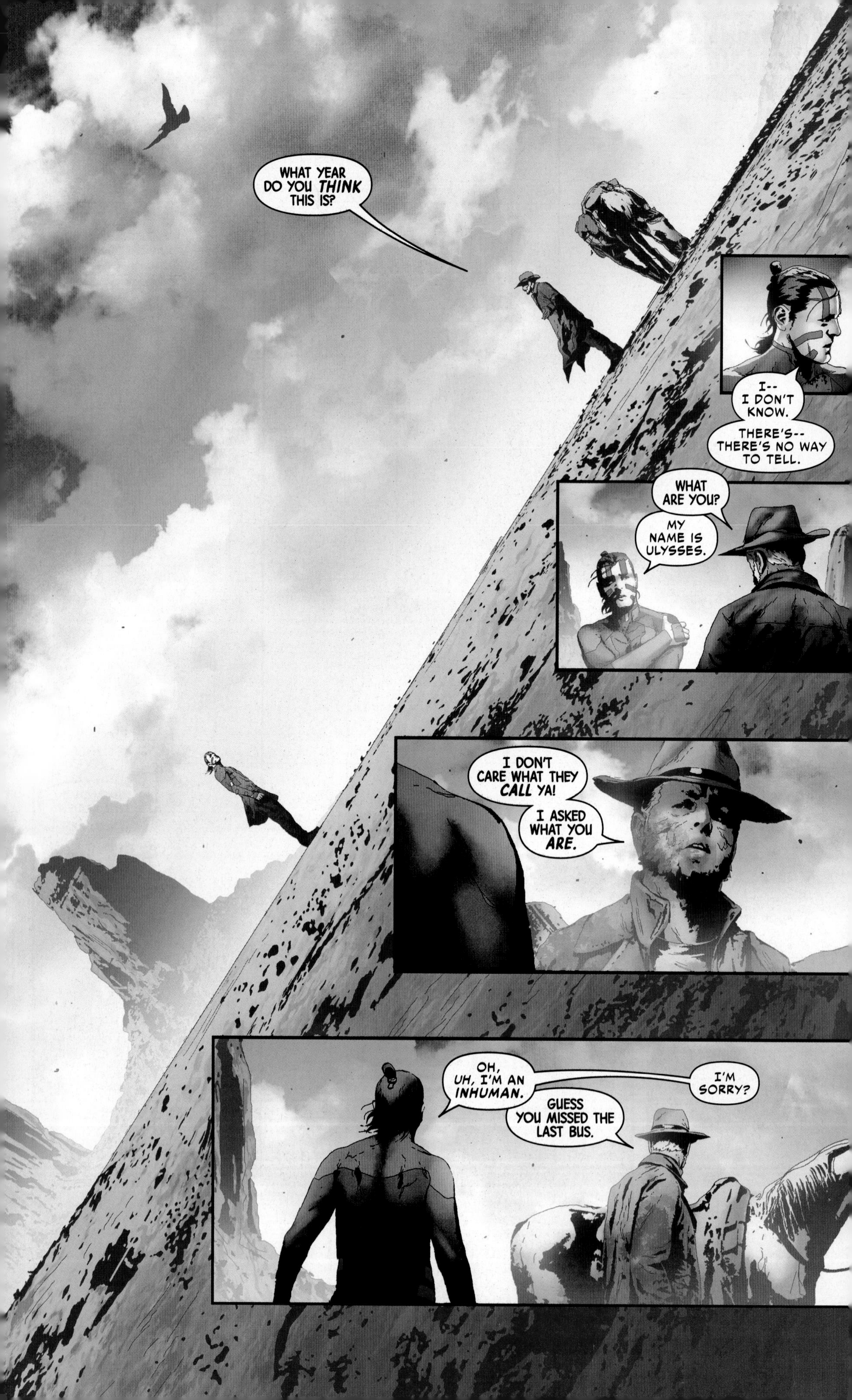
WHAT YEAR DO YOU THINK THIS IS?
I-- I DON'T KNOW.
THERE'S-- THERE'S NO WAY TO TELL.
WHAT ARE YOU?
MY NAME IS ULYSSES.
I DON'T CARE WHAT THEY CALL YA!
I ASKED WHAT YOU ARE.
OH, UH, I'M AN INHUMAN.
I'M SORRY?
GUESS YOU MISSED THE LAST BUS.

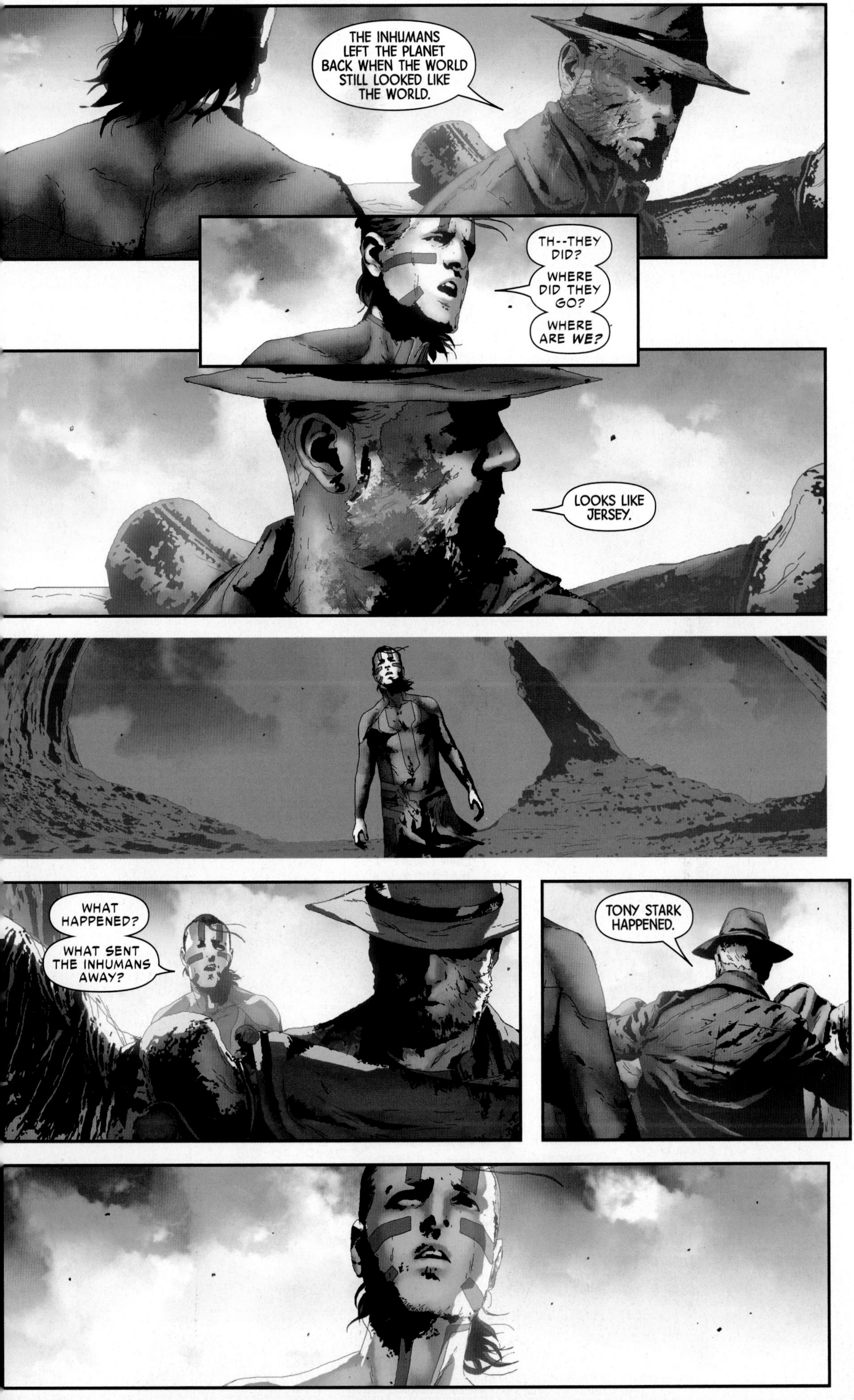
THE INHUMANS LEFT THE PLANET BACK WHEN THE WORLD STILL LOOKED LIKE THE WORLD.
TH--THEY DID?
WHERE DID THEY GO?
WHERE ARE WE?
LOOKS LIKE JERSEY.
WHAT HAPPENED?
WHAT SENT THE INHUMANS AWAY?
TONY STARK HAPPENED.

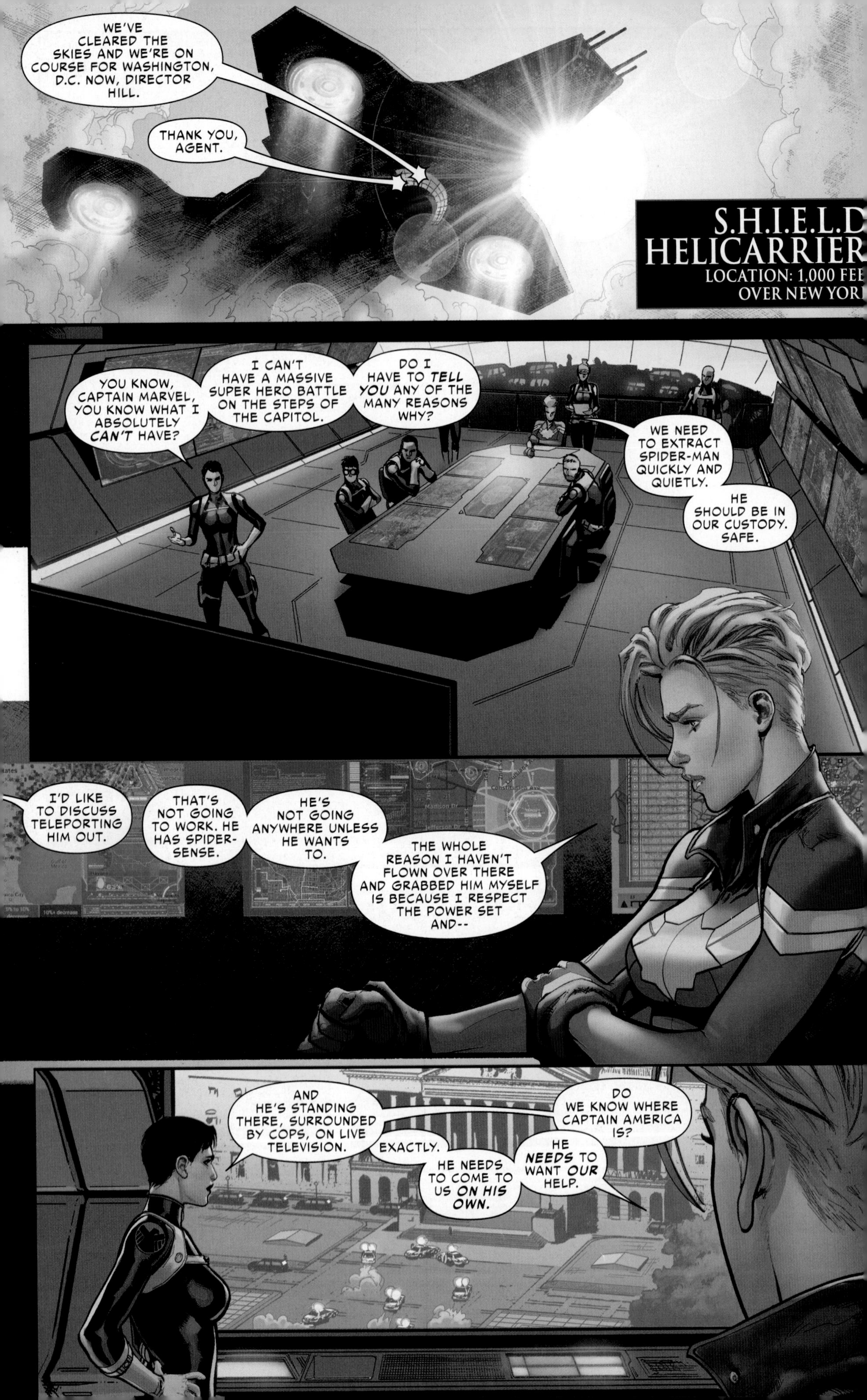

WE'VE CLEARED THE SKIES AND WE'RE ON COURSE FOR WASHINGTON, D.C. NOW, DIRECTOR HILL.
THANK YOU, AGENT.
S.H.I.E.L.D HELICARRIER
LOCATION: 1,000 FEE
OVER NEW YOR
YOU KNOW, CAPTAIN MARVEL, YOU KNOW WHAT I ABSOLUTELY CAN'T HAVE?
I CAN'T HAVE A MASSIVE SUPER HERO BATTLE ON THE STEPS OF THE CAPITOL.
DO I HAVE TO TELL YOU ANY OF THE MANY REASONS WHY?
WE NEED TO EXTRACT SPIDER-MAN QUICKLY AND QUIETLY.
HE SHOULD BE IN OUR CUSTODY. SAFE.
I'D LIKE TO DISCUSS TELEPORTING HIM OUT.
THAT'S NOT GOING TO WORK. HE HAS SPIDER-SENSE.
HE'S NOT GOING ANYWHERE UNLESS HE WANTS TO.
THE WHOLE REASON I HAVEN'T FLOWN OVER THERE AND GRABBED HIM MYSELF IS BECAUSE I RESPECT THE POWER SET AND--
AND HE'S STANDING THERE, SURROUNDED BY COPS, ON LIVE TELEVISION.
DO WE KNOW WHERE CAPTAIN AMERICA IS?
EXACTLY.
HE NEEDS TO COME TO US ON HIS OWN.
HE NEEDS TO WANT OUR HELP.

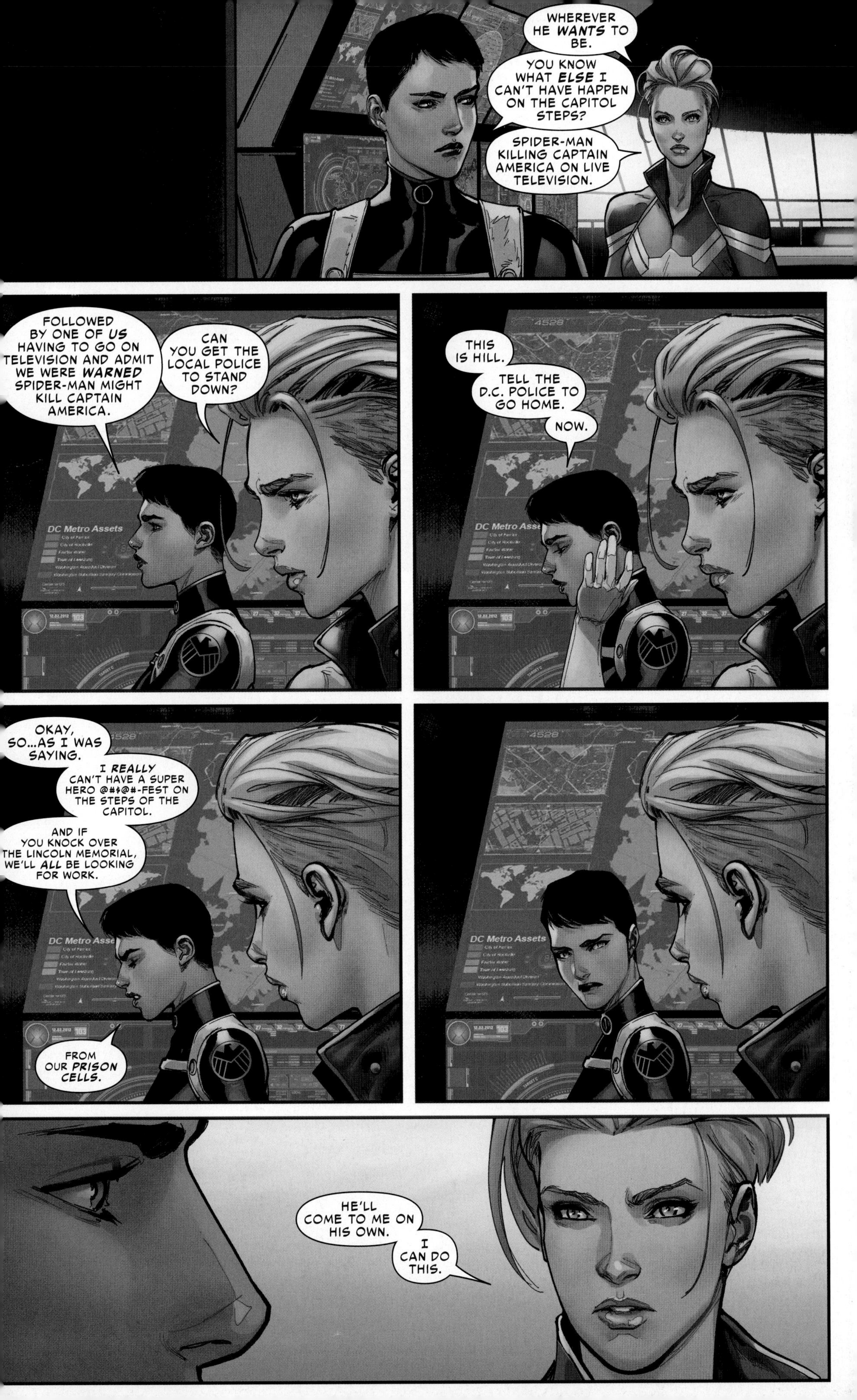
WHEREVER HE *WANTS* TO BE.
YOU KNOW WHAT *ELSE* I CAN'T HAVE HAPPEN ON THE CAPITOL STEPS?
SPIDER-MAN KILLING CAPTAIN AMERICA ON LIVE TELEVISION.
FOLLOWED BY ONE OF *US* HAVING TO GO ON TELEVISION AND ADMIT WE WERE *WARNED* SPIDER-MAN MIGHT KILL CAPTAIN AMERICA.
CAN YOU GET THE LOCAL POLICE TO STAND DOWN?
THIS IS HILL.
TELL THE D.C. POLICE TO GO HOME.
NOW.
OKAY, SO...AS I WAS SAYING.
I *REALLY* CAN'T HAVE A SUPER HERO @#$@#-FEST ON THE STEPS OF THE CAPITOL.
AND IF YOU KNOCK OVER THE LINCOLN MEMORIAL, WE'LL *ALL* BE LOOKING FOR WORK.
FROM OUR *PRISON CELLS*.
HE'LL COME TO ME ON HIS OWN.
I CAN DO THIS.

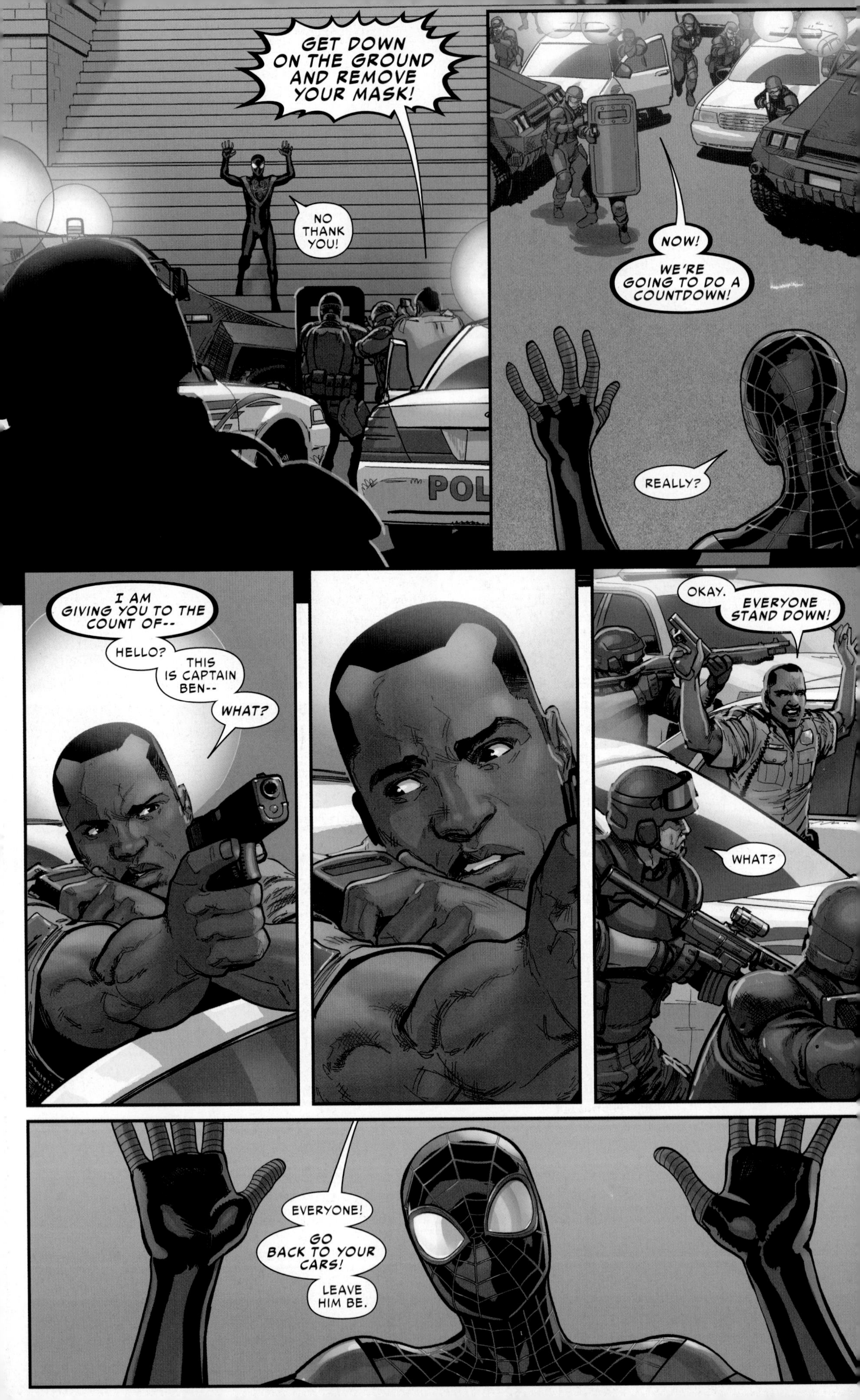
GET DOWN ON THE GROUND AND REMOVE YOUR MASK!
NO THANK YOU!
NOW!
WE'RE GOING TO DO A COUNTDOWN!
REALLY?
I AM GIVING YOU TO THE COUNT OF--
HELLO?
THIS IS CAPTAIN BEN--
WHAT?
OKAY.
EVERYONE STAND DOWN!
WHAT?
EVERYONE!
GO BACK TO YOUR CARS!
LEAVE HIM BE.

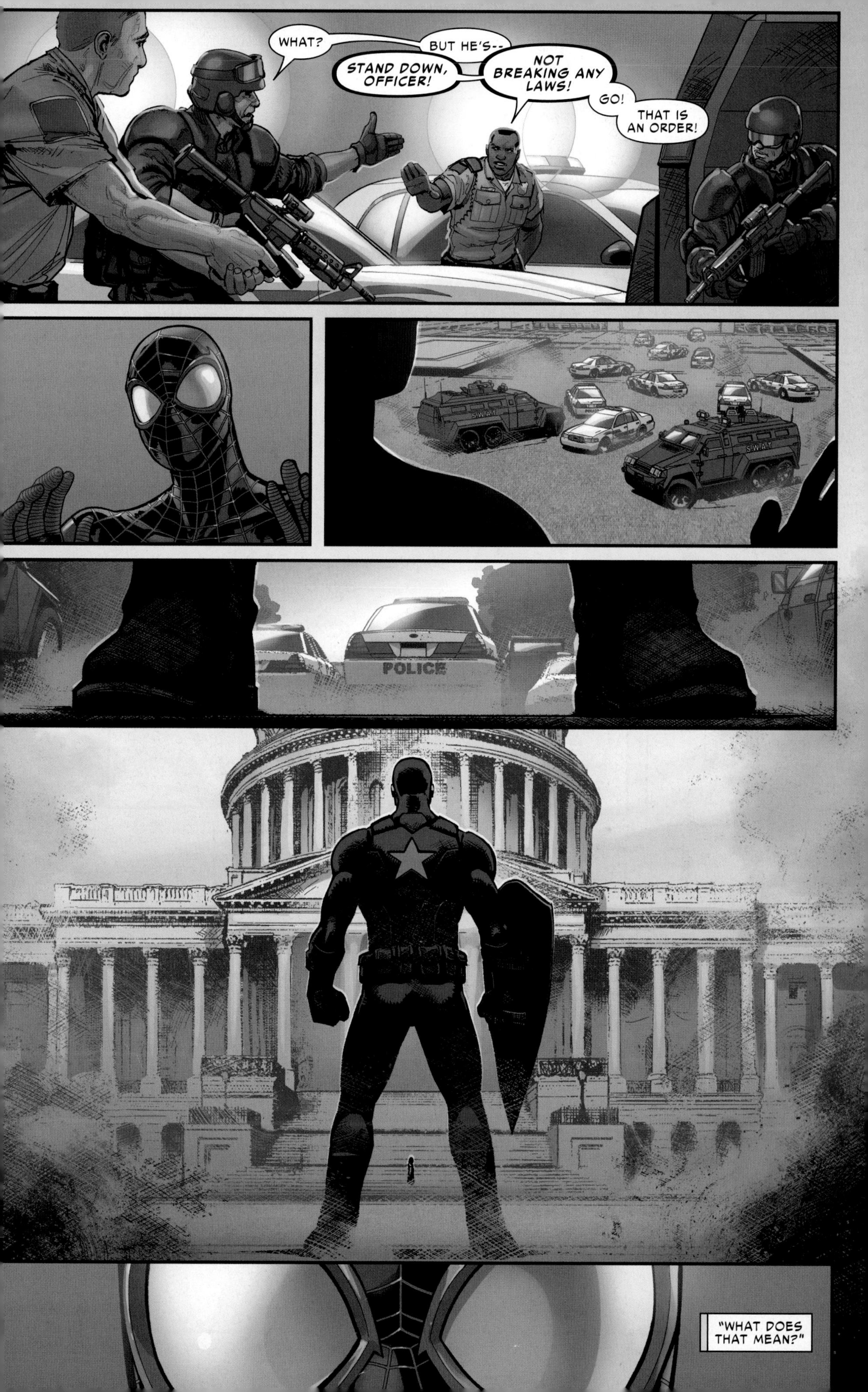
WHAT?
BUT HE'S--
STAND DOWN, OFFICER!
NOT BREAKING ANY LAWS!
GO!
THAT IS AN ORDER!
S.W.A.T
S.W.A.T
POLICE
"WHAT DOES THAT MEAN?"

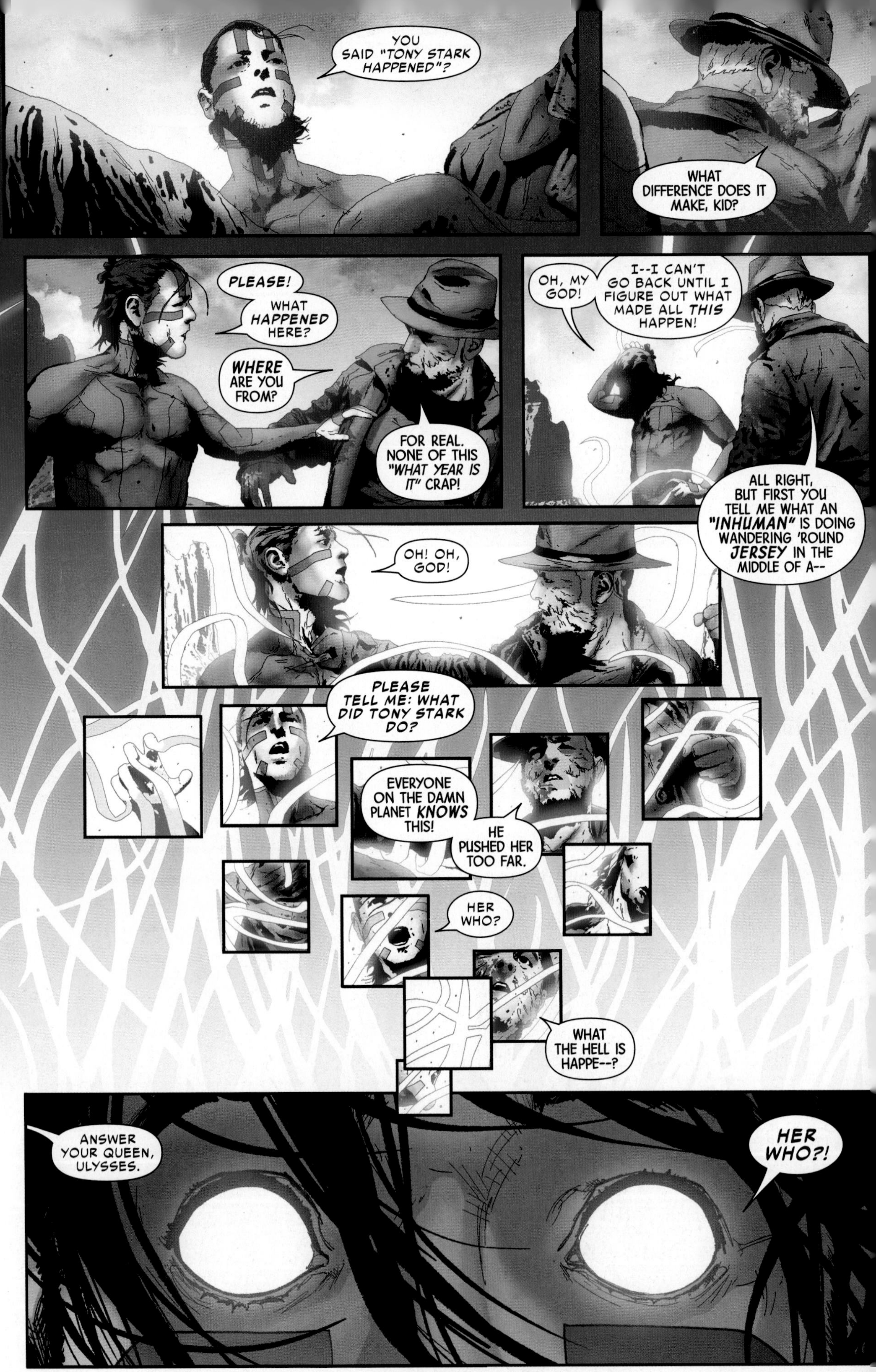
YOU SAID "TONY STARK HAPPENED"?
WHAT DIFFERENCE DOES IT MAKE, KID?
PLEASE!
WHAT HAPPENED HERE?
WHERE ARE YOU FROM?
FOR REAL. NONE OF THIS "WHAT YEAR IS IT" CRAP!
OH, MY GOD!
I--I CAN'T GO BACK UNTIL I FIGURE OUT WHAT MADE ALL THIS HAPPEN!
ALL RIGHT, BUT FIRST YOU TELL ME WHAT AN "INHUMAN" IS DOING WANDERING 'ROUND JERSEY IN THE MIDDLE OF A--
OH! OH, GOD!
PLEASE TELL ME: WHAT DID TONY STARK DO?
EVERYONE ON THE DAMN PLANET KNOWS THIS!
HE PUSHED HER TOO FAR.
HER WHO?
WHAT THE HELL IS HAPPE--?
ANSWER YOUR QUEEN, ULYSSES.
HER WHO?!

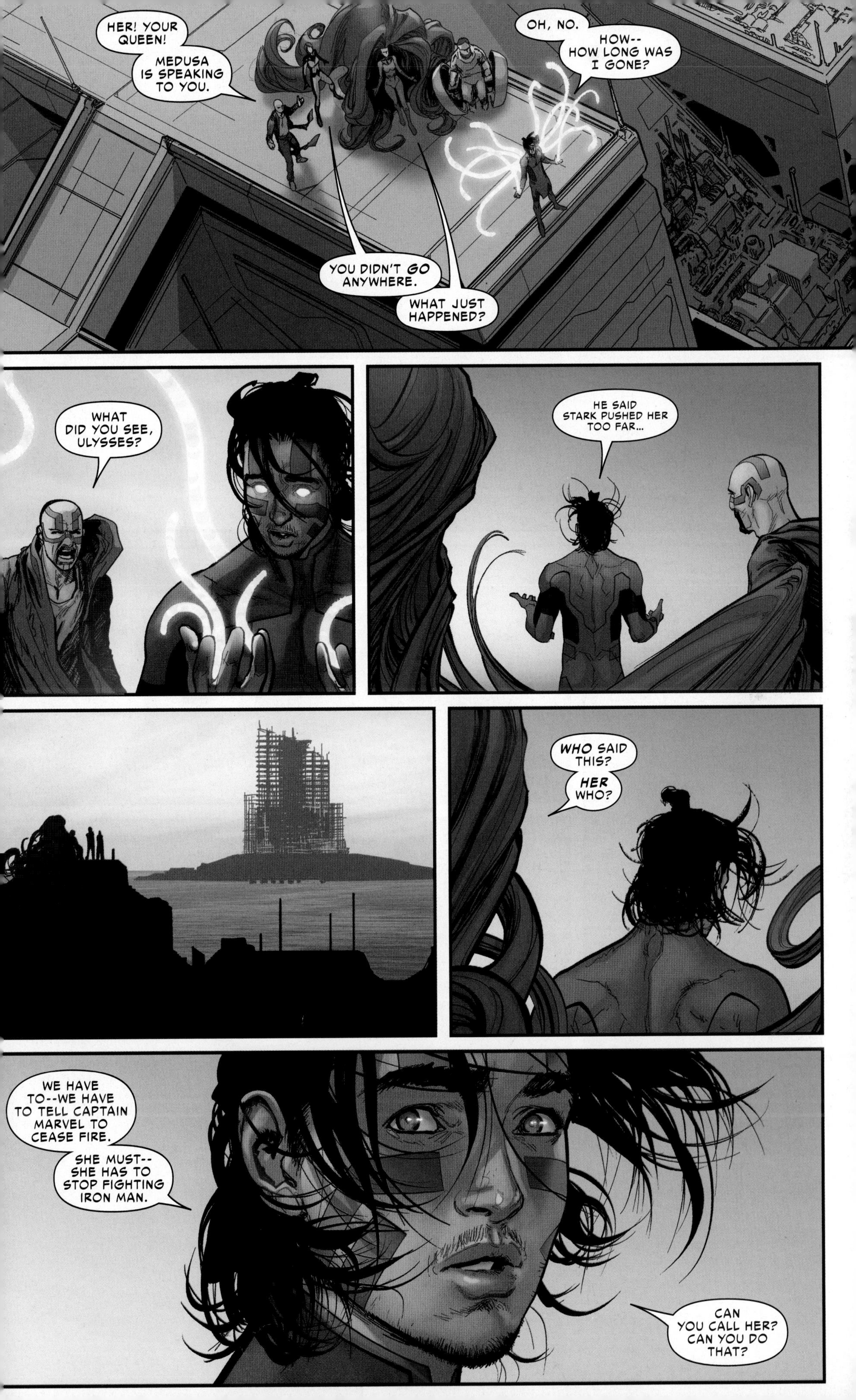
HER! YOUR QUEEN!
MEDUSA IS SPEAKING TO YOU.
OH, NO.
HOW-- HOW LONG WAS I GONE?
YOU DIDN'T GO ANYWHERE.
WHAT JUST HAPPENED?
WHAT DID YOU SEE, ULYSSES?
HE SAID STARK PUSHED HER TOO FAR...
WHO SAID THIS?
HER WHO?
WE HAVE TO--WE HAVE TO TELL CAPTAIN MARVEL TO CEASE FIRE.
SHE MUST-- SHE HAS TO STOP FIGHTING IRON MAN.
CAN YOU CALL HER? CAN YOU DO THAT?

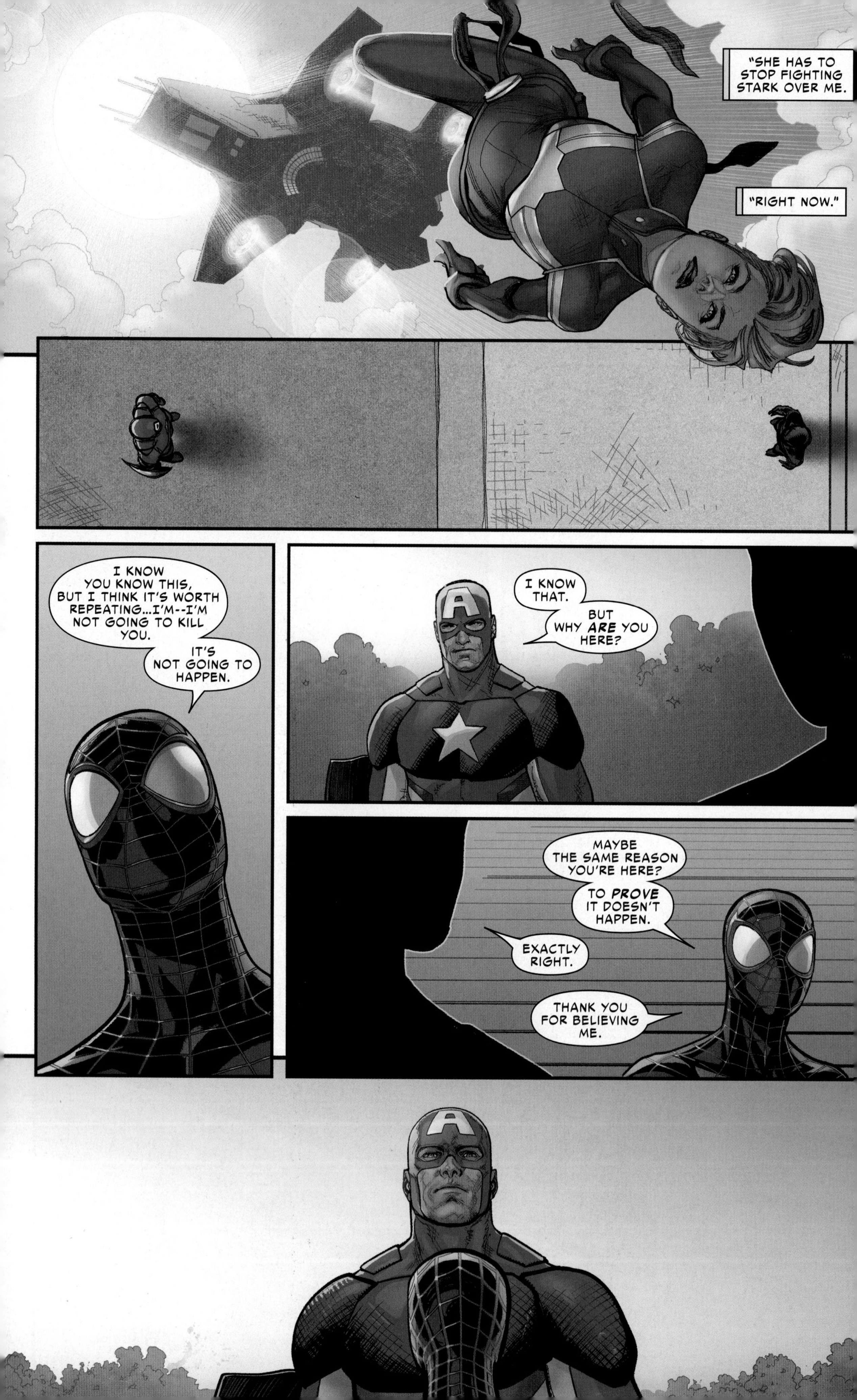
"SHE HAS TO STOP FIGHTING STARK OVER ME.
"RIGHT NOW."
I KNOW YOU KNOW THIS, BUT I THINK IT'S WORTH REPEATING...I'M--I'M NOT GOING TO KILL YOU.
IT'S NOT GOING TO HAPPEN.
I KNOW THAT.
BUT WHY ARE YOU HERE?
MAYBE THE SAME REASON YOU'RE HERE?
TO PROVE IT DOESN'T HAPPEN.
EXACTLY RIGHT.
THANK YOU FOR BELIEVING ME.

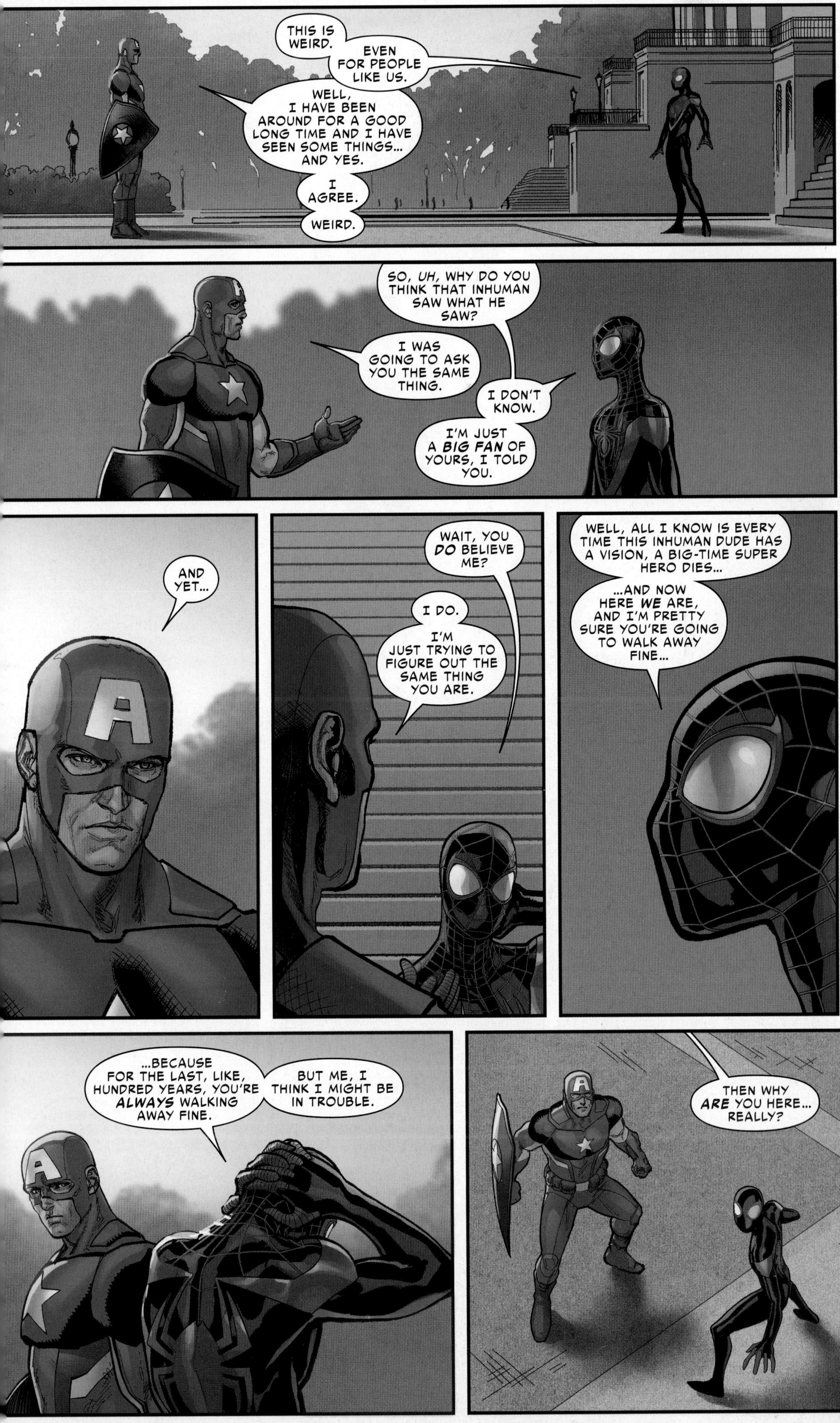
THIS IS WEIRD.
EVEN FOR PEOPLE LIKE US.
WELL, I HAVE BEEN AROUND FOR A GOOD LONG TIME AND I HAVE SEEN SOME THINGS... AND YES.
I AGREE.
WEIRD.
SO, *UH*, WHY DO YOU THINK THAT INHUMAN SAW WHAT HE SAW?
I WAS GOING TO ASK YOU THE SAME THING.
I DON'T KNOW.
I'M JUST A ***BIG FAN*** OF YOURS, I TOLD YOU.
AND YET...
WAIT, YOU ***DO*** BELIEVE ME?
I DO.
I'M JUST TRYING TO FIGURE OUT THE SAME THING YOU ARE.
WELL, ALL I KNOW IS EVERY TIME THIS INHUMAN DUDE HAS A VISION, A BIG-TIME SUPER HERO DIES...
...AND NOW HERE ***WE*** ARE, AND I'M PRETTY SURE YOU'RE GOING TO WALK AWAY FINE...
...BECAUSE FOR THE LAST, LIKE, HUNDRED YEARS, YOU'RE ***ALWAYS*** WALKING AWAY FINE.
BUT ME, I THINK I MIGHT BE IN TROUBLE.
THEN WHY ***ARE*** YOU HERE... REALLY?

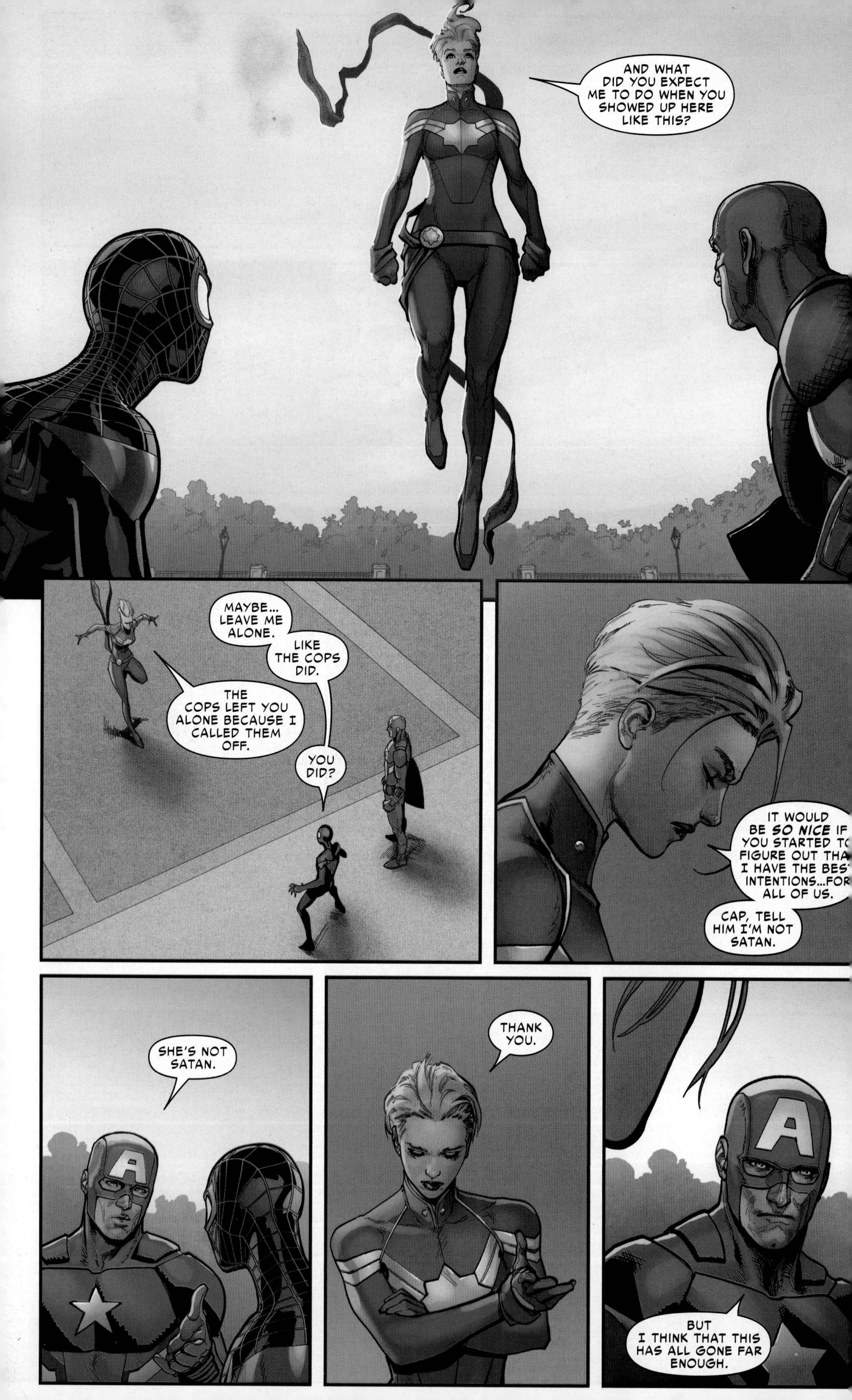
AND WHAT DID YOU EXPECT ME TO DO WHEN YOU SHOWED UP HERE LIKE THIS?
MAYBE... LEAVE ME ALONE.
LIKE THE COPS DID.
THE COPS LEFT YOU ALONE BECAUSE I CALLED THEM OFF.
YOU DID?
IT WOULD BE SO NICE IF YOU STARTED TO FIGURE OUT THAT I HAVE THE BEST INTENTIONS...FOR ALL OF US.
CAP, TELL HIM I'M NOT SATAN.
SHE'S NOT SATAN.
THANK YOU.
BUT I THINK THAT THIS HAS ALL GONE FAR ENOUGH.

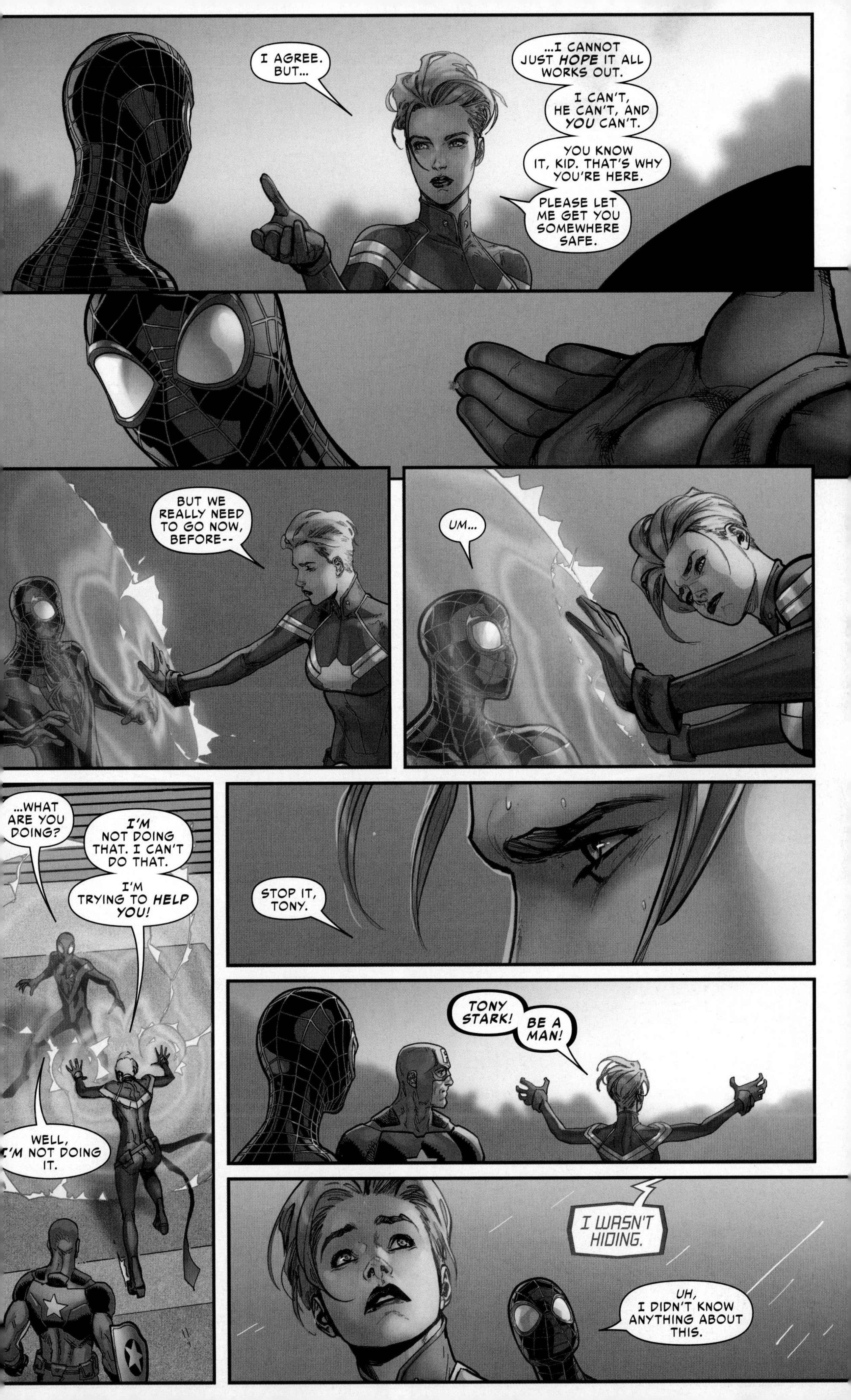
I AGREE. BUT...
...I CANNOT JUST HOPE IT ALL WORKS OUT.
I CAN'T, HE CAN'T, AND YOU CAN'T.
YOU KNOW IT, KID. THAT'S WHY YOU'RE HERE.
PLEASE LET ME GET YOU SOMEWHERE SAFE.
BUT WE REALLY NEED TO GO NOW, BEFORE--
UM...
...WHAT ARE YOU DOING?
I'M NOT DOING THAT. I CAN'T DO THAT.
I'M TRYING TO HELP YOU!
WELL, I'M NOT DOING IT.
STOP IT, TONY.
TONY STARK!
BE A MAN!
I WASN'T HIDING.
UH, I DIDN'T KNOW ANYTHING ABOUT THIS.

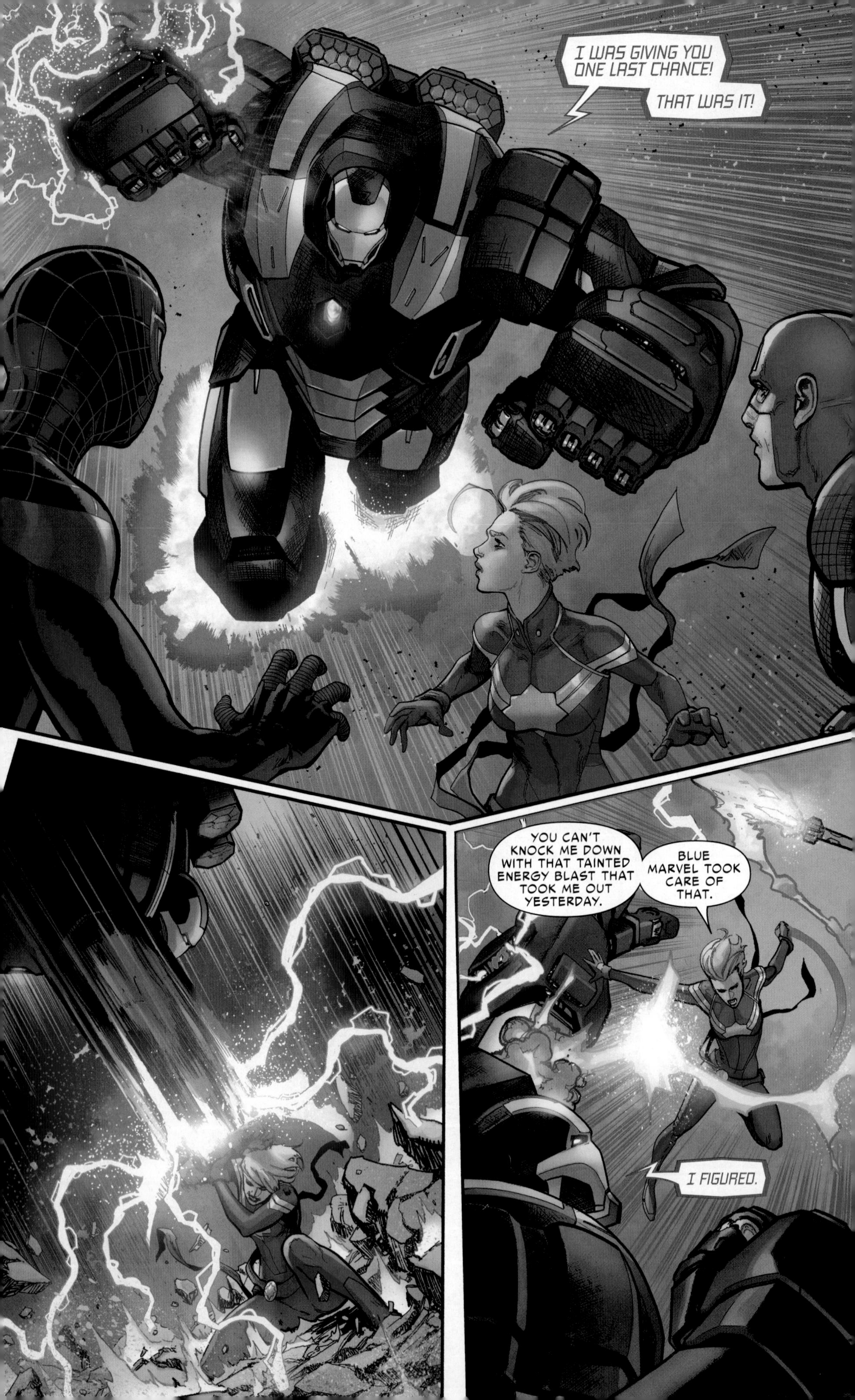
I WAS GIVING YOU ONE LAST CHANCE!
THAT WAS IT!
YOU CAN'T KNOCK ME DOWN WITH THAT TAINTED ENERGY BLAST THAT TOOK ME OUT YESTERDAY.
BLUE MARVEL TOOK CARE OF THAT.
I FIGURED.

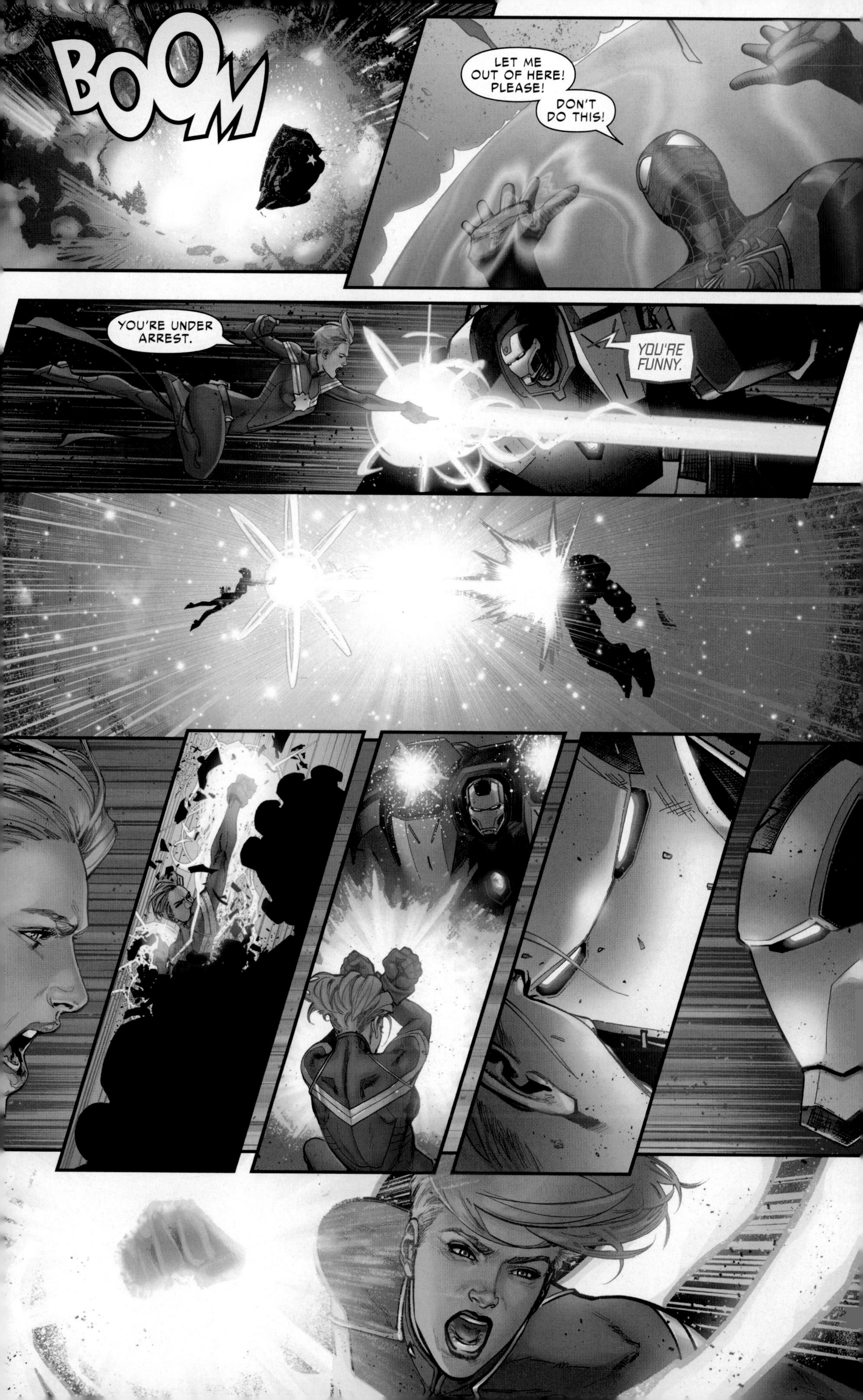
BOOM
LET ME OUT OF HERE! PLEASE!
DON'T DO THIS!
YOU'RE UNDER ARREST.
YOU'RE FUNNY.

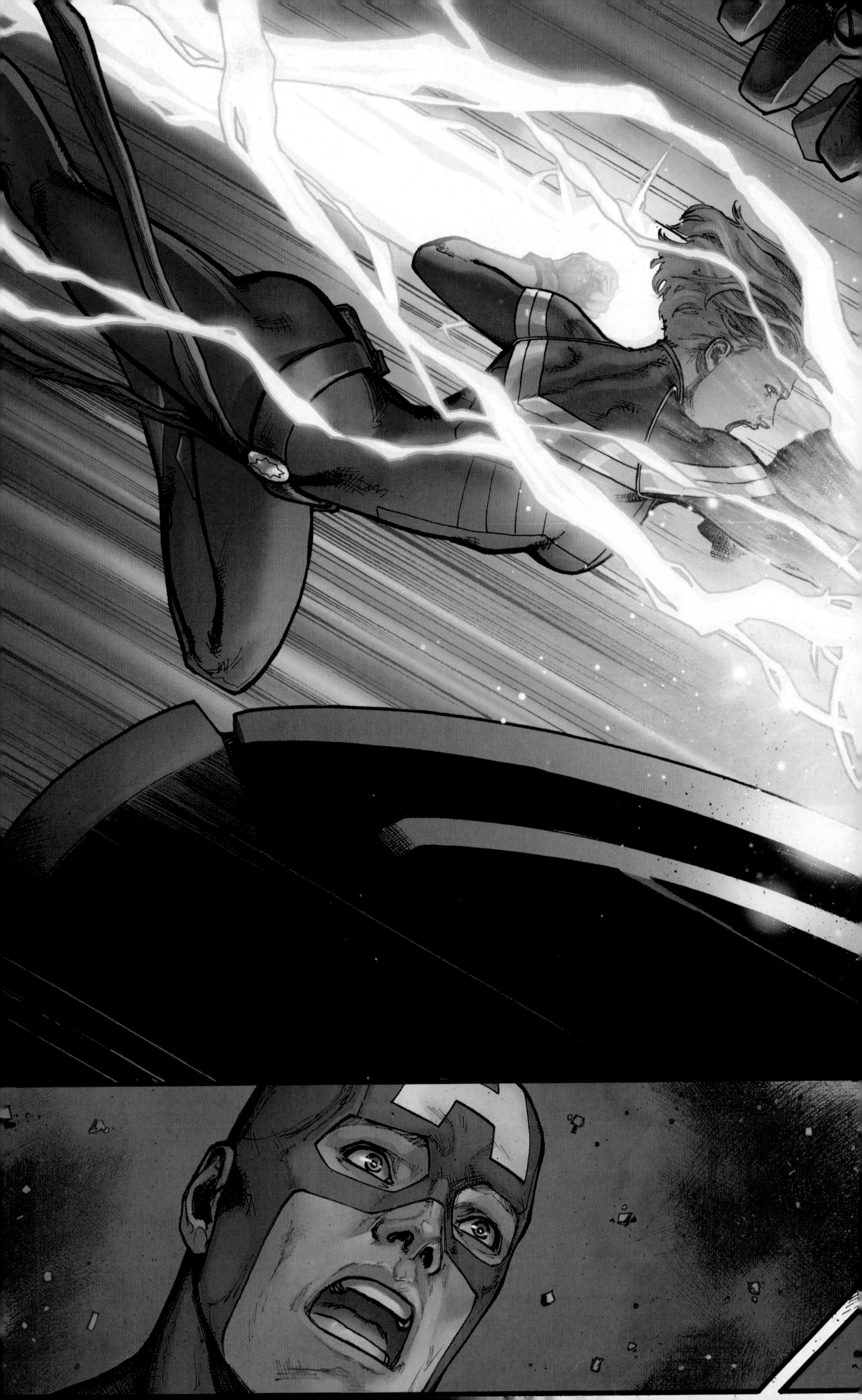

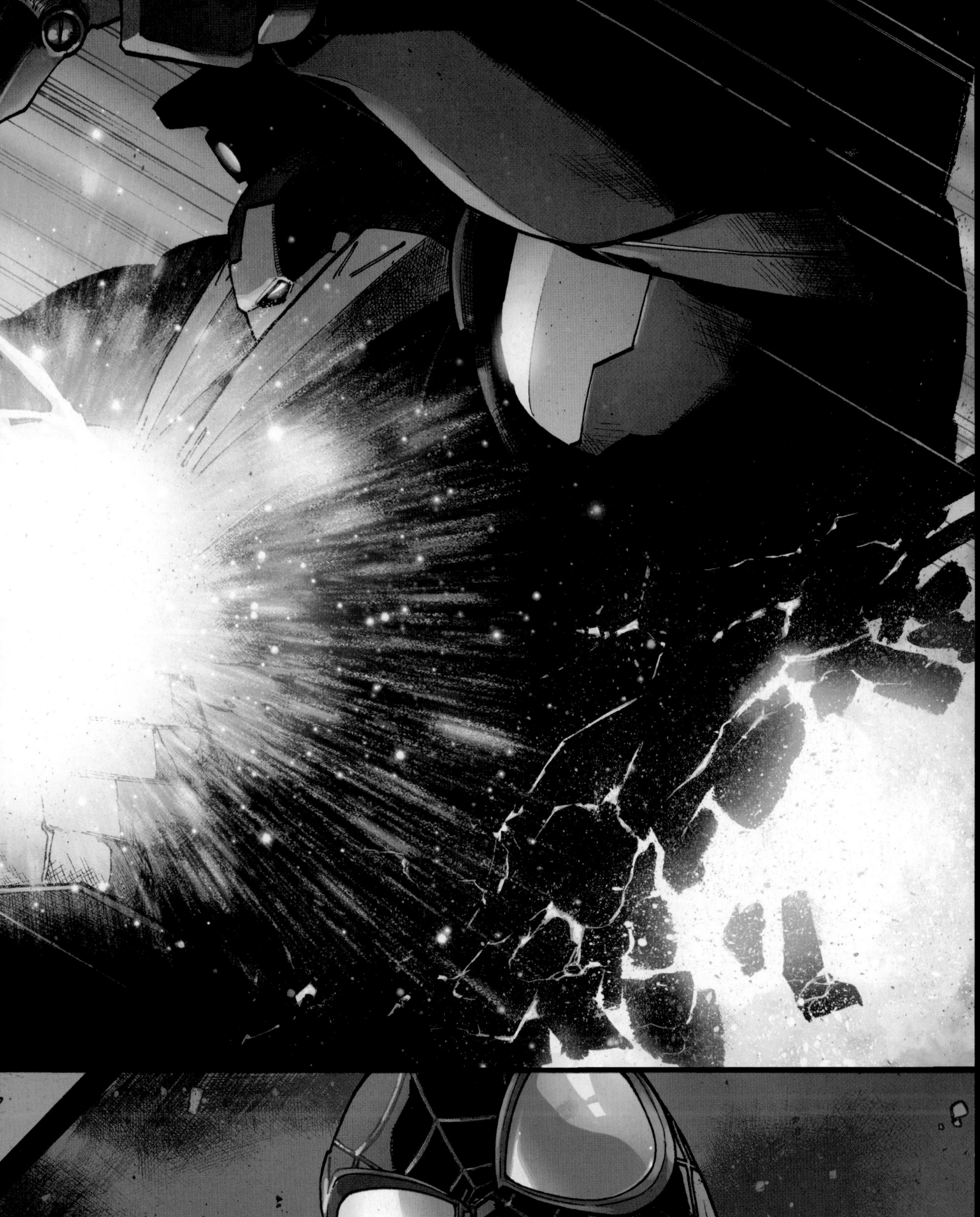

CIVIL WAR II #8

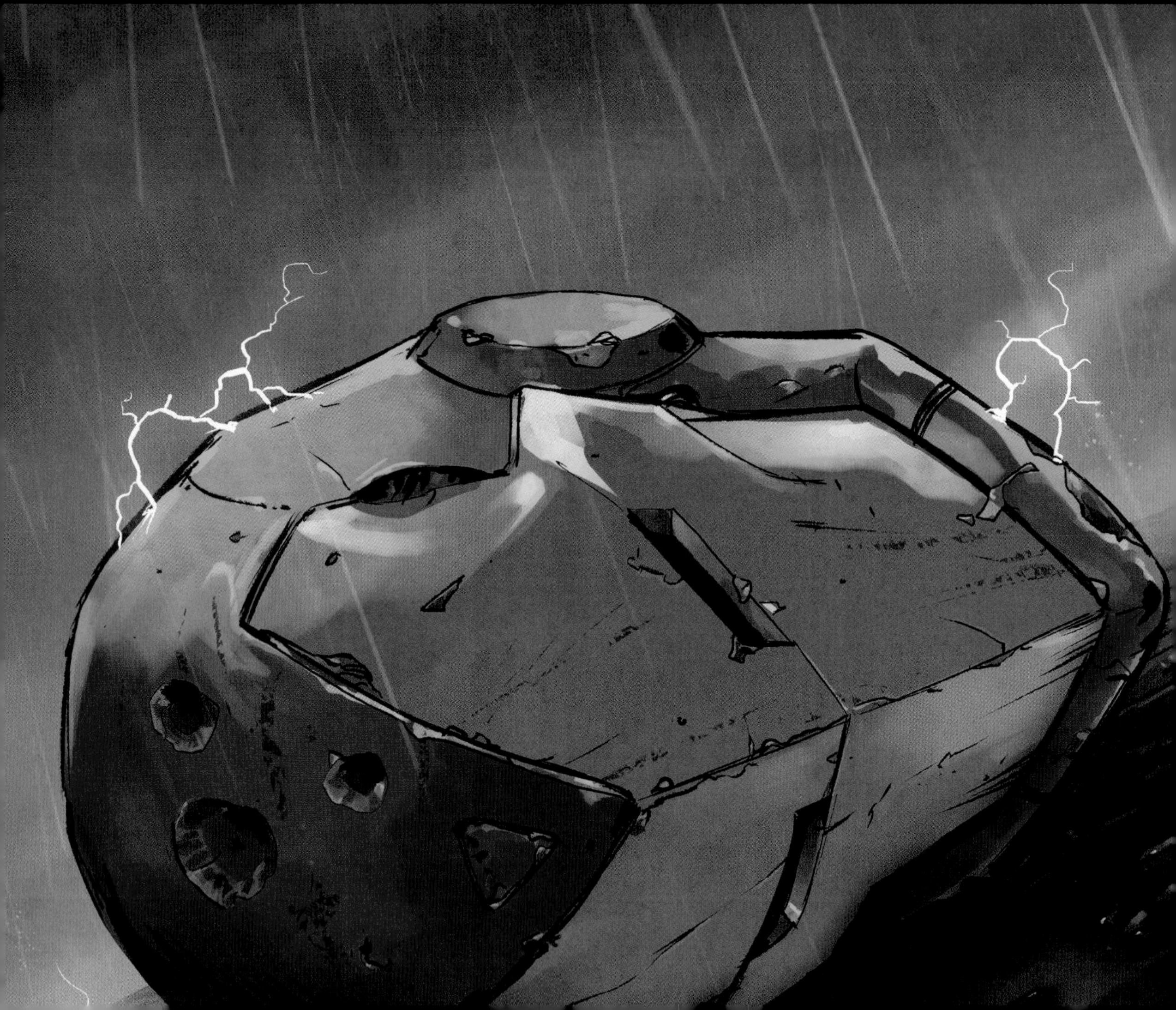

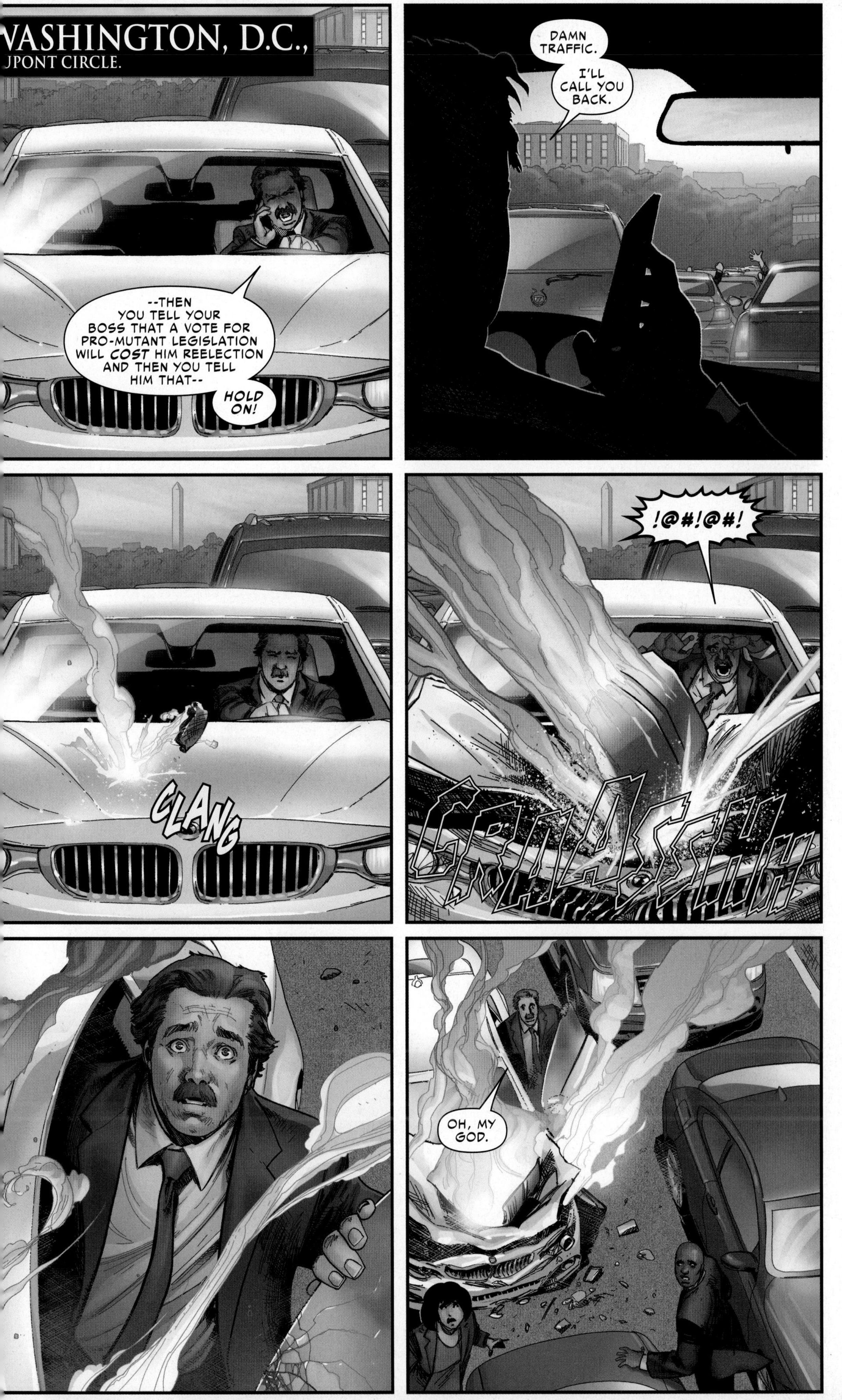

VASHINGTON, D.C.,
JPONT CIRCLE.
--THEN YOU TELL YOUR BOSS THAT A VOTE FOR PRO-MUTANT LEGISLATION WILL COST HIM REELECTION AND THEN YOU TELL HIM THAT--
HOLD ON!
DAMN TRAFFIC.
I'LL CALL YOU BACK.
CLANG
!@#!@#!
OH, MY GOD.

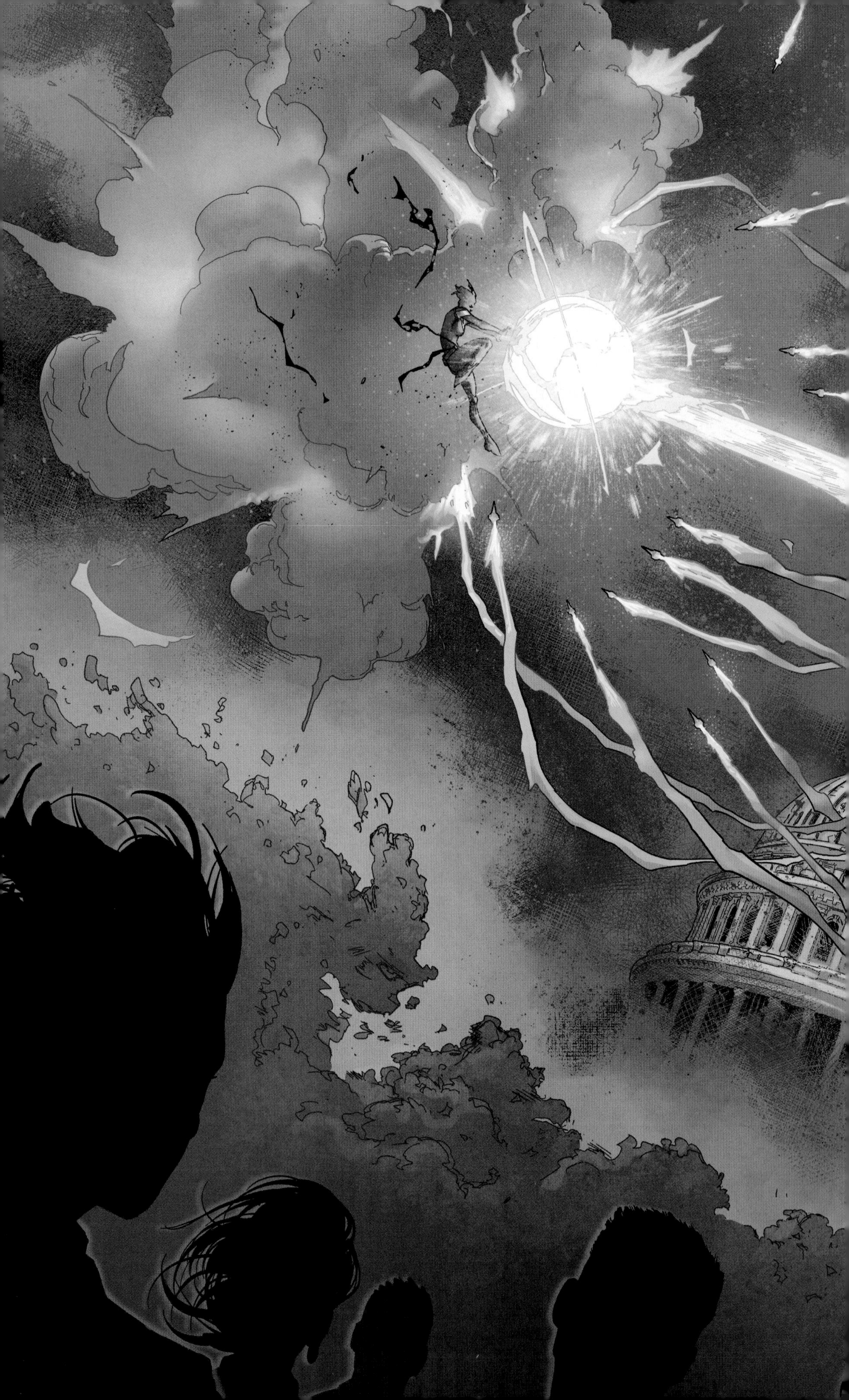

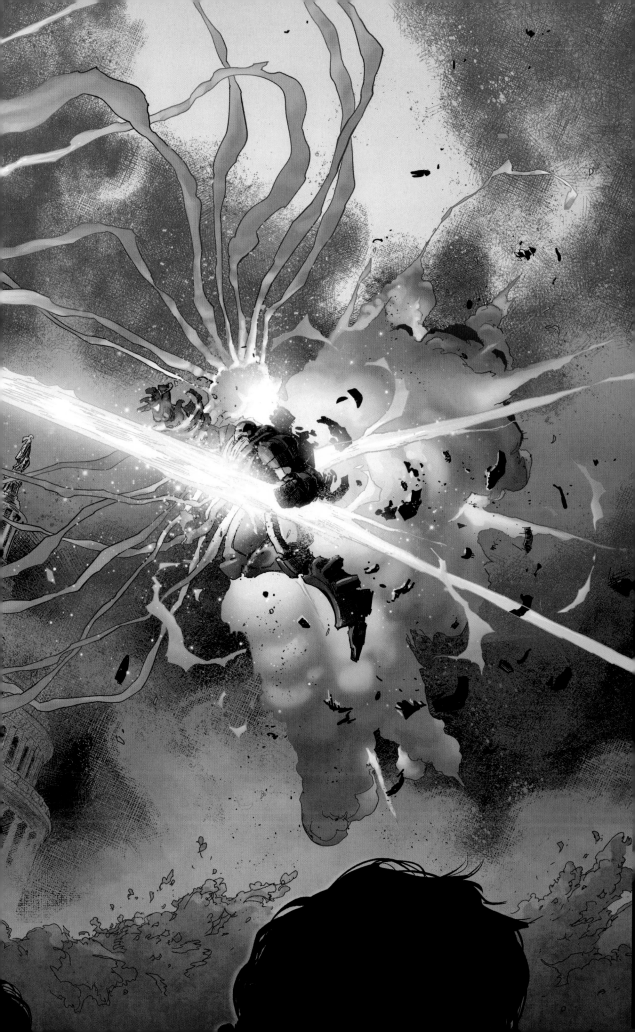

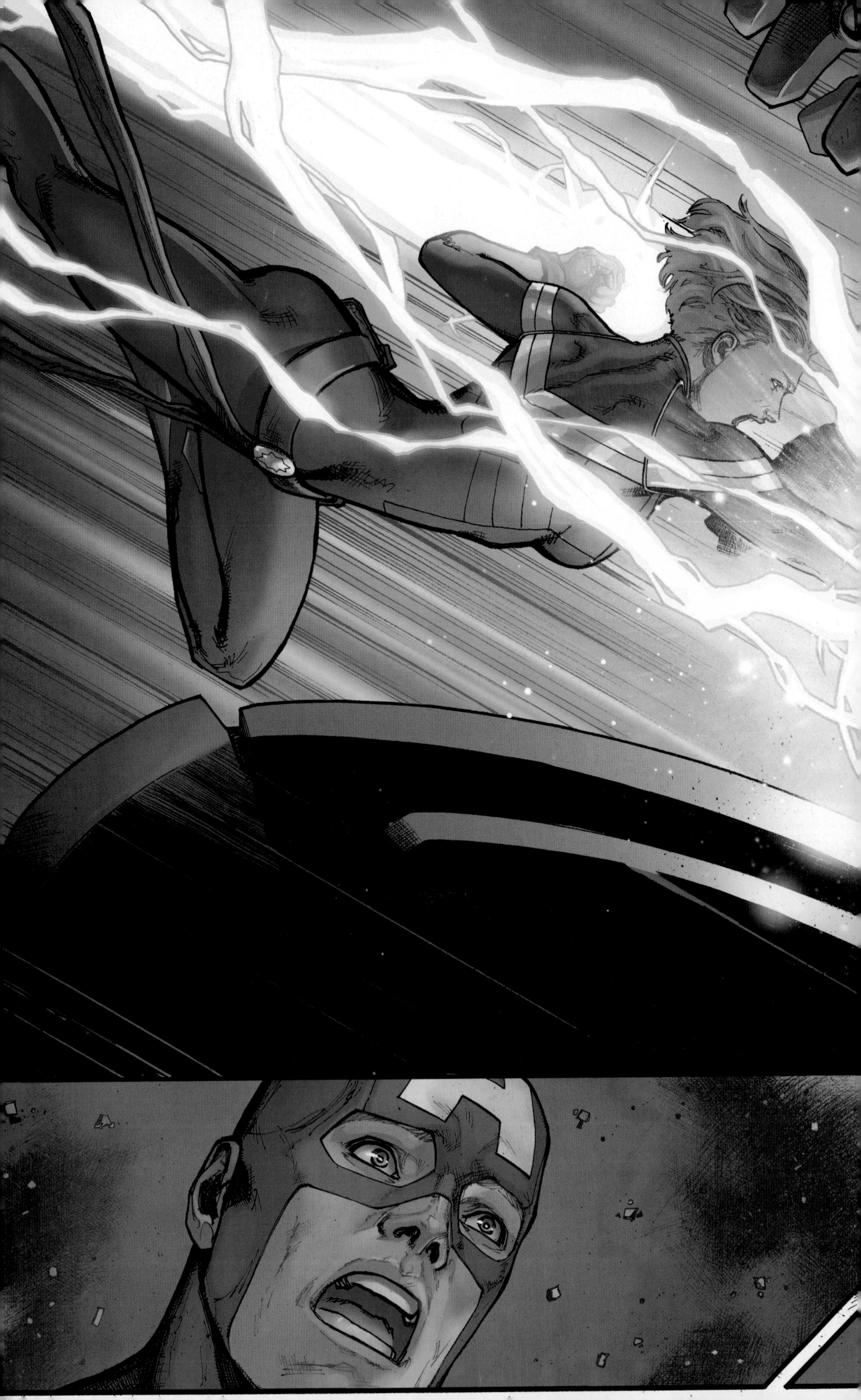

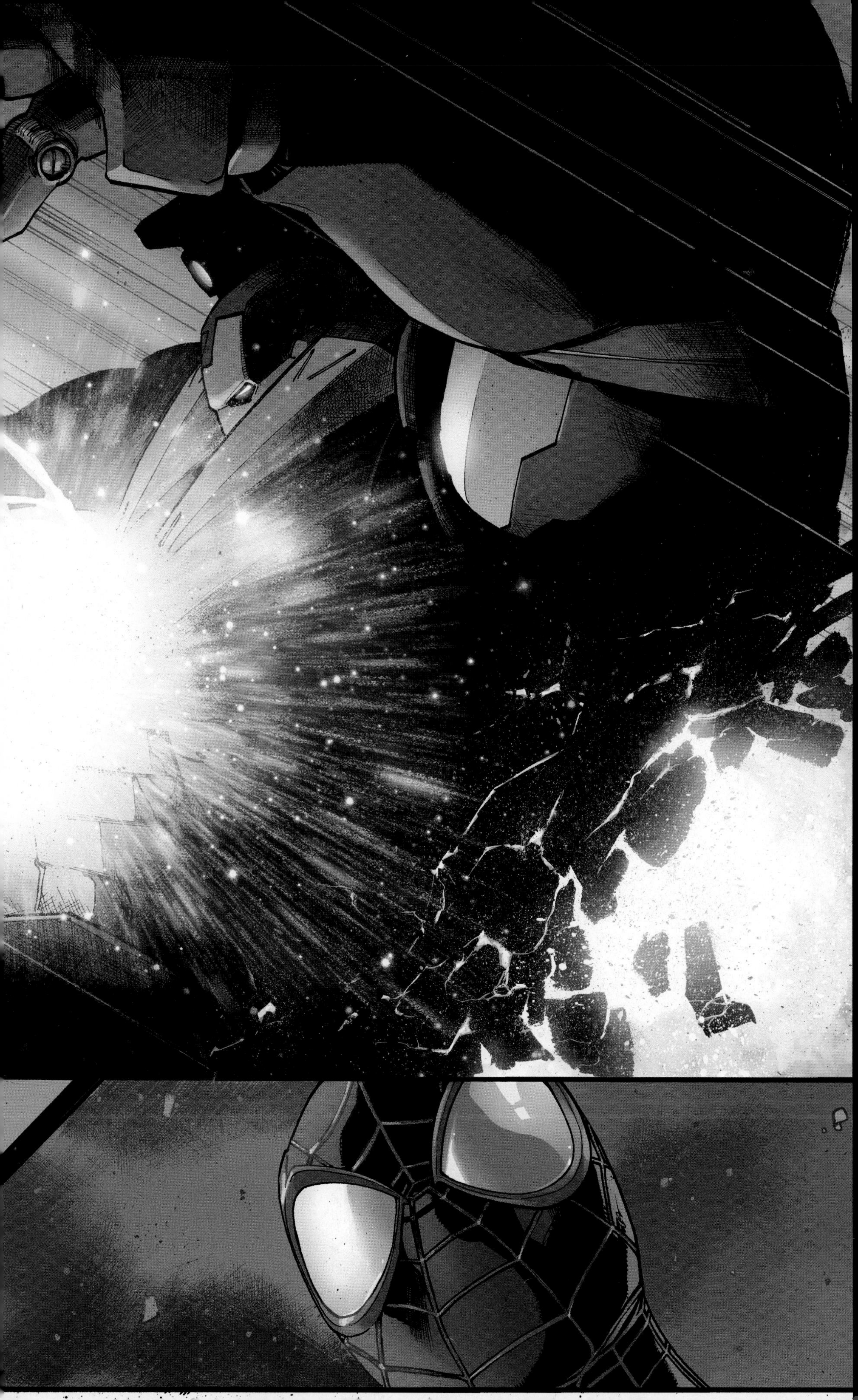

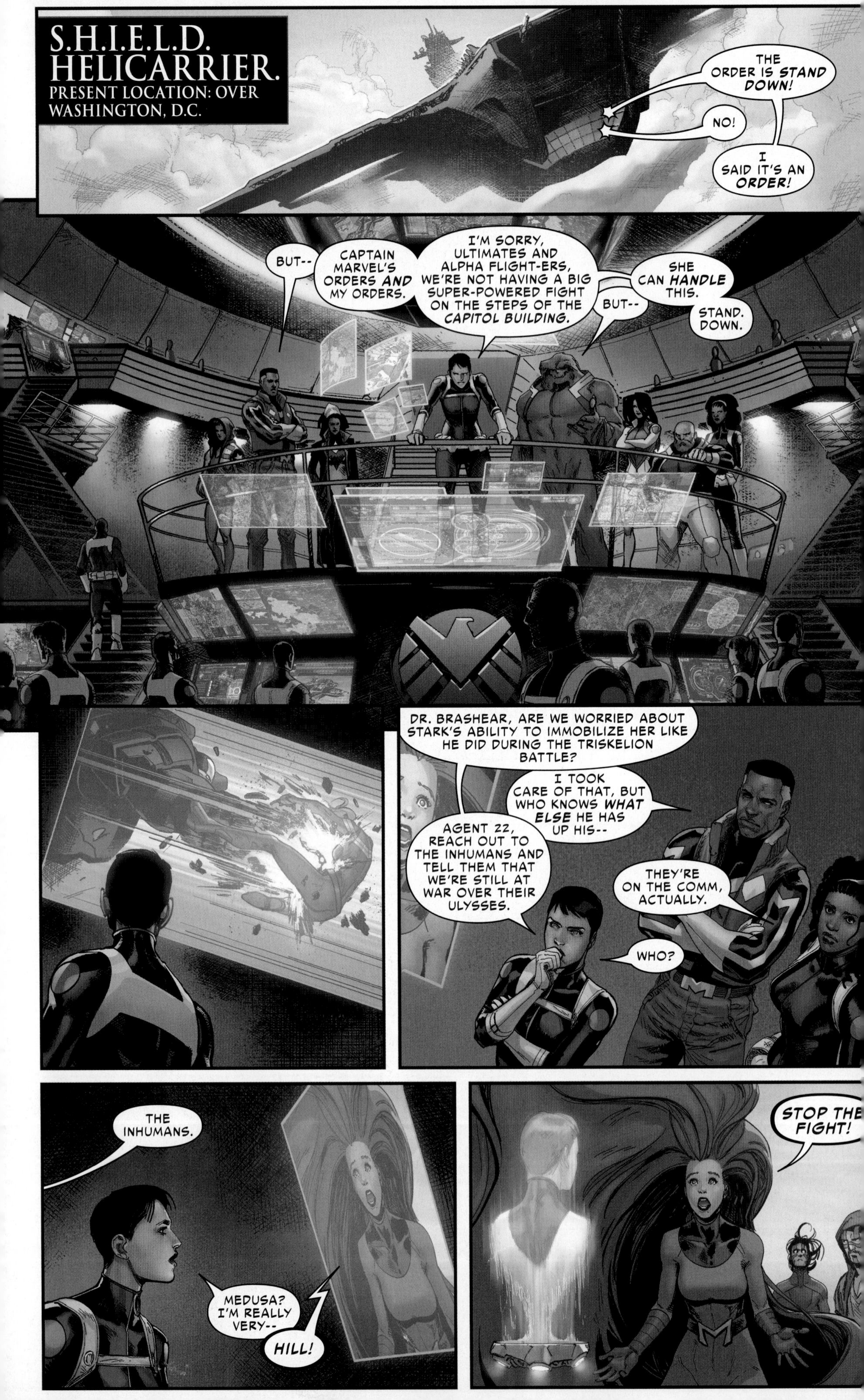
S.H.I.E.L.D. HELICARRIER.
PRESENT LOCATION: OVER WASHINGTON, D.C.
THE ORDER IS STAND DOWN!
NO!
I SAID IT'S AN ORDER!
BUT--
CAPTAIN MARVEL'S ORDERS AND MY ORDERS.
I'M SORRY, ULTIMATES AND ALPHA FLIGHT-ERS, WE'RE NOT HAVING A BIG SUPER-POWERED FIGHT ON THE STEPS OF THE CAPITOL BUILDING.
BUT--
SHE CAN HANDLE THIS.
STAND. DOWN.
DR. BRASHEAR, ARE WE WORRIED ABOUT STARK'S ABILITY TO IMMOBILIZE HER LIKE HE DID DURING THE TRISKELION BATTLE?
I TOOK CARE OF THAT, BUT WHO KNOWS WHAT ELSE HE HAS UP HIS--
AGENT 22, REACH OUT TO THE INHUMANS AND TELL THEM THAT WE'RE STILL AT WAR OVER THEIR ULYSSES.
THEY'RE ON THE COMM, ACTUALLY.
WHO?
THE INHUMANS.
MEDUSA? I'M REALLY VERY--
HILL!
STOP THE FIGHT!

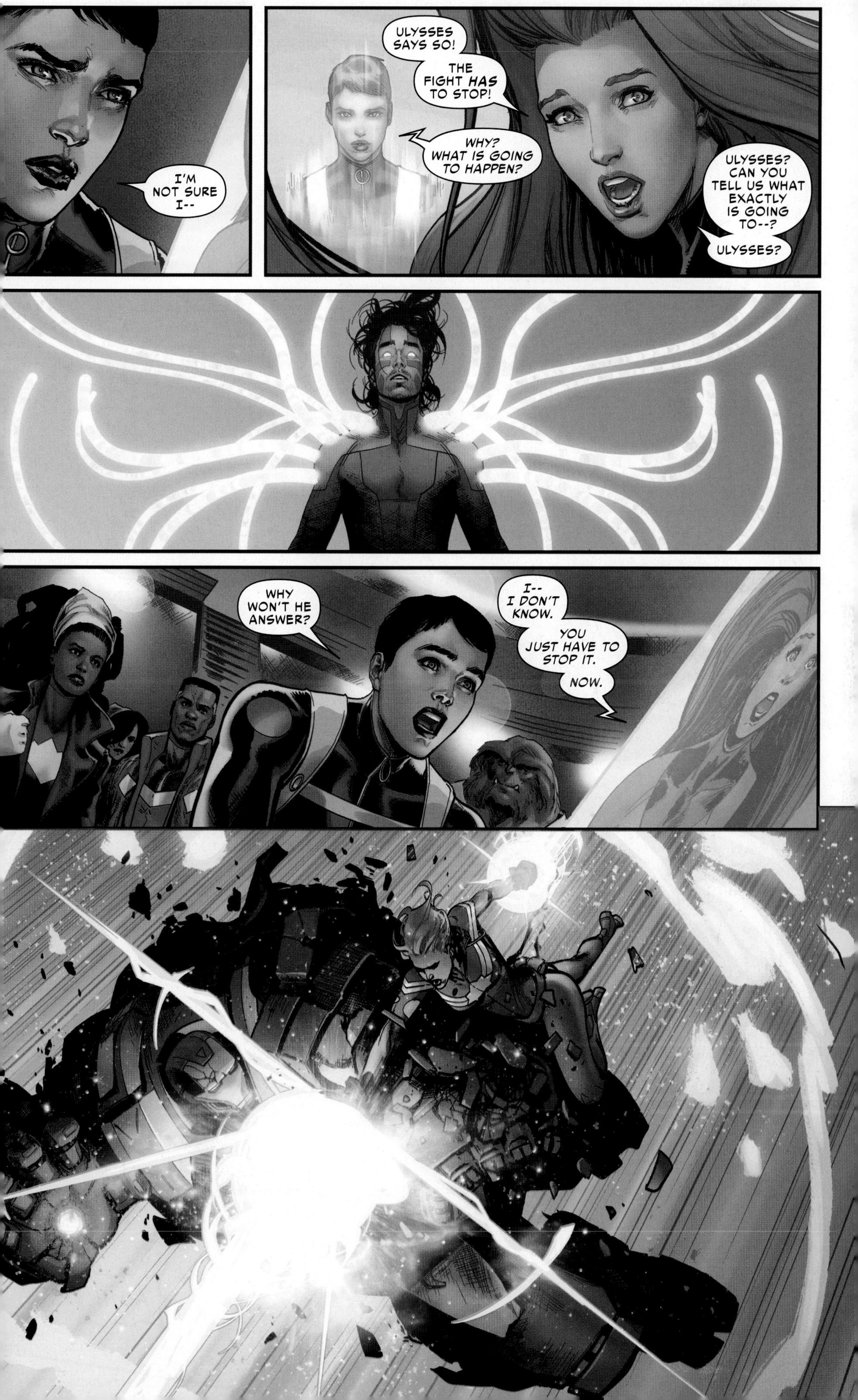
I'M NOT SURE I--
ULYSSES SAYS SO!
THE FIGHT HAS TO STOP!
WHY? WHAT IS GOING TO HAPPEN?
ULYSSES? CAN YOU TELL US WHAT EXACTLY IS GOING TO--?
ULYSSES?
WHY WON'T HE ANSWER?
I-- I DON'T KNOW.
YOU JUST HAVE TO STOP IT.
NOW.

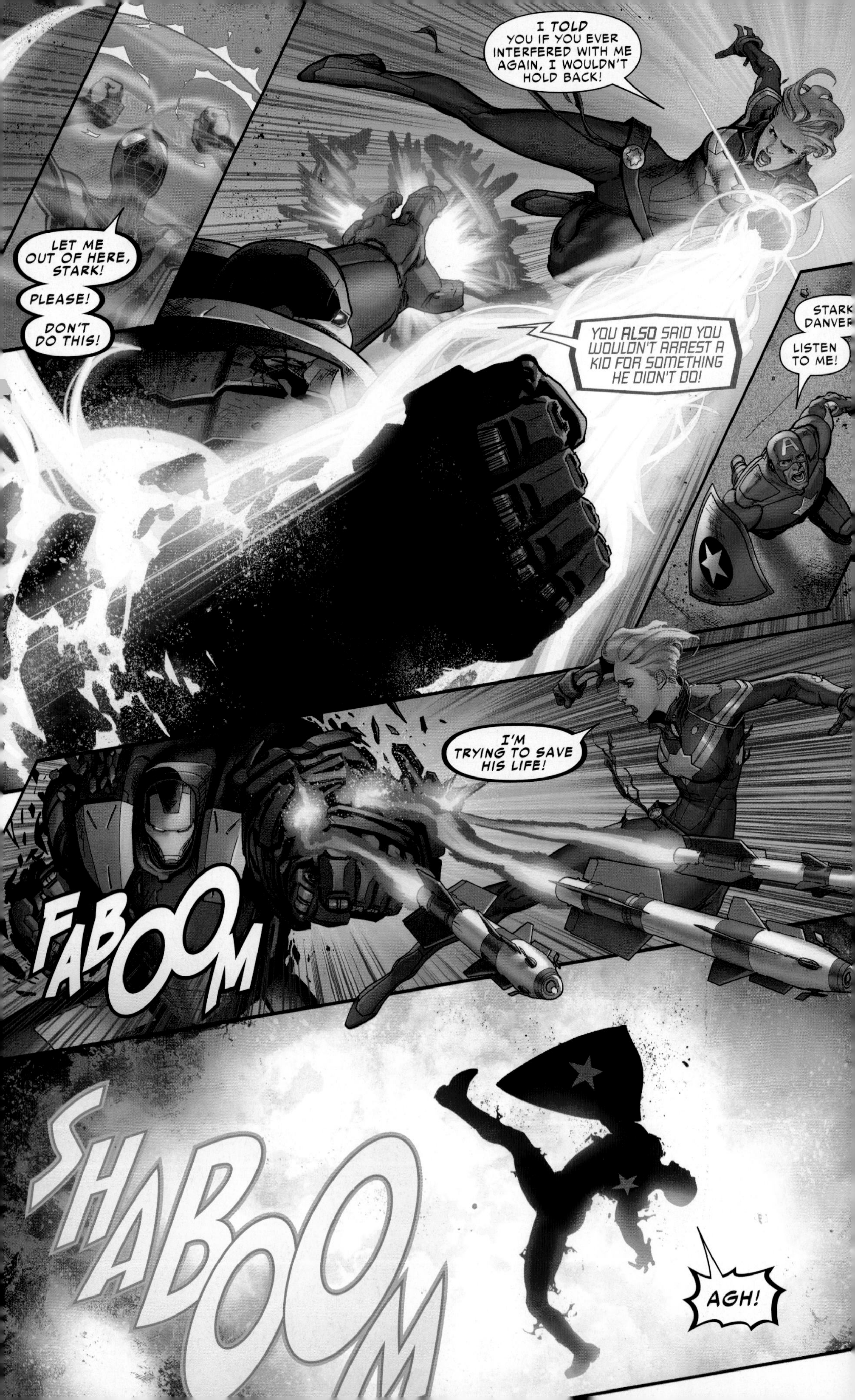
LET ME OUT OF HERE, STARK!
PLEASE!
DON'T DO THIS!
I TOLD YOU IF YOU EVER INTERFERED WITH ME AGAIN, I WOULDN'T HOLD BACK!
YOU ALSO SAID YOU WOULDN'T ARREST A KID FOR SOMETHING HE DIDN'T DO!
STARK
DANVER
LISTEN TO ME!
I'M TRYING TO SAVE HIS LIFE!
FABOOM
SHABOOM
AGH!

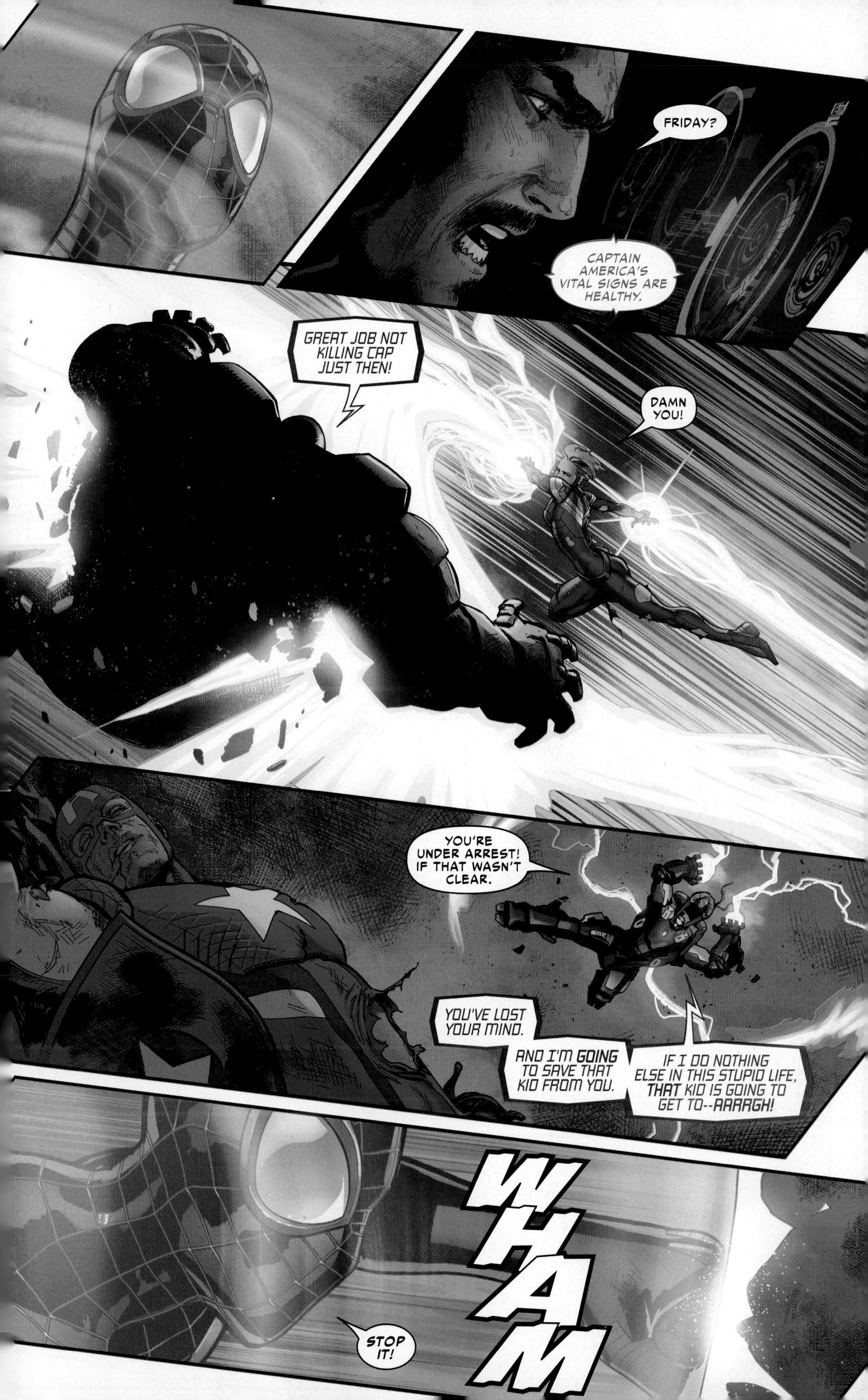
FRIDAY?
CAPTAIN AMERICA'S VITAL SIGNS ARE HEALTHY.
GREAT JOB NOT KILLING CAP JUST THEN!
DAMN YOU!
YOU'RE UNDER ARREST! IF THAT WASN'T CLEAR.
YOU'VE LOST YOUR MIND.
AND I'M GOING TO SAVE THAT KID FROM YOU.
IF I DO NOTHING ELSE IN THIS STUPID LIFE, THAT KID IS GOING TO GET TO--ARRRGH!
WHAM
STOP IT!

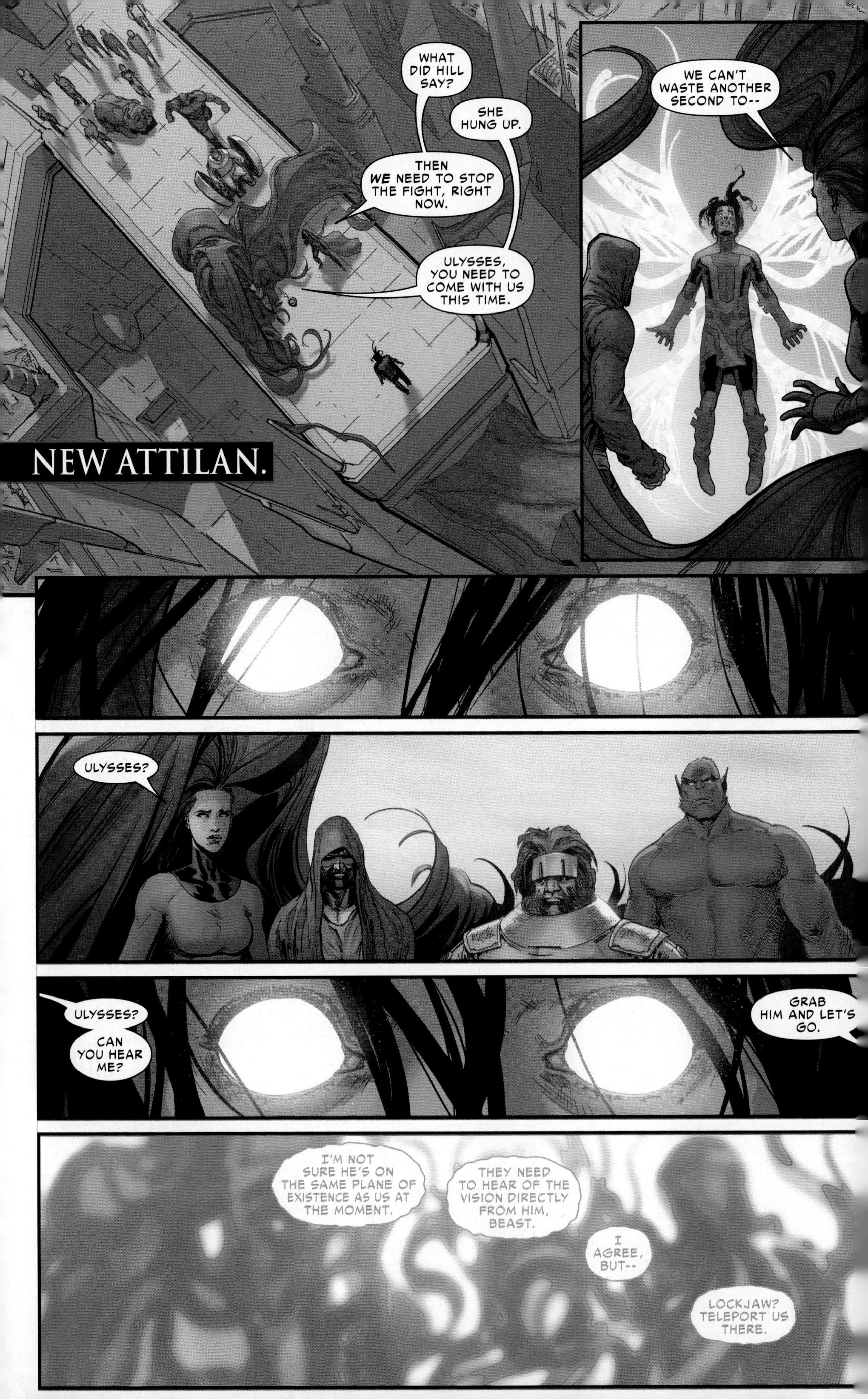
NEW ATTILAN.
WHAT DID HILL SAY?
SHE HUNG UP.
THEN WE NEED TO STOP THE FIGHT, RIGHT NOW.
ULYSSES, YOU NEED TO COME WITH US THIS TIME.
WE CAN'T WASTE ANOTHER SECOND TO--
ULYSSES?
ULYSSES?
CAN YOU HEAR ME?
GRAB HIM AND LET'S GO.
I'M NOT SURE HE'S ON THE SAME PLANE OF EXISTENCE AS US AT THE MOMENT.
THEY NEED TO HEAR OF THE VISION DIRECTLY FROM HIM, BEAST.
I AGREE, BUT--
LOCKJAW? TELEPORT US THERE.

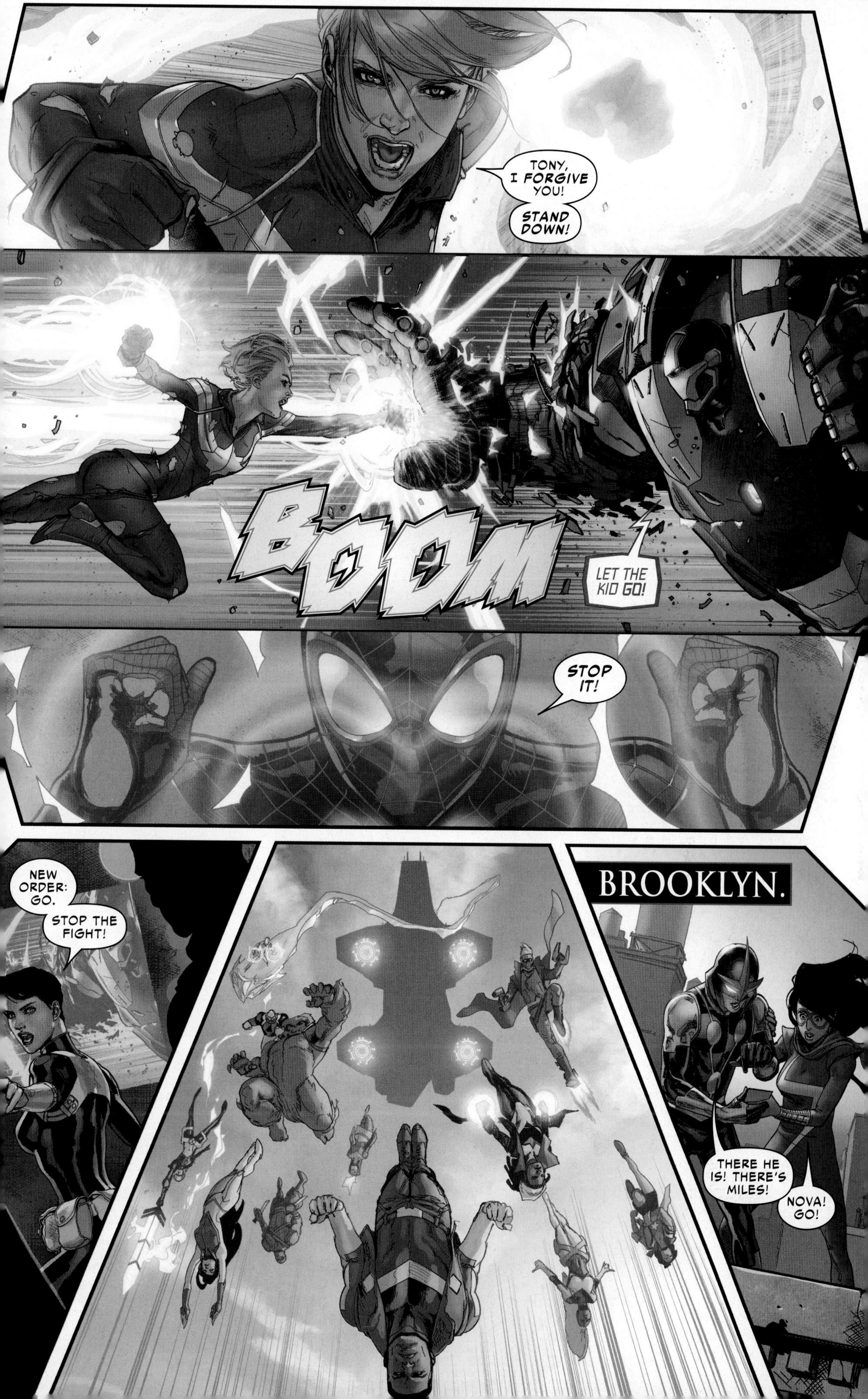
TONY, I FORGIVE YOU!
STAND DOWN!
BOOM
LET THE KID GO!
STOP IT!
NEW ORDER: GO.
STOP THE FIGHT!
BROOKLYN.
THERE HE IS! THERE'S MILES!
NOVA! GO!

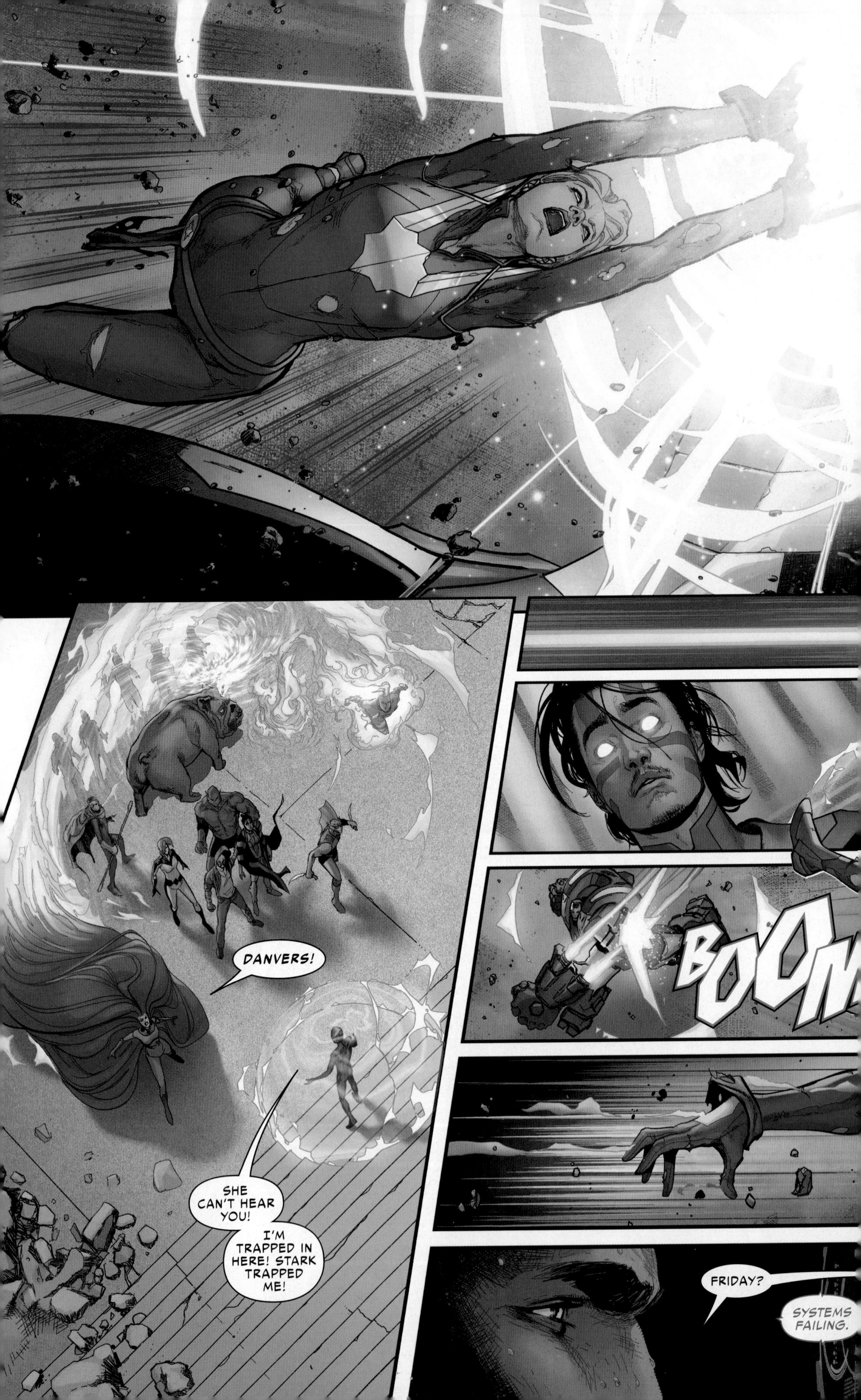
DANVERS!
SHE CAN'T HEAR YOU!
I'M TRAPPED IN HERE! STARK TRAPPED ME!
BOOM
FRIDAY?
SYSTEMS FAILING.

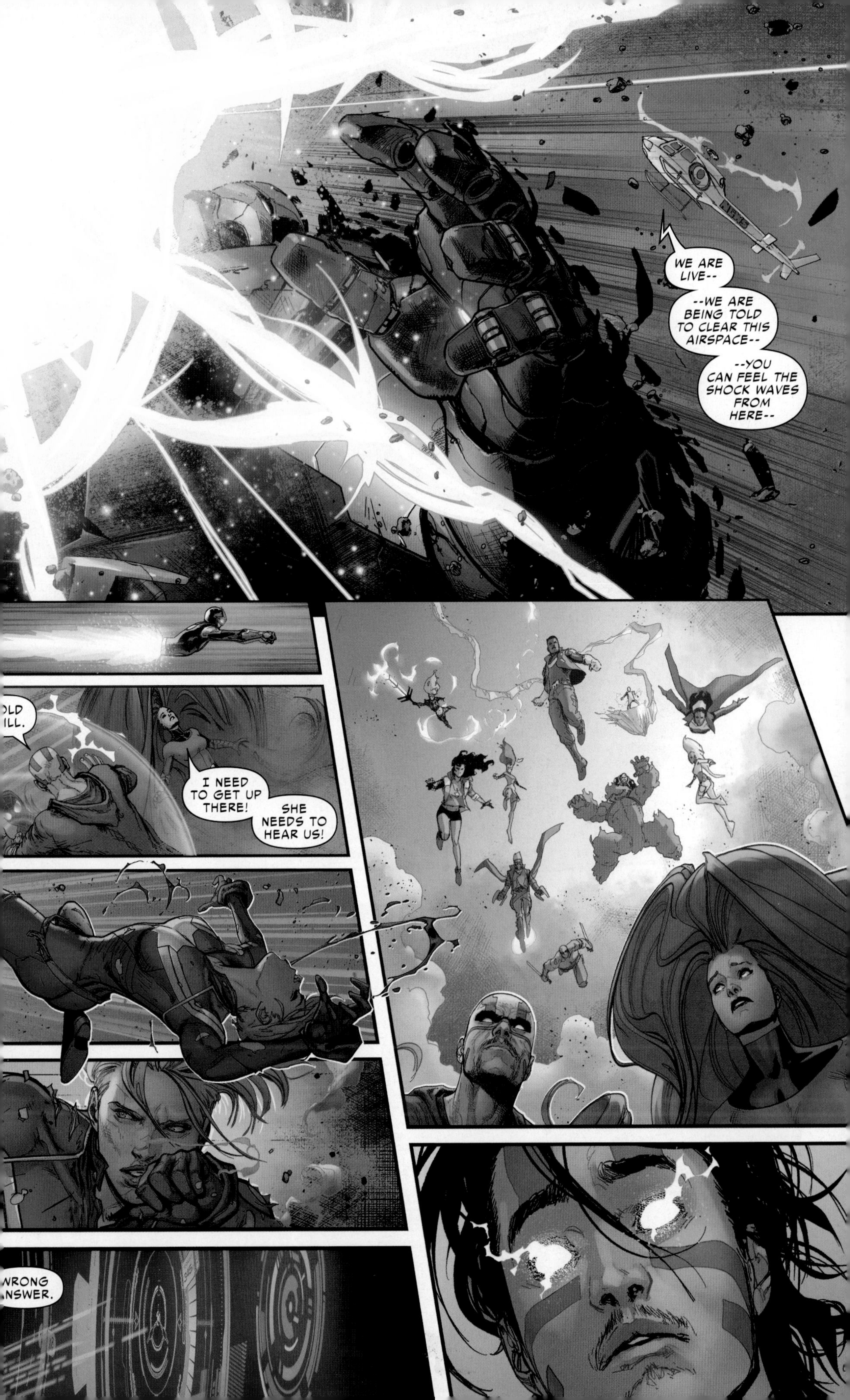
WE ARE LIVE--
--WE ARE BEING TOLD TO CLEAR THIS AIRSPACE--
--YOU CAN FEEL THE SHOCK WAVES FROM HERE--
OLD ILL.
I NEED TO GET UP THERE!
SHE NEEDS TO HEAR US!
WRONG NSWER.

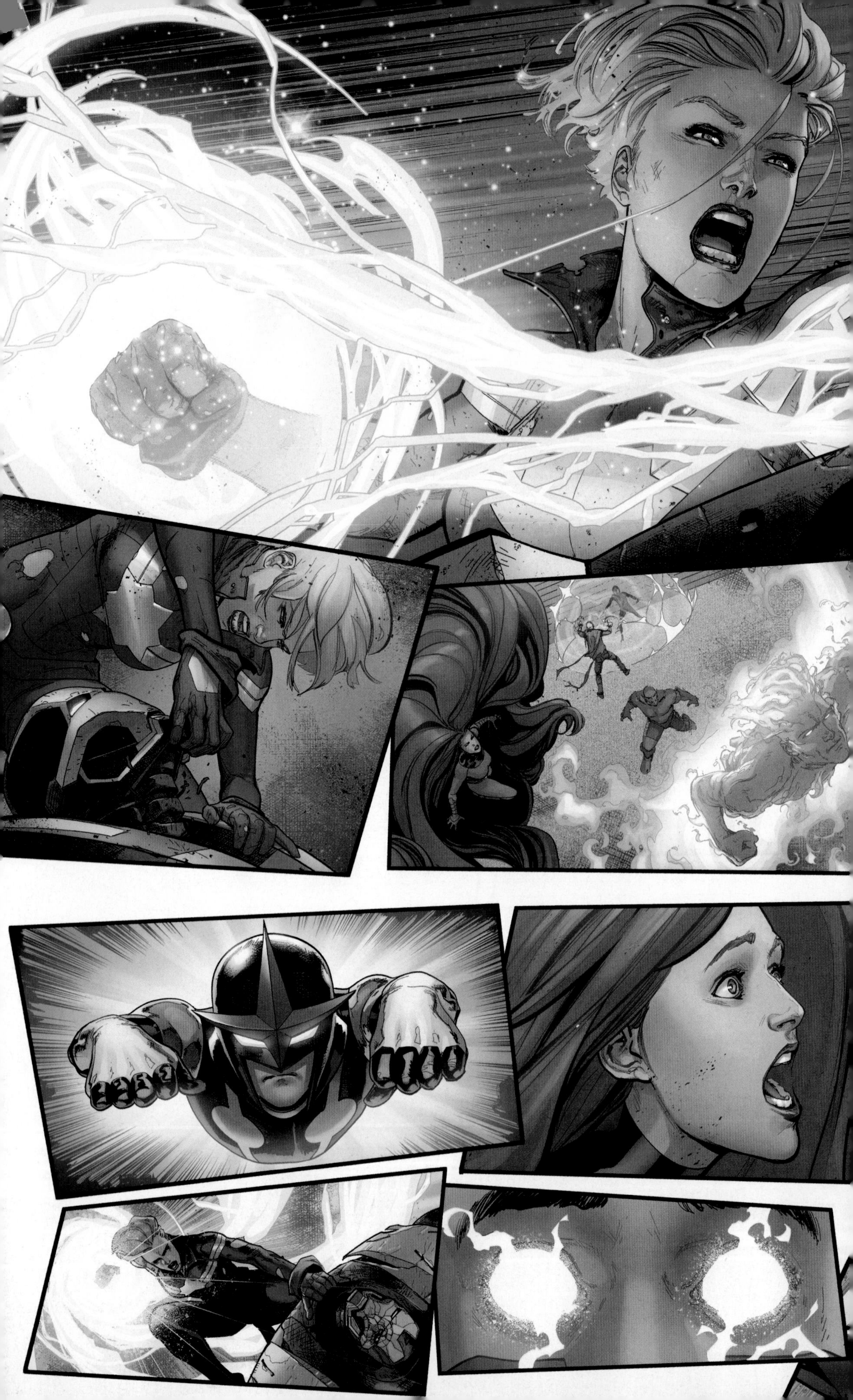

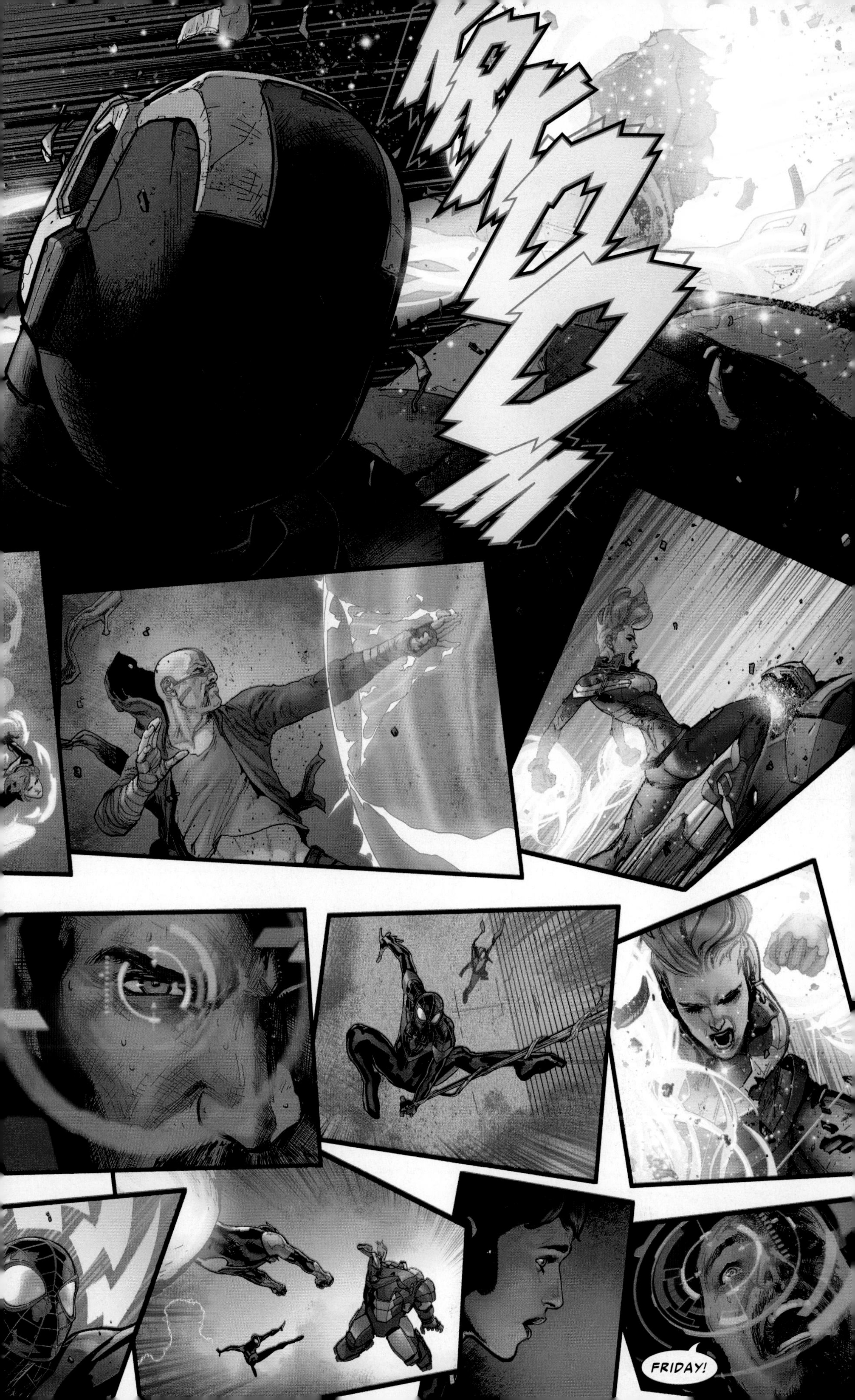
FRIDAY!

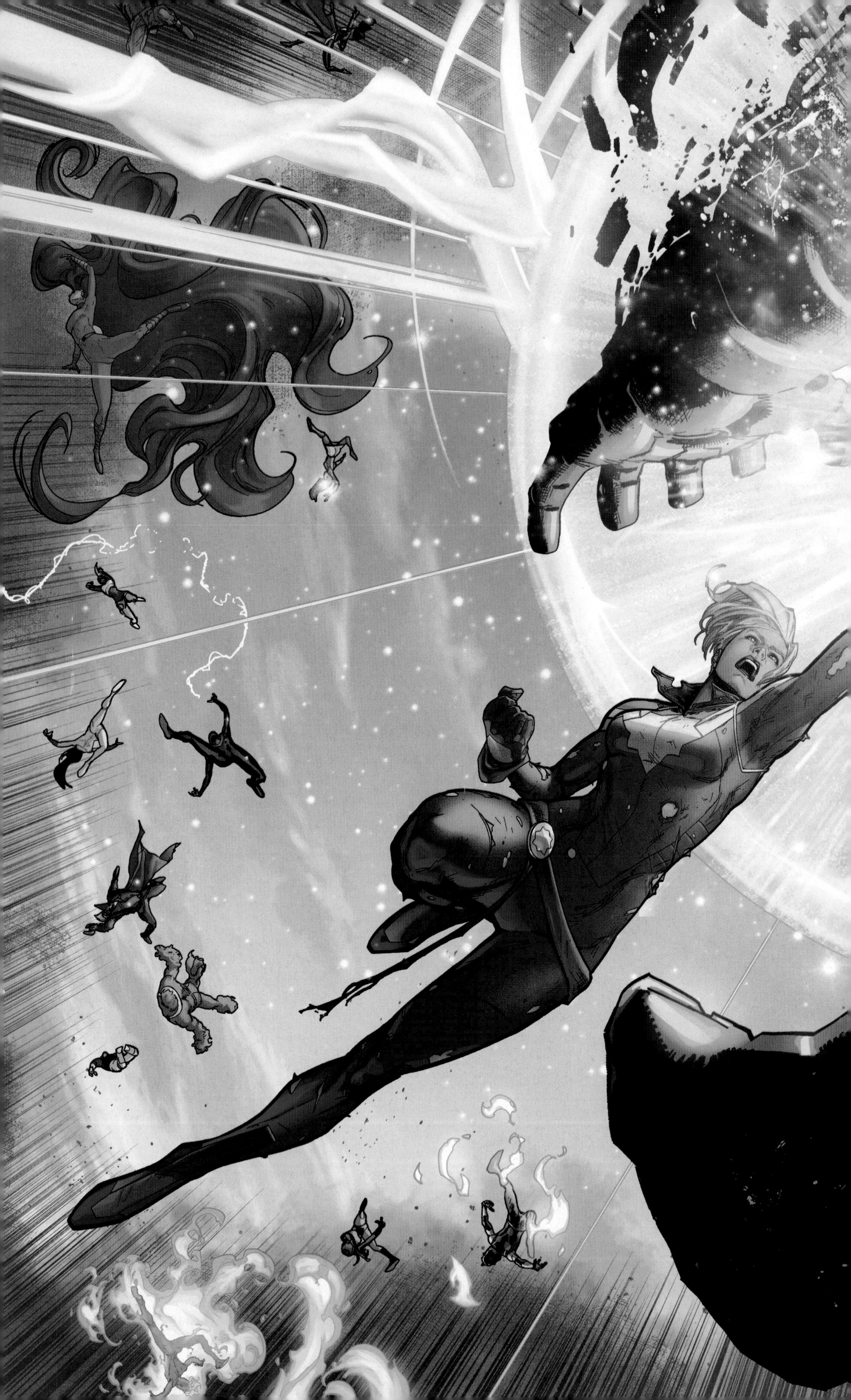

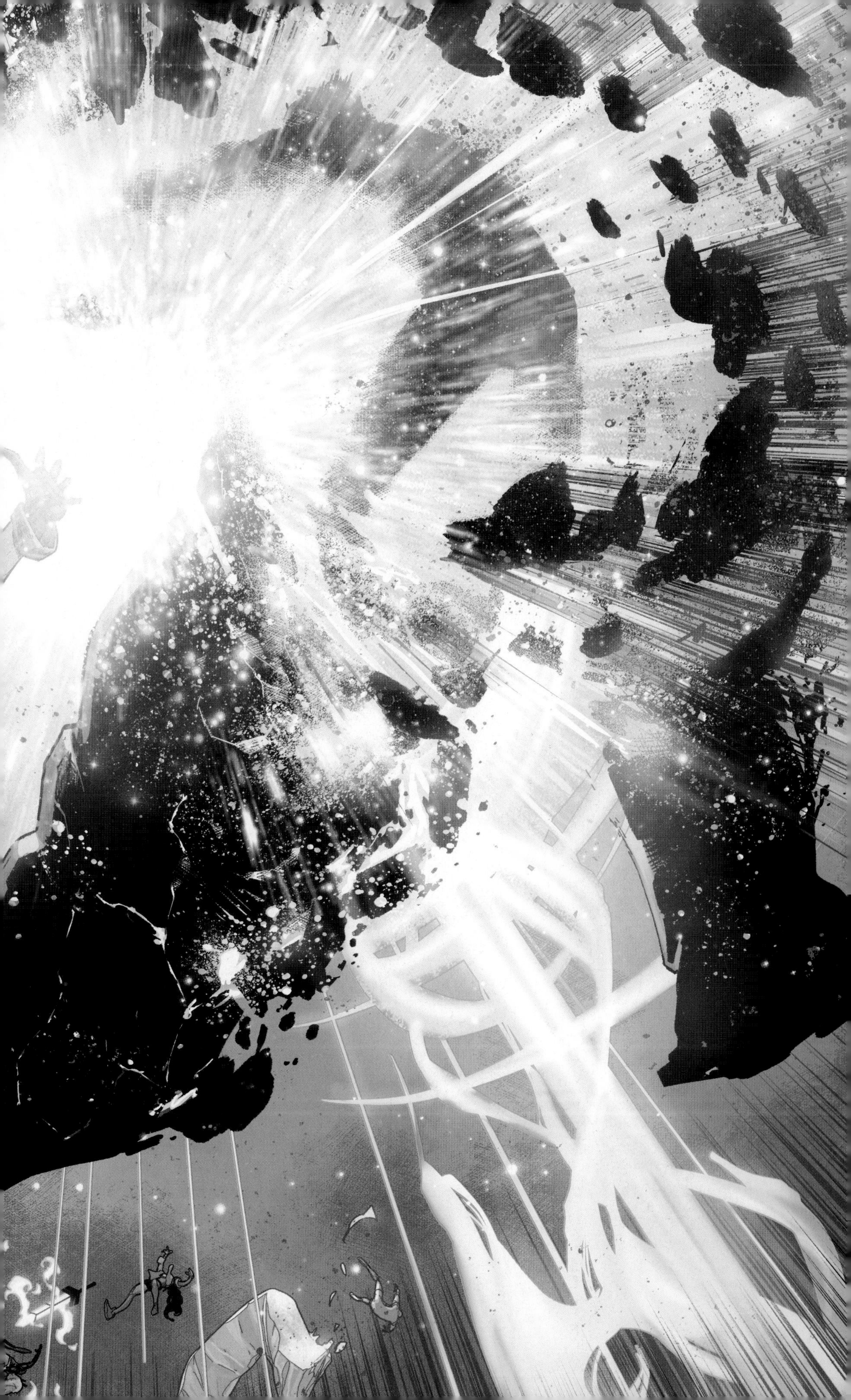

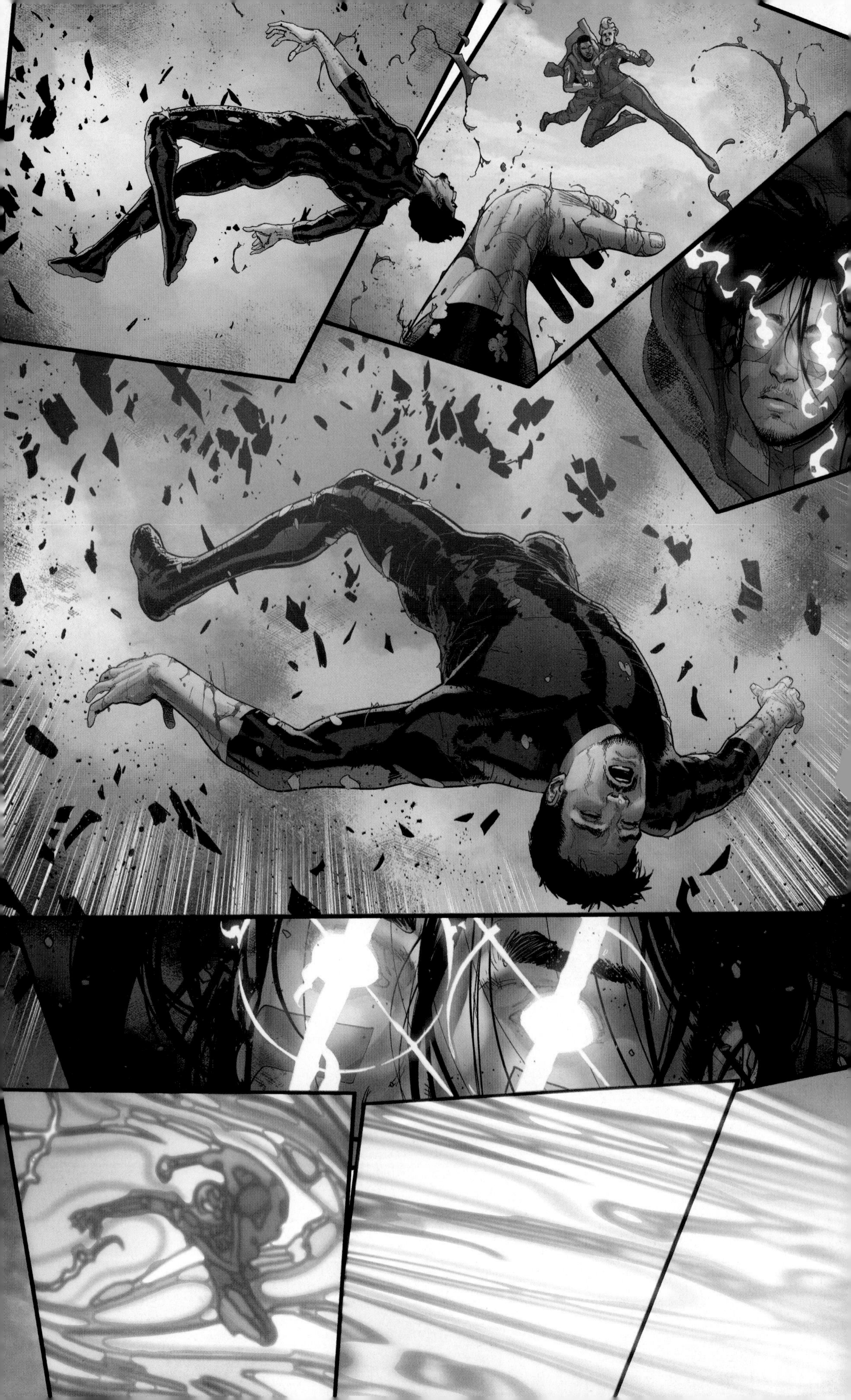

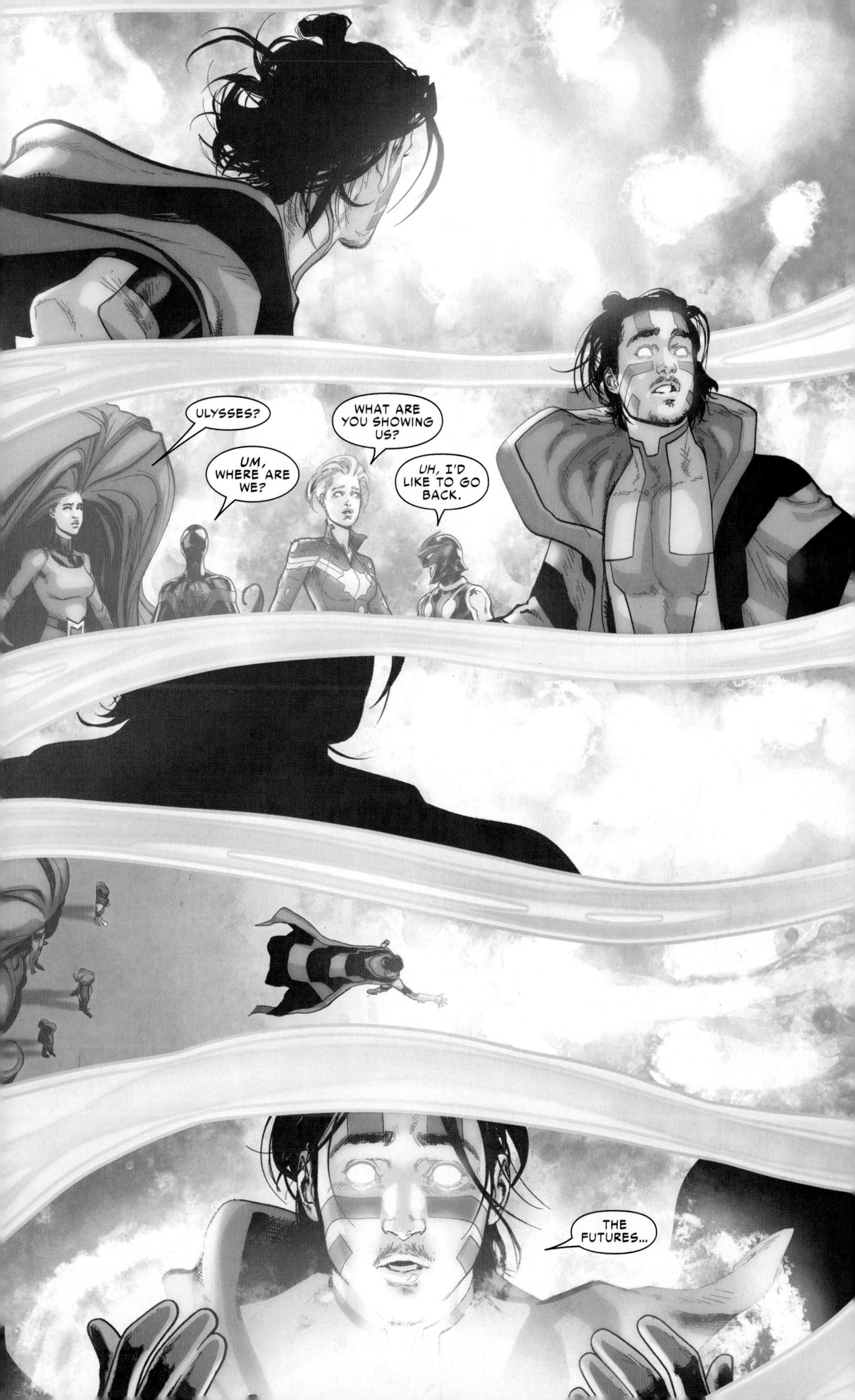
ULYSSES?
UM, WHERE ARE WE?
WHAT ARE YOU SHOWING US?
UH, I'D LIKE TO GO BACK.
THE FUTURES...

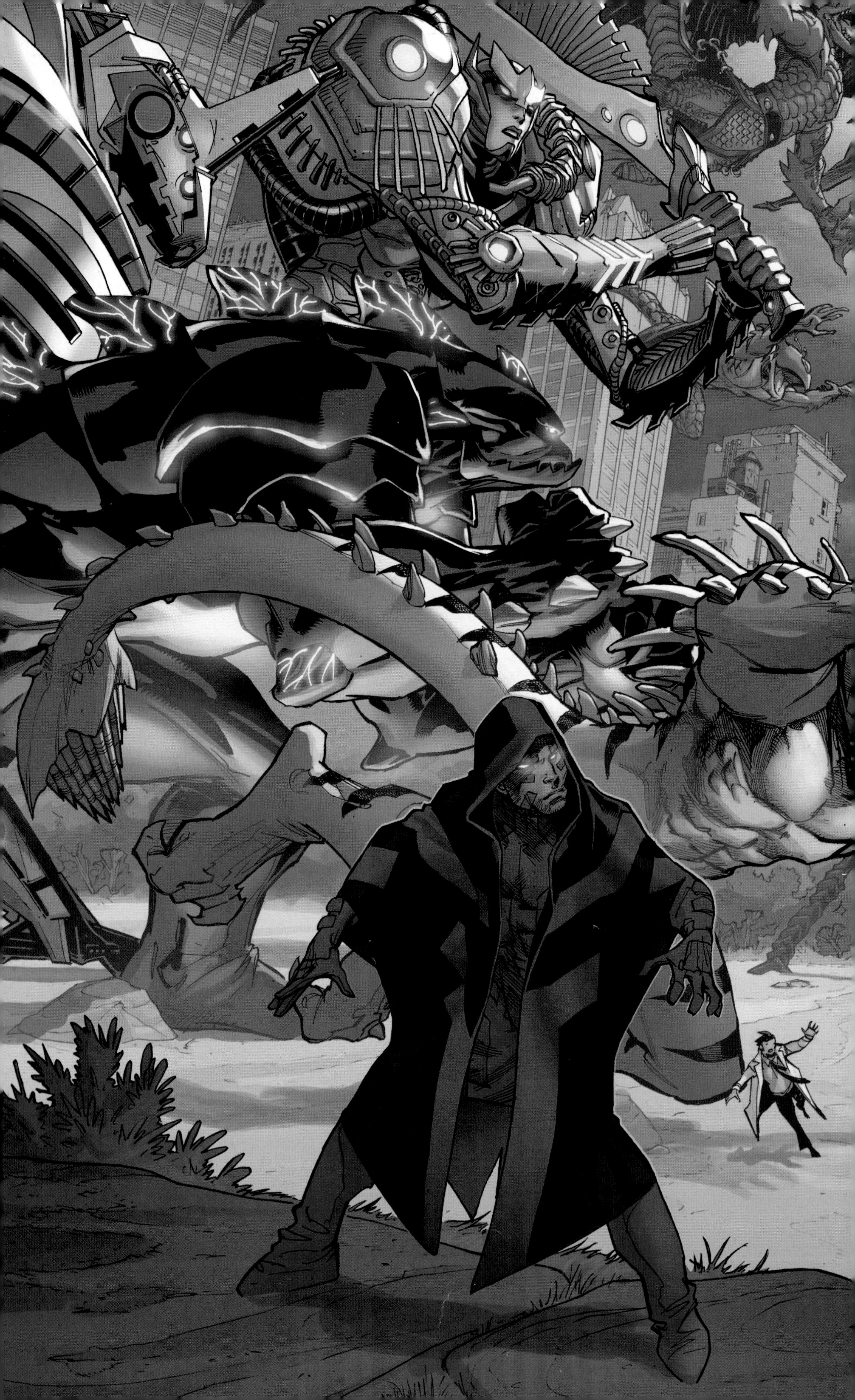

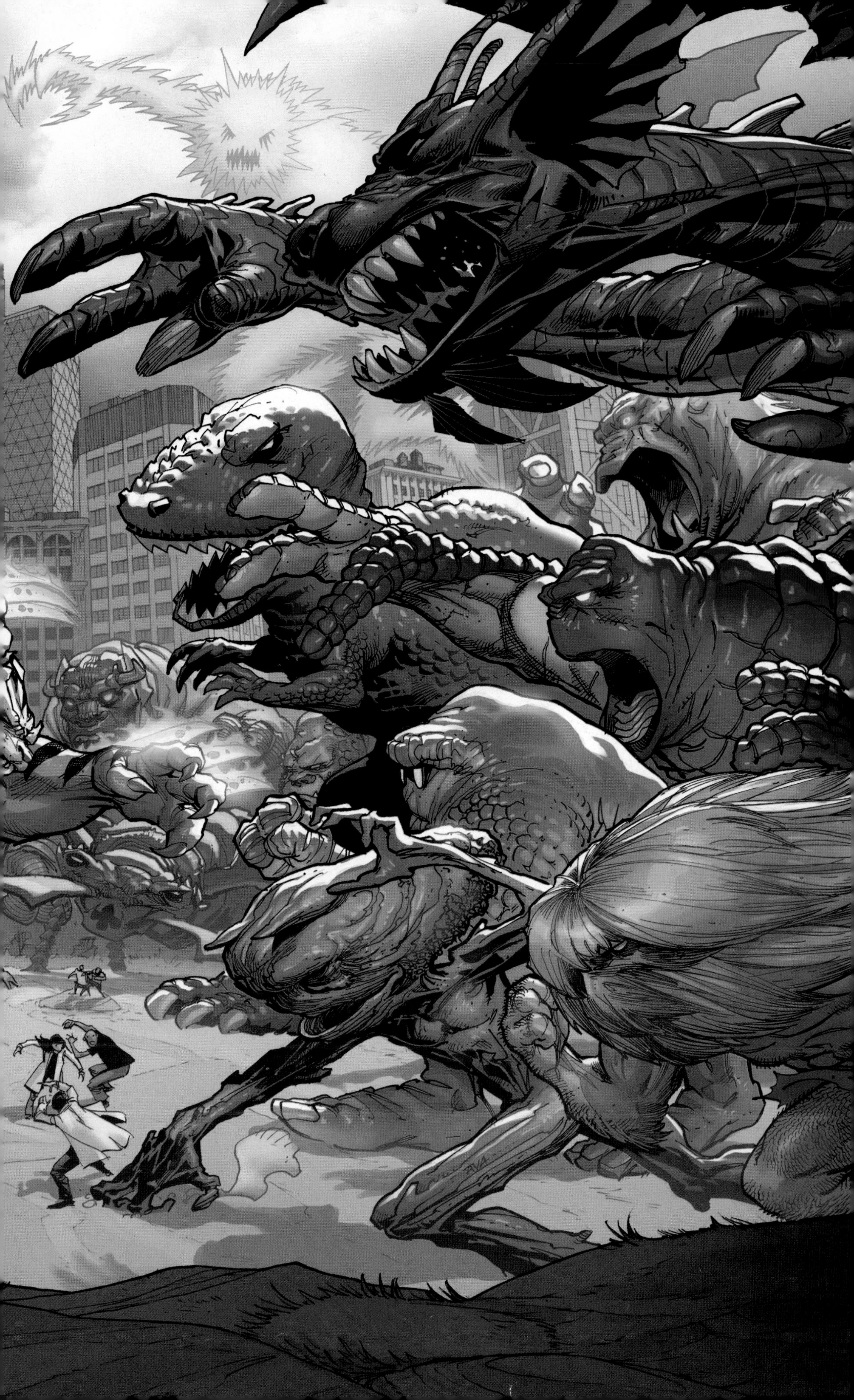

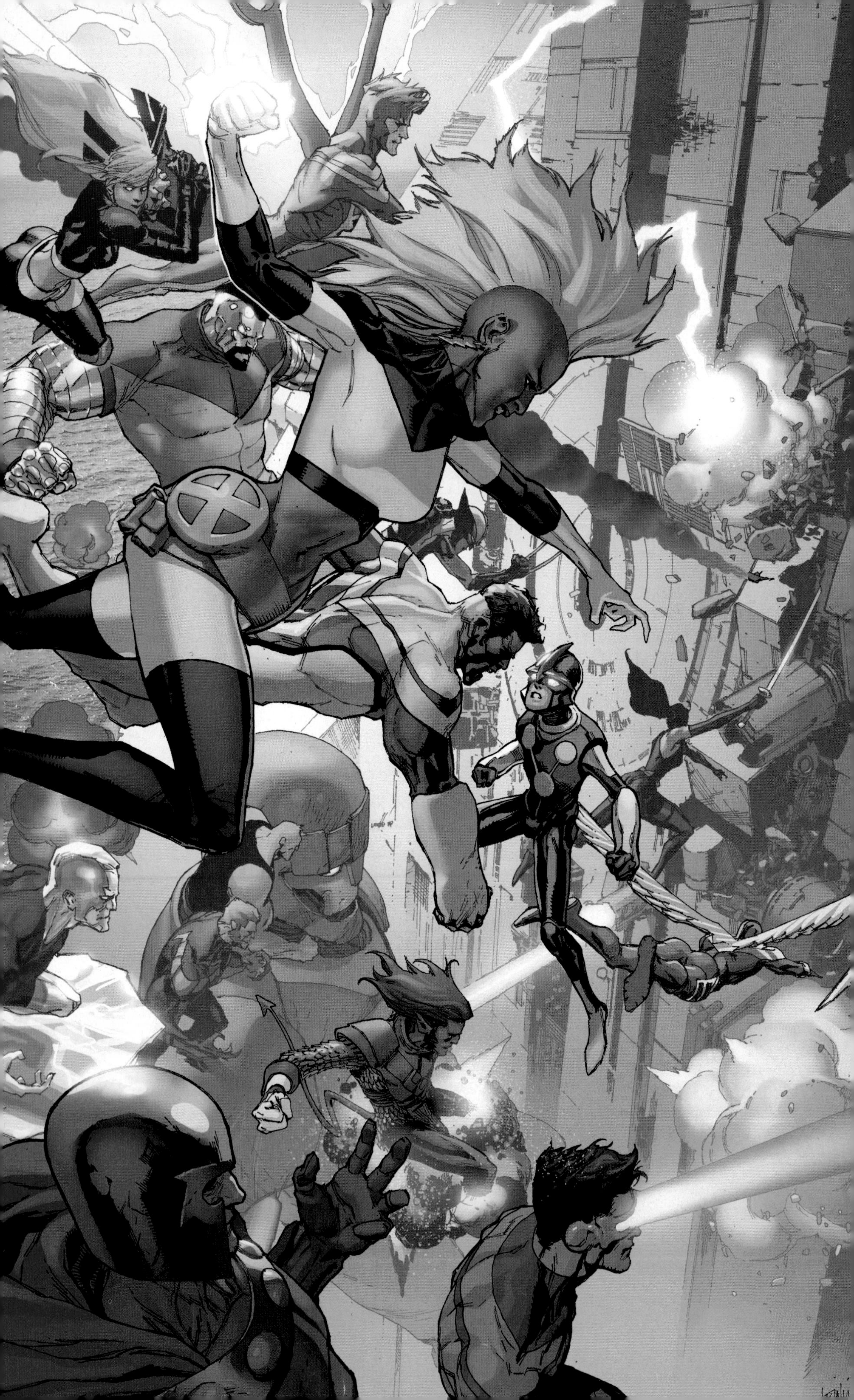

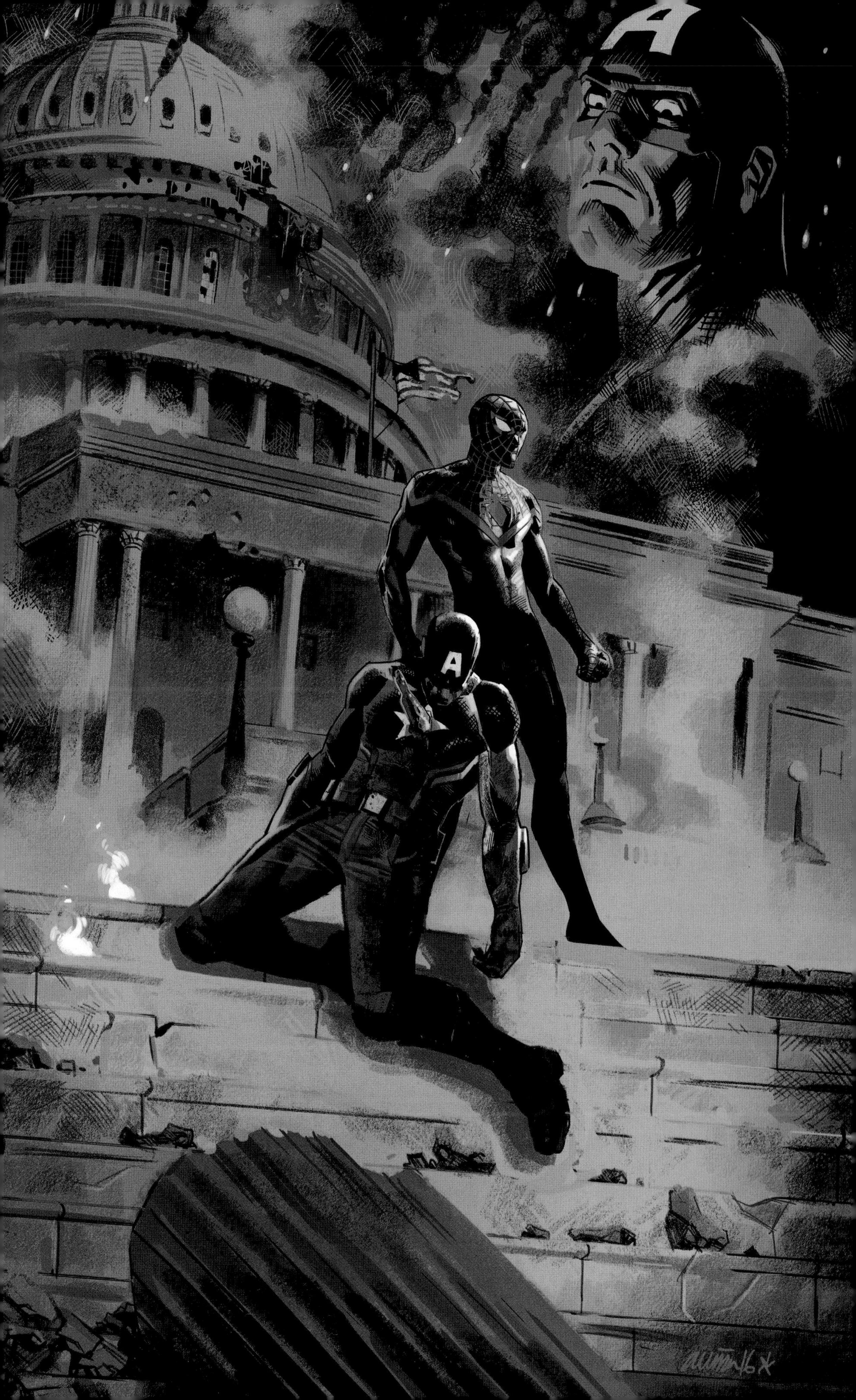

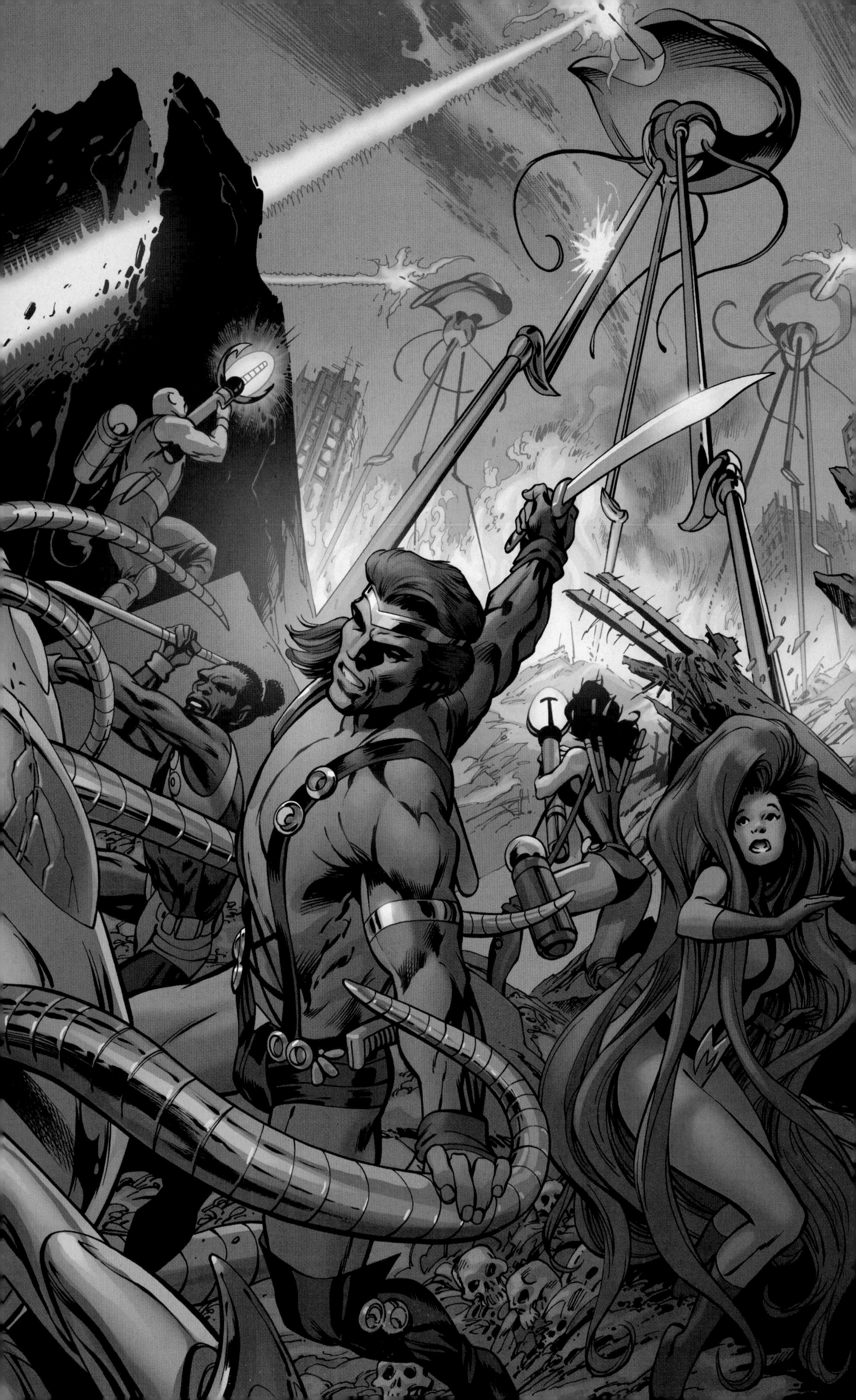

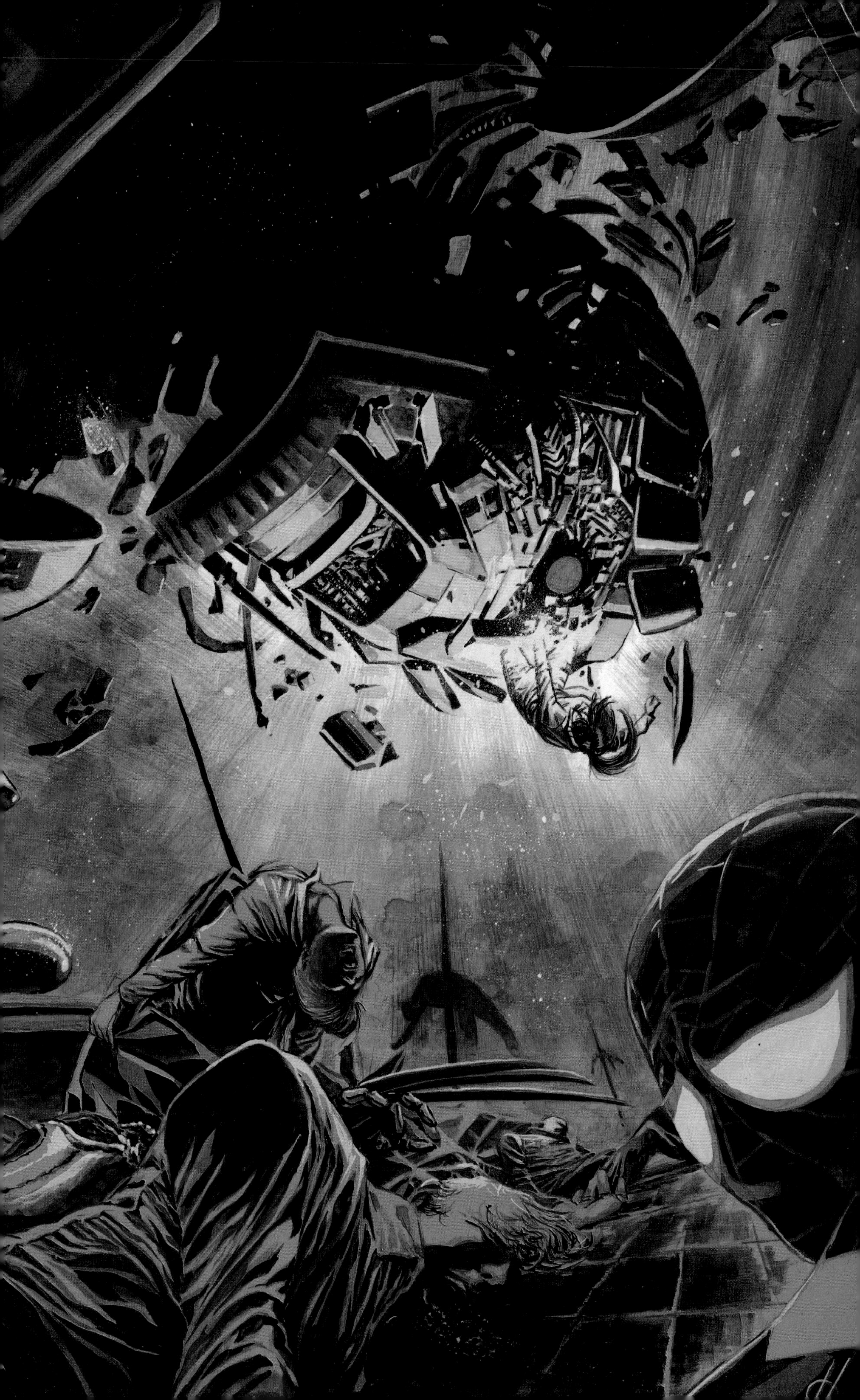

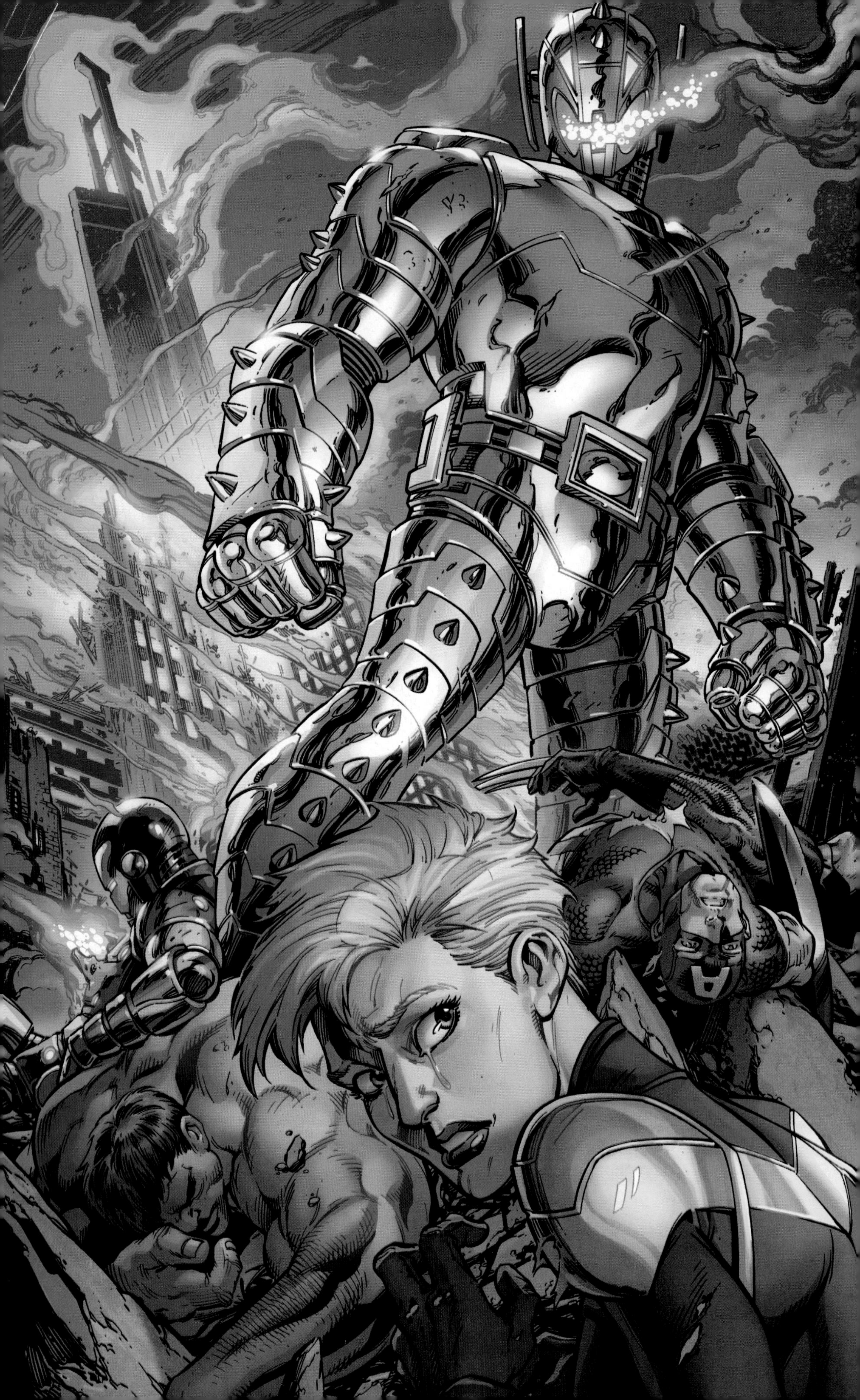

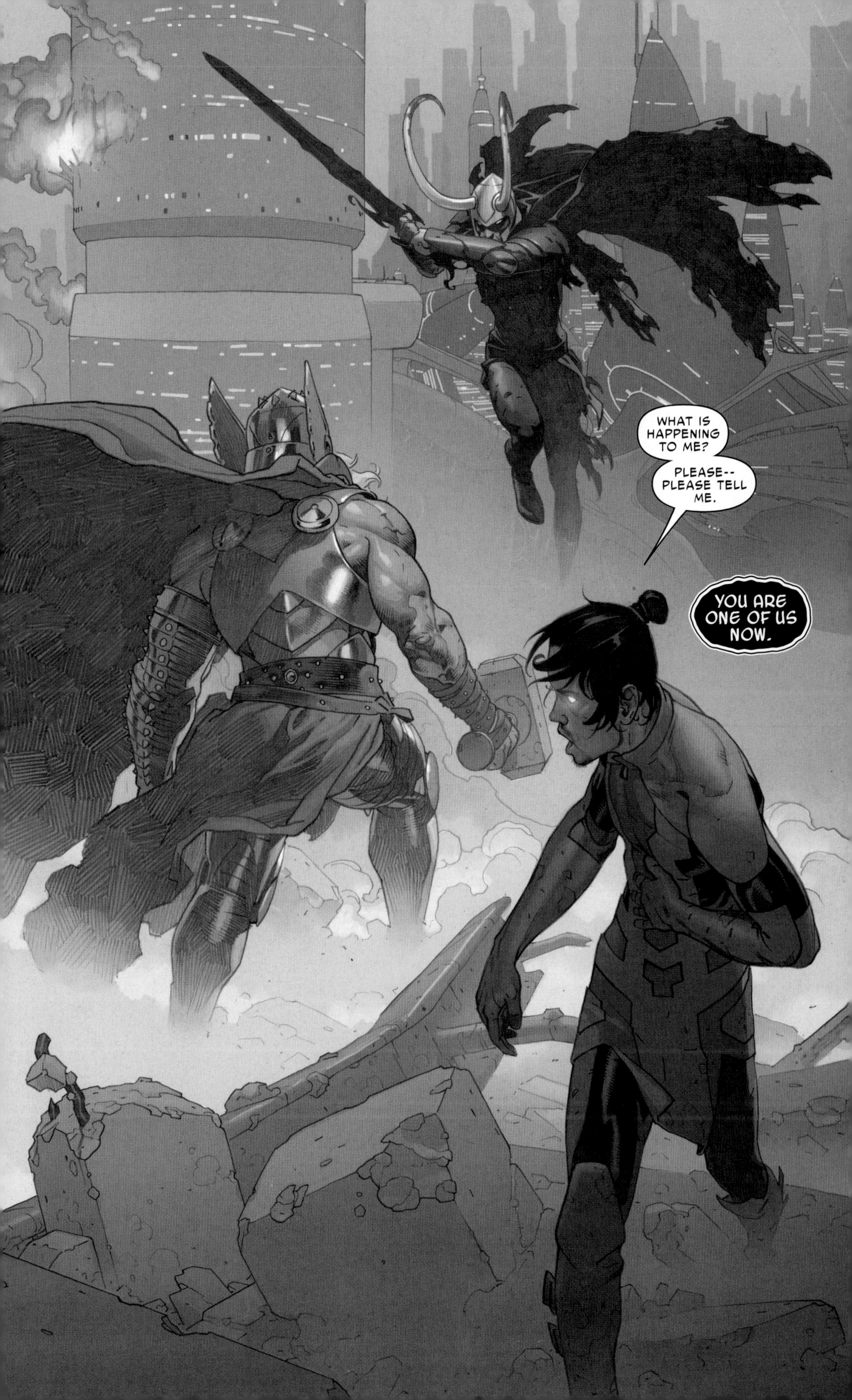
WHAT IS HAPPENING TO ME?
PLEASE-- PLEASE TELL ME.
YOU ARE ONE OF US NOW.

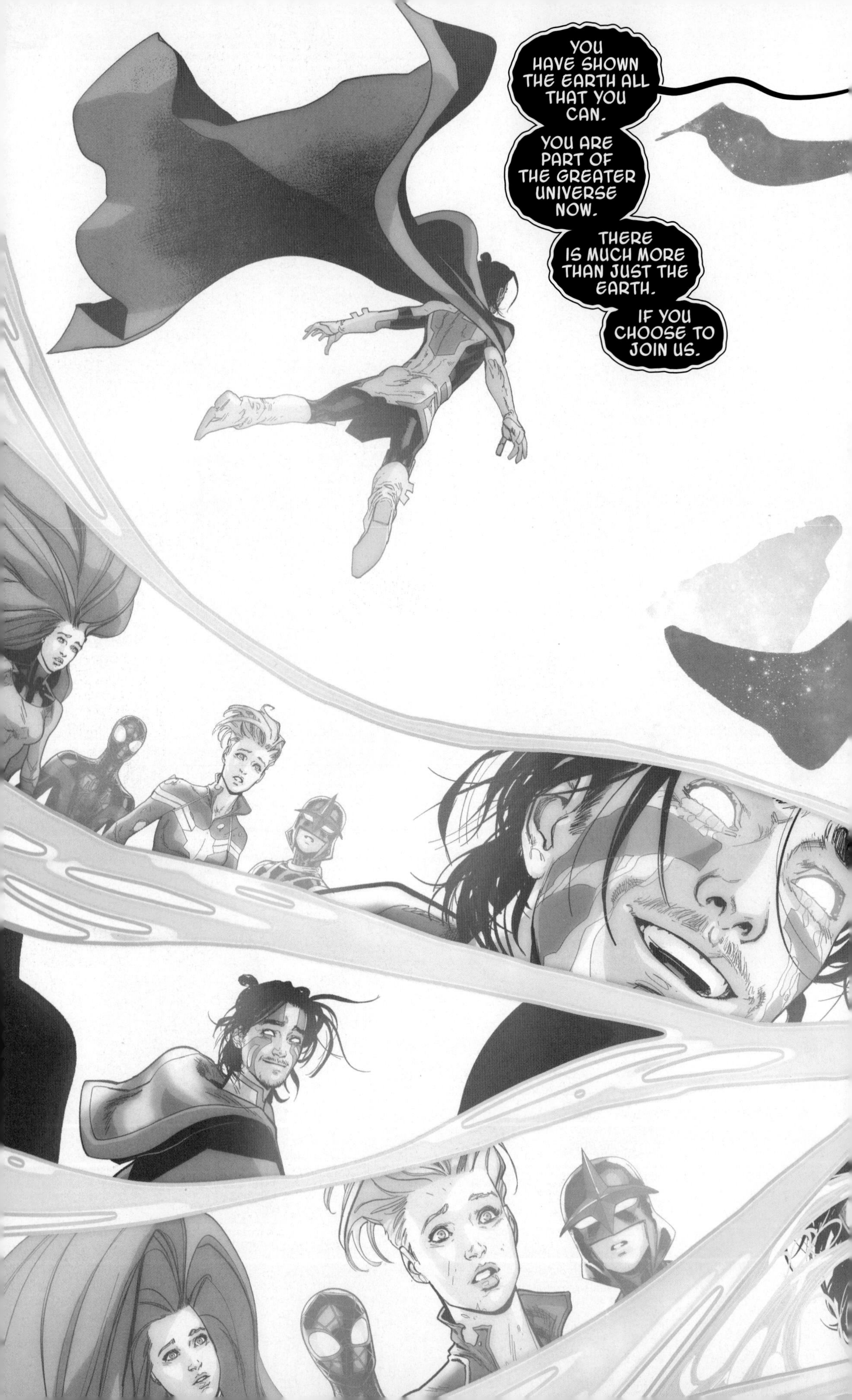
YOU HAVE SHOWN THE EARTH ALL THAT YOU CAN.
YOU ARE PART OF THE GREATER UNIVERSE NOW.
THERE IS MUCH MORE THAN JUST THE EARTH.
IF YOU CHOOSE TO JOIN US.

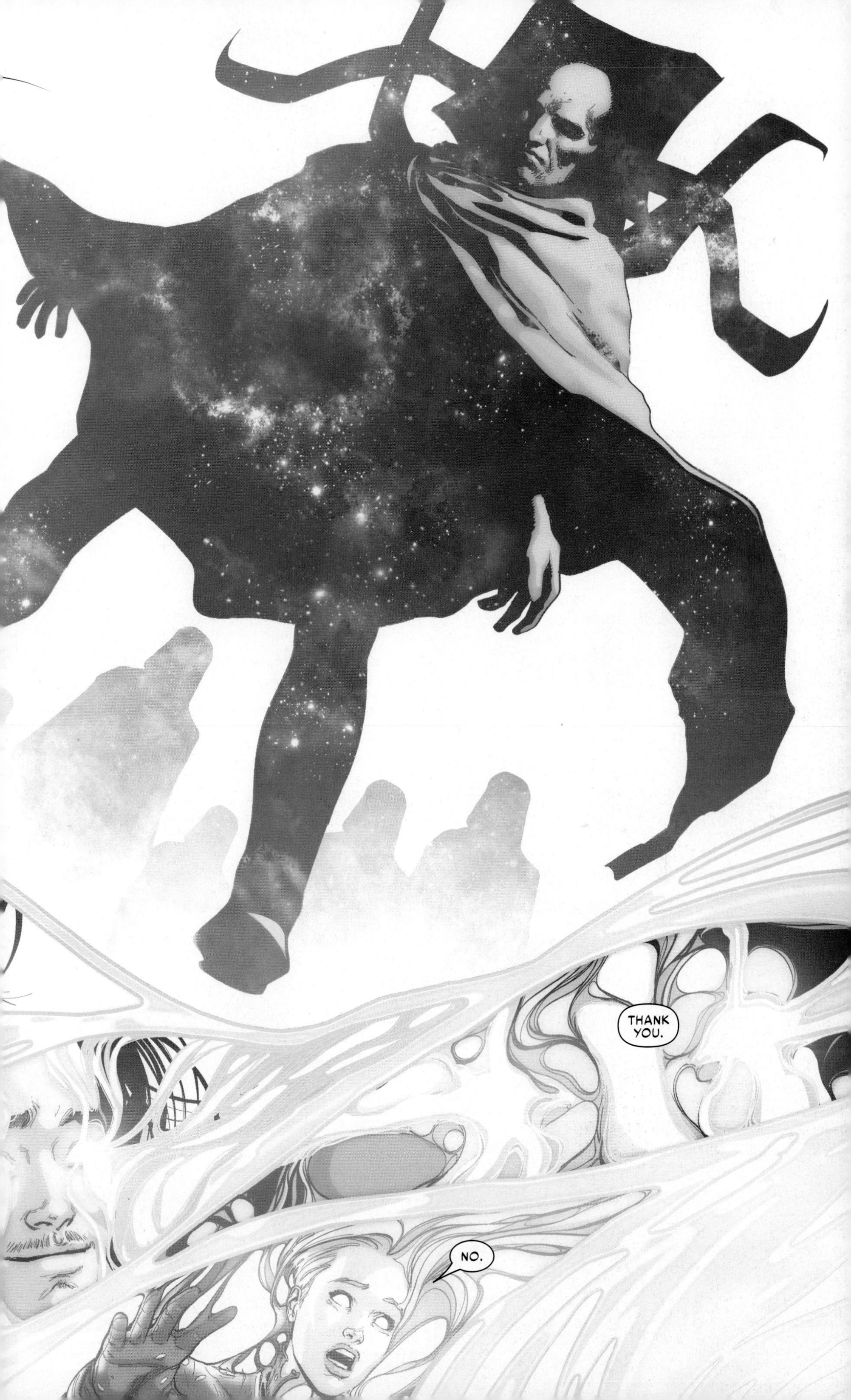
THANK YOU.
NO.

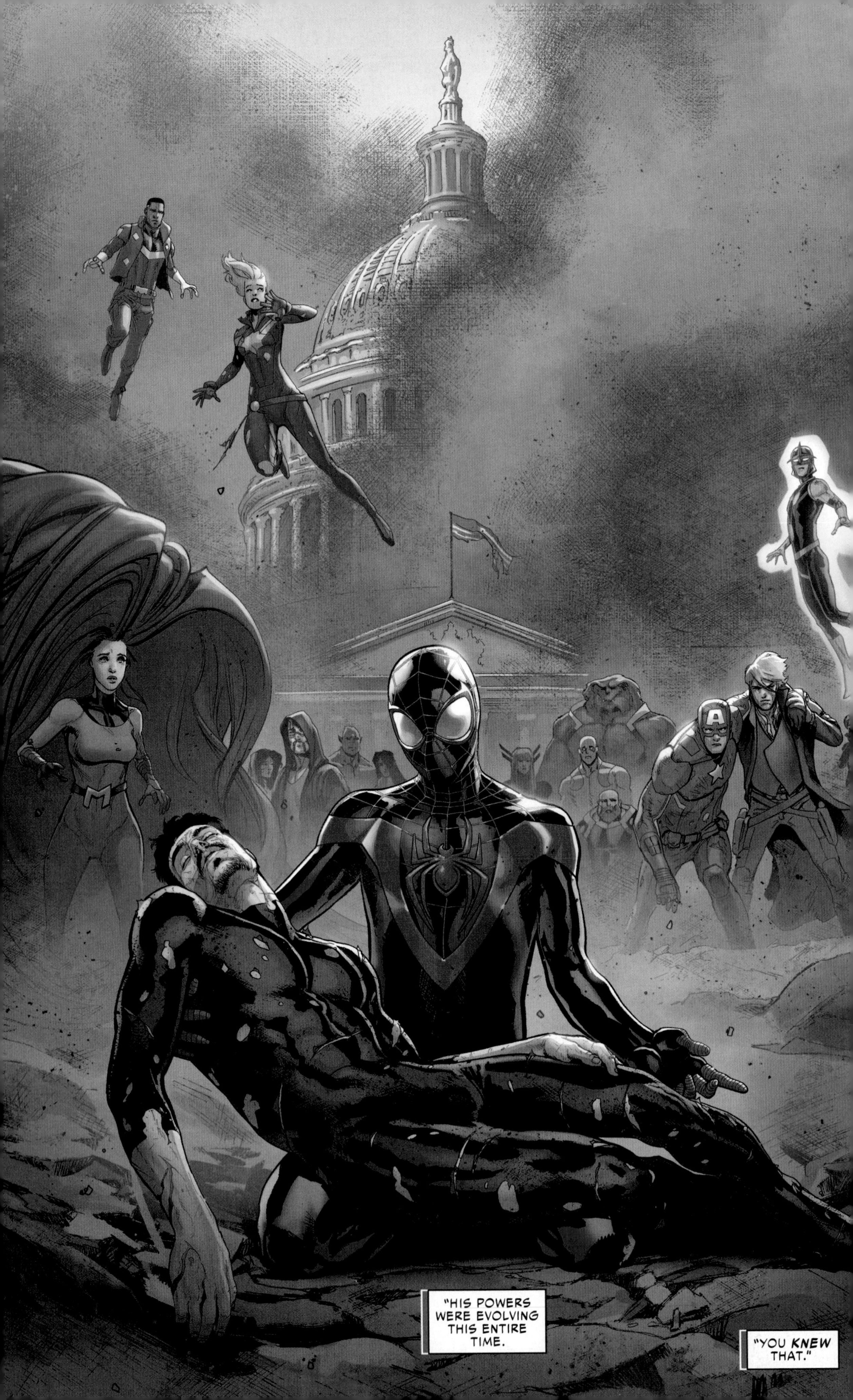
"HIS POWERS
WERE EVOLVING
THIS ENTIRE
TIME.
"YOU KNEW
THAT."

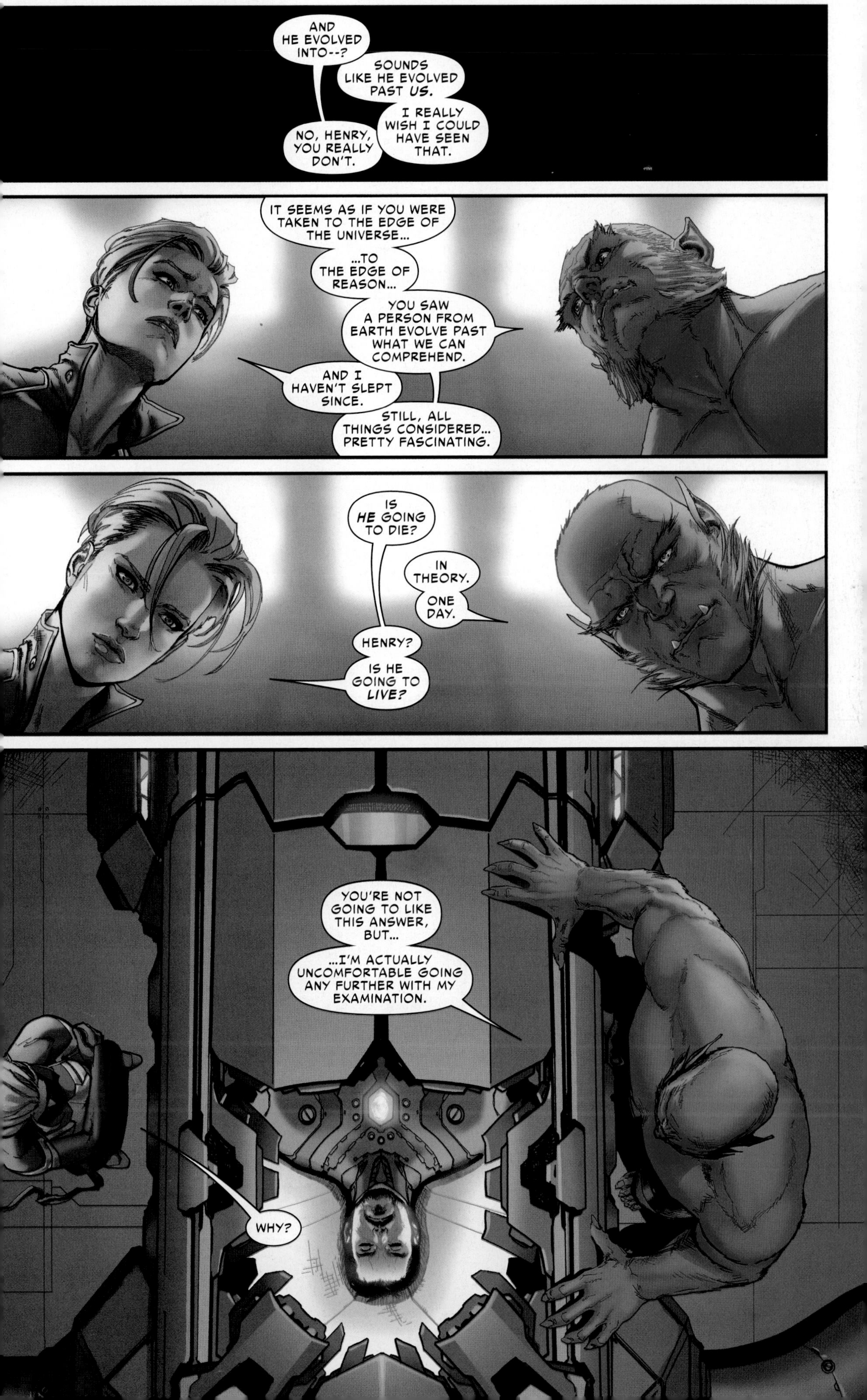
AND HE EVOLVED INTO--?
SOUNDS LIKE HE EVOLVED PAST US.
I REALLY WISH I COULD HAVE SEEN THAT.
NO, HENRY, YOU REALLY DON'T.
IT SEEMS AS IF YOU WERE TAKEN TO THE EDGE OF THE UNIVERSE...
...TO THE EDGE OF REASON...
YOU SAW A PERSON FROM EARTH EVOLVE PAST WHAT WE CAN COMPREHEND.
AND I HAVEN'T SLEPT SINCE.
STILL, ALL THINGS CONSIDERED... PRETTY FASCINATING.
IS HE GOING TO DIE?
IN THEORY.
ONE DAY.
HENRY?
IS HE GOING TO LIVE?
YOU'RE NOT GOING TO LIKE THIS ANSWER, BUT...
...I'M ACTUALLY UNCOMFORTABLE GOING ANY FURTHER WITH MY EXAMINATION.
WHY?

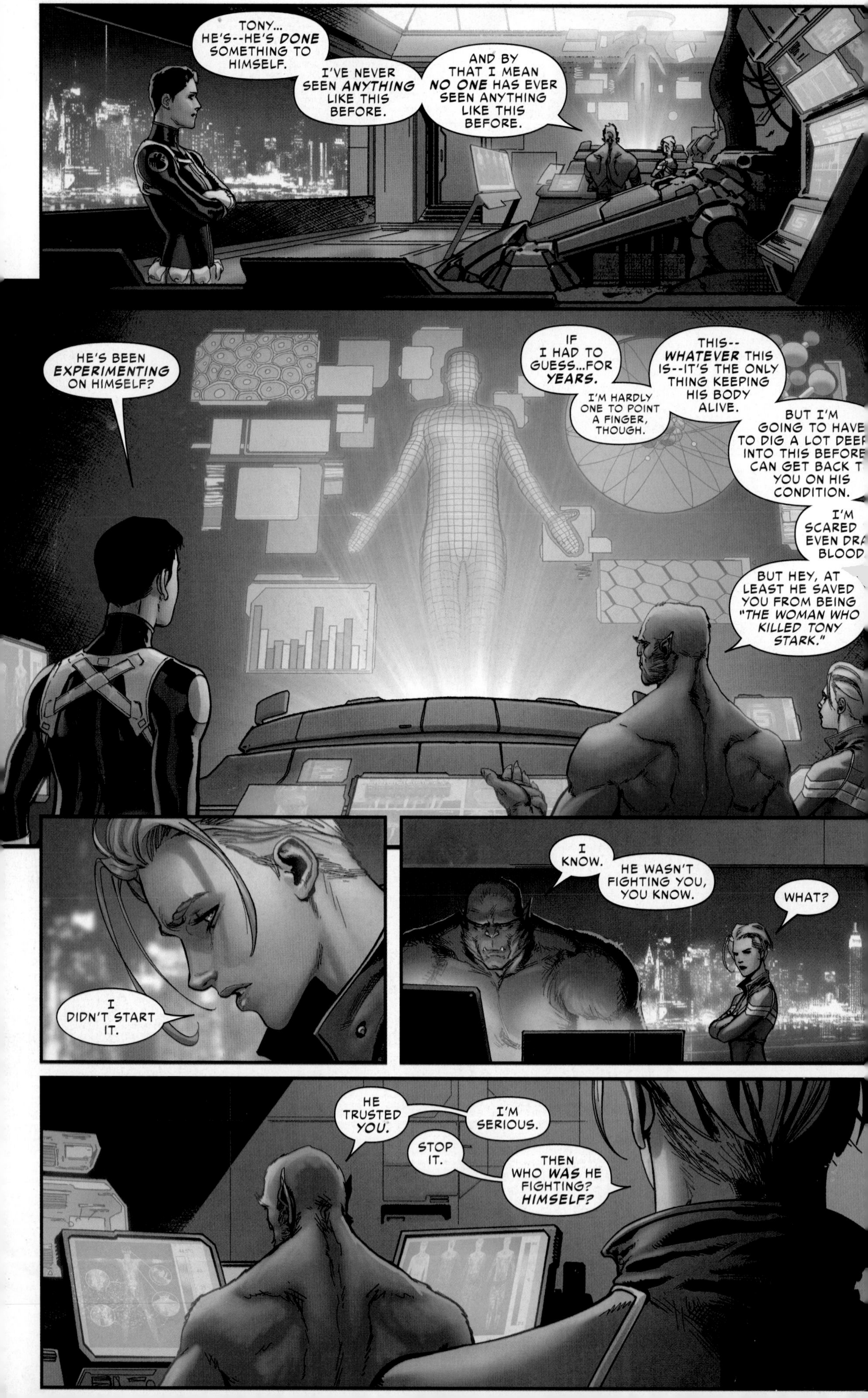
TONY... HE'S--HE'S DONE SOMETHING TO HIMSELF.
I'VE NEVER SEEN ANYTHING LIKE THIS BEFORE.
AND BY THAT I MEAN NO ONE HAS EVER SEEN ANYTHING LIKE THIS BEFORE.
HE'S BEEN EXPERIMENTING ON HIMSELF?
IF I HAD TO GUESS...FOR YEARS.
I'M HARDLY ONE TO POINT A FINGER, THOUGH.
THIS-- WHATEVER THIS IS--IT'S THE ONLY THING KEEPING HIS BODY ALIVE.
BUT I'M GOING TO HAVE TO DIG A LOT DEEP INTO THIS BEFORE CAN GET BACK T YOU ON HIS CONDITION.
I'M SCARED EVEN DRA BLOOD.
BUT HEY, AT LEAST HE SAVED YOU FROM BEING "THE WOMAN WHO KILLED TONY STARK."
I DIDN'T START IT.
I KNOW.
HE WASN'T FIGHTING YOU, YOU KNOW.
WHAT?
HE TRUSTED YOU.
I'M SERIOUS.
STOP IT.
THEN WHO WAS HE FIGHTING? HIMSELF?

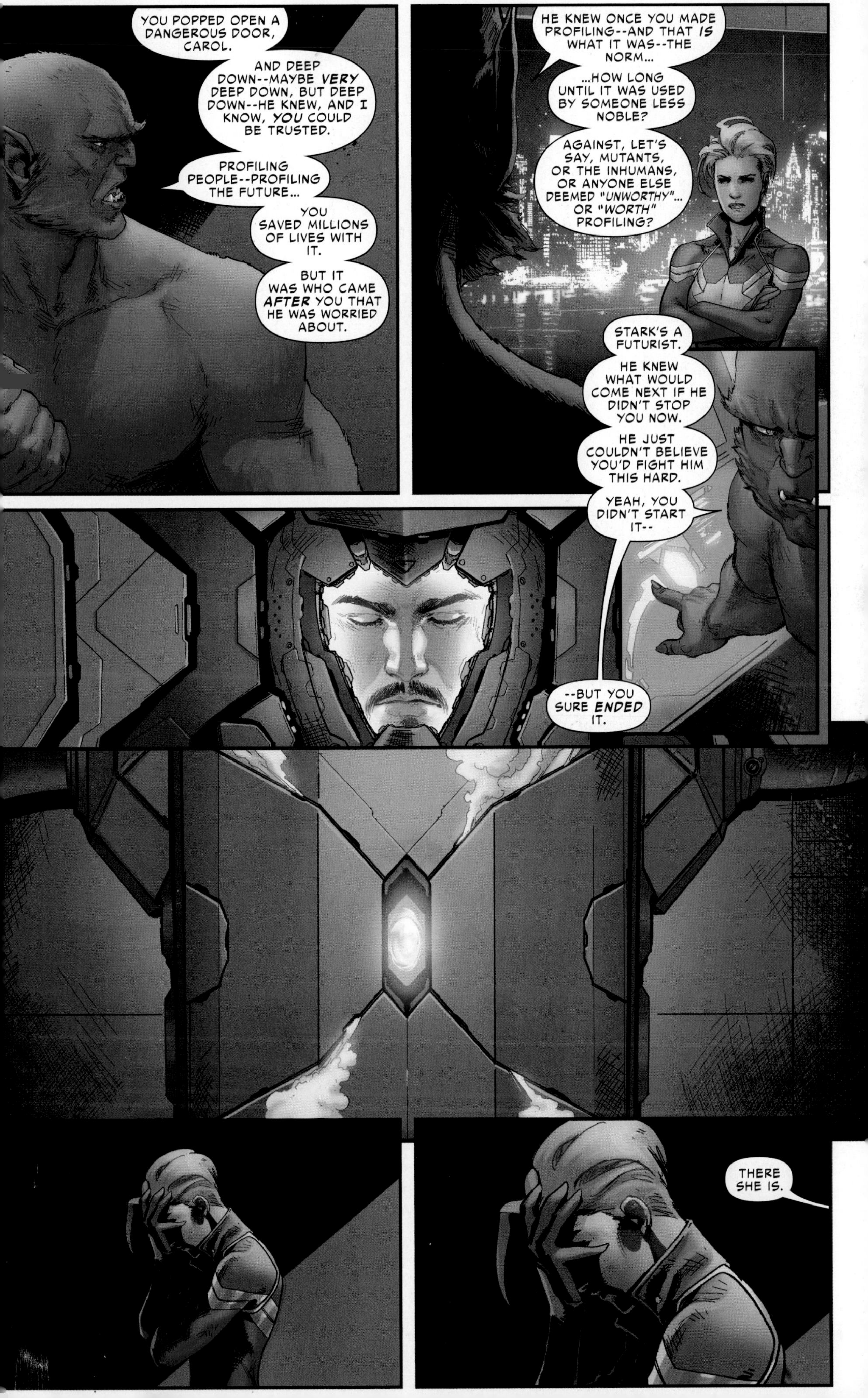
YOU POPPED OPEN A DANGEROUS DOOR, CAROL.
AND DEEP DOWN--MAYBE *VERY* DEEP DOWN, BUT DEEP DOWN--HE KNEW, AND I KNOW, *YOU* COULD BE TRUSTED.
PROFILING PEOPLE--PROFILING THE FUTURE...
YOU SAVED MILLIONS OF LIVES WITH IT.
BUT IT WAS WHO CAME *AFTER* YOU THAT HE WAS WORRIED ABOUT.
HE KNEW ONCE YOU MADE PROFILING--AND THAT *IS* WHAT IT WAS--THE NORM...
...HOW LONG UNTIL IT WAS USED BY SOMEONE LESS NOBLE?
AGAINST, LET'S SAY, MUTANTS, OR THE INHUMANS, OR ANYONE ELSE DEEMED *"UNWORTHY"*... OR *"WORTH"* PROFILING?
STARK'S A FUTURIST.
HE KNEW WHAT WOULD COME NEXT IF HE DIDN'T STOP YOU NOW.
HE JUST COULDN'T BELIEVE YOU'D FIGHT HIM THIS HARD.
YEAH, YOU DIDN'T START IT--
--BUT YOU SURE *ENDED* IT.
THERE SHE IS.

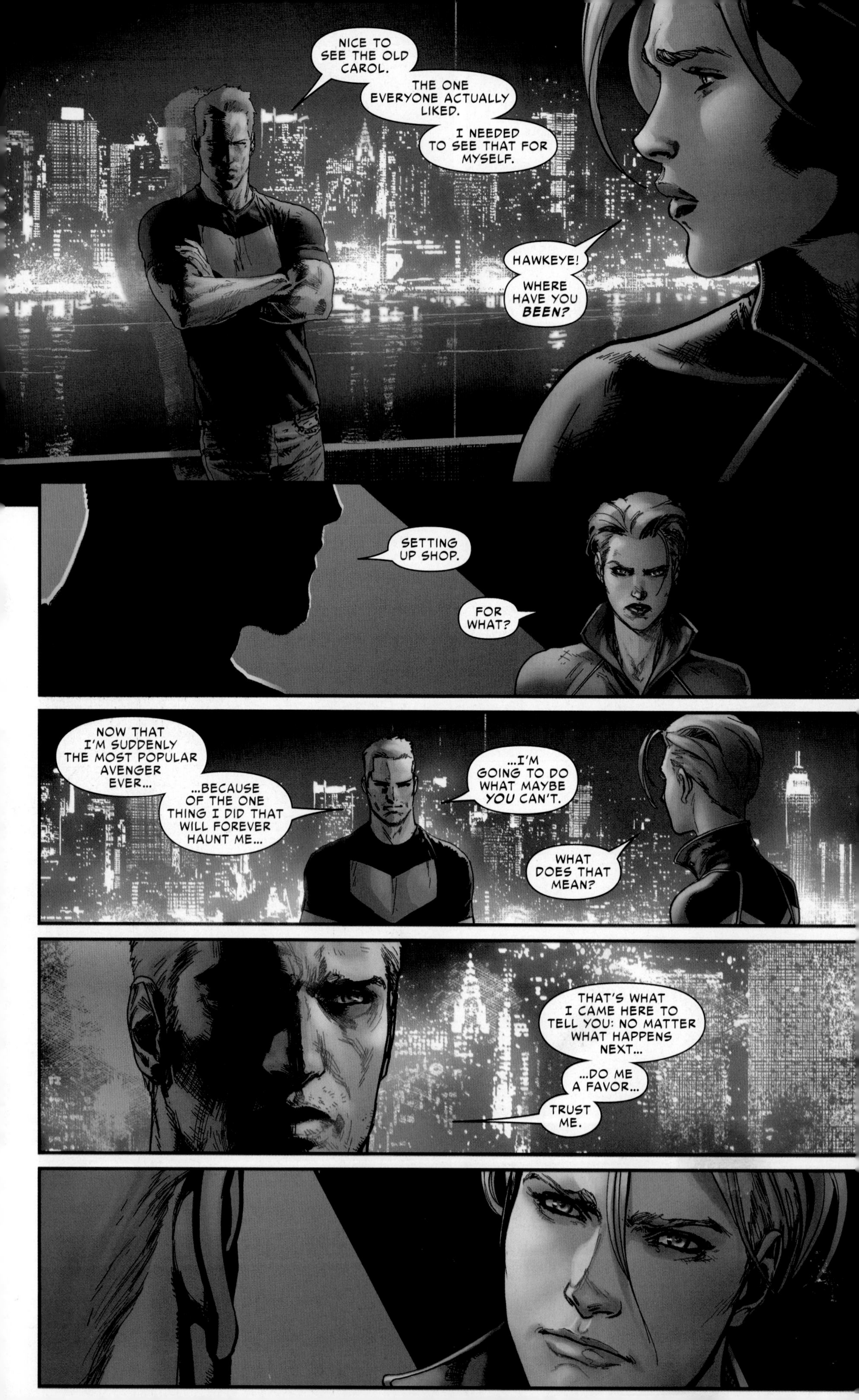
NICE TO SEE THE OLD CAROL.
THE ONE EVERYONE ACTUALLY LIKED.
I NEEDED TO SEE THAT FOR MYSELF.
HAWKEYE!
WHERE HAVE YOU *BEEN?*
SETTING UP SHOP.
FOR WHAT?
NOW THAT I'M SUDDENLY THE MOST POPULAR AVENGER EVER...
...BECAUSE OF THE ONE THING I DID THAT WILL FOREVER HAUNT ME...
...I'M GOING TO DO WHAT MAYBE *YOU* CAN'T.
WHAT DOES THAT MEAN?
THAT'S WHAT I CAME HERE TO TELL YOU: NO MATTER WHAT HAPPENS NEXT...
...DO ME A FAVOR...
TRUST ME.

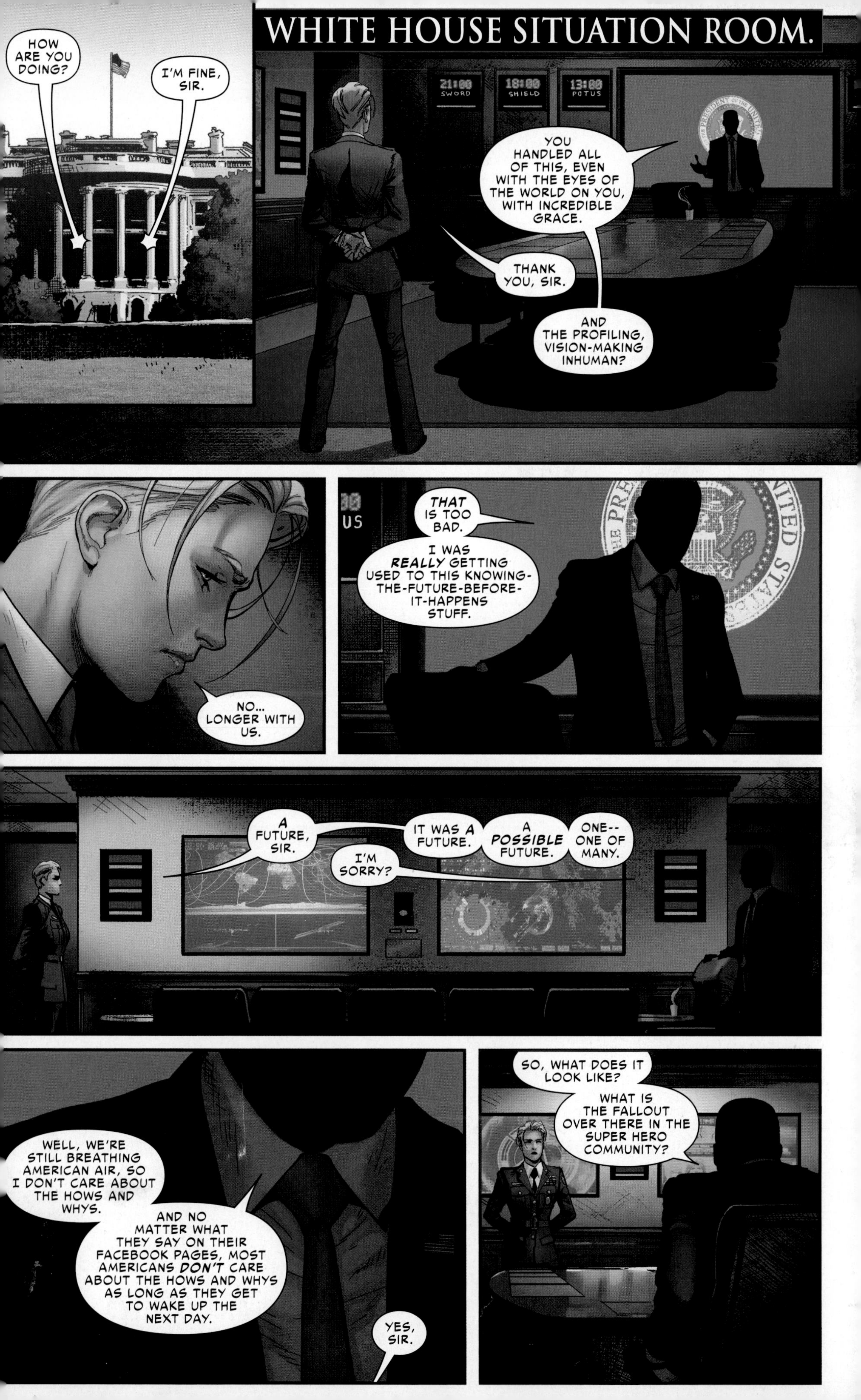
WHITE HOUSE SITUATION ROOM.
HOW ARE YOU DOING?
I'M FINE, SIR.
21:00 SWORD
18:00 SHIELD
13:00 POTUS
YOU HANDLED ALL OF THIS, EVEN WITH THE EYES OF THE WORLD ON YOU, WITH INCREDIBLE GRACE.
THANK YOU, SIR.
AND THE PROFILING, VISION-MAKING INHUMAN?
NO... LONGER WITH US.
THAT IS TOO BAD.
I WAS REALLY GETTING USED TO THIS KNOWING-THE-FUTURE-BEFORE-IT-HAPPENS STUFF.
A FUTURE, SIR.
IT WAS A FUTURE.
A POSSIBLE FUTURE.
ONE-- ONE OF MANY.
I'M SORRY?
WELL, WE'RE STILL BREATHING AMERICAN AIR, SO I DON'T CARE ABOUT THE HOWS AND WHYS.
AND NO MATTER WHAT THEY SAY ON THEIR FACEBOOK PAGES, MOST AMERICANS DON'T CARE ABOUT THE HOWS AND WHYS AS LONG AS THEY GET TO WAKE UP THE NEXT DAY.
YES, SIR.
SO, WHAT DOES IT LOOK LIKE?
WHAT IS THE FALLOUT OVER THERE IN THE SUPER HERO COMMUNITY?

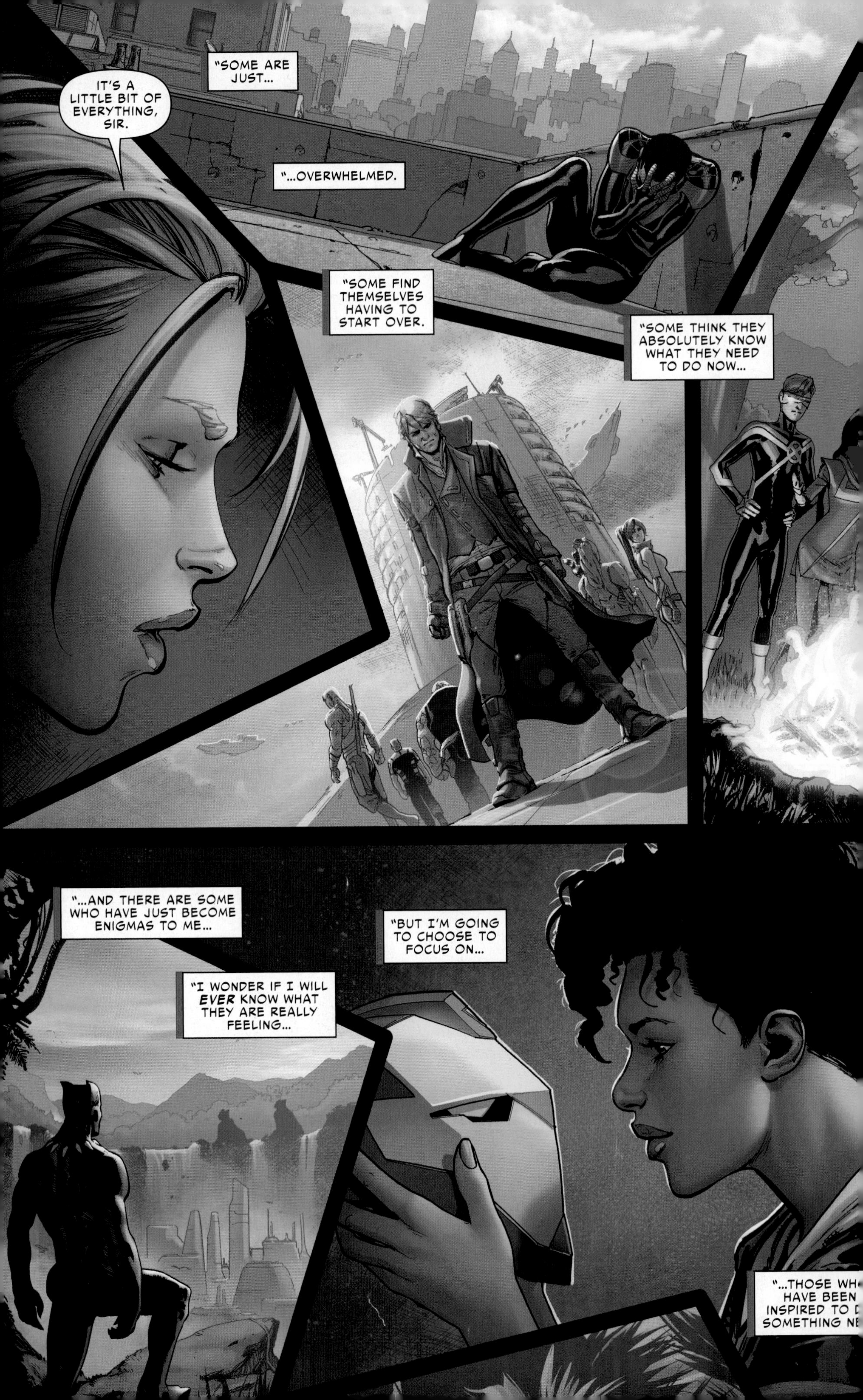
IT'S A LITTLE BIT OF EVERYTHING, SIR.
"SOME ARE JUST...
"...OVERWHELMED.
"SOME FIND THEMSELVES HAVING TO START OVER.
"SOME THINK THEY ABSOLUTELY KNOW WHAT THEY NEED TO DO NOW...
"...AND THERE ARE SOME WHO HAVE JUST BECOME ENIGMAS TO ME...
"I WONDER IF I WILL EVER KNOW WHAT THEY ARE REALLY FEELING...
"BUT I'M GOING TO CHOOSE TO FOCUS ON...
"...THOSE WH HAVE BEEN INSPIRED TO SOMETHING NE

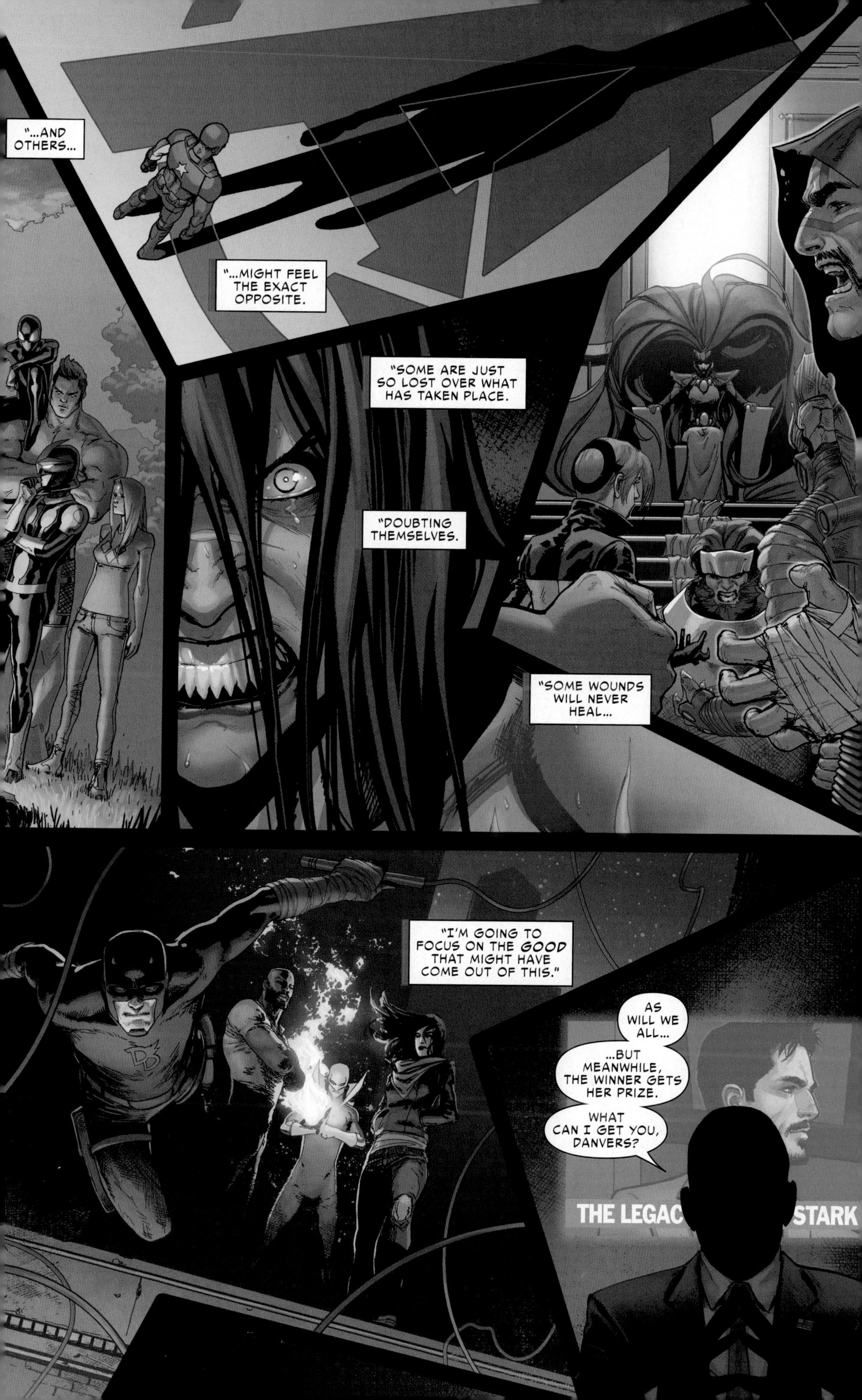
"...AND OTHERS...
"...MIGHT FEEL THE EXACT OPPOSITE.
"SOME ARE JUST SO LOST OVER WHAT HAS TAKEN PLACE.
"DOUBTING THEMSELVES.
"SOME WOUNDS WILL NEVER HEAL...
"I'M GOING TO FOCUS ON THE GOOD THAT MIGHT HAVE COME OUT OF THIS."
AS WILL WE ALL...
...BUT MEANWHILE, THE WINNER GETS HER PRIZE.
WHAT CAN I GET YOU, DANVERS?
THE LEGAC
STARK

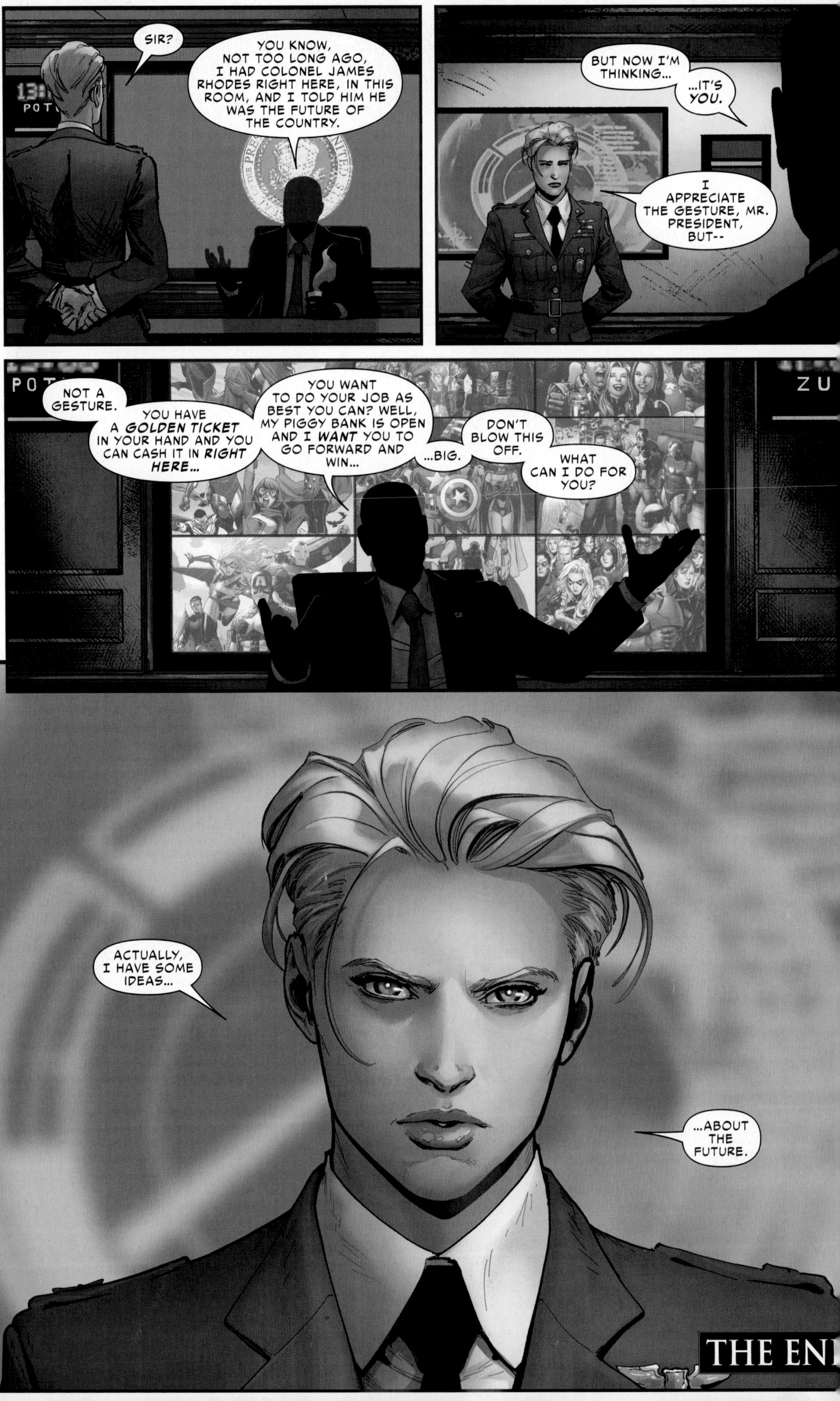
SIR?
YOU KNOW, NOT TOO LONG AGO, I HAD COLONEL JAMES RHODES RIGHT HERE, IN THIS ROOM, AND I TOLD HIM HE WAS THE FUTURE OF THE COUNTRY.
BUT NOW I'M THINKING...
...IT'S *YOU.*
I APPRECIATE THE GESTURE, MR. PRESIDENT, BUT--
NOT A GESTURE.
YOU HAVE A ***GOLDEN TICKET*** IN YOUR HAND AND YOU CAN CASH IT IN ***RIGHT HERE...***
YOU WANT TO DO YOUR JOB AS BEST YOU CAN? WELL, MY PIGGY BANK IS OPEN AND I ***WANT*** YOU TO GO FORWARD AND WIN...
...BIG.
DON'T BLOW THIS OFF.
WHAT CAN I DO FOR YOU?
ACTUALLY, I HAVE SOME IDEAS...
...ABOUT THE FUTURE.
THE EN

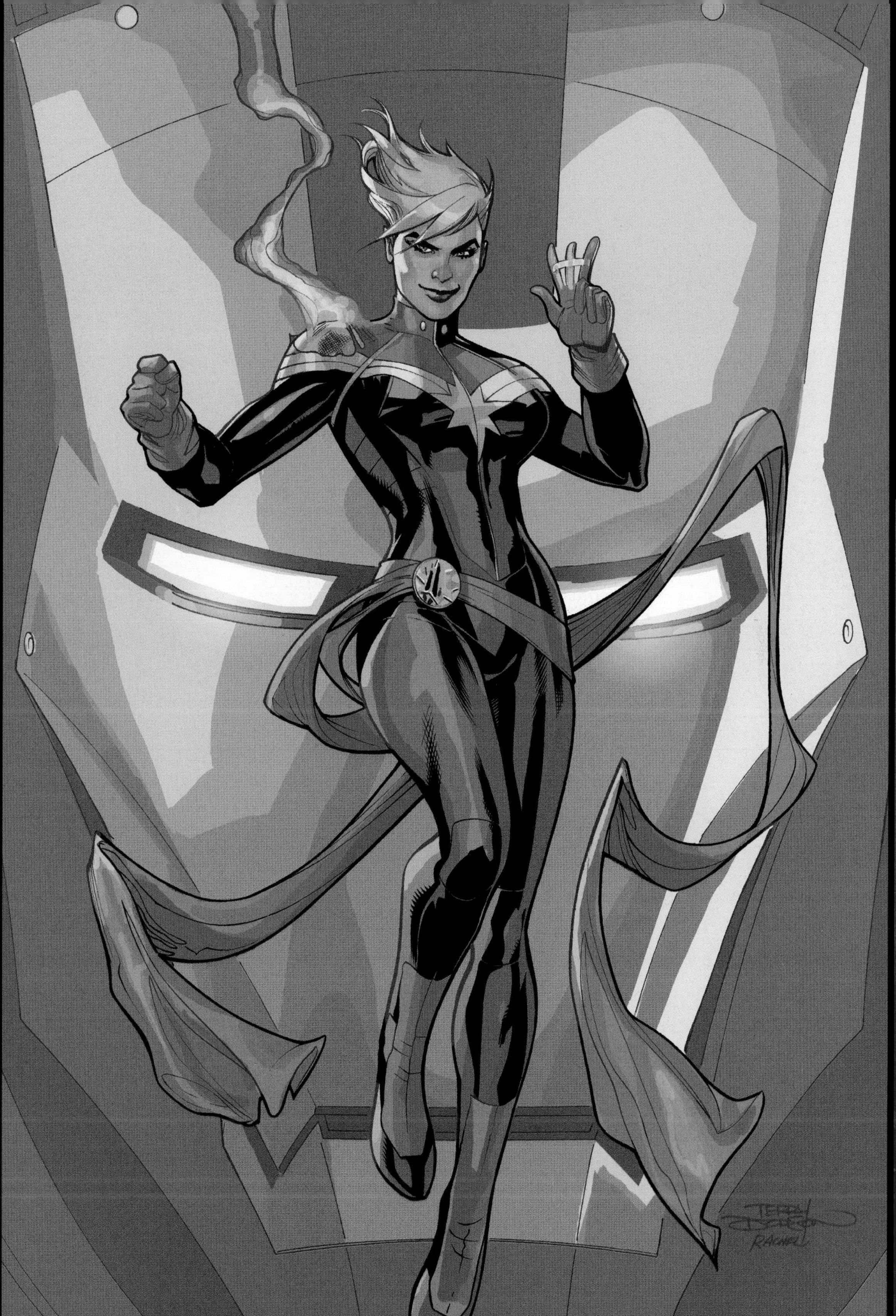

#0 VARIANT
BY TERRY DODSON & RACHEL DODSON

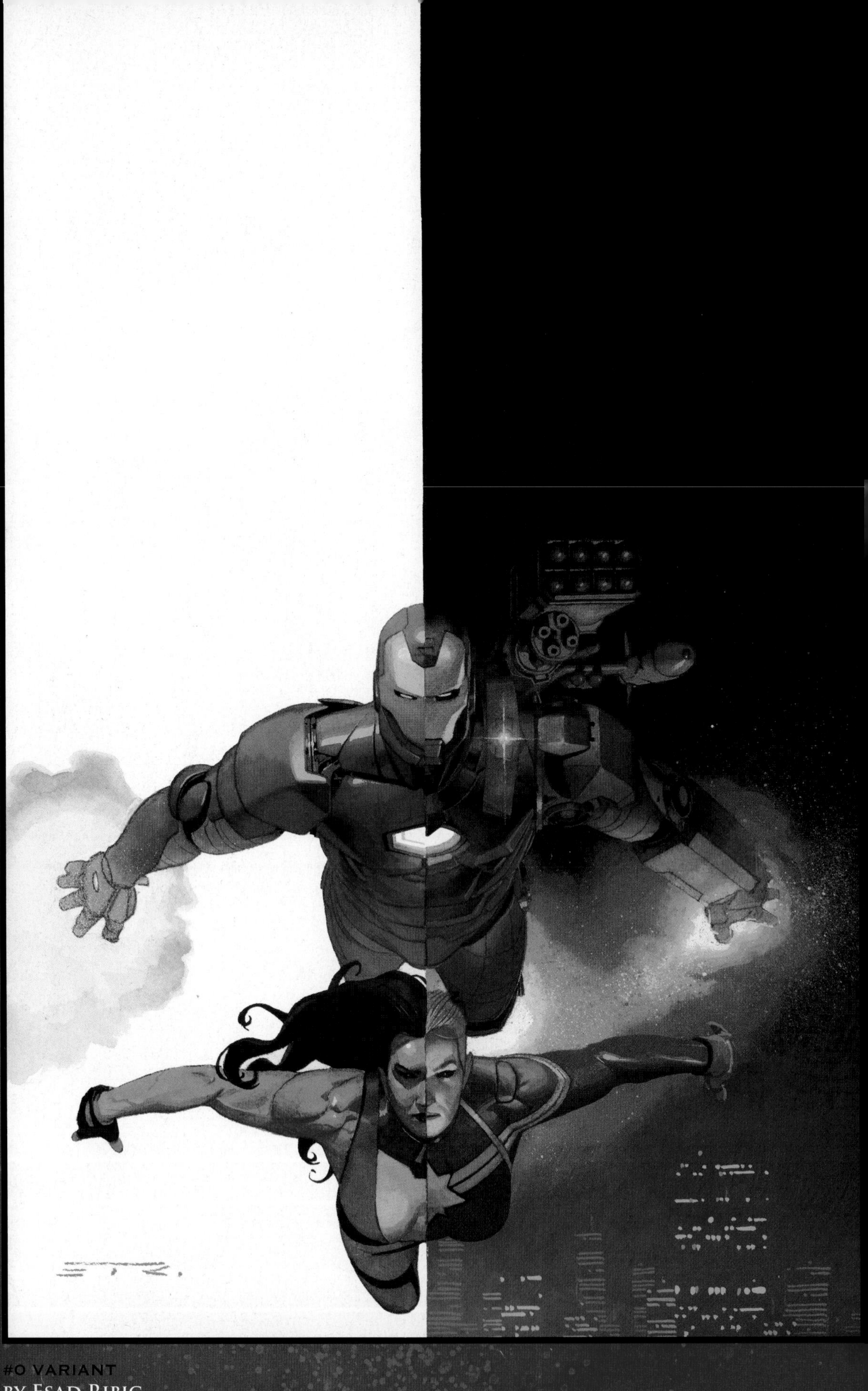

#0 VARIANT
BY ESAD RIBIC

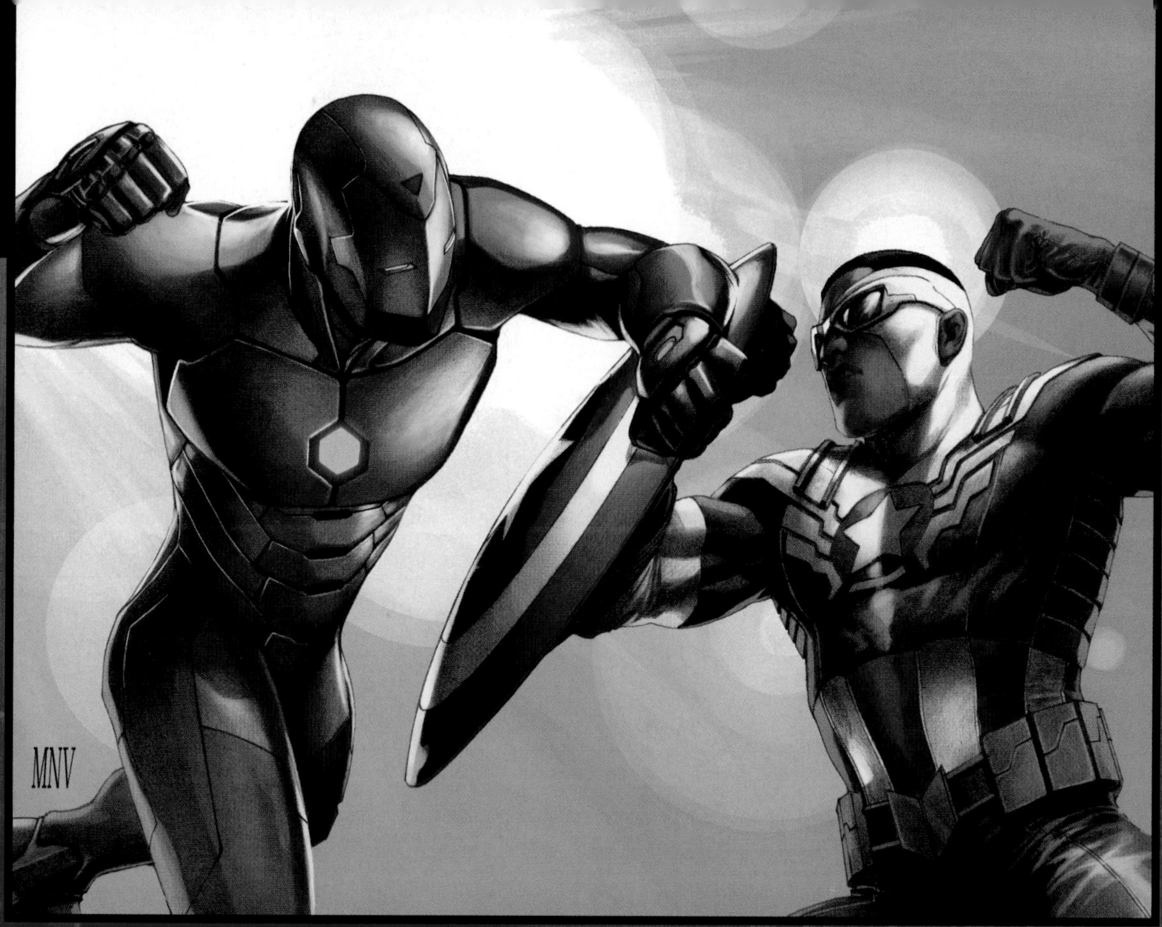
MNV

#1 VARIANT
BY STEVE MCNIVEN

#1 VARIANT
BY MARQUEZ

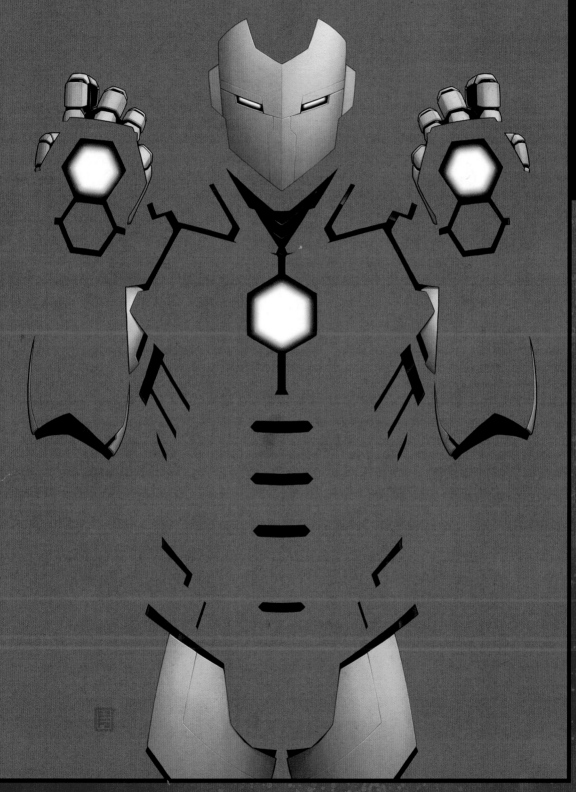

civil war II
001
jtc negative space
variant edition

rated t+
$5.99 usd
direct edition
marvel.com

#1 NEGATIVE SPACE VARIANT
BY JOHN TYLER CHRISTOPHER

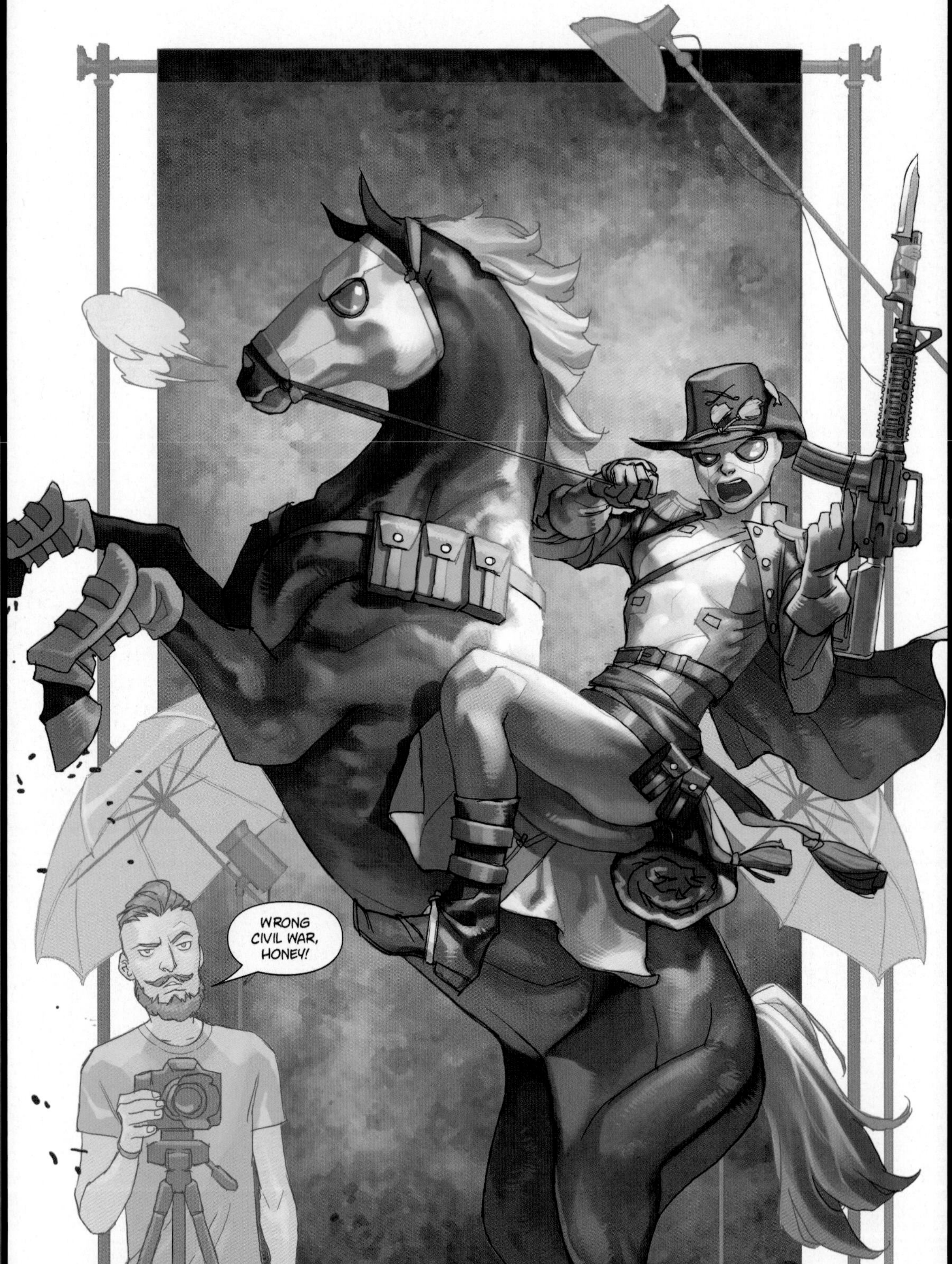
WRONG CIVIL WAR, HONEY!

#1 PARTY VARIANT
BY YASMINE PUTRI

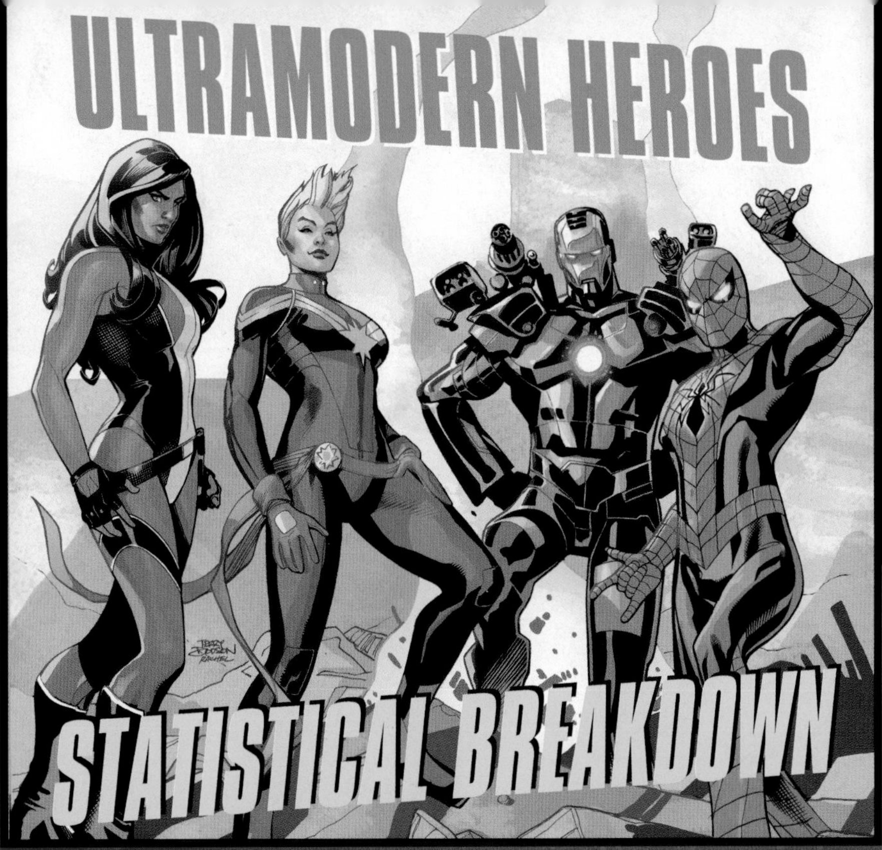
ULTRAMODERN HEROES
STATISTICAL BREAKDOWN

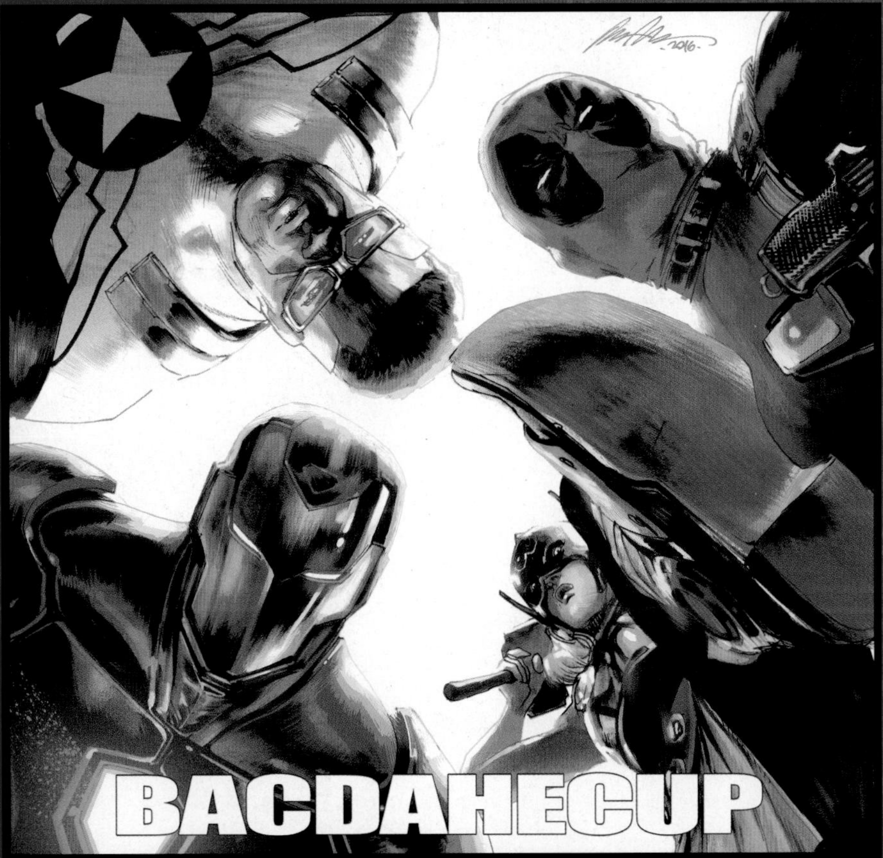
BACDAHECUP

#1 HIP-HOP VARIANT
BY RAFAEL ALBUQUERQUE

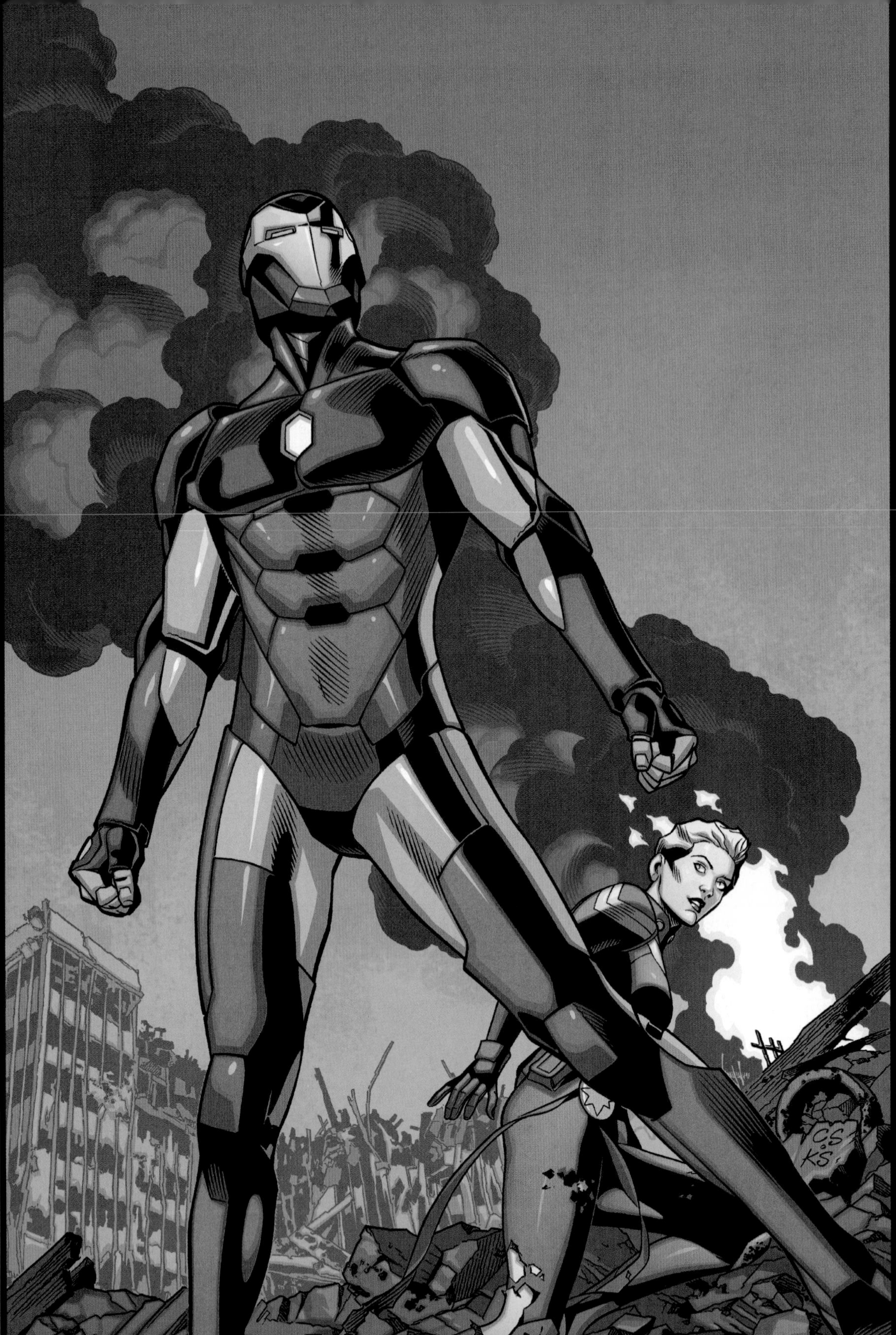
C.S.
K.S.

#1 BATTLE VARIANT
BY CHRIS SPROUSE, KARL STORY & DAVE McCAIG

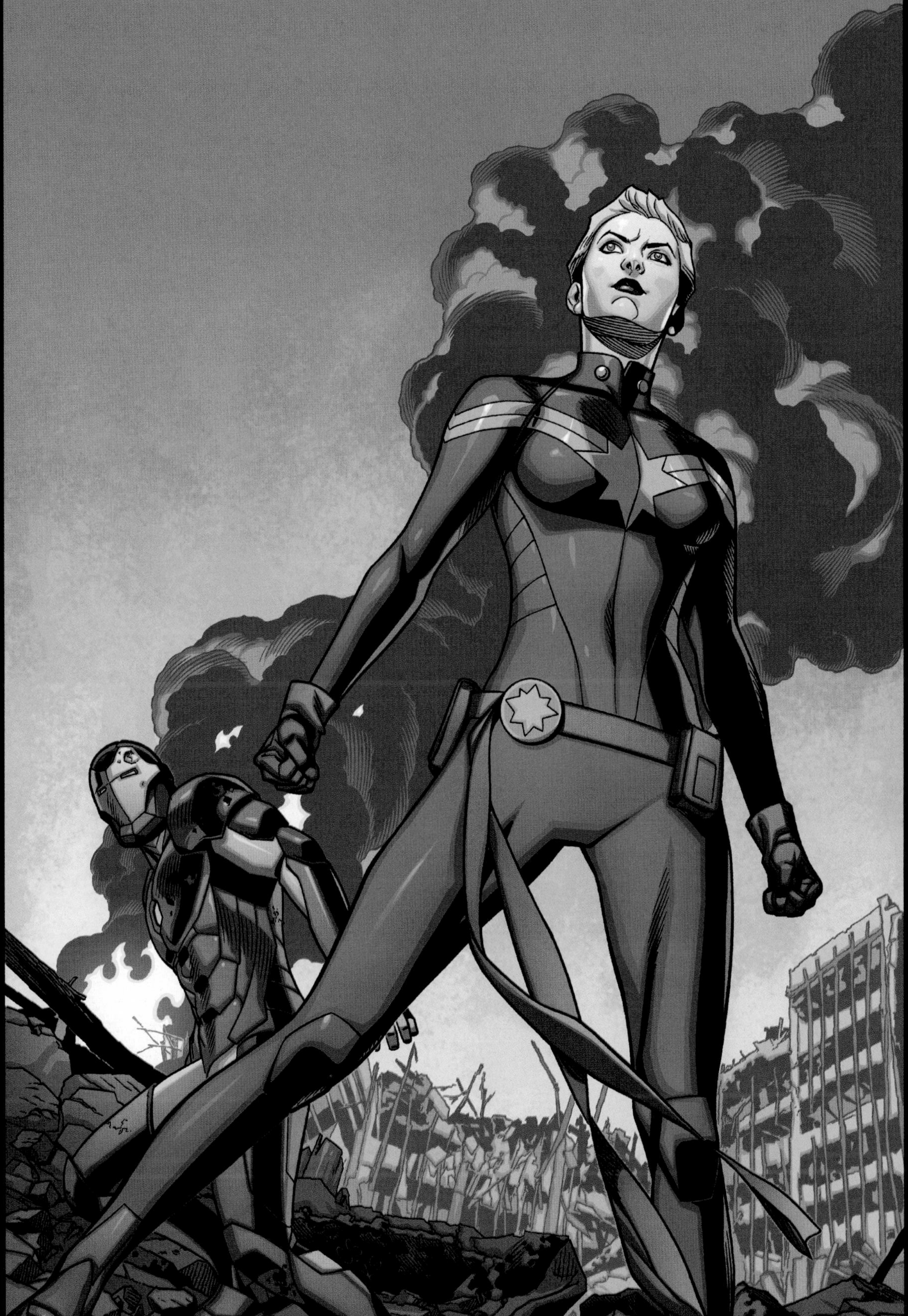

#7 BATTLE VARIANT
BY CHRIS SPROUSE, KARL STORY & DAVE MCCAIG

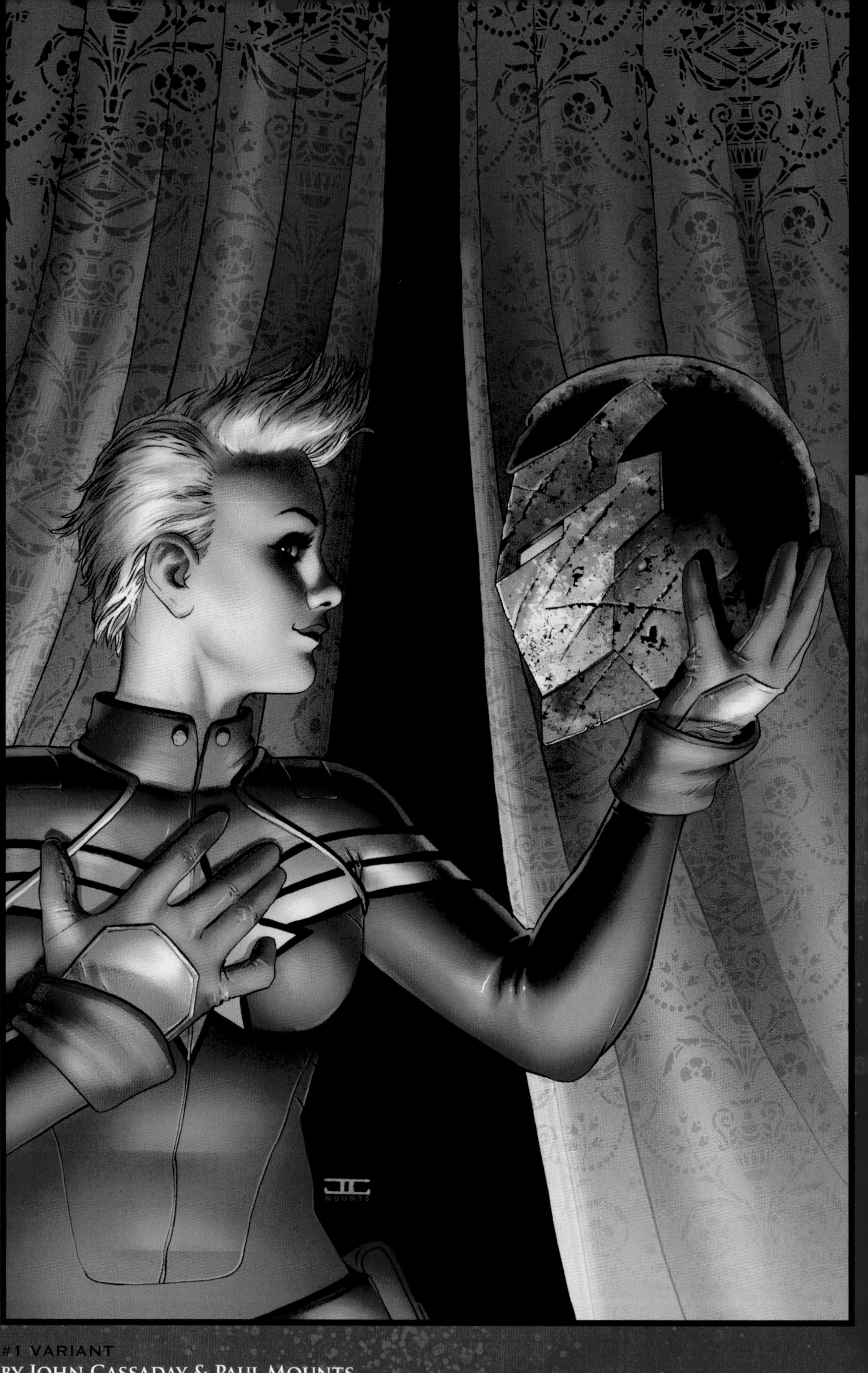
MOUNTS

#1 VARIANT
BY JOHN CASSADAY & PAUL MOUNTS

#8 VARIANT
BY JOHN CASSADAY & LAURA MARTIN

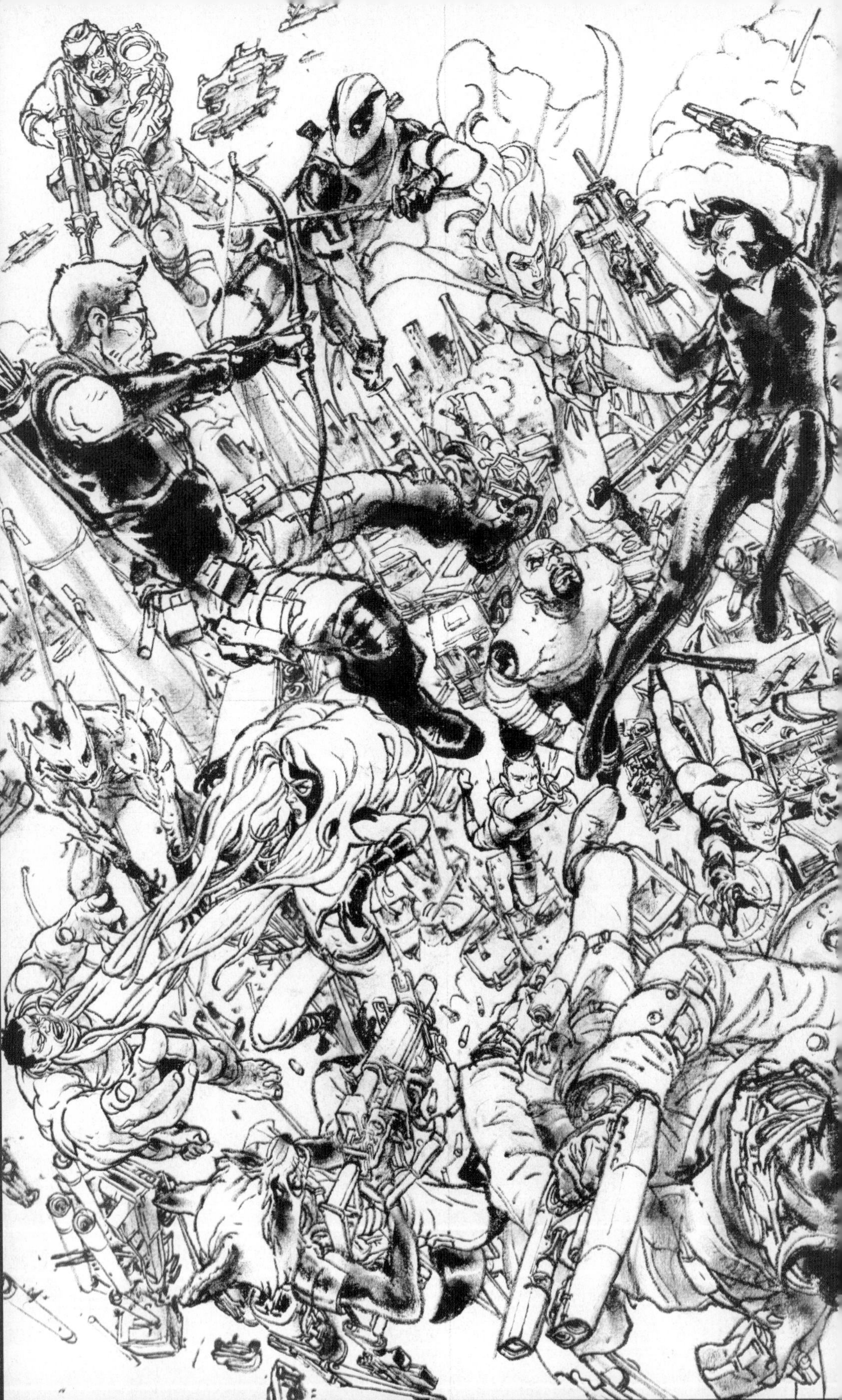

COMBINED #0-7 VARIANTS
BY KIM JUNG GI

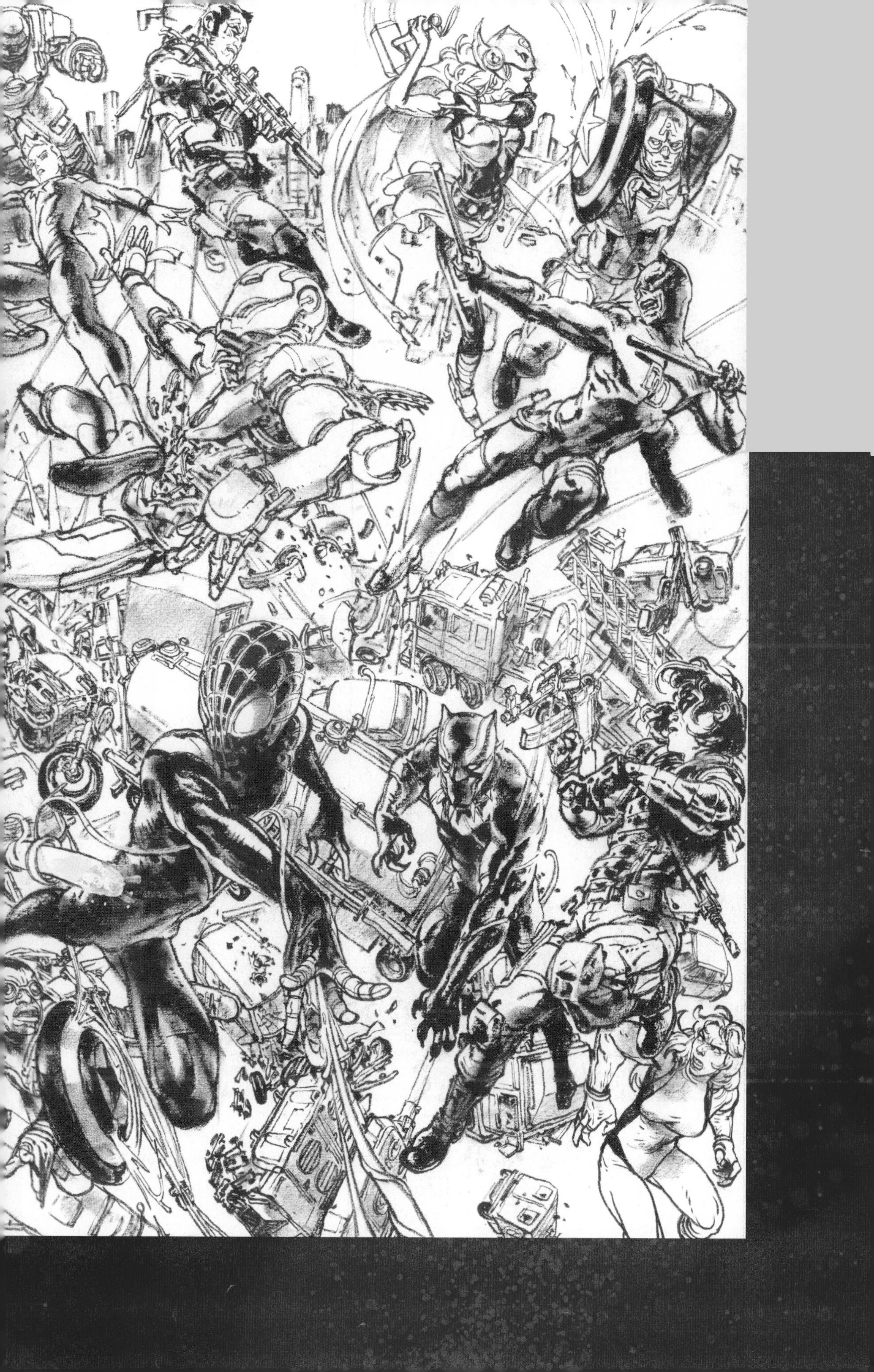

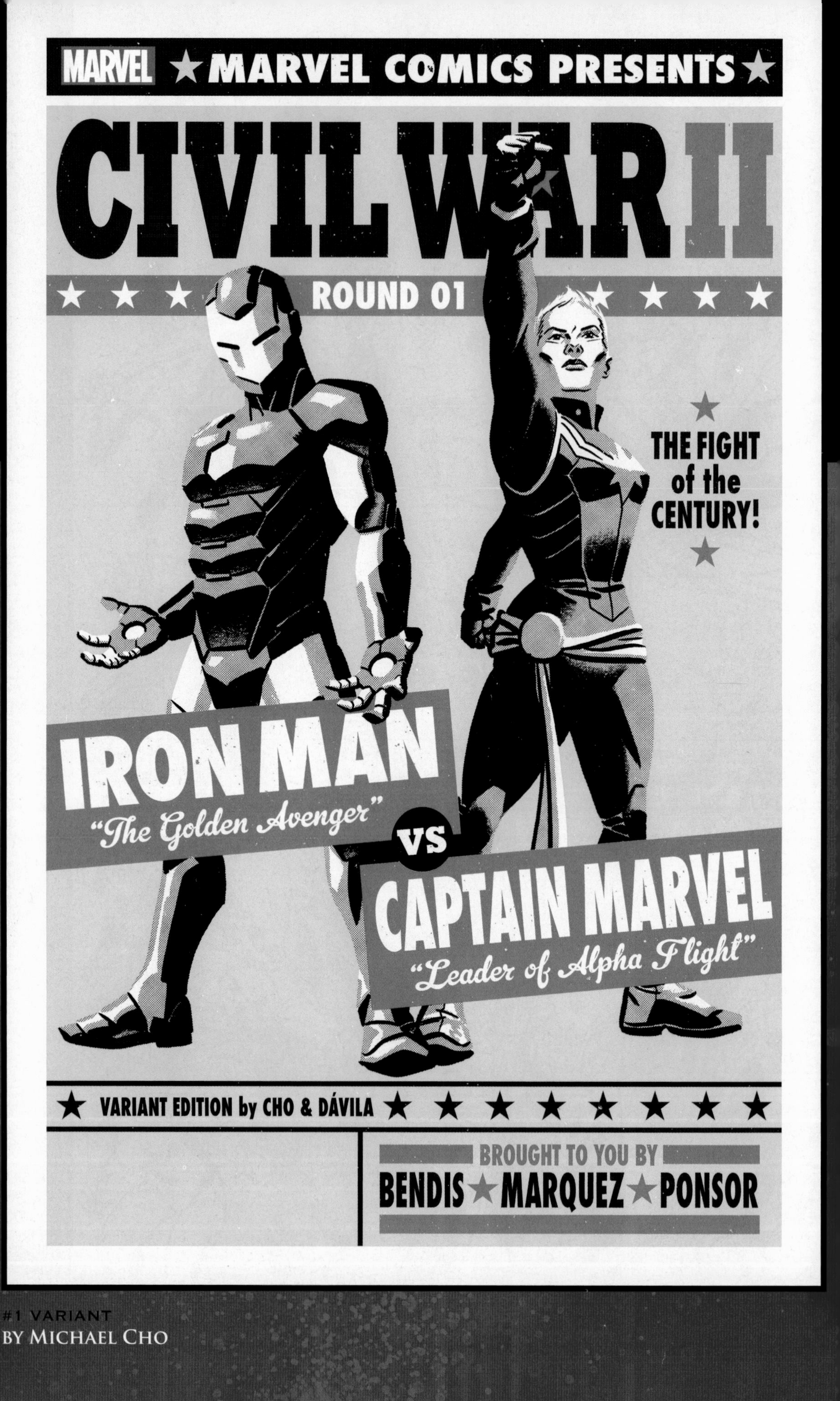
MARVEL
★ MARVEL COMICS PRESENTS ★
CIVIL WAR II
ROUND 01
THE FIGHT of the CENTURY!
IRON MAN
"The Golden Avenger"
VS
CAPTAIN MARVEL
"Leader of Alpha Flight"
VARIANT EDITION by CHO & DÁVILA
BROUGHT TO YOU BY
BENDIS ★ MARQUEZ ★ PONSOR

#1 VARIANT
BY MICHAEL CHO

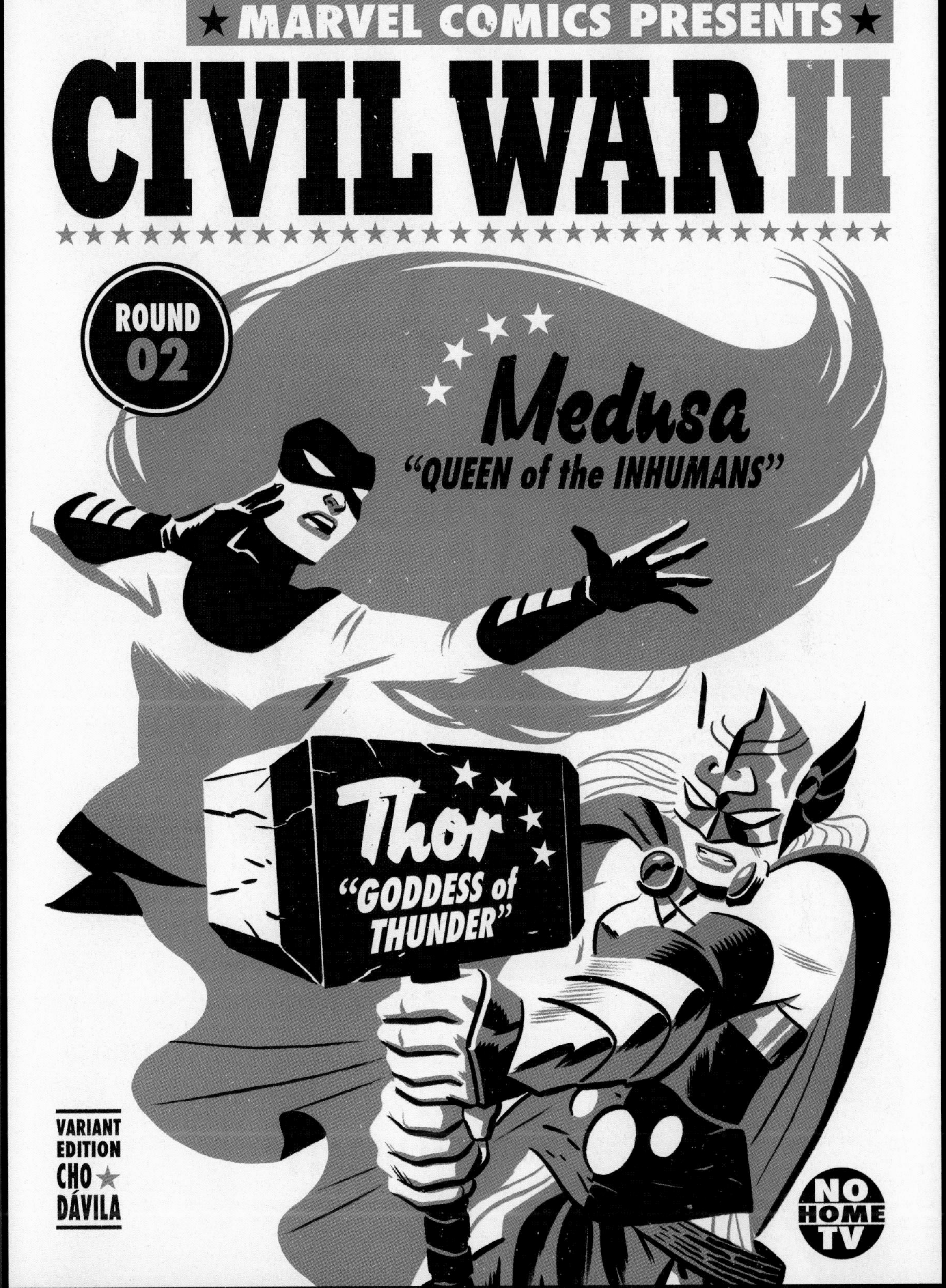
★MARVEL COMICS PRESENTS★
CIVIL WAR II
ROUND 02
Medusa
"QUEEN of the INHUMANS"
Thor
"GODDESS of THUNDER"
VARIANT EDITION CHO★DÁVILA
NO HOME TV
BROUGHT TO YOU BY
BENDIS★MARQUEZ★PONSOR

#2 VARIANT
BY MICHAEL CHO

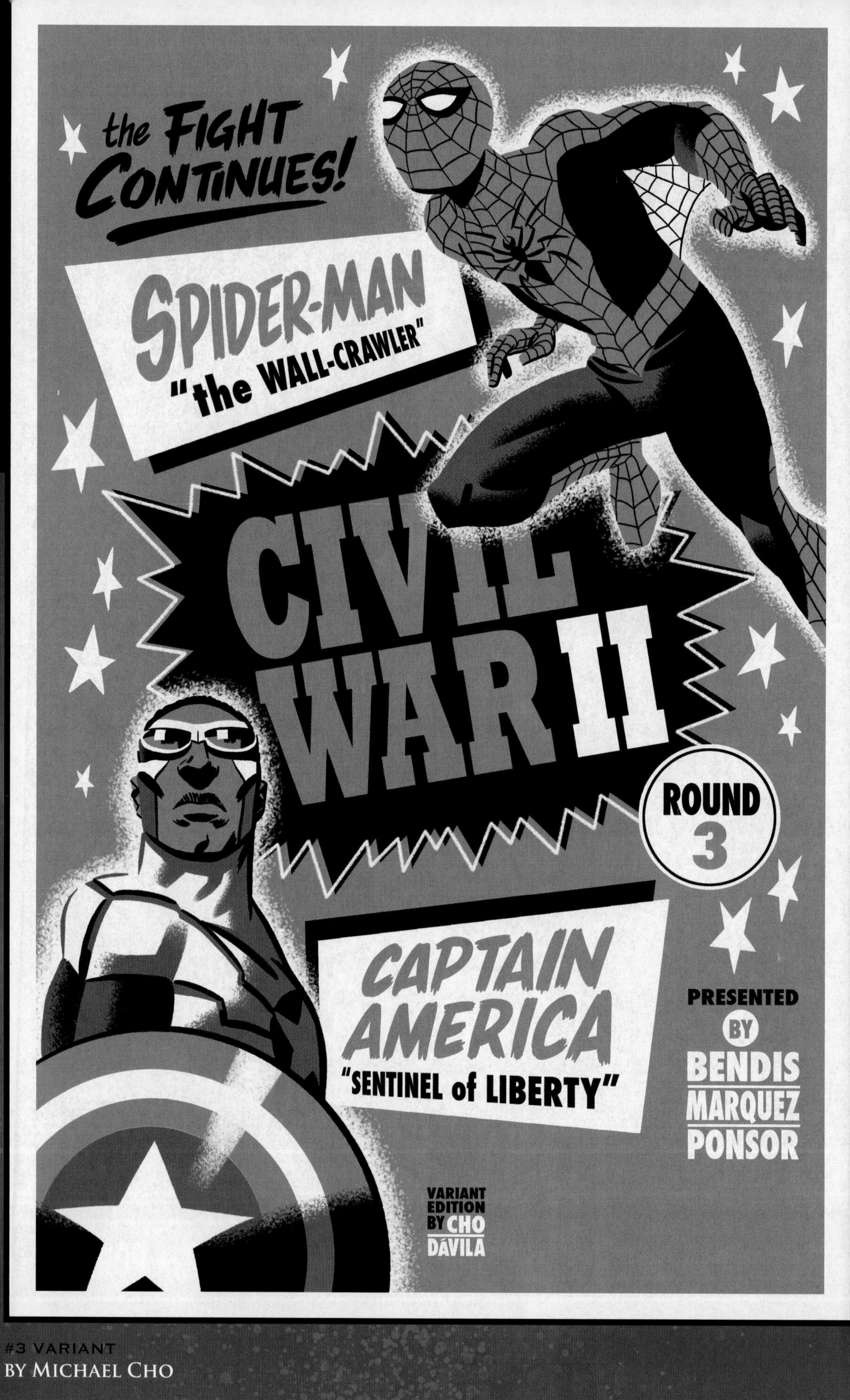

the FIGHT CONTINUES!
SPIDER-MAN
"the WALL-CRAWLER"
CIVIL WAR II
ROUND 3
CAPTAIN AMERICA
"SENTINEL of LIBERTY"
PRESENTED BY
BENDIS
MARQUEZ
PONSOR
VARIANT EDITION BY CHO DÁVILA

#3 VARIANT
BY MICHAEL CHO

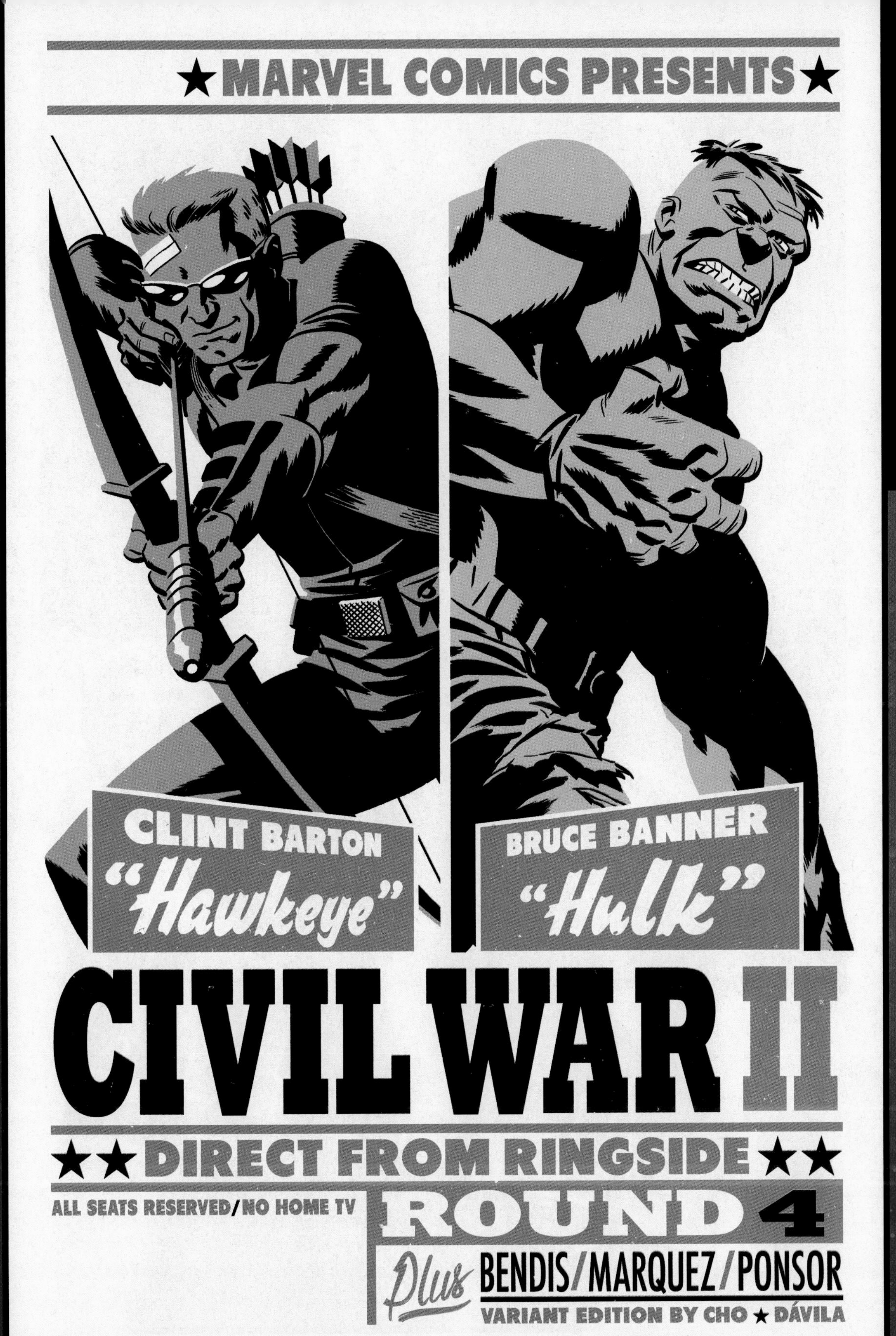
★MARVEL COMICS PRESENTS★
CLINT BARTON
"Hawkeye"
BRUCE BANNER
"Hulk"
CIVIL WAR II
★★DIRECT FROM RINGSIDE★★
ALL SEATS RESERVED/NO HOME TV
ROUND 4
Plus BENDIS/MARQUEZ/PONSOR
VARIANT EDITION BY CHO ★ DÁVILA

#4 VARIANT
BY MICHAEL CHO

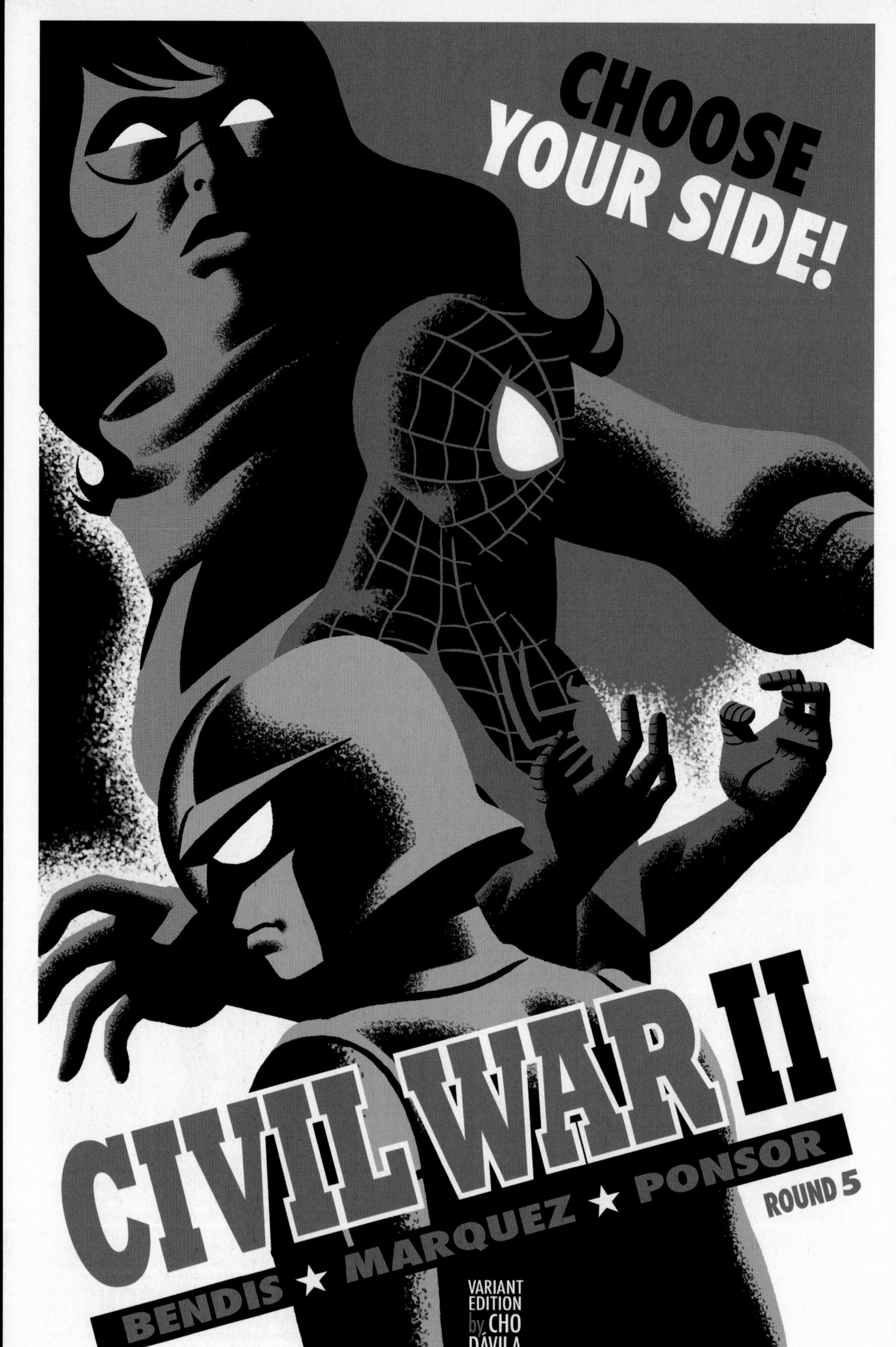
CHOOSE YOUR SIDE!
CIVIL WAR II
BENDIS ★ MARQUEZ ★ PONSOR
ROUND 5
VARIANT EDITION by CHO DÁVILA

#5 VARIANT
BY MICHAEL CHO

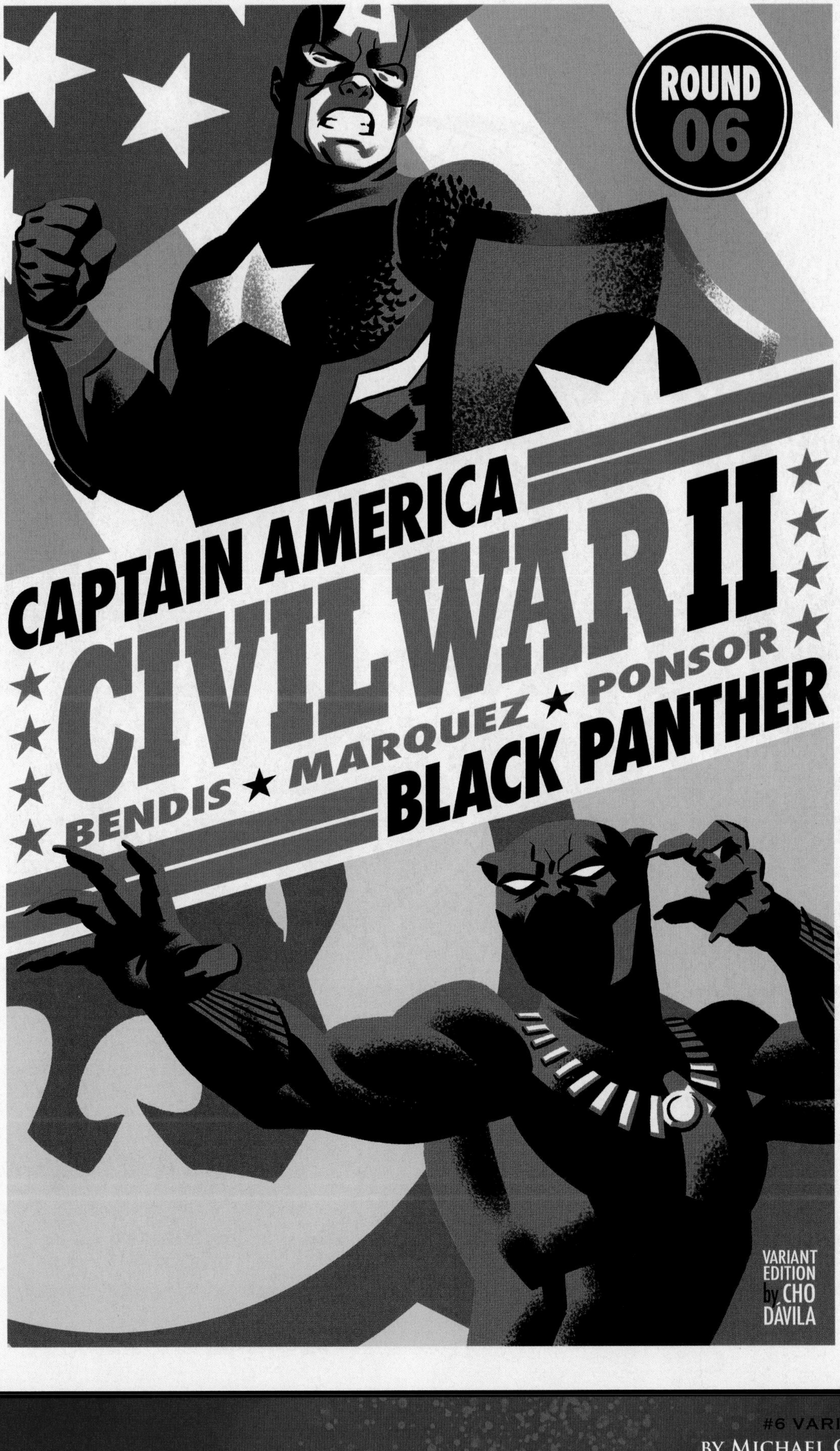
ROUND 06
CAPTAIN AMERICA
CIVIL WAR II
BENDIS ★ MARQUEZ ★ PONSOR
BLACK PANTHER
VARIANT EDITION by CHO DÁVILA

#6 VARIANT
BY MICHAEL CHO

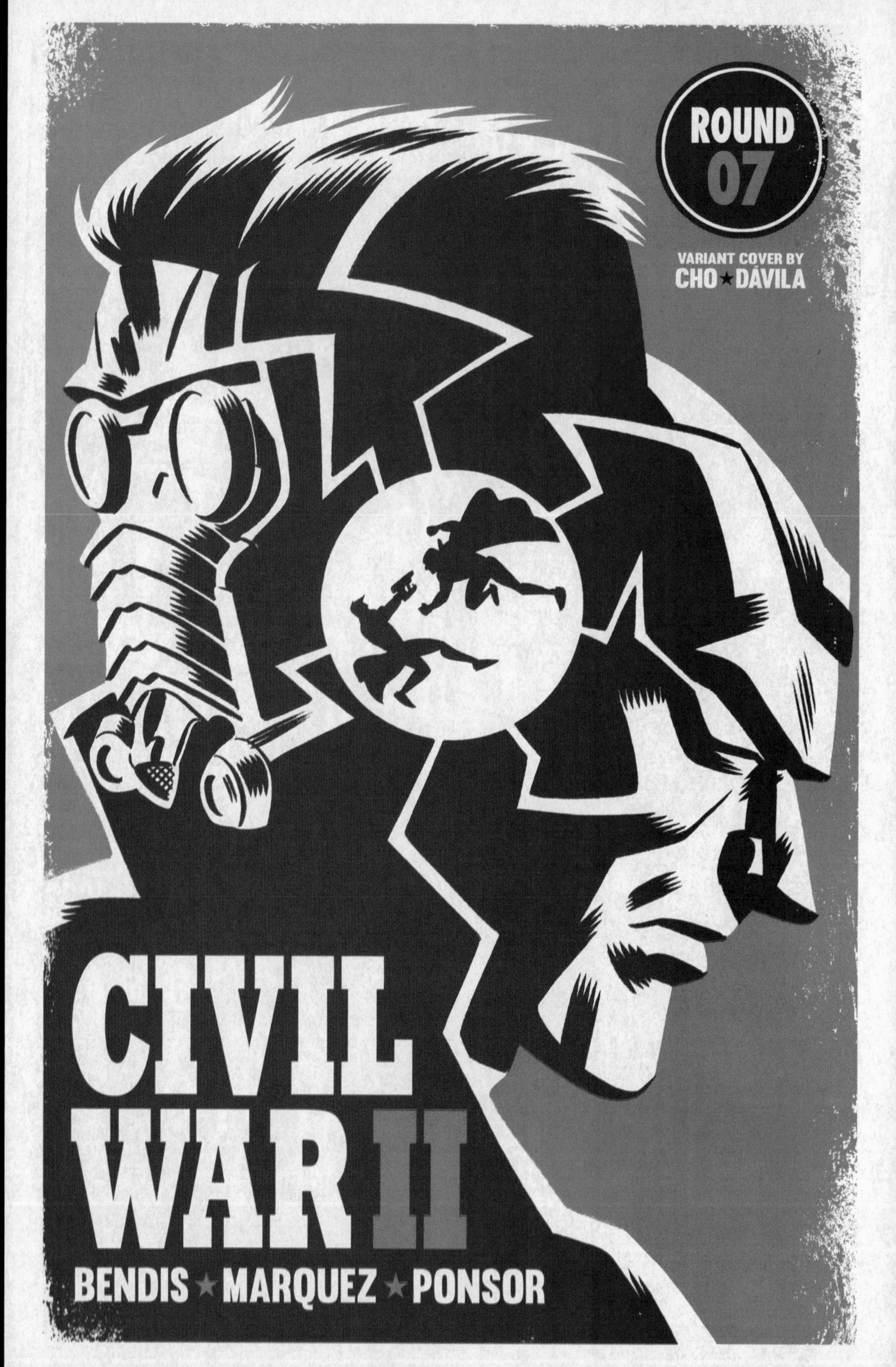
ROUND
07
VARIANT COVER BY
CHO★DÁVILA
CIVIL
WAR II
BENDIS★MARQUEZ★PONSOR

#7 VARIANT
BY MICHAEL CHO

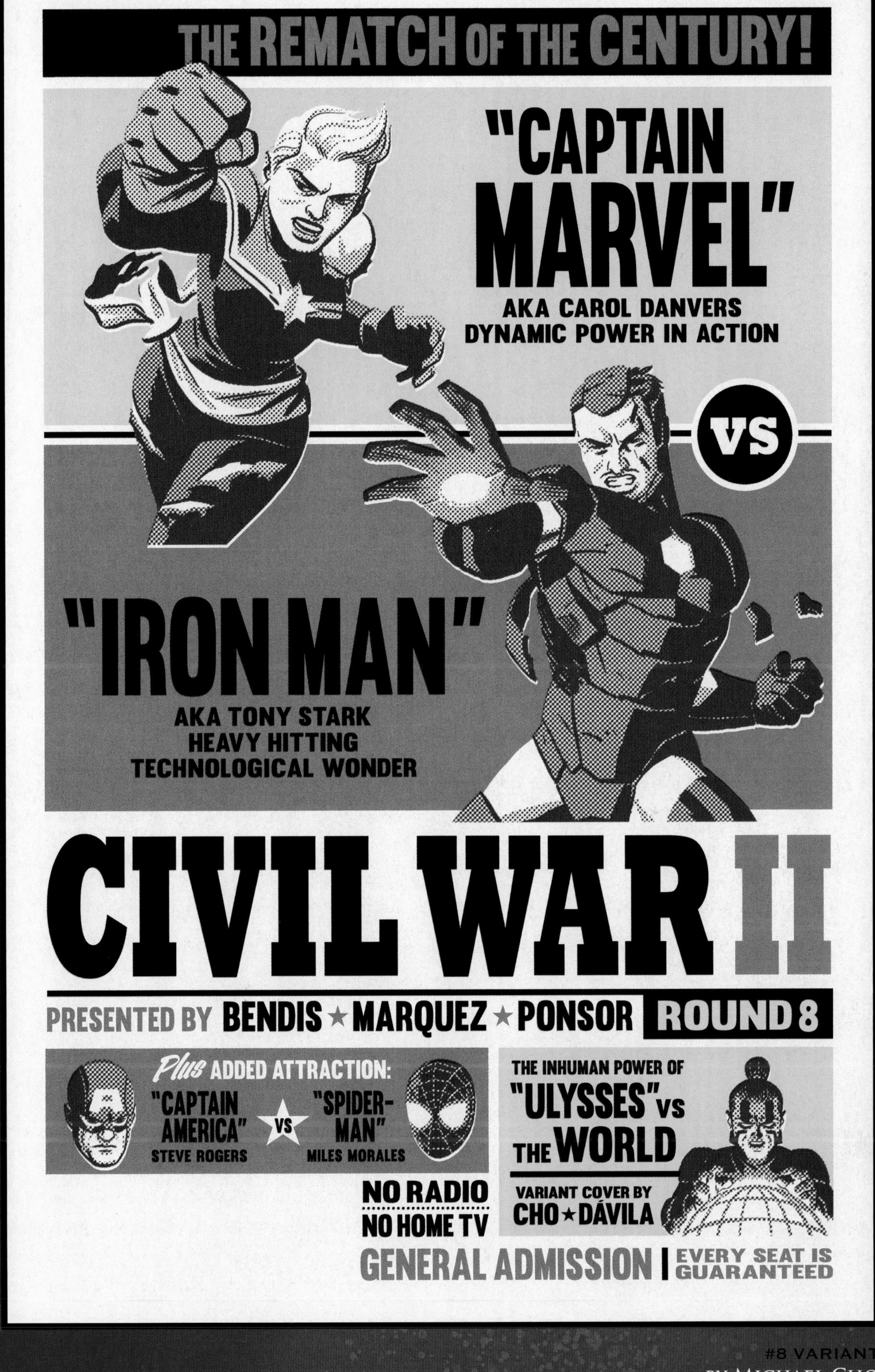
THE REMATCH OF THE CENTURY!
"CAPTAIN MARVEL"
AKA CAROL DANVERS
DYNAMIC POWER IN ACTION
VS
"IRON MAN"
AKA TONY STARK
HEAVY HITTING
TECHNOLOGICAL WONDER
CIVIL WAR II
PRESENTED BY BENDIS ★ MARQUEZ ★ PONSOR
ROUND 8
Plus ADDED ATTRACTION:
"CAPTAIN AMERICA"
STEVE ROGERS
VS
"SPIDER-MAN"
MILES MORALES
THE INHUMAN POWER OF
"ULYSSES" VS THE WORLD
NO RADIO
NO HOME TV
VARIANT COVER BY
CHO ★ DÁVILA
GENERAL ADMISSION
EVERY SEAT IS GUARANTEED

#8 VARIANT
BY MICHAEL CHO

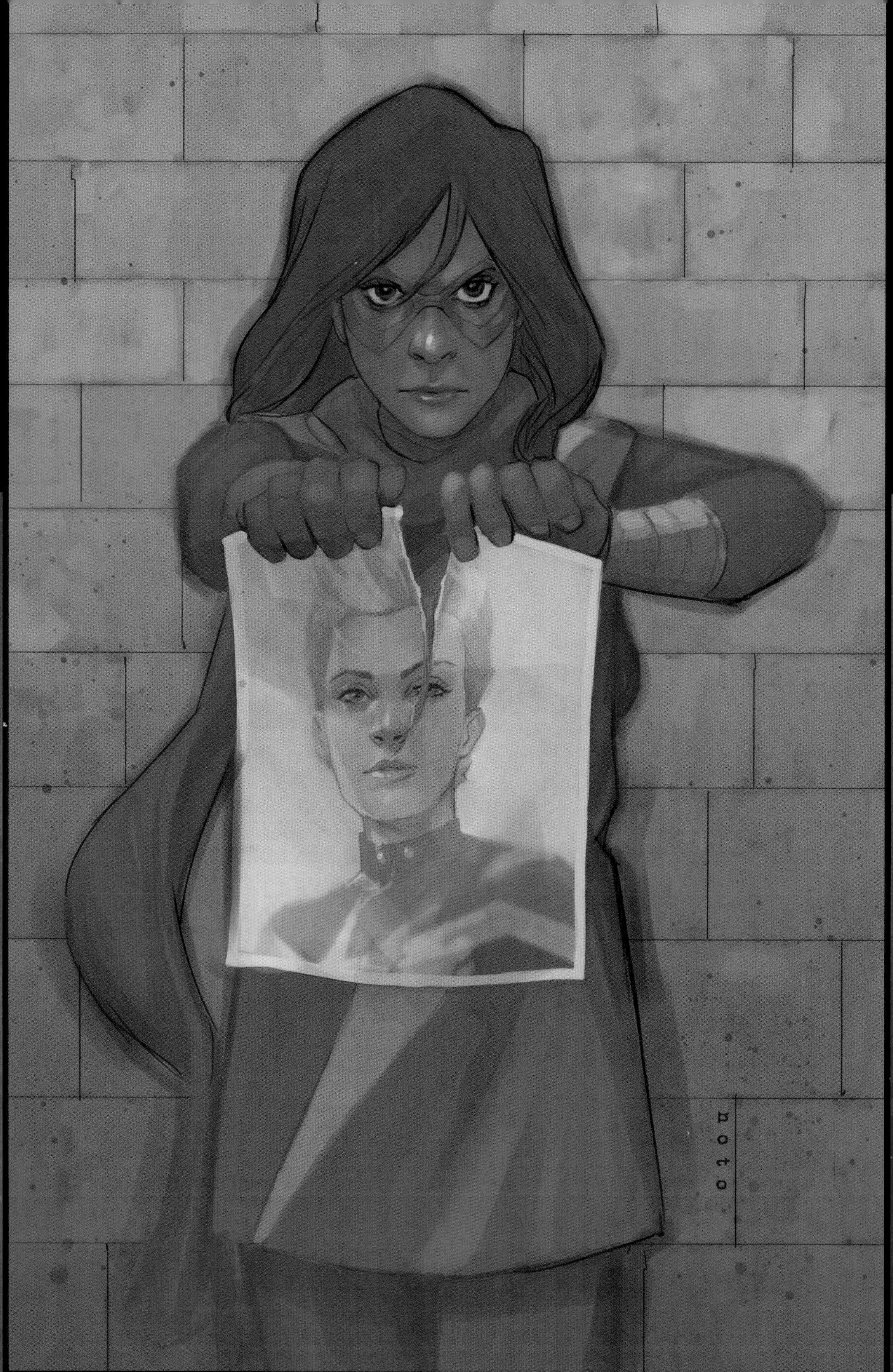
noto

#0 VARIANT
BY PHIL NOTO

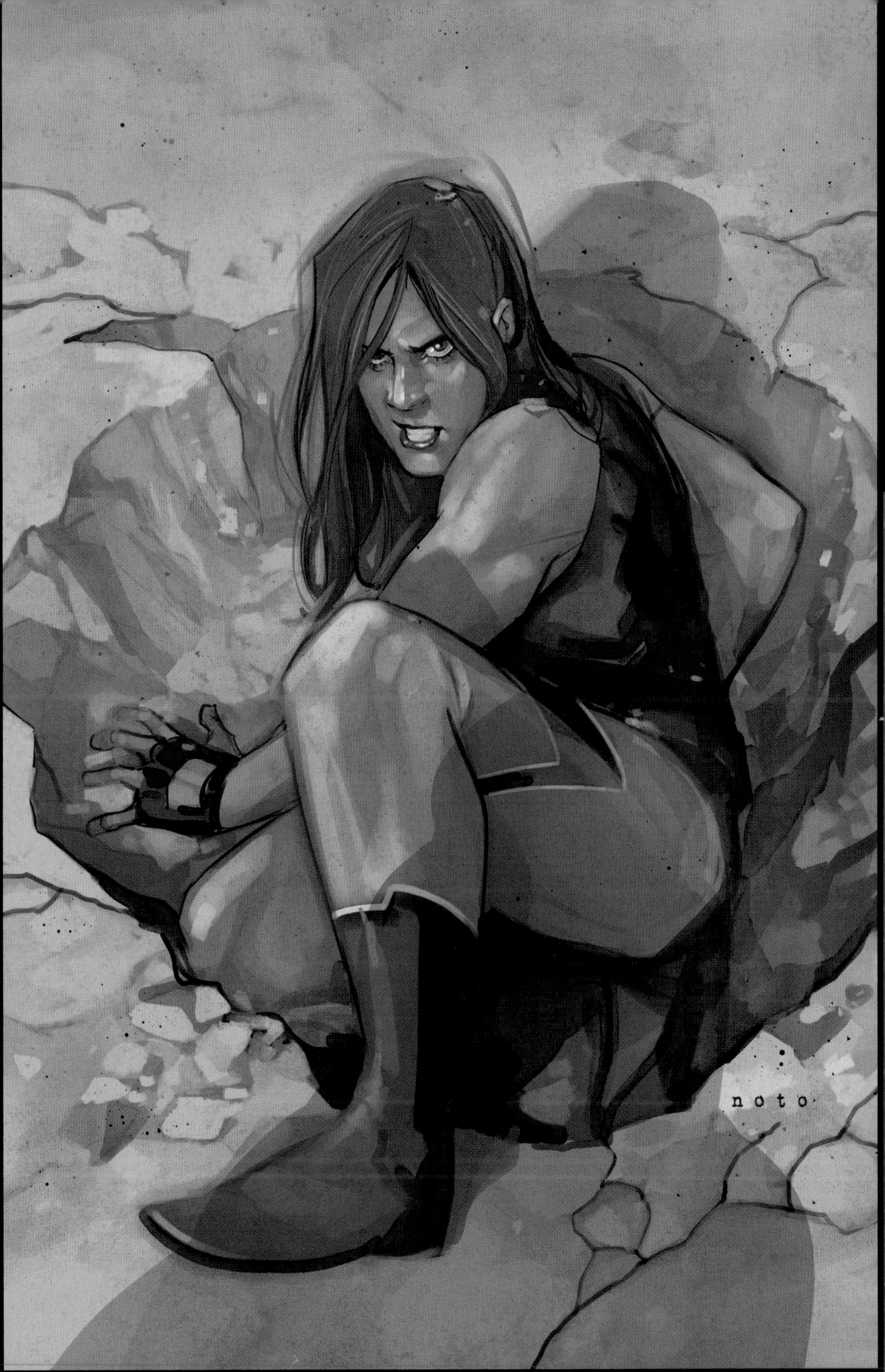
noto

#1 VARIANT
BY PHIL NOTO

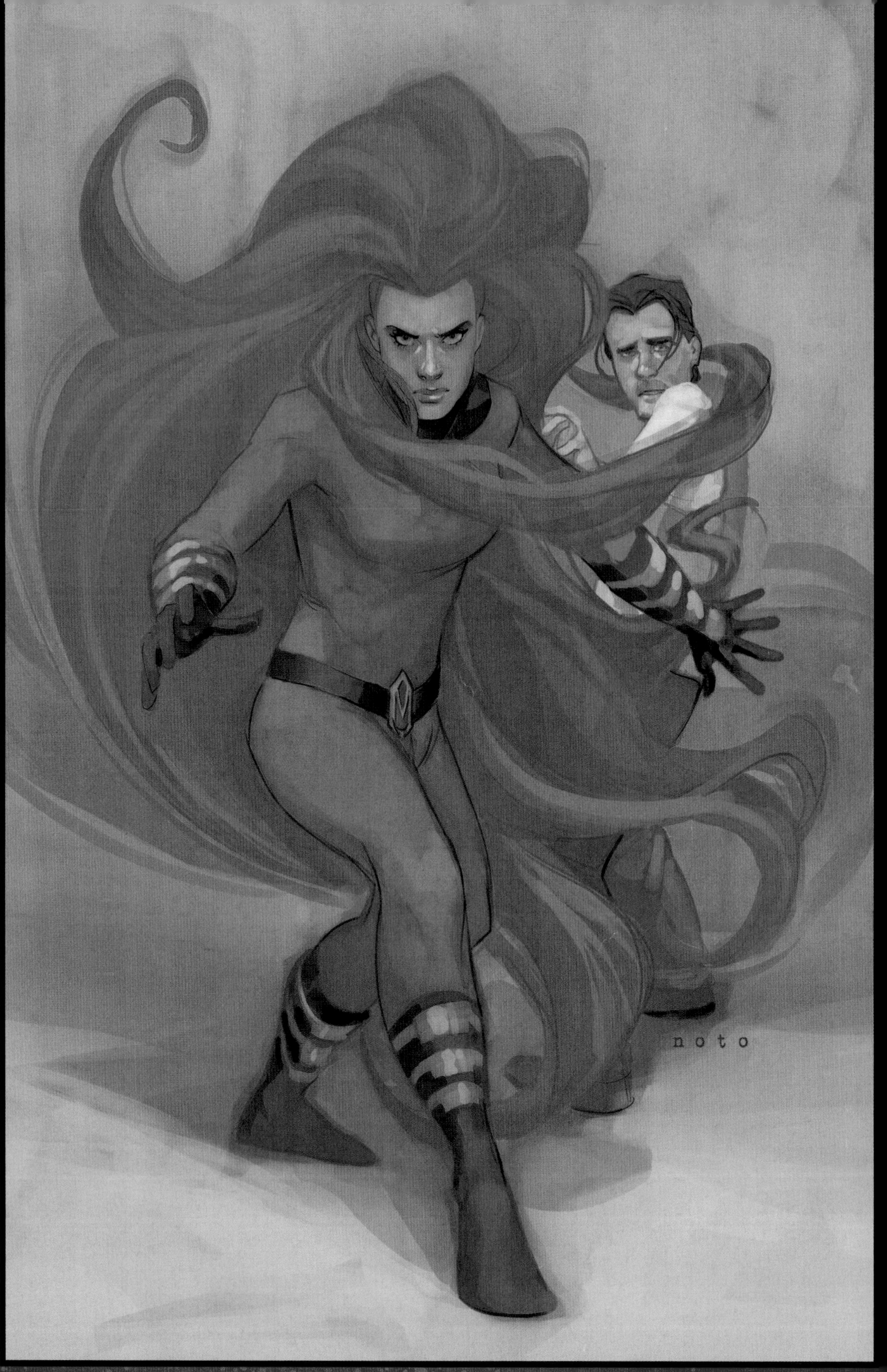
noto

#2 VARIANT
BY PHIL NOTO

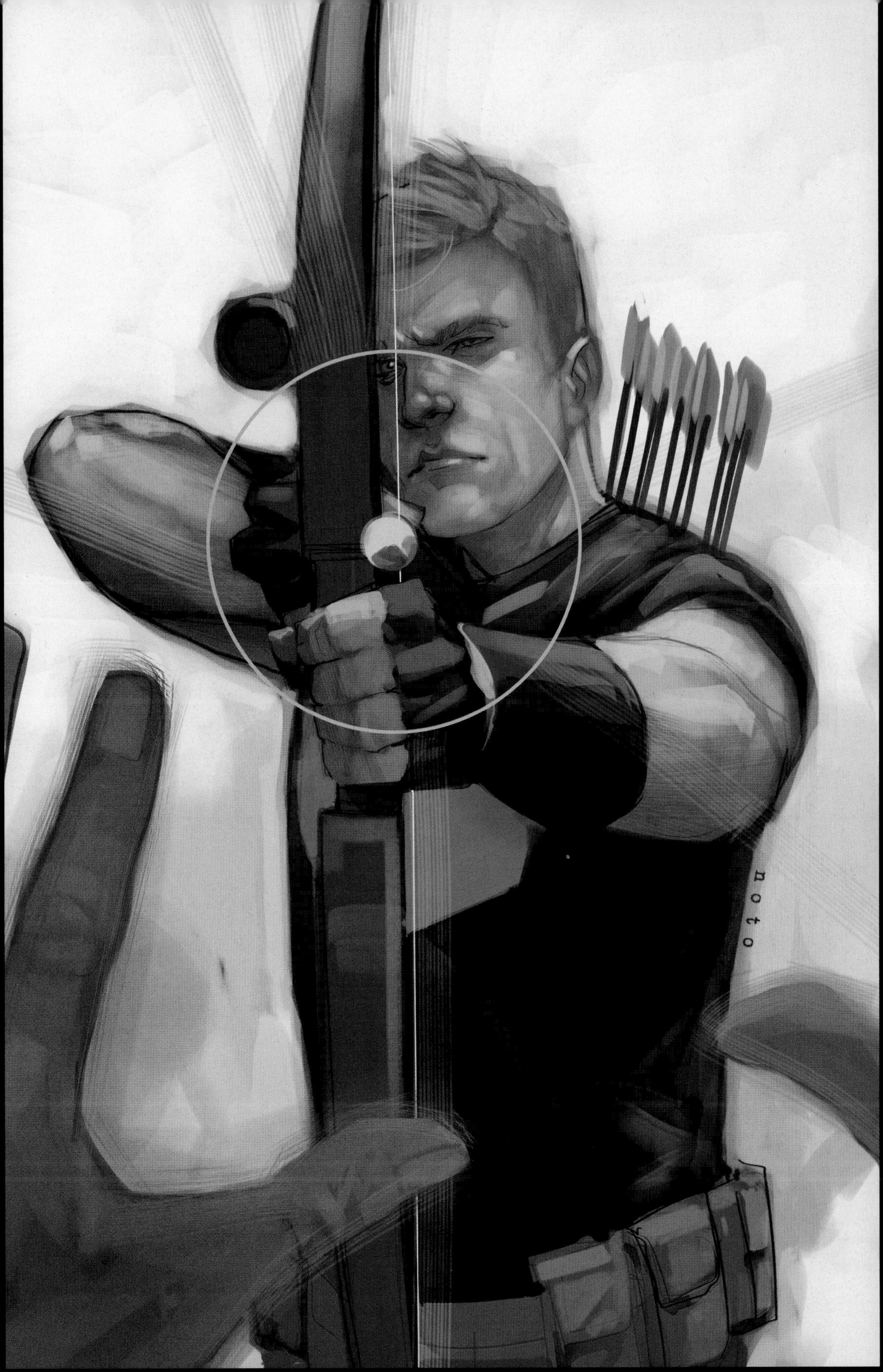
noto

#3 VARIANT
BY PHIL NOTO

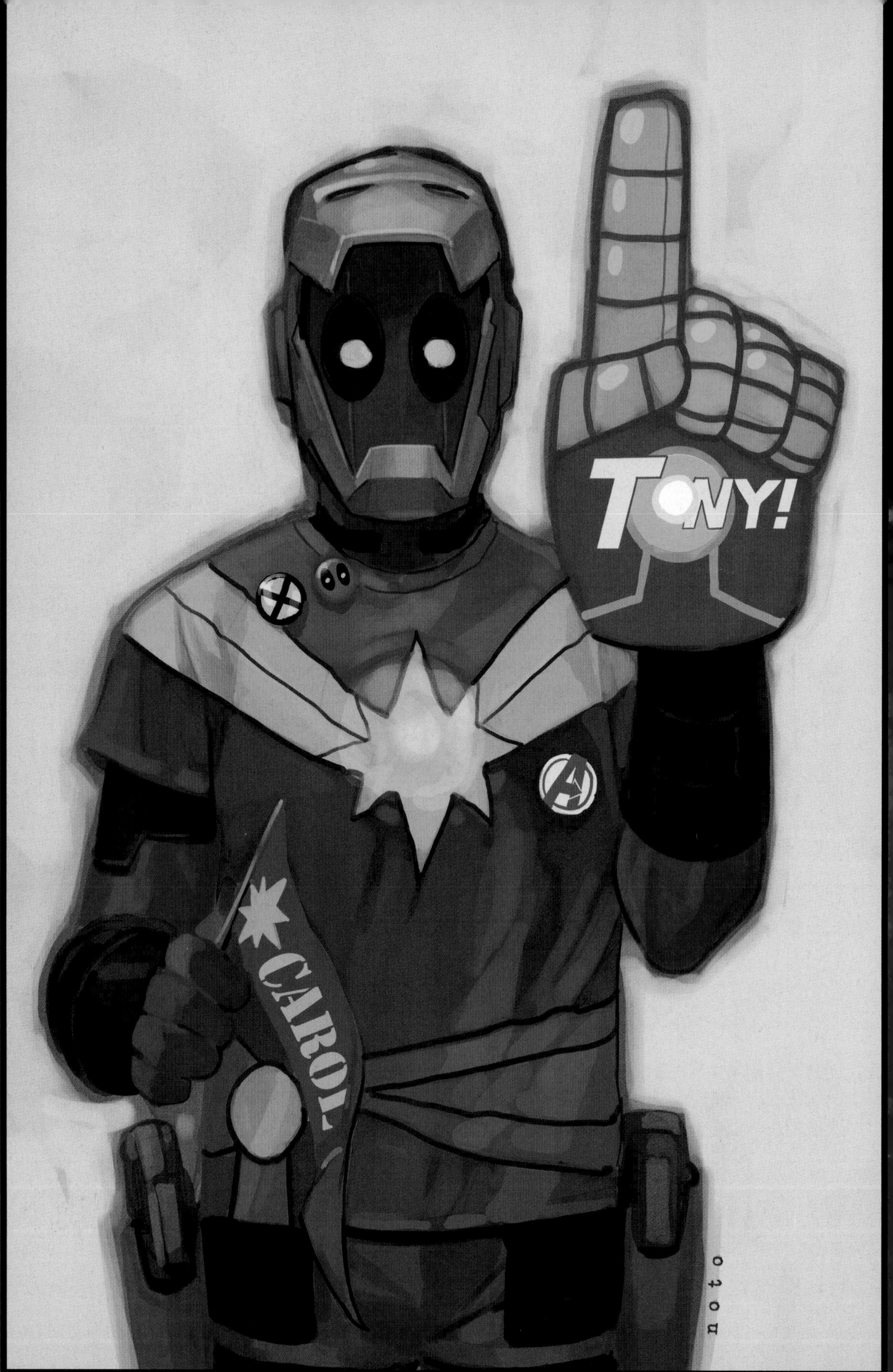
TONY!
CAROL
noto

#4 VARIANT
BY PHIL NOTO

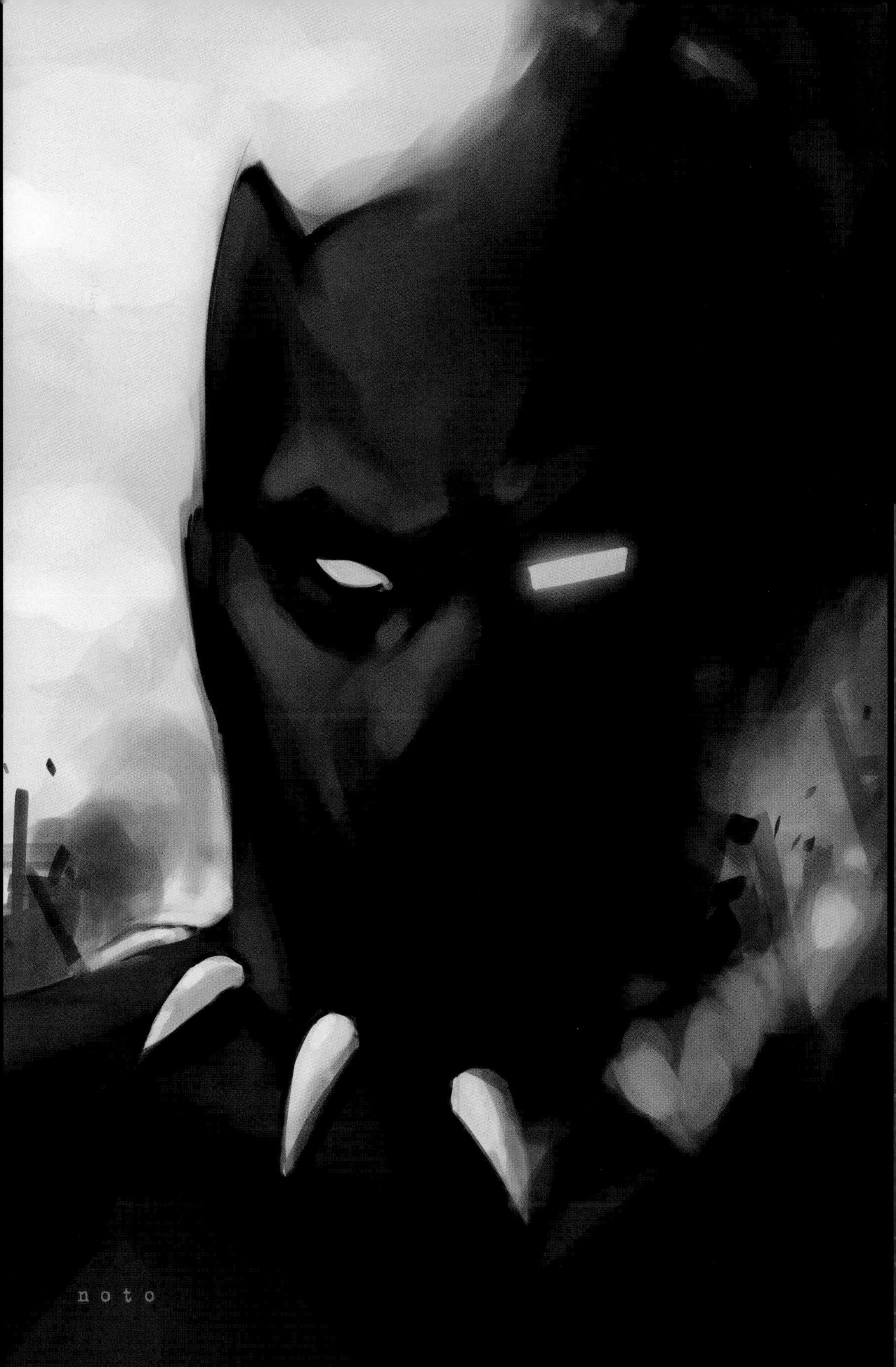
noto

#5 VARIANT
BY PHIL NOTO

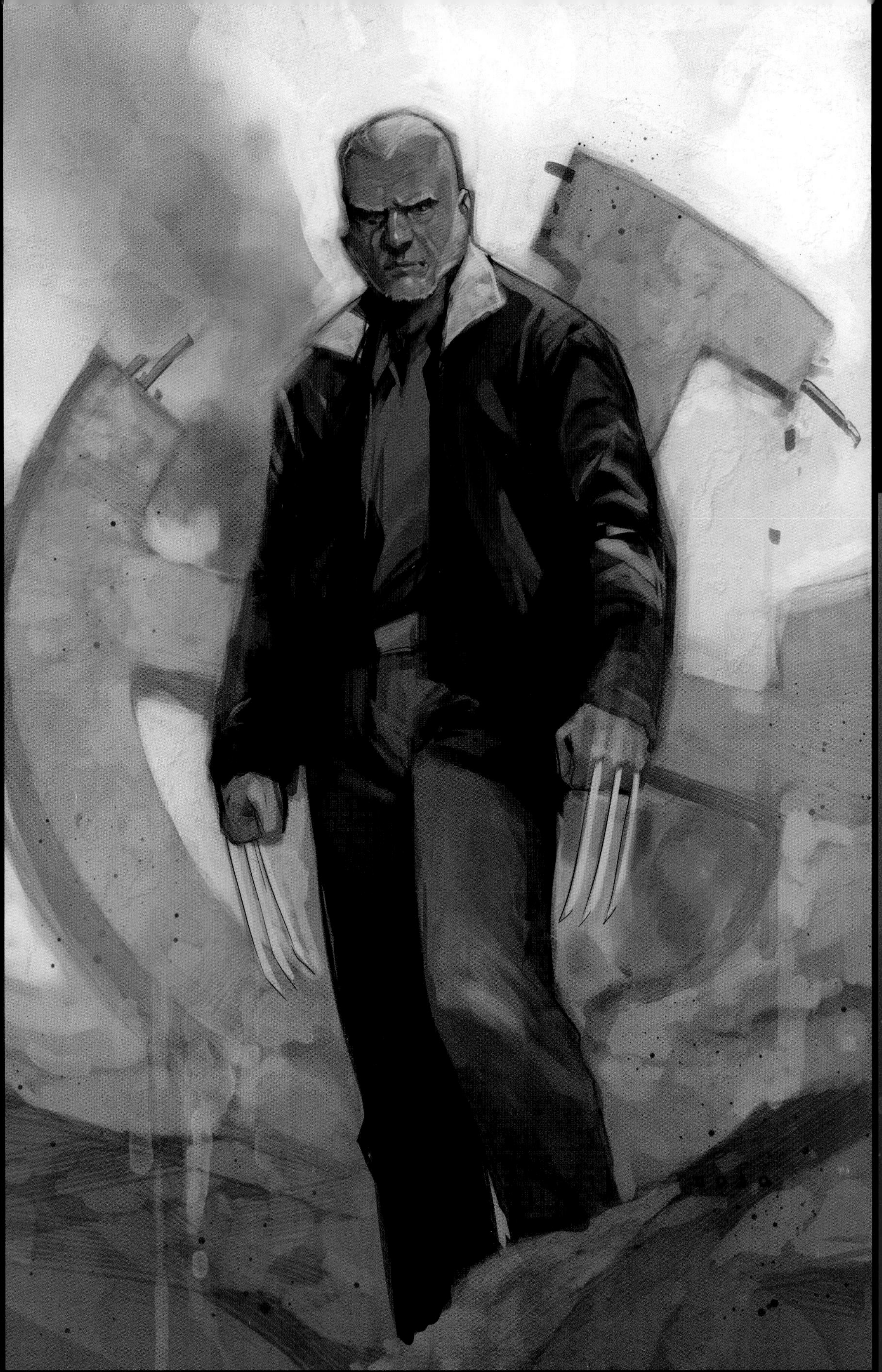

#6 VARIANT
BY PHIL NOTO

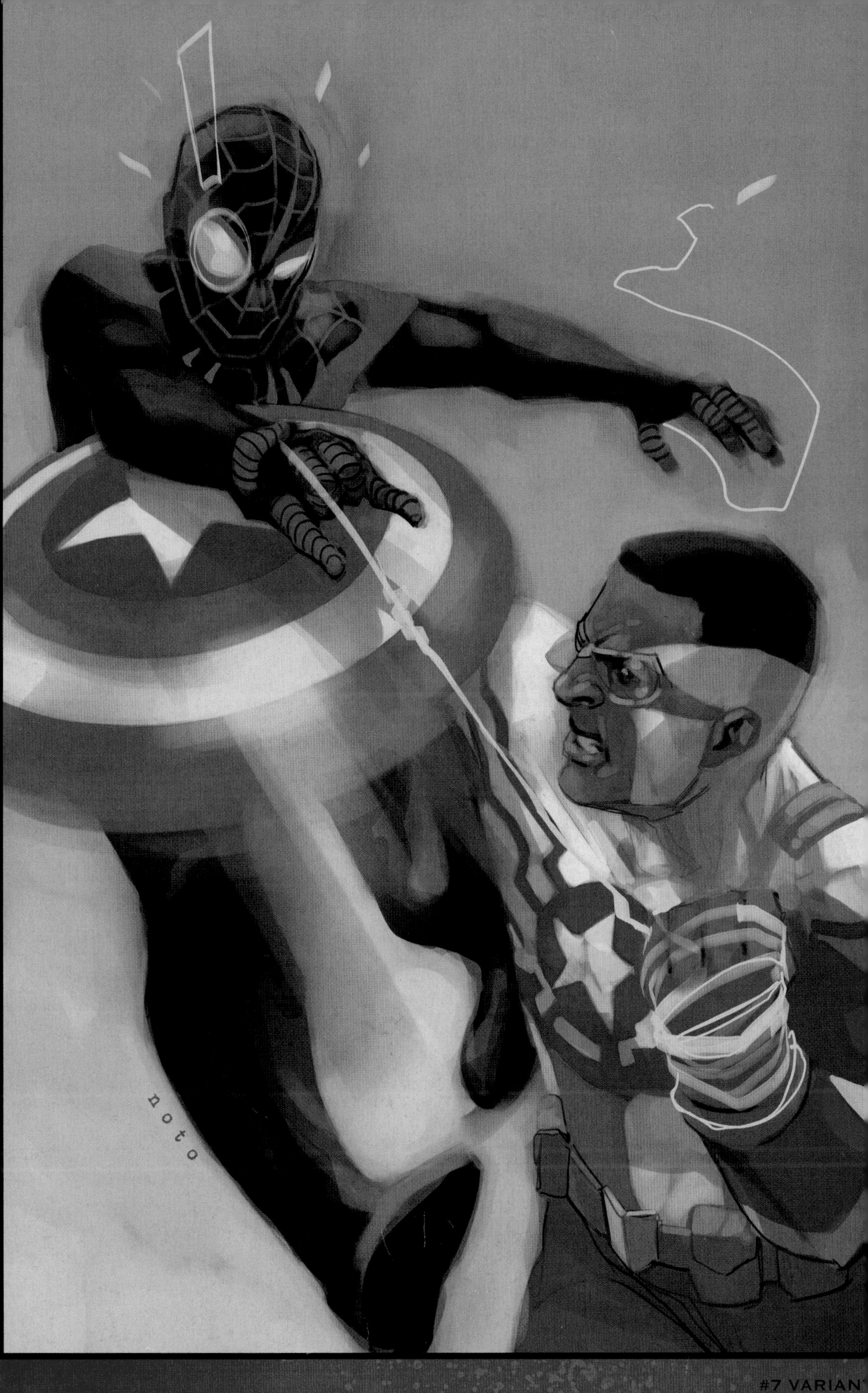
noto

#7 VARIANT
BY PHIL NOTO

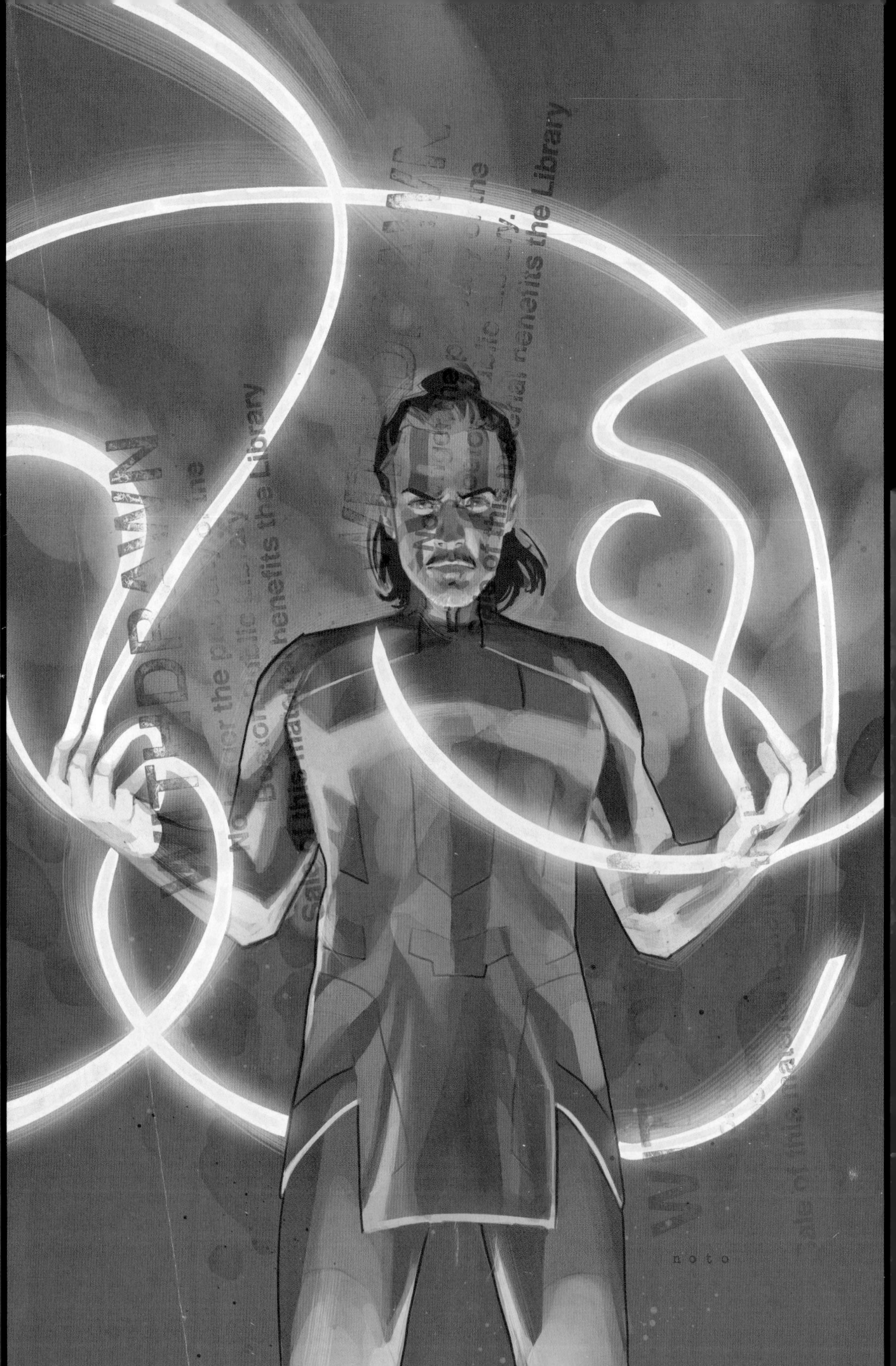
noto

#8 VARIANT
BY PHIL NOTO